Century 21 Jr.™
INPUT TECHNOLOGIES & COMPUTER APPLICATIONS

JACK P. HOGGATT, ED.D.
PROFESSOR OF BUSINESS COMMUNICATION
UNIVERSITY OF WISCONSIN – EAU CLAIRE
EAU CLAIRE, WISCONSIN

●

JON A. SHANK, ED.D.
PROFESSOR OF EDUCATION
ROBERT MORRIS UNIVERSITY
MOON TOWNSHIP, PENNSYLVANIA

●

KARL BARKSDALE
TECHNOLOGY CONSULTANT
FARRER MIDDLE SCHOOL
PROVO, UTAH

●

CONTRIBUTING AUTHOR

DIANNE S. RANKIN
EDUCATIONAL MEDIA DEVELOPMENT

THOMSON

SOUTH-WESTERN

Australia · Brazil · Canada · Mexico · Singapore · Spain · United Kingdom · United States

THOMSON

SOUTH-WESTERN

Century 21 Jr., Input Technologies and Computer Applications
Jack Hoggatt, Jon Shank, Karl Barksdale

VP/Editorial Director:
Jack W. Calhoun

VP/Editor-in-Chief:
Karen Schmohe

Acquisitions Editor:
Jane Congdon

Project Manager:
Dave Lafferty

Consulting Editor:
Dianne S. Rankin

Fee Writer:
Suzanne Knapic Schuetter
SKS Marketing & Publishing Services

VP/Director of Marketing:
Carol Volz

Production Project Manager:
Diane Bowdler

Production Manager:
Patricia Matthews Boies

Marketing Manager:
Mike Cloran

Marketing Coordinator:
Linda Kuper

Manager of Technology, Editorial:
Liz Prigge

Technology Project Editor:
Scott Hamilton

Web Coordinator:
Ed Stubenrauch

Sr. Manufacturing Buyer:
Charlene Taylor

Production House:
GEX Publishing Services

Art Director:
Stacy Jenkins Shirley

Internal Designer:
Joseph Pagliaro Graphic Design

Cover Designer:
Joseph Pagliaro Graphic Design

Photo Manager:
John Hill

Photo Researcher:
Darren Wright

Printer:
Quebecor World, Versailles
Versailles, KY

Mission Information Guide

Use this Mission Information Guide to help you travel through the various features of *Century 21™ Jr.* Launch your middle school students into a new galaxy of computer instruction ....

Century ....5, 4, 3, 21 Jr. Lift off!

Perfect for your introductory course in middle school, **Century 21 Jr. Input Technologies & Computer Applications** is a much-anticipated arrival that brings lots to celebrate! This exciting new book introduces keyboarding, computer basics, the Internet, and computer applications. Students are also introduced to new grade-level-appropriate computer skills based on the National Educational Technology Standards (NETS).

This is the first book for middle school students that addresses an array of new input technologies. Coverage of the latest input technologies includes handwriting recognition, speech recognition, Tablet PCs, Personal Digital Assistants (PDAs), scanning, electronic photos, and digital imaging.

Computer applications instruction prepares students to work with word processing, spreadsheets, presentations, databases, file maintenance, Windows, computer concepts, ethics, programming, and Web sites.

Also available is **Century 21 Jr. Input Technologies** for a shorter course when applications have already been covered.

Century 21 Jr. Input Technologies & Computer Applications
Student text for 2-semesters
(Top-Bound, 640 pgs, 4-color) 0-538-44265-4

Century 21 Jr. Input Technologies
Student text for 1-semester
(Top-Bound, 368 pgs, 4-color) 0-538-44263-8

Wrap-around Teacher's Edition for *Century 21 Jr. Input Technologies & Computer Applications*
(Top-Spiral Bound, 672 pgs, 4-color) 0-538-44264-6

Teacher's Manual for *Century 21 Jr. Input Technologies*
(Soft cover, 192 pgs, 1-color) 0-538-44262-X

Instructor's Resource CD-ROM
- For *Century 21 Jr. Input Technologies & Computer Applications* 0-538-44260-3
- For *Century 21 Jr. Input Technologies* 0-538-44259-X

ExamView® Electronic Testing Software CD-ROM
0-538-44261-1

Adobe® eBook
- For *Century 21 Jr. Input Technologies & Computer Applications* 0-538-44255-7
- For *Century 21 Jr. Input Technologies* 0-538-44266-2

CheckPro for *Century 21 Jr.*
- Windows site license CD, User's Guide 0-538-44269-7

Technology Bundle
- *MicroType™ 4 & CheckPro for Century 21 Jr.* Windows Site Licenses 0-538-44327-8
(Macintosh version of MicroType 3.0 is also available.)

Out of This World Features!

Units are divided into chapters, which are then divided into daily lessons for learning segments that progress at your students' pace.

The **Web Resources** provided on the chapter openers direct students to specific learning support including games, review activities, flash cards, and much more on the text's dedicated support Web site.

Step-by-step instructional design teaches students concepts and then encourages them to practice and apply the concepts to real-life situations.

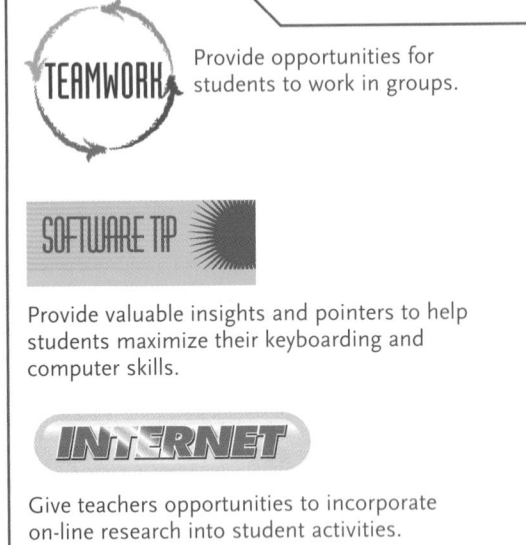

TEAMWORK Provide opportunities for students to work in groups.

SOFTWARE TIP Provide valuable insights and pointers to help students maximize their keyboarding and computer skills.

INTERNET Give teachers opportunities to incorporate on-line research into student activities.

Reviewing What You Have Learned questions at the end of the chapter test students' understanding of the material covered.
Applying What You Have Learned exercises provide activities for reinforcing content from the chapter.

About Business features at the end of each chapter address entrepreneurship, economics, ethics, and workplace trends and issues.

Career and Life Skills Success Builders at the end of each chapter provide activities focused on careers, leadership, and teamwork.

Academic Success Builders at the end of each chapter cover math review, communication and reading review, personal finance, and youth organizations.

Thomson South-Western provides all the tools necessary for a rewarding classroom experience.

Wrap-around Teacher's Edition for **Century 21 Jr. Input Technologies & Computer Applications**—Reduced pages from the student text are surrounded with teaching comments and invaluable teaching tips and resources.

Teacher's Manual for **Century 21 Jr. Input Technologies**—The Teacher Manual contains teaching notes and printed solutions.

Bring a Universe of Technology to Your Classroom

Instructor's Resource CD
This CD includes student data files, unit tests, solution files, chapter tests, PowerPoint presentations, and teaching notes all in one place for easy access.

ExamView® Electronic Testing Software
Create printed or online quizzes, study guides, and tests easily and quickly with this computerized testing tool. Ideal for building tests, worksheets, and study guides (practice tests), this assessment solution also saves grading time and improves student results by focusing on specific learning objectives.

Adobe eBooks for Century 21 Jr.
Take learning to a new level with this dynamic, interactive text material available digitally.

MicroType
This engaging, easy-to-use program teaches new-key learning and skill building, with lessons that correlate to the Century 21 Jr. texts. MicroType features 3-D animations, videos, and fun, interactive games.

CheckPro for Century 21 Jr.
Save time as you instantly check documents keyed from the text! This new software works with Microsoft Word and Excel for Windows and can even check completion of PowerPoint activities. The Web reporting feature allows students to provide their results to the instructor using the Internet.

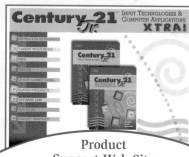

Product Support Web Site
Discover teaching and learning resources that you won't find anywhere else when you adopt Century 21 Jr. The password-protected Teacher Resources Center includes a wealth of downloadable solutions, files, and teaching resources. The Student Resource Center offers supplemental materials, activities, games, enrichment materials, and much more. Visit **www.c21jr.swlearning.com** to see for yourself.

Preface

Step into the Future

You are about to use some very high-tech computer tools. Learning them is essential to your success in school and at work. You may be wondering whether or not you will be able to learn these tools. Don't worry. Instead, think about this: At first, no one was sure if scientists could build spaceships safe enough for travel to the moon. These space pioneers gave their best efforts and worked through problems step-by-step. Eventually, the United States succeeded in landing people on the moon. This is one of the greatest accomplishments in history.

By taking small, steady steps, space scientists took a giant leap forward, creating technologies that helped all mankind. Just like the space scientists of the past, you must always take the next step forward. They never gave up. Don't you give up, either. Learn a lesson from their example. If you give your best efforts and take things one step at a time, you, too, can accomplish great things.

About this Textbook

Units in the Textbook

This textbook is organized in 5 units that contain 17 chapters. The chapters have several lessons that will take you step-by-step along many computer adventures. The lessons have examples and activities to make learning fun, interesting, and exciting. The units in the textbook are described below.

Unit 1 Digital Communication Tools

Any digital device used to communicate with others is a digital communications tool. These devices are also called *DigiTools*. You will begin by learning some of the history of DigiTools and how they work. You will learn how computers are changing the way we live, work, and play. You will learn to use the basic features of programs such as *Microsoft Word*, *Windows Explorer*, and *Internet Explorer* in this unit.

Unit 2 Keyboarding

You may already know how to key properly by touch, or you may be a beginner. In either case, you can improve your touch keyboarding techniques,

speed, and control to input letters, figures, and symbols. The better your keying skills are, the more quickly you will be able to input information into your computer. After all, you don't want to spend any more time than is needed to key documents, such as a short story for school. You will use *Microsoft Word* in this unit to learn or improve keying skills.

Unit 3 Alternative Input Technologies

In this unit, you will learn some new ways to input information into a computer. Using speech recognition, you can talk and have your computer type for you. In many instances, you can dictate faster than you can key. You will find that speech recognition is an important input skill to learn, practice, and apply. Handwriting recognition, another important input skill, will allow you to input data simply by using your own handwriting. You can also take notes and draw using handwriting tools. Other input technologies, such as scanners and digital cameras, are covered in this unit. You will also learn about handheld computers, called PDAs, and smart phones in this unit.

Unit 4 Word Processing, Desktop Publishing, and Document Formatting

In Unit 4, you will learn to prepare attractive documents such as reports, letters, tables, and newsletters using *Microsoft Word*. As you complete this unit, you will become skilled with word processing, desktop publishing, and formatting documents. You will also learn to use your e-mail software in this unit.

Unit 5 Computer Applications

The goal of this unit is to acquaint you with *PowerPoint*, *Excel*, and *Access*. These are the names of the presentation, spreadsheet, and database programs you will learn to use in this unit. You will also learn to create Web pages in Unit 5.

Chapter Organization

Each chapter contains chapter objectives, an introduction that tells you what the chapter is about, lessons with illustrations and activities, and end-of-chapter activities. Each lesson also contains objectives to guide your learning.

In some lessons, you will use data files. Data files contain additional instructions or documents that you are to complete. All data files needed for a lesson are listed at the beginning of the lesson.

Activities are placed throughout the lessons to help you learn, practice, and apply the concepts presented in the chapter. New learning is presented with step-by-step instructions in the *Learn* activities. Practice of new learning, with some detailed instructions or reminders, is provided in the *Practice* activities. In the *Apply* activities, only general instructions are provided. These activities allow you to apply the skills and knowledge you have learned.

Various message boxes, Help Words, and icons appear along the left side of pages in the textbook. Instant Messages and Software Tips provide information related to the lesson. Help Words are words or terms that you can enter into the Help search feature of a software program. This lets you find additional information provided by the program's Help feature. Technique Tips and Spacing Tips appear along the left side of the page in lessons or activities that relate to keyboarding. These tips give you important information and reminders. Icons alert you to watch for certain instructions in an activity.

The disc icon tells you that you will need to use data files to complete an activity.

The Internet icon tells you that you will need to access the Internet to complete an activity.

The teamwork icon tells you that you will work in a team to complete an activity.

At the end of each chapter, you will apply what you have learned by answering review questions and completing additional activities. Beginning in Chapter 6, you will build keyboarding skill by completing drills and timed writings. At the end of each chapter, you will also study some important topics in sections titled:

- About Business
- Career and Life Skills Success Builder
- Academic Success Builder

A Web site related to this textbook is available at http://c21ji.swlearning.com. On this site, you can access data files, vocabulary flash cards, games, and slides that review chapter concepts, supplemental activities, reference materials, and links to other Web sites. The items available for each chapter are listed in the Web Resources box at the beginning of each chapter.

Learning to work with others in a team is an important skill.

Begin Your Adventure

You may discover that you already know something about the technologies you will study. Share your knowledge with those around you so that everyone can succeed together. As you learn more, you will become more self-confident. You will soon be applying your new skills in exciting ways. Remember, always take the next step. Soon, you will be surprised at how much you have achieved and how far you have journeyed.

Contents

UNIT 1
Digital Communication Tools

Chapter 1 **Computer Basics**
Chapter 2 **Finding and Managing Information**
Chapter 3 **Computers and Society**

Computers are an important part of the world around us. People use computers every day to get their work done. They are used to communicate with friends and family. They also play an important role in entertainment.

In Unit 1, you will learn basic information about computers and how they work. You will learn to find and manage data using computers. You will also learn about some of the effects computers have on society.

The activities provided at the end of each chapter will help you:

↗ Review the concepts you have learned

↗ Apply the software skills you have learned

↗ Learn about business trends and issues

↗ Improve math and communication skills

↗ Develop career-related skills

Developing your interviewing skills is critical to your success. So how do you prepare for an interview? You need to know your skills, and you need to practice answering typical interview questions.

In this activity, you will research and develop a list of interview questions. Then, you will practice your interview skills in a mock interview. With two additional classmates, you will have the opportunity to be an interviewer, interviewee, and evaluator. Each of you will play each role.

1. Open *CD-C17-Instructions*. Read the instructions for conducting the mock interview. Use the data files *CD-C17-Questions* and *CD-C17-Evaluation* to complete this exercise.

2. Remember to include a sample of your best work from this chapter in your portfolio.

↗ Academic Success Builder

STUDENT ORGANIZATIONS: WEB PAGE CREATION Organizations such as FBLA's Middle Level Achievement Program have competitive events for students. One competitive event is Web page creation. Students in this event use Web design software or HTML to create a Web site. The topic for the Web site is usually assigned by the organization. Other requirements for the Web site may be given. For example, a Web site with two or more pages and at least one working link may be required.

Web sites are often judged against criteria such as the following:

- Overall appeal—Does it gain and hold the attention of your audience?
- Layout—Are the format, text, colors, and graphics used readable, appropriate, and appealing?
- Navigation—Are the links appropriate, functional, and logical?

In this activity, you will practice skills needed to create a Web site. These skills will help you do well in a competitive event.

1. Plan a Web site with two or more pages. The Web site topic should relate to the student club used for your slide show in the Academic Success Builder for Chapter 14 on p. 511. The Web site should promote the club and its activities. The audience for the Web site is middle school students.

2. Create the Web site. Include at least one link and an appropriate graphic in the Web pages. Use appropriate folder names and filenames for the site.

Chapter 1

Lessons 1–4

Computer Basics

OBJECTIVES

In Chapter 1, you will:

↗ Learn how computers communicate with machines, people, and groups.

↗ Explore hardware and software.

↗ Explore and use a computer's operating system.

↗ Use a login name and password.

↗ Open and close programs and save files.

↗ Use Help to find information about software.

↗ Use basic commands and enter text in *Microsoft Word*.

↗ Apply acceptable use rules.

President John F. Kennedy had an idea. His dream would challenge everyone's imaginations. On May 25, 1961, he asked scientists to build a spacecraft. The ship had to carry people to the moon and bring them home safely.

Such a trip would require a computer. A **computer** is a machine that follows a set of instructions to change and store data. However, the computer needed to do the job didn't exist in 1961! It had to be invented. That computer cost $150,000 to make. However, it was far less powerful than today's cell phones. Would you trust your life to such a weak computer in deep space?

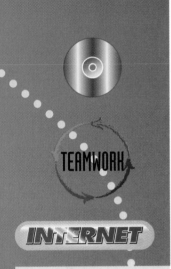

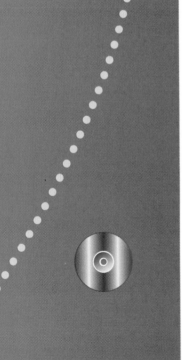

Data Files

- CD-C17-Business
- CD-C17-Instructions
- CD-C17-Questions
- CD-C17-Evaluation

↗ About Business

U.S. WORKERS AND THE WORLD ECONOMY Have you ever thought about how events around the world can affect workers in the United States? In Chapter 3, you learned that many U.S. companies compete in the global marketplace. These companies and their U.S. workers are affected by changes in the global economy. For example, developing countries, such as China, Brazil, and Mexico, now allow U.S. companies to export more goods to their countries than in the past. To **export** means to send goods to another country for sale there. This can create jobs for U.S. workers who make products for export. However, if the economy in countries where U.S. goods are sold becomes weak, these countries may not purchase as many U.S. goods. Some U.S. workers who produce goods for export may lose their jobs.

NAFTA (North American Free Trade Agreement), which was enacted in 1994, has made moving goods between the U.S., Canada, and Mexico easier. Some U.S. companies now sell more products in Canada and Mexico. This benefits U.S. workers by creating more job opportunities. However, some goods that were produced in the U.S. are now produced in plants owned by U.S. companies in Canada or Mexico. Some U.S. workers may lose jobs as production of goods moves to another country.

Many companies from foreign countries have plants that make goods in the U.S. This creates jobs for U.S. workers. The goods produced may be sold in the U.S. and other countries. If sales of these goods decline, the company's U.S. workers may be laid off or lose their jobs. This is another example of how the world economy affects U.S. workers.

1. Work with a classmate to complete this activity. Start *Word*. Open *CD-C17-Business* from the data files.

2. Follow the instructions in the file to research a foreign company that makes goods and employs workers in the U.S.

↗ Career and Life Skills Success Builder

INTERVIEWING SKILLS Imagine that after years of going to school, researching a career plan, and developing skills, the time has come to apply for a job. You develop your resume, apply for the job, and get called for an interview. You arrive for the interview on time in your new suit. You shake hands with the interviewer. When the first question is asked, you freeze! You can be the best, most-qualified person for a position. However, if you don't interview well, you probably won't get the job.

Digital image © 1996 CORBIS; Original image courtesy of NASA/CORBIS

This computer had important work to do. The *Apollo 11* spaceship would reach the moon on July 20, 1969. It would release a lunar module called the *Eagle*. The computer would need to land the *Eagle* within a few feet of a selected spot on the moon. The computer also had to calculate the use of fuel. The ship could not carry enough fuel for a second try. The landing was a success. With less than 30 seconds of fuel remaining, the *Eagle* landed.

The *Eagle* had a very primitive computer. Still, it helped fulfill President Kennedy's dream of landing on the moon. Imagine what today's powerful computers can do for your ideas and dreams!

Keypad Practice

Use the *Calculator* program to complete the problems shown below.

Drill 1 Addition

A	B	C	D	E
381	495	567	308	820
+ 620	+ 207	+ 498	+ 122	+ 467
1,001	702	1,065	430	1,287

Drill 2 Subtraction

A	B	C	D	E
590	817	908	760	514
- 359	- 264	- 324	- 429	- 238
231	553	584	331	276

Drill 3 Multiplication

A	B	C	D	E
90	24	87	89	406
x 13	x 56	x 21	x 30	x 52
1,170	1,344	1,827	2,670	21,112

Drill 4 Division

A	B	C	D	E
40.33	145	92.75	133	91.33
15/605	27/3,915	40/3,710	52/6,916	30/2,740

Speed Building

Key a 2' timed writing on the two paragraphs. Determine *gwam*.

 all letters used

	gwam 2'
When saying hello to someone is the correct	4
thing to do, make direct eye contact and greet the	10
person with vitality in your voice. Do not look	14
down or away or speak only in a whisper. Make the	20
person feel happy for having seen you, and you	24
will feel much better about yourself.	28
Similarly, when you shake hands with another	32
person, look that person in the eye and offer a	37
firm but not crushing shake of the hand. Just a	42
firm shake or two will do. Next time you meet a	47
new person, do not puzzle over whether to shake	52
hands. Quickly offer your hand with confidence.	57

gwam 2' | 1 | 2 | 3 | 4 | 5 |

Lesson 1

Computers as Digital Communication Tools

Objectives

In Lesson 1, you will:

⬇ Learn how computers help us communicate with machines, each other, and groups.

⬇ Learn about the main parts of information processing.

⬇ Explore and discuss hardware.

⬇ Learn about two types of software.

Communicating with Computers

Learning to use computers can help you share information with others. Computer skills can help you work with imagination. They will also help you with your schoolwork. If you need to create or share a message, chances are a computer can help!

Computers help people communicate with machines, with another person, and with groups. The list below gives some examples:

- Computers guide vehicles that explore the land on Mars.
- Computers control lighting, air-conditioning, and security systems in buildings.
- Cell phones have computers that allow users to make calls, store phone numbers, and send text messages.
- Musicians use computers to share music with fans.
- Animated films such as *Finding Nemo* and *Shrek* are created using computers.
- Movies can be viewed on computers, video game consoles, or DVD players.

Stockdisc

Figure 1.1 Computers in cell phones make them powerful DigiTools.

Building Keying Skill

Warmup Practice

Key each line twice. If time permits, key the lines again.

Alphabet

1 Jack Vance helped Maryann with six bags of quartz.

Figure/Symbol

2 Orlando paid $35,690 on Account #84917 on June 23.

Speed

3 Pamela may go visit with the neighbor by the lake.

gwam 1' | 1 | 2 | 3 | 4 | 5 | 6 | 7 | 8 | 9 | 10 |

Improve Keying Technique

Key each line twice. If time permits, key the lines again.

SPACE BAR

1 it is be no box zap six ace save nice make ill joy
2 up in to and tax yes help gone face down quit were

Shift keys

3 Rio de Janeiro; Port of Spain; Mount Saint Helens;
4 Jan and Seth left on Monday to go to Mt. Rushmore.

Adjacent keys

5 union open oil cash here wet where brass part bids
6 Wes Marti was the last guy to weigh before dinner.

Long direct reaches

7 my ice any run sum nut gum hut many curb vice nice
8 Bob Cox broke my record to receive a bronze medal.

Word response

9 girl down coal held paid land rush odor iris hands
10 Pamela may wish to make a bid for their auto maps.

gwam 1' | 1 | 2 | 3 | 4 | 5 | 6 | 7 | 8 | 9 | 10 |

Discuss Computers and Communication

Discuss with your class or team how people use computers. How do they use computers to communicate with machines? with individuals? with groups? List three examples of each.

DigiTools

Computers are digital communication tools—called DigiTools for short. **Digital devices** are those that share data in electronic form (streams of the digits 1 and 0). The physical parts of a computer are called **hardware**. The computer case, keyboard, mouse, and monitor are examples of hardware.

Software gives instructions to a computer. Word processing and drawing programs are examples of software. Software is also called *programs* or *applications*. The hardware and software work together to allow you to process data and to communicate.

Information Processing

A primary use of computers is processing information. **Information processing** means putting facts or numbers into a meaningful form. Information processing has five main parts: input, processing, output, distribution, and storage.

- **Input** refers to the way you give data to a computer. You might use a keyboard or drawing tablet to input data.

- **Processing** refers to how data is changed or used. You might add numbers, sort a list of names, or change the color of a drawing. These are all examples of processing.

- **Output** refers to the way you get data from a computer. You might print a letter or view photos on a monitor.

- **Distribution** refers to sending information to the people who need it. For example, you might post information about a school event on the school web site.

- **Storage** refers to saving the data for later use. You might store data on a floppy disk, on a CD, or on the computer's hard drive.

Applying

What You Have Learned

Create a Web Page Using Excel

Work in a team with two or three classmates to complete this activity. You will use your *Excel* skills to create a spreadsheet about the Apollo missions.

1. Brainstorm ideas with your teammates for a spreadsheet about the Apollo missions. For example, your team may wish to compare the six lunar landings. Your spreadsheet could include data such as the:

   * Number of astronauts on each trip

   * Amount of time spent on the lunar surface

   * Amount of material collected on the surface

   * Time spent in space travel to and from the moon

2. Access the Internet. Research the Apollo missions and find data suitable for the spreadsheet you have decided to create. Do your research with your team.

3. Use your collective imaginations to design the spreadsheet. Enter the data you have found.

4. Save the file as a Web page in the *myapollo17* folder. Use an appropriate page title. Name the file *webpage13*.

5. View the page in a browser. Open the file again in *Excel* to make corrections, if needed. Remember to save the updated file.

Update Web Pages

1. Start *Notepad*. Open the *index.html* file from the *myapollo17* folder.

2. Add a link to the *webpage13* file. Be sure to use the correct file extension. Save the *index* page using the same name. View the page in a browser and test the link. Make corrections, if needed.

3. Open each Web page file that you created a link to on the *index* page. On each Web page, create a link that will take users to the *index* page.

Supplemental activities for this chapter can be found at www.c21jr. swlearning.com.

Relate Information Processing to E-mail

When you create and send an e-mail message, you may do all the steps of information processing described. Match the tasks listed below with the information processing steps.

a. input   ___ 1. Viewing the message you have created on the screen

b. processing   ___ 2. Keying the message

c. output   ___ 3. Saving a copy of the message in your Sent folder

d. distribution   ___ 4. Using the Send feature to send the message

e. storage   ___ 5. Formatting the message in a large type size

✓ CHECK POINT Exchange papers with a classmate and discuss your answers.

Hardware

Only in the last 10 to 15 years have computers become part of our daily lives. Early computers were too large and expensive to be used by most people. Early computers were also very slow compared to modern computers. Today, computers come in a variety of shapes and sizes. Figure 1.2 shows six very different DigiTools in different styles.

Courtesy of Suunto

SPOT Wristwatch (with internal computer)

Courtesy of palmOne Inc.

Handheld computer

Courtesy of palmOne Inc.

Smart phone

Tablet PC

Hewlett-Packard

Hewlett-Packard

Laptop PC

Hewlett-Packard

Desktop PC

Figure 1.2 DigiTools come in a variety of sizes.

Reviewing *What You Have Learned*

Answer these questions to review what you have learned in Chapter 17.

1. Who invented the World Wide Web?

2. In what year was the early Web browser *Netscape* introduced? What did this mean for the Web?

3. What is the difference between a Web page and a Web site?

4. What is the purpose of a hyperlink on a Web page?

5. What is the code or language used to create Web pages called?

6. What symbols are used to enclose HTML tags?

7. What is a file extension?

8. What dialog box can users access to display file extensions?

9. What file extension can you use for a Web page that you create using *Notepad*?

10. What HTML tag begins a new line in a Web page?

11. What pair of HTML tags is used to place a title for a Web page in the title bar of a browser?

12. Nested HTML tags are arranged how?

13. What two pairs of tags are used to create a bulleted list?

14. An anchor tag is used to create what feature on a Web page?

15. What three parts are needed for a color tag?

16. What type of computer interface displays pictures, icons, and other images?

17. Why should you use graphic files that are compressed or small in size for a Web page?

18. Describe how to save a picture displayed on a Web page to the computer's hard drive.

19. What commands can be used in *Word* to save a *Word* document as a Web page?

20. Give three examples of Web page creation programs.

Computers are also found in other devices. Televisions, DVD players, digital cameras, microwave ovens, and cars have them. All of these tools are also considered DigiTools.

Personal Computers

As you study this book, you will probably use some type of personal computer. A **personal computer** (PC) is a small computer designed for an individual user. The PC may be a desktop model, a laptop, or a Tablet PC. You may also use a handheld computer for some activities.

At the center of every computer is a microprocessor. A **microprocessor** is a small circuit board that controls all work done by the computer. It is found inside the computer case. In PCs, it is commonly called the *CPU*, which stands for *central processing unit*. Examine the parts of a typical desktop PC in Figure 1.3. Do you have all of these parts in your computer system?

1C LEARN: Survey Your Computer System

1. Study the typical computer system shown in Figure 1.3. Then study the computer system you will use for this class.

2. List the parts of your computer system.

3. What parts do you have in your system that are not shown in Figure 1.3?

4. What parts are shown in Figure 1.3 that are not in your system?

Figure 1.3 Parts of a Desktop Personal Computer

```
<P><B>Web Site Index </B></P>
<A HREF="webpage7.html">Mission Overview</A><BR>
<A HREF="webpage8.html">Photo Gallery</A><BR>
<A HREF="webpage9.mht">Astronaut Bio, Cernan</A><BR>
<A HREF="webpage10.mht">Astronaut Bio, Evans</A><BR>
<A HREF="webpage11.mht"> Astronaut Bio, Schmitt
</A><BR>
<A HREF="webpage12.mht">Apollo 17 Slide Show</A><BR>
</BODY>
</HTML>
```

2. Save the file in the *myapollo17* folder as *index.html*.

3. Start your Web browser and open the *index.html* file. Try each link. Do they all work? Open the file in *Notepad* and make corrections if needed.

Web Creation Programs

Several programs for designing and creating Web sites are available. Some of the most popular ones are *Macromedia Dreamweaver*, *Adobe GoLive*, and *Microsoft FrontPage*. These programs eliminate the time-consuming task of entering HTML tags. They also contain tools for designing the structure and links among Web pages. In *FrontPage*, you can view both the HTML code and a preview of the Web page. If you are very interested in designing and creating Web pages, you may want to learn to use a Web page creation program.

Figure 17.16 Web Page Displayed in *FrontPage*

Peripherals

A computer can't do everything by itself! It needs help. Many DigiTools can connect to a computer. Other devices that can work with your computer are called **peripherals**. Printers, digital tablets, and scanners are examples of these devices.

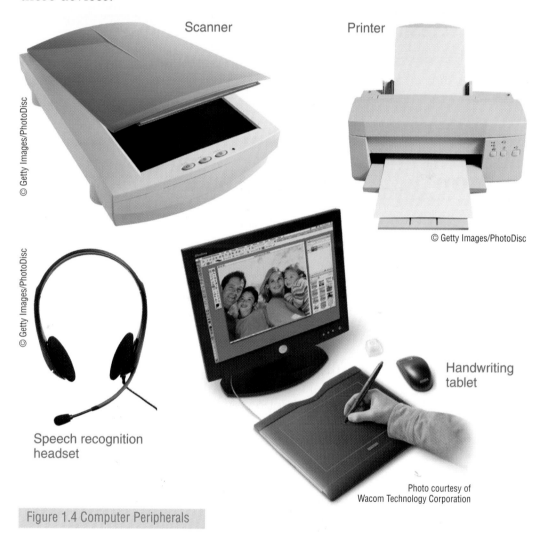

Scanner

Printer

© Getty Images/PhotoDisc

© Getty Images/PhotoDisc

© Getty Images/PhotoDisc

Speech recognition headset

Handwriting tablet

Photo courtesy of Wacom Technology Corporation

Figure 1.4 Computer Peripherals

1D APPLY:

Discuss DigiTools

1. Discuss with your class or team different DigiTools. Which ones do you know about? Which ones have you used? Have you seen anyone use the following devices: smart phone, desktop PC, laptop PC, Tablet PC?

2. Have you used tools such as a scanner, speech headset, writing tablet, or digital camera? If yes, describe the work or activity you did.

Create a Web Page Using Excel

1. Start *Excel*. Open *presidents* from the data files. You created a file similar to this in Chapter 15.

2. To save the file, choose **File** from the menu bar. Choose **Save as Web Page**. Create a new folder named *mypresidents*. Choose the new *mypresidents* folder in the Save in box.

3. Enter an appropriate title for the page. Name the file *mypresidents*. *Excel* will automatically add the file extension. Click **Save**.

4. Close *Excel*. Start your Web browser and open the *mypresidents* file. The file extension will likely be .mht. Close the browser after viewing the page.

> **Help Words**
>
> Web page
>   Put *Excel* data on a
>   Web page

Lesson 125 — Linking Web Pages

Objectives

In Lesson 125, you will:
↘ Create an index Web page.
↘ Link related Web pages to create a Web site.

Linking Web Pages to Create a Web Site

In the previous lessons, you have created several Web pages about the Apollo missions. You have learned a lot about using HTML tags. However, you do not have a Web site. To create a Web site, you must link your pages. This can be done in several ways. An easy way is to create an index page with links to other pages you have created.

125A PRACTICE:

Create an Index Web Page

> **SOFTWARE TIP**
>
> Make sure you know the exact filename and file extension for each file. It may be htm, html, mht, or mhtml.

1. Start *Notepad*. Enter the following text and tags as shown below:

```
<HTML>
<HEAD>
<TITLE> Apollo 17 Mission Log Index </TITLE>
</HEAD>
<BODY BGCOLOR= WHITE TEXT=BLUE LINK=RED VLINK=GREEN>
<A HREF="http://www.nasa.gov/"><IMG
SRC="images/title.gif" WIDTH="627" HEIGHT="148"> </A>
<HR>
```

Lesson 125   Linking Web Pages   613

Software

Computers need instructions to work properly. These instructions are called software. Software tells the computer hardware what to do. For example, if you play a video game, the game console is hardware. The game you are playing is a software program.

Do you write e-mail? Do you send instant messages? Do you visit web sites? If the answer is yes, you are already using software.

Source: http://www.nasa.gov.

Figure 1.5 *Internet Explorer* is browser software that lets you access web sites.

You will use two types of software: an operating system and application programs. **Operating system** software controls basic operations of the computer. It also allows the computer to use other types of software. You will learn more about operating system software in Lesson 2.

Application programs help you perform tasks. Word processing and drawing programs are examples of these programs. You will learn to use application programs in Lesson 3 and in many other lessons in this book.

4. Close *PowerPoint*. Start your Web browser and open the *mystates* file. The file extension will likely be .mht.

5. An outline of the slide show will appear at the left of the window as shown in Figure 17.15. The first slide will appear at the right of the window.

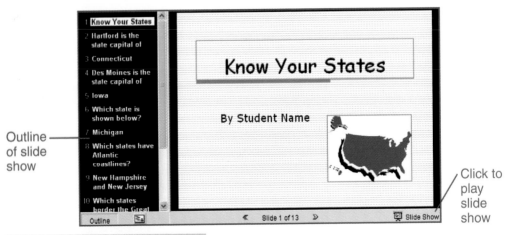

Outline of slide show

Click to play slide show

Figure 17.15 Slide Show Web Page

6. Click the **Slide Show** button to play the show. Click the mouse to progress through the slides. Close the browser after viewing the slides.

124E APPLY:

Create a Slide Show for the Web

In this activity, you will use your *PowerPoint* skills to create a slide show about the *Apollo 17* mission.

1. Access the Internet. Research *Apollo 17* using the NASA site or other Web sites.

2. Use *PowerPoint* to create a slide show about the *Apollo 17* mission. Limit the length of your slide show to 10 to 15 slides. Add graphics and format the slides for an attractive presentation.

3. Save the file as a Web page in the *myapollo17* folder. Name the file *webpage12*. *PowerPoint* will automatically add the file extension (.mht or .mhtml).

4. View the pages in a browser. Open the file again in *PowerPoint* to make corrections if needed. Remember to save the updated file.

Software Uses

You can often guess the uses of a program from its name. Six commonly used programs are listed below. Match the program name with its use. Your teacher will tell you the correct answers.

a. *Microsoft Word*   ___ 1. Accounting program

b. *Microsoft FrontPage*   ___ 2. Drawing program

c. *Solitaire*   ___ 3. Web browser

d. *Paint*   ___ 4. Word processing

e. *Internet Explorer*   ___ 5. Web page creation

f. *QuickBooks*   ___ 6. Popular game

Lesson 2   Operating System and Login Basics

Objectives

In Lesson 2, you will:

⇘ Learn about the role of an operating system.

⇘ Log into your computer with a login name and password.

⇘ Change your password.

⇘ Study the parts of the typical operating system desktop.

⇘ Turn off or restart your computer properly.

Operating Systems

An operating system (OS) is the most important software on a computer. The OS controls the hardware. It turns your instructions into the numbers the computer hardware understands. The OS also makes it possible to run other types of software. The OS will give you important messages about your computer. It may remind you to save before you turn off the computer. It may ask you to choose between several available printers. The OS may also ask you to enter your password. You will learn to use an operating system called *Microsoft Windows*. It is a commonly used OS.

Login Names and Passwords

Before you can use your computer, you may need to know your login name and password. A **login name** is a series of letters and/or numbers that identify you to the computer. A **password** is a series of letters and/or

3. Insert the picture of Eugene Cernan found in the *images* folder. The file is named *cernan.jpg*.

4. Save the file as a Web page in the *myapollo17* folder. Name the file *webpage9*. *Word* will automatically add the file extension. Close *Word*.

5. Start your Web browser and open *webpage9*. The file extension will likely be .mht (*webpage9.mht*).

CHECK POINT How does your page look? If you are not satisfied with the appearance, open the file in *Word* and make changes. Then save the file again.

124C APPLY: Research and Create Biographical Web Pages

1. Two astronauts besides Eugene Cernan were on the *Apollo 17* mission. Research their names and personal histories on the Internet. Begin your research at the NASA Web site. (Pictures of both men can be found in the *images* folder, but you must learn their names before you can find the proper files.)

2. Prepare two biographical Web pages, one for each astronaut, using *Word*. Use the information you find about each astronaut to prepare their biographies. You must do your own original writing.

3. Save your two astronaut biographies using the File, Save as Web Page commands. Use the filenames *webpage10* and *webpage11*. Save the files in the *myapollo17* folder. View the pages in a browser. Make corrections if needed.

124D LEARN: Create a Slide Show for the Web

1. Start *PowerPoint*. Open *states* from the data files. You created a file similar to this in Chapter 14.

2. To save the file, choose **File** from the menu bar. Choose **Save as Web Page**. Create a new folder named *states*. Choose the new *states* folder in the Save in box.

3. Name the file *mystates*. *PowerPoint* will automatically add the file extension. Click **Save**.

numbers that you enter to gain access to a computer. Login names and passwords provide security for your computer.

Just like a traffic cop checks a driver's license when making a traffic stop, your OS will check for your login and password. *Windows* will guide you through the login process. *Windows* will warn you if you log in improperly.

Login names and passwords are often assigned by your school. Sometimes, you will be allowed to invent your own. At home, you may be able to create your own login name and password. Passwords protect your data, files, pictures, e-mail, and other information from use by others. Your password is your main security device. Follow these rules related to passwords:

- Keep your password secure. Never share your passwords with your friends. Only a parent or teacher should know your passwords.

- Respect others. Do not ask them for their passwords.

- Don't sneak someone's password, even as a prank. Using another person's assignments and password is not right.

- Think of a password that you will remember. However, don't make your password too long. The more letters or numbers it has, the greater the chance for errors.

- Don't create a password that someone can guess easily. For example, don't use your first name or your birthday.

2A LEARN: Log In to Your Computer

Instant Message

If your computer is on a network or has an older version of *Windows*, your login steps may be different. Follow your teacher's directions to log in.

1. Learn your login name and password from your teacher.

2. Turn on your computer. It may take a few seconds to warm up. After it does, you will normally see a welcome screen. See Figure 1.6. Your welcome screen may look a little different. However, the login steps are similar on most computers.

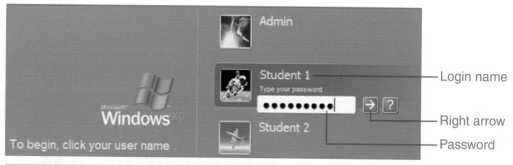

Figure 1.6 A Typical *Windows* Welcome Screen

Save a Word File as a Web Page

1. Start *Word*. Open *election* from the data files. You created a file similar to this in Chapter 13.

2. To save the file, choose **File** from the menu bar. Choose **Save as Web Page**. Create a new folder named *election*. Choose the new *election* folder in the Save in box as shown in Figure 17.14.

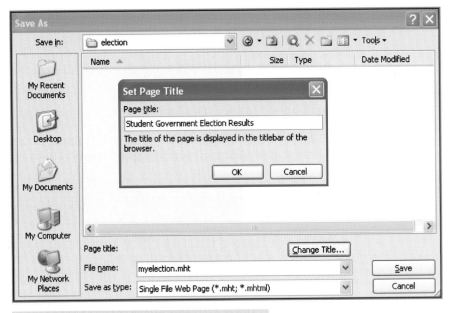

Figure 17.14 Set the Page Title for a Web Page

3. Name the file *myelection*. *Word* will automatically add the file extension.

4. Click the **Change Title** button. For the page title, key **Student Government Election Results**. Click **OK**. Click **Save**. You may see a message telling you that the formatting of some graphics will be changed. Click **Continue**.

5. Close *Word*. Start your Web browser and open the *myelection* file. The file extension will likely be .mht (*myelection.mht*). Close the browser after viewing the Web page.

Create an Astronaut Biography in Word

1. Start *Word*. Open the file *cernan* from your data files.

2. Using your *Word* skills, format the document. Use bold, centered text, bulleted lists, and any other techniques you have learned to create an attractive page.

3. Choose your login name from the list. (Or enter your login name as instructed.)

4. Enter your password (if required). Click or tap the right arrow to continue.

✓ CHECK POINT The *Windows* desktop should appear similar to Figure 1.7. If you have trouble with the login, ask your teacher for help.

Windows Desktop

After you log in, you will see the *Windows* computer interface. A **computer interface** is the means by which users get information and give commands to the computer. If the computer uses a text interface, users must type text to tell the computer what to do. *Windows* has a graphical user interface (GUI). This means that pictures, called icons, are used to stand for programs and commands. Users can start programs by selecting an icon. Users can give commands by clicking buttons or other options.

In *Windows*, the main screen for the computer interface is called the desktop. The **desktop** is an on-screen work area on which windows, icons, menus, and dialog boxes appear. You can start programs and give other commands from the desktop. Your desktop screen may look a little different from the one shown in Figure 1.7. However, there will be many similarities.

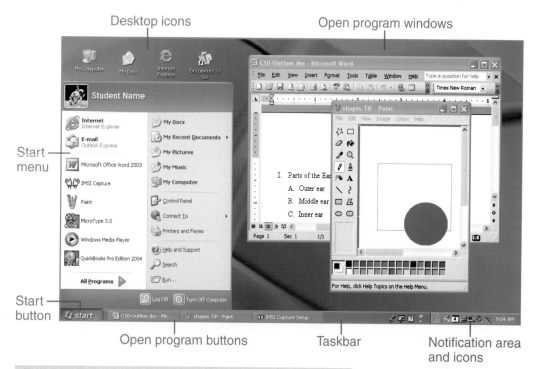

Figure 1.7 *Windows* Desktop, Start Menu, and Open Windows

```
<BODY BGCOLOR= WHITE TEXT=BLUE LINK=RED VLINK=GREEN>
<A HREF="http://www.nasa.gov/"><IMG
SRC="images/title.gif" WIDTH="627" HEIGHT="148"> </A>
<HR>
<H2>Photo Gallery</H2>
<IMG SRC="images/rover2.gif" WIDTH="300" HEIGHT="300">
<IMG SRC="images/rover3.gif" WIDTH="300" HEIGHT="300">
<IMG SRC="images/patch.gif" WIDTH="300" HEIGHT="300">
<IMG SRC="images/cm.gif" WIDTH="300" HEIGHT="300">
<IMG SRC="images/dig.gif" WIDTH="300" HEIGHT="300">
<IMG SRC="images/far.gif" WIDTH="300" HEIGHT="300">
</BODY>
</HTML>
```

3. Save the page in the *myapollo17* folder as *webpage8.html*. View the Web page in a browser. Make corrections to the file, if needed.

Lesson 124 — Creating Web Pages Using Word, Excel, and PowerPoint

Objectives

In Lesson 124, you will:
↘ Create Web pages using *Microsoft Word*.
↘ Create Web pages using *Microsoft PowerPoint*.
↘ Create Web pages using *Microsoft Excel*.

Data files: *election, cernan, states*

As the Web became more and more popular, a problem arose. As you know by now, it can take a lot of time to create a Web page using HTML tags. There are literally billions of documents on the Web. Many of these documents have been created in *Microsoft Word*, *Microsoft PowerPoint*, or *Microsoft Excel*. Can you imagine how much time it would take to individually add the HTML tags to each of these documents?

To solve this problem, in 1997 Microsoft added features to many of its software programs. For example, if you have a *Word* document, you can save it as a Web page. The Save As Web Page command is located on the File menu. You will use this feature to create Web pages.

Discover Your OS's Desktop

1. Turn on your computer and log in if you have not already done so.

2. Find the program and folder icons marked in Figure 1.7. Now look at your desktop. List the program or folder icons shown on your desktop.

3. Find the taskbar in Figure 1.7. The taskbar contains the Start button. It also contains buttons for open programs. To the right on the taskbar is the notification area. It also contains icons. Now look at your desktop. List all of the items that appear on your taskbar.

4. Find the Start button shown in Figure 1.7. Now look at your desktop and find the Start button. Click or tap the **Start** button. This will open the Start menu. The Start menu gives you quick access to several programs and documents.

5. You will learn to open programs from the Start menu in a later exercise. Click a blank area of the desktop to close the Start menu.

Turning Off Your Computer Properly

Turning off a computer in the proper way will help you avoid losing important information. When *Windows* shuts down, it does tasks such as:

- Close any open programs.
- Save any unsaved data.
- Close open connections to networks.
- Save your current settings.

To turn off your computer, you will choose Start from the taskbar. Then you will choose Turn Off Computer. You will have three choices. Read about the choices in the table below. Then complete activity 2C to turn off your computer.

Windows Turn Off Computer Options	
Restart	If others will be using the computer shortly after you, choose Restart. This will clear your login information. The computer will be ready for the next user.
Turn Off	If the computer is being shut down for the day, choose Turn Off.
Stand By	This option puts the computer in a mode that saves power. The computer may look as if it is turned off. However, when you press a key, the login screen will appear. This will let you take a break and quickly pick up where you left off. (This option is rarely used in class.)

123E PRACTICE: Turn a Graphic into a Link

In this activity, you will make the graphic at the top of the Web page a hyperlink to NASA.

1. Start *Notepad.* Open the *webpage6.html* file that you created earlier.

2. Place the anchor tag and NASA Web site address around the image tag as shown below.

```
<A HREF="http://www.nasa.gov/"><IMG
SRC="images/title.gif" WIDTH="627" HEIGHT="148"> </A>
```

3. Save the file in the *myapollo17* folder as *webpage7.html*. Close *Notepad.* Open *webpage7.html* in a browser.

4. Test the graphic link to see if it works. If not, open the file in *Notepad* and make corrections.

Instant Message

You may see a thin line around the graphic link. The LINK= and VLINK= attributes determine the color of the line.

123F APPLY: Copy Graphics to the Images Folder

You will need more graphics to use in the activities to follow. In this activity, you will copy graphics from the data files to your *myapollo17\images* folder.

1. Start *Windows Explorer.* Follow the path to the folder where the data files are stored. Open the *apollo17* folder and then the *images* subfolder.

2. Select all the graphics in this folder except *title.gif*. Copy these files to your *myapollo17\images* folder.

3. Close *Windows Explorer.*

Instant Message

Review how to copy files to another folder in Lesson 9C on page 57.

123G APPLY: Create a Photo Gallery Web Page

In this activity, you will use what you know about displaying graphics on a Web page to create a photo gallery. Use five or six NASA images stored in the *images* folder.

1. Start *Notepad.* Refer to the sample text and tags shown below as you create a new Web page.

2. Choose the images you want to use from the *images* folder. Insert the filenames for those images and appropriate height and width attributes in the file instead of the sample ones shown below and on the following page.

```
<HTML>
<HEAD>
<TITLE> Apollo 17 Mission Log </TITLE>
</HEAD>
```

Turn Off Computer

Your logoff screen may look different from this example. However, your logoff steps will be very similar.

1. Click or tap the **Start** button. Click **Turn Off Computer** as shown at the left in Figure 1.8.

Figure 1.8 Turn Off Computer Options

2. Click or tap **Turn Off** as shown on the right in Figure 1.8. Your computer should now shut down.

Lesson 3   Windows Program Basics

Objectives

In Lesson 3, you will:
- Learn the parts of a program window.
- Sharpen your mouse skills.
- Open and close programs.
- Use menus and toolbar buttons to give commands.
- Minimize, maximize, restore, and resize windows.
- Switch between open programs.

Program Windows

Windows opens programs in separate windows on the desktop. Open windows are similar to each other. As you read about window parts, refer to Figure 1.9 and look at your screen. These parts can be found in most open windows.

Displaying Images

Displaying graphics in Web pages is fairly simple. The image search tag can be used to find a graphic and display it on the page. The tag is < IMG >, the attribute is SRC, and the value is the name of the file. The WIDTH and HEIGHT attributes control the size of the image displayed on the page.

Tag or Attribute	Action
<IMG SRC="filename">	Displays an image on a Web page.
WIDTH="number"	Attribute that defines how many pixels wide a picture will be.
HEIGHT="number"	Attribute that defines how many pixels high a picture will be.

123D LEARN:

Insert Tags to Display Graphics

1. Start *Notepad*. Open the *webpage5.html* file that you created earlier.

2. Delete the segment of HTML code shown below:

```
<CENTER><H2><P>Apollo 17 Mission Log</P></H2></CENTER>
```

3. Place the image search tag between the body < BODY > and the horizontal rule < HR > tags. Key the tags as shown below in bold.

```
<BODY BGCOLOR=WHITE TEXT=BLUE LINK=RED VLINK=GREEN>
<IMG SRC="images/title.gif" WIDTH="627" HEIGHT="148">
<HR>
```

4. Save the file in the *myapollo17* folder as *webpage6.html*. Close *Notepad*. Open *webpage6.html* in a browser.

 **CHECK POINT** The graphic should look like the one shown in Figure 17.13. If it does not, open the file in *Notepad* and make corrections.

WIDTH="627" ——

HEIGHT="148" ——

Figure 17.13 Web Page with Title Graphic

Parts of a Program Window	
Title Bar	Tells the name of the program and may show the name of the open file
Menu Bar	Provides access to commands and options
Toolbar	Provides quick access to commands
Control Buttons	Controls size and look of program window (Minimize, Maximize, and Restore)
Scroll Bars	Allows you to move other parts of the file into the viewing area
Working Area	Allows you to enter or change data
Status Bar	Provides helpful messages
Resize Handle	Allows you to change the window size

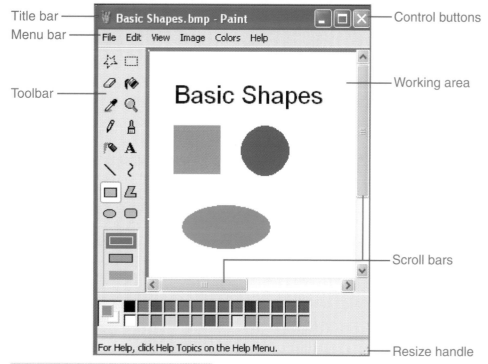

Figure 1.9 The *Paint* Open Window

Mouse Skills

The mouse is a hovering and pointing device. Just like a spaceship hovers above the surface of a planet, a mouse can hover on any part of the screen. After you move your mouse into position, you can use it to give commands.

The mouse has been the main pointing device on computers for many years. Today, many people use a digital pen in addition to a mouse. These pens are

3. Right-click the *Apollo 17* patch image at the top of the Web page. A pop-up window will appear. Different browsers have different commands. Pick the command that works for your browser. An example is shown in Figure 17.11. The command could be:

- Save Picture As
- Save Image As
- Download Image to Disk

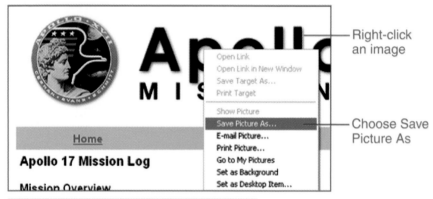

Figure 17.11 Save a Picture from a Web Page

4. The name of the graphic will automatically appear in the File name box as shown in Figure 17.12. Browse to the *images* folder and open it. Click the **Save** button. The file will be saved in the *images* folder. See Figure 17.12.

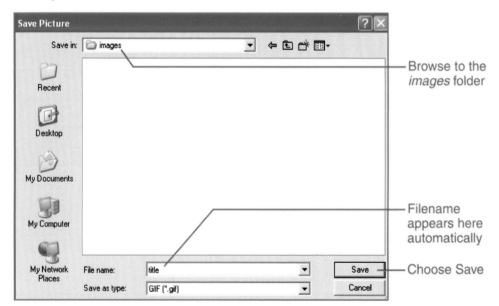

Figure 17.12 Save the file in the *images* folder.

used on Tablet PCs, PDAs, and digital tablets. Laptop users can also use trackpads. Fortunately, if you know how to use your mouse, pens and trackpads will be easier to learn. A typical mouse is shown in Figure 1.10.

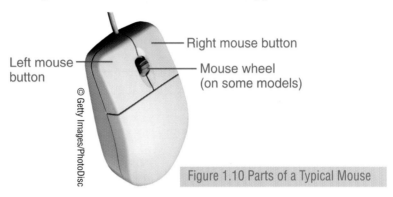

Figure 1.10 Parts of a Typical Mouse

To use a mouse, slide it over the surface of your desk or mouse pad. This way you can hover over any spot on the screen. After positioning the pointer, you can

- **Left-click.** Used to select something.
- **Double-click.** Often needed to open an application.
- **Click and drag.** Move windows and other objects around the screen.
- **Right-click.** Open pop-up menus.

The mouse pointer changes shape when you hover over different parts of a window. Each shape will give you a different clue. This clue will tell you what you can do while hovering on a certain spot. These shapes are also available for trackpad and digital pen users. Study the various mouse pointers in the table below. You will use your mouse as you open, close, and resize programs later in this lesson.

Instant Message

If your mouse pointer cannot be moved any farther, lift your mouse in the air. Move it backward a few inches. Place the mouse on the pad and continue.

Mouse and Pen Pointer Shapes	
⇖	**Arrow pointer.** Tells you where the mouse is located as you hover across the screen.
I	**Vertical bar.** Appears in areas where you can enter words or numbers.
⧖	**Hourglass.** Tells you to wait as *Windows* catches up and finishes following your instructions.
⬉	**Two-sided arrow.** Tells you when you're hovering over a resizing handle or window border. Click or tap and drag in and out to make a window bigger or smaller.
⬌	**Four-sided arrow.** Lets you know when you're hovering over an object that can be moved.
👆	**Pointing hand.** Appears where there is a link you can click.
✎	**Pen.** Used for handwriting recognition. When the pen appears, you can hand-type. (More information about this is given in Chapter 6.)

123B PRACTICE: Change Colors

In this activity, you will apply your skills to change the Web page colors to ones that will make the page easier to read.

1. Start *Notepad*. Open the *webpage4.html* file that you created earlier.

2. Change the background color to white, the text color to blue, the link color to red, and the visited link color to green. Use the attributes and values shown below.

```
<BODY BGCOLOR=WHITE TEXT=BLUE LINK=RED VLINK=GREEN>
```

3. Save the file in the *myapollo17* folder as *webpage5.html*. Close *Notepad*. Open *webpage5.html* in a browser. If the colors are not correct, open the file in *Notepad* again and make corrections.

Web Graphics and Folders

The World Wide Web uses a graphical user interface (GUI). A **graphical user interface** displays pictures, icons, and other images. It allows users to give commands and navigate by clicking the mouse or tapping a digital pen rather than by keying commands. In 1993, *Mosaic*, a browser with a GUI, started to attract a lot of attention. Today, browsers with a graphical user interface are common.

Graphics can make the difference between an exciting Web page and a dull one. Remember to use graphic files that are compressed or small in size as explained in Chapter 7. A compressed JPEG or GIF graphic will load faster on Web pages than uncompressed files like those in TIFF format. The graphics must also be placed in the correct folder.

123C LEARN: Save Images to a Special Folder

In this activity, you will create a new folder. Then you will save images to this new folder.

1. Start *Windows Explorer*. Open the *myapollo17* folder. Inside the *myapollo17* folder, create a new folder. For the new folder name, key **images**.

2. Start your browser. Use your Favorites list to open the *Apollo 17* Mission Log Web site. (Or choose **File**, **Open** and browse to the data files. Open the *apollo17* folder and the *index* file.)

Instant Message

See Lesson 6 on page 39 to review how to create folders.

Opening and Closing Programs

A program such as *Paint* can be opened in different ways. If the program has an icon on the desktop, you can click or tap the icon to open it. If the program is listed on the Start menu, you can click its name to open it. You can also open a program by choosing it from the All Programs list from the Start menu.

You can close an open program in different ways. You can click or tap the Close control button on the program window. You can choose Close from the Control menu. You can also choose a command such as Close or Exit from the program's menu bar. You will practice opening and closing programs in the following activities.

3A LEARN:

Open and Close Paint

1. Turn on your computer and log in. In the steps that follow, you will open the *Paint* program.

2. Click or tap the **Start** button on the taskbar. (See Figure 1.7 on page 12 to review the location of the Start button.)

3. Click or tap **All Programs**. Click or tap **Accessories**. Click or tap **Paint**. The *Paint* window should open and look similar to Figure 1.9 on page 15.

Figure 1.11 Start Menu Options to Open *Paint*

Instant Message

If you're using a digital pen, hover about ¼ inch above the surface of your tablet. Hover and pause over each part of the screen.

4. Look again at Figure 1.9 on page 15. On your screen, find all the parts of the *Paint* window that are marked in the figure.

5. Move your mouse or digital pen over the different parts of the *Paint* window. Watch carefully as the pointer changes shape. How many different mouse shapes do you see?

6. Point to different icons on the *Paint* toolbar. Hesitate for a few seconds over each tool icon. The name of each tool should appear on screen. In Figure 1.12 on page 18, the name of the Eraser tool is shown on screen.

7. Click the *Paint* window **Close** control button in the upper-right corner of the window to close the *Paint* program. See Figure 1.12 to find the Close button.

Use the attributes in the following table to change the various color options on a Web page.

Tag of Attribute	Action
<BODY insert attributes and values> </BODY>	Body tag. Contains attributes and values.
BGCOLOR=value	Background color attribute.
TEXT=value	Text color attribute.
LINK=value	Hypertext link color attribute.
VLINK=value	Visited hypertext link color attribute.

123A LEARN: Add Color to a Web Page

1. Start *Notepad*. Open the *webpage3.html* file that you created earlier.

2. Add the attributes and values to the open body tag exactly as shown below in bold.

`<BODY BGCOLOR=BLACK TEXT=YELLOW LINK=WHITE VLINK=BLUE>`

3. Save the file in the *myapollo17* folder as *webpage4.html*. Close *Notepad*. Open *webpage4.html* in a browser.

 **CHECK POINT** The *webpage4.html* file should look like Figure 17.10. If it does not, open the file in *Notepad* and make corrections.

Apollo 17 Mission Log

Mission Overview

- Launched with a Saturn V rocket on December 7, 1972.
- Landed on the moon on December 11, 1972.
- Lunar Module blasted from the moon on December 14, 1972.
- Linked up with the Command Module near midnight on December 15, 1972, and began the long trip home to Earth.
- Splashdown took place on December 19, 1972.
- Link to NASA.

Figure 17.10 Web Page with Color Changes

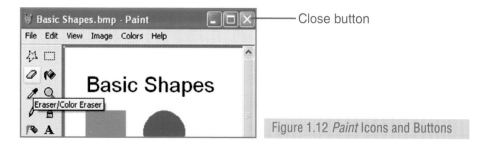

Close button

Figure 1.12 *Paint* Icons and Buttons

3B PRACTICE: Open and Close Notepad

Notepad is a simple program that allows users to enter and format text. In this activity, practice what you have learned about opening and closing programs.

1. Open *Notepad*. (Choose **Start**, **All Programs, Accessories, Notepad.**)

2. Look at the *Notepad* window. Which window parts shown in Figure 1.9 on page 15 are part of the *Notepad* window?

3. Close *Notepad* by clicking or tapping the window's **Close** control button.

CHECK POINT Did you locate the title bar, menu bar, and toolbar?

Using Menus and Toolbars

Most programs that work with *Windows* have a menu bar. The menu bar allows you to choose commands and options. To use the menu bar, click or tap an item on it. A list of options will appear. You can then click or tap the option you want.

The menu may appear at first with only a few items shown. Such a menu will have a double arrow (also called chevrons) at the bottom. You can click this arrow to see all the menu options. The *Microsoft Word* Help menu is shown in Figure 1.13.

Click chevrons to show full menu

Full menu

Figure 1.13 *Microsoft Word* Help Menu

Lesson 123 Adding Color and Graphics

Objectives

In Lesson 123, you will:
- Add color values and attributes to Web pages.
- Save graphics from Web pages.
- Display graphics in Web pages.
- Set height and width attributes for graphics in Web pages.

Data files: *index*, all files in the *myapollo17\images* folder

Adding Color to Web Pages

The first Web pages were a boring black and white. Now, however, Web page creators can use tags that allow browsers to display color. Tags can be used to control the background color of a page and the text color. There are three parts to a color tag:

1. The tag itself. The < BODY > < /BODY > tag is an example.

2. An attribute. An **attribute** is a characteristic you want the Web page to have. For example, if you want to change the background color, in the body tag you can add the attribute BGCOLOR, like this:
   < BODY BGCOLOR > .

3. A value. A **value** can be a number or a word assigned to an attribute. For example, you can change the background colors by using numbers or words to create the color you want, like this:
   < BODY BGCOLOR = WHITE > .

The following table lists common color values.

Color Values		
#FF0000	=	RED
#00FF00	=	GREEN
#0000FF	=	BLUE
#FFFFFF	=	WHITE
#000000	=	BLACK
#FFFF00	=	YELLOW

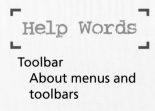

Help Words

Toolbar
    About menus and
    toolbars

Some menu items are followed by three dots. When you select one of these menu options, a dialog box will appear. A dialog box provides more information. It may allow you to make choices or enter data. If a menu item appears dimmed, you cannot choose that option.

Toolbars also allow you to give commands. Using a toolbar option is often faster than using the menu bar. However, the menu bar may give you more options. To use a toolbar, simply click a button on the bar. The *Microsoft Word* Standard toolbar is shown in Figure 1.14. You could click the Save button, which looks like a floppy disk, to save a document.

Figure 1.14 *Microsoft Word* Standard Toolbar

Moving and Changing the Size of Windows

Program windows can be made different sizes and placed in different areas of the screen. You may want to size or move windows when you have two or more programs open at once. To move a window, click the title bar and drag the window to where you want it. To resize a window, click and drag the resize handle in the bottom-right corner of the window. Look at Figure 1.17 on page 20 to see a resize handle.

You can also "hide" a window by sending it to the taskbar. This is called minimizing the window. When you minimize a window, the program is not closed. It is simply moved off the screen. You minimize a window by clicking its Minimize button. See Figure 1.15. To bring the window back to the screen, you can click the program name on the taskbar.

To make the window fill the entire screen, you can click the Maximize button. To restore a window to its previous size, you can click the Restore button. You will practice using these buttons in the next activity.

Minimize   Restore   Maximize   Close

Figure 1.15 Control Buttons

3C LEARN: Give Commands and Change Windows

1. Turn on your computer and log in if you have not already done so.

2. Start the *Paint* program. (Click **Start, All Programs, Accessories, Paint**.)

3. Save the file in the *myapollo17* folder as *webpage3.html*. Start your Web browser and open the *webpage3.html* file.

 **CHECK POINT** The Web page list should look similar to Figure 17.8. If it does not, open the file in *Notepad* and make corrections.

<H2> tags create heading ——

<CENTER> tags center —— text heading
<HR> tag creates a line ——
<B> tag creates bold text ——

<UL> and <LI> tags —— create a bulleted list

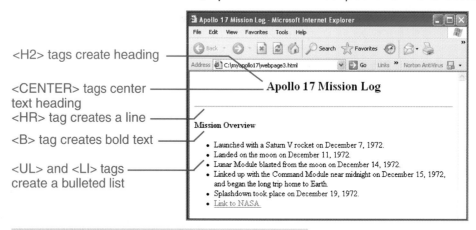

Figure 17.9 Web Page with Headings and Bulleted List

4. Click the **Link to NASA** link. The browser should access the NASA Web site. Close the browser.

122C PRACTICE: Create a Web Page

In this activity, you will create a Web page related to a camping trip for students.

1. Access the Internet. Use a search engine to find sites with information about camping safety. Make a note of the Web site address for the site you think is most appropriate for students.

2. Start *Notepad*. Using the *webpage3.html* document as a model, enter text and HTML tags to create a new Web page as directed below.

3. For the Web page title, key **Class Camping Trip**. Enter a horizontal rule below the main title.

4. Below the horizontal rule, key **Items to Pack** and make the text bold. Leave one blank line and begin a bulleted list. Enter five or more items that you think are appropriate to pack for a camping trip such as a sleeping bag, hiking boots, a jacket, or a swimsuit.

5. Below the bulleted list, key the text **Click here for camping safety information**. Make this text a link to the Web site you found that has camping safety information.

6. Save the file in a new folder named *camping*. For the filename, key *camping1.html*. Close *Notepad*. View the Web page in a browser. If you find errors or want to change the formatting, open the file in *Notepad* and make corrections.

3. Select (click or tap) the **Pencil** on the *Paint* toolbar. Use the pencil to write your first name.

4. Select (click or tap) **View** on the menu bar. Select **Zoom**. Select **Large Size**.

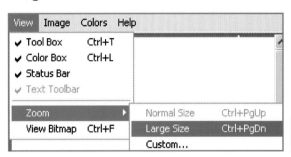

Figure 1.16 Select a command from the menu bar.

5. Click or tap the arrows on the scroll bar to view your name. Select **View** on the menu bar. Select **Zoom**. Select **Normal Size**.

6. Click the *Paint* title bar and drag the *Paint* window into the top right corner of your desktop.

7. Move your mouse or pen over the window's resize handle (in the bottom right corner). The pointer should change to a double arrow. See Figure 1.17. Click and drag the *Paint* window resize handle to resize the *Paint* window.

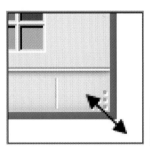

Figure 1.17 Drag the resize handle to change a window's size.

8. Click or tap the **Maximize** button. (See Figure 1.15 to locate the button.) The *Paint* window will become very large. It may cover nearly all of the screen.

9. Click or tap the **Restore** button. (See Figure 1.15 to locate the button.) The window will shrink back to its normal size.

10. Click or tap the **Minimize** button. (See Figure 1.15 to locate the button.) Look at the taskbar. The program name should appear on a button on the taskbar. Click or tap the **Paint** button on the taskbar. The window will appear on the screen.

untitled - Paint

Figure 1.18 A Minimized Program Button on the Taskbar

Adding Hyperlinks

Hyperlinks are an important feature of Web pages. They make it easy for the user to move to related material on the same page or on a different page. Hyperlinks are created with an anchor tag < A HREF = " " > < /A > . Look at this sample that links to the NASA Web site:

< A HREF = "http://www.nasa.gov/" > Link to NASA < /A >

The anchor tag allows the hypertext reference (HREF = "") to be inserted between the quotation marks. The reference is then anchored to the text. Clicking the text will take the user to the Web page indicated.

122B LEARN:

Create Headings, Bulleted Lists, and Hyperlinks

1. Start *Notepad* and open the *webpage2.html* file that you created earlier.

2. Delete all of the **< BR >** tags in the document. Add the tags shown below in bold.

```
<HTML>
<HEAD>
<TITLE>Apollo 17 Mission Log</TITLE>
</HEAD>
<BODY>
<CENTER><H2><P>Apollo 17 Mission Log</P></H2></CENTER>
<HR>
<B><P>Mission Overview </P></B>
<UL>
<LI> Launched with a Saturn V rocket on December 7,
1972.</LI>
<LI>Landed on the moon on December 11, 1972.</LI>
<LI>Lunar Module blasted from the moon on December 14,
1972.</LI>
<LI>Linked up with the Command Module near midnight on
December 15, 1972, and began the long trip home to
Earth.</LI>
<LI>Splashdown took place on December 19, 1972.</LI>
<LI><A HREF="http://www.nasa.gov/">Link to NASA.</A>
</LI>
</UL>
</BODY>
</HTML>
```

11. Now you will work with two open programs at once. Start the *Calculator* program. (Select **Start, All Programs, Accessories, Calculator**.)

12. Click the *Calculator* title bar and drag the window below the *Paint* window.

13. Maximize the *Paint* program. It should now cover the *Calculator* program.

14. You can work only in an active window. Only one window at a time can be active. To make the *Calculator* window active, click the **Calculator** button on the taskbar. To make the *Paint* program active, click the **Paint** button on the taskbar.

15. Now you will use a menu option to close a program. Make *Paint* the active window. Select **File** from the menu bar. Select **Exit**. Choose **No** if you are asked to save.

16. *Calculator* should now be the active window. Click the **Close** control button to close the program.

Lesson 4   Microsoft Word Basics

Objectives

In Lesson 4, you will:
- Give commands and enter text in *Word*.
- Open, save, and close files.
- Learn to use Help in *Word*.
- Print a document in *Word*.
- Discuss rules for acceptable computer use.

Data files: *CD-04-Word, CD-04-Acceptable Use, CD-C01-Practice*

Microsoft Word

Microsoft Word is a word processing program. You may use this program as you learn to key and to create reports and letters. The program window for *Word* has the window parts you learned about earlier. It also has some other parts you may not have seen before. For example, the status bar at the bottom of the screen tells you the page number. Rulers help you position text on the page. The parts of the *Word* window are marked in Figure 1.19 on page 22.

Headings and Bulleted Lists

The revised Web page *webpage2.html* is now easier to read. It is much more organized. However, it still isn't very interesting. Centered headings and a bulleted list would improve the page.

The center tag < CENTER > can be used to center text horizontally on the page. Heading tags, such as < H2 >, can be used to create a bold heading in a font that is larger than the body text. The bold tag < B > can be used to create bold text.

Notice that the tags in the first example below are nested. **Nested** means the tags are organized in pairs moving from the outside in. For example, the < CENTER > </CENTER > tags are on the outside. The < H2 > </H2 > tags come next. Then the < P > </P > are placed on both sides of the text. Look at these examples:

Example of correctly nested tags:

```
<CENTER><H2><P>Apollo 17 Mission Log</P></H2></CENTER>
```

Example of tags that are **not** correctly nested:

```
<CENTER><H2><P>Apollo 17 Mission Log</CENTER></P></H2>
```

Tags that create bulleted lists must also be nested properly. Bulleted lists start with the unordered list tag < UL >. Each item in the list is identified by list item tags < LI > < /LI > before and after the text. At the end of the list, the close unordered list tag < /UL > appears. Review the actions of tags listed in the following table.

Tag	Action
<CENTER> </CENTER>	Centers text and graphics on a Web page.
<H1> </H1> <H2> </H2> <H3> </H3> <H6> </H6>	The heading tag is used to create headings in documents. Makes text larger or smaller, depending on the number used.
<HR>	Creates a horizontal line, also called a horizontal rule. Tag is used alone, not as part of a pair.
<UL> <LI></LI> </UL>	Begins a bulleted (unordered) list. Marks the beginning and end of each item in a bulleted list. Ends a bulleted (unordered) list.
<B> </B>	Applies bold to text.

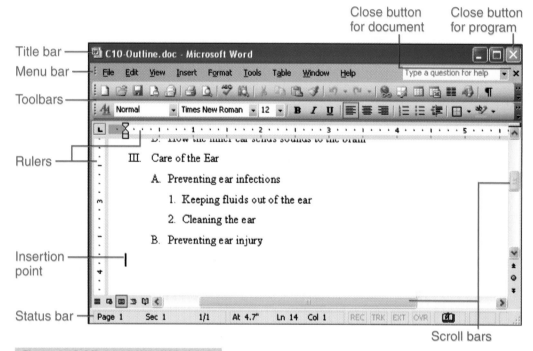

Close button for document

Close button for program

Title bar

Menu bar

Toolbars

Rulers

Insertion point

Status bar

Scroll bars

Figure 1.19 *Microsoft Word* Window

Instant Message

You will learn to key properly by touch in Chapter 4.

Entering Text

When you enter text using a keyboard, it is entered at the insertion point. In *Word* the insertion point appears as a vertical line. The insertion point is marked in Figure 1.19. When a line is full, the text will automatically move to the next line. This feature is called **wordwrap**. To begin a new paragraph, you must tap the ENTER key.

You can use the Show/Hide command to help you see when you have keyed spaces or pressed the ENTER key. Each space is shown as a dot on the screen. When you tap ENTER, a paragraph symbol (¶) appears. To display or hide formatting marks, you will click the Show/Hide button on the Standard toolbar. Showing these formatting marks on the screen can be helpful when you enter text.

4A LEARN: Enter Text in Word

1. Begin by starting the *Word* program. Select **Start, All Programs, Microsoft Office, Microsoft Office Word**. A new blank document should appear.

2. Click the **Show/Hide** button to show the formatting marks on the screen if they do not already appear. See Software Tip on page 23.

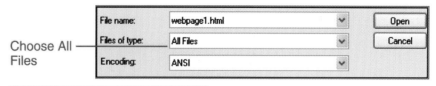

Choose All Files

Figure 17.7 Open a file in *Notepad*.

3. Add the tags and title text exactly as shown below in bold.

```
<HTML>
<HEAD>
<TITLE>Apollo 17 Mission Log</TITLE>
</HEAD>
<BODY>
<P>Apollo 17 Mission Log</P>

<P>Mission Overview</P>

Launched with a Saturn V rocket on December 7, 1972.<BR>
Landed on the moon on December 11, 1972.<BR>
Lunar Module blasted from the moon on December 14,
1972.<BR>
Linked up with the Command Module near midnight on
December 15, 1972, and began the long trip home to
Earth.<BR>
Splashdown took place on December 19, 1972.<BR>
Link to NASA.<BR>
</BODY>
</HTML>
```

4. Save the file in the *myapollo17* folder as *webpage2.html*. Close *Notepad*. Start your Web browser and open the *webpage2.html* file.

 **CHECK POINT** The *webpage2.html* page should look similar to Figure 17.8. If it does not, open the file in *Notepad* and make corrections.

Title appears in title bar

<P></P> tags create double spacing

 tags create single spacing

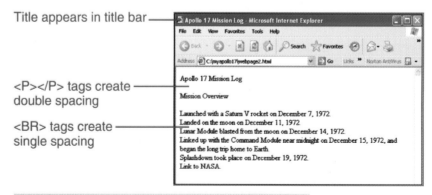

Figure 17.8 Web Page with Line and Paragraph Breaks

5. Close the browser.

3. Using your keyboard, key the text shown below. Press the SPACE BAR at the bottom of the keyboard to space between words. Hold down a SHIFT key as you tap another letter to make a capital letter. Tap ENTER at the end of a paragraph.

   ```
   Text is keyed in the program window.  To change or
   edit text, move the insertion point.
   ```

4. Now you will practice using the mouse and the arrow keys to move the insertion point. Move to just after *the* in line 1.

5. Tap the BACKSPACE key three times to delete the word. Key **a**.

6. Move to the end of the text. Tap the ENTER key four times. Key your first name.

7. Practice using the scroll bars and the PAGE UP and PAGE DOWN keys to move around in the document.

8. Close the document by selecting **File** and then **Close** from the menu bar. Select **No** if asked whether you want to save the document.

Saving and Opening Documents

You can save documents you create in *Word* to use again later. If you close a document without saving it, it will be lost. The first time you save a document, you must give it a filename. Filenames should give a clue about the content of the document. For example, a letter to Mr. Wilson might be named *Wilson Letter*.

The **Save As** command on the File menu is used to save a new document. You can also create a special folder in which to place your document using this command.

You can open a document that you or someone else has created earlier. The **Open** command on the File menu is used to open documents. In *Word*, you can have two or more documents open at once.

Data Files

Throughout this book you will need to open data files. A data file contains information you will use to complete an activity. Data files will save you lots of time. With a data file, part of the work has already been done for you. In the next activity, you will learn how to locate these valuable files.

Lesson 122   Formatting Web Pages

Objectives

In Lesson 122, you will:
- Add paragraph and line breaks to a Web page.
- Insert a title for the title bar of a Web page.
- Create headings in a Web page.
- Add bulleted lists to a Web page.
- Create hyperlinks in a Web page.
- Properly nest HTML tags in a Web page.

Basic Formatting Tags

Your *webpage1.html* file is hard to read because there are no line breaks. What happened? You tapped enter to create new paragraphs in the text file. The answer is that you must insert tags to define everything in an HTML file.

Formatting tags add interest and make Web pages appear organized. Formatting tags will tell a Web browser how to display a page of information in an interesting way. For example, if you want your paragraphs to be formatted properly, you must use paragraph < P > or break < BR > tags. Every well-formatted Web page needs a title. Text you place between the < TITLE > tags will appear in the title bar of the Web browser when the page is displayed. Read the tag descriptions in the table below.

Tag	Action
\<P> \</P> or \<P>	Leaves one blank line and begins a new paragraph. (Like pressing the ENTER key twice in *Word*.)
\ \</BR> or \ 	Begins a new line. (Like pressing the ENTER key once in *Word*.) Doesn't always need a pair.
\<TITLE> \</TITLE>	Places a title for a Web page in the title bar of the Web browser.

122A LEARN: Format Paragraphs and Enter Titles

1. Start *Notepad*. Choose **File**, **Open**. In the Look in box, navigate to the *myapollo17* folder.

2. In the Files of type box, click the down arrow and select **All Files**. The *webpage1.html* file that you created earlier should be displayed. Choose it and click the **Open** button.

Most data filenames begin with **CD**. The lesson number where you will use the file, such as **04** for Lesson 4, comes next. The final part is a word or name that relates to the file content. The data file *CD-04-Word* is a document you will use in Lesson 4. This document is about *Microsoft Word*.

4B LEARN: Open and Save Documents

1. Start *Word* if it is not already open. Select **File** and then **Open** from the menu bar. The Open dialog box will appear.

2. In the Look in box, click the down arrow. Then select the drive or folder where your teacher has told you the data files are stored.

3. Click the filename *CD-04-Word*. Click **Open**. The document will appear on the screen.

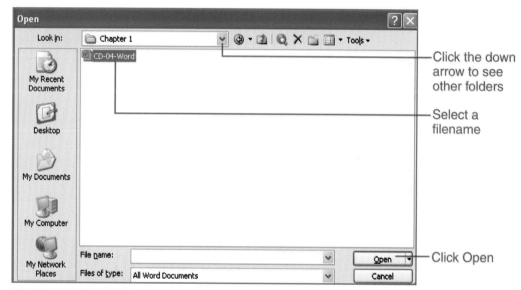

Figure 1.20 Open Dialog Box

4. Move to the end of the document. Key the sentence shown below.

   I will learn to use all of these types of programs as I study this book.

5. Select **File** and then **Save As** from the menu bar. The Save As dialog box will appear.

6. Your teacher will tell you where to save your work. Choose that folder (such as My Documents) in the Save in box.

121E LEARN: Save File as Web Page

Instant Message

Generally, you should use simple filenames and lowercase letters when saving Web pages. Web addresses must be entered exactly as written. Many people find lowercase letters easier to enter into a browser's address window.

1. Start *Notepad*. (Choose **Start**, **All Programs**, **Accessories**, **Notepad**.)

2. Open the file *webpage1* that you created earlier.

3. Choose **File** from the menu bar. Choose **Save As**. When the Save As dialog box appears, click the **New Folder** icon. Place the new folder in the folder where you save work for this class. For the name of the new folder, key **myapollo17**.

4. Open the new *myapollo17* folder. Save the file in this folder. For the filename, key **webpage1.html**. Click **Save**. Close *Notepad*.

5. Start your Web browser. Choose **File**, **Open** and browse to find the *webpage1.html* file. Open the file.

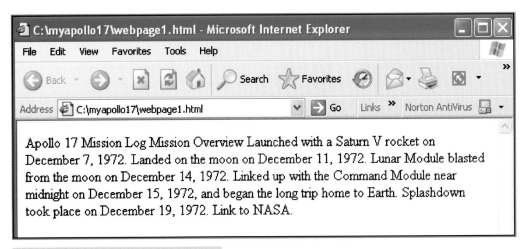

Figure 17.6 View your first Web page.

CHECK POINT Your Web page should look similar to Figure 17.6. If it does not, open the file in *Notepad*. Compare the text and tags with those in the textbook. Make corrections, if needed.

6. Close the browser after viewing the Web page. You will learn to format the Web page in the next lesson.

7. Your teacher may ask you to create a new folder for your work. To create a new folder for your work, click the **Create New Folder** button. Key a name for the folder in the Name box and click **OK**. The new folder name will appear in the Save in box.

8. In the File name box, key the filename *04-Word*. Click **Save**. The new filename should appear on the *Word* title bar.

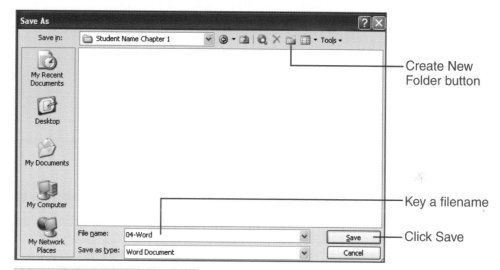

Figure 1.21 Save As Dialog Box

9. Close the file by selecting **File** and then **Close** from the menu bar.

Getting Help

Many programs have a Help feature. The Help feature gives you information about how to use commands and do tasks while using the program. You can find the information by choosing Help from the menu bar. Like *Word*, many programs have a Help button on a toolbar. *Word* also has a text box near the top right of the screen. You can use this box to find Help information. You simply key a word or two that relates to the topic you want to learn about and tap ENTER.

4C LEARN: ## Use Word Help

1. Start *Word* if it is not already open.

2. Open the file you created earlier, *04-Word*. (Select **File** and then **Open** from the menu bar.)

3. Key **save a file** in the Help search box and tap ENTER. A list of Help topics related to your search words will appear. See Figure 1.22 on page 26.

File Extensions

Web pages must be saved carefully with either an *htm* or an *html* file extension. A **file extension** is a three- or four-letter code that identifies a particular file type. The filename and the file extension are separated by a period. For example, *Word* files have a *doc* file extension. *Excel* files have an *xls* extension. *PowerPoint* files have a *ppt* extension. Web pages are usually saved with an *htm* or *html* file extension.

To create documents using HTML, you will need to know the exact name of each file, including the file extension. By default, file extensions are hidden. Settings in the Folder Options dialog box can be changed to display file extensions.

121D LEARN: Display File Extensions

1. Choose **Start**, **Control Panel**, **Appearance and Themes**, **Folder Options**.

2. Choose the **View** tab. Scroll down the list to find the **Hide extensions for known file types** option. Click the box beside this option to remove the check mark as shown in Figure 17.5.

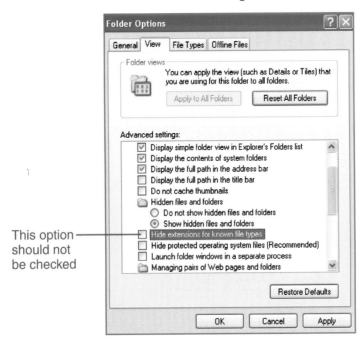

This option should not be checked

Figure 17.5 Folder Options Dialog Box

3. Choose **Apply** and then **OK**. Close the Appearance and Themes window.

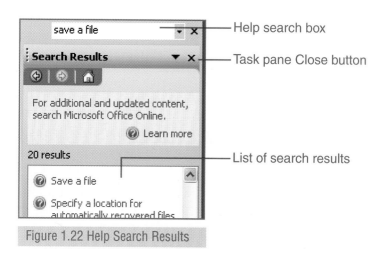

Help search box

Task pane Close button

List of search results

Figure 1.22 Help Search Results

4. Locate the topic **Save a file**. Click this topic. Another window will open that contains information about saving files. Read the text in the Help window. Click the **Close** button on the Help window to close it.

5. Move to the end of the document. Key the following sentence.

   I have learned how to use Help.

6. Click or tap the **Save** button on the Standard toolbar to save the document using the same name.

7. Close *Word* by selecting **File** and then **Exit** from the menu bar.

Printing Files

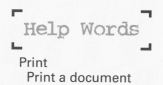

Help Words

Print
   Print a document

The Print command allows you to print a document. You can print by clicking the Print button on the Standard toolbar. Clicking the Print button causes the document to print using the default settings. To view or change print settings, you can choose Print from the File menu. This command will open the Print dialog box as shown in Figure 1.23 on page 27. In this box, you can choose a printer, select the number of copies you want to print, and choose other options.

You have created and saved a *Word* file, *04-Word*. Now you will learn to print this file. Your teacher will tell you which printer you can use to print your work. Your teacher will also give you any special instructions for your printer or network.

4D LEARN: Print a Word File

1. Start *Word* if it is not already open. Open the *04-Word* file that you saved earlier.

Tag	Action
<HTML> </HTML>	Begins and ends a Web page.
<HEAD> </HEAD>	Creates a header for a Web page. Used to place the title of a Web page. Also holds hidden information normally not displayed on a Web page.
<TITLE> </TITLE>	Places a title for a Web page in the title bar of the Web browser.
<BODY> </BODY>	Words and pictures placed between the BODY tags appear in the main viewing area of the Web browser.

Any text or graphics that you want to appear in the Web browser window must be placed between the BODY tags.

121C LEARN: Enter Tags Using a Text Editor

To enter tags, you must use a text editor. A **text editor** is a simple word processing program. *Notepad* is a text editor that should be on your computer if you use *Microsoft Windows*. You will use *Notepad* in this activity.

1. To start *Notepad*, choose **Start**, **All Programs**, **Accessories**, **Notepad**.

2. Key the following HTML tags. Key carefully. Accuracy is important.

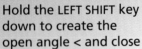

Instant Message

Hold the LEFT SHIFT key down to create the open angle < and close angle > brackets.

```
<HTML>
<HEAD>
<TITLE></TITLE>
</HEAD>
<BODY>
Apollo 17 Mission Log

Mission Overview

Launched with a Saturn V rocket on December 7, 1972.
Landed on the moon on December 11, 1972.
Lunar Module blasted from the moon on December 14, 1972.
Linked up with the Command Module near midnight on
December 15, 1972, and began the long trip home to
Earth.
Splashdown took place on December 19, 1972.
Link to NASA.
</BODY>
</HTML>
```

3. Save the file as *webpage1* in the folder where you save work for this class. Later, you will create a new folder and save the document as a Web page.

2. Click **File** on the menu bar. Choose **Print**. The Print dialog box will appear as shown in Figure 1.23. Click the down arrow by **Printer Name** and select the printer you wish to use if it is not already selected.

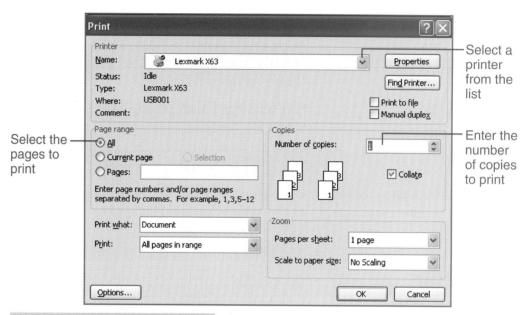

Select a printer from the list

Select the pages to print

Enter the number of copies to print

Figure 1.23 *Word*'s Print Dialog Box

3. Enter **1** for the number of copies to print if that number does not already appear. Click **OK**. Your document should now print. Close *Word*.

Following the Rules

The *Apollo 11* astronauts were able to land on the moon because they followed rules. They studied and practiced for years before their trip. They worked through every possible problem. They prepared. They learned that they had to follow certain rules. These rules were put in place for their own safety. If they didn't follow them exactly, the hostile environment of space could take their lives.

When you're using a computer, you need to follow certain rules as well. Chances are, your school has rules you should follow. These rules are usually called **acceptable use policies**. An example of an acceptable use policy is shown in Figure 1.24 on page 28.

3. Use your Favorites list to open the Apollo Lunar Surface Journal page on the NASA Web site. After the page fully opens, choose **View** on the menu bar. Select **Source** or **Page Source**. Do you see the tags? Close the window that shows the tags by clicking its **Close** button.

4. Use your Favorites list to open the Web page about Tim Berners-Lee that you bookmarked earlier. Look at the HTML source tags that created this page. Close the window that shows the tags by clicking its **Close** button.

5. You will learn more about how HTML tags work in later activities. Close the browser.

How HTML Tags Work

HTML tags make up the code that Web browsers understand. Here are a few facts you should know about HTML tags:

- There are two kinds of tags: **open** and **close**.
- **Open HTML tags** start commands. Open tags are easy to spot. They are enclosed in angle (< >) brackets. The first is called an open angle bracket (<), and the second is called a close angle bracket (>).
- **Close HTML tags** stop commands. Close tags have a slash (/) after the first bracket (< / >).
- Tags normally work in pairs, although a few tags work alone.
- Tags can be written in uppercase < CENTER > or lowercase < center > letters. In this chapter, uppercase letters will be used so you can see the tags more clearly.

Study the example below to see how tags work. The < CENTER > tag displays any text between the tags in the horizontal center of the page, like this:

< CENTER > Apollo 17 Mission < /CENTER >

The open < CENTER > tag starts centering the words and pictures, and the close < /CENTER > tag stops centering. When creating a new Web page, write the most important tags first. These tags give structure to Web pages. Other tags, text, and pictures fit around these basic tags.

NORTHSIDE SCHOOL _____

ACCEPTABLE USE POLICY
FOR COMPUTER CLASSES AND LABS

Rule

1. Never share your password with others.

2. Do not let other people use your computer account without permission.

3. Never use your computer to lie, distort, or offend another person.

4. Use your computer only for official school purposes. Personal use is not allowed.

5. Do not forward any e-mail or other messages that appear suspicious.

6. Do not steal information from the computer files of others.

7. Do not download graphics, music, videos, or other information from the Internet without permission.

8. Always log out of your computer at the end of the day and either restart or shut down your computer.

9. Do not bring food or drink into the lab. This will prevent accidents.

10. Always organize and clean your workstation area before you leave at the end of each day.

Figure 1.24 Sample Acceptable Use Policy

4E APPLY: Discuss Acceptable Use Policies

1. Work in a group with two other students. Talk about the rules for using computers at your school.

2. Start *Word*. Open the data file *CD-04-Acceptable Use*.

3. Read the rules in the data file. Compare the rules to the ones you must follow at your school. Under each rule, key **yes** if the rule is the same at your school. Key **no** if the rule is not the same.

4. Save the file as *04-Acceptable Use* in the folder with your earlier work. Close *Word*.

How Web Pages Were First Made

Tim Berners-Lee created a new computer language called HTML. **HTML (HyperText Markup Language)** is the language of the Web. It is what browsers (such as *Netscape* and *Internet Explorer*) interpret to display documents and pictures.

Markup is a key term in the language name. Web pages are *marked up* by command tags that are placed in angle brackets < >. These command tags tell Web browsers how to display Web pages so you can read them. For example, the < B > command causes words to be displayed in **bold**. The command tags are normally hidden from the user. However, they can be displayed as shown in Figure 17.4. In the next activity, you will display the command tags in a Web page.

Close button

HTML tags

Figure 17.4 HTML tags for a Web page can be displayed in a separate window.

121B LEARN: View HTML Tags

The Web page you will view was created by Ryan as a special project. Like you, Ryan is a student learning more about the Web each day. Peek inside his Web pages to see the tags he used to create his project.

1. Use your Favorites list to open the *Apollo 17* Mission Log Web site. (Or choose **File, Open** and browse to the data files. Open the *apollo17* folder and the *index* file.)

2. Click **View** on the menu bar. Select **Source** or **Page Source**. The source tags that create this page will appear in a separate window as shown in Figure 17.4. Close the window that shows the tags by clicking its **Close** button.

Reviewing What You Have Learned

Answer these questions to review what you have learned in Chapter 1.

1. A(n) _____ is a machine that follows a set of instructions to change and store data.

2. Give an example of how computers help people communicate with another person and with a group.

3. The physical parts of a computer are called _____.

4. Programs that give instructions to a computer are called _____.

5. What are the five main parts of information processing?

6. A small computer designed for an individual user is called a _____ _____.

7. A(n) _____ is a small circuit board that controls all work done by the computer.

8. What are computer peripherals? Give two examples.

9. Software that controls basic operations of the computer is called a(n) _____ _____.

10. Give two examples of applications software and tell what you can do with each one.

11. A(n) _____ is a series of letters and/or numbers that you enter to gain access to a computer

12. The _____ is an on-screen work area on which windows, icons, menus, and dialog boxes appear.

13. List the three *Windows* Turn Off Computer options.

14. List two parts of a program window that can be used to give commands.

15. Describe two ways to close a program.

16. What happens when you click the Minimize button on a program window?

17. When a line is full in *Word*, the text automatically moves to the next line. This feature is called _____.

18. The _____ feature gives you information about how to use commands and do tasks while using the program.

19. You can store documents you create in *Word* to use again later. To do so, use the _____ command.

20. A document giving a school's rules related to computer use is called a(n) _____ _____ _____.

Visit Web Sites

Before you start creating Web pages, access a few Web pages and preview what you are going to create. The first Web site you will visit was created by a student named Ryan. Ryan used his ideas and creativity to design his Web site.

1. Start your browser software such as *Internet Explorer* or *Netscape*.

2. Choose **File**, **Open** and browse to the data files. Open the *apollo17* folder. Then choose and open the *index* file.

3. After the page opens, add this Web page to your Favorites list. You will return to it later.

4. Scroll down the first page. Read the short story about the Apollo Lunar Surface Journal and how some of the first NASA Web pages came about in 1995.

5. Scroll to the top of the page and click several links. Visit the Photo Gallery and the Astronaut Bios pages. Can you see why this can be called a Web site? Ryan has linked together several pages on a single topic.

6. Ryan has created a hypertext link to another Web site at NASA. Click the **Home** link to return to the Home Web page. Click the link **Link to NASA** (or enter **http://www.nasa.gov** in the browser's Address box).

7. Ryan's Web site has only a few pages. The NASA Web site has many pages. A good way to find information on a big Web site is by using a provided search tool. Use the NASA Web site search tool to find the Apollo Lunar Surface Journal that Ryan wrote about on his Web site. Enter the search words **Apollo Lunar Surface Journal** as shown in Figure 17.3. After you find this resource, add this Web page to your Favorites list.

Source: http://www.nasa.gov/home/index.html

Figure 17.3 Search the NASA Web Site

8. In the browser's Address box, enter **http://www.w3c.com** to visit the World Wide Web Consortium (WC3) Web site. After you arrive at the site, use the search tool to find information about Tim Berners-Lee. Add any important pages you find about this famous inventor to your Favorites list. Close the browser.

Instant Message

Review how to add a site to a Favorites list in Lesson 12 on page 76.

Instant Message

You may need to click a link such as **Enter NASA.gov** to find a page with the search tool.

Applying *What You Have Learned*

Data File

CD-C01-Practice

Update a Data File

1. Start *Word*. Open *CD-C01-Practice* from your data files.

2. Follow the directions in the report to create fun faces in the document.

3. Leave *Word* open. Start the *Calculator* program.

4. In *Calculator*, select **Help** on the menu bar. Select **Help Topics**. On the Contents tab, select **Calculator**. Read the following Help topics:

   • Calculator overview

   • Perform a simple calculation

5. Close the *Calculator* Help window. Use *Calculator* to find answers to the math problems in the *Word* document.

6. Minimize *Calculator*. Make *Word* the active window. Key the answers to the problems in the document.

7. Save the *Word* document as *C01-Practice*. Print the document and then close *Word*. Close *Calculator*.

 **CHECK POINT** Compare your answers to the math problems to a classmate's answers. If the answers are not the same, do the math problems again to find the correct answers.

Create a Drawing in Paint

1. Open the *Paint* program.

2. Sketch a picture of the first landing on the moon, or pick another topic and create a drawing.

3. Experiment with the different tools on the toolbar such as Pencil and Airbrush. Use Help to learn how to add color to shapes. If you don't like something you have drawn, use the Eraser tool.

4. Save your drawing in the folder with your other work. Name the file *C01-Drawing*. Close *Paint*.

Supplemental activities for this chapter can be found at www.c21jr. swlearning.com.

Building a Better Browser

The creation of Web browser software led to greater interest in and use of the Web. A *Web browser* is a program that allows users to find and view Web pages. They make using the Web interesting and easy. On December 15, 1994, the *Netscape 1.0* browser became available. *Netscape* was the first commercial browser for viewing Web pages. This program could be downloaded free of charge.

Netscape and the Web became a popular hit. Many important organizations, such as NASA, began posting information on the Web. To **post** a Web page means to upload a page to the Web for sharing. *Netscape 1.0* was released 22 years after the *Apollo 17* crew began their voyage home from the moon. A great way to share the story of the moon missions was finally available. People began to visit the NASA Web site to view images from space. *Netscape* is still a popular Web browser.

Figure 17.2 *Netscape* is a popular Web browser.

From the moment important organizations such as NASA went online, the Web became an essential research tool. Since 1994, many schools and libraries have connected to the Internet and the World Wide Web. Today, millions of students use the Web for research.

Creating Web Pages and Web Sites

Students can use the Web for more than just researching information. Students like you can create their own Web sites. A **Web site** is a collection of related Web pages. The pages on a Web site are connected using hyperlinks. A hyperlink is text or a graphic that, when clicked, takes you to a new location. The new location can be a different place on the same Web page. The new location can also be a different Web page or site.

Data Files

- *CD-C01-Business*
- *CD-C01-Leadership Skills*
- *CD-C01-End Marks*
- *CD-C01-Check*

↗ About Business

BUSINESS BASICS A **business** is an entity that sells or rents products or services. The main goal of a business is to make a profit. **Income** is money a business receives for products or services. A business may also have income from investments, selling property, or other activities. **Expenses** are items for which money is paid, such as rent, utilities, or labor. **Profit** is the amount of income that remains after expenses are paid.

A business may have other goals in addition to making a profit. A few examples of these goals are:

- Helping people
- Educating people
- Entertaining people
- Protecting the environment
- Advancing medical or scientific knowledge

A business may be organized in one of three primary ways: as a sole proprietorship, a partnership, or a corporation. In a sole proprietorship, one person owns the business. The owner gets all the income from the business. The owner is also responsible for paying all debts of the business. In a partnership, two or more people own the business. The partners share in the income from the business. They are responsible for the debts of the business. In a corporation, the company is owned by people who buy shares (called stock) in the company. The stockholders may share some of the income of the business. Stockholders are not personally responsible for the debts of the business.

1. Work in a team with two other students to complete this activity. Choose one of the forms of business discussed above (sole proprietorship, partnership, or corporation). Identify three businesses in your area that are this type of business. For each business, give the business name, the location, and the primary products or services the business provides.

2. Start *Word*. Open and print *CD-C01-Business* from your data files. Complete the crossword puzzle to review terms you learned in this activity.

↗ Career and Life Skills Success Builder

LEADERSHIP SKILLS Do you remember playing *Follow the Leader* when you were a child? It's a fun game in which everyone takes turns being in charge while others follow. In the business world, being a leader is no game. Basic leadership skills are necessary tools for success in the workplace.

Lesson 121 | History of the World Wide Web

Objectives

In Lesson 121, you will:
- Learn about the creation of the World Wide Web.
- Learn how HTML tags work.
- Write HTML tags.
- Save and view a Web page.

Data file: *index*

Invention of the World Wide Web

It all started in 1989. The place was the European Particle Physics Laboratory (CERN) in Geneva, Switzerland. While working at CERN, a computer programmer came up with a revolutionary idea. He called his invention the World Wide Web. The programmer's name was Tim Berners-Lee. Berners-Lee was as important to the history of the Internet as Neil Armstrong was to the first moon landing. He once said of his creation:

> The dream behind the Web is of a common information space in which we may communicate by sharing information. Its universality is essential: the fact that a hypertext link can point to anything, be it personal, local or global, be it draft or highly polished.[1]

Figure 17.1 Tim Berners-Lee invented the World Wide Web.

The World Wide Web was not an overnight success. After years of hard work, Berners-Lee had only a small Web running on just a few computers. His Web was hardly "worldwide." It was limited to a handful of scientists sharing scientific documents about high-energy physics.

---

[1] Tim Berners-Lee, "The World Wide Web: A Very Short Personal History," *World Wide Web Consortium*, http://www.w3.org/People/Berners-Lee/ShortHistory.html (accessed December 24, 2004).

What makes a good leader? Have you ever been part of a group led by someone everyone admired? Do you have what it takes to be a good leader? The dictionary defines a **leader** as a person who guides, directs, or commands. Good leaders usually have these traits in common:

- Good leaders are trusted by others in the group.
- Good leaders are dependable and do what they say they will do.
- Good leaders are good communicators—they keep everyone informed and give clear feedback.
- Good leaders can adapt to new situations.
- Good leaders use sound judgment to make decisions.
- Good leaders listen to everyone's opinions and do not prejudge others' ideas.
- Good leaders stand up for what they believe in and resist peer pressure.
- Good leaders are honest when working with others.

1. Start *Word*. Open and print the data file *CD-C01-Leadership Skills*.

2. Follow the directions given to determine if you have the skills to be a good leader.

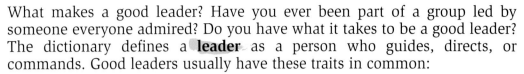

↗ Academic Success Builder

COMMUNICATIONS: END MARKS An *end mark* is used to indicate the end of a sentence. End marks signal the reader that a complete thought has been made. There are three end marks:

- Period (.)—used at the end of a sentence that is a statement
- Question mark (?)—used at the end of a sentence that asks a direct question
- Exclamation point (!)—used at the end of a statement or sentence that is a command or expresses strong feelings

1. Start *Word*. Open *CD-C01-End Marks* found in your data files. Print the file and then close it. Study the Guides and the Learn line(s) for each Guide.

2. For the Practice lines and the Apply lines, read the sentences and add the correct end marks.

READING: READ A CHECK Have you ever received a check instead of cash as a gift? Have you ever received a rebate check from a company for something you purchased? A **check** is a written order to a bank to make a payment from an account. Can you read a check correctly? Let's find out!

1. Start *Word*. Open *CD-C01-Check*. Print the file and then close it.

2. Match the letter by the check part to the correct check part description. Compare your answers to those of a classmate. If you disagree, decide which answer is most likely to be correct and make any changes needed. Give your answers to your teacher.

Courtesy of NASA

Meanwhile, back on Earth, a new way to share information was being invented. It was called *cyberspace* by many of its early fans. Today, we call this information-sharing space the Internet and the World Wide Web. In this chapter, you will learn about how the World Wide Web was created. You will also learn to create and link Web pages.

Chapter 2

Lessons 5–9

Finding and Managing Information

Web Resources:
www.c21jr.swlearning.
com/studentresources

- Data Files
- Vocabulary Flash Cards
- Test Your Knowledge, Managing Files and Folders
- *PowerPoint* Reviews
- More Activities

OBJECTIVES

In Chapter 2, you will:

↗ Learn about devices for storing computer files.

↗ Learn how files are organized in folders in *Windows Explorer*.

↗ Create folders and subfolders.

↗ Rename and delete folders and files.

↗ Move folders, subfolders, and files.

↗ Follow file paths to save and find files.

↗ Open and save *Excel* and *Word* files.

↗ Open and use multiple documents and applications.

↗ Preview and print *Word* and *Excel* files.

↗ Delete, rename, copy, and move files.

Apollo 13 was speeding to the moon. Suddenly, something went terribly wrong. An unexpected explosion crippled the ship. The astronauts sent a brief message: "Houston, we've had a problem here." [1]

Mission Control in Houston, Texas, quickly assembled a team of experts. They analyzed the problem. The computers flashed that the ship was rapidly losing electrical power. Much of the oxygen supply was lost. The main engine was also damaged. Mission Control sent the bad news. A moon landing was impossible. Getting home safely was the only goal.

---

[1] James A. Lovell, "Houston, We've Had a Problem," *Apollo Expeditions to the Moon, Chapter 13.1,* http://www.hq.nasa.gov/office/pao/History/SP-350/ch-13-1.html (accessed December 29, 2004).

Chapter 17

Lessons 121–125

Creating and Linking Web Pages

OBJECTIVES

In Chapter 17, you will:

↗ Learn about the creation of the World Wide Web.

↗ Write HTML tags and create Web pages.

↗ Format Web page HTML tags.

↗ Create hypertext links.

↗ Capture, copy, and insert images on Web pages.

↗ Save *Word, Excel,* and *PowerPoint* documents as Web pages.

↗ Link Web pages to create a Web site.

It was 4:27 p.m. on December 14, 1972. Eugene Cernan and Harrison Schmitt finished their last exploration of the moon. They returned to the Lunar Module and prepared to leave. Near midnight, they blasted off. Early the next morning, the astronauts docked with the Command Module and hurried home. It was the last Apollo adventure into lunar space.

The astronauts collected many pictures and a great deal of data about the moon. Unfortunately, only a few people could view everything the astronauts had brought home. NASA did not have an easy way to share what they had learned with everyone on Earth.

Mission Control provided instructions for the astronauts.

The astronauts followed Mission Control's instructions to the letter. They began a race against time. Flinging their damaged ship around the moon like a slingshot, they made a beeline for Earth. They organized supplies and turned their lunar module into a deep-space life raft.

They saved every spark of electricity. It was needed for the computer. The computer had to make the calculations for a safe path to Earth. Without these calculations, the ship could skip off the Earth's atmosphere.

Vital links to Mission Control aided the astronauts on their journey home. As a result, *Apollo 13* landed safely. You also have a journey ahead. Your computer can link you to a galaxy of information. This information is critical to your success.

Instant Message

To be *linked* means to be connected to resources and information.

↗ Career and Life Skills Success Builder

MODEL EMPLOYABILITY SKILLS Do you have the skills that employers are looking for? What does it mean to have *employability* skills? In recent chapters, you have practiced communication skills, identified your personal strengths, and developed a career plan. But how do you know if you have the basic skills that *all* employers are looking for?

To be a good employee, you will need to have certain skills that will benefit any employer. You need to have excellent communication skills and the ability to talk easily with customers. You must work well with a team and be able to take the lead on group projects. You should be able to adapt easily to new situations. You should be willing to continue learning to be better at your job. You must be responsible, honest, and dependable. You should be able to prioritize your work to meet important deadlines. And, of course, you need to have the technical skills needed to do your job.

In this activity, you will have the opportunity to model your skills. You will work as part of a team to develop a presentation about employability skills. You and your classmates will use your communication skills to share ideas. You will demonstrate your willingness to work by taking on tasks. You will display your ability to be dependable and meet deadlines. You will also demonstrate your ability to work as part of a team.

1. Start *Word*. Open the data file *CD-C16-Skills*. Work with three classmates. Follow the instructions for developing a presentation about employability skills.

2. Remember to include a sample of your best work from this chapter in your portfolio.

↗ Academic Success Builder

COMMUNICATIONS: AVOIDING GENDER BIAS Your language should reflect the role of men and women in today's society. The role of women in the United States has changed over the years. Women were not employed in the workforce in the early years. Because of this, many job names reflect a gender bias. For example, *businessman* was used to describe people who worked in business. *Policeman* and *serviceman* were used to refer to people in the police or armed forces. These terms do not reflect the role of women in these jobs. Terms such as *businessperson*, *police officer*, and *soldier* should be used instead. Avoid using pronouns and terms that reflect male gender when referring to both men and women.

1. Start *Word*. Open and print *CD-C16-Bias* found in your data files.

2. Follow the instructions given to practice writing sentences that avoid gender bias.

Lesson 5   Exploring Your Digital Space

Objectives

In Lesson 5, you will:

↘ Learn about common storage devices.

↘ Use files to store data.

↘ Use folders to organize files.

↘ Navigate folders with *Windows Explorer*.

Instant Message

Digital information is data saved and displayed in ways that computers understand.

The *Apollo 13* astronauts asked Mission Control for guidance and help. Your *Windows* operating system (OS) is like Mission Control for your computer. The OS controls all of the software, folders, and files on your computer. You will use the toolbars and menus provided to navigate the folders and files on your computer. Your OS makes online journeys possible.

Storing Data

You will want to save some of the important information you find on your digital journeys. You can save information on a variety of devices. Some of these devices are inside the computer case. Others are pieces of equipment that you can connect to your computer.

Instant Message

USB Flash drives are also called pen drives, jump drives, thumb drives, key drives, and memory sticks.

A **hard drive** is a common storage device located inside a computer. A hard drive can also be a separate piece of equipment that you connect to the computer. **Compact discs (CDs)**, **digital video discs (DVDs)**, **floppy disks**, and **USB Flash drives** are other types of storage devices.

Figure 2.1 Floppy disks, CDs, and USB Flash drives are common storage devices.

You can store different amounts of data on different devices. The following table compares the data that can be stored.

ACROSS THE CURRICULUM

Data Files

- *CD-C16-Business*
- *CD-C16-Skills*
- *CD-C16-Bias*

↗ About Business

OUTSOURCING Companies must react quickly to changes in customers' needs and wants in order to be successful. Outsourcing is a practice that helps companies do this. **Outsourcing** means that a company hires another company or a person to do work. This is done rather than having the work performed by company employees.

Outsourcing work lets a company focus on its primary business. Other jobs that are not related to the primary business of the company may be handled by outside firms. For example, a company that makes bicycles may want to focus on the jobs that relate directly to producing bicycles. Other jobs, such as providing building security, preparing the payroll, and providing technical support for the company's computers, may be outsourced to other firms.

A company may outsource work for reasons such as the following:

- The company does not have enough employees who are trained to do the work.

- The company does not have the buildings or equipment needed to do the work.

- The company cannot do the work quickly enough to meet the need for the product or service.

- The company finds that having another company do the work costs less than doing the work in-house.

- The company does not have enough need for the work to justify having a full-time employee to do it.

Many companies specialize in doing work that is outsourced by other companies. In this activity, you will identify some companies that do outsourced work.

1. Start *Word*. Open *CD-C16-Business* from the data files. Read the examples of the types of work that companies often outsource.

2. Follow the instructions to identify companies that do outsourced work. Share the findings of your research with the class.

Storage Device	Can Hold
Floppy disk	Documents from several folders in a file cabinet
CD or DVD	Documents from one drawer in a file cabinet
Hard drive for a single computer or USB Flash drive	Documents from four or five file cabinet drawers
Hard drive on a network	Documents from a room full of file cabinets

As you learned in Chapter 1, **files** are used to store digital information. You can store text, pictures, video, and sound in computer files. **Folders** are used to store and organize files. Using a logical system of files and folders will help you find stored data quickly.

5A LEARN: Survey Your Storage Devices

Work with a classmate to complete this activity. Consider the computer system you will use for this class. Survey the storage devices you can use with this system.

1. List all the local storage devices you have for use with the computer.

2. List any other places you can store data, such as on a network drive.

Windows Explorer

Windows Explorer is the program you will use to manage files and folders. Using this program, you can see the folders and files stored on your computer. By default, many programs save files in the *My Documents* folder. However, you can tell the software to save in another place.

The *My Documents* folder is the center of your digital activities. This is your home base, where you save valuable information. You will locate this important folder as you learn to use *Windows Explorer*.

5B LEARN: Explore Folders in Windows Explorer

SOFTWARE TIP

If your Standard Buttons toolbar does not appear, choose **View, Toolbars, Standard Buttons** from the menu bar.

1. To open *Windows Explorer*, choose **Start, All Programs, Accessories, Windows Explorer**.

2. Click the **Folders** button on the Standard Buttons toolbar. This will reveal a list of folders in the left pane as shown in Figure 2.2 on page 37. The *Desktop* folder contains all the items that appear on your desktop. The *My Computer* folder contains all the files and folders on your computer.

Timed Writing

Key each paragraph once. DS between paragraphs. Key a 1' timed writing on each paragraph; determine *gwam*. Key a 2' timed writing on both paragraphs; determine *gwam*.

A all letters used

gwam | 2'

```
          •    2    •    4    •    6    •    8
     You are nearly at the end of your computer           4
  •   10   •   12   •   14   •   16   •   18
applications class.  The keyboarding skill level          9
  •   20   •   22   •   24   •   26   •
you attained is much better now than when you            13
 28   •   30   •   32   •   34   •   36   •
were given keying instruction for the first time.        19
 38   •   40   •   42   •   44   •   46   •
During the early period of your training, you            23
      48   •   50   •   52   •   54   •   56   •
were taught to key the letters of the alphabet as        28
      58   •   60   •   62   •   64   •   66   •
well as the figures by touch.  During the initial        33
      68   •   70   •   72   •   74   •   76
time of learning, the emphasis was placed on             38
      •   78   •
keying technique.                                        39

          •    2    •    4    •    6    •    8
     After you learned to key the alphabet and           43
  •   10   •   12   •   14   •   16   •
the figures, your next job was to learn how to           47
 18   •   20   •   22   •   24   •   26   •
format documents.  The various types of documents        52
 28   •   30   •   32   •   34   •   36   •
you learned to format included letters, tables,          57
   38   •   40   •   42   •   44   •   46
and reports.  During this time of training, an           62
  •   48   •   50   •   52   •   54   •   56
emphasis also was placed on increasing the rate          67
   •   58   •   60   •   62   •   64   •   66
at which you were able to input.  You should now         72
   •   68   •   70   •   72   •
recognize the value of a keying skill.                   75
```

gwam 2' | 1 | 2 | 3 | 4 | 5 |

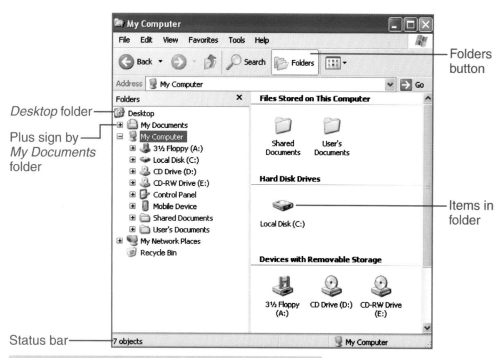

Desktop folder—

Plus sign by—
My Documents
folder

Folders button

Items in folder

Status bar—

Figure 2.2 *Windows Explorer* File and Folder Organization

3. Click the **plus sign** (+) beside the *My Documents* folder. The folders and files in the *My Documents* folder will be shown in a list below the folder name. The plus sign is changed to a minus sign (–).

4. Click the **minus sign** beside the *My Documents* folder. The list of folders and files is hidden.

5. Click the **Desktop** folder icon. The folders and files that are available on the desktop of your PC are shown in the right pane of the window.

6. Display the folders in the right pane differently. Click the **Views** button on the toolbar and choose **List** as shown in Figure 2.3. The items in the right pane appear as a list.

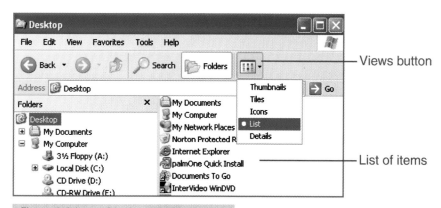

Views button

List of items

Figure 2.3 Items Displayed in List View

Building Keying Skill

Warmup Practice

Key each line twice. If time permits, key the lines again.

Alphabet
1 Jack Betz will give us the equipment for six days.

Figure/Symbol
2 I paid Invoice #508 ($346.79 with a 12% discount).

Speed
3 The chair by the chapel in the city is an antique.

gwam 1' | 1 | 2 | 3 | 4 | 5 | 6 | 7 | 8 | 9 | 10 |

Improve Keying Technique

Key each line twice.

One-hand words
1 in we no be up as on you was him are get only rate
2 case only best upon area you water oil great after

One-hand phrases
3 you were|at my best|get set|set rate|as few|no tax
4 water rate|my only date|my tax case|my care|as few

gwam 1' | 1 | 2 | 3 | 4 | 5 | 6 | 7 | 8 | 9 | 10 |

TECHNIQUE TIP

Don't stop or pause between words.

Improve Tab Technique

Set tabs at 2.5" and 4.5". Key the text below, tapping TAB to place text in columns. Key three 1' timings, trying to increase the amount keyed on each timing.

Alabama	Alaska	Arizona
Montgomery	Juneau	Phoenix
California	Colorado	Connecticut
Sacramento	Denver	Hartford
Florida	Georgia	Hawaii
Tallahassee	Atlanta	Honolulu
Illinois	Indiana	Iowa
Springfield	Indianapolis	Des Moines

7. Click the **Views** button again and choose each option in turn to see how items appear in that view. Close *Windows Explorer* or continue to the next activity.

5C PRACTICE: List the Contents of Folders

1. Start *Windows Explorer*. (Choose **Start, All Programs, Accessories, Windows Explorer**.)

2. View the folders in the left pane. (Click the **Folders** button on the toolbar.)

3. Click the icon beside the *Desktop* folder in the left pane. Make a list of *Desktop* folder items that appear in the right pane.

4. Click the icon beside the *My Computer* folder (not the plus or minus sign). Make a list of *My Computer* folder items that appear in the right pane.

5. Click **View** on the menu bar and choose **Status Bar**. The Status bar will appear at the bottom of the *Windows Explorer* window. See Figure 2.2 if you have trouble locating the Status bar. What information is shown on your Status bar? Close *Windows Explorer*.

 **CHECK POINT** Compare your answers to a classmate's answers. Discuss any answers that are different. Is one answer wrong or are there different items on the two computers?

Lesson 6   Organizing Your Digital Space

Objectives

In Lesson 6, you will:
* Create folders.
* Rename, delete, and move folders.
* Create subfolders.

Working with Folders

As you learned earlier, a folder is a container used to store files. You can create as many new folders as you need. You can also create folders within folders. In Chapter 1, you learned to create a new folder from the Save As dialog box. In this lesson, you will learn to create folders using *Windows Explorer*.

Applying *What You Have Learned*

Edit a Database

1. Start *Windows Explorer*. Open the folder where you store your files for this class. Make a copy of the *117-Composers* database file. Place the copy in the same folder. Name the copy of the file *C16-Composers*. Close *Windows Explorer*.

2. Start *Access*. Open the *C16-Composers* database file. Open the *Composers (1600-1799)* table. Make the changes listed below. Print and then close the table.

   * Enter **Joseph** for Franz Hayden's middle name.

   * Enter **Amadeus** for Wolfgang Mozart's middle name.

   * The complete title for Beethoven's composition is **Symphony No. 5 in C minor**, **Op. 67**. Update the field.

   * Correct the dates for Franz Hayden. They should be **1732-1809**.

Design and Create a Database

You and two of your classmates have been asked by your principal to design a database that will allow the school to:

* Locate a student at any time during the school day

* Send information to the home address of a student's parent(s) or legal guardian

* Contact a student's parent(s) or guardian during the school day for an emergency

1. Work with two classmates to plan the fields that will be needed in a database table to store this information. Read steps 2 through 5 below to see how the data will be used.

2. Working alone, create a new database file. Name the file *C16-School Records*. Create a table for the database, using the fields you planned with your classmates. Remember to use an appropriate data type and enter a description for each field. Set a field for the primary key. Save the table using an appropriate name.

3. Enter data in the table for five students. Make up names, addresses, and other data so you do not share real personal information.

4. Create a query that is based on your database table. Include fields that result in a table showing the student's first name, the student's last name, and the number where a student's parent or guardian may be contacted during the day. Save the query using an appropriate name.

5. Create a report based on your query. Include all the fields in the report. Sort the data in the report by the student's last name. Choose a layout and style to create an attractive report. Save the report using an appropriate name. Print the report. Close *Access*.

Supplemental activities for this chapter can be found at www.c21jr. swlearning.com.

You should give each folder a name that will tell you the type of information in the folder. This way you can find files more easily. For example, you would place a file called *All About Moon Rocks* in the *Moon Rocks* folder. You would *not* place it in a folder called *Maps to Mars*. You can rename a folder if you decide later that another name would be more helpful.

You probably have notes and other information for your school classes recorded on paper in notebooks or folders. When you finish a class and no longer need the papers, you throw them away. If you did not, you would soon have too much paper to handle. You need to manage your computer records in the same way. When you no longer need a file or a folder, you can delete it. You will learn to delete folders in this lesson.

In this lesson, the steps direct you to save in folders within *My Documents*. Your teacher may direct you to use another folder. If this is the case, use the name of the folder given by your teacher instead of *My Documents* as you follow the steps.

6A LEARN: Create Folders with Windows Explorer

In this activity, you will create several folders inside the *My Documents* folder. The first folder you create will be named *Computers*. This is where you will save your completed projects.

1. Start *Windows Explorer*. Click the **Folders** button on the toolbar, if needed, to view the folders in the left pane. Click **My Documents** in the left pane. (You may need to scroll up to find it.)

2. Click **File** on the menu bar. Click **New** and then click **Folder**. See Figure 2.4.

Figure 2.4 Choose New, Folder from the File menu to create a new folder.

3. A new folder named *New Folder* will appear. Look for it in both the left and right panes of the *Windows Explorer* window. The new folder name will be highlighted in the right pane as shown in Figure 2.5 on the left.

Figure 2.5 Name a Folder

Reviewing　What You Have Learned

Answer these questions to review what you have learned in Chapter 16.

1. A database is a collection of information that is stored in database objects. Name four database objects that you used in this chapter.

2. A database _____ contains all the information about one person or item.

3. A database _____ holds one piece of information from a database record.

4. The _____ determines the kind of data a field can hold.

5. Double clicking on the column border will increase or decrease the column _____ in a database table.

6. Data can be entered into a database table in Datasheet view or using a database _____.

7. The data type used for letters or numbers that do not require calculations is _____.

8. The data type used for dollar values is _____.

9. You create an AutoForm based on a table that has 12 fields in each record. Which of those fields will be included in the form?

10. When you create a form using the Form Wizard, which fields can you include in the form?

11. Explain the difference between landscape and portrait orientations.

12. To add a field to an existing table, open the table in _____ view.

13. What is the purpose of a query?

14. What is the purpose of a filter?

15. What software feature can be used to arrange the data in a column in a database table in ascending order?

16. What is a database report? How does it differ from a database table?

17. You have a database with the names of all the people in San Francisco. You want to display only the records of the people with the last name *Halverson*. How will you display these records?

18. A field chosen to identify each record in an *Access* database table is called the _____. *Access* will not allow duplicate data to be entered in this field.

19. Data can be entered in an *Access* table in _____ view. Changes can be made to an *Access* table in _____ view.

20. In a field with the field type _____, you do not enter data in the field. *Access* automatically assigns a number in this field to each record you create.

4. Key a new name **Computers** for the folder as shown in Figure 2.5. Tap ENTER. Notice that the new folder name now appears in both panes.

5. Close *Windows Explorer* or continue to the next activity.

6B PRACTICE: Create More Folders

If you make a mistake, you can rename the folder. Right-click on the folder. Choose Rename. Key the new name. Tap ENTER.

1. Start *Windows Explorer*. Click the **Folders** button on the toolbar, if needed, to view the folders in the left pane. Click **My Documents** in the left pane.

2. Create eight new folders in your *My Documents* folder. Use the following names for the folders:

   Space

   Moon Rocks

   Maps to Mars

   Saturn

   Stars

   Perfect Planets

   Comets

   Asteroids

3. Close *Windows Explorer* or continue to the next activity.

 Do you have nine new folders? One folder should be named *Computers*. The others should have the names shown in step 2 above.

6C LEARN: Delete Folders

Using *Windows Explorer*, you can delete unwanted folders in several ways. You will learn three ways to delete folders in this activity.

1. Start *Windows Explorer*. Click the **Folders** button on the toolbar, if needed, to view the folders in the left pane. Click **My Documents** in the left pane.

2. To see the File and Folder Tasks pane, click the **Folders** button on the toolbar. This will reveal a list of commands in the left pane as shown in Figure 2.6 on page 41.

3. Click the **Comets** folder to select it. Click **Delete this folder** in the File and Folder Tasks pane. Answer **Yes** when asked whether you want to send the folder to the *Recycle Bin* folder.

Create a Query and a Report

For this activity, you will create a report showing the first name, last name, class, and instructor for all students taking a class from Mr. Johnson during the first period. Before creating the report, you will need to create a query to get the data for the report.

1. Start *Access*. Open the *120-Lincoln* database file.

2. Create a query in Design view. Base the query on the *Student Schedules* table. Include these fields in the query: *First Name*, *Last Name*, *Class Period 1*, *Instructor 1*. In the *Instructor 1* column on the *Criteria* row, enter **Johnson**. The design grid should look like Figure 16.31.

Field:	First Name	Last Name	Class Period 1	Instructor 1	
Table:	Student Schedules	Student Schedules	Student Schedules	Student Schedules	
Sort:					
Show:	☑	☑	☑	☑	
Criteria:				Johnson	
or:					

Figure 16.31 Query Design Grid

3. Save the query using the name **Period 1 Johnson**. Run the query. Look over the query results. There should be six records. Close the query results table.

4. Create a report using the Report Wizard. Base the report on the *Period 1 Johnson* query. Include all the fields in the report.

5. Group the report by the *Class Period 1* field. Sort the report by the Last Name field in Ascending order. Choose **Align Left 1** for the layout and **Portrait** for the orientation.

6. Choose **Formal** for the style. Enter **Period 1 Johnson** for the report title. Preview the report. Print the report. Close *Access*.

 **CHECK POINT** Compare your printed report with the one shown in Figure 16.27 on page 578.

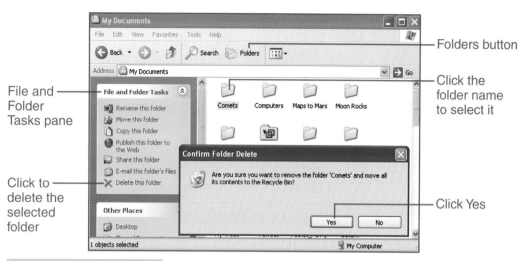

Folders button

Click the folder name to select it

File and Folder Tasks pane

Click to delete the selected folder

Click Yes

Figure 2.6 Delete a Folder

Instant Message

Tablet PC users, hold the pen on the folder. When the mouse appears, lift up to reveal the pop-up menu.

4. Right-click the **Maps to Mars** folder to open a pop-up menu. Choose **Delete** from the menu. Choose **Yes** in the Confirm Folder Delete box.

5. Click the **Asteroids** folder to select it. Tap DELETE on the keyboard. Choose **Yes** in the Confirm Folder Delete box.

6. Close *Windows Explorer* or continue to the next activity.

6D LEARN: Rename Folders

In this activity, you will learn two ways to rename a folder.

1. Start *Windows Explorer*. Click the **Folders** button on the toolbar, if needed, to view the folders in the left pane. Click **My Documents** in the left pane.

2. Click the **Folders** button to reveal the File and Folder Tasks pane.

3. To rename the *Perfect Planets* folder, click the folder to select it. Click **Rename this folder** in the File and Folder Tasks pane. Key the new name **Planets**. Tap ENTER.

Click to rename the selected folder

Select the folder

Figure 2.7 Rename a Folder

SOFTWARE TIP

You can also rename a file by choosing **Rename** from the File menu.

4. To rename the *Moon Rocks* folder, right-click the folder to display a pop-up menu. Choose **Rename** from the menu. Key the new name **Moon**. Click a blank area outside the folder name.

5. Close *Windows Explorer* or continue to the next activity.

6. The next prompt asks for the sort order you want for detail records. Click the down arrow in the first box and select **Last Name**. The default order, **Ascending**, should be shown beside the box. If it is not, select it. See Figure 16.29. Click **Next** to continue.

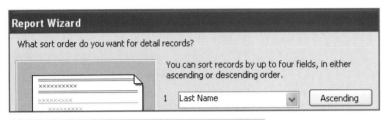

Figure 16.29 Report Wizard Sort Order Screen

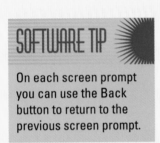

SOFTWARE TIP

On each screen prompt you can use the Back button to return to the previous screen prompt.

7. The next screen allows you to select a report layout. Select **Stepped** for the layout and **Portrait** for the orientation. Click **Next** to continue.

8. The next screen allows you to select a report style. Select **Corporate** for the style. Click **Next** to continue.

9. On the last screen, key **Lincoln Junior High Students** for the report name. Select **Preview the report**. Click **Finish**.

10. The report will be saved and opened in Print Preview. Compare your report with the top portion of the report shown in Figure 16.30.

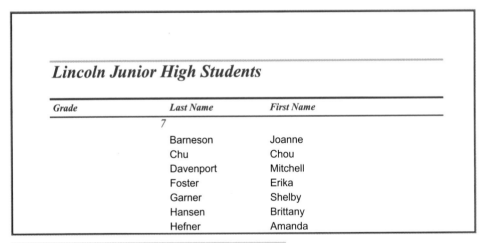

Lincoln Junior High Students

Grade	Last Name	First Name
7		
	Barneson	Joanne
	Chu	Chou
	Davenport	Mitchell
	Foster	Erika
	Garner	Shelby
	Hansen	Brittany
	Hefner	Amanda

Figure 16.30 Lincoln Junior High Students Report

11. Print the report and then close it. Close *Access* or continue to the next activity.

Working with Subfolders

When one folder is inside another, it may be called a **subfolder**. Subfolders often hold information related to the topic of a main folder. For example, Figure 2.8 shows the subfolders *Moon, Planets, Saturn,* and *Stars* in the *Space* folder. In this lesson you will reorganize your folders by topic.

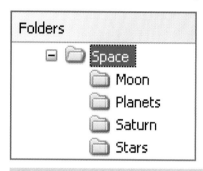

Figure 2.8 Subfolders inside the *Space* Folder

6E LEARN: Move Subfolders by Dragging

You can move subfolders into other folders by selecting and dragging them. Learn how in the steps that follow.

1. Start *Windows Explorer*. Click the **Folders** button on the toolbar, if needed, to view the folders in the left pane. Click **My Documents** in the left pane.

2. In the right pane, click and drag the *Moon* folder and drop it onto the *Space* folder. See Figure 2.9. The *Moon* folder should now be a subfolder in *Space*.

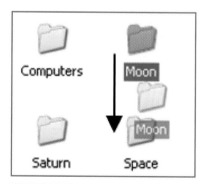

Figure 2.9 Move a Folder by Dragging to a New Location

3. Practice by dragging the **Stars** subfolder into the *Space* folder in the same way.

4. Close *Windows Explorer* or continue to the next activity.

- Way fields will be grouped in the report
- Way records will be sorted in the report
- Style and layout of the report

If you do not like the results of your choices, you can delete the report and create a new one using different choices. You can also make changes to a report in Design view.

120A LEARN: Create a Report with the Report Wizard

1. Start *Windows Explorer*. Open the folder where you store your files for this class. Make a copy of the *119-Lincoln* database file. Place the copy in the folder where you save your work for this class. Name the copy of the file *120-Lincoln*. Close *Windows Explorer*.

2. Start *Access*. Open the *120-Lincoln* database file. You will create a report to show data from the *Student Schedules* table. In the Objects list, click **Reports**. Double-click **Create report by using wizard**.

3. Select the *Student Schedules* table under Tables/Queries. See Figure 16.27.

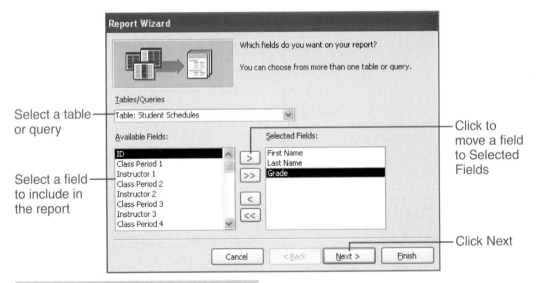

Figure 16.28 Report Wizard Opening Screen

SOFTWARE TIP

If you move the wrong field to the *Selected Fields* column, highlight the field name and click the left arrow to move the field back to the *Available Fields* column.

4. Click on the **First Name** field in the list under Available Fields. Click the right arrow button to move the field to the Selected Fields box. Do the same for the other fields to be included in the report: *Last Name* and *Grade*. Your screen should look like Figure 16.28. Click **Next**.

5. The next prompt asks if you want to add any grouping levels. Select *Grade* and click the right arrow button to move the field name to the next column. Click **Next** to continue.

Move Subfolders in Different Ways

Moving folders by dragging them is easy when the folders appear in the same window. When folders are not in the same window, you can use the Move Items box to choose a new location and move a folder. Practice this method by following the steps below.

1. Start *Windows Explorer*. Click the **Folders** button on the toolbar, if needed, to view the folders. Click **My Documents** in the left pane.

2. Click the **Folders** button to reveal the File and Folder Tasks pane.

3. Click the **Planets** folder to select it. Click **Move this folder** in the File and Folder Tasks pane. See Figure 2.10.

Figure 2.10 Select a Folder to Move

4. The Move Items dialog box will appear as shown in Figure 2.11. Scroll up, if needed, to see the *My Documents* folder. Click the **My Documents** folder. Click the **Space** subfolder to select it. Click the **Move** button. The *Planets* folder will be moved into the *Space* subfolder.

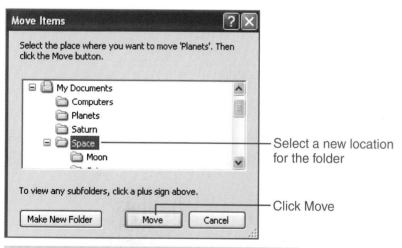

Figure 2.11 Select a New Location and Move a Folder

5. Use the same method to move the *Saturn* subfolder into the *Space* folder. Close *Windows Explorer* or continue to the next activity.

Lesson 120   Working with Database Reports

Objectives

In Lesson 120, you will:
- ⬂ Create reports using the Report Wizard.
- ⬂ Print database reports.

Reports

A **report** is a database object used to display data. Reports can be formatted to show data in a format that is easy to read. The top part of a report is shown in Figure 16.27. Reports can contain data from tables or queries. You can create an AutoReport from an open table or query. You can use the Report Wizard to create a report or mailing labels. In this lesson, you will create a report using the Report Wizard.

Period 1 Johnson

Class Period 1 History

Last Name	First Name	Instructor 1
Chu	Chou	Johnson
Foster	Erika	Johnson
Garner	Shelby	Johnson
Hansen	Brittany	Johnson
Hennessy	Matthew	Johnson
Martinez	Ricardo	Johnson

Figure 16.27 Database Report

The Report Wizard

The Report Wizard allows you to create a report by making a series of choices. You can choose the:

- Table or query on which the report is based
- Fields to include in the report

✔ CHECK POINT Do you have four subfolders (*Moon, Planets, Saturn,* and *Stars*) in your *Space* folder?

6G APPLY: Move and Create Folders

You can put subfolders into other subfolders. For example, the *Saturn* subfolder can become a subfolder inside *Planets*. All you have to do is move the *Saturn* subfolder into the *Planets* subfolder. Follow the steps below to practice moving and creating folders.

1. Start *Windows Explorer*. Click the **Folders** button on the toolbar, if needed, to view the folders. Click **My Documents** in the left pane. Click **Space** in the left pane to open the folder. Its contents will appear in the right pane.

2. Drag the **Saturn** folder to move it into the *Planets* folder.

3. Click **Planets** in the left pane to open the folder. Create a new folder for each planet in the solar system. (Choose **New, Folder** from the File menu.) Name the folders:

   Mercury

   Venus

   Earth

   Mars

   Jupiter

   Uranus

   Neptune

   Pluto

4. Click **Computers** in the left pane to open the folder.

5. Create a new folder in the *Computers* folder. Name the new folder **Chapter 1**.

6. Create another new folder inside the *Computers* folder. Name the new folder **Chapter 2**. You can use these folders to store files you create for this class. Close *Windows Explorer*.

Sort Ascending button ─┤ ├─ Sort Descending button

Figure 16.26 Sort Buttons

3. Now you will use the Sort feature to arrange the records by the *Grade* field in ascending order. Click in any cell in the *Grade* field. Click the **Sort Ascending** button. The data will be shown with all seventh graders first and then all eighth graders.

4. Now you will arrange the records by the *Grade* field in descending order. Click in any cell in the *Grade* field. Click the **Sort Descending** button. The button is shown in Figure 16.26. The data will be shown with all eighth graders first.

5. Close the Student Schedules table. Choose **No** if asked if you want to save design changes to the table. Close *Access* or continue to the next activity.

119D PRACTICE: Query, Filter, and Sort Records

In this activity, you will create a query in a database that contains information for a newspaper delivery route.

1. Start *Windows Explorer*. Open the folder where your data files for this class are stored. Make a copy of the *CD-119-Newspaper* database file. Place the copy in the folder where you save your work for this class. Name the copy of the file *119-Newspaper*. Close *Windows Explorer*.

2. Start *Access*. Open the *119-Newspaper* database file. Create a query in Design view. Base the query on the *Customer Information* table. Include the *First Name, Last Name,* and *Address* fields in the query. Save the query using the name **Customer Addresses**.

3. Run the query. Select (highlight) the word **Hyacinth** in the *Address* field in the first record in the results table. Click the **Filter by Selection** button on the toolbar. Only records that have the word *Hyacinth* in the street address should be displayed.

4. Click in a cell in the *Address* field. Click the **Sort Ascending** button to arrange the customers by their street address in ascending order.

   ✓ **CHECK POINT** Does your query results table have 11 records? The address of the first record should be 13400 Hyacinth Court, and the address of the last record should be 13452 Hyacinth Court.

5. Print the query results table that has been filtered and sorted. Use portrait orientation. Close the query results table without saving changes. Close *Access*.

Lesson 7   Working with Application Files

Objectives

In Lesson 7, you will:
↘ Create and save a file in *Word*.
↘ Follow file paths to save and find files.
↘ Open a *Word* file and save using a new name.
↘ Open an *Excel* file and save using a new name.
↘ Copy and paste information between files.

Data files: *CD-07-Orbit, CD-07-Distances, CD-07-Moon*

Your *Windows* OS serves as Mission Control for your application programs. Your applications help you solve different problems and complete tasks in different ways. Programs such as *Paint, Word, Excel,* and *Calculator* are very different from one another. Depending on the tasks you need to do, you will need to use all of them from time to time.

Creating and Saving Files

In this lesson you will use programs to gather information and solve problems. The information will be saved in files. In Chapter 1, you learned to save a file in *Word*. In this lesson, you will learn to navigate to a particular folder to save a file. You will use the folders you created in the previous lesson to keep your files organized and easy to find.

You should give the files and folders you create names that are logical and easy to understand. Current versions of *Microsoft Windows* allow you to use long filenames of up to 255 characters. This does not mean, however, that all of your filenames should be really long. Use a name that suggests the content of the file with as few words as possible. The following characters cannot be used in file or folder names: \ / : * ? " < > |. Some programs do not allow you to use long filenames. For those programs, only eight characters can be used in a filename.

7A LEARN: Create and Save a File

1. Start *Word*. Open *CD-07-Moon* from the data files.

Help Words

Filter
  Create a filter
  Remove a filter

1. Start *Access*. Open the *119-Lincoln* database file. Open the *Student Schedules* table.

2. Click in a cell in the *Class Period 1* column that contains **History**. Click the **Filter by Selection** button on the toolbar. See Figure 16.25. Only records with *History* in the *Class Period 1* field will display.

Filter by Selection   Remove Filter
button   button

Figure 16.25 Filter Buttons

3. Click in a cell in the *Grade* column that contains **7**. Click the **Filter by Selection** button. Only records for seventh graders will display.

4. Leave *Access* open. Start *Word*. Open *CD-119-Memo* from your data files. Save the file as *119-Memo* in the location where you store files for this class.

5. Make *Access* the active window. In the *Student Schedules* filtered table, select the following columns: *ID, Last Name, First Name, Grade, Class Period 1*, and *Instructor 1*. (Point to the first column head and drag across to select the columns.) Click the **Copy** button on the toolbar.

6. Make *Word* the active window. Click on the blank line below the paragraph of the memo. Click the **Paste** button on the toolbar. The table will appear in your memo. Center the table horizontally.

7. Change **Student Name** to your name in the memo heading. Add the current date in the heading. Save the memo again, using the same name. Print and close the memo. Close *Word*.

8. Make *Access* the active window. Click the **Remove Filter** button on the toolbar. See Figure 16.25.

9. All records should now be displayed in the table. Close *Access* or continue to the next activity.

119C LEARN: Sort Records

In this activity, you will use the Sort feature to arrange records in the *Student Schedules* table in various ways.

1. Start *Access*. Open the *119-Lincoln* database file. Open the *Student Schedules* table.

2. Click in any cell in the *Last Name* field. Click the **Sort Ascending** button on the toolbar. The Sort toolbar buttons are shown in Figure 16.26. The *Last Name* field should be alphabetized starting with *Barneson*.

2. The following questions appear in the data file. You will answer these questions in a later activity.

In kilometers, how far is the Earth from the moon?

What word is used to describe the moon at its closest point to Earth?

What word is used to describe the moon at its farthest point from Earth?

In kilometers, how far away is the moon when it is at its closest point to Earth?

In kilometers, how far away is the moon when it is at its farthest point away from Earth?

What is the difference in kilometers between the farthest and nearest points?

Instant Message

If you have been told to save in a different folder, choose the folder that your teacher has directed you to use instead of *My Documents*.

3. Click **File** on the menu bar. Choose **Save As**. The Save As dialog box will appear. Click **My Documents** in the left pane as shown in Figure 2.12.

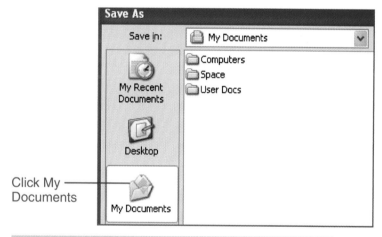

Figure 2.12 Click My Documents on the Save As dialog box.

Help Words

Save
Save a file

4. A list of folders stored in *My Documents* will appear. Double-click the **Computers** folder to open it. Then double-click the **Chapter 2** folder to select it. This folder name will appear in the Save in text box. See Figure 2.13.

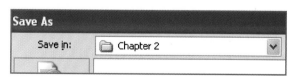

Figure 2.13 Select a folder to appear in the Save in box.

5. In the File name box at the bottom of the dialog box, key the name **Moon Project**. Click the **Save** button. See Figure 2.14 on page 47.

4. Click in the query design grid in the first column by *Field*. Click on the down arrow that appears in the cell to show a list of field names. Select **ID**.

5. Tab to the next column. Click the down arrow and select **Last Name**.

6. Tab to the next column. Click the down arrow and select **First Name**.

7. Tab to the next column. Click the down arrow and select **Grade**. In the *Criteria* row for this column, key **8**. Your design grid should look like the one in Figure 16.24.

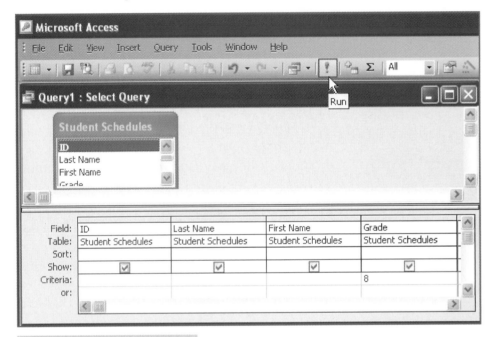

Figure 16.24 Query Design Grid

8. Click the **Save** button to save the query. For the query name, key **Students Grade 8**. Click **OK**.

9. Click the **Run** button on the toolbar. The Run button is shown in Figure 16.24. The query results will display in a table.

10. Read the Check Point below. Close the query window. Close *Access* or continue to the next activity.

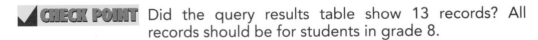 **CHECK POINT** Did the query results table show 13 records? All records should be for students in grade 8.

119B LEARN:

Use Filter By Selection

The principal at Lincoln Junior High has requested some information from the database. He wants to know which eighth-grade students have history during first period. In this activity, you will use the Filter by Selection feature to answer this question.

Key a
name for
the file

Click Save

Figure 2.14 Name the file and click Save.

6. Your document will be saved in the *Chapter 2* folder. Choose **File** on the menu bar. Select **Exit** to close *Word*.

File Paths

The *Apollo 13* astronauts had to follow a precise flight path to Earth. If they came in too shallow, the ship would bounce off the atmosphere. If *Apollo* came in too steep, the ship would burn up in a ball of fire.

You must also follow a precise path through the folders to the files that you need. How do you find the exact file you are looking for? You find a file by following its path. The drive and series of folders and subfolders that describe the location of your document is called the **path.**

The file path begins with the drive on which your file is saved. Drive C is usually a hard drive located inside a computer. When you save on a floppy disk, *A* is usually the drive for the floppy disk. Other drives, such as a CD drive, may have other letters such as *D, E,* or *F.* A network drive might have other letters such as *G, U,* or *Z.*

You followed a precise path to save your *Moon Project* file. That path statement can be written in a shorthand way from folder to subfolders to your file:

C:*My Documents\Computers\Chapter 2\Moon Project*

When you locate a file using *Windows Explorer*, the path for the file is shown in the Address box. The path for your file should look similar to the one shown in Figure 2.15. Notice that the *Documents and Settings* and *User Name* folders have been placed in front of the folders you chose for the file location. This is the way *Windows* automatically organizes files placed in the *My Documents* folder. You may see your login name in the path instead of *User Name*.

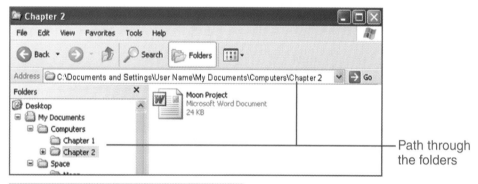

Path through
the folders

Figure 2.15 Path to the *Moon Project* File

Database Filters

Another way to find information is by using a filter. A **filter** hides records in a table that do not match your criteria. For example, suppose you want to find all the records for students who have Johnson for history in first period. You can apply a filter that will hide all other records. Filtered records are not deleted, just hidden. They will be displayed again when the filter is removed.

Sorting in a Database

The **Sort** feature allows you to arrange the information in a table or query in a certain order. The information can be sorted in ascending order (0 to 100 or A to Z) or descending order (100 to 0 or Z to A).

Create a Query in Design View

In this activity, you will create a query to show the *Last Name*, *First Name*, and *Grade* fields for records for eighth-grade students.

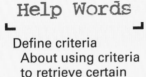

Help Words

Define criteria
  About using criteria
  to retrieve certain
  records

1. Start *Windows Explorer*. Open the folder where your data files for this class are stored. Make a copy of the *CD-119-Lincoln* database file. Place the copy in the folder where you save your work for this class. Name the copy of the file *119-Lincoln*. Close *Windows Explorer*.

2. Start *Access*. Open the *119-Lincoln* database file. Click **Queries** in the Objects list. Double-click **Create query in Design view**. A window containing the query design grid will open as shown in Figure 16.23. The Show Table dialog box will be open.

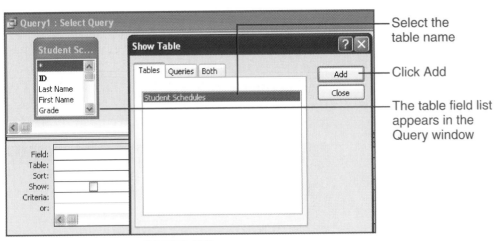

Figure 16.23 Show Table Dialog Box

3. The table *Student Schedules* will be selected. Click **Add**. The *Student Schedules* fields list box will appear in the query window. Click **Close** on the Show Table dialog box.

In the next activity, you will follow a different path to locate the folder that holds data files for use in this class. Here is a sample path to a file named *CD-07-Orbit*. Can you follow this path?

C:\Shared Documents\Data Files\Chapter 2\CD-07-Orbit

7B PRACTICE: Open and Save Files in Word

You learned about data files in Chapter 1. Practice using data files and following a path to find files in this activity.

1. Start *Word*. Choose **File** from the menu bar. Choose **Open**.

2. Follow the path to the folder that holds your data files as instructed by your teacher.

Instant Message

If you need a reminder of how to open a data file, review Chapter 1, Activity 4B.

3. Select the *CD-07-Orbit* file. Click **Open**. This report has answers to some of the questions in your *Moon Project* file. You'll definitely want to save a copy.

4. Choose **File, Save As**. Save the file in the *Moon* folder. Follow this path by opening each folder in turn: *My Documents\Space\Moon*

5. Name the file *07-Orbit* and then choose **Save**. Close the file.

6. You need to change the name of the *Moon Project* file so that it begins with the lesson number. Open the *Moon Project* file. (The path is *My Documents\Computers\Chapter 2\Moon Project.*)

7. Save the file in the same location using the name *07-Moon Project*. Close *Word*.

7C PRACTICE: Open and Save Files in Excel

At first glance, *Microsoft Excel* looks very different from *Microsoft Word*. But take another look! The menu and toolbars are very similar. The main portion of the *Excel* window is organized into columns, rows, and cells. These parts are marked in Figure 2.16. In the cells, you can enter words or numbers. You can also enter formulas to do math calculations.

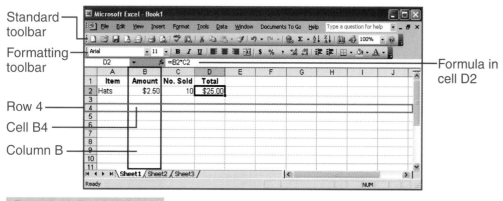

Figure 2.16 *Excel* Window

1. Start *Access*. Open the *118-Lincoln* database file. Open the *Student Schedules* table in Design view.

2. Insert a new row after the *First Name* field. In the new row, key **Grade** for the field name. Select **Number** as the data type. For the description, key **Grade level of student**. Save the table and switch to Datasheet view.

3. The four new students you added to the database (Ferrero, Chang, Bjorkman, and Guillermo) are in grade 8. Enter **8** in the *Grade* field for these students.

4. All the other students in the database are in grade 7. Enter **7** in the *Grade* field for these students.

5. You should have 12 records in your *Student Schedules* table. Close *Access*.

Lesson 119 Working with Database Queries, Filters, and Sorts

Objectives
In Lesson 119, you will:
↘ Create a query in Design view.
↘ Create a filter by selection.
↘ Sort a table.

Data files: *CD-119-Lincoln, CD-119-Newspaper, CD-119-Memo.doc*

Data is stored in a database so that it can be recalled later. The data may be needed to answer a question or complete a listing. In this lesson, you will learn to use queries and filters to find data.

Database Queries

A **query** is a database object that displays certain data that you describe. You describe the data by entering criteria. The criteria might be the field name, data in a certain field, or data that is not in a field. For example, the database for Lincoln Junior High has records for students in both grade 7 and grade 8. You can create a query that will display only records for students in grade 8. A query allows you to include all the fields included in a table or only selected ones. When you create the query to show only records for eighth-grade students, for example, you may want only their first name, last name, and grade included.

1. To start *Excel*, choose **Start**, **All Programs**, **Microsoft Office**, **Microsoft Excel**.

2. Choose **File** from the menu bar. Choose **Open**.

3. Follow the path to the folder that contains data files for this class as instructed by your teacher. Select the *CD-07-Distances* file. Click **Open**.

4. *Excel* has a Standard toolbar and a Formatting toolbar like *Word* does. Make sure the Standard and Formatting toolbars are on two separate rows as shown in Figure 2.16. If they are not, click the down arrow at the end of the toolbar and choose **Show Buttons on Two Rows**. See Figure 2.17.

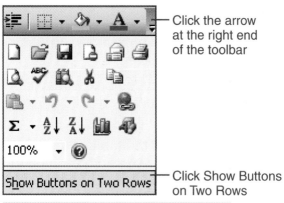

Click the arrow
at the right end
of the toolbar

Click Show Buttons
on Two Rows

Figure 2.17 Show Buttons on Two Rows

5. Do you see any answers to the questions found in your *07-Moon Project* file in this document? You will want to save the document under a new name for later use. Choose **File** from the menu bar. Choose **Save As**. Save the file in the *Moon* folder. Follow this path by opening each folder in turn: *My Documents\Space\Moon*.

6. Key **07-Distances** for the filename as shown in Figure 2.18. Choose **Save**.

Figure 2.18 Save a File in *Excel*

7. Choose **File** from the menu bar. Choose **Exit** to close *Excel* and the *07-Distances* file.

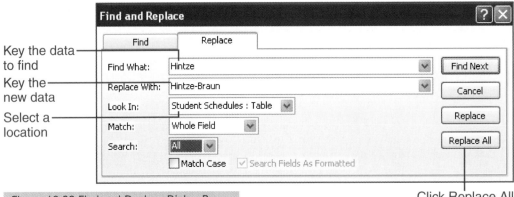

Key the data
to find

Key the
new data

Select a
location

Figure 16.22 Find and Replace Dialog Box

Click Replace All

13. In the Find What box, key **Hintze**. In the Replace With box, key **Hintze-Braun**. In the Look In box, **Student Schedules: Table** should appear. If it does not, select it.

14. Click **Replace All**. A dialog box will appear telling you that you won't be able to undo this operation. Click **Yes** to continue. Click **Cancel** to close the Find and Replace box.

15. Widen the columns in the table as needed to display the new name. Close the table. Close *Access* or continue to the next activity.

118B PRACTICE: Update Records in a Database

Four of the students in the database for Lincoln Junior High have no instructor names recorded. Also, four new students must be added to the table.

1. Start *Word*. Open and print the file *CD-118-Names* found in your data files. Close *Word*.

2. Start *Access*. Open the *118-Lincoln* database file. Open the *Student Schedules Form 3* form. Use the form to add or update the records with the data from the printout.

3. Close the database. Close *Access* or continue to the next activity.

 Switch seats with one of your classmates. Check to see whether they have made the edits for 118A and 118B correctly.

118C APPLY: Add a New Field to a Table

The database for Lincoln Junior High was not designed to include the grade level of the students. In this activity you will add a field and update the records.

Lesson 8 — Find Information and Print Files

Objectives

In Lesson 8, you will:

↘ Open two programs at once.

↘ Switch between active and inactive programs.

↘ Find information in *Word* and *Excel* files.

↘ Copy and paste answers from one program to another.

↘ Preview and print *Word* and *Excel* files.

Open Documents to Find Information

As you learned in Chapter 1, the *Windows* OS allows you to have several documents open at the same time. This can help you find information in one file while reading questions in another.

Remember that you can work only in the active program. A program is active when it has a darkened title bar. Tap or click inside an inactive program window to make it active. You can also click the program name on the taskbar to make it active.

8A PRACTICE: Use a Word Document to Find Information

In this activity, you will switch between active and inactive windows to find information and answer questions.

Instant Message

If you need a reminder of how to restore and resize your *Word* window, review Chapter 1, Moving and Changing the Size of Windows, page 19.

⌐ ¬
 Help Words
L ⌐

Copy
 Move or copy text
 and graphics

1. Start *Word*. Open the *07-Moon Project* file that you saved earlier. Follow this path to the file: *My Documents\Computers\Chapter 2\07-Moon Project*.

2. Resize the *Word* window so that it occupies only about half of the screen.

3. Open the file *07-Orbit* that you saved earlier. Follow this path to the file: *My Documents\Space\Moon\07-Orbit*.

4. Resize the *07-Orbit* file window so it occupies the other half of the screen.

5. Click in first one *Word* window then the other a few times. Watch how the color of the title bars changes to show the active window.

6. Read the *07-Orbit* file and find the answers to the first five questions in the *07-Moon Project* file.

7. In the *07-Orbit* file, select the text that answers the first question. Click **Edit** on the menu bar. Choose **Copy**.

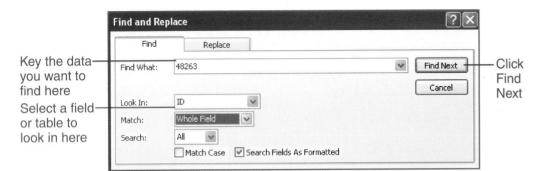

Key the data you want to find here

Select a field or table to look in here

Click Find Next

Figure 16.21 Find Dialog Box

5. Click **Cancel** to close the Find box. Use the mouse or the TAB key to move to the *First Name* field. Change the name from Rico to **Ricardo**.

6. Use Find to move to the record for Felipe Santos, ID 25781. He has changed science instructors. He has switched from Baker to **Boyer**. The class still meets during the fourth class period. Update his record.

7. Use Find to move to the record for Brittany Hansen, ID 35981. She has **History** during the first class period and **English** during the second class period. Her English teacher is **Fenn**, not Ramos. Her history teacher is **Johnson**. Update her record.

8. Use Find to move to the record for Mary Castello. You do not know Mary's ID number, so you will use her name to find her record. Click in the *Last Name* field of any record that appears in the form.

9. Choose **Edit**, **Find**. Key **Castello** in the Find What box. **Last Name** should appear in the Look In box. Click **Find Next**. Mary's record will display.

10. Mary Castello moved last week. You need to delete her record from the table. Click in any field of the record for Mary Castello. Click the **Delete Record** button on the toolbar. Choose **Yes** when asked if you are sure you want to delete the record.

11. Close the *Student Schedules Form 3* form. Open the *Student Schedules* table. Notice that the changes you made in the form appear in the table.

12. Miss Hintze, who teaches math, was recently married. Her new name is Hintze-Braun. You will use the Replace feature to update the table with her new name. Click **Edit** on the menu bar. Click **Replace**. The Find and Replace dialog box will appear as shown in Figure 16.22.

SOFTWARE TIP

Click the **Delete Record** button to delete a selected record.

Delete Record button

8. Make the *07-Moon Project* file the active window. Click the blank line under the first question where you want the answer to appear. Click **Edit** on the menu bar. Choose **Paste**. This will paste your answer into the file. Tap ENTER to insert a blank line before the next question.

9. Repeat the copy and paste process to paste answers to the second, third, fourth, and fifth questions into the *07-Moon Project* file.

10. Save the *07-Moon Project* file using the new name *08-Moon Project*. Place the file in the *My Documents\Computers\Chapter 2* folder.

11. Close the *07-Orbit* file. Leave the *08-Moon Project* file open for the next activity if you have time to continue working. If not, close the file.

 Compare your answers with a classmate's answers. If they are different, read the *07-Orbit* file again to see which answers are correct.

8B PRACTICE: Use an Excel Document to Find Information

1. Start *Word* if it is not already open. Open the *08-Moon Project* file. Resize the window so that it occupies one half of the screen.

2. Start *Excel*. Choose **File** from the menu bar. Choose **Open**. Find the *07-Distances* file that you saved earlier. The path is *My Documents\ Space\Moon*. Open the file.

3. Resize the *07-Distances* file so it occupies the other half of the screen.

4. The *07-Distances* file shows the answers to the last question in the *08-Moon Project* file.

5. Select the answer (50,345 km) in the *Excel* file. Click **Edit** on the menu bar. Choose **Copy**.

6. Make the *08-Moon Project* file the active window. Click the blank line under the last question where you want the answer to appear. Click **Edit** on the menu bar. Choose **Paste**. This will paste your answer into the file.

7. Make the *Excel* file the active window. Choose **File** from the menu bar. Choose **Exit** to close *Excel* and the *07-Distances* file.

8. The *08-Moon Project* file should now be the active window. Click the **Save** button on the Standard toolbar to save the file. Close the file.

Previewing and Printing Files

The **Print Preview** command allows you to see how a document will look before you print it. Buttons on the Print Preview toolbar allow you to change view settings and other options. The **Zoom** feature lets you see your document

Reasons for Editing Records

Information changes over time. Errors are sometimes made when entering data. As a result of these errors and changes, the data in a database may need to be corrected or updated. **Edits** (changes and corrections) may be needed for a variety of reasons. For example, a person may move to a new house. This person's address data would need to be updated. A student may change classes. An incorrect address may be entered. All these situations require edits to the database.

Methods for Editing Records

Editing database records is similar to editing word processing documents. You begin by moving to the location where the change is to be made. You can use the DELETE or BACKSPACE keys to delete data. You can also delete entire records.

When you have a small database table, you can locate records easily by simply scrolling through the rows. However, many databases are large, and scrolling to find a certain record to edit is not so easy. You can use the Find feature to locate a record quickly. You can use the Replace feature to change several occurrences of data in a table. You can make edits to records in Datasheet view or using a form.

118A LEARN: Edit Records in a Database

1. Start *Windows Explorer.* Open the folder where you save work for this class. Make a copy of the *117-Lincoln* database file. Place the copy in the same folder. Name the copy of the file *118-Lincoln*. Close *Windows Explorer.*

2. Start *Access.* Open the *118-Lincoln* database file.

3. You need to edit the record for the student with ID 48263. Open the *Student Schedules Form 3* form. Click in the *ID* field for the first record that appears.

4. Click **Edit** on the menu bar. Click **Find**. In the Find What box, key **48263**. In the Look In box, **ID** should appear. If it does not, select it. See Figure 16.21. Click **Find Next**. The record for the student with this ID, Rico Martinez, will be displayed.

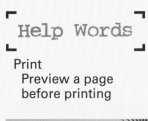

Help Words

Print
    Preview a page
    before printing

in smaller or larger sizes. This can be helpful when checking a document that is several pages long. You can also magnify a part of the page. Make a habit of using Print Preview to check documents before you print.

As you learned in Chapter 1, the **Print** command allows you to print a document. Clicking the Print button on the Standard toolbar causes the document to print using the default settings. To view or change print settings, you can choose Print from the File menu. This command will open the Print dialog box as shown in Figure 2.20 on page 53. In this box, you can choose a printer, select the number of copies you want to print, and choose other options.

You have found information and answered the questions in your *08-Moon Project* file. Now you will learn to preview and print this file. Your teacher will tell you which printer you can use to print your work. Your teacher will also give you any special instructions for your printer or network.

8C LEARN: Preview and Print a Word File

1. Start *Word* if it is not already open. Open the *08-Moon Project* file that you saved earlier in the *My Documents\Computers\Chapter 2* folder.

2. Click the **Print Preview** button on the Standard toolbar. The document will appear in the Print Preview window as shown in Figure 2.19.

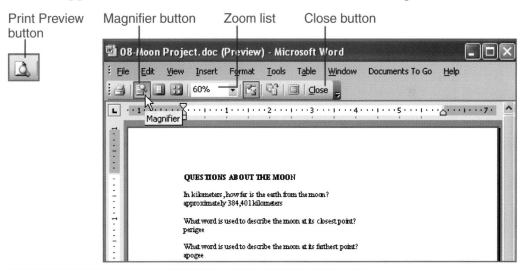

Figure 2.19 Use Print Preview to check a document before printing.

3. The **Magnifier** button should be selected. See Figure 2.19. If it is not, click the button. Move the magnifier glass pointer over the page and click the page. The area you click will be enlarged. Click the page again to return to the original view.

Delete Fields in a Database Table

The *Composers (1600-1799)* table has data in the *Teachers* field for only one record. You have decided that this data is not really needed. You will delete the *Teachers* field in this activity.

1. Start *Access*. Open the *117-Composers* database file. Open the *Composers (1600-1799)* table in Design view.

2. Right-click in the row that has *Teachers* for the field name. Choose **Delete Rows** from the pop-up menu. See Figure 16.20.

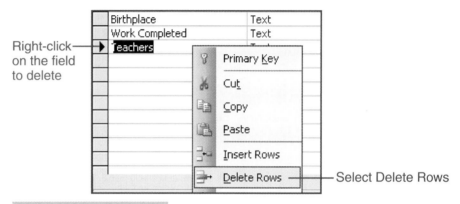

Figure 16.20 Delete a Field

3. You will be asked whether you want to delete the field and all the data in the field. Choose **Yes**. The field will be deleted.

4. Click the **Save** button to save the table. Switch to Datasheet view. Print the table in portrait orientation. Close *Access*.

Congratulations! You now know how to edit records as well as add and delete fields to an existing database table.

Lesson 118   Editing Records

Objectives

In Lesson 118, you will:
⬎ Edit records and enter new records.
⬎ Use the Find feature to locate records.
⬎ Delete records.
⬎ Add a field to a table.
⬎ Use the Replace feature to update records.

Data file: *CD-118-Names*

4. The Zoom feature lets you see your document in smaller or larger sizes. To practice using Zoom, click the down arrow for the **Zoom** list. Choose **50%** from the list. Click the **Zoom** list arrow again and choose **150%**. Click the **Close** button to close Print Preview.

5. Click **File** on the menu bar. Choose **Print**. The Print dialog box will appear as shown in Figure 2.20. Click the down arrow by **Printer Name** and select the printer you wish to use if it is not already selected. See Figure 2.20.

Select a printer from the list

Select the pages to print

Enter the number of copies to print

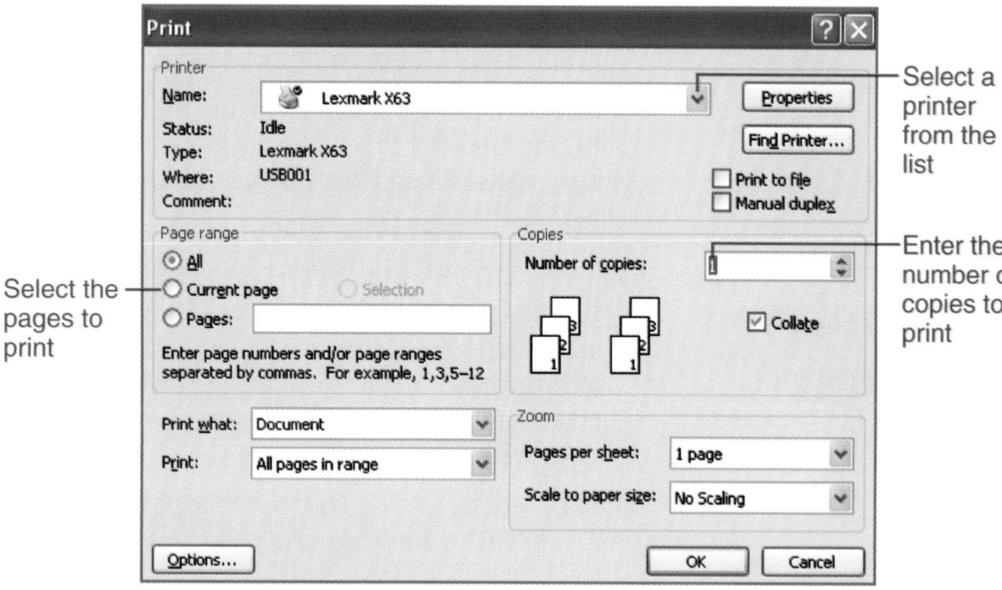

Figure 2.20 *Word's* Print Dialog Box

6. Enter **1** for the number of copies to print if that number does not already appear. Click **OK**. Your document should now print. Close *Word*.

8D PRACTICE: Print an Excel File

1. Start *Excel*. Choose **File** from the menu bar. Choose **Open**. Find the *07-Distances* file that you saved earlier. The path is *My Documents\Space\Moon*. Open the file.

2. Click the **Print Preview** button on the Standard toolbar. The document will appear in the Print Preview window as shown in Figure 2.21 on page 54. Notice that the buttons on the toolbar are different from those found in *Word*.

Add Fields to the Composers Database

In this activity, you will open a database from your data files and practice adding a field.

1. Start *Windows Explorer*. Open the folder where your data files for this class are stored. Make a copy of the *CD-117-Composers* database file. Place the copy in the folder where you save your work for this class. Name the copy of the file *117-Composers*. Close *Windows Explorer*.

2. Start *Access*. Open the *117-Composers* database file. Open the *Composers (1600-1799)* table in Design view.

3. Add a field to the table. Insert the new field after the *Life* field. Key **Birthplace** for the field name. Select **Text** for the data type. For the description, key **Composer's birthplace**.

4. Save the table and switch to Datasheet view. Print the table in landscape orientation. Close *Access*.

5. Work with another student to find the country where each composer was born. For example, Bach was born in Germany. Access the Internet and find the birth country for three of the remaining composers. Your classmate should find data for the other three composers. Share your data with each other.

6. Start *Access*. Open the *117-Composers* database file. Open the *Composers (1600-1799)* table. Update the table with the birthplaces you found in your research.

7. Print the table again in landscape orientation. Complete the Check Point and then close the table. Close *Access* or continue to the next activity.

 **CHECK POINT** Exchange tables with a classmate and check each other's work. Make corrections to your table, if needed.

Instant Message

Enter the composer's name in a search engine or online encyclopedia to find data about him.

Deleting Fields in a Database Table

After a database table has been created, you might want to delete fields from the table. You might find that the data you intended to enter is not available. You might also find that the information you entered in a table is no longer needed.

To delete fields from a table, you begin by opening the table in Design view. Then you can select and delete the field. You will learn to delete a field in the next activity.

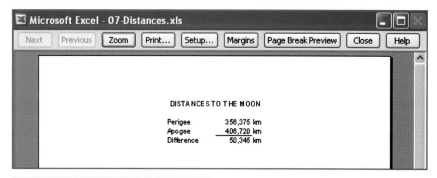

Figure 2.21 Print Preview in *Excel*

3. Click the **Zoom** button. A larger view of the worksheet will appear. Click the **Zoom** button again to return to the original view.

4. Click the **Close** button to close Print Preview. You will learn how to set options using this toolbar in a later chapter.

5. Click **File** on the menu bar. Choose **Print**. The Print dialog box will appear as shown in Figure 2.22. Notice that some options are different than in the *Word* Print dialog box and some are the same.

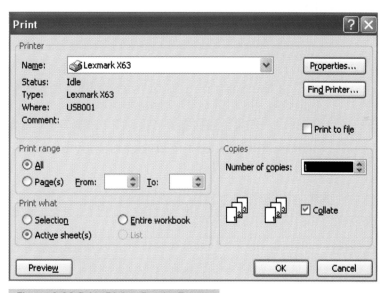

Figure 2.22 Print Dialog Box in *Excel*

6. Click the down arrow by **Printer Name** and select the printer you wish to use if it is not already selected.

7. Enter **1** for the number of copies to print if that number does not already appear. Click **OK**. Your document should now print. Close *Excel*.

4. A new row will be inserted above the selected row. In the new row, key **Instructor 1** for the field name. Choose **Text** for the data type. For the description, key **Name of Instructor for period 1 class**. See Figure 16.19.

5. Repeat the procedure to insert a row for the name of the instructor for each class period. For the last class (Period 6) enter the data in the blank row under Class Period 6. See Figure 16.19.

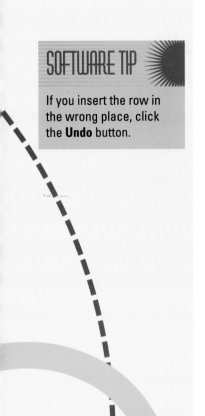

Student Schedules : Table

	Field Name	Data Type	Description
🔑	ID	Text	Student's ID number
	Last Name	Text	Student's last name
	First Name	Text	Student's first name
	Class Period 1	Text	Name of period 1 class
	Instructor 1	Text	Name of instructor for period 1 class
	Class Period 2	Text	Name of period 2 class
	Instructor 2	Text	Name of instructor for period 2 class
	Class Period 3	Text	Name of period 3 class
	Instructor 3	Text	Name of instructor for period 3 class
	Class Period 4	Text	Name of period 4 class
	Instructor 4	Text	Name of instructor for period 4 class
	Class Period 5	Text	Name of period 5 class
	Instructor 5	Text	Name of instructor for period 5 class
	Class Period 6	Text	Name of period 6 class
▶	Instructor 6	Text	Name of instructor for period 6 class

Figure 16.19 Table with Fields Added

6. Click the **Save** button on the toolbar to save the changes to the table design. Switch to Datasheet view.

7. Create an AutoForm. Using the form, enter the names of the instructors for each class for the students shown below. Data for other students will be entered later.

	Chu	Santos	Hansen	Martinez	Castello
Instructor 1	Johnson	Fenn	Ramos	Johnson	Baker
Instructor 2	Fenn	Hintze	Johnson	Hintze	Strauss
Instructor 3	Hamilton	Hamilton	Hamilton	Vasquez	McDowell
Instructor 4	Boyer	Baker	Wallace	D'Angelo	Vasquez
Instructor 5	Hintze	Burdette	Strauss	Ramos	Fenn
Instructor 6	Burdette	McDowell	Boyer	Baker	Wallace

8. Click the **Save** button to save the form. For the form name, enter **Student Schedules Form 3**. Close the form. Close the *117-Lincoln* database. Close *Access* or continue to the next activity.

Lesson 9   Managing Files

Objectives

In Lesson 9, you will:

↘ Delete files.

↘ Rename files.

↘ Copy files from one folder to another.

↘ Move files from one folder to another.

Deleting Files

Apollo 11 left much of the lunar module and its equipment behind on the moon. Some call this equipment space junk! Many of the satellites that have been sent into space are now broken. That's more space junk just floating around!

You don't need to leave any "junk" on your computer! You should delete files that you no longer need so they do not take up valuable space on your hard drive. This will free space for other files. Deleting unused files will also make it easier to find the files you are looking for.

You can delete files in several ways. You can delete files in *Windows Explorer* using the File and Folder Tasks pane or the pop-up menu. You can also delete files from an Open or Save As dialog box in some programs. You will learn to delete files in the next activity.

9A LEARN: Delete Files

SOFTWARE TIP

You can also choose **Delete this file** in the File and Folder Tasks pane to delete a selected file.

1. Start *Windows Explorer*. Follow the path to find your *Excel* file *07-Distances*. The path is *My Documents\Space\Moon*.

2. Click the **Views** button and choose the **Icons** option.

3. Click the **07-Distances** file icon in the right pane to select the file. See Figure 2.23. Tap the DELETE key on the keyboard.

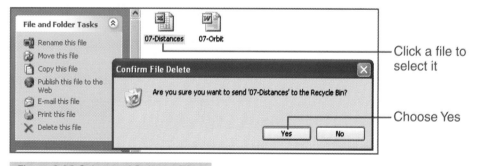

Figure 2.23 Select and Delete a File

Adding Fields to a Database Table

After a database table has been created, you might want to add fields to the table. For example, in the *Student Schedules* database table, it might be helpful to record the instructor for each of the class periods. To add fields to a table, you begin by opening the table in Design view. You insert a new row in the table where you want the field to appear. Then you enter a field name, data type, and description. After you save the table, you are ready to enter data in the new field for the existing records or for new records.

117A LEARN:

Add Fields to a Database Table

Access does not have a Save As command like the one you may have used in other programs to save files using a new name. You need to copy and rename database files in *Windows Explorer*. You will do so in this activity. You will also learn to add fields to a database table.

Instant Message

To review copying files in *Windows Explorer*, refer to Chapter 2, Lesson 9C.

1. Start *Windows Explorer*. Open the folder where you save work for this class, such as *C:\My Documents\Chapter 16*. Make a copy of the *116-Lincoln* database file. Place the copy in the same folder. Name the copy of the file *117-Lincoln*. Close *Windows Explorer*.

2. Start *Access*. Open the *117-Lincoln* database file. Open the *Student Schedules* table in Design view.

3. Right-click anywhere in the row with the field name **Class Period 2**. Choose **Insert Rows** from the pop-up menu. See Figure 16.18.

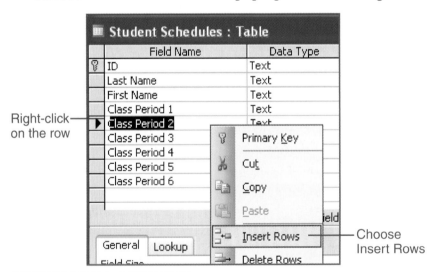

Figure 16.18 Insert a New Row

4. Choose **Yes** when asked whether to send the folder to the *Recycle Bin* folder.

5. Close *Windows Explorer* or continue to the next activity.

Renaming, Copying, and Moving Files

Sometimes, keeping your files organized will require you to rename, move, or copy files. There are several ways to rename files. First you must select the file. Then you can right-click and choose Rename on a pop-up menu. You can also choose an option in the File and Folder Tasks pane. The File and Folder Tasks pane also has options to help you move or copy a file. In the next few activities, you will learn how to complete these actions.

9B LEARN: Rename a File

1. Start *Windows Explorer*. Follow the path to find your *Word* file *07-Orbit*. The path is *My Documents\Space\Moon*.

2. Click the **Views** button and choose the **Icons** option. Display the File and Folder Tasks pane.

3. Click the file icon for *07-Orbit* to select the file. Choose **Rename this file** from the File and Folder Tasks pane. See Figure 2.24.

Click to rename a selected file

Click a file to select it

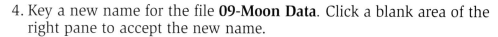
Figure 2.24 Rename a File

4. Key a new name for the file **09-Moon Data**. Click a blank area of the right pane to accept the new name.

5. Follow the path to find your *Word* file *08-Moon Project*. The path is *My Documents\Computers\Chapter 2*.

6. Right-click the **08-Moon Project** file. Choose **Rename** from the pop-up menu.

7. Key a new name for the file **09-Moon Project**. Click a blank area of the right pane to accept the new name.

SOFTWARE TIP

Tablet PC users, hold the pen on the file icon. When the mouse appears, lift up to display a menu.

Instant Message

If you have trouble creating the form, refer to Lesson 116B.

2. Create a new form using the Form Wizard. The form should include all the fields available in the *Student Schedules* table. Choose the **Justified** layout and the **Blends** style. For the form title, key **Student Schedules Form 2**.

3. Open the form and go to a new blank record. Enter data for the two records shown below, using the form.

ID	22854	23927
Last Name	Hefner	Davenport
First Name	Amanda	Mitchell
Class Period 1	Math	Science
Class Period 2	History	History
Class Period 3	Physical Ed	English
Class Period 4	Science	Math
Class Period 5	English	Chorus
Class Period 6	Chorus	Keyboarding Apps

4. After you have entered the data, close the form. Open the *Student Schedules* table.

5. Choose **File**, **Page Setup** to open the Page Setup dialog box. On the Page tab, select **Landscape** as shown in Figure 16.17. Click **OK**.

SOFTWARE TIP

Double-click on the right border line of each column heading to adjust the width of the columns.

Figure 16.17 Select Landscape orientation in the Page Setup dialog box.

6. Use Print Preview to see whether the *Student Schedules* table will print on one page. Adjust column widths or the page margins, if needed, so the table prints on one page and all the data is shown. Print the table. Close *Access*.

Lesson 117 Adding and Deleting Fields

Objectives

In Lesson 117, you will:
- Add fields to a database table.
- Delete a field in a database table.
- Update database records.

Data file: *CD-117-Composers*

9C LEARN: Copy a File

1. Start *Windows Explorer*. Follow the path to find your *Word* file *09-Moon Data*. The path is *My Documents\Space\Moon*.

2. Click the **Views** button and choose the **Icons** option. Display the File and Folder Tasks pane.

3. Click the file icon for *09-Moon Data* to select the file. Choose **Copy this file** from the File and Folder Tasks pane. See Figure 2.25.

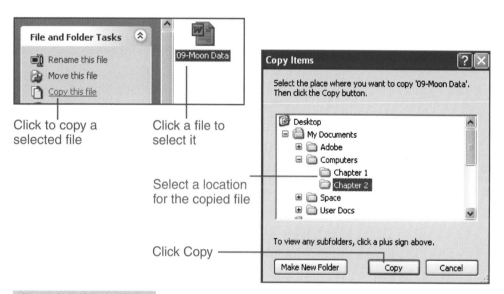

Figure 2.25 Copy a File

4. In the Copy Items box, select the folder where you want the copy of the file placed. For this activity, select the *My Documents\Computers\Chapter 2* folder. Click **Copy**.

5. Complete the Check Point below. Then close *Windows Explorer* or continue to the next activity.

✔ **CHECK POINT** In *Windows Explorer*, navigate to the *My Documents\Computers\Chapter 2* folder. A copy of the file *09-Moon Data* should be in this folder.

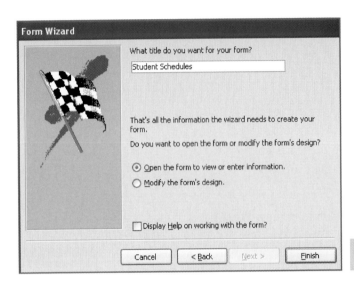

Figure 16.16 Enter a title for the form on the Form Wizard.

8. The form will appear on your screen with the five records that you entered earlier. Your form should look like the one shown in Figure 16.13.

9. Move to a new blank record. Enter data for the two records shown below.

ID	52798	63156
Last Name	Schuricht	Talbot
First Name	Jessica	Dane
Class Period 1	Math	Keyboarding Apps
Class Period 2	History	History
Class Period 3	Physical Ed	English
Class Period 4	Chorus	Math
Class Period 5	English	Chorus
Class Period 6	Science	Science

10. Close the form and open the *Student Schedules* table. Notice that the records you added using the form are now included in the table. Complete the Check Point below and then close *Access*.

 **CHECK POINT** Starting with Record 1, check each record for spelling and keying errors. Make the necessary corrections and close the table.

116D PRACTICE: Create a Form

1. Start *Access*. Open the database file *116-Lincoln* that you created in Lesson 116A.

9D LEARN: Move a File

1. Start *Windows Explorer*. Follow the path to find your *Word* file *09-Moon Data*. The path is *My Documents\Space\Moon*.

2. Click the **Views** button and choose the **Icons** option. Display the File and Folder Tasks pane.

3. Rename the file *09-Moon Data*. Key **09-Earth's Moon** for the new filename.

4. Click the file icon for *09-Earth's Moon* to select the file. Choose **Move this file** from the File and Folder Tasks pane. See Figure 2.26.

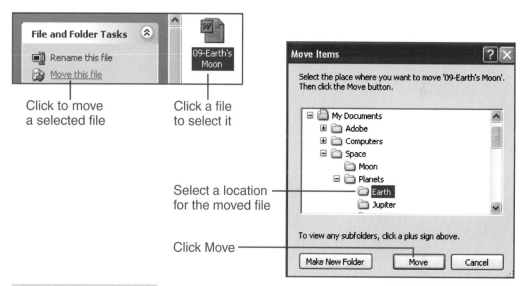

Figure 2.26 Move a File

5. In the Move Items box, select the folder where you want the file placed. For this activity, select the **My Documents\Space\Planets\Earth** folder. Click **Move**.

6. Complete the Check Point below and then close *Windows Explorer*.

CHECK POINT In *Windows Explorer*, navigate to the *My Documents\Space\Planets\Earth* folder. The file *09-Earth's Moon* should be in this folder.

Create a Form Using a Wizard

1. Start *Access*. Open the database file *116-Lincoln* that you created in 116A.

2. Click **Forms** on the Objects list in the database window. Double-click **Create form by using wizard**. The Form Wizard will open as shown in Figure 16.15.

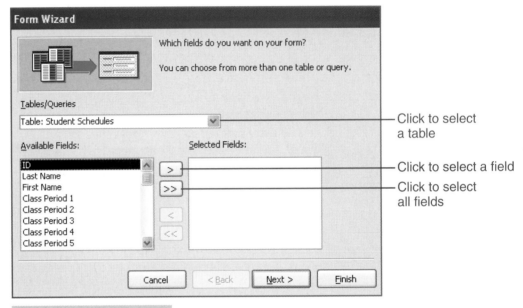

Figure 16.15 Forms Wizard

SOFTWARE TIP

The > button moves only the highlighted field over to the *Selected Fields* window.

3. Because you have only one table, the name of that table (Student Schedules) appears in the Tables/Queries box. If you had several tables, you could select the table from which you want to prepare the form. (To select a table, click the down arrow and choose the desired table.)

4. Click the double-arrow button to select all the fields and include them in the form. Click **Next**.

5. The next prompt is for selecting the form layout. Select **Columnar** and then click **Next**.

6. You will be prompted to choose a style for the form. Select **Expedition** for this form and then click **Next**.

7. Finally, you will be prompted to give the form a title. Key **Student Schedules** for this form (if it is not already displayed). Select the option **Open the form or enter information** if it is not already selected. See Figure 16.16. Click **Finish**.

Reviewing What You Have Learned

Answer these questions to review what you have learned in Chapter 2.

1. Your computer's _____ controls all of the software, folders, and files on your computer.

2. List three common devices used to store computer files. What computer storage devices can hold documents from four or five file cabinet drawers?

3. *Windows Explorer* is the program used to _____ _____.

4. By default, many *Windows* programs save files in the _____ folder.

5. The _____ folder contains all the files and folders on your computer.

6. In *Windows Explorer*, you can click the plus sign (+) beside a folder to reveal _____.

7. List five options available from the Views list in *Windows Explorer*.

8. Why should you delete files and folders you no longer need?

9. List three folder or file tasks you have practiced using the File and Folder Tasks pane in *Windows Explorer*.

10. To delete a file or folder in *Windows Explorer,* you can select the file or folder and tap the _____ key on the keyboard.

11. To display a pop-up menu with options for deleting, renaming, and moving files and folders, _____ the file or folder in *Windows Explorer.*

12. The drive and series of folders and subfolders that describe the location of a file is called the _____.

13. Drive _____ is usually a hard drive located inside a computer. Drive A is usually a _____ drive.

14. When you locate a file using *Windows Explorer*, the path for the file is shown in the _____ box.

15. The main portion of the *Microsoft Excel* window is organized into _____, _____, and _____.

16. When working with two or more *Windows* programs open, how can you tell which window is the active window? How can you make another window the active window?

SOFTWARE TIP

When you press TAB in the last field of a record, a new blank record will appear.

3. A form will be created and the first record will be displayed as shown in Figure 16.14. The arrows at the bottom of the screen can be used to move to a record. Click on each of the arrows in turn. As you click on each arrow, notice the record that is displayed before and after clicking on the arrow.

Click	To Go
I◄	To the first record
►	Forward one record
◄	Back one record
►I	To the last record
►*	To a new blank record

4. Click on the *Student Schedules* table window. Click the window's **Close** button to close the table.

5. Click on the *Student Schedules* form window. Go to a new blank record. Enter the data for two students as shown below. Press TAB or use the mouse to move from field to field in the form.

ID	11583	25781
Last Name	Chu	Santos
First Name	Chou	Felipe
Class Period 1	History	English
Class Period 2	English	Math
Class Period 3	Keyboarding Apps	Keyboarding Apps
Class Period 4	Science	Science
Class Period 5	Math	Art
Class Period 6	Art	History

6. When you finish entering the data, close the form by clicking its **Close** button. Choose **No** when asked if you want to save changes to the form.

7. Open the *Student Schedules* table. Notice that the new records are in the table. Read the Check Point below, and then close the table. Close *Access* or continue to the next activity.

CHECK POINT You should now have five records in the *Student Schedules* table.

17. The _____ command allows you to see how a document will look before you print it.

18. In *Word*, clicking the _____ button causes a document to print using the default settings. To view or change print settings, choose Print from the _____ menu.

19. Which characters cannot be used in file or folder names?

Applying *What You Have Learned*

Create Subfolders

Your *Computers* folder has subfolders to hold your work for Chapters 1 and 2. You need to create subfolders for the remaining 15 chapters. This way, all your assignments will have a home.

1. Start *Windows Explorer*. Click the **Folders** button on the toolbar, if needed, to view the folders in the left pane. Click the **plus sign** by the *My Documents* folder in the left pane to reveal the items in that folder.

2. Click the icon by the *Computers* folder to show its contents in the right pane.

3. Create 15 subfolders inside your *Computers* folder. Name them this way: **Chapter 3, Chapter 4, Chapter 5,** and so on to **Chapter 17.**

4. Close *Windows Explorer.*

Rename and Move Files

Filenames should be descriptive. This means that a filename should give you an idea of what is in the file. Some of the files in you created in Chapter 1 are not very descriptive. For example, it's hard to know what is inside the *C01-Practice* file. You will rename files and move them into your *My Documents\Computers\Chapter 1* folder.

1. Start *Windows Explorer*. Locate and open the folder in which you saved files you created in Chapter 1.

2. In the right pane, select the file **04-Word**. Rename the file **04-Office Suite**.

3. Move the file into your *My Documents\Computers\Chapter 1* folder.

4. In the right pane, select the file **C01-Practice**. Rename the file **C01-Symbols**.

5. Move the file into your *My Documents\Computers\Chapter 1* folder. Close *Windows Explorer.*

Supplemental activities for this chapter can be found at www.c21jr. swlearning.com.

table and includes all the fields from the table. You can also create a form using the Form Wizard. The Form Wizard will ask you a series of questions and create the form based on your answers. A form created with the Form Wizard is shown in Figure 16.13.

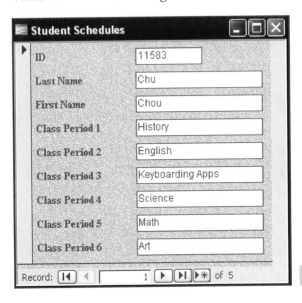

Figure 16.13 Form in Expedition Style

Using AutoForm is a quick way to create a form, but the Form Wizard gives you more choices about how the form will look. You will create forms in both ways in the activities that follow.

116B LEARN:

Create an AutoForm

1. Start *Access*. Open the database file *116-Lincoln* that you created in 116A. Open the *Student Schedules* table.

2. Click the down arrow on the **New Objects** button on the toolbar and select **AutoForm**. See Figure 16.14.

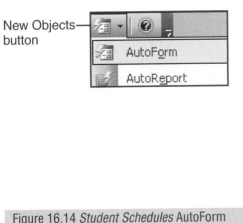

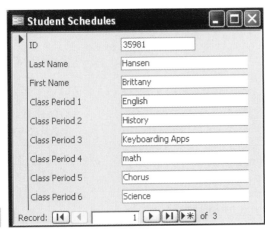

Figure 16.14 *Student Schedules* AutoForm

Across the Curriculum

Data Files

- *CD-C02-Business*
- *CD-C02-Teamwork Skills*
- *CD-C02-Teamwork Suggestions*
- *CD-C02-Budget*

↗ About Business

BUSINESS AND GOVERNMENT Businesses and governments affect one another in various ways. A **government** is an authority that rules or controls the affairs of a nation, state, city, or other area. One way governments affect businesses is by passing laws. These laws say how businesses can deal with others. For example, laws state the lowest amount a company must pay its workers. Laws forbid companies from selling unsafe products to consumers. Laws state that a company cannot make a product that was patented by another company for a certain number of years. Laws state the kinds of taxes businesses must pay. A **tax** is an amount of money that must be paid to support a government.

Governments also affect where companies can sell products. For example, the United States makes trade agreements with other countries. A **trade agreement** gives rules for business dealings. For example, a trade agreement might state how many cars from another country can be sold in the United States each year.

Businesses affect governments by paying taxes. These taxes help support the programs and activities of the government. For example, the taxes paid by companies in your area may help pay for running your school. Businesses also try to influence the laws and rules governments pass. For example, companies may try to get a state to lower its sales tax in an effort to increase product sales.

1. Start *Word*. Open and print *CD-C02-Business* from your data files. Complete the problems related to sales tax.

2. Compare your answers with those of a classmate. If the answers are different, recheck your work to find the correct answers.

↗ Career and Life Skills Success Builder

TEAMWORK What does it mean to be a team player? In the world of work, a **team** is a group of people working together to achieve a common goal. People working as teams can usually accomplish more than people working alone. In fact, job success often depends on your ability to work well with others. Here are some points to remember when working with a team:

- **Be part of the team.** Work hard to get along with others, and listen to what others have to say.

Field Name	Data Type
ID	Text
Last Name	Text
First Name	Text
Class Period 1	Text
Class Period 2	Text
Class Period 3	Text
Class Period 4	Text
Class Period 5	Text
Class Period 6	Text

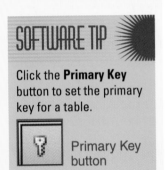
3. Click in the *ID* field row. Click the **Primary Key** button on the toolbar to set this field as the primary key.

4. Save the table. Key **Student Schedules** for the table name. Switch to Datasheet view.

5. Three student records are shown below. Enter the records into the *Student Schedules* table. After you enter the data, adjust the column widths to fit the longest entry in each column.

ID	35981	48263	52596
Last Name	Hansen	Martinez	Castello
First Name	Brittany	Rico	Mary
Class Period 1	English	History	Science
Class Period 2	History	Math	Chorus
Class Period 3	Keyboarding Apps	Physical Ed	History
Class Period 4	Math	Chorus	Physical Ed
Class Period 5	Chorus	English	English
Class Period 6	Science	Science	Math

6. Close the table. Click **Yes** to the prompt asking you if you want to save the changes to the layout. Close *Access* or continue to the next activity.

Database Forms

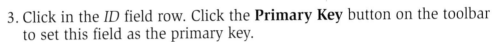

You have already learned how to enter data into the database table using Datasheet view. You can also enter data using a database form. A **form** is an object used to enter or display data. You can create a form quickly using the AutoForm feature. The **AutoForm** feature creates a form based on an open

Help Words

Form
    Create a form

- **Be considerate.** When working with a team, think about how the things you do or say will affect others. Give compliments for good work or ideas. In general, treat others the way you want to be treated.

- **Be helpful and do your part.** Always do your share of the work and help others with their work, when appropriate.

1. Open and print the data file *CD-C02-Teamwork Skills*. Complete the questions to see if you are ready to be part of a team. Give the completed form to your teacher.

2. Open and print the data file *CD-C02-Teamwork Suggestions*. Read the list and put a check mark next to the five suggestions you think are the most important. Then, meet with two or three classmates and discuss which items they think are the most important. After the discussion, look at your list again. Would you make any changes? If yes, correct your list, explain why you made your changes, and give the list to your teacher.

↗ Academic Success Builder

MATH AND PERSONAL FINANCE: BUDGETS A **budget** is an itemized spending plan. Budgets help you plan your future spending and determine the amount of money you need for a certain period of time. You can prepare budgets for any period of time, such as a week, a month, six months, or a year. To prepare a useful budget for any length of time, you need to know some basic information such as:

- Your recent history of spending for the budget period you use

- The amount of money you expect to have for the upcoming budget period

- Your financial needs (what you need to spend) for the upcoming budget period

Once you have this information, you can plan a budget. Planning a budget requires making choices. Some items you want to buy may cost more money than you will have in your budget period. You need to save to buy those items in the future. If your budget shows you have more money than you plan to spend, you can increase the amount you will save. However, if your budget shows you have less money than you think you need, you must reduce your spending or increase the money you will have. For example, do not buy clothes you want but do not need. You could also take a part-time job after school to make extra money. In this activity, you will create a budget for one week.

1. Start *Word*. Open *CD-C02-Budget*. Print the document and then close it. Follow the directions given to record your spending and plan a budget.

2. To build your math skills, complete the math activities related to preparing a budget. Compare your answers with those of a classmate.

8. Choose **File** on the menu bar. Choose **Print**. Select a printer if needed. Choose **All** for the print range. Select **1** for the number of copies. Click **OK**. Close *Access* after printing the table.

✓ **CHECK POINT**　Check your printed table. Have you included all your instructors? Are their names spelled correctly? Great job! You now know how to create a database and enter records.

Lesson 116　Creating a Database Form

Objectives

In Lesson 116, you will:

↘ Learn about database design issues.
↘ Create a database file.
↘ Create a database table.
↘ Create a database form.
↘ Add records to a database.

Planning Database Design

Planning the design of a database to make using the data easy is important. The database you created in Lesson 115 is not designed in the best way for storing and using the data. For example, a new table would have to be set up for each student. Schedules would have to be viewed one at a time. Searching or sorting the data would be difficult. A database with one table that includes all student schedules in the same table would be more useful. It would allow users to search and sort the data more easily. In the next activity, you will create a database to store schedule data for students at Lincoln Junior High.

116A APPLY:　 Create a Database for Student Schedules

Instant Message

To review creating a table, see Activity 115B.

1. Start *Access*. Create a blank database. Name the database file *116-Lincoln*.

2. Create a table in Design view. Enter the field names and data types shown below. Include an appropriate description for each field.

Chapter 3

Computers and Society

OBJECTIVES

In Chapter 3, you will:

↗ Learn how computers influence the way we live.

↗ Study a brief history of computers.

↗ Learn about computer networks and the Internet.

↗ Use a browser to access and navigate Web pages.

↗ Use the History and Favorites feature of a browser.

↗ Search the Internet for information.

↗ Learn about computer ethics and netiquette.

↗ Consider security and privacy issues related to Internet use.

↗ Explore copyright issues related to Internet use.

The *Apollo 11* astronauts spent 21 hours and 36 minutes on the moon. They collected 21.7 kg (less than 48 pounds) of rocks and soil to carry home. You can see some of these rocks at the National Air and Space Museum in Washington, D.C.

Some people said that flying to the moon was silly. They believed it was too expensive. They joked that it was a long way to go for 48 pounds of rocks and dirt! After all, we have plenty of rocks here on Earth.

The value of the space program cannot be measured in moon rocks. As with many things in life, it's the journey of discovery that matters most. It is *not* all about reaching a destination. It is *what we learn along the way* that makes the biggest difference.

In this chapter, you will think about how computers and their use affect daily life in our society. The Internet is one aspect of computer use that has affected society greatly in recent years. You will learn to access and find information on the Internet. You will also learn about using the Internet in a safe way.

© Roger Ressmeyer/CORBIS

2. Create a new table in Design view. (Double-click **Create a new table in Design view**.) Enter the following field names, data types, and descriptions:

Field Name	Data Type	Description
Class	Text	Name of Class
Teacher	Text	Name of Teacher

3. Click the **Save** button on the toolbar. The Save As box will appear. Key your name in the Table Name box and click **OK**. Choose **Yes** when asked if you want to create a primary key.

4. When you are setting up a table, you use Design view. When you want to enter data in a table, you use Datasheet view. Click the **Datasheet View** button on the toolbar to switch to Datasheet view.

5. Enter data for your class schedule in the table.

6. After entering all the data, click the **Print Preview** button on the toolbar. Click the **Zoom** button on the toolbar a couple of times to switch between a full-page and a close-up view of the table. Notice that the table name (your name) and the current date appear at the top of the table. See Figure 16.12. *Page 1* appears at the bottom of the page.

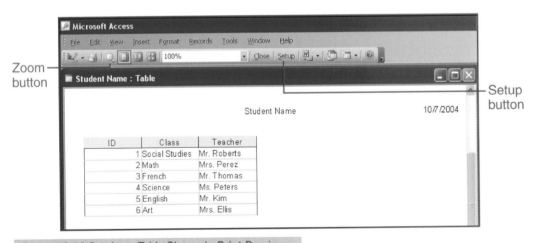

Figure 16.12 Database Table Shown in Print Preview

7. When you have a large table to print, you may need to change the margins or set the page orientation. Click the **Setup** button on the toolbar. You can change margins for a database document on the Margins tab. Click the **Page** tab. You can set the page for landscape or portrait orientation on this tab. Click **Cancel**. Click the **Close** button on the toolbar to close Print Preview.

Lesson 10   Computers and Daily Life

Objectives

In Lesson 10, you will:

⟩ Learn how the development of computers was influenced by the space program.

⟩ Study the history of computers.

⟩ Consider how computers are part of everyday life.

The space program led to a wave of invention. Senator Kay Bailey Hutchison spoke about this topic.[1] She told the U.S. Senate that the space program has improved our lives. According to the Texas senator, space-related breakthroughs have been made in:

- Global positioning satellite systems (GPS)

- Weather prediction

- Heating and cooling for homes

- Hazardous chemical storage

- Air and water purification

- Recycling

- Scratch-resistant sunglasses

- Laser treatment of arteriosclerosis

- Medical devices such as the pacemaker and defibrillator

- Computer hardware and software

MICHAEL KLEINFELD/UPI /Landov

Senator Kay Bailey Hutchison

The PC Race

The rush to reach the moon in the 1960s was called the *space race*. The race to space gave birth to another pursuit—the race for better PCs. As Senator Hutchison said, "The personal computers we all use are the direct result of NASA's development of smaller computers needed for space travel."

Computers have probably always been a part of your everyday life. For older people, this is not true. Before the last 15 to 20 years, computers were not commonplace. The first electronic computers were introduced in the mid-1900s. These computers were very big. Some computers covered large rooms and weighed hundreds of pounds.

---

[1] "Space Program Deserves Lawmakers' Support," *Daily News*, Senator Kay Bailey Hutchison Web site, October 4, 1999, http://hutchison.senate.gov/speech29.htm (accessed January 17, 2005).

ID	Class	Teacher
1	History	Mr. Chen
2	Math	Ms. Boston
3	Chorus	Mr. Fields
4	English	Ms. Ramirez
5	Keyboarding Applications	Mr. Dexter
6	Physical Education	Ms. Gomez

3. Look at record 5 that contains *Keyboarding Applications.* The column width is not wide enough to show all the information. You can adjust column widths to fit the data.

4. Place the cursor on the column border (vertical line) to the right of the word **Class** (the column head). The cursor will appear as a double arrow with a vertical line. See Figure 16.11. Double-click the column border. The column width will adjust to fit the longest item in the column.

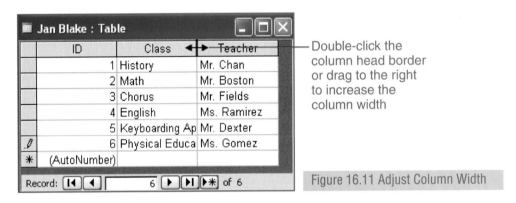

Double-click the column head border or drag to the right to increase the column width

Figure 16.11 Adjust Column Width

5. Close the table. You will be asked whether you want to save changes to the layout of the table. Click **Yes**.

6. Complete the Check Point below and then close *Access*.

 **CHECK POINT** Switch seats with one of your classmates. Check to see if your classmate's *Jan Blake* table is set up correctly. Make sure all classes are included. Check for keying and spelling errors.

115E PRACTICE: Create Table and Add Records

Practice what you have learned. Create another table and enter data as directed below.

1. Start *Access* and open the *115-Schedules* database file.

Figure 3.1 Early computers were large and heavy.

Early computers could do only basic operations. For example, they could add, subtract, divide, and multiply. They could do these tasks many times faster than a person could. However, they were painfully slow compared with today's computers. To change the tasks the computer could do, the computer had to be rewired.

Advances in computers came slowly at first. Once computers had a way to store information, the demand for computers grew. People started building smaller computers. In 1977, the Apple PC personal computer was introduced. Since that time, computers have steadily been changed and improved. Some important milestones in the history of computing are shown in the table below.

Computing History Milestones	
1946	The first large-scale electronic computer called ENIAC was created.
1951	UNIVAC, one of the first commercial computers, was bought by the U.S. Census Bureau.
1963	The computer mouse was developed by Douglas Engelbart.
1965	Minicomputers were introduced. These were the first computers to use integrated circuits.
1969	Small computers helped astronauts land on the moon.
1977, 1981	Apple PCs and IBM PCs were introduced. Personal computers became practical for business and personal use.
1983	Notebook computers were introduced.

8. A prompt will appear asking whether you want to create a primary key. Click **Yes**. *Access* will create a field named *ID* to be the primary key. *Access* will prevent any duplicate values from being entered in the primary key field.

9. You have created your first database table. Click the **Close** button on the *Access* window to close *Access*.

115C LEARN: Add Records to a Table

┌────────────┐
│ Help Words │
└────────────┘
Enter data
  Add or edit data

Earlier you created the *115-Schedules* database file. You also created the *Jan Blake* table. In this activity, you will add records to the table.

1. Start *Access* and open the *115-Schedules* database file.

2. Click **Tables** in the Objects list in the database window. Double-click the table name **Jan Blake** to open the table.

3. The cursor will be in the *ID* field. Press TAB once to move the cursor to the *Class* field. Key **History**, which is Jan Blake's first class. See Figure 16.10.

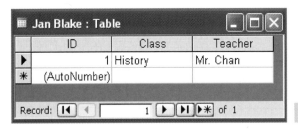

Figure 16.10 *Jan Blake* Database Table

SOFTWARE TIP

The data is automatically saved when a table is closed.

4. Press TAB to move the cursor to the *Teacher* field. Key **Mr. Chan**, which is the name of Jan Blake's history teacher.

5. Click the **Close** button on the table window to close the table. Close *Access* or continue to the next activity.

115D PRACTICE: Add Records to a Table

SOFTWARE TIP

Move from column to column by pressing TAB, by clicking in a cell, or by using the arrow keys.

Practice what you have learned by entering other records in the Jan Blake table. Remember that the *ID* field in the table was created automatically when you chose to create a primary key. The field type is AutoNumber. This means that you do not enter data in this field. *Access* will automatically assign a number in this field to each record you create.

1. Start *Access* and open the *115-Schedules* database file if it is not already open.

2. Open the *Jan Blake* table. Enter the remaining classes shown in the table below. Remember that *Access* will fill in the *ID* field automatically.

1984	Macintosh computers were introduced. The mouse and icons became important tools for computer users.
1991	The World Wide Web was developed. Internet use began to increase rapidly.
1993	PDAs were introduced. PDAs and other handheld computers are popular today.
2001	Tablet PCs were introduced. Handwriting and speech continue to become more popular as input methods.

From the 1970s, computer makers have been in intense competition. Each seeks to create faster, smaller, and less expensive computers. The results have been a huge success. The power of computers has more than doubled every two years for the past 35–40 years. That's a lot!

Today's fast, tiny, and powerful computers are finding their way into the most unlikely places. Often without knowing it, we use dozens of computers every day. They have become more important in our lives with every passing year. As a result, they now influence the way we work, live, and play.

Video Game Controller

Flat Screen Television

Digital Clock

Figure 3.2 Computers are part of many common devices.

10A LEARN: Describe How Computers Improve Productivity

People worked and lived for thousands of years without computers. So why have we become so dependent upon them now? The simple answer is that computers help us get more done. They increase our productivity. **Productivity** is a measure of how much work can be done in a certain amount of time.

1. Work in a group with three or four classmates. Identify as many ways as you can that computers make people more productive. Make a list of the ways.

2. Discuss your list with another group of students in your class. What ways did you identify that they did not? What ways did the other group identify that you did not?

2. In the *115-Schedules* database window, double-click **Create table in Design view**. See Figure 16.7.

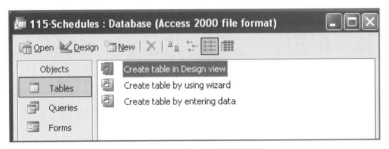

Figure 16.7 Double-click the option you want.

3. When the Table window opens, the cursor will blink under Field Name. Key **Class** for the first field name. See Figure 16.8.

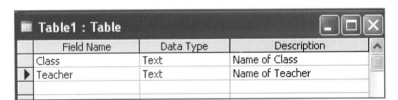

Figure 16.8 Table in Design View

4. Press TAB. *Text* will automatically appear under Data Type. Press TAB again to move the cursor to the Description column. Key **Name of Class** for the description.

5. Press TAB once. Key **Teacher** for the second field name. Press TAB twice. Key **Name of Teacher** for the description.

6. Click the **Close** button on the Table window. When you click the **Close** button, a prompt asks whether you want to save the table. Click **Yes**.

7. Key **Jan Blake** in the Table Name box. Click **OK** to save the table. See Figure 16.9.

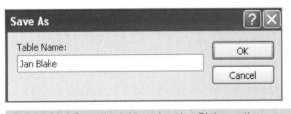

Figure 16.9 Save the table using Jan Blake as the name.

Impact of Computers on Society

Here is a great way to understand the impact of computers on society. Imagine all computers disappearing in an instant. As you walk around today, think about how things would be different if computers suddenly disappeared.

School

Think about your school. Most likely the heating, cooling, emergency, and communication systems all use computers. Obviously the computer labs would disappear. Most modern clocks would stop, and the lights wouldn't turn on. Fire alarms might not work properly. In addition, your teacher probably takes roll and enters your grades with the help of a computer. How many of your assignments require a computer?

Transportation

Think about transportation. Without computers, most modern cars would stop working! Many of the safety, pollution control, and starter systems on cars use computers. Traffic lights and warning systems use computers. The Amber Alert warns motorists to be on the lookout for missing children. Many lives have been saved as a result of this and other computer alert systems.

Home

Think about your home. Many appliances, clocks, and other electronic devices would stop working. Your televisions, radios, DVD players, and computer games would quit working, too! No more Internet, e-mail, or instant messaging! Your home security alarm probably would not work. Your digital phone would not exist.

Figure 3.3 Many security alarms would not work without computers.

Data Types

Choosing the data type for each field is an important step in designing a database. The **data type** determines the kind of data a field can hold. You can use several types of data, some of which are shown in the table below.

Data Type	Description
Text	For letters or numbers that do not require calculations
Number	For numbers to be used in calculations
Date/Time	For dates and times
Currency	For dollar values
AutoNumber	Numbers assigned in order by *Access*
Yes/No	For data that can only be Yes or No

Primary Key

When you create an *Access* table, you can select one field in the table to be the primary key. A **primary key** is a field chosen to identify each record in a table. *Access* will not allow duplicate data to be entered in the primary key field. For example, a table can hold data for students at a school. Each student would have a student ID number. Each student's ID number would be different from all others. The field that holds the student's ID number can be set as the primary key. This would prevent a user from accidentally entering the same ID number for two different students. You can choose a field to set as the primary key. You can also let *Access* create a primary key field for you.

115B LEARN:

Create a Table in Design View

The purpose of the *115-Schedules* database that you created earlier is to store data about class schedules. For now, this simple database will have one table. The table will have three fields: *ID*, *Class*, and *Teacher*. The data type for *ID* field will be AutoNumber. This means that *Access* will automatically number each record entered.

1. Start *Access*. In the Getting Started pane, click the *115-Schedules* database name to open the database. See Figure 16.6. (If the *115-Schedules* database does not appear on a list of files, click **More** or **Open**. Open the folder where you saved the database file and select the file. Click **Open**.)

Figure 16.6 Choose the filename from the list of files.

Money and the Mall

Think about your money and shopping at the mall. The financial system as we know it would not exist. Money transactions are routed and recorded by computers. All ATMs require computers to help distribute cash. Credit card systems would cease to work. You wouldn't be able to buy anything at the mall or superstore because the registers would quit working. Besides that, the mall's elevators and escalators would stop working. There would be no lighting, no air-conditioning, and no security systems!

The Space Program

Think about the space program. Without computers, spaceships would never get off the ground. Satellites would quit working. The international space station would crash to the Earth. And we might never discover new opportunities in our expanding universe.

10B LEARN: Identify Computer Uses

You read about how computers are used in many areas of our everyday lives. Some other areas where computers are important include:

- Science
- Medicine
- Business and industry
- Arts and entertainment
- Protecting the environment

1. Work in a group with three or four classmates. Choose one of the categories of computer use listed above. Identify as many ways as you can that computers are used in this area. Make a list of the ways.

2. Discuss your list with another group of students in your class.

Lesson 11   Internet Basics

Objectives

In Lesson 11, you will:
↗ Learn about networks and the Internet.
↗ Learn about connecting to the Internet.
↗ Explore the parts of a Web browser window.
↗ Access and navigate Web pages.

Data files: *CD-11-History, CD-11-Questions*

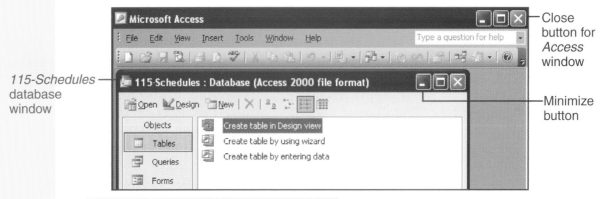

Close button for *Access* window

Minimize button

Figure 16.4 *115-Schedules* Database Window

5. You will create a database table in a later activity. For now, click the **Close** button on the *Access* window to close *Access*. See Figure 16.4.

Database Design

Once you have created a database file, you can create tables to store data. First, you should take some time to plan the design of the database. The database should be designed to make the data easy to use. You should consider the types of data (names, amounts, descriptions) that will be stored. You should also consider how the data will be used. For example, sorting data by state can be easy or hard, depending on how you enter the data.

Tables

A **table** is a database object used for organizing and storing data. A table is made up of records. A **record** contains all the information about one person or item. For example, a record might contain a person's name, address, and phone number. Records are made up of fields. A **field** is one piece of information about a person or item. For example, a person's last name might be one field. Tables are set up in columns and rows of information. In a database table, fields appear in columns, and records appear in rows, as shown in Figure 16.5.

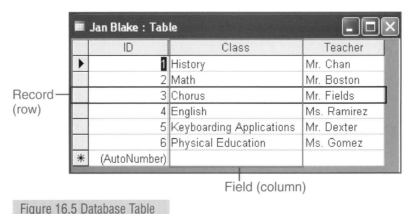

Record (row)

Field (column)

Figure 16.5 Database Table

One important way that computers affect society is by making information easy to find and access. For example, you learned to use the Help feature in *Word* to find information about using *Word*. You can also use your computer to find information stored in other locations. For example, you might find information about your class schedule on your school's local network.

Networks

When one computer links to another computer, a **network** is created. A small network may have only a few computers. A large network can include thousands of computers. A network with computers located within a short distance (such as within the same building) is called a local area network (LAN).

When many LANs link to each other, a web of networks is created. The **Internet** is a web of computer networks that spans the Earth. The Internet is often called simply the Net. Files on the Internet are stored on powerful computers called **servers**.

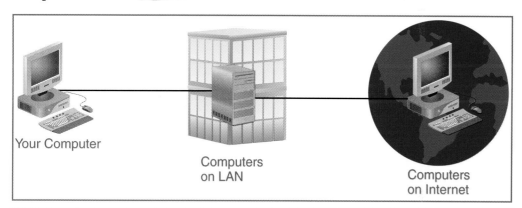

Your Computer

Computers on LAN

Computers on Internet

Figure 3.4 Using your computer, you can find information on a local network or on the Internet.

The Internet

The Internet has affected our society greatly by providing new ways for people to communicate. People use the Internet to research topics, exchange messages, buy and sell products, and promote organizations and ideas.

Electronic mail, commonly called e-mail, is a popular use of the Internet. **E-mail** is the electronic transfer of messages. It allows users to exchange information quickly and easily. You will learn to use e-mail in Chapter 11.

Newsgroups and chat rooms are also popular uses of the Internet. A **newsgroup** allows users to post messages for others to read. Newsgroups are organized around a topic, such as music or sports. There are newsgroups for thousands of different topics. A **chat room** allows users who are online to type text messages. The messages are displayed for others in the chat room almost instantly.

Help Words

Create database
Create an *Access*
database

2. Now you will create a blank database. At the right side of the screen in the Getting Started pane, click **Create a new file**. See Figure 16.2. Then click **Blank database**. (*Word 2002* users, just click **Blank database**.)

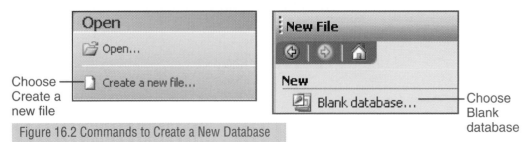

Figure 16.2 Commands to Create a New Database

3. Choose a folder from the Save in drop-down list or create a new folder to hold the file. In the File name box, key **115-Schedules**. Click **Create**.

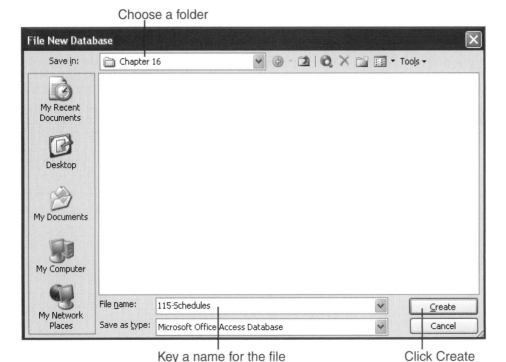

Figure 16.3 Steps to Save a New Database File

Instant Message

See Chapter 1
Lesson 3C to review
minimizing and
restoring windows.

4. The *115-Schedules* database window will appear inside the *Access* window. See Figure 16.4. You can create objects, such as tables, to place in the database. When you do so, you may need to move or minimize the database window so you can see other windows. Practice moving the *115-Schedules* database window by clicking its title bar and dragging the window. Practice minimizing and restoring the database window by clicking its **Minimize** and **Restore** buttons.

An important part of the Internet is the World Wide Web. It is also called simply the Web. The **World Wide Web** is a system of computers that can handle documents formatted in a special language. This language is called HTML (HyperText Markup Language). HTML documents, also called Web pages, can display text as well as graphics. They allow users to move from one document to another using hyperlinks. A group of related Web pages is called a Web site.

Web sites are created for many reasons. One reason is to sell products. The selling and buying of products on the Internet is called **e-commerce**. Billions of dollars' worth of products are sold each year by e-commerce. E-commerce has allowed businesses to reach customers in areas far from where the company's goods are made or sold in retail stores. E-commerce has made buying products more convenient for many consumers. Clothes, cars, groceries, medicine, movie tickets, books, and music are just a few of the items customers can buy online.

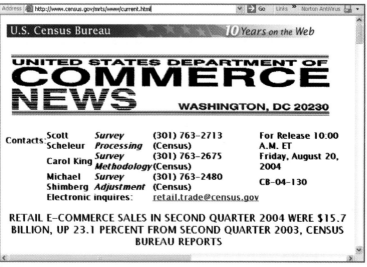

Source: U.S. Census Bureau Web site at http://www.census.gov/mrts/www/current.html.

Figure 3.5 E-commerce sales continue to grow.

Web sites are also used by people, companies, governments, and other groups to provide information. For example, you can access a Web site provided by the White House. On this site, you can find articles about current news events related to the U.S. President. You may also find entertaining articles about topics such as the President's dog.

Accessing the Internet

To access the Internet from a home computer, you may need to set up an account with an Internet service provider. An **Internet service provider (ISP)** is a company that provides customer connections to the Internet. Earthlink and America Online are popular ISPs. Many schools provide ISP service through their LANs.

Lesson 115 Creating a Database

Objectives

In Lesson 115, you will:
- Create a database.
- Create and save a database table.
- Add records to a database table.
- Print a database table.

Database Objects

In this chapter, you will use *Microsoft Access* to create electronic databases. The first step in creating a database is to save a new database file. Within the database file, you can create database **objects**. Some common objects are shown in the Objects list in Figure 16.1. *Tables* can be created to store data. *Queries* can be used to find data to answer questions. *Forms* can be used to enter and view data. *Reports* can be used to arrange data in a way that is easy to understand.

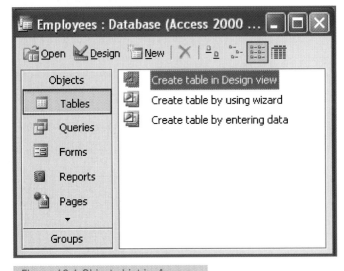

Figure 16.1 Objects List in *Access*

In this lesson, you will create a database to store data for a student's school schedule. You will learn to use forms, queries, and reports in other lessons.

Create a Database

1. To start *Microsoft Access*, click **Start**, **All Programs**, **Microsoft Office**, **Microsoft Access**.

Instant Message

Wireless connections are often called **Wi-Fi**. Sometimes they are called **802.11** connections. Another short-range wireless connection is called **Bluetooth**.

SOFTWARE TIP

If you do not see your Standard buttons or Address bar, choose **View, Toolbars, Standard Buttons** or **Address Bar**.

In the past, most computers were connected to their networks by wires. People had to sit in the same place every day so that their computers could connect to the Internet. Wireless Internet connections now allow more freedom of movement. Computers can be linked to the Internet without wires through a device called an access point. The area around an access point is called a hot spot. With the proper equipment, you can connect to the Internet when you are in a hot spot. Hot spots can be created in schools, restaurants, airports, hotels, or even some public parks.

Web Browsers

A **Web browser** is a program that lets you find and view Web pages. *Internet Explorer* is a popular Web browser. Look at the *Internet Explorer* window shown in Figure 3.6. You will see a title bar, menu bar, toolbar buttons, scroll bars, and control buttons like those you have learned about in other *Windows* programs.

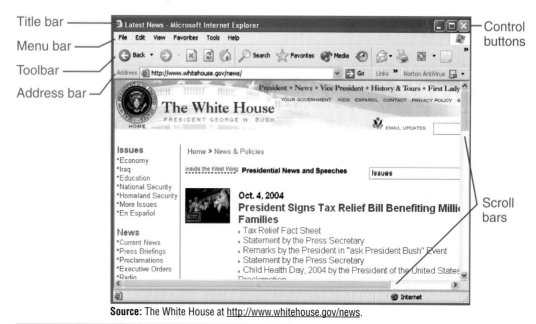

Source: The White House at http://www.whitehouse.gov/news.

Figure 3.6 The Internet Explorer Browser Window

Web Addresses

In Chapter 2, you learned to follow a path to locate a file on your computer. In a similar way, you must locate Web pages you wish to view. A **uniform resource locator (URL)** is an address for a Web site. A URL can be entered into the Address bar of a Web browser. After you enter a URL and give the appropriate command, the browser will look for the address you have entered. If the address is found, a Web page will be displayed.

© Getty Images/PhotoDisc

A **database** is an organized collection of facts and figures. You probably have used a phone book to find someone's phone number. A phone book is an example of a database in printed form. The data in a phone book are arranged by name in alphabetical order. This makes the data easy to find and use.

A database can also be in electronic form. You may have used a computer to look up data about books in your school library. You may have searched for a book by author, title, or subject. This data is probably stored in a database.

People use databases to store and arrange data. They use the data to answer questions and to help them make decisions. In this chapter, you will learn how to create an electronic database and store data. You will also learn how to find and arrange the data in a useful way.

CHAPTER 16   Database

URLs contain domain names. For example, the domain name *nasa.gov* is part of the address for the National Aeronautics and Space Administration Web site. The *.gov* at the end of the URL stands for *government*. Domain names can give you some insight into the purpose of the sites you visit. Here are a few examples:

.edu	United States educational institutions	.gov	United States government
.mil	United States military	.net	Network providers
.org	Organizations	.us	United States country code
.biz	Businesses	.mx	Mexico country code
.com	Commercial use	.uk	United Kingdom country code

11A LEARN: Access a Web Page

In this activity, you will use a URL to find the NASA welcome page. Instructions given are for *Internet Explorer*. If you have a different browser, the directions should be similar.

1. Follow your teacher's instructions to log on to the Internet.

2. Start *Internet Explorer*. Click in the Address box. The current address should be highlighted. If it is not, click and drag over the address to select it. In the Address box, enter **www.nasa.gov**. See Figure 3.7.

Figure 3.7 Internet Explorer Address Box

Instant Message

In a URL, **http://** is short for Hypertext Transfer Protocol. HTTP is the means by which information is shared over the Web.

3. Click the **Go** button to the right of the Address box or press the ENTER key. The characters *http://* will be automatically added to the beginning of the address you enter. Other characters may be added automatically after the text you enter. A welcome page similar to Figure 3.8 should appear (see page 73).

Chapter 16
Database

Web Resources:
www.c21jr.swlearning.
com/studentresources

- Data Files
- Vocabulary Flash Cards
- Beat the Clock, Database
- *PowerPoint* Reviews
- More Activities

OBJECTIVES

In Chapter 16, you will:

↗ Learn the purpose of a database and database objects.

↗ Create a database file.

↗ Create a database table.

↗ Add records to a database table.

↗ Create a database form.

↗ Enter data using a database form.

↗ Add fields and delete fields in a database table.

↗ Edit, add, and delete records in a database.

↗ Use a database to answer questions.

↗ Create queries.

↗ Filter data by selection.

↗ Sort data in database tables and reports.

↗ Create and print database reports.

Data are facts and figures. Your name is an example of data. The price of a car is an example of data. People have more data to deal with today than ever before. For data to be of value, it must be easy to find and understand.

Source: NASA at http://www.nasa.gov.

Figure 3.8 The NASA Welcome Page

4. Use the scroll bar to move down the NASA welcome page.

5. To visit another Web site, enter **www.nasm.si.edu** in the Address box and click **Go**. The Smithsonian National Air and Space Museum welcome page should display.

6. Using the scroll bars, examine the welcome page. Click the **Close** button on the browser window to close *Internet Explorer*.

Hyperlinks

Many Web pages have hyperlinks. A **hyperlink** is text or a graphic that, when clicked, takes you to a new location. The new location can be a different place on the same Web page. The new location can also be a different Web page or site.

Not all the pictures or words on a Web page are hyperlinks. How can you find hyperlinks on a Web page? Simply move the cursor around the page with your mouse or digital pen. When the cursor changes to a pointing hand, you have found a hyperlink. Hyperlink text often appears in a different color than other text on the page.

When you click a hyperlink, the browser will move to a new location. If you want to move back to the previous location, click the **Back** button on the browser toolbar. This will return you to the previous page. To return to the next page, click the **Forward** button. To return to your home page, click or tap the **Home** button.

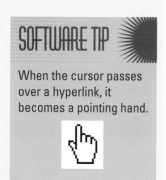

↗ Career and Life Skills Success Builder

DEVELOP PERSONAL FINANCE SKILLS You may be dreaming about it...the day you finish school and move out on your own. Maybe you even have an idea of where you will live and what type of work you will do. Of course, with every dream comes reality. Your perfect place will cost money every month, and you will have other bills that must be paid as well.

With planning and the right career, you can live in the place of your dreams. Depending on your income, you might live in a house, condominium, or apartment. Maybe you will have roommates to help pay your rent and bills, or maybe you will have that responsibility on your own. In this exercise you will develop a personal monthly budget. You will need to determine your monthly income and expenses. Expenses will include items such as rent, car payments and gas, utilities, food, and entertainment.

1. Open and print the data file *CD-C15-Expenses*. Close the file. Read the instructions to fill out the monthly expenses table.

2. Once you have finished your table, open the *Excel* worksheet *CD-C15-Personal Finances*. Complete the worksheet using your data. Save the file as *C15-Personal Finances*, and print the worksheet.

3. Remember to include a sample of your best work from this chapter in your portfolio.

↗ Academic Success Builder

YOUTH ORGANIZATIONS, SPREADSHEET COMPETITIONS Organizations such as FBLA's Middle Level Achievement Program include events that measure your knowledge of spreadsheet software. Students who enter this event use spreadsheet software to solve problems. The problems may include the use of various functions and formulas. Students may need to format and edit worksheets, sort data, and prepare a chart. Students' work is judged on accuracy, so entering information correctly and proofreading are very important.

To help you prepare for a spreadsheet competition, you will open and make the changes to a worksheet. Refer to Chapter 15 and the payroll formulas in the Academic Success Builder for Chapter 4, page 143, as needed.

1. Start *Word*. Open *CD-C15-Directions* from your data files. Print and then close the file.

2. Start *Excel*. Follow the printed directions to enter and copy formulas, sort data, and format the worksheet.

11B PRACTICE:

Access a Web Page and Use Hyperlinks

1. Log on to the Internet. Start *Internet Explorer*. In the Address box, enter **c21jr.swlearning.com**.

2. A Web site that contains Web pages related to your textbook should appear. Move the cursor around the welcome page. Watch the pointer become a pointing hand when it passes over a hyperlink.

3. Click a hyperlink, such as **Student Resources**. Quickly scan the new page to see the information that it provides. Click the **Back** button. See Figure 3.9. This will take you back to the previous page.

Figure 3.9 *Internet Explorer* Buttons

4. Click the **Forward** button. This will take you to the page you just left. Click the **Home** button. This will take you to your starting home page.

5. Click the **Close** button on the browser window to close *Internet Explorer*.

11C APPLY:

Access a Local Web Page

You have accessed Web pages stored on other computers using the Internet. Web pages can also be stored on a computer's hard drive or on a local network. In this activity, you will access a Web page that has been provided with your data files. The Web page has information about computer history. You will copy and paste data from the Web page into a *Word* file.

Instant Message

See activity 4B on page 24 to review browsing to find files.

1. Start *Internet Explorer*. Choose **File** from the menu bar. Choose **Open**. Click the **Browse** button. Navigate to the folder where your data files are stored.

2. From your data files, select *CD-11-History* and click **Open**. Click **OK** on the Open dialog box to open the Web page.

3. Start *Word*. Open *CD-11-Questions* from your data files. Read each question about computer history. Then read the Web page.

ACROSS THE CURRICULUM

↗ About Business

ECONOMIC INDICATORS "The economy is growing." "Unemployment rates are down." "The stock market was up today with moderate trading." Why do news reporters, politicians, and the man on the street talk so much about the economy? People talk about the economy because it affects their everyday lives. When the economy is strong or growing, people who want to work are more likely to be able to find jobs. In a growing economy, people tend to spend more and save less. This means that retail sales are usually higher. That's good news for entrepreneurs and other businesspeople.

The measurements that people use to describe how well the economy is doing are called **economic indicators**. Some economic indicators are listed below:

- New orders for durable goods such as appliances and cars

- Sales of new homes

- New claims for unemployment benefits

- Trends in the stock market

- Changes in the overall unemployment rate

- Personal income (the amount of money people have to spend)

- Industrial production (the number of products companies have produced for sale)

- Retail sales (for example, department store sales)

Noting the changes in economic indicators can help you plan for the future. For example, suppose you work for a department store. If retail sales have been decreasing, you may see a decrease in the number of hours you will be working. This might not be a good time for you to buy a new car or make any other large purchases.

1. Start *Word*. Open *CD-C15-Business* from your data files. Print and then close the file.

2. Follow the directions provided in the document to graph data for an economic indicator. Save your worksheet as *C15-Rates*.

Instant Message

Data on Web pages found on the Internet may be protected by laws that restrict their use. You will learn more about this in Lesson 14.

4. When you find the answer to a question, use your mouse to select the text in the Web page. Choose **Edit**, **Copy** from the menu bar.

5. Move to your *Word* document. Click below the question you want to answer. Choose **Edit**, **Paste** from the menu bar.

6. When you have answered all the questions, print the completed *Word* document. Save the file as *11-Questions*. Close *Word* and *Internet Explorer*.

✓ CHECK POINT Compare your answers with those of a classmate. If they differ, check the Web page again to find the right answers.

Lesson 12   Browser Features

Objectives

In Lesson 12, you will:
↘ Use the History feature of a browser.
↘ Add a Web site to a Favorites list.
↘ Access a Web site from the Favorites list.
↘ Use the Search feature on a browser.

History and Favorites Features

Browser programs, such as *Internet Explorer* and *Netscape*, have features you can use to help you find and revisit Web sites. The **History** feature shows you a list of links for sites you have visited recently. You can choose a time frame, such as *Today* or *This Week*. Then you can see links to sites visited during that time.

The **Favorites** feature allows you to create a list of links for sites. (In *Netscape*, this feature is called Bookmarks.) You can use these links to move quickly to a site you wish to visit again. You can organize these links into folders to make it easier to locate the link you want.

12A LEARN:  View History and Add Favorites

You will practice using the History and Favorites features in this activity.

1. Log on to the Internet. Start *Internet Explorer*.

2. Click the **History** button on the toolbar. See Figure 3.10 on page 76.

Timed Writing

Key each paragraph once. DS between paragraphs. Key a 1' timed writing on each paragraph; determine *gwam*.

A all letters used

gwam 2'

	•	2	•	4	•	6	•	8	

Before choosing a career, learn as much as 4

| • | 10 | • | 12 | • | 14 | • | 16 | • | 18 |

you can about what individuals in that career do. 9

| • | 20 | • | 22 | • | 24 | • | 26 | • |

For each job classification, there are job 13

| 28 | • | 30 | • | 32 | • | 34 | • | 36 | • |

qualifications that must be met. Analyze these 18

| 38 | • | 40 | • | 42 | • | 44 | • | 46 | • |

tasks very carefully in terms of your personality 23

| 48 | • | 50 | • |

and what you like to do. 26

| | • | 2 | • | 4 | • | 6 | • | 8 | |

Many of today's jobs require more formal 30

| • | 10 | • | 12 | • | 14 | • | 16 | • |

education or training after high school. The 34

| 18 | • | 20 | • | 22 | • | 24 | • | 26 | • |

training may be very specialized. This requires 39

| 28 | • | 30 | • | 32 | • | 34 | • | 36 | • |

intensive study or interning for a year or two. 44

| 38 | • | 40 | • | 42 | • | 44 | • | 46 |

You must decide if you are willing to expend so 49

| • | 48 | • | 50 |

much time and effort. 51

| | • | 2 | • | 4 | • | 6 | • | 8 | |

After you have chosen a career to pursue, 56

| • | 10 | • | 12 | • | 14 | • | 16 | • |

discuss the choice with parents, teachers, and 60

| 18 | • | 20 | • | 22 | • | 24 | • | 26 | • |

others. Such people can help you design a plan 65

| 28 | • | 30 | • | 32 | • | 34 | • | 36 |

to help you achieve your goals. Keep the plan 70

| • | 38 | • | 40 | • | 42 | • | 44 | • |

flexible and change it whenever necessary. 74

gwam 2' | 1 | 2 | 3 | 4 | 5 |

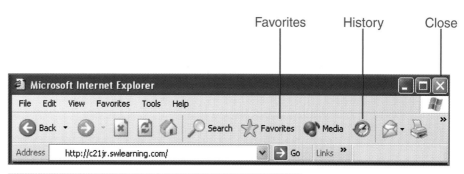

Figure 3.10 History and Favorites Buttons on Toolbar

3. A History pane will open. It should be similar to the one shown in Figure 3.11. Click **Today** if you visited the Century 21 Jr. Web site today. If you visited this site earlier, click the link that matches that time.

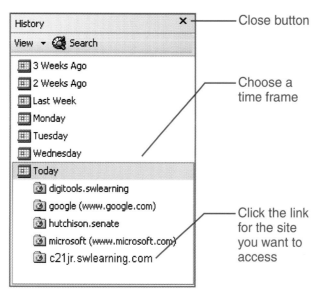

Figure 3.11 History Pane in *Internet Explorer*

4. Click the link for **c21jr.swlearning.com**. Your browser will move to this site. Click the **Close** button on the History pane to close it.

5. The Century 21 Jr. Web site contains data files, games, links, and other information that you will use as you complete the activities in this textbook. You will probably visit this site often. To make visiting the site easy, you will add the site to your Favorites list. Click the **Favorites** button on the toolbar. See Figure 3.10.

6. The Favorites pane will open. Click the **Add** button. The Add Favorite dialog box will appear with the site name. See Figure 3.12 on page 77. Click **OK**.

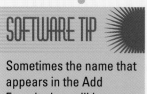

SOFTWARE TIP

Sometimes the name that appears in the Add Favorite box will be very long. You can key a different name for the site if you wish.

Building Keying Skill

Warmup Practice

Key each line twice. If time permits, key the lines again.

Alphabet

1 Jack Gable explained most of his very low quizzes.

Figure/Symbol

2 He used checks #259 and #308 to pay invoice #1647.

Speed

3 The eight busy men did the problems for the girls.

Improve Keying Speed

Key a 1' timed writing on each line. Your rate in gross words a minute (*gwam*) is shown below the lines.

TECHNIQUE TIP

Quickly tap the SPACE BAR after the last letter in each word. Immediately begin keying the next word.

1 He may go to the city to fix the bus for the city.

2 He is to go to the city with us to sign the forms.

3 The six girls paid for the auto to go to the city.

4 She is to go with them to the city to see the dog.

5 Diane may go to the dock to visit the eight girls.

6 The sign is on the mantel by the antique ornament.

7 Pamela kept the food for the fish by the fishbowl.

8 I paid the man by the dock for the bushel of corn.

9 The box with a shamrock and an iris is by the car.

10 To the right of the big lake is the dismal shanty.

gwam 1' | 1 | 2 | 3 | 4 | 5 | 6 | 7 | 8 | 9 | 10 |

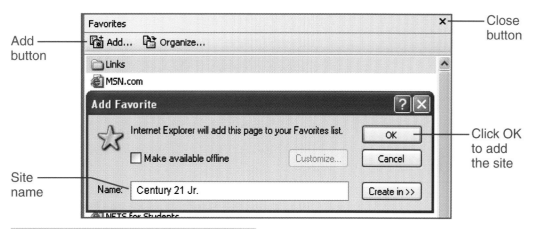

Add button

Close button

Site name

Click OK to add the site

Figure 3.12 *Internet Explorer* Favorites Pane

7. Scroll down your Favorites list and look for the name of the site. It may appear at the end of the list. Click the **Close** button on the Favorites pane. Continue to the next activity or close *Internet Explorer*.

12B PRACTICE: Use History and Favorites

1. Log on to the Internet and start *Internet Explorer*.

2. Use the History feature to go to the NASA site (http://www.nasa.gov) that you visited earlier. (If you are using a different computer, the NASA site might not be on the History list. In that case, enter the URL in the Address box.)

3. Add the NASA site to your Favorites list.

4. Locate the link on your Favorites list for the Century 21 Jr. site. Click the link to go to this site.

5. Click the **Student Resources** link. Click one or two of the links on this page to see the activities that are available for this chapter. Use the Back button to move back as needed. Close *Internet Explorer*.

Searching for Information on a Web Site

Once you find the Web site you want, you may be able to follow links to find the information you need. Sometimes, however, no link appears to offer the information you seek. Many Web sites have a search feature. You can use the **Search** feature to look for information. In Chapter 1, you learned to search for information in *Word*'s Help system. That process is similar to searching for data on a Web site. You enter a word or term in a search text box and give a command to start the search. The command is usually *Go* or *Search*. An example of a search box is shown in Figure 3.13.

9. In cell B27, enter a formula to find the lowest test score for Test 1. Copy the formula to cells C27:F27. Format the cells for one decimal place.

10. Apply a bottom border to cells A3:H3 and to cells B24:F24. Apply bold to cells A25:A27. Set the column width for all columns to 9.

11. Delete row 14 that contains data for Homziak.

12. Sort the data in rows 4 through row 23 by the Average column in descending order and then by the Student column in ascending order.

13. Select cells B3:F3 and cells B24:F24. (Hold down CTRL to select the second group of cells.) Create a column chart from this data. For the chart title, enter **AVERAGE TEST GRADES**. Do not show a legend. For data labels, use **Value**. Place the chart on the worksheet page below the data.

14. Set the top margin to 2 inches. Select the option to center the data horizontally on the page. Print the worksheet.

15. Save the worksheet as *C15-Grades*. Close the file.

Research Data and Create a Worksheet

In this activity, you will find precipitation data for one of the U.S. states and create a worksheet.

1. Work with a classmate to do the research portion of this activity. Access the NOAA (National Oceanic and Atmospheric Administration) Web site at http://www.noaa.gov. Follow the *Climate* links to find archived weather data for the United States.

2. Choose one of the U.S. states other than Kansas, or use a state assigned by your teacher. Find the precipitation in inches for the months January, February, and March for the last five years. Record the data. Record the URL of the site you are using. Close your browser.

3. Working individually, create a worksheet to hold the data. Use the worksheet *113-Precipitation* that you edited earlier as a guide for the layout and format of the worksheet.

4. Include formulas to show the low and high precipitation years as in *113-Precipitation*. Add the source of your data as in *113-Precipitation*.

5. Set the top margin to 2 inches. Select the option to center the data horizontally on the page. Print the worksheet. Save the worksheet as *C15-Research*.

6. Select the years and the precipitation data for the five years (not the Low and High rows). Sort this data in ascending order by the March column. Print the worksheet. Save the worksheet as *C15-Research by March*. Close *Excel*.

SOFTWARE TIP

An easy way to record a URL is to copy it to a *Word* file. To do so, click in the Address bar of the browser. The URL should be highlighted. Press CTRL + C. Go to a *Word* document and click **Paste**.

Supplemental activities for this chapter can be found at www.c21jr. swlearning.com.

Figure 3.13 NASA Web Site Search Feature

When the search is complete, the browser may move to a new page that contains information you seek. However, there might be several pages that relate to the search term. In this case, a list of links may appear. You can scroll through the links and choose the one you think will be most likely to have the information you need. Search results for the NASA search are shown in Figure 3.14. The numbers to the right of the links tell how likely it is that the article or page will have information you seek. Note that 200 document links are in the list of a possible 55,202 hits. **Hits** are items in a search results list. To access an item from the list, click the link. If you want to go back to the list to try another link, use the Back button.

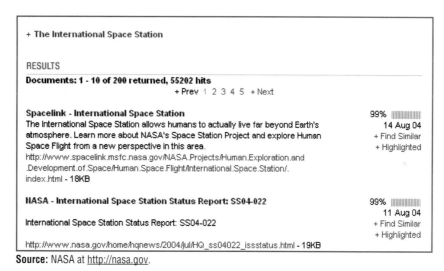

Source: NASA at http://nasa.gov.

Figure 3.14 Search Results on the NASA Web Site

12C LEARN:
Search on a Web Site

1. Log on to the Internet and start *Internet Explorer*. Use the Favorites link to go to the NASA Web site.

2. On the welcome screen, you may need to click a link such as **Enter the Main Site** to move past the welcome screen. Move ahead, as needed, until you reach a screen with a search box. It should be similar to the one shown in Figure 3.13.

3. Enter the term **space station** in the search box. Click **Go** or the button provided to begin the search.

23. Charts that have titles should not have a legend.

24. Column charts present information in vertical columns.

25. Cells selected as a range must be in adjacent rows and columns.

Applying *What you Have Learned*

Data File

CD-C15-Grades

Create Worksheet and Chart

1. Start *Excel*. Open *CD-C15-Grades* from your data files.

2. Insert a row above row 1. In cell A1, key **HEALTH TEST GRADES** for the worksheet title. Apply bold and a 12-point font to the title. Center the title across columns A through H.

3. Apply bold and center alignment to the column heads in row 3.

4. Insert rows so the following data can be keyed beginning with row 14. Key the data as shown.

	A	B	C	D	E	F
14	Homziak	95	98	98	97	98
15	Macy	80	75	83	90	95
16	Mahli	95	96	100	97	100
17	Rice	95	92	100	93	95
18	Robins	68	92	92	93	93
19	Tarzia	77	94	90	80	95
20	Vazza	71	88	96	85	93
21	Wayne	84	96	96	98	95
22	Wehner	67	72	85	92	88
23	Zehnder	86	94	94	80	100
24	Zigerell	80	96	94	90	95

5. In column G, use AutoSum to calculate the total points for all the test scores for each student.

6. In column H, enter a formula to calculate an average point score for each student. Format the cells for one decimal place.

7. In cell B25, enter a formula to find the average test score for Test 1. Copy the formula to cells C25:F25. Format the cells for one decimal place.

8. In cell B26, enter a formula to find the highest test score for Test 1. Copy the formula to cells C26:F26. Format the cells for one decimal place.

4. Scroll through the hits to find an item that interests you. Click the link and read the first paragraph of the article. Use the **Back** button, if desired, and read one or two more articles.

5. Print one of the articles. Remember to use Print Preview first to see how the page will print. Continue to the next activity or close *Internet Explorer*.

12D PRACTICE: Search on a Web Site

1. Log on to the Internet and start *Internet Explorer*. In the Address box, enter **nps.gov**. This is the URL for the U.S. National Parks Service Web site.

2. On the welcome screen, look for a search box. (Move ahead, if needed, until you reach a screen with a search box.) Enter the name of a U.S. national park in the search box. For example, you could enter **Yosemite**. Click **Search** or the button provided to start the search.

3. Scroll through the hits to find an item that interests you. Click the link and read the first paragraph of the article. Use the **Back** button, if desired, and read one or two more articles.

4. Print one of the articles. Remember to use Print Preview first to see how the page will print. Continue to the next activity or close *Internet Explorer*.

12E APPLY: Use History, Favorites, and Search

1. Log on to the Internet and start *Internet Explorer*. Use the History feature to go to the U.S. National Parks Service Web site (http://nps.gov).

2. Add this site to your Favorites list.

3. In the site's search box, enter **Yellowstone**. Click **Search** or the button provided to start the search.

4. Read the items in the search results as needed to answer the following questions:

   • In what state(s) is the park located?

   • What is the size of the park?

   • When was the park established as a park?

   • What are some of the main attractions of the park?

5. Close *Internet Explorer*.

 **CHECK POINT** Compare your answers with those of a classmate. If the first two answers differ, check the Web site again for accurate information.

Reviewing   *What You Have Learned*

Answer True or False to each question to review what you have learned in Chapter 15.

1. Spreadsheet software is used to create a worksheet, and word processing software is used to create a table.

2. Each spreadsheet file can contain only one worksheet.

3. Spreadsheet software is easier to use than word processing software to solve complex math problems.

4. A worksheet has rows that run vertically and columns that run horizontally.

5. Letters are used to identify worksheet columns.

6. Cells can be merged in a table but not in a worksheet.

7. The ENTER key must be used to move from one cell to another in a worksheet.

8. Formulas can be used to solve math problems.

9. By default, numbers are automatically right-aligned when entered.

10. A worksheet can be printed with borders on some or all of the cells.

11. A comma is used to separate the beginning cell from the ending cell in a range of cells.

12. A cell that has bold formatting applied can be changed to remove the bold by selecting **Edit**, **Clear**, **Formats** from the menu bar.

13. Clearing a cell and deleting cell contents are the same.

14. Text in a range of cells can be copied or moved to different locations.

15. The contents of one cell cannot be copied to more than one other cell.

16. The widths of columns do not need to be the same.

17. More than one row or column can be inserted or deleted at the same time.

18. When solving a math problem, spreadsheet software adds and subtracts before it multiplies and divides.

19. Formulas can be edited by changing the information in the formula bar.

20. A function is a predefined formula.

21. Words in a worksheet can be sorted only in ascending order.

22. The following are functions: SUM, AVERAGE, and MAX.

Lesson 13   Computer Ethics and Crime

Objectives

In Lesson 13, you will:

↘ Learn about ethics and netiquette rules.

↘ Evaluate an e-mail message for netiquette.

↘ Learn about computer crime.

↘ Find articles about computer crime.

Data file: *CD-13-Opportunity*

Computer users are expected to act responsibly. They must be concerned with ethics related to information and networks. **Ethics** are moral standards or values. They describe how people should behave. **Netiquette** is a term often used to describe rules for proper online behavior. People should also act in accordance with laws when using computers. You will learn about netiquette and computer crime in this lesson.

Netiquette

To communicate successfully, you follow certain rules of behavior. For example, you would not answer a telephone and start shouting at someone. This would be considered rude. You should also follow rules of polite behavior when communicating online. These rules are called netiquette. The word *netiquette* is formed from the words *etiquette* (the requirements for proper social behavior) and *Net* (from the word *Internet*).

Some netiquette rules relate to e-mail or instant messages sent to others. For example, when keying an e-mail message, do not key in ALL CAPS. This is like shouting your message and is considered rude. You will learn more guidelines for using e-mail messages in Chapter 11. Some other netiquette rules that you should know are listed below.

- Do not give out phone numbers or other personal information unless you are sure the site is safe.

- Never give out personal information about others without their permission.

- Consider all private e-mail to belong to the original author. Do not forward it or post it without permission.

- Send information only to those who need it. Busy people do not want to spend time reading messages that do not relate to them.

- Do not send large attachments without the receiver's permission.

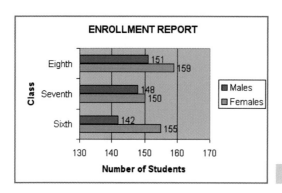

Figure 15.25 Enrollment Report Bar Chart

6. Select the chart and print it. Save the worksheet as *114-School*. Close the file. Close *Excel* or continue to the next activity.

114C PRACTICE: Pie Charts

In this activity, you will create an embedded pie chart with a legend at the right.

1. Start *Excel*. Open *CD-114-Expenses* from your data files.

2. Select cells A4:B8. Click the **Chart Wizard** button. Select **Pie** as the chart type. Select the chart in row 1, column 1 of the Chart sub-type samples. Click **Next**.

3. Click **Next** again to accept the defaults in step 2 of the Chart Wizard. In step 3 of the Chart Wizard, click the **Titles** tab. Key **MONTHLY EXPENSES** for the chart title.

4. Click the **Legend** tab. Select the **Show legend** option. Under Placement, select the **Right** option. Click the **Data Labels** tab. Select the **Percentage** option. Click **Next**.

5. Select the **As object in** option. Click the **Finish** button. The chart should look similar to Figure 15.26.

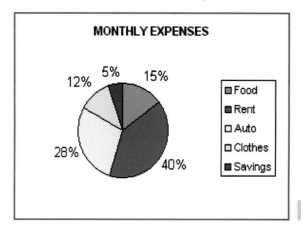

Figure 15.26 Pie Chart

6. Select the chart and print it. Save the worksheet as *114-Expenses*. Close *Excel*.

- Do not send spam. **Spam** is an e-mail message sent to many addresses. It is similar to hard-copy junk mail. The sender hopes to find a few people who are interested in the message.
- Make an effort to keep your computer virus-free to avoid spreading viruses to others.
- Be courteous to others in all online messages and on Web pages. Do not use offensive or biased language.
- Respect the privacy of others. Do not read e-mail or other material that is meant for someone else.
- Assume that messages (e-mail, instant messages, newsgroup postings) are not secure. Do not include private information.
- Be ethical. Do not copy material from the Web and use it as your own. Pay for shareware or other material you download when that is a stated policy.
- Do not use another person's computer or resources (such as online service) without permission.
- Do not use the Internet for anything that is illegal.

13A APPLY: Evaluate a Message for Netiquette

1. Start *Word*. Open *CD-13-Opportunity* found in your data files. Read the e-mail message contained in this document.
2. Work with one or two classmates to evaluate the e-mail message. Does the message follow netiquette rules (listed in the section above)? Make a list of any rules this message violates.

Computer Crime

Crime related to computers or committed by using computers can take many forms. Victims of computer-related crime can be individuals or businesses. People and companies must be careful to protect their private data. They must also protect the data gathered from others. For example, companies may have medical records or credit card numbers of customers. These records are often stored on computers. This makes them vulnerable to computer crime.

Computer Viruses and Hackers

One type of illegal activity related to computing is spreading computer viruses. A **computer virus** is a destructive program. A virus can be loaded onto a computer and run without the computer owner's knowledge. Viruses are dangerous. They can quickly destroy data. They can also cause a computer or network to stop working properly. Some viruses can travel across networks and get past security systems. Antivirus programs can be used to find and remove viruses before they do harm. These programs can be set to scan incoming data to look for viruses. Users should back up

6. Select the **Data Labels** tab. In the Label Contains section, select the **Value** option as shown in Figure 15.23. Choose **Next** to continue.

7. In step 4 of the Chart Wizard, click the radio button for the **As object in** option. *Sheet 1* should appear by this option. Click the **Finish** button.

Figure 15.24 Chart Wizard, Step 4

SOFTWARE TIP

You can print the worksheet and chart together. To do so, do not select the chart. Print the worksheet as usual.

8. The chart should appear on your worksheet. Click the chart border to select the chart. Click on a blank area of the chart and drag the chart under the data. Place the top-left corner of the chart in about cell A9.

9. Click and drag the lower-right corner of the chart border to resize the chart. Make the chart appear similar to the one shown in Figure 15.20 on page 538.

10. To print the chart without the worksheet, click the chart to select it. Choose **File, Print** from the menu bar. The **Selected Chart** option should be selected in the Print What section. Click **OK**.

11. Save the file as *114-Sales*. Close the file. Close *Excel* or continue to the next activity.

114B PRACTICE: Create a Bar Chart

1. Start *Excel*. Open *CD-114-School* from your data files.

2. Select the data in cells A3:C6. Click the **Chart Wizard** button to create a chart. Select **Bar** as the chart type.

3. Key **ENROLLMENT REPORT** for the chart title. Key **Class** for the Category (X) axis. Key **Number of Students** for the Value (Y) axis. Select **Value** for the data labels.

4. Select the **As object in** option to have the chart placed in the worksheet page with the data.

5. Select the chart and resize it, if needed, so it looks similar to Figure 15.25.

(make a copy of) important data and keep it in a safe place. For example, copies of important files could be saved on a CD-ROM. If a virus destroys the data stored on a computer, the backup copy can be used.

Another related type of computer crime is called **hacking**. Hacking is accessing computers or networks without the proper permission. People who do this are called **hackers**. Hacking is both unethical and illegal. Penalties for hacking can be up to 20 years in prison!

Hackers may be able to access and misuse information that belongs to others. For example, a hacker might steal a customer's credit card number. Using a credit card number that does not belong to you to buy products over the Internet is illegal. This is an example of computer fraud.

Identity Theft

Sometimes a criminal may steal more than a credit card number. He or she may steal a person's identity. The criminal will find as much personal information about a victim as possible. For example, bank account numbers, social security numbers, job information, family information, and spending records may be hacked. Personal information may also come from a stolen purse or wallet.

Once a criminal has this type of information, he or she can pretend to be the victim. This is called **identity theft**. Money may be moved out of the victim's bank account. A new credit card account, using the victim's name, may be opened. Vacations, cars, and other expensive items may be charged to the victim. When the credit card bills are not paid, the overdue account is reported on the victim's credit report. The victim may be turned down for loans or not hired for jobs because of the bad credit report. The victim may not know at first what is happening or that the credit report is bad. An identity thief may give the victim's name to the police during an arrest. If the person is released from police custody, but does not show up on the court date, an arrest warrant is issued for the victim.

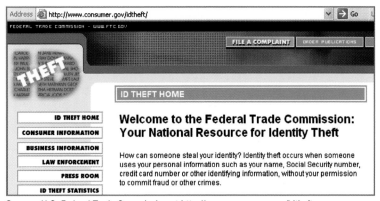

Source: U.S. Federal Trade Commission at http://www.consumer.gov/idtheft.

Figure 3.15 The U.S. Federal Trade Commission provides resources for victims of identity theft.

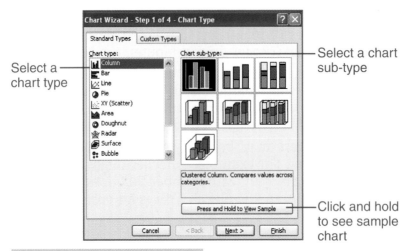

Figure 15.21 Chart Wizard, Step 1

4. Step 2 of the Chart Wizard shows the data range you selected. **Columns** is selected to show that data will be plotted from the columns in the cell range. Choose **Next** to continue.

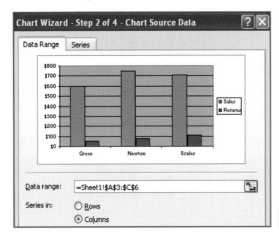

Figure 15.22 Chart Wizard, Step 2

5. In step 3 of the Chart Wizard, select the **Titles** tab. Key **SALES REPORT** in the Chart title box. Key **Salesperson** in the Category (X) axis box. Key **Sales** in the Value (Y) axis box.

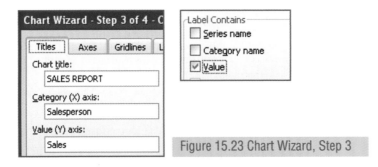

Figure 15.23 Chart Wizard, Step 3

Millions of Americans have been victims of identity theft. Businesses and victims have lost billions of dollars to this type of crime. The U.S. Federal Trade Commission provides resources for victims of identity theft. They also provide tips for reducing this crime. To reduce the chances of being a victim of identity theft you can:

- Request a copy of your credit report every year.
- Use strong passwords on credit card, bank, and phone accounts.
- Secure personal information in the home.
- Ask about information security procedures in your workplace.
- Avoid giving out personal information on the phone, through the mail, or over the Internet unless the site is reputable.
- Shred charge receipts, credit records, checks, and bank statements before throwing them away.
- Keep your Social Security card and number in a safe place.
- Protect access to home computers and guard against computer viruses.

Scams

Some criminals run scams using the Internet. A **scam** is a scheme used to take money under false pretenses or for a product that does not work as advertised. For example, a criminal might deceive consumers who respond to an ad on a Web page. The ad promises a computer for $700. The computer is to be delivered after the first payment of $199. After the first payment is made, the story changes. The criminal now tells consumers that they must pay the full amount before getting a computer. Even when the full amount is paid, only very old or damaged computers are delivered.

To avoid being the victim of a scam, buy only from reputable companies. Do not give out personal information or credit card numbers unless you are certain the company is honest and the Web site is safe.

13B APPLY: Access the Cybercrime Web Site

In this activity, you will access a Web site that has information about computer crimes. You will follow hyperlinks to find an article about one crime case and print the article.

1. Log on to the Internet. Start *Internet Explorer*. In the Address box, enter **www.cybercrime.gov**. This site is hosted by the U.S. Department of Justice.
2. Click hyperlinks related to computer crime and computer crime cases. Read about one computer crime case.
3. Choose **File** and then **Print Preview** from the menu bar to see how the document will appear when printed. Close Print Preview.

Parts of a Chart

Charts can be placed on a separate worksheet in the same workbook. Charts can also be placed on the same worksheet as the data used to create the chart. This is called an embedded chart. The parts of a column chart are described below and shown in Figure 15.20.

- The **titles** are headings that identify chart contents.
- The **category axis**, sometimes called the x-axis, is used to plot categories of data. The **value axis**, usually called the y-axis, is used to plot values associated with the categories of data.
- **Data points** are the bars, columns, or pie slices that represent the numerical data in a chart.
- **Data labels** are numbers or words that identify values displayed in the chart.
- **Gridlines** are lines through a chart that identify points on the axes.
- A **legend** is a key (usually with different colors or patterns) used to identify the chart's data categories.

Figure 15.20 Column Chart Parts

Create a Column Chart

SOFTWARE TIP

Use the Chart Wizard button to create charts.

Chart Wizard button

1. Start *Excel*. Open *CD-114-Sales* found in your data files. You will create an embedded column chart using the data in this worksheet.
2. Select cells A3:C6. Click the **Chart Wizard** button on the Standard toolbar.
3. Select the **Standard Types** tab as shown in Figure 15.21. Select **Column** from the Chart type list. Select the chart in row 1, column 1 of the Chart sub-type samples. Click and hold the **Press and Hold to View Sample** button to preview your chart. Choose **Next** to continue.

4. Choose **File**, **Print** from the menu bar. Select your printer if needed. Choose to print 1 copy of all pages. Click **Print**.

5. Read the case again from your printed copy. Use a marker or pen to highlight the main points of the article. Be prepared to share the main points of the case with the class.

Lesson 14   Safety and Copyright Issues

Objectives

In Lesson 14, you will:
- ↘ Learn about safety issues related to using the Internet.
- ↘ Use a search engine to find information on the Internet.
- ↘ Learn about copyright issues.

Online Safety

Using the Internet is a great way to communicate and interact with other people. Just as in the real world, many people you meet will be honest and kind. They will have no intention of harming you or cheating you. However, just as in the real world, some people in the virtual world try to cheat or harm others. For this reason, computer users must be concerned about safety.

Personal Safety

As a computer user, you should be concerned about your personal safety. When you meet someone on the Internet, you have only this person's word about who he or she is. You probably cannot see the person. The person may say his or her age is 14 when it is really 40. The person may say she is a woman, when he is really a man. The person may pretend to be interested in the things that interest you to gain your trust. The person's real motive may be to deceive you or harm you.

To protect yourself, never give out your full name, personal address, phone number, school address, or other private information to individuals you do not know personally. Never send your picture to someone you do not know personally. Never agree to meet in person someone you have met on the Internet unless you have a parent or guardian present. The person you meet might really be your age and share your interest in a hobby or sport. In this case, Mom or Dad can wait at the next table while you and your new friend talk and enjoy pizza. Your new friend probably brought Mom or Dad along, too. If the person you meet turns out to be different than you expected, you will be glad you have Mom or Dad nearby.

Insert a Worksheet in a Word Processing Document

In this activity, you will complete a worksheet in *Excel* and copy it into a *Word* document.

1. Start *Excel*. Open *CD-113-Children* from your data files. Enter this data to complete the worksheet.

Cell G4	**25.6**	Cell H4	**27.5**
Cell G5	**24.4**	Cell H5	**26.9**
Cell G6	**24.4**	Cell H6	**26.0**

2. In cell A7 enter **Total**. Enter formulas to find the total number of children for each year in cells B7:H7. Save the worksheet as *113-Children*.

3. Start *Word*. Open *CD-113-Memo* from your data files.

4. In the worksheet, select cells A1:H9. Click the **Copy** button. Go to the memo in *Word*. Position the insertion point between the two paragraphs of the memo. Click the **Paste** button.

5. Set the table alignment to center. (Choose **Table**, **Table Properties** from the menu bar. Select **Center** alignment and click **OK**.)

6. Compose and key a paragraph placed after the table. In the paragraph, tell whether the total number of children is predicted to increase or decrease from 2000 to 2020. Describe what is expected to happen with the children in age group 6 to 11 from 2000 to 2020.

7. Save the document as *113-Memo*. Print the memo. Close *Word*. Close *Excel*.

Lesson 114   Worksheets with Charts

Objectives

In Lesson 114, you will:

⭘ Create column, bar, and pie charts using worksheet data.

⭘ Embed charts on a worksheet page.

Data files: *CD-114-Sales, CD-114-School, CD-114-Expenses*

┌ ─ ─ ─ ┐
Help Words
└ ─ ─ ─ ┘
Chart
   About charts

Charts

You can create many different kinds of charts with spreadsheet software. Charts are important because they show information graphically. This allows readers to better understand the data. You can create column, bar, and pie charts, among others. **Column charts** and **bar charts** compare values across categories of data. **Pie charts** show how much each value is of a total value.

Safety of Data

Computer users should be concerned about the safety of their private data. Many people buy products from Web sites. Some doctors have patients fill out medical history forms online. Banks allow customers to make transactions online. All these situations require entering personal information. How can you be sure your data will be safe when using these Web sites?

Reputable companies that collect personal data on their Web sites take measures to ensure that the data will be safe. Safety is a concern as the data is transmitted and when it is stored on computers. When you enter an area of a secure Web site that requires private data, you will typically see a dialog box like the one shown in Figure 3.16.

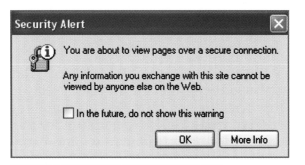

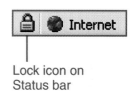

Lock icon on
Status bar

Figure 3.16 Security Alert Dialog Box

After you click OK and continue on the site, a locked Lock icon will appear on the status bar at the bottom of the window. This Lock icon assures you that your data is reasonably safe during transmission.

Once a company has your private data, it should take measures to keep it safe. Companies can use special hardware and software called **firewalls** to help prevent unauthorized users from getting to your data.

You should be aware of what a company plans to do with your data. Many companies post a privacy policy on their Web sites. A **privacy policy** is a document that tells how personal data will be used. Links such as *Privacy Statement* or *Privacy Policy* are often shown at the bottom of a site's welcome page. The first part of a typical privacy statement is shown in Figure 3.17.

Privacy Statement

This Privacy Statement relates solely to the online information collection and use practices of our Web site located at www.thomson.com (this "Web Site"), and not to any subdomains of this Web Site. We recognize that many visitors and users of this Web Site are concerned about the information they provide to us, and how we treat that information. This Privacy Statement, which may be updated from time to time, has been developed to address those concerns.

Figure 3.17 Privacy Statement for Web Site

7. Now you will sort the list by the Period column so the reader can easily see a complete list of students for each class. Go to cell A4. Click **Data** on the menu bar. Select **Sort.** Select **Period** from the Sort by list. From the first Then by list, select **Last Name**. From the second Then by list, select **First Name. Ascending** should be selected for all columns. Select the **Header row** option and click **OK**.

8. The data should now be arranged with the students in Period 2 listed in alphabetical order and then the students in Period 3 in alphabetical order. Save the file as *113-Art by Period*.

9. You can use the Selection option on the Print dialog box to print just the students from Period 2. Select cells A1:C19. Choose **File, Print** from the menu bar. In the Print what section, choose **Selection**. Select other options such as your printer, if needed. Click **OK**. The printed worksheet should contain only the students from Period 2.

10. To print the list for Period 3, you will first sort the list by Period in descending order. Go to cell A4. Choose **Data, Sort** from the menu bar. Select **Period** from the Sort by list. Select **Descending** by Period. From the first Then by list, select **Last Name**. From the second Then by list, select **First Name**. Select **Ascending** for the Last Name and First Name columns. Select the **Header row** option and click **OK**.

11. Select cells A1:C17. Follow the process from step 9 to print the selection. Save the file, using the same name. Close the file.

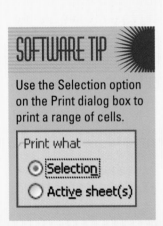

SOFTWARE TIP

Use the Selection option on the Print dialog box to print a range of cells.

113D PRACTICE: Sort a Guest List

1. Start *Excel*. Open *CD-113-Dinner*. Save the file as *113-Dinner by Ticket*.

2. Sort the data below the column heads in ascending order by ticket number. Check to see that the sorted list is in ascending order by ticket number (lowest to highest).

3. Select cells A3:F50. Apply the **All Borders** border style.

4. This worksheet is too long to print on one page using a 2-inch top margin. You will use different print settings. Choose **File, Page Setup**. Select the **Margins** tab. Under Center on page, select **Horizontally** and select **Vertically**. Click **OK**. Print the worksheet.

5. Sort the data below the column heads in ascending order by last name and then by first name. Check to see that the sorted list has the names in alphabetical order.

6. Save the worksheet as *113-Dinner by Name*. Print the worksheet. Complete the Check Point below and then close the file.

 **CHECK POINT** Compare your printed worksheet with that of a classmate. Make corrections if needed.

To protect your private data, enter your information only on sites that are secure and only with your parent's or guardian's permission. Read the site's privacy policy to see if you approve of how your data will be used before entering your data.

Internet Search Engines

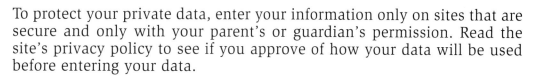

The Internet contains millions of sites and millions of pages of information. How can you find the information you need? In some cases you may know or be able to guess the URL for a site. For example, http://www.nasa.gov is an easy URL to remember for the NASA site. When you don't know the URL for a site, you can use a search engine. A **search engine** is a Web site that allows you to enter search criteria and find Web sites. You may have heard of some of these sites such as Google, Yahoo!, and MSN.

In Lesson 12, you learned to use the search feature of a Web site. Using a search engine is a similar process. You enter a word or phrase in a search box and click a button such as Go or Search. Then you receive a list of hits from which you can choose.

Search engines are powerful tools and can be a great help in finding information. However, there are some negatives. First, you will often receive more hits than you can possibly read. Second, some of the hits are paid for by advertisers. They may appear at the top of the list even though they are not the most likely to have the information you want. These hits are often labeled with words such as *Sponsored Sites*. Third, some sites may have inaccurate information. You'll need to take special care to find the sites with the best and most accurate information.

Knowing the source of information on a Web site can be important. Knowing the source can help you judge whether the information is likely to be correct. For example, suppose you read about a treatment for an illness on a Web site. You should see if the person giving the information is someone who is likely to know about the treatment, such as a doctor. You can read news stories and articles on many Web sites. You should be concerned about whether the facts in a story have been reported objectively. Knowing the source of the news story helps you judge whether or not to believe the story. Choose links such as *About Us* on Web sites to learn about the person or organization sponsoring the site.

14A LEARN: Use a Search Engine

1. Log on to the Internet and start *Internet Explorer*. In the Address bar, enter one of the URLs shown below or one given to you by your teacher.

   www.google.com
   www.yahoo.com
   www.msn.com

lowest number to the highest. **Descending** order means Z to A for words. For numbers, descending order means from the highest to the lowest number.

You may want to rename and save a worksheet before doing a sort. This lets you keep a copy of the information in its original order.

113C LEARN: Sort a Class List

1. Start *Excel*. Open *CD-113-Art* from your data files. Save the file as *113-Art by Name*.

2. To sort the data by name in ascending order, click cell A4.

3. Click **Data** on the menu bar. Select **Sort**. In the Sort dialog box, select **Last Name** from the Sort by list. **Ascending** should be selected as shown in Figure 15.19.

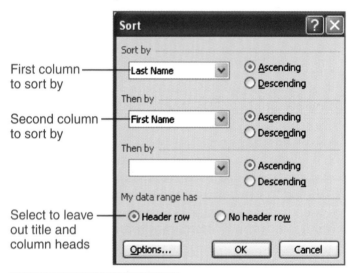

First column to sort by

Second column to sort by

Select to leave out title and column heads

Figure 15.19 Sort Dialog Box

4. Some people in the list have the same last name. Their names will be sorted by first name. Select **First Name** in the first Then by list. **Ascending** should be selected by First Name. In the My data range has section, select the **Header row** option if it is not already selected. Click **OK**.

5. Check to see that the names are sorted in alphabetical order. Check to see that the first names are also in alphabetical order when the last names are the same.

6. Set the top margin to 2 inches. Select the option to center the data horizontally on the page. Print the worksheet. Save the worksheet, using the same name.

2. In the search box, enter **online safety**. Click the button such as **Go** or **Search** to begin the search.

3. Scroll down the list of hits. Choose a hit that you think will have an article or tips for online safety. Look at several sites until you find one with good information about online safety for kids or teens.

4. Add the best site you found to your Favorites list. For this site, list the information given below. You may need to follow links such as *About Us* to find the company or organization that sponsors the site.

   - URL for the Web site
   - Web site name
   - Organization that sponsors or posts the site
   - The type of information you found (article, guidelines or rules, videos, and so on)

5. Share information about the site with your class or a group of classmates as directed by your teacher.

Copyright Issues

People or companies that create works that are new, useful, and potentially profitable may be granted a copyright for those works. A **copyright** is a form of protection granted by the U.S. government. Copyright laws and rules tell how copyrighted works can be legally used. Works such as books, articles, music, plays, movie scripts, and artwork can be copyrighted. Copyrighted material may carry the © symbol. However, you should assume that material may be copyrighted even if you do not see this symbol.

As a general rule, you may not legally use copyrighted material unless you have the owner's permission. However, you may be able to use a small portion of a copyrighted work for educational purposes. The rules that relate to this type of use are called the fair use doctrine.

Fair use doctrine does not allow plagiarism. The term **plagiarism** refers to using material created by another person and claiming it as your own. For example, suppose you find a report on the Internet that just fits the assignment you were given. You print the report and turn it in with your name as the writer. This is plagiarism and it is illegal. Plagiarism in schoolwork may result in serious punishment.

Much of the information found on Web pages on the Internet is copyrighted. This means that it may be illegal to reprint or post the material without permission. For example, suppose you see a really great picture on a Web site you visit. You decide to save the picture and use it on the desktop of your computer. You also send the picture to three friends. The picture may be copyrighted. If so, you may be breaking the law by copying and using the picture without the owner's permission. Look for copyright statements and

2. To insert a column between columns B and C, click a cell in column C. Click **Insert** on the menu bar. Select **Columns**. Key the following data in the appropriate cells:

Cell C3   **Trailers**
Cell C4   **13**
Cell C5   **17**
Cell C6   **21**

3. To insert two rows between rows 4 (Holt) and 5 (Nedro), point to the row 5 heading area. When the pointer changes to a right arrow, click and drag down to select two rows. Release the mouse button. Selected rows are shown in Figure 15.18.

	A	B	C	D	E
1	VEHICLE RECORDS				
2					
3	**Name**	**Cars**	**Trailers**	**Vans**	
4	Holt	225	13	115	
5	Nedro	243	17	97	
6	Peters	212	21	87	
7					

Click and drag over row headings to select rows

Figure 15.18 Selected Rows

4. Click **Insert** on the menu bar. Select **Rows**. Two rows will be inserted. (*Excel* inserts the number of rows you selected before giving the Insert command.)

5. Key the following information in the rows:

	A	B	C	D
5	James	211	11	83
6	Long	197	7	71

6. To delete column B, point to the column heading and click to select the column. Click **Edit** on the menu bar. Click **Delete**. Click the **Undo** button to restore the column.

7. To delete row 7, point to the row heading and click to select the row. Click **Edit** on the menu bar. Click **Delete**. Click the **Undo** button to restore the row.

8. Save the file as *113-Vehicles*. Close *Excel*.

Sorting Data in a Worksheet

Sort means to arrange or group items in a particular order. You can sort information in a worksheet in ascending or descending order. Ascending order means A to Z for words. For numbers, **ascending** order means from the

links such as *Legal Notices* on Web sites you visit. These notices help you determine whether the material is copyrighted.

Copyright rules also affect what you can do with some works after you purchase them. For example, movies and music are often sold with certain terms and conditions. These terms may limit how you can use the movie or music. For example, you may be able to make one or two copies of a song for backup purposes or to use on a portable music player. However, you may not be allowed to make copies of the song to give to friends. You will explore some terms of use for music purchased online in the next activity.

14B APPLY: Find Terms of Use Statements

1. Log on to the Internet and start *Internet Explorer*. In the Address bar, enter one of the URLs shown below or one given to you by your teacher.

   www.google.com
   www.yahoo.com
   www.msn.com

2. In the search box, enter **music download**. Click the button such as **Go** or **Search** to begin the search.

3. Choose links in the results list to find a site that sells music online. For example, Walmart.com sells music online that you can download. Access the site.

4. If the site has many departments, you may need to choose a link such as *Music.* You may need to choose another link such as *Download Music.* Follow links as needed to reach a page where you can buy and download songs.

5. Follow links such as *Terms of Sale* or *Usage and License Rules* to learn how you may use the music you purchase from this site. These links are often located at the bottom of the Web page.

6. Make a list of the main points given in the terms of use. What copies are you allowed to make? What copying is specifically not allowed? Be prepared to discuss your findings with the class.

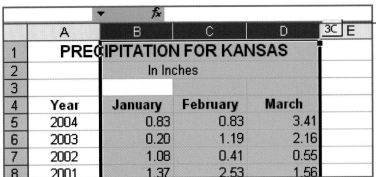

Click and drag over column heads to select columns

Figure 15.17 Selected Columns

7. Choose **Format**, **Column**, **Width**. Key **10** in the Column Width dialog box. Click **OK**.

8. Apply center alignment to the column heads in row 4. Apply a bottom border to cells B11:D11.

9. In cell A12, enter **Low**. Apply center alignment to cell A12. In cells B12:D12, enter formulas to display the lowest precipitation amount for each month.

10. In cell A13, enter **High**. Apply center alignment to cell A13. In cells B13:D13, enter formulas to display the highest precipitation amount for each month.

11. Set the top margin to 2 inches. Select the option to center the data horizontally on the page. Print the worksheet.

12. Save the file as *113-Precipitation*. Close the file.

Inserting and Deleting Rows and Columns

┌ ┐
Help Words
└ ┘
Insert
   Insert blank cells,
   rows, or columns

When you create or edit worksheets, you may find that you need to delete a row or column of data. You may also find that you need to insert a row or column of data. One or more rows or columns can be inserted at a time. Columns may be added at the left or within worksheets. Rows may be added at the top or within worksheets.

113B LEARN:

Insert and Delete Rows and Columns

1. Start *Excel*. Open *CD-113-Vehicles* from your data files.

Reviewing | *What You Have Learned*

Answer these questions to review what you have learned in Chapter 3.

1. The development of small and fast computers was a result of needs in what industry?

2. Describe early computers in terms of size and what they could do.

3. When were notebook computers introduced?

4. A measure of how much work can be done in a certain amount of time is called _____.

5. List three ways that computers are used in everyday life.

6. When one computer links to another computer, a _____ is created.

7. What is the Internet?

8. Name three popular uses of the Internet.

9. What is e-commerce?

10. What is an Internet service provider? Give two examples of an ISP.

11. A program that lets you find and view Web pages is called a
_____ _____.

12. To go to a certain Web site, what can you enter in the browser's Address bar?

13. What happens when a user clicks a hyperlink on a Web page?

14. Explain what the History feature and the Favorites feature of a browser allow you to do.

15. Items in a search results list are called _____.

16. Define the terms *ethics* and *netiquette*.

17. Give examples of three different types of computer-related crime.

18. What can you do related to computer use to protect your personal safety?

19. What can you do related to computer use to protect the safety of your personal data?

20. A Web site that allows you to enter search criteria and find related Web sites is called a _____ _____.

21. What is a copyright?

Change Column Widths

1. Open *CD-113-Precipitation* from your data files.

2. To set the width of column A to 10 characters, click any cell in column A. Click **Format** on the menu bar. Choose **Column**. Choose **Width**. Key **10** in the Column Width dialog box as shown in Figure 15.15. Click **OK**.

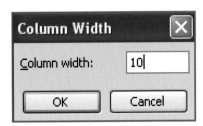

Figure 15.15 Column Width Dialog Box

3. To resize column B, move your pointer to the right border of the column B heading area. The pointer will change to a four-sided arrow as shown in Figure 15.16. Double-click the left mouse button. The column width will be adjusted to be as wide as the longest item in the column.

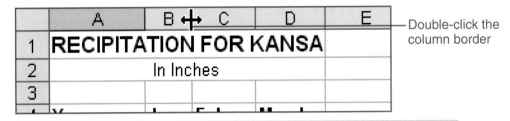

Figure 15.16 Double-click the right column border to fit the contents in the column.

4. Double-click the right column border of column C to fit the contents in the column.

5. You can also change a column width by clicking and dragging the right column border. Click and drag the right column border for column B so it appears to be about the same width as column A. Repeat the process for columns C and D.

6. You can set the width for several columns at one time. Point to the column B heading. When the cursor becomes a down arrow, click and drag to the right to select columns B, C, and D. The selected columns are shown in Figure 15.17.

Applying   *What You Have Learned*

Research Spyware

Have you ever heard the term *spyware*? In this activity, you will research this term on the Internet. You will use a search engine to find an online dictionary. You will also find articles related to spyware. Your goal is to find online resources to help you answer the following questions:

- What is spyware and what does it do?
- How can you protect your computer system so spyware is not loaded onto it?

1. Log on to the Internet and start *Internet Explorer*. In the Address bar, enter one of the URLs shown below or one given to you by your teacher.

   www.google.com
   www.yahoo.com
   www.msn.com

2. In the search box, enter **computer dictionary**. Choose one of the sites from the results list. On the dictionary site, search using the term **spyware**. Read the information provided.

3. Go back to the search results list. Access another online dictionary and find a definition for spyware. Read the information provided

4. Go back to the search engine you used in step 1. Key **spyware** in the search box. Click the button such as **Go** or **Search** to begin the search. Another search term you may wish to use is **spyware blocker**.

5. Choose links in the results list to find articles about spyware. Read two or three articles.

6. In your own words, write an answer for each question given above step 1. Be prepared to discuss your answers with the class.

Supplemental activities for this chapter can be found at www.c21jr. swlearning.com.

8. Delete cells A11:B11. Select cells A12:E16. Use Cut and Paste to move the data to A11:E15 (up one row).

9. Apply a bottom border to cells B15:E15. Enter formulas in cells B16:E16 to find the sum of the numbers in columns B, C, D, and E.

10. Select cells B4:E16 and apply the Currency Style format.

11. Go to cell F3 and enter **March %**. Apply bold and center alignment if it is not applied automatically.

12. In cell F4, enter a formula to find the percent the March Savings amount is of the Budget Savings amount. Format cell F4 for Percent Style. Copy the formula to cells F5:F16.

13. Apply a bottom border to cell F15. Select cells B16:F16 and apply a bottom double border to the cells.

14. Set the top margin to 2 inches. Select the option to center the data horizontally on the page. Print the worksheet.

15. Save the file as *112-Budget*. Close *Excel* or continue to the next activity.

✔ **CHECK POINT** Which expense items were over budget? Which ones were under budget? Compare your answers with those of a classmate.

Lesson 113 Formatting Cells and Columns

Objectives

In Lesson 113, you will:
- ↘ Change column widths in worksheets.
- ↘ Insert and delete columns and rows in worksheets.
- ↘ Sort data in a worksheet.
- ↘ Use formulas and functions in worksheets.
- ↘ Copy data from a worksheet to a *Word* document.

Data files: *CD-113-Precipitation, CD-113-Vehicles, CD-113-Art, CD-113-Dinner, CD-113-Children, CD-113-Memo*

┌ ┐
Help Words
└ ┘
Column
 Change column
 width and row
 height

Changing the Width of Columns

Often, the data you want to place in a cell will be longer than the standard column width. You change the column width by clicking and dragging the column heading right border. You can set a specific column width using the Column Width dialog box. You can also adjust the column width to fit the longest entry in that column.

Across the Curriculum

INTERNET

Data Files

- *CD-C03-Business*
- *CD-C03-Health Services*
- *CD-C03-Career*
- *CD-C03-Comma*
- *CD-C03-Reading*

⤴ About Business

THE GLOBAL MARKETPLACE Businesses sell products and services to their customers. **Market** is another term used to refer to a company's customers. The geographical area in which a company sells products is called its **marketplace**. Some businesses sell products in a limited marketplace. For example, a company may have two stores in one city. That city is the company's marketplace. Other companies may have a broad marketplace. Such companies may sell products in several cities or states. Companies that buy or sell products around the world operate in the **global marketplace**.

Many companies gather information about their market (customers). They want to know things such as:

- What are my customers like (age, gender, income level)?
- Why do they want or need our products?
- What is the best way to give them information about our products?

Using this market data, companies try to make products they think customers will want to buy. Companies who sell in the global marketplace may find it harder to understand their customers than those who sell in a more limited area. This is because the customers may be from different countries or cultures. Getting products to customers around the world can be harder than in a local market. Handling payments in foreign currencies may also require more work.

In this chapter, you learned about the Internet and e-commerce. The Internet has made selling in the global marketplace easier for many companies, especially small companies. Even a small company that sells in only one city may be competing in the global marketplace. Foreign companies may be trying to sell their products to the same customers as this local store. When consumers buy goods from other countries, they, too, are taking part in the global marketplace.

1. Start *Word*. Open and print *CD-C03-Business* from your data files. Complete the activity to learn more about products sold in the global marketplace.

2. Compare the answers to your currency problems with those of a classmate. If the answers differ, check the numbers again to see which are correct.

⤴ Career and Life Skills Success Builder

HEALTH AND PHYSICAL EDUCATION VS. YOUR CAREER Do you know what you want to be when you grow up? Trying to identify a career can be an overwhelming task. There are so many choices, and the number of job

INTERNET

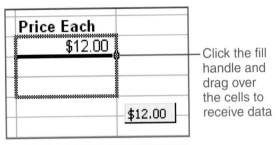 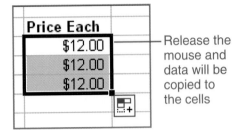

Click the fill handle and drag over the cells to receive data

Release the mouse and data will be copied to the cells

Figure 15.14 Copy Data in Cells

9. Go to cell C32. Enter **12.00** in the cell. Use the fill handle to copy the amount to cells C33:C36.

10. The Red Team has a new student. Enter the name **Clarice Moore** in cell A27.

11. All the students except Clarice sold **5** bags of bulbs at $12.00 per bag. Clarice sold **3** bags. Enter this data in the appropriate cells in the worksheet. Use the Copy command or the fill handle to make entering the data faster. Be sure to enter a Price Each amount for Clarice.

12. Go to cell C8. Click the **Borders** button on the toolbar and select **Bottom Border**. In cell C9, use AutoSum to find the total of the Price Each amounts. Apply a bottom border to cells C16, C28, and C36. Use AutoSum to find the total for Price Each amounts in cells C17, C29, and C37.

13. Set the top margin to 2 inches. Select the option to center the data horizontally on the page. Print the worksheet.

14. Save the worksheet as *112-Sales*. Close the file. Close *Excel* or continue to the next activity.

112D PRACTICE: Edit a Budget Worksheet

1. Start *Excel*. Open *CD-112-Budget* from your data files.

2. Edit cell A1 to read **BUDGET AND MONTHLY EXPENSES**. Change the font to 12 point and apply bold. Center the title over columns A through F.

3. Apply center alignment and bold to the column heads in row 3.

4. Use Cut and Paste to move the data in cells A19:B19 to cells A4:B4.

5. Clear the contents of cells A17:F18.

6. Change the value in cell E16 to **95**.

7. Copy cell B4 to cells C4:E4. Copy cell B5 to cells C5:E5.

possibilities doubles every few years. No matter what path you decide to follow, there are steps you can take to help you succeed at whatever you choose to do.

Did you know that the classes you are taking in school now can help you prepare for a future career? For example, your classes in health and physical education are related to many health care careers. If you want to help people live healthy lives, you may someday be a doctor or nurse. If you want to help people get fit, you might become a sports trainer or coach. Careers in this field also include jobs such as cancer researchers and medical assistants. These careers are all about helping people live life better.

1. Is a career in health care for you? Open and print the data file *CD-C03-Health Services*. Read the information to see if you are interested in this career path.

2. Open the data file *CD-C03-Career*. Follow the directions given to access the Internet and research a career in health care or wellness.

↗ Academic Success Builder

COMMUNICATIONS: COMMA A comma is used to separate words or groups of words to help the reader understand the meaning of a sentence. Commas are frequently misused. Sometimes they are not used when they need to be used, and they are frequently used when they are not needed. Common uses of the comma are listed below.

- Commas are used to join sentences.
- Commas are used to separate items in a series.
- Commas are used after introductory phrases and clauses.
- Commas are used to separate parallel adjectives.

1. Start *Word*. Open *CD-C03-Comma* from your data files. Print the file and then close it. Study the Guides and the Learn line(s) for each Guide.

2. For the Practice lines and the Apply lines, read the sentences and add commas where they are needed.

READING: READ A MAP Have you ever visited a new city and had difficulty finding your way to the places you wanted to visit? Did you have a map of the city? Could you read the map to locate the buildings you wanted to visit and the information you needed? Could you read the map to find directions to the places you wanted to go?

In this activity, you will answer questions related to finding your way around Greensboro, North Carolina, using a city map.

1. Start *Word*. Open *CD-C03-Reading* from your data files. Print the file and then close it.

2. Follow the directions given to access a map online. Read the map to answer the questions in the data file. Compare your answers with those of a classmate and decide on answers you both agree are correct.

Copying and Moving Data

Help Words

Move
Move or copy cells

The contents of a cell or range of cells can be copied or moved to another location. To move data, select the cell or range of cells to be moved. Click the Cut button on the Formatting toolbar. Move to the new location and click the Paste button. To copy data, select the cell or range to be copied. Click the Copy button. Move to the cell (or first cell in the range) where the information is to be copied and click the Paste button.

112C LEARN:

Cut, Copy, and Paste Data

In this activity, you will use the Cut, Copy, and Paste commands and formulas to complete a worksheet. The worksheet contains fund-raising records for a school club.

1. Start *Excel*. Open *CD-112-Sales* found in your data files.

2. The Price Each amount is the same for all candles. You will copy the price to rows 6, 7, 8, 13, 14, and 15. Go to cell C5 that contains the candle price. Click the **Copy** button on the Standard toolbar. Click and drag to select cells C6:C8. Click the **Paste** button on the Standard toolbar. Press the ESC key on the keyboard to remove the copy selection from cell C5.

3. Go to cell C13 and click **Copy**. Click and drag to select cells C14:C16. Click the **Paste** button. Press the ESC key.

4. The club is also selling fall bulbs (tulips, hyacinths, daffodils) to raise money. You will copy and edit the team data to record information for this new project. Select cells A1:C16. Click the **Copy** button. Go to cell A20 and click the **Paste** button. Press the ESC key.

5. In cell A20, edit the title to read **FALL BULBS SALES RECORDS**.

6. Select cells B24:C27. Hold down the CTRL key and select cells B32:C35. Press the DELETE key to remove the cell contents. (The cell formats will remain.)

7. For the bulbs sales project, Julian Bevins will be on the Blue Team. To move his name, go to cell A27. Click the **Cut** button on the Standard toolbar. Go to cell A36 and click the **Paste** button.

8. Go to cell C24. Enter the amount **12.00**. (It will appear as $12.00, as shown in Figure 15.14, because the cell format was copied along with the contents.) To copy this amount to cells C25:C26, go to cell C25. The small square in the bottom-right corner of the cell is called the **fill handle**. Point to the fill handle until the cursor becomes a plus sign. Click and drag over cells C25:C26 and release the mouse button. The amount will be copied to these cells.

SOFTWARE TIP

By dragging the fill handle of a cell, you can copy the contents of a cell to other cells in the same row or column.

UNIT 2
Keyboarding

Chapter 4 **Letter Keys**

Chapter 5 **Number and Symbol Keys**

Before you can use the computer to help you manage or share information, you must place or *input* data into the computer. Data can be input in several different ways. The most common way is by using a keyboard. In Chapter 4, you will learn to input data using the letter keys on the keyboard. In Chapter 5, you will learn to use the number and symbol keys.

The activities provided at the end of each chapter in this unit will help you:

↗ Review the concepts you have learned.

↗ Apply the software skills you have learned.

↗ Improve your keyboarding skills.

↗ Learn about business trends and issues.

↗ Improve math and communication skills.

↗ Develop career-related skills.

Clearing and Deleting Cell Contents and Formats

When you click in the formula bar and edit cell contents, only the text or numbers are changed. If the cell had bold text, any new text you key in the cell will be bold. If the cell had numbers that were centered, the new text you key will be centered. You can use the **Clear** command to clear the contents of a cell, the format of a cell, or *both*.

112B LEARN:

Clear and Delete Cell Contents

SOFTWARE TIP

To select several cells, hold down the CTRL key. Click on each cell you want to select.

1. Start *Excel*. Open *CD-112-Schedule* found in your data files.

2. Go to cell F3. Press the DELETE key on the keyboard. This clears (deletes) the cell contents only; the cell format remains. In cell F3, key **Friday** and tap ENTER. Notice that the text appears in bold because the format was not deleted.

3. Go to cell B6. Hold down the CTRL key and click cell B8. Both cells should be selected. Still holding down the CTRL key, click cell D6. All of these cells should be selected (highlighted). Release the CTRL key.

4. Click **Edit** on the menu bar. Choose **Clear**. Choose **Formats** as shown in Figure 15.13. The data will remain, but the bold format will be removed from these cells.

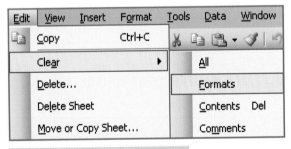

Figure 15.13 Clear Cell Formats

5. Select cells A11:F12. To clear the contents and formats in these cells, choose **Edit**, **Clear**, **All**.

6. Select the remaining names that have bold or italic format. Clear the cell formats.

7. Save the file as *112-Schedule*. Print the worksheet. Close *Excel*.

 **CHECK POINT** Compare your printed copy with that of a classmate to see if the contents and formats have been deleted or cleared correctly.

Chapter 4

Lessons 15–34

Letter Keys

Web Resources:
www.c21jr.swlearning.
com/studentresources

- Data Files
- Vocabulary Flash Cards
- Sort It Out, Keying
  Position and
  Technique
- *PowerPoint* Reviews
- More Activities

OBJECTIVES

In Chapter 4, you will:

↗ **Learn to key the letter keys.**

↗ **Learn to use ENTER, TAB, and BACKSPACE.**

↗ **Practice correct and safe keying techniques.**

↗ **Improve speed and accuracy using the letter keys.**

↗ **Use basic features of *Microsoft Word*.**

© Roger Ressmeyer/CORBIS

In the 1950s, the U.S. space program began with only a few scientists, engineers, and pilots. Soon, it had grown to include thousands of people working at many companies and government agencies. To work together, these people had to share information.

Messages can be delivered in person or by phone. Many times, however, they are in written form. Being able to key messages quickly and accurately is an important skill for everyone who uses computers. Whether you work in the space program or just want to finish your homework before dinner, good keying skills can help you be more productive.

Lesson 112   Editing, Moving, and Copying Cells

Objectives

In Lesson 112, you will:

⟶ Edit data in cells.

⟶ Clear the contents and formats of cells.

⟶ Move, copy, and paste cells.

⟶ Use formulas and functions in worksheets.

Data files: *CD-112-Schedule*, *CD-112-Sales*, *CD-112-Budget*

Editing Cell Content

You can edit (change) text or numbers you have keyed in a cell. To edit data, go to the cell that contains the data. Click in the formula bar. Use the DELETE or BACKSPACE keys to delete old data. Key the new data. Tap ENTER or click the Enter icon on the formula bar. You can also select the data to be changed and key the new text or numbers to replace it.

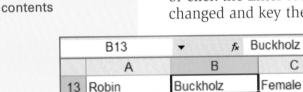

Go to the cell you wish to change   Click in the formula bar and delete data   Click the Enter icon or tap the ENTER key   Key new data

Figure 15.12 Edit data in the formula bar.

112A LEARN: Edit Cell Content

1. Start *Excel*. Open *110-Lockers* that you created earlier.

2. Go to cell 5C. Click in the formula bar. Use the BACKSPACE or DELETE key to delete **7**. Key **8**. Tap ENTER.

3. Go to cell A7. Key **Jane**, which will automatically replace **Dora**. Tap ENTER.

4. Go to cell B9. Click in the formula bar. Delete the digit **4** in the locker number. Key a **6** in its place so the number is 86620. Tap ENTER.

5. Save the worksheet as *112-Lockers*. Print the worksheet. It should print with a 2-inch top margin and be centered horizontally because these options were selected earlier. Close the file.

Lesson 15   Home Keys (fdsa jkl;)

Objectives

In Lesson 15, you will:

⬊ Learn control of home keys **(fdsa jkl;)**.

⬊ Learn control of the SPACE BAR and ENTER key.

15A LEARN: Work-Area Arrangement

Arrange your work area as shown in Figure 4.1. Place the:

- Keyboard directly in front of the chair, front edge of the keyboard even with the edge of the desk
- Monitor for easy viewing
- Disk drives for easy access
- Book at the right of the keyboard

South-Western

Figure 4.1 Properly Arranged Work Area

15B LEARN: Keying Position

The way you sit when you use the keyboard is very important. You can key more accurately when you sit properly. You will also be less likely to feel tired or strained when you sit properly. When you use a keyboard, keep your:

- Fingers curved and upright over the home keys
- Wrists low, but not touching the keyboard

Help Words

Cell reference
About cell and
range references

11. Go to cell B10 and click the **Copy** button. Select the range C10:G10 and click the **Paste** button. The formula will be copied to the other columns. Notice that the cell addresses have changed for each column.

12. Go to cell A11 and key **MAX**. Go to cell B11. Key **=MAX(B4:B9)** and tap ENTER. The highest score (100) will display in cell B11. Copy the formula to cells C11:G11.

13. Select cells A9:G9. Click the **Borders** button on the Formatting toolbar and select **Bottom Border**.

14. Go to cell A1. Click the **Merge and Center** button. Select cells A1:I1. Click the **Merge and Center** button. The title should now be centered over columns A through I.

15. Choose **File**, **Page Setup** to access the Page Setup dialog box. Change the top margin to 2 inches. Select the option to have the table centered horizontally on the page. Print the worksheet.

16. Save the file as *111-Quiz*. Complete the Check Point below and then close *Excel*.

 Ask a classmate to check your printed worksheet. Make corrections and print again if errors are found.

111C PRACTICE: Use Formulas and Functions

Use the Increase Decimal or Decrease Decimal button to change the number of decimal places displayed for a number.

Decrease Increase
Decimal   Decimal

1. Start *Excel*. Open *CD-111-Stats* found in your data files.

2. Enter a formula in cell F4 to calculate the individual batting averages (Hits/At Bats). Click the **Decrease Decimal** button on the Formatting toolbar until only two decimal places display in the answer. Copy this formula to cells F5:F11.

3. In cell B12, use the AutoSum function to calculate the total for cells B4:B11. Copy this formula to cells C12:E12.

4. In cell F13, enter a formula using the MIN function to display the lowest average. Adjust the format for two decimal places if needed.

5. In cell F14, enter a formula using the MAX function to display the highest average. Adjust the format for two decimal places if needed.

6. In the Page Setup dialog box, change the top margin to 2 inches. Select the option to have the table centered horizontally on the page. Print the worksheet.

7. Save the worksheet as *111-Stats*. Close *Excel*.

- Forearms parallel to the slant of the keyboard
- Body erect, sitting back in the chair
- Feet on the floor for balance

Proper keying position is shown in Figure 4.2.

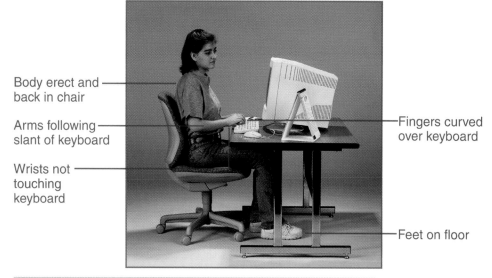

Body erect and back in chair

Arms following slant of keyboard

Wrists not touching keyboard

Fingers curved over keyboard

Feet on floor

Figure 4.2 Sitting properly when using a keyboard is very important.

15C LEARN: Home-Key Position

When using a keyboard, you need a place to begin. The keys where you place your fingers to begin keying are called the **home keys**. The home keys are **a s d f** for the left hand and **j k l ;** for the right hand.

1. Find the home keys on the keyboard chart shown below: **a s d f** for the left hand and **j k l ;** for the right hand.

2. Locate and place your fingers on the home keys on your keyboard. Keep your fingers well curved and upright (not slanting).

3. Remove your fingers from the keyboard. Place them in home-key position again. Curve and hold your fingers lightly on the keys.

Use Functions

1. Start *Excel*. On a new blank worksheet, key the data below. Apply bold and a 12-point font size to the title. Center the title across columns A through G. Apply center alignment and bold to the column heads in row 3.

	A	B	C	D	E	F	G
1	COMPUTER CLASS QUIZ SCORES						
2							
3	Name	Quiz 1	Quiz 2	Quiz 3	Quiz 4	Quiz 5	Quiz 6
4	Joe	90	90	90	100	90	90
5	Mary	89	90	90	79	90	90
6	Paul	100	100	100	100	100	100
7	Carl	100	80	90	100	90	90
8	Sue	90	100	100	100	100	80
9	Twila	90	90	90	80	80	80

2. Go to cell H3 and key **Total**. Apply bold and center alignment.

3. Go to cell H4. Key **= SUM(B4:G4)** and tap ENTER. The sum of the numbers in cells B4:G4 (550) should appear in cell H4.

4. When the numbers you want to add are in adjacent rows or columns, you can use the AutoSum function to quickly add the numbers. Go to cell H5. Click the **AutoSum** button on the Standard toolbar. Tap ENTER.

5. Select cells B6:H6 and click AutoSum. Repeat, using the AutoSum button to find totals in cells H7, H8, and H9.

6. Go to cell I3 and key **Average**. Apply bold and center alignment.

7. Go to cell I4. Key **= AVERAGE(B4:G4)** and tap ENTER. The average of the numbers in cells B4:G4 (91.66667) should appear in cell I4.

8. You can copy formulas to nearby cells. The formula will adjust to contain cell addresses for the nearby cells. Go to cell I4 and click the **Copy** button on the Standard toolbar. Select the range I5:I9. Click the **Paste** button on the Standard toolbar.

9. Go to cell I5 and then I6. Notice that the cell locations in the formula have changed for each row.

10. Go to cell A10 and key **MIN**. Go to cell B10. Key **= MIN(B4:B9)** and tap ENTER. The lowest score (89) will display in cell B10.

SOFTWARE TIP

Use the AutoSum feature to add all numbers in adjoining cells in a row or column.

Σ AutoSum button

SOFTWARE TIP

If you do not want cell references to change when you copy a formula, key a $ before the column letter and the row number. This is called an *absolute reference*. For example: A1 will always refer to cell A1, even if the formula is copied to another row or column.

15D LEARN: Keystroking and SPACE BAR

When you key, tap each key lightly with the tip of the finger. Keep your fingers curved as shown in Figure 4.3. The **SPACE BAR** is used to place a space between words. Tap the SPACE BAR with the right thumb. Use a quick down-and-in motion (toward the palm). Avoid pauses before or after spacing. The correct way to space is shown in Figure 4.3.

Curve fingers and
tap the keys

Tap the SPACE BAR with a
quick down-and-in motion

Figure 4.3 Keying and Spacing Technique

15E PRACTICE: Keystroking and SPACE BAR

1. Place your fingers in home-key position.

2. Key the line below. Tap the SPACE BAR once at the point of each arrow.

3. Review proper position at the keyboard (15B). Key the line again.

a s d f j k l ; aa jj ss kk dd ll ff ;;

15F LEARN: ENTER Key

ENTER key reach

The **ENTER** key is used to return the insertion point to the left margin and move it down one line. The **margin** is the blank space between the edge of the paper and the print. Tap the ENTER key once to **single-space** (**SS**). This moves the insertion point down one line. Tap the ENTER key twice to **double-space** (**DS**). This moves the insertion point down two lines. Tap the ENTER key four times to **quadruple-space** (**QS**). This moves the insertion point down four lines.

1. Reach the little finger of the right hand to the ENTER key. Tap the key. Return the finger quickly to home-key position.

2. Practice tapping the ENTER key several times.

3. The T-shirts cost $3.00 each. In cell D5, key **= 25*3** and tap ENTER. The answer (75) should appear in the cell.

4. You want to find the total receipts from games, food, and T-shirts. Go to cell E4. In cell E4, key **= B4 + C4 + D4** and tap ENTER. The answer (763.25) should appear in the cell.

5. Go to cell E5. Key a formula to find the total expenses for games, food, and T-shirts. (Hint: The answer should be 276.33.)

6. Profit is the amount of money from receipts that is left after expenses are paid. To find the profit for games, go to cell B6. In cell B6, key **= B4-B5** and tap ENTER. The answer (239.5) should appear in the cell.

7. In cell C6, enter a formula to find the profit for food. In cell D6, enter a formula to find the profit for T-shirts. In cell E6, enter a formula to find the total profit. (Hint: The total profit should be 486.92.)

8. Go to cell F3 and key **T-Shirts %**. Apply bold and center alignment if it is not applied automatically.

9. You want to know what percent of the total profit comes from T-shirt sales. To find this answer, you should divide the profit for T-shirts (50) by the total profit (486.92). In cell F6, key **= 50/E6** and tap ENTER. The answer (0.102686) should appear in the cell.

10. Now you will format the worksheet to make it easier to understand. Select cells B4:E6. Click the **Currency Style** button on the Formatting toolbar.

11. Go to cell F6. Click the **Percent Style** button on the Formatting toolbar.

12. Select cells B5:E5. Click the down arrow on the Borders button. Select **Bottom Border**.

13. Choose **File**, **Page Setup** to access the Page Setup dialog box. Change the top margin to 2". Select the option to have the table centered horizontally on the page. Print the worksheet.

14. Your worksheet should look like Figure 15.10. Save the file as *111-Festival*. Close *Excel*.

Functions

Help Words

Worksheet function
About functions

Spreadsheet software has built-in functions. A **function** is a predefined formula that can be used to perform calculations. For example, the SUM function is used to add numbers. Some other commonly used functions are described below.

- The AVERAGE function finds the average of the numbers in a range of cells.

- The COUNT function counts the numbers in a range of cells.

- The MIN function finds the smallest number in a range of cells.

- The MAX function finds the largest number in a range of cells.

Home Keys and SPACE BAR

Key each line once single-spaced; double-space between 2-line groups. Do not key the line numbers.

Tap the ENTER key twice to insert a DS between 2-line groups.

```
1  j jj f ff k kk d dd l ll s ss ; ;; a aa jkl; asdf
2  j jj f ff k kk d dd l ll s ss ; ;; a aa jkl; asdf
```
Tap the ENTER key twice to double-space (DS).
```
3  a aa f ff j jj ; ;; l ll s ss d dd k kk f ff jkl;
4  a aa f ff j jj ; ;; l ll s ss d dd k kk f ff jkl;
```
DS
```
5  fj fj dk dk sl sl a; a; jf jf kd kd ls ls ;a ;a j
6  fj fj dk dk sl sl a; a; jf jf kd kd ls ls ;a ;a j
```
Tap the ENTER key four times to quadruple-space (QS).

ENTER Key

Reach out with the little finger and tap the ENTER key quickly. Return your finger to home key.

Use MicroType Lesson 1 for additional practice.

Key each line twice single-spaced; double-space between 2-line groups.

```
1  aa kk dd jj
2  ll ss ff ;; jj k
3  fj fj dk dk sl sl a;a
4  kd ls ;l kj a; sl dk fj ;a
5  ss kk dd jj aa ;; ff ll sls kfk
```

✓ CHECK POINT Does your **J** finger remain in place as you tap the ENTER key? If not, make an effort to improve your reach technique.

Formulas

Formulas are equations that perform calculations on values in a worksheet. You can use formulas to add, subtract, multiply, and divide numbers. To solve math problems, select the cell in which the answer is to appear. Key an equal (=) sign to indicate that the following text and numbers will be a formula. Enter the formula and tap ENTER. The formula will appear in the formula bar, and the answer will appear in the cell as shown in Figure 15.10.

Formula bar

Results displayed in cell

	B6	▼	f_x =B4-B5		
	A	B	C	D	E	F
1		JACKSON SCHOOL FALL FESTIVAL				
2						
3		Games	Food	T-Shirts	Total	T-Shirts %
4	Receipts	$ 289.50	$ 348.75	$ 125.00	$ 763.25	
5	Expenses	$ 50.00	$ 151.33	$ 75.00	$ 276.33	
6	Profit	$ 239.50	$ 197.42	$ 50.00	$ 486.92	10%
7						

Figure 15.10 Formulas appear in the formula bar.

Formulas are solved in this order:

1. Calculations inside parentheses are done before those outside parentheses.

2. Multiplication and division are done next in the order they occur.

3. Addition and subtraction are done last in the order they occur.

111A LEARN:

Use Formulas

In this activity, you will use formulas to calculate money amounts and percentages related to games, food, and T-shirt sales at a school festival.

1. Start *Excel*. Open *CD-111-Festival* from your data files.

2. At the festival, 25 T-shirts were sold at $5.00 each. In cell D4, key = **25*5**. As you key the formula, it will appear in both the cell and the formula bar. See Figure 15.11. Tap ENTER or click the **Enter** icon on the formula bar. The answer (125) should appear in the cell.

SOFTWARE TIP

If you realize you have made an error when entering a formula, click the **Cancel** icon or press the ESC key.

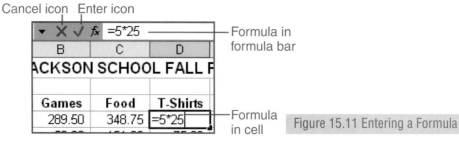

Cancel icon   Enter icon

Formula in formula bar

Formula in cell

Figure 15.11 Entering a Formula

Lesson 16 Review

Objectives

In Lesson 16, you will:
↘ Review control of home keys (**fdsa jkl;**).
↘ Review control of SPACE BAR and ENTER.

16A REVIEW: Work-Area Arrangement and Keying Position

Arrange your work area as shown in Figure 4.4 below. Place the:

- Keyboard directly in front of the chair, front edge of the keyboard even with the edge of the desk
- Monitor for easy viewing
- Disk drives for easy access
- Book at the right of the keyboard

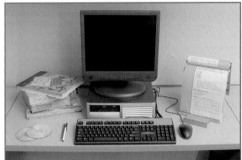

South-Western

Figure 4.4 Properly Arranged Work Area

Review Figure 4.5 for keying position. Sit properly at the keyboard with:

- Fingers curved and upright over home keys
- Wrists low, but not touching the keyboard
- Forearms parallel to the slant of the keyboard
- Body erect, sitting back in the chair
- Feet on the floor for balance

Figure 4.5 Proper Keying Position

7. Click the **Save** button on the Standard toolbar to save the file, using the same name. Close the file. Close *Excel* or continue to the next activity.

✔ **CHECK POINT** Compare your printed worksheet table with that of a classmate. If they differ, review the activity steps to decide which one is correct.

110C PRACTICE: Create and Print a Worksheet

SOFTWARE TIP

If you are continuing from an earlier activity, you may need to click the **New** button on the Standard toolbar to open a new blank worksheet.

New button

1. Start *Excel*. A blank worksheet should open. Key the data below in the worksheet in the cells as shown. (Do not key the row numbers and column letters.)

	A	B	C	D	E	F
1						
2						
3	**Month**	**Gregg**	**Maria**	**Luiz**	**Charles**	**Sandra**
4	January	5567	6623	7359	4986	6902
5	February	2457	7654	3569	2093	6432
6	March	6930	3096	5792	4607	7908
7	April	4783	6212	4390	5934	5402
8	May	5042	5092	4500	9453	5321
9	June	5430	6098	5781	5009	6023

2. In cell A1, key the title **MONTHLY SCORES**. Apply bold and a 12-point font size to the title. Center the title across columns A through F.

3. Apply center alignment and bold to the column heads in row 3. Select the range A3:F9. Apply a single line border to the cells.

4. Change the top margin to 2". Select the option to have the table centered horizontally on the page. Print the worksheet.

5. Save the worksheet as *110-Scores*. Close the worksheet. Close *Excel*.

Lesson 111   Using Formulas and Functions

Objectives
In Lesson 111, you will:
↘ Use formulas and functions in worksheets.
↘ Apply number formats such as currency and percent.
↘ Change the number of decimal places displayed in a number.

Data files: *CD-111-Festival, CD-111-Stats*

16B REVIEW: Home-Key Position

1. Find the home keys on the chart shown below: **a s d f** for the left hand and **j k l ;** for the right hand.

2. Locate and place your fingers on the home keys on your keyboard with your fingers well curved and upright (not slanting).

3. Remove your fingers from the keyboard; then place them in home-key position again, curving and holding them lightly on the keys.

16C PRACTICE: Home Keys and SPACE BAR

Keying technique

Spacing technique

SPACING TIP

Tap the ENTER key twice to insert a DS between 2-line groups.

When you key, remember to tap each key lightly with the tip of the finger. Tap the SPACE BAR with the right thumb. Use a quick down-and-in motion (toward the palm). Avoid pauses before or after spacing.

Key each line once single-spaced; double-space between 2-line groups. Do not key the line numbers.

```
1  a s d f aa ss dd ff j k l ; jj kk ll ;; af j; klkl
2  a s d f aa ss dd ff j k l ; jj kk ll ;; af j; klkl
```
Tap the ENTER key twice to double-space (DS).
```
3  ja ja kf kf sd sd ;l ;l ak ak sj sj d; d; lf lf ;;
4  ja ja kf kf sd sd ;l ;l ak ak sj sj d; d; lf lf ;;
```
                                                     DS
```
5  fjf kdk sls ;a; jfj dkd lsl a;a flf kak ;d; lsl ;;
6  fjf kdk sls ;a; jfj dkd lsl a;a flf kak ;d; lsl ;;
```
                                                     DS
```
7  jj ll aa dd kk ;; ss ff jj ll aa dd kk ;; ss ff ;;
8  jj ll aa dd kk ;; ss ff jj ll aa dd kk ;; ss ff ;;
```
Tap the ENTER key four times to quadruple-space (QS).

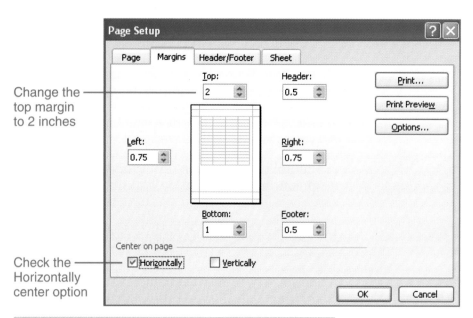

Change the top margin to 2 inches

Check the Horizontally center option

Figure 15.8 The Margins Tab of the Page Setup Dialog Box

4. Check the **Horizontally** option under Center on page. Click **OK**.

5. Click **Print Preview** to see the format of the worksheet table. Click the **Zoom** button, if needed, to view the entire page. Click the **Print** button on the toolbar.

6. In the Print dialog box, select the name of your printer. Under Print range, **All** should be selected as shown in Figure 15.9. For Number of copies, **1** shoud be selected. Under Print what, **Active sheet** should be selected. Click **OK**. The worksheet should print.

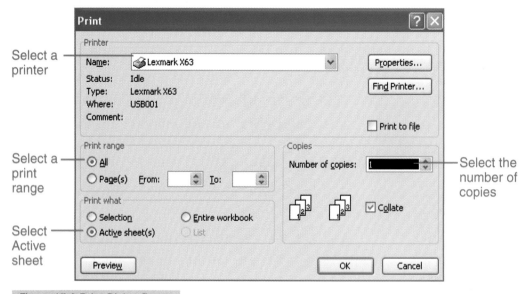

Select a printer

Select a print range

Select Active sheet

Select the number of copies

Figure 15.9 Print Dialog Box

16D PRACTICE: ENTER Key

ENTER *Right little* finger

Use the correct reach for the ENTER key. Reach the little finger of the right hand to the ENTER key. Tap the key. Return the finger quickly to home-key position.

Key each line once single-spaced; double-space between 2-line groups.

```
 1 a aa j jj;
 2 a aa j jj;

 3 s ss k kk f ff;
 4 s ss k kk f ff;

 5 l ll d dd j jj a aa;
 6 l ll d dd j jj a aa;

 7 k kk d dd s ss l ll f ff;
 8 k kk d dd s ss l ll f ff;

 9 d dd a aa f ff s ss j jj k kk;
10 d dd a aa f ff s ss j jj k kk;
```

16E PRACTICE: Key Words

SOFTWARE TIP

Click the **Show/Hide** button on the Standard toolbar to display formatting marks for spaces and paragraphs.

 Show/Hide button

Key each line once single-spaced; double-space between 2-line groups. Do not key the red lines between groups of words.

```
1 as; as;|ask ask|ad; ad;|add add|all all|fall fall;
2 as; as;|ask ask|ad; ad;|add add|all all|fall fall;

3 a sad lass; a sad lass;|all fall ads all fall ads;
4 a sad lass; a sad lass;|all fall ads all fall ads;

5 add a; add a;|ask a lad ask a lad|a salad a salad;
6 add a; add a;|ask a lad ask a lad|a salad a salad;
```

16F LEARN: End-of-Class Routine

Use MicroType Lesson 2 for additional practice.

Each day before you leave the classroom, do the following:

- Exit the software.
- Remove your disk from the disk drive.
- Turn off equipment if directed to do so.
- Clean up your desk area and push in your chair.

6. Click in cell A3 and drag over cells B3 and C3. Release the mouse button. The cells in the range A3:C3 should now be selected. Click the **Bold** button on the Formatting toolbar. With the cells still selected, click the **Center** button on the Formatting toolbar. (See Figure 15.5.)

7. Click and drag to select cells in the range B4:C10 as shown in Figure 15.6. Click the **Center** button on the Formatting toolbar. (See Figure 15.5.)

8. Sometimes it is easier to read data in a printed worksheet if the cell borders are displayed. Click and drag to select cells in the range A1:C10. Click the down arrow on the **Borders** button on the Formatting toolbar. Select the **All Borders** option as shown in Figure 15.7.

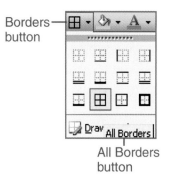

Borders button

All Borders button

Cells with single line borders

	A	B	C
1	LOCKER ASSIGNMENTS		
2			
3	**Name**	**Locker**	**Grade**
4	Ann	13579	7
5	Barb	24680	7
6	Connie	14703	8
7	Dora	25814	8
8	Eve	97532	7
9	Flora	86420	7
10	Grace	63074	8
11			

Figure 15.7 Worksheet with single line cell borders.

9. Click **File** on the menu bar. Click **Save as**. In the Save in box, select the folder where you save work for this class. In the File name box, key **110-Lockers**. Click **Save**. Close the file. Close *Excel*.

Printing Worksheets

Before you print a worksheet, you should use Print Preview to see how the printed worksheet table will look. You can set options to center the data on the page or change the margins before printing.

110B LEARN:

Print a Worksheet

1. Start *Excel*. Open *110-Lockers* that you created earlier.

2. Click the **Print Preview** button on the Standard toolbar to view the worksheet. Notice that the data is placed in the upper-left corner of the page. Click the **Close** button to close Print Preview.

3. Click **File** on the menu bar. Choose **Page Setup**. Choose the **Margins** tab. Enter **2** in the Top box as shown in Figure 15.8.

Lesson 17 New Keys h and e

Objectives

In Lesson 17, you will:

- Learn reach technique for **h** and **e**.
- Combine **h** and **e** smoothly with home keys.

Data file: *CD-17-Checksheet*

17A PRACTICE: Warmup

Key each line twice single-spaced; double-space between 2-line groups.

All keystrokes learned

```
1 ff jj dd kk ss ll aa ;; ff jj dd kk ss ll aa ;; jj
2 add; fad; lads; asks; dad; lass; fall; salad; sad;
3 a fall ad; ask dad; a salad; add a lad; a sad lass
```

Tap ENTER four times to quadruple-space (QS) between lesson parts.

17B LEARN: Plan for Learning New Keys

All the remaining keys that you will learn require the fingers to reach from the home keys to tap other keys. Follow the Standard Plan given below to learn the reach for each new key.

STANDARD PLAN FOR LEARNING NEW KEYS

1. Find the new key on the keyboard chart provided.
2. Look at your keyboard and find the new key on it.
3. Study the picture at the left of the practice lines for the new key. Note which finger is used for the key.
4. Curve your fingers; place them in home-key position (over fdsa jkl;).
5. Watch your finger as you reach to the new key and back to home position a few times. Keep your finger curved.
6. Key the set of drill lines according to the directions provided.

You can format one cell at a time. You can also format a range of cells. A **range** is a group of two or more cells on a worksheet. A range is identified by the cell in the upper-left corner and the cell in the lower-right corner. A colon is used to separate the two cell locations. For example, B4:C10 is the range of cells from cell B4 through C10. A cell range is highlighted in Figure 15.6.

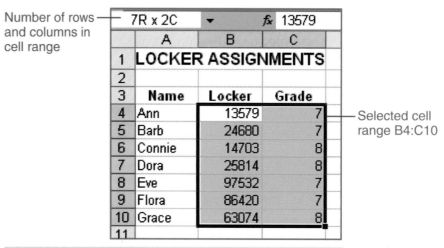

Figure 15.6 You can select a range of cells to apply formatting.

110A LEARN: Format Data

In this activity, you will add a title and column headings to complete the worksheet you started earlier. You will also format the data to create a worksheet that is attractive and easy to read. Refer to Figure 15.5 if you need help finding buttons on the Formatting toolbar.

1. Start *Excel*. Open *109-Data* that you created earlier.

2. Go to cell A1. Key **LOCKER ASSIGNMENTS** and press TAB. The text will extend into column B. Click cell A1. Click the **Bold** button on the Formatting toolbar.

3. Go to cell A1. Click the down arrow for the **Font Size** on the toolbar. Select **12** for the font size.

4. Click and drag over cells A1 through C1. Click the **Merge and Center** button on the toolbar as marked in Figure 15.5. The title will be centered over the data in columns A through C.

5. Go to cell A3. Enter **Name**. Go to cell B3 and enter **Locker**. Go to cell C3 and enter **Grade**.

17C LEARN: New Keys h and e

Use the Standard Plan for Learning New Keys (p. 103) for each key to be learned. Review the plan now. Relate each step of the plan to the illustrations and copy shown below. Then key each line twice. Do not key the line numbers, the vertical lines separating word groups, or the labels.

h *Right index* finger

e *Left middle* finger

Learn **h**

1 j h j h|ha ha|had had|ash ash|dash dash|half half;
2 jh jh|has has|had had|ash ash|half half|hash hash;
3 hall hall|shall shall|half half|dash dash|had had;

Learn **e**

4 d e d e|elf elf|sell sell|desks desks|flake flake;
5 ed ed|sales sales|deeds deeds|safe safe|jell jell;
6 a seed; a lead; a jade; a desk; seek a; see a lake

Combine **h** and **e**

7 he he|shed shed|shelf shelf|shell shell|held held;
8 a flash; a shed; she held; he has jade; has a desk
9 sea shell; he has ash; she had jade; he had a sale

Tap ENTER 4 times to quadruple-space (QS) between lesson parts.

17D PRACTICE: Technique Review

Techniques are very important. In the early stages of learning to key, it is helpful to have others observe your techniques and tell you how you are doing. Sometimes your teacher will provide the feedback; other times you will receive feedback from one of your classmates.

1. Open *CD-17-Checksheet* from your data files. Print the document. Close the file.

2. Work with a classmate. Ask your classmate to key lines 7–9 (above) as you watch for proper techniques. Mark notes on your checksheet. Share your comments with your classmate.

3. Ask your classmate to rate your techniques as you key lines 7–9. Discuss your ratings with your classmate.

Lesson 110 | Formatting and Printing Worksheets

Objectives

In Lesson 110, you will:
- ⭷ Learn guidelines for formatting worksheets.
- ⭷ Format worksheets.
- ⭷ Print worksheets.

Worksheet Guidelines

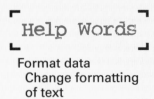

Worksheets that are for your own use can be very informal. You may enter data quickly and think little about the format. Worksheets that will be attached to reports or letters or shared with others, however, should be formatted carefully. The worksheet should present data in a format that is easy to read. Follow these general guidelines for worksheet tables:

- A **worksheet title** describes the content of a worksheet table. Key the title in all capital letters using a 12-point or 14-point font. Apply bold and center the title across the columns that have data. Leave one blank row after the title.

- A **column head** appears at the top of a column and describes the data in the column. Key column heads in the default font size or a 12-point font. Apply bold and center alignment to column heads.

- Key data in cells using the default font or a 12-point regular font. Data in cells can be aligned left, aligned right, or centered. Usually, numbers are aligned right and words are aligned left.

- Center worksheet tables horizontally on the page. Center worksheet tables vertically on a page or set a 2-inch top margin.

┌─────────────┐
Help Words
└─────────────┘

Format data
Change formatting
of text

You can use buttons on the Formatting toolbar to format a worksheet table. Font size, font effects such as bold, and alignment options are provided as shown in Figure 15.5. Many of these options are the same ones you have used to format word processing documents.

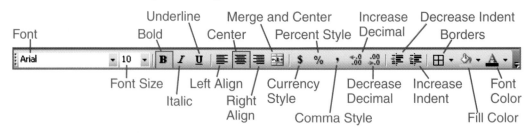

Figure 15.5 Use options on the Formatting toolbar to create an attractive worksheet.

17E PRACTICE: Key Mastery

Use MicroType Lesson 3 for additional practice.

Key each line twice.

```
1 ask ask|seek seek|half half|leaf leaf|halls halls;
2 ask dad; he has jell; she has jade; he sells leeks
3 he led; she has; a jak ad; a jade eel; a sled fell
4 she asked a lass; she led all fall; she has a lead
5 he led; she had; she fell; a jade ad; a desk shelf
```

17F APPLY: Compose Sentences

Read the sentences below. From the list at the left, choose the word that best completes the sentence. Key the word and tap the ENTER key.

add

dad

fall

fell

hall

held

jade

lake

salad

shelf

1. Tom _____ down the stairs.

2. Please wait outside in the _____.

3. She will start school in the _____.

4. Miguel went to the _____ to swim.

5. Shannon may ask her _____ for the money.

6. Tim had a _____ for lunch.

7. The stone in the ring was _____.

8. If you _____ 8 plus 6, you get 14.

9. Please put the books on the _____.

10. He _____ the door open for her.

✔ **CHECK POINT** Trade papers or places with a classmate. Check your classmate's answers as he or she checks your answers.

3. Notice that the text in column A is left aligned. The numbers in columns B and C are right aligned.

4. Enter the remaining data shown below in the worksheet beginning in cell A5.

	A	B	C
1			
2			
3			
4	Ann	13579	7
5	Barb	24680	7
6	Connie	14703	8
7	Dora	25814	8
8	Eve	97532	7
9	Flora	86420	7
10	Grace	63074	8

5. Now you will save the worksheet. Click **File** on the menu bar. Click **Save as**. The Save As dialog box will appear as shown in Figure 15.4.

Select a folder for your file

Enter a name for the file

Click Save

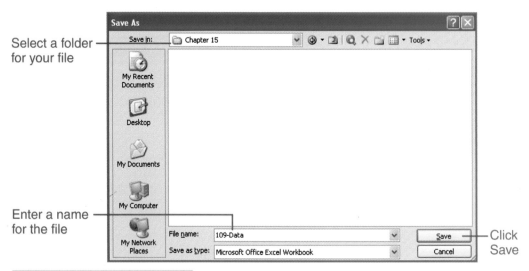

Figure 15.4 Save As Dialog Box

6. In the Save in box, select the folder where you save work for this class. In the File name box, key **109-Data**. Click **Save**. Close *Excel*.

Lesson 18 New Keys i and r

Objectives

In Lesson 18, you will:
↘ Learn reach technique for **i** and **r**.
↘ Combine **h** and **e** smoothly with home keys.

18A PRACTICE: Warmup

Instant Message

- Key the line at a slow, steady pace.
- Tap and release each key quickly.
- Key the line again at a faster pace.

Key each line twice.

Home keys

```
1 a f d s k j ; l ask fad all dad sad fall lass jj ;
```

h/e

```
2 j h ha has had ash hash d e led fed fled sled fell
```

All keys learned

```
3 she had a sale; ask a lad; she sells jade; a lake;
```

18B LEARN: New Keys i and r

TECHNIQUE TIP

Keep your fingers curved and upright.

Follow the plan for learning new keys shown on page 103. Key each line twice. If time permits, key lines 7–9 on the next page again.

i *Right middle* finger

r *Left index* finger

Learn i

```
1 k i|ki ki|is is|if if|ill ill|aid aid|kid kid|hail
2 ki ki|like like|jail jail|file file|said said|dial
3 if a kid; he did; a lie; if he; his file; a kid is
```

Learn r

```
4 f r|fr fr|far far|her her|are are|ark ark|jar jars
5 fr fr|jar jar|red red|her her|lark lark|dark dark;
6 a jar; a rake; read a; red jar; hear her; are free
```

Entering Data

To enter data in a worksheet, go to the desired cell and key the data. Tap TAB or ENTER to record the data in the cell. You can also click the Enter icon on the formula bar to record the data. The Enter icon is shown in Figure 15.3.

You might begin keying data and wish to stop, perhaps because you realize you are in the wrong cell. Press the ESC key before tapping TAB or ENTER to cancel data entry. You can also click the Cancel icon on the formula bar to cancel data entry. The Cancel icon is shown in Figure 15.3.

Text and numbers (including times and dates) can be entered in a worksheet cell. Formulas, which are made up of text and numbers, can also be entered. By default, text is aligned at the left, and numbers are aligned at the right. However, you can change the alignment for both text and numbers. You can also center a title over several columns in a worksheet.

Figure 15.3 Text and numbers can be entered in a worksheet.

If you make a mistake when entering data, use the DELETE and BACKSPACE keys to remove text or numbers. If you find an error after you have left the cell, go to the cell that has the error. Key the correct data and tap TAB or ENTER. The new data you key will replace the error.

109C LEARN:

Enter Data

1. Start *Excel*. A new blank worksheet should appear.

2. Go to cell A4. Enter the text **Ann** in the cell. Tap TAB to move to cell B4. Enter the number **13579** in cell B4. Tap TAB to move to cell C4. Key the number **7** in cell C4. Tap ENTER. Tap HOME to move to cell A5 if the cursor does not move there automatically.

Combine i and r

```
7 ride ride|fire fire|risk risk|hire hire|hair hairs
8 her hair; hire her; a fire; is she fair; is a risk
9 a ride; if her; is far; red jar; his are; her aide
```
Quadruple-space (QS) between lesson parts.

18C PRACTICE: Key Mastery

Key each line twice.

Reach review
```
1 hj ed ik rf hj de ik fr hj ed ik rf jh de ki fr hj
2 he he|if if|all all|fir fir|jar jar|rid rid|as ask
```

h/e
```
3 she she|elf elf|her her|hah hah|eel eel|shed shelf
4 he has; had jak; her jar; had a shed; she has fled
```

i/r
```
5 fir fir|rid rid|sir sir|kid kid|ire ire|fire fired
6 a fir; is rid; is red; his ire; her kid; has a fir
```

All keys learned
```
7 jar jar|deal deal|fire fire|shelf shelf|lake lakes
8 he is; he did; ask her; red jar; she fell; he fled
```

All keys learned
```
 9 if she is; he did ask; he led her; he is her aide;
10 she has had a jade sale; he said he had a red fir;
```

Use MicroType Lesson 4 for additional practice.

18D APPLY: Enrichment Activity

Unscramble the letters shown below to create eight words. If you have difficulty, key the letters in different orders to unscramble the words.

ksa	lase	djea	eifr
ajr	alde	iads	lhesf

changes when you move from cell to cell. You can identify the active cell by looking at its border. The active cell is the cell with the thick border around it. (See Figure 15.1.)

To move to a new cell with the mouse, move the pointer over the desired cell and click the mouse. You can also use the arrow keys and the TAB key to move to a new cell.

To move the active cell from one spot to another quickly, you can use keyboard shortcuts. For example, to move to the first cell in a row and make it the active cell, tap HOME. To move to cell A1, press CTRL + HOME. To move the active cell up one page, tap PGUP.

109B LEARN:　Move Around a Worksheet

In this activity, you will practice moving in a worksheet using the mouse and the keyboard.

1. Start *Excel*. A new blank worksheet should appear. Use the mouse to click in cell C4. Cell C4 is now the active cell. Note that the cell address appears in the cell reference box as shown in Figure 15.2.

Figure 15.2 The active cell is shown in the cell reference box.

2. Use the mouse to make cell A12 active. Use the mouse to make cell B24 active. You may need to use the scroll bars to display on screen the area you want.

3. Use the arrow keys to make cell D11 active. Use the arrow keys to make cell F30 active. Use the arrow keys to make cell P30 active.

4. Use PAGE DOWN and arrow keys to make J100 active. Use PAGE UP and arrow keys to make L40 active.

5. Tap the **F5** key (found in the row of function keys at the top of the keyboard). Enter **H100** in the Reference box. Click **OK**. H100 should now be the active cell. Using the F5 key is often the quickest way to move to a cell that is far from your current location.

6. Hold the CTRL key down and tap the HOME key to make cell A1 active. Tap the TAB key once to make cell B1 active.

7. Close the file without saving it by clicking the workbook **Close** button (see Figure 15.1) or choosing **File**, **Close** from the menu bar. Close *Excel*.

Lesson 19 Review

Objectives

In Lesson 19, you will:

⭲ Improve reachstroke control and keying speed.

⭲ Improve technique on SPACE BAR and ENTER.

19A PRACTICE: Warmup

TECHNIQUE TIP

- Keep your wrists low, but not touching the frame of the keyboard.
- Keep your forearms parallel to the slant of the keyboard.

Key each line twice.

Home keys

```
1 aa jj ff kk ss ll dd ;; aj fk sl d; dd ff jj ll kk
```

h/e

```
2 he fee she ash deed deaf shed held head half easel
```

i/r

```
3 fire rile risk hire rail dial rake like raid rider
```

QS

19B PRACTICE: SPACE BAR Technique

TECHNIQUE TIP

Quickly space after each word and immediately begin the next word without pausing.

Key each line twice.

Short, easy words

```
1 is as if he hi has ask had are her jar kid lad sad
2 jail half lake sail side rail leaf desk fade flair
3 his like reel fails laser seeks lease hired safari
```

DS

Short-word phrases

```
4 he is|if she|a jar|he did|as he is|has had|she did
5 red jar|a lake|red hair|her desk|as a lark|as dark
6 he said|she has had a|here he is|all fall|are free
```

QS

Use a down-and-in motion for spacing.

Refer to Figure 15.1 as you read about the basic parts of a worksheet screen in the list below.

- The **title bar** displays the application and current worksheet name.
- The **menu bar** contains the drop-down menu commands.
- The Standard and Formatting **toolbar**s provide easy access to frequently used commands.
- The **cell reference box** identifies the active cell(s) by the letter of the column and the number of the row where they cross. In Figure 15.1, cell E10 is the active cell.
- The **formula bar** displays the contents of the active cell and is used to enter or edit text or numbers.
- **Scroll bars** are used to move horizontally or vertically within a worksheet.
- The **active cell** is the current location of the insertion point. It stores information that is entered. It is highlighted with a thick border.
- **Worksheet tabs** identify the worksheets in the workbook.
- The **status bar** gives you a variety of information. For example, NUM appears when the number lock feature is active.
- The *Excel* **Close button** closes the program.
- The **workbook Close** button closes the open workbook. *Excel* remains open.

109A LEARN:

Identify Worksheet Parts

1. To start *Excel*, choose **Start**, **All Programs**, **Microsoft Office**, **Microsoft Excel**.

2. Refer to Figure 15.1. Locate each item marked in the figure on your screen.

3. Start *Word*. Open *CD-109-Worksheet Parts* found in your data files. Complete the activity as directed to identify worksheet parts. Save the file as *109-Worksheet Parts*.

4. Close *Word*. Close *Excel* by clicking the **Close** button or choosing **File**, **Exit** from the menu bar. The Close button is marked in Figure 15.1.

Moving Around in a Worksheet

When you enter data in a worksheet, it is placed in the active cell. The active cell is the current location of the insertion point. Thus, the active cell

19C PRACTICE: ENTER Technique

Key each line twice.

TECHNIQUE TIP

Keep up your pace to the end of the line. Tap ENTER quickly and begin the new line without a pause or stop.

1 if he is;

2 as if she is;

3 he had a fir desk;

4 she has a red jell jar;

5 he has had a lead all fall;

6 she asked if he reads fall ads;

7 she said she reads all ads she sees;

8 his dad has had a sales lead as he said;

QS

19D PRACTICE: Key Mastery

Key each line twice.

h/e

1 he she heel shelf held heed shed heal hire herself

2 he had a sled; she hired a; he has had; she held a

i/r

3 air sir fire liar hair iris ride fair dried desire

4 hire her; she is a risk; his airfare; he fired her

All keys learned

5 he is; he has a red sled; like jade; if he is free

6 is a; he has a jar; a lake; she is safe; fried eel

7 he is free; here she is; she has a jade; like her;

8 he had a; red jars; fire risk; fall ads; sled ride

QS

MicroType

Use MicroType Lesson 5 for additional practice.

Lesson 109   Spreadsheet and Worksheet Basics

Objectives

In Lesson 109, you will:
- ⬎ Learn about spreadsheet software and worksheets.
- ⬎ Enter information in a cell and move around in a worksheet.

Data files: *CD-109-Worksheet Parts*

Worksheets and Workbooks

Workbook
  Create a new
  workbook

A **workbook** is a spreadsheet file. It contains one or more worksheets, usually with related data. A **worksheet** is one section in a workbook (spreadsheet file). It is where you enter information. When spreadsheet software is opened, a worksheet will appear on the screen. Other worksheets in the workbook are indicated by worksheet tabs at the bottom of the screen. If needed, more worksheets can be added to a workbook. Worksheets can also be deleted from a workbook.

A worksheet contains columns, rows, and cells. Columns run up and down a worksheet. Each column has a heading (letters from A to Z, AA to AZ, etc.) running left to right across the worksheet. Rows run across a worksheet. Each row has a heading (a number such as 1, 2, 3). The headings run up and down the left side of the worksheet. A cell is formed where a column and row cross. Cells are where information is keyed. A worksheet is shown in Figure 15.1.

Figure 15.1 *Excel* Worksheet

Lesson 20 New Keys o and t

Objectives

In Lesson 20, you will:
⭲ Learn reach technique for **o** and **t**.
⭲ Combine **o** and **t** smoothly with all other learned keys.

20A PRACTICE:

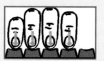

Keep fingers curved and upright.

Warmup

Key each line twice.

Home row
```
1 jskj; dlaf; sad fall; had a hall; a fall ad; ask a
```
3rd row
```
2 a fire; if her aid; he sees; he irks her; fish jar
```
All keys learned
```
3 he had half a jar; as she fell; he sells fir desks
```

20B LEARN:

New Keys o and t

Follow the plan for learning new keys shown on page 103. Key each line twice.

o *Right ring* finger

t *Left index* finger

Learn o
```
1 l o|l o|lo lo|do do|of of|so so|old old|fold fold;
2 fork fork|soak soak|hold hold|sold sold|joke joke;
3 a doe; old fork; solid oak door; old foe; oak odor
```
Learn t
```
4 f t|f t|it it|fat fat|the the|tied tied|lift lift;
5 ft ft|fit fit|sit sit|hit hit|kite kite|talk talk;
6 lift it; tie the; hit it; take their test; is late
```
Combine o and t
```
7 to to|too too|took took|hot hot|lot lot|tort tort;
8 hook hook|told told|fort fort|sort sort|jolt jolt;
9 told a joke; jot or dot; took a jolt; took a look;
```

Web Resources:
www.c21jr.swlearning.
com/studentresources

- Data Files
- Vocabulary Flash Cards
- Beat the Clock, Worksheet
- *PowerPoint* Reviews
- More Activities

OBJECTIVES

In Chapter 15, you will:

↗ Use *Microsoft Excel* spreadsheet software to create worksheets.

↗ Use formatting and editing features to make worksheets attractive and easy to read.

↗ Use functions and formulas to prepare worksheets.

↗ Create charts using worksheet data.

Comstock Images

Spreadsheet software is a computer program used to record, report, and analyze data in worksheets. You can use it to add, subtract, divide, and multiply numbers. You can use formulas to find answers. Spreadsheet software solves repetitive math problems correctly, quickly, and easily. Also, it allows you to use charts to show data graphically.

One reason to use spreadsheet software is that when a number in a problem is changed, all related "answers" are changed for you. For example, you can quickly see how the amount of money you will earn from selling candy bars can go up or down by changing the number sold or the selling price in the formula.

In this chapter you will create worksheets. You will edit and format them so they are correct, attractive, and easy to read. You will use formulas to solve easy, hard, and repetitive math problems. You will create charts to show your information.

20C PRACTICE: Key Mastery

Key each line twice.

TECHNIQUE TIP

- Keep your fingers curved and upright.
- Keep your wrists low, but not resting on the desk.
- Use a down-and-in spacing motion.
- Keep your eyes on the copy as you key.

MicroType

Use MicroType Lesson 6 for additional practice.

h/e

1 the the | lead lead | held held | hear hear | heart heart;

2 he heard | ask their | here the | has fled | hide the jars

i/t

3 its its | hit hit | tie tie | sit sit | kite kite | fit fit;

4 a tire | a fire | tied to it | it fits | it sits | it is fit

o/r

5 or or | for for | fort fort | oar oar | soar soar | rot rot;

6 three doors | a red rose | for a fort | he rode | for free

SPACE BAR

7 of he or it is to if do el odd off too are she the

8 off of it | does the | if she | to do the | for the | she is

All keys learned

9 if she is; ask a lad; to the lake; off the old jet

10 he or she; for a fit; if she did; the jar; a salad

20D APPLY: Enrichment Activity

Unscramble the letters shown below to create eight words. If you have difficulty, key the letters in different orders to unscramble the words.

ejt	hfla
rae	krfo
feas	sseha
eilk	isftr

can lead to a career in film or radio. Also, you read that if you love science and problem solving, a career in technology might be for you. Through your research, you have probably found a few careers that interest you.

In this activity, you will use what you have learned to develop a career plan. A good place to start is to review the career information sheets from Chapters 3, 4, 6, 8, and 9. For example, in Chapter 4, you researched careers in arts and communications. Review the information sheet from that chapter (data file *CD-C04-Arts and Music*). Do the interests and abilities of the career area fit your personality? Are there careers on the list that interest you? Follow the steps below to create a career plan presentation.

1. Make a list of your current interests and skills. Then, review the career information sheets from Chapters 3, 4, 6, 8, and 9. Identify the career area that most closely matches your interests and skills.

2. Visit career Web sites to research careers in your interest area. Some sites you might want to visit are the U.S. Department of Labor (http://www.bls.gov) and America's Career InfoNet (http://www.acinet.org/acinet/). Choose a career and summarize the skills and abilities needed for that career.

3. Start *PowerPoint* and open *CD-C14-Career Plan* from your data files. Using this sample plan as a guide, create your own career plan. Save your presentation as *C14-My Career Plan*.

↗ Academic Success Builder

STUDENT ORGANIZATIONS: PRESENTATION COMPETITION Student organizations, such as FBLA's Middle Level Achievement Program, hold presentation competitions. Individuals or teams of students may enter these events. Students use presentation software to create slide shows to use in delivering presentations. The topic of the presentation may be assigned by the organization sponsoring the event. The organization usually gives a certain amount of time for the slide show. In this activity, you will review information about creating effective slides. You will also practice your skills by creating a presentation.

1. Start *Word*. Open *CD-C14-Presentations* found in your data files. Read the information about preparing slides found in this document. Close the file.

2. Open *CD-C14-Competition*. Print and then close the file. Follow the instructions provided in this document to create a presentation.

3. Save the presentation as *C14-Club*. Deliver the presentation to a group of classmates.

Lesson 21   New Keys n and g

Objectives
In Lesson 21, you will:
↘ Learn reach technique for **n** and **g**.
↘ Combine **n** and **g** smoothly with all other learned keys.

21A PRACTICE: Warmup

Key each line twice.

h/e
1 he has a hoe; he has her heart; her health; he had
o/t
2 took the toad; it is hot; a lot; her toes; dot it;
i/r
3 a tire; it is fair; their jar; their skis; ride it

21B LEARN: New Keys n and g

Follow the plan for learning new keys shown on page 103. Key each line twice. If time permits, key lines 7–9 again.

Learn n
1 j n|jn jn|an an|and and|end end|ant ant|land lands
2 jn jn|and and|den den|not not|end end|and and|sand
3 not a train; hand it in; near the end; nine or ten

Learn g
4 f g|fg fg|go go|jog jog|got got|frog frog|get gets
5 fg fg|get get|egg egg|dig dig|logs logs|golf golf;
6 good eggs; eight dogs; a frog; a goat; golf gadget

Combine n and g
7 gone gone|nag nag|ago ago|gnat gnat|dragon dragons
8 green grass; nine ants; need glasses; ten gallons;
9 go golfing; not again; long ago; ten frogs; a gang

n *Right index* finger

g *Left index* finger

INTERNET

Data Files

- *CD-C04-Arts and Music*
- *CD-C14-Career Plan*
- *CD-C14-Presentations*
- *CD-C14-Competition*

↗ About Business

EMPLOYEE BENEFITS Employers want to attract good workers and keep them after they have been hired and trained. One way companies attract and keep good workers is by offering them employee benefits. **Employee benefits** are payments made to workers in the form of cash, goods, or services. These payments are in addition to basic wages or salaries. These payments are also called fringe benefits. Employee benefits are designed to help fulfill the safety and security needs of employees.

Employee benefits offered by many companies may include:

- Health insurance for the employee and family
- Life insurance for the employee (sometimes for family members also)
- Paid holidays
- Paid vacations (amount usually increases with years of service)
- An employee pension plan (money paid to retired employees based on years of service)
- A retirement savings plan (401K plan)
- Disability income insurance (provides income to an employee who is injured away from the job and can no longer work)
- Tuition paid to help employees continue their education
- Employee discounts on items purchased from the company

The type of employee benefits offered usually varies with the size of the company. Many small companies cannot afford to offer employee benefits. The rising cost of health care has also caused many companies to change the type and amount of health care coverage offered to employees.

1. Use your browser software to find an Internet job site (such as Monster.com, Yahoo Hotjobs, or America's Job Bank). Use the job site's search feature to look for job ads in a career field that interests you.

2. Review online job ads to see the types of employee benefits offered. For three jobs, list the job title, salary, and benefits offered for the job.

↗ Career and Life Skills Success Builder

DEVELOPING YOUR CAREER PLAN In recent chapters, you researched various careers. You searched the Internet and explored how your classes relate to careers. For example, you may have discovered how your art classes

21C PRACTICE:

ENTER Key Technique

Tap ENTER quickly and start a new line without pausing.

Key each line twice.

1 here she is;
2 he is at the inn;
3 she goes to ski there;
4 he is also to sign the log;
5 he left the egg on the old desk;
6 he took the old dog to the ski lodge;

✓ **CHECK POINT** Does your **J** finger remain in place as you tap the ENTER key? If not, make an effort to improve your reach technique.

21D PRACTICE:

Key Mastery

TECHNIQUE TIP

- Keep your wrists low, but not resting on the desk.
- Keep your eyes on the copy as you key.

Use MicroType Lesson 7 for additional practice.

Key each line twice.

n/g
1 gone gone|sing sing|long long|sing sing|gang gangs
2 sing a song; log on; sign it; and golf; long songs

SPACE BAR
3 is is|go go|of of|or or|he he|it it|the the|and an
4 if it is a jar|he has a dog|like to go|to do signs

All keys learned
5 an old oak desk; a jade ring; at her side; of the;
6 he goes there at night; she has left for the lake;

7 he took her to the lake; take the hooks off; he is
8 the old jet; sign the list on the; go to the right

21E APPLY:

Compose Sentences

Read the sentences below. From the list at the left, choose the word that best completes the sentence. Key the word and tap the ENTER key.

first
grass
jade
lake
oak

1. *Rae took her boat to the* _____ .
2. *I used a chain saw to cut down the* _____ *tree.*
3. *You need to cut the* _____ .
4. *Rafael bought a* _____ *ring.*
5. *Blake finished* _____ *in the race.*

Speed Forcing Drill

Key a 30" timed writing on each line. Your rate in gross words a minute (*gwam*) is shown below the lines.

1 He bid on the chair.
2 Pamela may make the sign.
3 The busy girls made the signs.
4 Rodney may pay them for their work.
5 She dismantled the bicycle in the field.
6 Jay and I may suspend work on the big island.
7 Dick and I may work on the problems with the firm.

gwam 30" | 2 | 4 | 6 | 8 | 10 | 12 | 14 | 16 | 18 | 20 |

TECHNIQUE TIP

Reach out with your little finger and tap the ENTER key quickly. Return your finger to the home key.

Statistical Copy

Key each paragraph once. DS between paragraphs. Key the paragraphs again, trying to increase your speed.

The latest quarterly sales report (January 1 through March 31) shows that sales for the first three months of the year were down about 12% from the previous quarter. This is due in large part to the strike (January 1 through February 25) at our Atlanta plant. Total sales for the quarter were $890,684.

All of our regions had decreases in sales except the Southern Region. The Southern Region had sales of $290,675 (+7.46%), the Northern Region had sales of $275,218 (-9.05%), the Eastern Region had sales of $140,381 (-3.87%), and the Western Region had sales of $184,410 (-12.7%). On a more positive note, our sales look much more promising for this quarter.

Lesson 22   New Keys LEFT SHIFT and period (.)

Objectives

In Lesson 22, you will:

↘ Learn reach technique for **LEFT SHIFT** and . **(period)**.

↘ Combine **LEFT SHIFT** and . **(period)** smoothly with all other learned keys.

22A PRACTICE: Warmup

TECHNIQUE TIP

1. Hold down the LEFT SHIFT key with the little finger on the left hand.
2. Tap the letter with the right hand.
3. Return finger(s) to home keys.

Key each line twice.

Reach review

1 rf ol gf ki hj tf nj ed fr lo fg ik jh ft jn a; de

SPACE BAR

2 as if go at it is in he or to of so do on jet lake

All keys learned

3 a jar; if an; or do; to go; an oak door; she told;

22B LEARN: New Keys LEFT SHIFT and . (period)

Key each line twice.

Learn **LEFT SHIFT**

1 a J|Ja Ja|Ka Ka|La La|Hal Hal|Kal Kal|Jan Jan|Jane
2 Jan did it; Kent took it; Ida said; Jane has a dog
3 I see that Kate is to aid Hans at the Oakdale sale

Learn . (period)

4 l .|l. l.|fl. fl.|ed. ed.|ft. ft.|rd. rd.|hr. hrs.
5 l. l.|fl. fl.|hr. hr.|e.g. e.g.|i.e. i.e.|in. ins.
6 a. s. d. f. j. k. l. ;. h. e. i. r. o. t. n. g. o.

Combine **LEFT SHIFT** and . (period)

7 I do. Ian is. Olga did. Jan does. Ken is gone.
8 Hal did it. I shall do it. Kate left on a train.
9 Jan sang a song. Linda read it. Ken told a joke.

LEFT SHIFT *Left little* finger

. **(period)** *Right ring* finger

Building Keying Skill

Warmup Practice

Key each line twice. If time permits, key the lines again.

Alphabet

1 Jacki Vizquel played six ball games for the Twins.

Figure/Symbol

2 John sold 20 boxes @ $48.57 and 30 boxes @ $69.10.

Speed

3 The goal of the tutor is to do the problems right.

gwam 1' | 1 | 2 | 3 | 4 | 5 | 6 | 7 | 8 | 9 | 10 |

Improve Keying Technique

Key each line twice. If time permits, key the lines again.

Third row

1 to yet peer quit were pout pepper terror tire rope
2 Our pups were too little to take to your pet show.

Bottom row

3 extinct, zebra, moving, vans, numb, moon, vacation
4 Zeno had a six-month smallpox injection on Monday.

gwam 1' | 1 | 2 | 3 | 4 | 5 | 6 | 7 | 8 | 9 | 10 |

Tabulation Practice

Set tabs at 2.5 inches and 4.5 inches. Key the text below. Key three 1' timings. Try to increase amount of text keyed on each timing.

Arkansas	Kentucky	Louisiana
Little Rock	Frankfort	Baton Rouge
Delaware	Massachusetts	Michigan
Dover	Boston	Lansing
Idaho	Missouri	Montana
Boise	Jefferson City	Helena
Kansas	New Hampshire	New Jersey
Topeka	Concord	Trenton

22C PRACTICE: ENTER Key Technique

TECHNIQUE TIP

Quickly tap ENTER at the end of each line and immediately begin the next line.

Key each line twice.

1 I like the dog.
2 Janet is at the inn.
3 Jake is to take the test.
4 Hank and Jo left for the lake.
5 Hans took the girls to a ski lodge.
6 Jeff took the old desk to the ski lodge.
7 Jason and Jeff like to listen to those songs.

22D PRACTICE: Key Mastery

SPACING TIP

• Do not space after . within abbreviations.
• Space once after . following abbreviations and initials.
• Space twice after . at end of a sentence except at the end of a line. There, tap ENTER without spacing.

Key each line twice.

Abbreviations/initials

1 He said ft. for feet; rd. for road; fl. for floor.
2 Lt. Hahn let L. K. take the old gong to Lake Neil.

Short words

3 a an or he to if do it of so is go for got old led
4 go the off aid dot end jar she fit oak and had rod

Short phrases

5 if so|it is|to do|if it|do so|to go|he is|to do it
6 to the|and do|is the|got it|if the|for the|ask for

All letters learned

7 Ned asked her to send the log to an old ski lodge.
8 J. L. lost one of the sleds he took off the train.

22E APPLY: Enrichment Activity

Use MicroType Lesson 8 for additional practice.

Unscramble the letters shown below to create eight words. If you have difficulty, key the letters in different orders to unscramble the words.

ndse	ordo
solt	ahsd
eatk	iarnt
eetf	dogle

Applying

What You Have Learned

Planets Presentation

In this activity, you will plan, prepare, and deliver a presentation about the planets in our solar system. The purpose of the presentation is to inform your listeners about the planets. The audience will be your classmates.

1. In a *Word* document, key the name of the presentation. Under the name, key the heading **Purpose**. Under the heading, key two or three goals for the presentation. Key the heading **Audience Profile**. Under the heading, key a bulleted list of four or five points that describe the audience. Save the document as *C14-Planets Outline*.

2. Do research about the solar system. Your talk should include the names of the planets, the order in which they are placed from the Sun, and two or three interesting facts about each planet. Also include some basics facts about the Sun. Key an outline of the content of the presentation in the *C14-Planets Outline* document. Save the file again, using the same name.

3. Plan and create a slide show to use in your presentation. You should have at least 11 slides (a title slide and a slide for each planet and the Sun). Create the slides based on the content of your outline. Find clip art of the planets and include it on the slides. Use an appropriate design template. Save the slide show as *C14-Planets*.

4. Practice delivering your presentation using the slides.

5. Deliver the presentation to a group of your classmates. Ask your listeners to complete a feedback form immediately after your presentation. (The form is in the file *CD-108-Feedback*). Review the completed forms to see how you can improve when giving presentations in the future.

States Slide Show

In this activity, you will create a slide show with information about U.S. states. The purpose of the slide show is to allow students to review geography facts using the slides.

1. Start *Word*. Open and print *CD-C14-States* from your data files. Close *Word*.

2. Create the slides shown in the printed document. Use the *Profile.pot* design template or a similar design. Use the *Clip Art on Office Online* link to find clip art or photos to use on the slides.

3. Play the show to make sure it displays as you want. Click the **Spelling** button on the Standard toolbar to check the spelling. Proofread the slides carefully and correct all errors. Save the file as *C14-States*. Close the file.

Data Files

- *CD-108-Feedback*
- *CD-C14-States*

Supplemental activities for this chapter can be found at www.c21jr.swlearning.com.

Lesson 23   Review

Objectives

In Lesson 23, you will:

↘ Improve use of SPACE BAR, LEFT SHIFT, and ENTER.

↘ Improve keying speed on words, phrases, and sentences.

Data file: *CD-23-Checksheet*

23A PRACTICE: ## Warmup

TECHNIQUE TIP

To use the LEFT SHIFT key:
1. Hold down the LEFT SHIFT key with the little finger on the left hand.
2. Tap the letter with the right hand.
3. Return finger(s) to home keys.

Key each line twice.

Reach review

1 ki fr lo de jn fg jh ft l. l.lo i.o. r.e. n.g. h.t

SPACE BAR

2 a as ask|h he hen|n no not|t to too took|d do dot;

LEFT SHIFT

3 Kent left. Lana is not here. Jake sang the song.

23B PRACTICE: ## Key Mastery

Key each line twice.

n/g

1 jn jn|fg fg|slang slang|lingo lingo|jargon jargon;
2 Nate sang eight or nine songs; Lana sang one song.

o/t

3 lo lo|ft ft|to to|foot foot|lots lots|tooth tooth;
4 John has lost the list he took to that food store.

i/r

5 ki ki|fr fr|ire ire|risk risk|ring ring|tire tire;
6 Ida is taking a giant risk riding their old horse.

LEFT SHIFT/.

7 Jason K. Hanselt; Katie O. Higgins; Kirk N. Jones;
8 J. L. Johnson is going to Illinois to see her son.

CHECK POINT Did you space once after periods following initials?

Reviewing What You Have Learned

Answer these questions to review what you have learned in Chapter 14.

1. Presentations are given for three general purposes. What are these purposes?

2. What is an audience profile? Why should you prepare an audience profile when planning a presentation?

3. What are the three parts of a good presentation and what does each part do?

4. Is reading from a script when you deliver a presentation a good idea? Why or why not?

5. What is a visual aid? Give two examples of visual aids.

6. What task does *Microsoft PowerPoint* help the user do?

7. What does the Slide pane display and allow the user to do?

8. What are placeholders?

9. What does the Notes pane allow the user to do?

10. What is the task pane?

11. What is the Slide Sorter view used for?

12. What slide layout is usually used for the first slide in a slide show? What slide layout should you use if you want to include a bulleted list on the slide?

13. What is a slide design template?

14. Describe how to insert clip art in a slide.

15. What is the purpose of the Drawing toolbar?

16. Describe how to change the background color for slides.

17. Why might you want to drag a sound icon off the slide?

18. What is included on a notes page? What view can you use to see how the notes page will appear?

19. What color choices do you have when printing notes pages?

20. List five tips or guidelines you should follow when giving a presentation.

23C PRACTICE: ENTER Key Technique

Key each line twice.

TECHNIQUE TIP

Quickly tap ENTER at the end of each line and immediately begin the next line.

1 Jon has gone to ski;
2 he took a train at eight.
3 Karen asked for the disk;
4 she is to take it to the lake.
5 Joe said he left the file that
6 has the data he needs at the lodge.
7 Janine said she felt ill as the ski
8 lift left to take the girls to the hill.

23D PRACTICE: Increase Speed

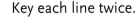

Key each line twice.

Key words (Think, say, and key the words.)
1 is and the if she of air did dog risk forks eight
2 rifle signs their then title ant aisle dials dish
3 shall signal tight shelf rigid right soaks island

Key phrases (Think, say, and key the phrases.)
4 is to|or do|to it|if he is|to do|it is|of an|if he
5 he did|of the|to all|is for|is a tie|to aid|if she
6 he or she|to rig it|if she did|is to sit|is to aid

Key sentences (Tap keys at a brisk, steady pace.)
7 Jake is to go to the lake to get her old red skis.
8 Hal asked for a list of all the old gold she sold.
9 Helen said she left the old disk list on his desk.

Are your fingers curved and upright?

MicroType

Use MicroType Lesson 9 for additional practice.

23E PRACTICE: Technique Review

TEAMWORK

Your techniques are an important part of learning to key. You should continue to work to refine your techniques.

1. Open *CD-23-Checksheet* from your data files. Print the document. Close the file.

2. Work with a classmate. Ask your classmate to key lines 7–9 (above) as you watch for proper techniques. Mark notes on your checksheet. Share your comments with your classmate.

3. Ask your classmate to rate your techniques as you key lines 7–9. Discuss your ratings with your classmate.

- **Look confident.** Stand erect and show that you want to communicate with the audience.

- **Let your personality come through.** Be natural; let the audience know who you are. Show your enthusiasm for the topic you are presenting.

- **Use gestures and facial expressions.** A smile, frown, or puzzled look, when appropriate, can help communicate your message. Make sure your gestures are natural.

108B APPLY:

Add Notes and Deliver the School Presentation

1. Start *PowerPoint.* Open *107-School Show* that you created earlier.

2. Add notes to the slides to create notes pages that are appropriate to use as audience handouts. Print the notes pages. Click the **Spelling** button on the Standard toolbar to check the spelling. Proofread and correct all errors.

3. Review the information you have prepared for the presentation. Decide which information will be presented by each team member. Practice delivering the presentation.

4. Deliver the presentation to the class or a group of classmates. At the beginning of the presentation, give the audience copies of *CD-108-Feedback* found in your data files. Ask each listener to complete the form immediately after your presentation. Also give the listeners the handouts before you begin the presentation.

5. Review the feedback forms completed by the listeners with your teammates. List points on which the team did particularly well. List ways that you can improve when giving presentations in the future.

Lesson 24   New Keys u and c

Objectives

In Lesson 24, you will:

⬦ Learn reach technique for **u** and **c**.

⬦ Combine **u** and **c** smoothly with all other learned keys.

24A PRACTICE: Warmup

Key each line twice.

Reach review

1 fg jn lo fr ki de 1. ft jh gf ij tf nj ed ol rf .1

SPACE BAR

2 if so to of no go is in it as see are art jet lake

LEFT SHIFT

3 Ken has a horse. Jan has a dog. He is going too.

24B LEARN: New Keys u and c

Key each line twice. If time permits, rekey lines 7–9.

Learn u

1 j u|ju ju|just just|rust rust|dust dust|used used;
2 ju ju|jug jug|jut jut|turn turn|hug hug|sure sure;
3 turn it; due us; the fur; use it; fur rug; is just

Learn c

4 d c|dc dc|can can|tic tic|catch catch|clock clock;
5 dc dc|ice ice|cat cat|car car|care care|dock docks
6 a can; the ice; she can; the dock; the code; a car

Combine u and c

7 cut cute duck clue cuff cure luck truck curd such;
8 such luck; a cure; to cut; the cure; for the truck
9 Janet and Jack told us to take four cans of juice.

u *Right index* finger

c *Left middle* finger

6. To see how the notes pages will look, click **View** on the menu bar. Choose **Notes Page**. Click the **Next Slide** button several times to view all the notes pages. Go to slide 1 and play the show. Notice that the notes do not display.

7. Now you will print the notes pages. Click **File** on the menu bar. Choose **Print**. Select a printer. Under Print range, select **All**.

8. Under Print what, select **Notes Pages** as shown in Figure 14.20.

Select Notes Pages

Select a color choice

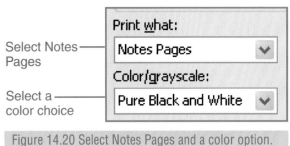

Figure 14.20 Select Notes Pages and a color option.

9. Slides or notes pages can be printed in color, grayscale, or pure black and white. Select **Pure Black and White** because it uses the least amount of ink. Click **OK** to print the pages. Close the file.

Presentation Delivery

Planning and preparing a presentation is only half the task of giving a good presentation. The other half is the delivery. Positive thinking is a must for a good presenter. Prepare and practice before the presentation. This will help you be confident that you can do a good job. Don't worry that the presentation will not be perfect. Set a goal of being a better speaker each time you give a speech, not of being a perfect speaker each time. Practice the presentation tips below to improve your presentation skills.

- **Know your message.** Knowing the message well allows you to talk with the audience rather than read to them.

- **Look at the audience.** Make eye contact with one person briefly (for two to three seconds). Then move on to another person.

- **Know how to use the visuals.** Practice using the visual aids you have chosen for the presentation. Glance at each visual as you display it. Then focus on the audience.

- **Vary the volume and rate at which you speak.** Slow down to emphasize points. Speed up on points that you are sure your audience is familiar with.

24C PRACTICE: Key Mastery

Key each line twice.

3rd/1st rows

1 no to in nut run cue tot cot nun urn ten turn cute

2 Nan is cute; he is curt; turn a cog; he can use it

LEFT SHIFT and .

3 Jett had a lead. Kate ate the cake. Lane let us.

4 I said to use Kan. for Kansas and Ore. for Oregon.

Short words

5 if the and cue for end fit rug oak she fur due got

6 an due cut such fuss rich turn dock curl such hair

Short phrases

7 a risk|is fun|to rush|for us|a fit|the dog|such as

8 just in|code it|turn it|cure it|as such|is in luck

All keys learned

9 He told us to get the ice. Joe called her for us.

10 Hal is sure that he can go there in an hour or so.

24D APPLY: Critical Thinking Activity

Landov

President Lyndon Johnson

You have learned to key the letters shown below. Notice that only the letters keyed with the right hand are shown as capitals. Key as many United States Presidents' last names as you can, using only these letters.

a c d e f g H I J K L N O r s t U

To key notes, click *Click to add notes* in the Notes pane. Key the note for the slide. Format the note text as desired. For example, you can apply bold, change the text alignment, or create a bulleted list. After keying the note for the first slide, click the **Next Slide** button and key the note for the second slide. You may wish to click and drag the top border of the Notes pane to make the Notes pane larger. This makes entering notes easier and does not affect the slide.

108A LEARN: Create Notes and Print Notes Pages

1. Start *Word*. Open *CD-108-National Script* from the data files. This file contains a script the presenter can use to practice delivering the presentation.

2. Start *PowerPoint*. Open *107-National*. You will create notes to be printed with the slides as handouts for the audience.

3. Select **Normal** view and go to slide 1. In the Notes pane, key **Contact Information** and apply bold to the text. Begin a new line. Key your name, your school name, and your school address on separate lines. An example is shown in Figure 14.19.

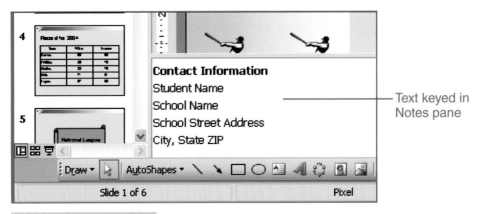

Figure 14.19 Notes Pane

4. Go to slide 2. In the Notes pane, key **Goals**. Apply bold to the text. On the two following lines, list two goals of the presentation. Find the goals by reading the script for slide 2. Copy key phrases from the script to the Notes pane. Edit as needed and format the two goals as a bulleted list.

5. On slides 3, 4, 5, and 6, create notes to emphasize information that will be presented with that slide. Copy key phrases from the script and edit as needed to create two or three key points that will help the audience remember the information. Format the information as a bulleted list. Save the file as *108-National*.

Lesson 25   New Keys w and RIGHT SHIFT

Objectives

In Lesson 25, you will:

⭷ Learn reach technique for **w** and **RIGHT SHIFT**.

⭷ Combine **w** and **RIGHT SHIFT** with all other learned keys.

25A PRACTICE: Warmup

Key each line twice.

Reach review

 1 fr fg de ju ft jn ki lo dc ki rf l. ed jh ol gf tf

u/c

 2 luck used cure such cute cause lunch accuse actual

All letters learned

 3 Jefferson just took the huge lead in the election.

25B LEARN: New Keys w and RIGHT SHIFT

w *Left ring* finger

RIGHT SHIFT *Right little* finger

TECHNIQUE TIP

Depress the SHIFT key, tap the key, and release the SHIFT key in a quick 1-2-3 count.

Key each line twice. If time permits, rekey lines 7–9.

Learn **w**

 1 s w|sw sw|two two|wet wet|low low|how how|was was;
 2 sw sw|were were|what what|snow snow|worker worker;
 3 to show; to watch; to win; when we; wash and wear;

Learn **RIGHT SHIFT**

 4 ;A ;A;|A1 A1;|Dan Dan;|Ann Ann;|Ron Ron;|Gene Gene
 5 Chicago; San Diego; Santa Fe; Atlanta; Eau Claire;
 6 Richard left for San Diego; Fran left for Chicago.

Combine **w** and **RIGHT SHIFT**

 7 Charla and Wanda will watch the show with Willard.
 8 We will want to show the award to Walt and Andrew.
 9 Wes wished he was in Washington watching the show.

3. Choose to have the sound play automatically when the slide is displayed. Drag the sound icon off the slide. Play the show to make sure the sound is appropriate and plays correctly.

4. Save the file as *107-School Show*. Close *PowerPoint*.

Lesson 108   Delivering a Presentation

Objectives

In Lesson 108, you will:

⬎ Add notes to a presentation.

⬎ Print slide notes pages.

⬎ Practice and deliver a presentation.

Data files: *CD-108-National Script, CD-108-Feedback*

Slide Notes

⌐ Help Words ⌐

Notes
  About notes

Notes can be added to slides using the Notes pane in Normal view. You can also key notes in the Notes Page view. Notes do not display when you play a slide show. However, you can print the notes on notes pages. A notes page shows the slide and the notes below the slide. The notes can be used to help you remember details as you give the presentation. The printed notes pages can also be used as handouts for the audience. The top portion of a notes page is shown in Figure 14.18.

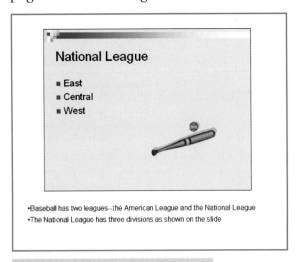

Figure 14.18 Sample Notes Page

25C PRACTICE: Key Mastery

Key each line twice.

w and RIGHT SHIFT

1 Dr. Wade works here; Dr. Weeks left two weeks ago.
2 Will Whitt get a watch when his is in town on Wed.

n/g

3 sing a song|long gone|wrong sign|and got|a gallon;
4 Glenda signed the wrong check. Jen is gone again.

Short words

5 is and the she sir for rid cut got rug oak end dog
6 wet red oil ear inn gas ink car on ace look no sea

Short phrases

7 he did|a jet ride|she is|if she can go|take a look
8 as soon as|to go to|if it is|when he is|has done a

All keys learned

9 Jason and Chuck are going. Laurie thinks she can.
10 Frank worked eight hours; Linda worked four hours.

SPACING TIP

Space quickly after keying each word.

25D APPLY: Spacing with Punctuation

SPACING TIP

Do not space after an internal period in an abbreviation. Space once after each period following initials.

Key each line twice.

1 Dr. Hoag said to use wt. for weight; in. for inch.
2 J. R. Chen has used ed. for editor; Rt. for Route.
3 Sue said Jed Ford got an Ed.D. degree last winter.
4 Use i.e. for that is; cs. for case; ck. for check.

25E APPLY: Critical Thinking Activity

Use MicroType Lesson 11 for additional practice.

You have learned to key the following letters. You also know how to use the LEFT SHIFT and RIGHT SHIFT keys. Key the last names of as many United States Presidents as you can, using only these letters.

a c d e f g h i j k l n o r s t u w

A computer must have speakers and a sound card to play music and sounds. You must have a microphone to record sounds. When music or sounds are added to a slide, a sound icon appears on the slide. You can drag the sound icon off the slide if you don't want it to appear when the show is played. You can set sounds to start automatically when the slide displays or to start on a mouse-click.

107E LEARN: Add Sound to Slides

Instant Message

If no sound files related to baseball hits or a roaring crowd are found, click the **Clip art on Office Online** link. Find and download sound files from this site. Then repeat the file search.

1. Start *PowerPoint*. Open *107-National* that you edited earlier. Select Normal view and go to slide 2. You will find and add sound files to this slide.

2. Click **Insert** on the menu bar. Choose **Movies and Sounds**. Choose **Sound from Clip Organizer**. In the task pane, key **baseball** in the Search for box. Click **Go**. Look for a file that plays the sound of a baseball being hit. Click the sound file to add it to the slide.

3. Click **Automatically** in the box that asks how you want the sound to start. A sound icon will display on the slide. Click and drag the icon to the left off the slide as shown in Figure 14.17.

Figure 14.17 Slide with Sound Icon

SOFTWARE TIP

To remove a sound from a slide, select and delete the Sound icon.

4. Repeat steps 2 and 3 to find and add a sound file that plays the roar of a crowd. Use search terms such as *crowd*, *cheer*, or *applause*. After inserting the sound, play the show to see how the sounds play.

5. Save the file using the same name, *107-National*. Close the file.

107F PRACTICE: Add Sound to Slides

1. Start *PowerPoint*. Open *106-School Show* that you created earlier.

2. Add an appropriate sound file to at least one slide. For example, you might use a file with sounds from a restaurant when you talk about the school cafeteria. You might add sounds of a crowd or the school song when you talk about sports events.

Lesson 26   New Keys b and y

Objectives
In Lesson 26, you will:
> ↘ Learn reach technique for **b** and **y**.
> ↘ Combine **b** and **y** with all other learned keys.

26A PRACTICE: Warmup

Keep fingers curved
and upright.

Key each line twice.

Reach review
```
1 ft. de lo ju sw ki fr dc jn jh l. fg rt. ws ol ed.
```
c/n
```
2 nice coin cent cane niece dance ounce check glance
```
All letters learned
```
3 Jack Elgin had two hits in the first four innings.
```

26B LEARN: New Keys b and y

Key each line twice. If time permits, rekey lines 7–9.

b *Left index* finger

y *Right index* finger

Learn b
```
1 f b f b|fb bf|fib fib|big big|book book|bank bank;
2 fb fb fb|bugs bugs|oboe oboe|label label|bird bird
3 Bob bid; Rob bunted; black rubber ball; brief job;
```
Learn y
```
4 j y|jy jy|jay jay|yes yes|eye eye|day day|rye rye;
5 yiy yiy|eye eye|only only|yellow yellow|your yours
6 why did you; yellow cycle; only yesterday; he says
```
Combine b and y
```
7 buy buy|boy boy|busy busy|buddy buddy|byway byway;
8 by the bay; you buy a; big burly boy; a yellow bus
9 Bobby went by way of bus to buy the big blue belt.
```

107C LEARN:

Rearrange Slide Order

1. Start *PowerPoint*. Open *107-National* that you created earlier.

2. Slide 6 with the National League banner should appear before the slide showing the results of the league playoffs. Click the **Slide Sorter View** button.

3. Click and drag slide 6 one slide to the left. Now the slides should appear in the order shown in Figure 14.16. Save the file using the same name, *107-National*. Close the file.

107D APPLY:

Add Content and Rearrange Slides

1. Start *PowerPoint*. Open *106-Presidents* that you created earlier.

2. Use the Internet to learn three facts about each President listed below.

   - President Abraham Lincoln
   - President Thomas Jefferson
   - President Franklin Roosevelt
   - President Theodore Roosevelt

3. Create a slide similar to the one you created for President Washington for each President listed above. Use the *Clip art on Office Online* link to find images of the Presidents.

4. When you have completed the slides, rearrange them. Place the title slide first and the table slide second. Place the slides about the Presidents next. Arrange those slides in order by years served in office.

5. Save the file as *107-Presidents*. Complete the Check Point below. Then close the file.

 Compare the order of your slides with those of a classmate. Make changes if needed.

Adding Sound to Slides

┌   ┐
  Help Words
└   ┘

Sound
  About music and
  sounds

Music and other sounds can enhance your presentation. You can add music and sounds from files to slides. You can also record sounds to use in a presentation. When you use sounds, make sure they are appropriate. The sound, also called audio, should not be overbearing or distracting. Sound can be used to introduce a topic, build excitement, or provide a transition between topics. Be sure the sound is played at a time when you will not be talking.

26C PRACTICE: SPACE BAR Technique

Key each line once.

1 Jason will be able to take the bus to the concert.
2 Gary is to sign for the auto we set aside for her.
3 Rey is in town for just one week to look for work.
4 Ted is to work for us for a week at the lake dock.
5 June said he was in the auto when it hit the tree.
6 Dan has an old car she wants to sell at this sale.

26D PRACTICE: ENTER Key Technique

Use MicroType Lesson 12 for additional practice.

Key each line once. At the end of each line, quickly tap the ENTER key and start the next line.

1 Gary will hit first.
2 Jan will be the second hitter.
3 Nick will be second and bat after Jason.
4 Roberto will be the center fielder and hit eighth.

| gwam | 1' | 1 | 2 | 3 | 4 | 5 | 6 | 7 | 8 | 9 | 10 |

26E LEARN: Find Words Keyed Score

A **standard word** in keyboarding is five characters. These five characters can be letters, numbers, symbols, or spaces. Each group of five characters is shown by the number scale under lines you key. For an example, look under line 4 in 26D above. One measure used to describe keying skill is the number of words you key in a certain amount of time, such as a minute. The number of standard words keyed in 1' is called **gross words a minute** (*gwam*).

1. Key line 4 of 26D again as your teacher times you for 1'. Then follow the steps below to find 1' *gwam* for the timing.

   • Note on the scale the figure beneath the last word you keyed. That is your 1' *gwam* if you key the line partially or only once.

   • If you completed the line once and started over, add 10 to the figure. The result is your 1' *gwam*.

2. Key line 4 of 26D again as your teacher times you for 30". Then follow the steps below to find 30" gwam:

   • Find 1' *gwam* (total words keyed).

   • Multiply 1' *gwam* by 2. The resulting figure is your 30" *gwam*.

2. Create the slide shown in Figure 14.15. Use the Horizontal Scroll AutoShape and add the text **National League**. In a text box, enter **Playoffs – 2004**. Format the slide approximately as shown.

3. Save the file using the same name, *107-National*. Close the file or continue to the next activity.

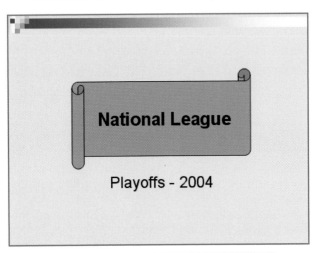

Figure 14.15 Slide with AutoShape and Text Box

Rearranging Slide Order

As you review your slides, you may find that you want them to be in a different order. Slides can be rearranged in the **Slide Sorter** view or on the Slides tab. To rearrange slides, click and drag a slide to a location. Slide Sorter view is shown in Figure 14.16.

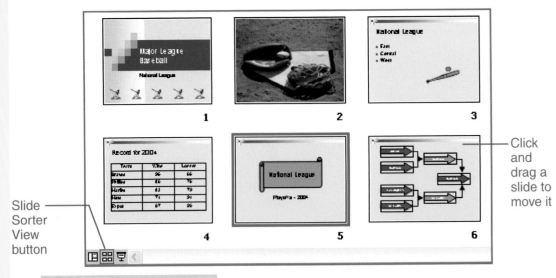

Slide Sorter View button

Click and drag a slide to move it

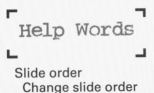

Figure 14.16 Slide Sorter View

Lesson 27 Review

Objectives
In Lesson 27, you will:
↘ Improve spacing, shifting, and entering.
↘ Increase keying control and speed.

27A PRACTICE: Warmup

Key each line twice.

Reach review
1 ton only beat teen week rich used nice count B. J.

b/y
2 buy yes boy year obey eyes been yield debate Bobby

All letters learned
3 Jason knew the gift you held was for Dr. Jacobson.

27B PRACTICE: SPACE BAR and SHIFT Keys

Key each line twice.

SPACE BAR (Space immediately after each word.)
1 in by we so do the and run yet ink low jet fun can
2 in the|when he|if she will|run to|yes you|can be a
3 Lance take a look at her car to see what is wrong.
4 Janet lost both of the keys to the car in the lot.

SHIFT keys (Hold down SHIFT key; tap key; release both quickly.)
5 Dr. Alou; Jose K. Casey; Sue A. Finch; Jon B. Bins
6 Della and I went to France in June to see her dad.
7 Roger and Carlos went to Salt Lake City on Friday.
8 The San Francisco Giants were in town on Thursday.

✔ CHECK POINT Do you reach up to keys without moving your hands away from your body?

7. Change the fill color for two of the arrows to red as shown in Figure 14.13. If you select the wrong object, click the **Undo** button and try again.

8. Add text to each arrow object, keying the name of the team as shown in Figure 14.13. Apply bold to the text. Change the font color to white.

9. Now you will change the background color for all the slides in this show. Click **Format** on the menu bar. Click **Background**. Click the down arrow for the background fill color as shown in Figure 14.14. Choose **More Colors**.

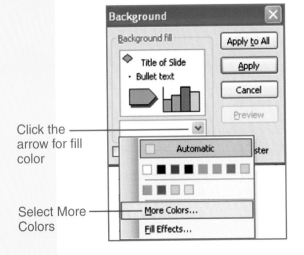

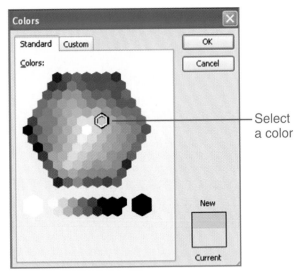

Click the arrow for fill color

Select More Colors

Select a color

Figure 14.14 Use Background and Colors dialog boxes to change the slide background.

10. Select a color on the Standard tab of the Colors dialog box. The new color and the current color are shown in the lower right of the dialog box. Click **OK** to return to the Background dialog box.

11. Click **Preview**. If you like the color applied to the sample slide, click **Apply to All**. If not, choose another color or lighten the color. Preview again. Click **Apply to All** when you are happy with the color.

12. Save the file as *107-National*. Close the file or continue to the next activity.

✔ **CHECK POINT** Ask a classmate to review your slide 5 and offer comments for improvement.

107B APPLY: Create a Slide with AutoShapes

1. Start *PowerPoint*. Open *107-National* that you created earlier. Go to slide 5. Insert a new slide at the end of the show. Use the Blank slide layout.

27C APPLY: Check Speed

Key each line once double-spaced. Key a 20" timing on each line. Your rate of gross words a minute (*gwam*) is shown word-for-word below the lines.

1 I will see her.

2 Janet has a new job.

3 Jack will go to the lake.

4 Karl is to go skiing with her.

5 Kara has two old oak doors to sell.

6 Faye and I took the test before we left.

7 Jessie said she will be in school on Tuesday.

8 Jay will go to the city to work on the road signs.

gwam 20" | 3 | 6 | 9 | 12 | 15 | 18 | 21 | 24 | 27 | 30 |

27D PRACTICE: Speed Building

TECHNIQUE TIP

- Keep your fingers curved and upright.
- Keep your hands and arms quiet.
- Space quickly without pausing between words.

Key each line once.

1 Judy had gone for that big ice show at Lake Tahoe.

2 Jack said that all of you will find the right job.

3 Cindy has just left for work at the big ski lodge.

4 Rudy can take a good job at the lake if he wishes.

5 Rob saw the bird on the lake by the big boat dock.

6 Ted knew the surf was too rough for kids to enjoy.

27E APPLY: Critical Thinking

Use MicroType Lesson 13 for additional practice.

Work with another student to complete this activity. Unscramble the letters shown below to create eight words. Work as quickly as you can. Raise your hand when you have all eight words.

usjt   ukcl

rgwon   aitng

ntcuo   kirnd

lbdiu   jnyoe

Create Graphics Using the Drawing Toolbar

In this activity, you will create a slide showing the results of baseball playoffs. The slide, shown in Figure 14.13, is created using features of the Drawing toolbar.

1. Start *PowerPoint*. Open *106-National* that you created earlier. Go to slide 4. Insert a new slide at the end of the show. Use the Blank slide layout.

2. Draw a rectangle box with no fill. Set the size for the box to 3 inches wide and 1 inch high. Use AutoShapes to draw a block arrow inside the rectangle as shown in Figure 14.13. Apply a blue fill to the arrow shape.

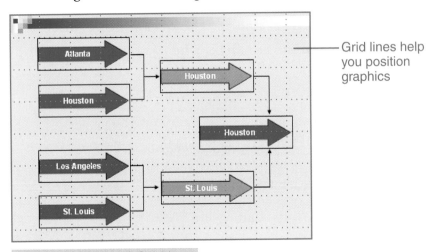

Grid lines help you position graphics

Figure 14.13 Slide with Graphics

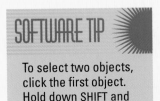

SOFTWARE TIP

To select two objects, click the first object. Hold down SHIFT and click the second object.

3. Select the rectangle and the arrow. Click **Draw** on the Drawing toolbar. Click **Group** from the pop-up menu. Now you can copy and move these two objects as though they were one. Copy and paste the box so you have six boxes, as shown in Figure 14.13.

4. You can display a grid on the slide to help you position graphics. Click **View** on the menu bar. Choose **Grid and Guides**. Select the **Display grid on screen** option and click **OK**. The grid will display as shown in Figure 14.13.

5. Position the rectangles on the screen approximately as shown in Figure 14.13. Use the grid lines to help you align objects and space them evenly.

6. Draw lines to connect the boxes as shown in Figure 14.13. Hold down the CTRL key while using the arrow keys to move the lines or other objects in small amounts. Increase the zoom for the Slide pane to help you see whether the lines are joining exactly. Play the show to see if the lines look correct. Remember that you can group and copy lines as well as other objects.

Lesson 28   New Keys m and x

Objectives
In Lesson 28, you will:
⬆ Learn reach technique for **m** and **x**.
⬆ Combine **m** and **x** with all other learned keys.

28A PRACTICE: Warmup

Key each line twice.

Reach review
```
1 fg jy lo fr jn de sw ft ki jh fb dc ju by us if ow
```
b/y
```
2 by bay buy big yes boy buy bit try bury ruby byway
```
All letters learned
```
3 Beth can win the gold if she will just key faster.
```

28B LEARN: New Keys m and x

Key each line twice. If time permits, rekey lines 7–9.

m *Right index* finger

x *Left ring* finger

Learn m
```
1 j m|jm jm|jams jams|make make|mail mail|most most;
2 jm jm|me me|may may|moon moon|grim grim|mean meant
3 to them; meet me; make a mark; mail it; mean to me
```
Learn x
```
4 s x|sx sx|six six|fix fix|exit exit|extend extend;
5 sx sx|six six|tax tax|hex hex|fix fix|exact exact;
6 to excel; to exile; an exit; by six; an excise tax
```
Combine m and x
```
7 mix fox six jam men box hoax coax maxim axle taxi;
8 to fix; mix it; six men; make an exit; make a box;
9 Maxine Cox took the exit exams in Texas on Monday.
```

3. Start *PowerPoint*. Open *105-School Show* that you created earlier. Working from your outline, develop a bulleted list slide that informs the audience about what the presentation will cover. Use **Today's Presentation** for the title of slide 2. Key a bulleted list telling what your presentation will cover.

4. Insert additional slides and key the main points and subpoints of your presentation. Include at least one slide that has a table that presents some information about your school. For example, you could create a table that shows the number of male and female students in each grade level.

5. Add appropriate clip art to at least two slides. Save the file as *106-School Show*. Play the show. Discuss ways to improve the show with your teammates. Make the desired changes and save the file again. Close *PowerPoint*.

Lesson 107   Adding Graphics to Slides

Objectives

In Lesson 107, you will:
- Use the Drawing toolbar features to create graphics.
- Change the background color for slides.
- Rearrange the order of slides.
- Add sound to slides.

Drawing Toolbar

The Drawing toolbar has tools that can be used to draw shapes and designs. In Chapter 13, you learned to create WordArt and insert text boxes and AutoShapes using the Drawing toolbar. You can use the same procedures to create these graphics in slides. Review the Drawing toolbar in Figure 14.12. It is usually displayed across the bottom of the screen.

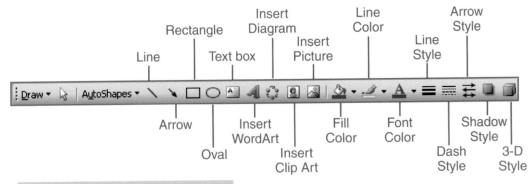

Figure 14.12 Drawing Toolbar in *Word*

Key each line twice.

3d/1st rows

1 men box but now cut gem rib ton yet not meet mired
2 cub oxen torn went time were note court worn owned

Short words

3 and own she box fix city duck held hair name their
4 art gas face honk milk draw junk aware extra start

Short phrases

5 you want|if she is|one of the|that is|they are not
6 make the call|for all the|and is|able to|they may;

All keys learned

7 Jacki is now at the gym; Lexi is due there by six.
8 Stan saw that he could fix my old bike for Glenda.

28D APPLY: Spacing with Punctuation

Key each line twice.

1 Rex has an Ed.D. in history; Mary Jane has a Ph.D.
2 Lexi may send a box c.o.d. to Ms. Cox in St. Paul.
3 Maxine will take a boat to St. Thomas in December.
4 Maria used Wed. for Wednesday and Mon. for Monday.

28E APPLY: Critical Thinking

Atlantic

California

Connecticut

Mt. McKinley

Mt. Rushmore

Pacific

Rhode Island

Wyoming

Key the sentences below. From the list at the left, choose the word that best completes the sentence. Do not key the numbers.

1. *The smallest state is* _____.

2. *The state with the least number of residents is* _____.

3. *The state with the most residents is* _____.

4. *The ocean off the east coast is the* _____.

5. *The highest mountain in the United States is* _____.

2. Click the **Slide Design** button on the Formatting toolbar. Choose a design template for the show. Choose a simple design that will allow you to add pictures later. Apply the design to the slide.

Instant Message

One good source of information about U.S. Presidents is the White House Web site at http://www.whitehouse.gov/history/presidents.

3. Insert a slide with the Title, Text, and Content layout. In the title placeholder, key **President Washington**. For the first bullet item, key **First President**. For the second bullet item, key **Commander of the Continental Army**. Key a third bullet item about President Washington. Search the Internet, if needed, to find more information about this President.

4. Find and insert clip art of President Washington. Use the *Clip art on Office Online* link if the clip art is not available on your computer. Resize the clip art, if needed, and place it in the Content placeholder.

5. Insert a new slide at the end of the file. Use the Title and Table layout. Create the slide as shown in Figure 14.11.

6. Save the file as *106-Presidents*. Close the file.

Term of Office

President	Years
George Washington	1789-1797
Thomas Jefferson	1801-1809
Abraham Lincoln	1861-1865
Theodore Roosevelt	1901-1909
Franklin D. Roosevelt	1933-1945

Figure 14.11 Slide 3 in the Presidents Show

106E APPLY: Continue Work on School Presentation

1. Continue to work with your teammates to complete this activity. Start *Word*. Open *105-School Outline* that you created earlier.

2. Now that you have had time to think about the presentation about your school, review the outline you and your teammates composed. Add two or more subpoints for each main topic in your outline.

Lesson 29   New Keys p and v

Objectives
In Lesson 29, you will:
↘ Learn reach technique for **p** and **v**.
↘ Combine **p** and **v** with all other learned keys.

29A PRACTICE: Warmup

Key each line twice.

One-hand words
1 gate link face moon extra hook base join beef milk
Phrases
2 if you will|take a look|when they|join us|to see a
All letters learned
3 Jo Buck won a gold medal for her sixth show entry.

29B LEARN: New Keys p and v

Key each line twice. If time permits, rekey lines 7–9.

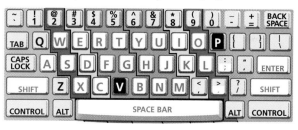

Learn p
1 ; p ;p|pay pay|put put|apt apt|kept kept|pack pack
2 ;p ;p|pain pain|paint paint|paper paper|soap soap;
3 a plan; a party cap; pick a place; a pack of paper
Learn v
4 f v f v|via via|live live|have have|vote vote|save
5 vf vf|van van|visit visit|liver liver|voice voice;
6 five vans; have a visit; very valid; vim and vigor
Combine p and v
7 pave hive open save plan jive soap very pain votes
8 apt to vote; pick a vase; pack the van; five pans;
9 Pam has a plan to have the van pick us up at five.

p *Right little* finger

v *Left index* finger

Create a Slide with a Table

1. Start *PowerPoint*. Open *106-National* that you created earlier. You will now create a slide to show the 2004 records for the Eastern Division teams.

2. Go to slide 3. Click the **New Slide** button. Choose the **Title and Table** layout in the Slide Layout task pane. You may have to scroll down to find this layout.

3. In the title placeholder, key **Record for 2004**.

4. Double-click where indicated in the table placeholder. The Insert Table box will appear as shown in Figure 14.10. Enter **3** in the Number of columns box. Enter **6** in the Number of rows box. Click **OK**.

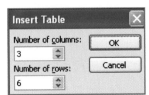

Figure 14.10 Insert Table Box

5. Key the data shown below in the table. Apply bold and center alignment to the column heads. Apply center alignment to the numbers.

Team	Wins	Losses
Braves	96	66
Phillies	86	76
Marlins	83	79
Mets	71	91
Expos	67	95

6. You now know how to create slides with bulleted lists and tables. Save the file using the same name *106-National*. Close the file.

Create Presidents Show

INTERNET

In this activity, you will begin creating a presentation about U.S. Presidents. You will include a title slide, a slide with a bulleted list, and a slide with a table.

1. Start *PowerPoint*. A new presentation with a blank title slide should appear. For the presentation title, key **My Favorite Presidents**. For the subtitle, key **By** and your name.

29C PRACTICE: Key Mastery

Key each line twice.

Reach review

```
1 jn fr ki ft lo dc jh fg ju fb fv ;p sx jm de jy sw
2 just dear sweat jump fever decade injury swat hush
```

3d/1st rows

```
3 born none mix bore curve more noon bunny comb vice
4 open exit were none trip crop brown money pine pin
```

Short phrases

```
5 go to a|they may keep|with your|and the|it will be
6 very much|sure to|a big|make a|too much|to view it
```

All letters learned

```
7 Kevin does a top job on your flax farm with Craig.
8 Dixon flew blue jets eight times over a city park.
```

29D PRACTICE: SHIFT and ENTER Key Technique

Key each line once. At the end of each line, quickly tap the ENTER key and immediately start the next line.

```
1 Dan took a friend to the game.
2 Jan had a double and a single.

3 Bob and Jose Hill will sing a song.
4 Sam and Jo took the test on Monday.

5 Laura sold her old cars to Sandra Smith.
6 Nicky left to play video games with Tim.
```

gwam 30" | 2 | 4 | 6 | 8 | 10 | 12 | 14 | 16 |

29E APPLY: Critical Thinking Activity

Use MicroType Lesson 15 for additional practice.

1. To key the names of 13 U.S. states, you have to know the letter *M*. How many of the 13 states can you key?

2. Only three U.S. state names include the letter *P*. How many of them can you key?

3. Only five U.S. state names include the letter *V*. Can you key them?

9. Click the **Insert Clip Art** button on the Drawing toolbar. Find and insert clip art related to baseball. Place the image in the lower-right corner of the screen. Resize the image if needed.

10. Save the National League show file as *106-National*. Close the file. Close the *CD-104-American* file without saving changes.

106B PRACTICE: Add Slides to Presentation

1. Start *Word* and open *CD-106-Effective Slides* from your data files. Read about how to use bulleted lists to create effective slides. Close *Word*.

2. Start *PowerPoint*. Open *105-Madison* that you created earlier.

3. Insert a new slide after the title slide. Use the Title and Text layout. Key a title that relates to one of the main topics in your *103-Outline*. Enter the main points and any subpoints related to the topic on the slide. You can rearrange the order of the slides later, if needed.

4. Capitalize the important words in the title. Capitalize the first word of each line in the bulleted list and all proper nouns. Use short phrases for the bullet points. Do not place punctuation at the end of the lines, because they are not complete sentences. An example slide is shown in Figure 14.9.

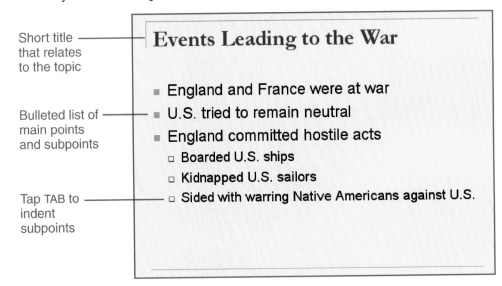

Short title that relates to the topic

Bulleted list of main points and subpoints

Tap TAB to indent subpoints

Events Leading to the War

- England and France were at war
- U.S. tried to remain neutral
- England committed hostile acts
  - Boarded U.S. ships
  - Kidnapped U.S. sailors
  - Sided with warring Native Americans against U.S.

Figure 14.9 Sample Slide from Madison Show

5. Add slides and enter the remaining data from your outline. Be careful not to place too much text on one slide. Add appropriate clip art to at least two slides.

6. Save the file as *106-Madison*. Close the file.

Lesson 30 New Keys q and comma (,)

Objectives

In Lesson 30, you will:
⬧ Learn reach technique for **q** and **, (comma)**.
⬧ Combine **q** and **, (comma)** with all other learned keys.

30A PRACTICE: ## Warmup

Key each line twice.

All letters learned
```
1 six buy jam ask dog call vote down fork crop there
```
p/v
```
2 five pups; to vote; pay for; very plain; her plan;
```
All letters learned
```
3 Jacki Farve played six games on Thursday with Ben.
```

30B LEARN: ## New Keys q and , (comma)

Key each line twice. If time permits, rekey lines 7–9.

SPACING TIP

Space once after **,** used as punctuation.

q *Left little* finger

,(comma) *Right middle* finger

Learn q
```
1 a q a q|aqua aqua|quote quote|quad quad|quit quits
2 aq|queen queen|quake quake|equip equip|quick quick
3 a square; the quote; a quart; to acquire; is equal
```
Learn , (comma)
```
4 k , k , k, k, ,k,|a,b c,d e,f g,h i,j k,l m,n o,p,
5 Monday, Tuesday, Wednesday, Thursday, and Saturday
6 Rob took Janet, Pam, Seth, and Felipe to the game.
```
Combine q and , (comma)
```
7 Key the words quit, squad, square, and earthquake.
8 I have quit the squad, Quen; Raquel has quit, too.
9 Quit, quiet, and quaint were on the spelling exam.
```

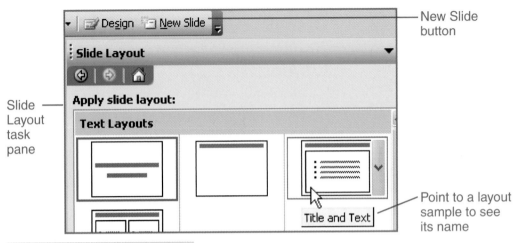

New Slide button

Slide Layout task pane

Point to a layout sample to see its name

Figure 14.8 Slide Layout Options

106A LEARN:

Insert Slides and Choose Layouts

In this activity, you will review the American League show to see the slide layouts used. You will update the National League show to add slides and choose layouts.

1. Start *PowerPoint*. Open *CD-104-American* from your data files.

2. Click slide 2 in the Slides tab. The layout for this slide is Blank. This layout provides space for the clip art that fills the slide.

3. Click the **Next Slide** button to go to slide 3. The layout for this slide is Title and Text. The text is formatted as a bulleted list. The slide also has clip art.

4. Go to slide 4. This slide has the Title and Diagram or Organizational Chart layout.

5. Leave this file open and open *105-National* that you edited earlier. In *105-National*, click the **New Slide** button. The Slide Layout task pane will open and a new slide will be inserted. Click the **Blank** slide layout found under Content Layouts.

6. You will copy the clip art from slide 2 of *CD-104-American* and paste it on this slide. Go to slide 2 in *CD-104-American*. Right-click the image on the slide and choose **Copy**. Go to slide 2 in *105-National*. Click the **Paste** button. Resize the image to fill the entire slide if needed.

7. In *105-National*, go to slide 2. Click the **New Slide** button. Click **Title and Text** in the Slide Layout task pane.

8. In the title placeholder, key **National League**. In the bulleted list placeholder, key **East** and tap ENTER. Key **Central** and tap ENTER. Key **West** and click outside the placeholder.

Key Mastery

Use MicroType Lesson 16 for additional practice.

Key each line twice. If time permits, key lines 7–8 again.

Double letters

1 add egg ill books access three effect otter cheese
2 Betty and Ross will help cook the food for dinner.

q/comma

3 Marquis, Quent, and Quig were quite quick to quit.
4 Quin, Jacqueline, and Paque quickly took the exam.

Short phrases

5 a box|if the call|when you go|if we can|look for a
6 if we go|it is our|up to you|do you see|she took a

All letters learned

7 Jevon will fix my pool deck if the big rain quits.
8 Verna did fly quick jets to map the six big towns.

30D PRACTICE:

Spacing with Punctuation Technique

Key each line once. At the end of each line, quickly tap the ENTER key and immediately start the next line.

Space once.

1 Quin, the artist, won; Qua, the pianist, also won.
2 Quince, keyed qt. for quart; also, sq. for square.
3 Ship the desk c.o.d. to Dr. Quig at La Quinta Inn.
4 Jay, Kay, and Sue were on my team; Gerald was not.

30E APPLY:

Critical Thinking

1. Key the sentences below. From the list at the left, choose the word that best completes the sentence. Do not key the numbers.

2. Use the Internet to learn about these six U.S. Presidents. Record the years that the person was President and the home state for each person.

John Adams
George Bush
Grover Cleveland
Herbert Hoover
Franklin Roosevelt
George Washington

1. *The President who served two terms that were not consecutive was* _____.
2. *The only President to serve more than two terms was* _____.
3. _____ *was referred to as the Father of His Country.*
4. _____ *and* _____ *had sons who became President.*
5. *The President during the 1929 crash of the stock market was* _____.

1. Work with two classmates to complete this activity. In a *Word* document, enter **SCHOOL PRESENTATION** at the top of the page.

2. Leave one blank line and then key the heading **Purpose**. Under this heading, key three or four goals that you will try to accomplish with this presentation.

3. Leave one blank line and key the heading **Audience**. Under this heading, create a bulleted list. Include several points that describe the audience for the presentation. Review Lesson 103 if needed.

4. Insert a page break to begin a new page. Working as a team, develop the main points for the presentation. Remember, the goal is to acquaint new students and their parents with your school and what it has to offer. Key the main points in an outline.

5. You will develop the subpoints for the outline later. Give the outline an appropriate title and format it correctly. Save the document as *105-School Outline*. Print the document.

6. Start *PowerPoint* and open a new blank presentation. Create a title slide for the School presentation. Include the name of your school and the date on the title slide. Select and apply a design template. Add appropriate clip art (such as a school logo) if desired.

7. Save the presentation file as *105-School Show*. Close *PowerPoint*.

Instant Message

Review how to format an outline in Lesson 86.

Lesson 106   Inserting and Formatting Slides

Objectives

In Lesson 106, you will:
- ⬊ Insert new slides and use different slide layouts.
- ⬊ Create a slide with a bulleted list.
- ⬊ Create a slide with a table.

Data files: *CD-104-American, CD-106-Effective Slides*

Slide Layouts

Help Words

Slide layout
   Insert a new slide

You can add slides to a presentation as you develop it. Slides are available in several different layouts. You can choose the layout that will work best for the content of the slide. For example, if you wish to include a bulleted list, insert a slide with the Title and Text layout. Examples of slide layouts are shown in Figure 14.8. To insert a new slide, click the New Slide button on the Formatting toolbar. To access the Slide Layout task pane, choose Slide Layout from the Format menu.

Lesson 31　Review

Objectives

In Lesson 31, you will:
↘ Learn to key block paragraphs.
↘ Improve keying technique and speed.

31A PRACTICE:　Warmup

Key each line twice.

All letters learned
1 Jared helped Maxine quickly fix the big wood vase.

SHIFT keys
2 Jake and Kathy went to New York City on Wednesday.

Easy
3 Pamela may hang the signs by the door in the hall.

31B LEARN:　Block Paragraphs

Key each paragraph once. Tap ENTER only at the end of the paragraph. Double-space between the paragraphs; then key the paragraphs again at a faster pace.

Instant Message

The paragraphs at the right are called "block" paragraphs. This is because all lines begin evenly at the left margin.

Paragraph 1
You already know that you can use the Enter key to space down and start a new line. If you don't use the Enter key, the insertion point will continue on the same line until it reaches the right margin. Then it will automatically space down to the next line.

Paragraph 2
Later in the textbook you will learn how to adjust the right and left margins to vary the line length. As you make the line length smaller, the margins become larger. As you make the line length larger, the margins become smaller.

4. Click the arrow for the Results should be box. Select **Clip Art**. Click the **Go** button. Thumbnails of the clip art found will appear in the Clip Art task pane. Choose an image from the search results that you think will look good on the title slide. Click the image to insert it.

5. Click and drag the image to place it in the lower-right corner of the screen. Right-click the image and choose **Format Picture**. On the Size tab, set the image height to 1 inch. Select the **Lock the aspect ratio** option so the width will change automatically to keep the picture in proportion when it is resized. Click **OK**.

6. Use the Copy and Paste commands to make four copies of the image. Place the five images along the bottom of the screen similar to Figure 14.7.

7. Play the show to see how the slide looks. Click the **Save** button to save the file using the same name, *105-National*. Close the file.

Figure 14.7 Title Slide with Clip Art

105D PRACTICE: Insert Clip Art

1. Start *PowerPoint*. Open *105-Madison* that you created earlier.

2. Find and insert clip art that relates to this presentation. For example, clip art of the U.S. flag or the American eagle symbol would be appropriate. Review the information in the *Clip art on Office Online* section on page 489 if appropriate clip art is not available on your computer.

3. Resize the clip art, if needed, and place it in a location that makes an attractive slide.

4. Save the file as *105-Madison*. Close the file.

105E APPLY: Plan Presentation and Create Title Slide

The principal of your school would like you and two of your classmates to develop a presentation. The goal of the presentation is to acquaint new students with your school. The audience will be new students and their parents.

31C PRACTICE: Check Keying Speed

Key a 30" timed writing on each line. Your rate in gross words a minute (*gwam*) is shown below the lines.

1 She owns all of the lake land.
2 The man with the sign may aid them.
3 I may make my goal if I work with vigor.
4 Six of the girls may make a bid for the gown.
5 Laurie and Orlando may make the map of the island.

gwam 30" | 2 | 4 | 6 | 8 | 10 | 12 | 14 | 16 | 18 | 20 |

31D PRACTICE: Build Speed

Use MicroType Lesson 17 for additional practice.

Key each line twice.

1 I may have six quick jobs to get done for low pay.
2 Vicky packed the box with quail and jam for Jason.
3 Max can plan to bike for just five days with Quig.
4 Jim was quick to get the next top value for Debby.
5 Jack B. Manly requested approval for extra weight.
6 Jacque may have plans for the big dance next week.

✔ CHECK POINT Do you reach down without moving your hands toward your body?

31E APPLY: Critical Thinking

Warren G. Harding

Thomas Jefferson

John F. Kennedy

Ronald Reagan

Harry S. Truman

1. Key the sentences below. From the list at the left, choose the word that best completes the sentence. Do not key the numbers.

2. Use the Internet to learn about these five U.S. Presidents. Record the years that the person was President and the home state for each person.

1. _____ *was the U.S. President during World War II when a nuclear bomb was dropped on Japan.*

2. *The Declaration of Independence was written by* _____.

3. *The Teapot Dome scandal took place when* _____ *was U.S. President.*

4. *The oldest U.S. President when he assumed the duties of President was* _____.

5. *The youngest U.S. President to assume the duties of President was* _____.

Clip Art on Office Online

When appropriate clip art is not available on your computer, you can find clip art on a Web site provided by Microsoft. To access these images, log on to the Internet. In *PowerPoint*, click the **Insert Clip Art** button. Click the **Clip art on Office Online** link at the bottom of the Clip Art task pane. This link will take you to the Microsoft Clip Art and Media page. Search for clip art using an appropriate term. For example, to find images of the U.S. flag, use the term *U.S. flag.*

Select and download the images that you want to use. The images will be placed in the Clip Organizer on your computer. They will be placed in the *Downloaded Clips* folder. When you search for clip art in the usual way, these images should appear.

105C LEARN: Insert Clip Art

The title slide for your National League presentation looks much more professional with the design template applied. In this activity, you will make it even more attractive by inserting clip art.

1. Start *PowerPoint*. Open *105-National* that you created earlier.

2. Click the **Insert Clip Art** button on the Drawing toolbar. The Clip Art task pane will open as shown in Figure 14.6.

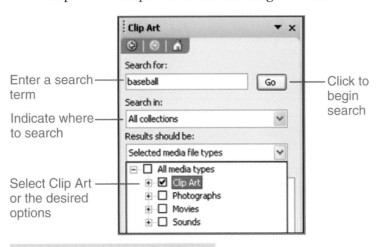

Figure 14.6 Insert Clip Art Task Pane

3. Key **baseball** in the Search for box. **All collections** should be selected in the Search in box. If this option is not selected, click the down arrow and select it.

Lesson 32   New Keys z and colon (:)

Objectives

In Lesson 32, you will:

⬎ Learn reach technique for **z** and **:** (**colon**).
⬎ Combine **z** and **:** (**colon**) with all other learned keys.

32A PRACTICE: Warmup

Key each line twice.

All letters learned
```
1 Max was a big star when he played for Jack Vasque.
```
SHIFT keys
```
2 Ramon Santos; Karl Jones; Kate Van Noy; Sue McMan;
```
Easy
```
3 Jan and Bob may work with the maid on the problem.
```

32B LEARN: New Keys z and : (colon)

Key each line twice. If time permits, rekey lines 7–9.

z *Left little* finger

: (colon) *Right little* finger +
LEFT SHIFT

SPACING TIP

Space twice after **:** used as punctuation.

Learn **z**
```
1 a z az za za|zap zap|zoo zoo|zone zone|azure azure
2 zip zip|zinc zinc|quiz quiz|zero zero|Zelda Zelda;
3 speed zone; a zigzag; a zoology quiz; puzzle size;
```
Learn **: (colon)**
```
4 ; : ;: :; :;|a:b c:d e:f g:h i:j k:l m:n o:p q:r :
5 To:  From:  Date:  Subject:  To:  Jason Kummerfeld
6 To:  Max Tobin|From:  Jerry Cole|Dear Mr. Maxwell:
```
Combine **z** and **: (colon)**
```
7 Please key these words:  amaze, seize, and zigzag.
8 Zane read:  Shift to enter : and then space twice.
9 Roz, use these headings:  City:  State:  ZIP Code:
```

4. Click two or three other designs to see how they look with your slide. Finally, click the **Pixel.pot** design sample. Your title slide should look like the one in Figure 14.4. This design is simple and allows the reader to focus on the content, rather than on a busy background.

5. Save the file as *105-National*. Close the file. Close *PowerPoint* or continue to the next activity.

Select a Design Template

1. Start *PowerPoint*. Open *104-Madison* that you created earlier.

2. Click the **Slide Design** button on the Formatting toolbar. Choose a design template for the show. Choose a simple design that will allow you to add pictures later. Click the design sample to apply it to the title slide.

3. Save the file as *105-Madison*. Close the file.

Adding Graphics to Slides

Help Words

Clip art
Find a clip

You will learn to use two types of graphics in presentations. A **graphic** is a drawn picture, a photo, or a chart. Drawing objects are graphics you draw that are part of your presentation file. For example, you might include a star or a circle graphic on a slide. A picture is a drawing or photo in a separate file that you insert into your document. Picture graphics include clip art (drawn pictures) that you will use in this chapter.

You learned to insert pictures, create graphics using AutoShapes, and create WordArt in Chapter 13. You will use the same commands and procedures to create graphics for slides. A slide with a photo, clip art, WordArt, and a star graphic is shown in Figure 14.5.

Figure 14.5 Slide with Graphics

32C PRACTICE: Key Mastery

Key each line twice. If time permits, key lines 5–6 again.

q/z

1 quiz quartz amaze quote Amazon mosque muzzle quick
2 Zane amazed us all on the quiz but quit the squad.

x/comma

3 six, box, tax, axle, next, extra, exhibit, example
4 Lexi, Rex, and Felix went to Texas to the exhibit.

v/m

5 move save moon visit imply valve most vain improve
6 Melvin, Kevin, or Matt drove the van to Las Vegas.

TECHNIQUE TIP

- Use curved, upright fingers.
- Use a steady keystroking pace.

32D PRACTICE: Key Block Paragraphs

1. Key each paragraph once. Tap ENTER only at the end of the paragraph.

2. Key a 1' timed writing on each paragraph. Use the numbers and dots above the words to determine *gwam*. Each dot indicates one additional word. For example, if you key to the beginning of *average* in line 1, you have keyed eight words.

Use MicroType Lesson 18 for additional practice.

Paragraph 1

```
        •     2     •     4     •     6     •     8     •
The space bar is used frequently.  On average,
  10    •    12    •    14    •    16    •    18    •
every fifth or sixth stroke is a space when you
  20    •    22    •    24    •    26    •    28    •
key.  If you use good techniques, you will be able
  30    •    32    •    34
to increase your speed.
```

Paragraph 2

```
        •     2     •     4     •     6     •     8     •    10
Just keep the thumb low over the space bar.  Move
        •    12    •    14    •    16    •    18    •    20
the thumb down and in quickly towards the palm of
        •    22    •    24    •    26    •    28    •
your hand to get the prized stroke you need to
  30    •    32
build top skill.
```

Lesson 105

Enhancing Slides

Objectives

In Lesson 105, you will:
- ⬎ Apply a design template.
- ⬎ Enhance the appearance of a slide with clip art.

Applying Design Templates

Help Words

Design template
Apply a design
template

If you and your classmates decided the title slide created for Lesson 104C looks a bit plain, you are exactly right. In this lesson, you will learn to make your slides more interesting. One way to make a slide more interesting is to apply a design template. A **design template** is a set of design elements that can be applied to slides. A design template includes things such as a background design, font, font size, and color scheme. Using design templates gives the slides a professional look.

105A LEARN:

Select a Design Template

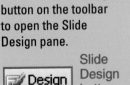

SOFTWARE TIP

Click the **Slide Design** button on the toolbar to open the Slide Design pane.

Slide Design button

1. Start *PowerPoint*. Open *104-National* that you created earlier.

2. Click the **Slide Design** button on the Formatting toolbar. Various design templates will appear in the task pane as shown in Figure 14.4. When you point to a sample design, the name of the design will display.

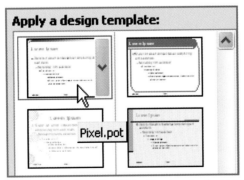

Sample designs in Slide Design task pane

Figure 14.4 Slide Design Task Pane

Title slide with Pixel design

3. Use the scroll bar to view the design templates. Choose a design that you find interesting. Click the design sample. Notice that the title slide now has the design that you clicked.

Lesson 33   New Keys CAPS LOCK and question mark (?)

Objectives

In Lesson 33, you will:

⬎ Learn reach technique for **CAPS LOCK** and **? (question mark)**.

⬎ Combine **CAPS LOCK** and **? (question mark)** with all other learned keys.

33A PRACTICE: Warmup

Key each line twice.

Alphabet

1 Jack P. Hildo may buy five quartz rings next week.

x/z

2 excess zebra fixture zoology exact zest extra zero

Easy

3 Jay is to turn to the right when the signal turns.

33B LEARN: New Keys CAPS LOCK and ? (question mark)

The **CAPS LOCK** key is used to key a series of capital letters. To key capital letters, tap the **CAPS LOCK** key. Key the letters that are to appear in capitals. Then tap the **CAPS LOCK** key again to turn off this feature.

Key each line twice. If time permits, rekey lines 7–9 on the next page.

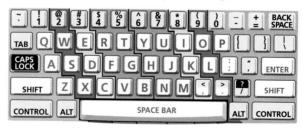

CAPS LOCK *Left little* finger

?(question mark)
LEFT SHIFT; then *right little* finger

Learn CAPS LOCK

1 Put CUBS and CARDS and METS and EXPOS on the sign.
2 OHIO STATE plays INDIANA on Wednesday or Thursday.
3 Microsoft is MSFT; Intel is INTC; Coca Cola is KO.

Learn ? (question mark)

4 ; ? ; ? ;? g?h i?j k?l m?n o?p q?r s?t u?v w?x y?z
5 Who? Who? What? What? When? When? Why? Why?
6 Ask who? Are you sure? What time? Where is she?

Create a Title Slide

The slide show that you viewed in activity 104A was for the American League. You will create a similar slide show for the National League. In this activity, you will create a title slide.

1. Start *PowerPoint*. A new blank presentation should appear. Click inside the placeholder box labeled *Click to add title*. Key **Major League Baseball** for the title of your presentation.

2. Click in the subtitle placeholder. Key **National League** in this box.

3. You will add other slides later. Now you will save the file. Click **File** on the menu bar. Click **Save as**. The Save As dialog box will appear as shown in Figure 14.3.

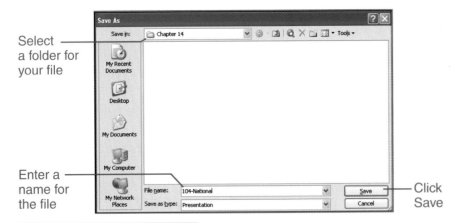

Select a folder for your file

Enter a name for the file

Click Save

Figure 14.3 Save As Dialog Box

4. In the Save in box, select the folder where you save work for this class. In the File name box, key **104-National**. Click **Save**.

5. Click the **Slide Show** button to view the slide.

CHECK POINT Working with two classmates, compare this title slide with the one from the *CD-104-American* show. Discuss which one looks better and why. Close the file.

Create a Title Slide

In this activity, you will create a title slide for the presentation about the War of 1812 that you planned earlier.

1. Start *PowerPoint*. A new blank presentation should appear. Click inside the title placeholder box. Key **James Madison and the War of 1812**.

2. Click in the subtitle placeholder. Key **By** and your name in this box.

3. Save the file using the filename *104-Madison*. Play the show to view the slide. Then close the file and *PowerPoint*.

Combine CAPS LOCK and ?

7 What symbol is DIS? What symbol is YHOO? Did he?
8 What does CPA stand for? What does CFO stand for?
9 Did your mother use NB, NE, or NEBR. for NEBRASKA?

33C PRACTICE: Key Mastery

TECHNIQUE TIP

- Use curved, upright fingers.
- Use a steady keystroking pace.

Key each line twice. If time permits, key lines 5–6 again.

z/v

1 David and Zack Valdez zipped through both quizzes.
2 Vizquel, Alvarez, Chavez, and Gonzalez have voted.

q/p

3 Quincy quickly put the papers next to the puppies.
4 Paul quickly keyed: quiz, opaque, parquet, equip.

x/c

5 Carl Drexler stood next to Connie Cox and Tex Cey.
6 Rex Cain and Max Carr paid the extra tax for Carl.

33D PRACTICE: Key Block Paragraphs

Use MicroType Lesson 19 for additional practice.

Key each paragraph once. Tap ENTER only at the end of the paragraph. Key a 1' timed writing on each paragraph. Determine your *gwam*.

Paragraph 1

```
            2        4        6        8
Before long you will key copy that is written in
10     12       14       16       18
script.  Script copy is copy that is written with
20     22       24       26       28
pen or pencil.  With practice, you will be able
  30      32       34
to key script at a rapid rate.
```

Paragraph 2

```
            2        4        6        8       10
A rough draft is a draft that is not yet in final
       12       14       16       18
form.  It is where the writer can get his or her
20     22       24       26       28
thoughts down on paper.  After the rough draft is
30     32       34       36       38
completed, it is ready to be edited.  It may take
40     42       44       46       48
several edits before it is put in final form.
```

- The **Status bar** displays helpful information such as the slide number and the design template name.
- The **Close button** closes the *PowerPoint* program.
- The **Help search box** provides quick access to program Help.
- The **task pane** displays commonly used commands for *PowerPoint*. This pane will display such things as slide layouts, slide designs, and clip art.
- The **scroll bar** allows you to move to slides by clicking and dragging the bar or clicking the arrow buttons.
- The **Previous Slide** and **Next Slide** buttons display the previous or next slide in the Slide pane.

PowerPoint Views

PowerPoint has different views that help you work in different ways. *Normal* view is shown in Figure 14.2. This view is used for creating and editing slides. *Slide Sorter* view displays thumbnails of the slides. This view is used to view several slides at a time and to sort or rearrange slides. *Slide Show* view is used to play the slide show. It displays full screen and shows the features and sounds applied to slides.

Help Words

View
  About *PowerPoint*
  views

104A LEARN:

View a PowerPoint Presentation

Before learning how to create a presentation, become familiar with *PowerPoint* by looking at a presentation that has already been created.

1. To start *PowerPoint*, click **Start**, **All Programs**, **Microsoft Office**, **Microsoft PowerPoint**.
2. Click **File** on the menu bar. Choose **Open**. In the Look in box, select the folder where your data files are stored for this class. Select *CD-104-American* from the data files. Click **Open**.
3. Look at the parts of the *PowerPoint* screen labeled in Figure 14.2. Find each part on your computer screen.
4. To play the slide show, click the **Slide Show** button in the lower left-hand corner of the *PowerPoint* window.
5. After viewing the title slide, advance to new slides by clicking the mouse or tapping the ENTER, SPACE BAR, or Right arrow keys to go to the next slide. (Tap the Left arrow key to go to a previous slide. To end a show before seeing all the slides, tap the ESC key.)
6. Click **File** on the menu bar. Choose **Close** to close this slide show. Exit *PowerPoint* (choose **File**, **Exit**) or continue to the next activity.

SOFTWARE TIP

Click the **Slide Show** button to play the show.

Slide Show button

Lesson 34 New Keys TAB and BACKSPACE

Objectives

In Lesson 34, you will:

↘ Learn reach technique for **TAB** key and **BACKSPACE**.

↘ Improve and check keying speed.

34A PRACTICE: Warmup

Key each line twice.

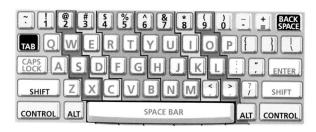

Alphabet

1 Quig just fixed prize vases he won at my key club.

CAPS LOCK

2 Find ZIP Codes for the cities in WYOMING and IOWA.

Easy

3 It may be a problem if both girls go to the docks.

gwam 1' | 1 | 2 | 3 | 4 | 5 | 6 | 7 | 8 | 9 | 10 |

34B LEARN: New Key BACKSPACE

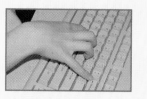

BACKSPACE *Right little* finger

The **BACKSPACE** key is used to delete characters. You should key the BACKSPACE key with your right little finger. Keep your index finger anchored to the **J** key as you tap BACKSPACE. Tap the BACKSPACE key once for each letter to be deleted. Then return the finger to the *;* key. When you hold down the BACKSPACE key, letters to the left of the insertion point will be deleted until the BACKSPACE key is released.

Use the BACKSPACE key to key the sentence as instructed.

1. Key the following.
   The delete

2. Use the BACKSPACE key to make the change shown below.
   The ~~delete~~ backspace

3. Continue keying the sentence as shown below.
   The backspace key can be

Instant Message

This symbol means to delete. ℘

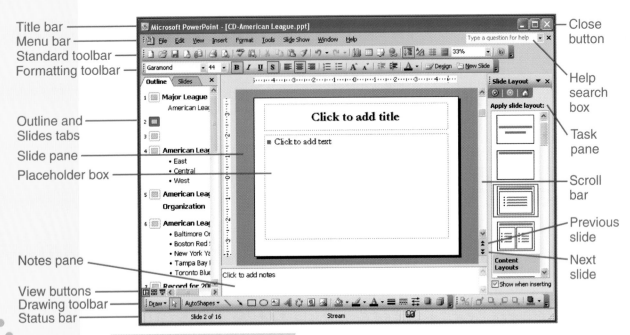

Figure 14.2 *PowerPoint* Window

Refer to Figure 14.2 as you read about the parts of the *PowerPoint* window.

- The **title bar** displays the program and filename.

- The **menu bar** displays menus that contain program commands.

- The Standard and Formatting **toolbars** provide quick access to commands.

- The **Outline tab** displays the number of each slide and the text that is included on each slide.

- The **Slides tab** displays small images of the slides that have been created.

- The **Slide pane** displays the current slide or the slide that you click on in the Slides tab.

- **Placeholders** are boxes with dotted borders that are part of most slide layouts. These boxes hold title and body text or objects such as charts, tables, and pictures.

- The **Notes pane** allows you to key notes about the slide.

- The **View buttons** allow you to view the slides in several different ways, depending on what you are doing.

- The **Drawing toolbar** contains buttons for commands that allow you to create and format drawing objects such as shapes, text boxes, and WordArt.

4. Use the BACKSPACE key to make the change shown below.
   The backspace key ~~can be~~ is

5. Continue keying the sentence as shown below.
   The backspace key is used to fix

6. Use the BACKSPACE key to make the change shown below.
   The backspace key is used to ~~fix~~ make

7. Continue keying the sentence shown below.
   The backspace key is used to make changes.

TAB *Left little* finger

Click the **Show/Hide** button on the Standard toolbar to display formatting marks. TAB appears as a right arrow (→).

 Show/Hide button

34C LEARN:

New Key TAB

The **TAB** key is used to move the insertion point to a specific location on the line. For example, TAB can be used to indent the first line of a paragraph. Word processing software has preset tabs called *default* tabs. Usually, the first default tab is set 0.5" to the right of the left margin. This tab setting is used to indent paragraphs as shown below.

Key each paragraph once. If time permits, key them again.

Tab → The tab key is used to indent blocks of copy such as these.

Tab → It should also be used for tables to arrange data quickly and neatly into columns.

Tab → Learn now to use the tab key by touch; doing so will add to your keying skill.

Tab → Tap the tab key very quickly. Begin keying the line immediately after you tap the tab key.

34D PRACTICE:

TAB and BACKSPACE

Key each paragraph once. Use the BACKSPACE key to correct errors as you key.

If time permits, key the paragraphs again.

Tab → George Washington was the first President of the United States. Before becoming President, he played a key role in helping the colonies gain their freedom.

Tab → Washington was the commander of the Continental Army. Much has been written about the winter he and his army spent at Valley Forge.

When you use the BACKSPACE key, keep the index finger anchored to the **J** key.

5. Consider the order in which the information is presented. Should any data be moved to earlier or later in the presentation? If yes, move the data.

6. Give the outline an appropriate title and format it correctly. (Review how to format an outline in Lesson 86.) Save the document as *103-Outline*. Print the outline.

 **CHECK POINT** Ask a classmate to review your outline for format and correct spelling. Make corrections if needed.

Lesson 104   Developing Visual Aids

Objectives

In Lesson 104, you will:
↘ Learn about using visual aids in a presentation.
↘ Learn to open and navigate through slides for a presentation.
↘ Create a title slide.

Data files: *CD-104-American*

Visual Aids

After creating the content for a presentation, you should consider visual aids you can use to help achieve your goals. A **visual aid** is something you show the audience to help them understand your message. A visual aid can be a sign or poster, perhaps with a drawing or photo. It can be a slide, either film or electronic. It can even be an object, such as a tool you are describing in your presentation.

Developing Slides Using PowerPoint

Microsoft PowerPoint is one of several software programs designed for developing electronic slides. These slides can be used as visual aids to help presenters communicate more effectively. In this chapter, you will use *Microsoft PowerPoint* to view a presentation and create presentations. You will find that many of the menus, commands, and toolbar buttons you learned to use in *Word* can also be used in *PowerPoint*. The *PowerPoint* opening screen appears in Figure 14.2.

34E APPLY: Check Speed

Instant Message

The **E** icon means that the difficulty level of this timed writing is *easy*.

Use MicroType Lesson 20 for additional practice.

Key each paragraph once. Double-space between paragraphs. Key a 1' timed writing on each paragraph; determine *gwam*.

 all letters used

```
          •    2    •    4    •    6    •    8    •
      How you key is just as vital as the copy you
    10   •   12   •   14   •   16   •   18   •
work from or produce.  What you put on paper is a
    20   •   22   •   24   •   26   •   28
direct result of the way in which you do the job.
          •    2    •    4    •    6    •    8    •
      If you expect to grow quickly in speed, take
    10   •   12   •   14   •   16   •   18   •
charge of your mind.  It will then tell your eyes
    20   •   22   •   24   •   26   •   28   •
and hands how to work through the maze of letters.
```

34F APPLY: Critical Thinking

Alaska

California

Chicago

Colorado

Delaware

Los Angeles

New York City

Sahara

Key the sentences below. From the list at the left, choose the word that best completes the sentence. Do not key the numbers.

1. *The largest city in the United States is* _____.
2. *The second largest city is* _____.
3. *The first state was* _____.
4. *The largest state is* _____.
5. *The largest desert in the world is the* _____.

© Getty Images/PhotoDisc

Developing the Content

Once you have considered the purpose and audience, decide on the main points you will cover in the presentation. All the main points should help you accomplish the goals of the presentation. Use the main points of your presentation to create an outline. Then add supporting points for each main point. Don't view the outline as final when you are creating it. Think of it as a starting point that can be changed or rearranged as needed.

As you develop the outline, keep in mind that a good presentation will have three parts. The **introduction** will tell listeners what your talk will be about. The **body** of the presentation will give the main and supporting points. The **conclusion** will give a summary of points you presented and tell the listeners again what action you want them to take.

For a beginning presenter, writing every word you plan to say in the presentation may be helpful. This allows you to think through every point carefully. It gives you time to express ideas in complete sentences. However, you should not read from a script when you deliver a presentation. Instead, use brief notes or the contents of slides to help you remember the points you want to discuss.

103C LEARN:

Create an Outline

You will plan content for a presentation about President James Madison and the War of 1812. The audience will be your classmates. The goal of the presentation is to inform your classmates about this important time in United States history.

1. Start *Word*. Open *CD-103-Madison* from the data files. This document contains information needed to prepare the outline.

2. Read the information. Identify five or six main points of the information.

3. Create an outline using the main points you have identified. Key the outline or copy the main points from the *CD-103-Madison* document.

4. Enter two or more supporting points under each main point. Choose only the most important information. You do not have to include every point in the document.

Reviewing | *What You Have Learned*

Answer these questions to review what you have learned in Chapter 4.

1. Describe how you should arrange your work area.

2. List five points that describe proper keying position.

3. What are the home keys for the left hand? What are the home keys for the right hand?

4. When you key, tap each key _____ with the tip of the finger, and keep your fingers _____.

5. Tap the ENTER key with your _____ finger.

6. Space _____ after a semicolon used as punctuation.

7. When keying, keep your wrist low, but not _____ on the keyboard or desk.

8. Quickly space after each word and immediately begin the next word with _____.

9. Keep your _____ on the copy as you key.

10. How many times should you space after a period within an abbreviation?

11. How many times should you space after a period following an abbreviation?

12. How many times should you space after a period at the end of a sentence?

13. To key a capital of the letter *P*, hold down the _____ key.

14. To key a capital of the letter *S*, hold down the _____ key.

15. A _____ in keyboarding is five characters.

16. The number of standard words keyed in 1' is called _____ *(gwam)*.

17. To key a series of capital letters, use the _____ key.

18. How many times should you space after a question mark at the end of a sentence?

19. When you hold down the _____ key, letters to the left of the insertion point will be deleted.

20. Word processing software has preset tabs called _____ tabs.

Supplemental activities for this chapter can be found at www.c21jr. swlearning.com.

Learning about the Audience

As you plan a presentation, you should consider the audience. The **audience** consists of the people who will listen to your talk. You need to develop a **profile** (description) of your audience.

To develop an audience profile, list some things you know about the people who will hear your talk. Answer questions such as:

- Does the audience know a lot or a little about the topic to be discussed? If they know a lot about the topic, you can skip basic information and move on to more advanced points.

- What are the ages of the people in the audience? You would not use the same words to talk to a third-grade class as you would to talk to a group of parents.

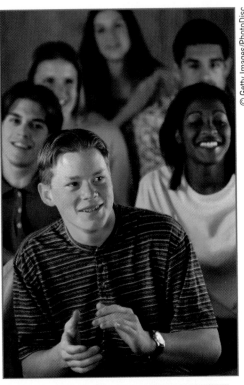

- Is the audience likely to be open to new ideas?

- Is the audience likely to resist taking the action you want them to take?

- Are the members of the audience listening by choice, or are they required to attend your talk?

Points such as these will affect how you approach your presentation.

Figure 14.1 Consider the audience when planning a presentation.

103B LEARN: Develop an Audience Profile

1. Start *Word* and open *CD-103-Profile* from the data files. Print and then close the file.

2. Read the description of a presentation and complete a profile for the audience.

TEAMWORK

Data Files

- *CD-C04-Business*
- *CD-C04-Art and Music*
- *CD-C04-Career*
- *CD-C04-Payroll*

INTERNET

↗ About Business

MARKET ECONOMY The United States has primarily a market economy. **Economy** refers to the business activities that take place in a region or country. These activities include things such as owning, producing, buying, and selling goods.

In some countries, the government owns or controls most of the country's resources. **Resources** are workers, goods such as lumber or oil, money, and things used in making products. Factories, buildings, machines, and trucks are examples of things used in making products. The government also plans the economic activities. This is an example of a centrally planned economy.

In the United States, however, most resources are owned by people or companies, not by the government. Consumers are free to choose the products they wish to buy. Companies are free to offer goods and services they think consumers want to buy. Thus, in a **market economy**, consumer buying choices determine, to a great extent, the goods and services that will be produced or offered.

The government also plays a role in the U.S. economy. The government owns or controls some of the resources. The government also passes laws or rules that affect what companies can sell. For example, drug companies must have their products approved by the U.S. Food and Drug Administration. Drugs that are not approved cannot be sold. A city government may pass rules about the type of companies that can operate in the city. For example, a company that uses dangerous chemicals might not be allowed.

1. Start *Word*. Open *CD-C04-Business* found in your data files. Work with one or two classmates. Follow the instructions provided to learn more about resources used in a market economy.

2. Discuss your answers with the class or another group of classmates.

↗ Career and Life Skills Success Builder

ART AND MUSIC VS. YOUR CAREER Have you ever wondered how studying art and music will prepare you for a future career? Studying art and music does not limit you to being a painter or a musician. The creative skills used in these classes can transfer to a wide range of careers.

Lesson 103   Planning Oral Presentations

Objectives

In Lesson 103, you will:
- ↘ Learn points to consider when planning a presentation.
- ↘ List goals for presentations.
- ↘ Create an audience profile.

Data files: *CD-103-Purpose, CD-103-Profile, CD-103-Madison*

A **presentation** is a talk or speech given to inform, persuade, and/or entertain. Good presentations do not just happen. A lot of planning and preparing for the presentation is needed. You have probably heard that "Those who fail to plan, plan to fail." This saying is particularly true with oral presentations. When planning a presentation, you need to consider the:

- Purpose of the presentation
- Audience for the presentation
- Content to present
- Visual aids, such as slides or posters, that you will use

You will learn more about the first three points to consider in this lesson. You will learn to use *Microsoft PowerPoint* to develop visual aids in the following lessons.

Determining the Purpose

Before you can plan and prepare a presentation, you must know the purpose of the presentation. You must know the goals you want to accomplish with the presentation. Do you want to inform or entertain? Do you want the people who hear the presentation to take some action? Do you want them to have different ideas or opinions after hearing the presentation? Answering questions such as these will help you determine your goals.

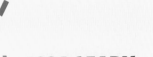

103A LEARN: Determine the Purpose of a Presentation

1. Start *Word*. Open *CD-103-Purpose* found in your data files. Print and then close the file.
2. Read the descriptions of presentations in the left column. In the right column, write one or more goals that you think the speaker would want to accomplish with the presentation.

If you like being creative, maybe you should work in film, radio, or television. Do you like to write? Maybe you will enjoy writing advertising copy, editing Web pages, or working for a newspaper. Are you artistic? Commercial artists can design anything from cereal boxes to billboard ads. Musicians can write TV jingles, teach music, or play for a symphony.

1. Is a career in art, design, music, or communications right for you? Open and print the data file *CD-C04-Art and Music.* Close the file. Read the information to see if you are interested in this career path.

2. Open the data file *CD-C04-Career.* Follow the directions given to access the Internet and research a career related to art or music.

↗ Academic Success Builder

MATH AND PERSONAL FINANCE: PAYROLL When you are paid money for a job, you need to see if the amount of money you receive for your work is correct. You may be paid an hourly amount called a *wage.* You are likely to receive a greater hourly wage if you work more than a regular workweek. A regular workweek is usually 40 hours. **Overtime** is the number of hours worked beyond 40 hours in a week. Some workers receive overtime hours and pay whenever they work more than 8 hours during one day.

Workers need to know how to compute regular pay, overtime pay rate, and overtime pay. **Regular pay** is the number of regular hours worked times your regular hourly rate. **Overtime pay** is the number of overtime hours worked times your overtime pay rate. The **overtime hourly rate** is usually given as a multiple of your regular pay rate. For example, it may be 1.5 or 2 times your regular pay rate.

The sum of the regular pay and overtime pay is called **gross pay**. You do not usually receive the gross pay. Your employer will subtract money from your gross pay for such things as taxes, insurance, and savings. The difference between gross pay and the deductions is called **net pay**. Net pay is the amount of money you actually receive for your work. You will practice math problems related to payroll in this activity.

1. Start *Word.* Open *CD-C04-Payroll* found in your data files. Print the document and then close it.

2. Complete the math activities as directed. Compare your answers with those of a classmate. Make corrections, if needed, and give your answers to your teacher.

Chapter 14

Presentations with Graphics and Multimedia

OBJECTIVES

In Chapter 14, you will:

↗ Identify the purpose of a presentation.

↗ Profile the audience for a presentation.

↗ Develop the content for a presentation.

↗ Create visual aids using *PowerPoint* software.

↗ Create electronic slides that have graphics and sound effects.

↗ Deliver a presentation.

In Chapters 10–13, you learned word processing skills to communicate by using written documents. In this chapter, you will focus on communicating orally. You will begin by learning how a good oral presentation is developed. You will identify the purpose of a presentation, profile the audience, and develop the content. You will use presentation software to create visual aids for a presentation. You will also practice delivering presentations.

© Wally McNamee/CORBIS

Chapter 5

Lessons 35-55

Number and Symbol Keys

Instant Message

To learn about U.S. Space Camp, visit the Web site at http://www.spacecamp.com.

OBJECTIVES

In Chapter 5, you will:

↗ Learn to key the number and symbol keys.

↗ Learn to use the numeric keypad to enter numbers.

↗ Practice correct and safe keying techniques.

↗ Improve keying speed and accuracy.

↗ Use basic features of *Microsoft Word*.

Numbers—how would people communicate without them? Numbers tell time, dates, distances, and amounts. They allow you to see how much you must pay for a new computer game. They let you give an exact street address. They tell you how to reach a friend on a cell phone. Numbers let you say how many miles you must travel if you plan to attend the U.S. Space Camp-Academy in Huntsville, Alabama.

Numbers let people learn and share information in a precise way. Because numbers are precise, keying them accurately is important. In this chapter, you will learn to key numbers using both the top row of the keyboard and the numeric keypad. You will also learn to key symbols found on the keyboard.

© Richard T. Nowitz/CORBIS

At the U.S. Space Camp-Academy in Huntsville, Alabama, young people learn about space travel.

UNIT 5
Computer Applications

The computer can be used to help you manage and share information in a variety of ways. Common applications are taught in this unit. In Chapter 14, you will learn to create and use electronic multimedia presentations to enhance oral presentations. In Chapter 15, you will learn to record, report, and analyze numerical information using worksheets. In Chapter 16, you will learn to organize facts and figures in a database. Finally, you will learn to create and link Web pages in Chapter 17.

The activities provided at the end of each chapter in this unit will help you: review the concepts you have learned, apply the software skills you have learned, improve your keyboarding skills, learn about business trends and issues, improve math and communication skills, and develop career-related skills.

Lesson 35　New Keys 8 and 1

Objectives
In Lesson 35, you will:
↘ Learn reach technique for **8** and **1**.
↘ Learn to key rough-draft copy.

35A PRACTICE:　Warmup

Key each line twice.

Alphabet
1 Levi Kintz packed my bag with six quarts of juice.

Spacing
2 is he | to me | and is | of us | to the | was it | it is | at my

Easy
3 A box with the forms is on the shelf by the bowls.

gwam 1' | 1 | 2 | 3 | 4 | 5 | 6 | 7 | 8 | 9 | 10 |

35B LEARN:　New Keys 8 and 1

TECHNIQUE TIP

Keep the fingers not being used to strike the number key anchored to the home keys.

Key each line twice. If time permits, rekey lines 7–9 on the next page.

Learn 8
1 k 8 k 8 | kk 88 kk 88 | k8k k8k | 88k 88k | 8k8 8k8 | k8 k8;
2 Add the figures 8 and 888. Only 8 of 88 finished.
3 Felipe lives at 88 Pine; Oscar lives at 88 Spruce.

Learn 1
4 a 1 a 1 | aa 11 aa 11 | a1a a1a | 11a 11a | 1a1 1a1 | a1 a1;
5 Key the figures 11 and 111. Read pages 11 to 111.
6 Travis keyed 1 instead of 11; I keyed 111, not 11.

8 *Right middle* finger

1 *Left little* finger

So your resume must capture the reader's attention quickly. It should show the job you are seeking, how you are qualified for the job, and how your experiences make you right for the position.

You may need to adjust your resume to relate your skills to the job you are seeking. For example, when seeking a job as an event photographer, you would highlight your photo skills. When seeking a job as an animal trainer at the zoo, you would show how you can care for animals. You will change information about the job you are seeking and how your skills match that job based on your current job search.

1. In this activity, you will create a resume to apply for a specific job. Start *Word*. Open the data file *CD-C13-Resume Instructions* found in your data files. Follow the instructions to create a resume. Save it as *C13-Resume*.

2. Remember to include a sample of your best work from this chapter in your portfolio.

⌐ Academic Success Builder

MATH AND PERSONAL FINANCE: ANALYZING NUMBERS Suppose your instructor tells you that two students in your class will be rewarded at the end of the grading period. They are:

• The student who has the highest mean quiz score during this grading period

• The student who makes the greatest percent gain from the previous grading period to this grading period

To be eligible for the reward, you must calculate your mean quiz score. The *mean score* is the arithmetic average. It is found by adding all the quiz scores and dividing by the number of quizzes. You must also find the percent of change. The *percent of change* is calculated using the following formula:

Percent of Change = (Ending Number – Beginning Number) / Beginning Number

If the ending number is greater than the beginning number, the percent is positive. This number is called the percent of increase. If the ending number is less than the beginning number, the percent of change will be negative. This number is called the percent of decrease. Ideally, your percent of change score for your quizzes will be positive!

1. Start *Word*. Open *CD-C13-Analysis* found in your data files. Print the file and then close it.

2. Complete the activities as directed to analyze numbers for quiz scores, personal savings, pay increases, and sales. Compare your answers with those of a classmate.

Combine **8** and **1**

```
7 His time was 8 min. 1 sec.; mine was 8 min. 8 sec.
8 June 18 was the day Ricardo Santo biked 181 miles.
9 Jane keyed 818 and 181; Michael keyed 811 and 118.
```

35C LEARN: Rough-Draft Copy

Study the proofreaders' marks shown at the left and in the sentences. Key each sentence DS, making all handwritten changes.

∧ = insert
= add space
⟋⟍ = transpose
ℐ = delete
⌣ = close up
≡ = capitalize
lc = lowercase

```
                          keyed copy
1  Rough draft is∧work with hand written change.
                    are               to be
2  Special marks∧used to show changes∧made.
   First lc
3  ∧Read a sentence notting changes; then key∧it.
   Next lc          that        all of
4  ∧Check to see∧if you made∧the changes correctly.
                   slightly           the
5  Read rough draft∧a bit ahead of∧keying point.
         so         you to   all
6  Doing∧this will help∧make∧the change right.
        soon                        rough
7  You∧will key often from script and∧draft.
```

✔ CHECK POINT Did you make each correction indicated?

35D PRACTICE: Balanced-Hand Sentences

TECHNIQUE TIP

Keep your fingers curved and upright.

Key each line twice.

```
1 Jane is to pay for the eight audit forms for them.
2 Rich is to go to the lake to fix the signs for us.
3 I may go to the city to do the work for the firms.
4 Profit is a problem for the big firms in the city.
5 The eight maps may aid them when they do the work.
```

gwam 30" | 2 | 4 | 6 | 8 | 10 | 12 | 14 | 16 | 18 | 20 |

Data Files

- *CD-C13-Business*
- *CD-C13-Resume Instructions*
- *CD-C13-Analysis*

⏶ About Business

BUSINESS ETHICS Ethics are standards of moral behavior. These standards or rules describe how people and companies should behave. Companies often have codes of conduct. These codes state how their employees should act in general and in certain situations. For example, employees are expected to be honest and fair in their dealings for the company. This is a general standard. Workers may not be allowed to accept gifts from customers. This is to prevent the employee from being tempted to give preferred treatment to the gift giver. This is a standard for specific behavior.

Many companies are showing a renewed interest in ethics. Companies are concerned about the image they portray. They want to be seen as honest and fair. They want customers and other companies to believe they can be trusted. Dealing fairly and honestly with others benefits the company as well as others. Honest employees are more likely to want to work for a company that they think follows ethical practices. Customers are more likely to buy from companies that they trust to treat them fairly. Other businesses are more likely to deal with a company that has a reputation for being honest.

Companies set the overall goals for how the company operates. However, individual employees are also responsible for acting in an ethical manner. An ethical employee:

- Treats coworkers and customers fairly and honestly
- Does not use company resources for personal use
- Gives a full day's work for a full day's pay
- Reports suspected wrongdoing to a company manager or government authorities

This behavior is in the best interest of the employee as well as the company. Ethical behavior helps a worker keep a job and find a new job.

1. Start *Word*. Open and print *CD-C13-Business* from your data files. Answer the questions to help you think about ethical issues.

2. Follow the directions in the data file to research cases related to business ethics.

⏶ Career and Life Skills Success Builder

DEVELOP A RESUME A *resume* is a one-page document that tells the story of you—the skills and qualifications that make you the best candidate for a job. Employers may spend as little as ten seconds glancing over a resume.

Lesson 36   New Keys 9 and 4

Objectives
In Lesson 36, you will:
↘ Learn reach technique for **9** and **4**.
↘ Learn to key from script copy.

36A PRACTICE: Warmup

Key each line twice.

Alphabet
1 By solving the tax quiz, Jud Mack won first prize.

CAPS LOCK
2 Jay used the CAPS LOCK key to key CAPITAL letters.

Easy
3 Six of the eight firms may make a bid for the bus.

gwam 1' | 1 | 2 | 3 | 4 | 5 | 6 | 7 | 8 | 9 | 10 |

36B LEARN: New Keys 9 and 4

Key each line twice. If time permits, rekey lines 7–9.

Learn 9
1 1 9 1 9|11 99 11 99|191 191|991 991|919 919|19 19;
2 My baseball number is 9; my football number is 99.
3 There were 999 racers; only 9 of the 999 finished.

Learn 4
4 f 4 f 4|ff 44 ff 44|f4f f4f|44f 44f|4f4 4f4|f4 f4;
5 He read pages 4 to 44. Janet has 44 extra points.
6 Tim added 4, 44, and 444. Jason scored 44 points.

Combine 9 and 4
7 Jay scored 44 of the 99 points; Joe had 49 points.
8 Is his average .449 or .494? Today it is at .449.
9 She keyed a 49 rather than a 94 in the number 494.

9 *Right ring* finger

4 *Left index* finger

Improve Keypad Speed

Use the *Calculator* program to complete the drills shown below.

Drill 1 Addition

A	B	C	D	E
576	902	489	766	470
+ 483	+ 110	+ 532	+ 152	+ 389
1,059	1,012	1,021	918	859

Drill 2 Subtraction

A	B	C	D	E
890	746	607	510	931
- 253	- 189	- 324	- 429	- 678
637	557	283	81	253

Drill 3 Multiplication

A	B	C	D	E
70	69	85	42	809
x 13	x 24	x 35	x 16	x 56
910	1,656	2,975	672	45,304

Drill 4 Division

A	B	C	D	E
22.92	124	211.64	134	150.86
13/298	54/6,696	39/8,254	67/8,978	36/5,431

Speed Forcing Drill

Key a 30" timed writing on each line. Your rate in gross words a minute (*gwam*) is shown below the lines.

1 He is to go with us.
2 Jay and I kept both pens.
3 Diane may work on their forms.
4 Orlando may go with me to the dock.
5 Jane and I may fix the signals for Kent.
6 Glen owns the lake land down by the big dock.
7 Helen is to go to the lake with the men to fix it.

| gwam | 30" | 2 | 4 | 6 | 8 | 10 | 12 | 14 | 16 | 18 | 20 |

36C LEARN: Handwritten Copy (Script)

Key each line twice.

1 *Script is copy that is written with pen or pencil.*
2 *Copy that is written poorly is often hard to read.*
3 *Read script a few words ahead of the keying point.*
4 *Doing so will help you produce copy free of error.*
5 *Leave proper spacing after punctuation marks, too.*
6 *With practice, you can key script at a rapid rate.*

36D PRACTICE: Keying Technique

TECHNIQUE TIP

- Reach up without moving hands away from you.
- Reach down without moving hands toward your body.

Use MicroType Numeric Keyboarding Lesson 2 for additional practice.

Key each sentence twice.

ol/lo
1 ol lo loaf cold sold hold lock loan fold long load
2 Lou told me that her local school loans old locks.

za/az
3 za az zap adz haze zany lazy jazz hazy maze pizzas
4 A zany jazz band played with pizzazz at the plaza.

ik/ki
5 ik ki kit ski kin kid kip bike kick like kiwi hike
6 The kid can hike or ride his bike to the ski lake.

ws/sw
7 ws sw was saw laws rows cows vows swam sways swing
8 Swin swims at my swim club and shows no big flaws.

ed/de
9 ed de led ode need made used side vied slide guide
10 Ned said the guide used a video film for her talk.

ju/ft
11 ju ft jug oft jet aft jug lift just soft jury loft
12 Ted said the guide used a video film for her talk.

Building Keying Skill

Warm-Up Practice

Key each line twice. If time permits, key the lines again.

Alphabet

1 Javy quickly swam the dozen extra laps before Gus.

Figure/Symbol

2 Blake's cell number was changed to (835) 109-2647.

Speed

3 The six men may work down by the lake on the dock.

gwam 1' | 1 | 2 | 3 | 4 | 5 | 6 | 7 | 8 | 9 | 10 |

Improve Keying Technique

Key each line twice.

TECHNIQUE TIP

Think, say, and key the words as words, not letter by letter.

Third row

1 it up tie yet toy put wet you true quiet were ripe

2 us we or pop top toe pew rope your pout ripe equip

3 our tar tip quip tour roar fret pretty puppy route

Home row

4 lad ask add had gas sad ash lash half sash haggles

5 has gaff asks fall glass hall lads adds gash lakes

6 dad fast wash last deals leafs dash jogs fish gasp

Bottom row

7 can zinc numb van oxen climb bronze buzz cave back

8 man exact bunk noun event vacancy convene minimize

9 verb nine burn neck zombie convict nonunion commit

gwam 1' | 1 | 2 | 3 | 4 | 5 | 6 | 7 | 8 | 9 | 10 |

Lesson 37 New Keys 0 and 5

Objectives
In Lesson 37, you will:
↘ Learn reach technique for **0** and **5**.
↘ Improve skill at keying copy with numbers.

37A PRACTICE: Warmup

Key each line twice.

Alphabet
1 Jewel amazed Vic by escaping quickly from the box.

Spacing
2 It will be fun for us to try to sing the old song.

Easy
3 He paid the men for the work they did on the dock.

gwam 1' | 1 | 2 | 3 | 4 | 5 | 6 | 7 | 8 | 9 | 10 |

37B LEARN: New Keys 0 and 5

Key each line twice. If time permits, rekey lines 7–9.

0 *Right little* finger

5 *Left index* finger

Learn 0
1 ; 0 ; 0|;; 00 ;; 00|;0; ;0;|00; 00;|0;0 0;0|0; 0;0
2 Reach from the ; to the 0. The license was 00H00.
3 Kia keyed 000 after the decimal; Tonya keyed 0000.

Learn 5
4 f 5 f 5|ff 55 ff 55|f5f f5f|55f 55f|5f5 5f5|5f 5f;
5 Ken had 55 points on the quiz; Jay also scored 55.
6 Of the 55 exhibits, only 5 won grand prize awards.

Combine 0 and 5
7 Debra told us the number was 505.550, not 550.505.
8 Lance hit .500 during July and .505 during August.
9 Orlando bought 500 pounds of grain on September 5.

9. Set the height of the text box to **0.5 inch** and the width to **2.5 inch**. Adjust the drawing canvas to be just slightly larger than the text box. Center the text box in the drawing canvas.

10. Format the text box border to be **2 ¼ point**, **single line**, **black**. For the fill color, select **blue**.

11. For the text in the box, choose these font settings: **12-point**, **bold**, **white**. Apply **Center** alignment to the text in the box.

12. Create another text box after the last line of the "Reputation and Choice" article. Key the text shown below in the text box. Use the same settings for the box and the text as for the box you created earlier.

    `Choices you make destroy or enhance your reputation.`

13. Create another text box after the last line of the first paragraph of the "Learning About People" article. Key the text shown below in the box. Use the same settings for the box and the text as for the box you created earlier.

    `Relating well to others is a major challenge.`

14. Create another text box after the last paragraph of the "Learning About People" article. Key the text shown below in the box. Use the same settings for the box and the text as for the box you created earlier.

    `Learn from experienced workers.`

15. Insert appropriate clip art near the middle of the second paragraph of the "Business Ethics" article. Use search terms such as *business* or *people working* to find clip art.

16. Set the height of the clip art to **0.7"**. Select **Tight** for the Wrapping style and **Right** for the Horizontal alignment.

17. Hyphenate the text. Review the line endings. If a word in a text box is hyphenated, insert a hard return before the word to make it all appear on the next line.

18. Insert a **Continuous** section break after the last paragraph to balance the columns.

19. Spell-check the document and proofread carefully. Correct all errors.

20. Save the document as *C13-Newsletter*. Print the document and then close it.

Supplemental activities for this chapter can be found at www.c21jr. swlearning.com.

37C PRACTICE: Keying Numbers

Key each line twice.

1 Mario dialed 594.1880 instead of dialing 495.1880.

2 He drove 598 miles one day and 410 miles the next.

3 He bowled 98, 105, and 94 the last time he bowled.

4 Orlando said the odometer read 58,940 on March 15.

5 Maryann was born in 1980; Marsha was born in 1954.

37D APPLY: Timed Writing

Use MicroType Numeric Keyboarding Lesson 3 for additional practice.

Key each paragraph once. DS between paragraphs. Key a 1' timed writing on each paragraph; determine *gwam*. Record your best timing.

E all letters used

```
        •    2    •    4    •    6    •    8    •
     You must realize by now that learning to key
   10   •   12   •   14   •   16   •   18   •
requires work.  However, you will soon be able to
   20   •   22   •   24   •   26   •   28   •
key at a higher speed than you can write just now.
        •    2    •    4    •    6    •    8    •
     You will also learn to do neater work on the
   10   •   12   •   14   •   16   •   18   •
computer than you can do by hand.  Quality work at
   20   •   22   •   24   •   26   •   28   •
higher speeds is a good goal for you to have next.
```

Applying | *What You Have Learned*

Data Files

- *CD-C13-Fitness*
- *CD-C13-Newsletter*

Flyer

1. Start *Word*. Open *CD-C13-Fitness* from your data files. Print the document and then close the file.

2. Open a new *Word* document. Using the handwritten notes (printed from *CD-C13-Fitness*), design and key a flyer. You decide the layout, but do the following:

   - Use one font with various sizes, styles, effects, and color.

   - Insert clip art related to physical fitness, exercise, or sports.

   - Use text boxes, borders, and shading.

   - Use WordArt and/or AutoShapes.

3. Spell-check the document and proofread carefully. Correct all errors.

4. Save the document as *C13-Fitness*. Print the document and then close it.

Newsletter

1. Start *Word*. Open *CD-C13-Newsletter* found in your data files.

2. Set the top, bottom, and side margins to **0.75 inch**. Set the page orientation to **Landscape**.

3. Format all text in a 12-point Times New Roman font.

4. Format the headings in a 14-point, bold, Times New Roman font. Center-align the headings.

5. Format all the paragraphs in the body for a first line indent of **0.25 inch**.

6. Insert two or three blank lines at the top of the document. Create WordArt for the text **Strategies for Success**. Position the WordArt as the main title at the top of the page and center it horizontally.

7. Format the body of the document in three columns of equal width.

8. Insert a text box between the first and second paragraphs. Key the following text in the text box:

   A bad reputation can result from one mistake.

Lesson 38   New Keys 7 and 3

Objectives

In Lesson 38, you will:
↘ Learn reach technique for **7** and **3**.
↘ Improve skill at keying copy with numbers.

38A PRACTICE: Warmup

Key each line twice.

Alphabet

1 Kevin can fix the unique jade owl as my big prize.

Punctuation

2 Al, did you use these words: vie, zeal, and aqua?

Easy

3 The small ornament on their door is an ivory duck.

gwam 1' | 1 | 2 | 3 | 4 | 5 | 6 | 7 | 8 | 9 | 10 |

38B LEARN: New Keys 7 and 3

Key each line twice. If time permits, rekey lines 7–9.

7 *Right index* finger

3 *Left middle* finger

Learn 7

1 j 7 j 7|jj 77 jj 77|j7j j7j|77j 77j|7j7 7j7|7j 7j;
2 Of the 77 computers, 7 are connected to a printer.
3 The highest score on the March 7 exam was only 77.

Learn 3

4 d 3 d 3|dd 33 dd 33|d3d d3d|33d 33d|3d3 3d3|3d 3d;
5 Dr. Ho used only 33 of the original 333 questions.
6 She scheduled quizzes on January 3 and on April 3.

Combine 7 and 3

7 Melanie scored only 73 on the July 3 exam, not 77.
8 Sandra answered 37 of the 73 questions in an hour.
9 Jessie bowled 73, Mike bowled 77, and I bowled 73.

Reviewing | *What You Have Learned*

Answer these questions to review what you have learned in Chapter 13.

1. Using a personal computer to produce high-quality printed documents is called _____ _____.

2. Desktop publishing uses _____ with text to make a good visual impression.

3. Two kinds of graphics used with *Word* are _____ _____ and _____.

4. Decorative text that you create in *Word* with predesigned font colors, shapes, and other effects is called _____.

5. A drawing object that is a container for text or graphics is a(n) _____ _____.

6. The _____ toolbar has a WordArt button and other options for working with graphics.

7. An area in which you can draw several shapes or place text boxes is called the _____ _____.

8. A drawing or photo in a separate file that you insert into your document is called a _____. One type of this graphic is called _____ _____.

9. One of the small circles or squares that appears on the border of a selected graphic and can be used to change its size is called a(n) _____ _____.

10. List five things you should do to make a flyer communicate a good visual message.

11. The ready-made shapes and lines that can be accessed from *Word's* Drawing toolbar are called _____.

12. Describe the steps used to add text to an AutoShape.

13. Search results for clip art will be displayed as miniature pictures called _____.

14. When you change the height of a graphic, you can lock the _____ _____ to make the width change automatically and prevent the graphic from being distorted.

15. Describe what *Word's* Columns feature does.

16. To balance text in two or more columns, insert a(n) _____ section break at the end of the last column.

38C PRACTICE: Tab Key

Click the Show/Hide button to see the TAB characters on your screen.

Key each line twice SS. DS between sets of lines.

```
1  5  Tab →   10  Tab →   394  Tab →   781  Tab →   908
2  9  Tab →   45  Tab →   703  Tab →   185  Tab →   731
3  4  Tab →   81  Tab →   930  Tab →   507  Tab →   405
4  7  Tab →   30  Tab →   585  Tab →   914  Tab →   341
5  3  Tab →   79  Tab →   485  Tab →   180  Tab →   789
```

38D PRACTICE: Keying Technique

Keep your wrists low, but not resting on the keyboard.

Key each line twice. Key 1' timings on lines 2, 4, and 6.

Letter response

```
1  milk milk|extra extra|pink pink|wage wage|oil oil;
2  Edward saw a deserted cat on a crate in my garage.
```

Word response

```
3  burn burn|hand hand|duck duck|rock rock|mend mend;
4  The eight signs are down by the lake by the docks.
```

Combination response

```
5  with only|they join|half safe|born free|goal rates
6  Dave sat on the airy lanai and gazed at the puppy.
```

gwam 1'| 1 | 2 | 3 | 4 | 5 | 6 | 7 | 8 | 9 | 10 |

38E APPLY: Compose Sentences

Use MicroType Numeric Keyboarding Lesson 4 for additional practice.

Key each sentence once. Use words of your choice to complete the sentences.

```
1  The name of my favorite baseball team is the
   _____ .
2  My favorite song is _____ .
3  My favorite teacher is _____ .
4  The class I enjoy the most is _____ .
5  If I had a million dollars, I would buy
   _____ .
6  The last movie I saw was _____ .
```

2. Click between words that are near the center of the Special Events paragraph. Insert clip art that is related to golf.

3. Right-click the clip art and select **Format Picture**. Click the **Size** tab. Change the height to **1 inch** and lock the aspect ratio. Click the **Layout** tab. Select the **Tight** option under Wrapping style. Select **Center** under Horizontal Alignment. Click **OK**.

4. In the Program paragraph, insert clip art related to a person speaking or to science-related topics. On the Size tab, make the graphic **1 inch** in height and lock the aspect ratio. On the Layout tab, select **Square** wrapping style. Select **Right** under Horizontal alignment.

5. Format the body text in two equal columns with a line between columns. Format the title for one column to extend across the text columns.

6. Spell-check, proofread, and correct errors. Save the document as *102-Conference*. Print and then close the document.

102E APPLY: Compose and Format a Newsletter Article

INTERNET

Instant Message

The Occupational Outlook Handbook can be found at the U.S. Bureau of Labor Standards at http://bls.gov/oco.

In this activity, you will do research and compose an article that presents information about desktop publishing careers.

1. Access the *Occupational Outlook Handbook* (OOH) on the Internet or in your school library. If using the online version, enter **desktop publisher** in the OOH Search/A-Z Index box. Read the information provided about desktop publishers.

2. Start *Word* and open a new blank document. Use the information you found to compose a newsletter article about desktop publishing careers. Include information that will persuade others to learn more about careers in or related to desktop publishing. You may want to include information about the type of work done, training and qualifications required, the job outlook, expected earnings, related occupations, and/or working conditions.

3. Arrange and format the information for an attractive newsletter that is easy to read. Use headings within the document to guide the reader. Use two or three columns and center the title over the columns. Save the document as *102-DTP*. Print the document and then close it.

Lesson 39   New Keys 6 and 2

Objectives

In Lesson 39, you will:
↘ Learn reach technique for **6** and **2**.
↘ Improve skill at keying copy with numbers.

Warmup

Key each line twice.

Alphabet
1 Wade Javey quickly found extra maps in the gazebo.

Spacing
2 am to | is an | by it | of us | an oak | is to pay | it is due

Easy
3 I am to pay the six men if they do the work right.

`gwam` 1' | 1 | 2 | 3 | 4 | 5 | 6 | 7 | 8 | 9 | 10 |

39B LEARN: New Keys 6 and 2

Key each line twice. If time permits, rekey lines 7–9.

6 *Right index* finger

2 *Left ring* finger

Learn 6
1 j 6 j 6 | jj 66 jj 66 | j6j j6j | 66j 66j | 6j6 6j6 | 6j; 6j
2 There were 66 entries. All 66 competed yesterday.
3 He said 76 trombones. I said that is not correct.

Learn 2
4 s 2 s 2 | ss 22 ss 22 | s2s s2s | 22s 22s | 2s2 2s2 | 2s; 2s
5 Of the 222 items, Charlton labeled 22 incorrectly.
6 The 22 girls may play 2 games against the 22 boys.

Combine 6 and 2
7 Monique has gone 262 miles; she has 26 more to go.
8 March 26, August 26, and October 26 are the dates.
9 Just 26 more days before Gilberto is 26 years old.

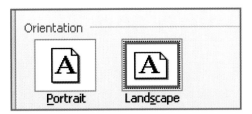

Figure 13.19 Select Landscape orientation in the Page Setup dialog box.

4. To select all the text in the document, choose **Edit**, **Select All** from the menu bar. Click the **Justify** button.

5. With the text still selected, choose **Tools**, **Language** from the menu bar. Choose **Hyphenation**. Select the **Automatically hyphenate document** option. See Figure 13.20. Click **OK**.

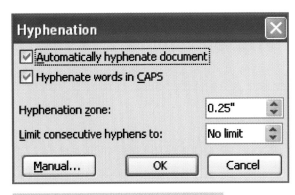

Figure 13.20 Hyphenation Dialog Box

6. Select the document title **Document Design**. Choose **Format**, **Columns** from the menu bar. Select **One** in the Presets section. Click **OK**. Apply **Center** alignment to the title. Add or delete hard returns after the title as needed so all of the columns begin on the same line. Leave one blank line after the title.

7. Save the document as *102-Design*. Print and then close the document.

CHECK POINT View the line endings in each column. Were hyphens inserted at the end of several lines? Is the document title centered over all the columns?

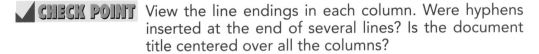

102D PRACTICE: Create a Newsletter

1. Start *Word*. Open *CD-102-Conference* found in your data files. Change the page orientation to **Landscape**.

39C PRACTICE: Keying Numbers

Key each line twice.

Straight copy

1 Jose moved from 724 Park Lane to 810 State Street.

2 Marcos was 3 minutes and 56 seconds behind Carlos.

Script

3 Call me at 195.438.9057 on Saturday, September 26.

4 The dates of the games are October 19, 20, and 23.

Rough draft

5 Mrs. kendall siad the prac tice willbe June 30.

6 Flihgt Nos. 3875 leave at 6:45 a.m. on Octobre 13.

39D APPLY: Timed Writing

Key each paragraph once. DS between paragraphs. Key a 1' timed writing on each paragraph.

 all letters used

```
        •        2    •      4    •      6    •      8
        Success does not mean the same thing to
   •       10    •      12   •      14   •      16   •      18
everyone.  For some, it means to get to the top at
   •       20    •      22   •      24   •      26   •      28
all costs:  in power, in fame, and in income.  For
   •       30    •      32   •      34   •      36   •      38
others, it means just to fulfill their basic needs
   •       40    •      42   •      44   •      46   •
or wants with as little effort as required.
            •       2    •      4    •      6    •      8    •
        Most people fall within the two extremes.  They
10   •       12   •      14   •      16   •      18   •
work quite hard to better their lives at home, at
20   •       22   •      24   •      26   •      28   •
work, and in the social world.  They realize that
30   •       32   •      34   •      36   •      38   •
success for them is not in being at the top but
   40   •       42   •      44   •      46   •      48   •
rather in trying to improve their quality of life.
```

6. If needed, switch to **Print Layout** view to see the text in columns. The text is all in the left column. To balance the text in two columns, click at the end of the last sentence. Click **Insert** on the menu bar. Choose **Break**. In the Break dialog box, choose **Continuous**. Click **OK**. The text should now be in two nearly equal columns.

7. Save the document as *102-Career Fair*. Close the document or continue to the next activity.

102B PRACTICE: ## Create a Three-Column Document

In this activity, you will change the number of columns in a document from two columns to three columns. You will also add a vertical line between the columns.

1. Start *Word*. Open *102-Career Fair* that you created earlier. Place the insertion point at the beginning of the document.

2. Choose **Format, Columns** from the menu bar. Select **Three** in the Presets section. Select the **Line between** option. See Figure 13.18 to locate the **Line between** option. Click **OK**.

3. Save the document as *102-Career Fair2*. Print and then close the document.

 **CHECK POINT** Compare your printed document with a classmate's document. If they are different, determine why. Make corrections if needed.

Page Orientation

Word documents can be designed with one of two page orientations. **Portrait orientation** places a document on the page with the short side of the paper at the top. **Landscape orientation** places a document on the page with the long side of the paper at the top. Portrait orientation is used for documents such as letters and reports. It is the default setting in *Word*. Landscape orientation may be used for wide tables, newsletters, or flyers.

102C LEARN: ## Create a Document in Landscape Orientation

1. Start *Word*. Open *CD-102-Design* found in your data files.

2. Format the document so it is arranged in three columns with vertical lines between the columns.

3. To set the page orientation, choose **File, Page Setup** from the menu bar. Click the **Margins** tab. Select **Landscape** in the Orientation section. See Figure 13.19. Click **OK**.

Lesson 40 Review

Objectives

In Lesson 40, you will:
↘ Improve your keying techniques.
↘ Increase keying speed.

40A PRACTICE: Warmup

Key each line twice. If time permits, key the lines again.

All letters learned

1 Jack viewed unique forms by the puzzled tax agent.

Shift keys

2 Keith left for San Diego, California, on Thursday.

Easy

3 Title to all of the lake land is held by the city.

`gwam` 1' | 1 | 2 | 3 | 4 | 5 | 6 | 7 | 8 | 9 | 10 |

40B PRACTICE: Keying Technique

Key each line twice. If time permits, key the lines again.

Reaches (Keep the fingers not used for reaching on home keys.)

1 bet not river cot next zebra open quite we yet you
2 Pete or Quinton will answer their seven questions.

SPACE BAR

3 an be go to at me if we no the and are did all big
4 Jo and I can get a cake on our way home from work.

Shift and number keys

5 December 15; July 24; May 30; February 6; March 7;
6 Jan and I took Monday off to go to Salt Lake City.

Number sentences

7 Jamal said 15 of the 34 team members were juniors.
8 He was born on May 26, 1987; I was born on May 30.

Spacing technique

`gwam` 30" | 2 | 4 | 6 | 8 | 10 | 12 | 14 | 16 | 18 | 20 |

Columns

Documents such as brochures and newsletters often have text in two or more columns on a page. The columns may be equal or unequal in width and length. A page may have a different number of columns. For example, a heading may be one column, and then two or more columns of text may be below it. The text within the multiple columns often uses Justify alignment and is hyphenated.

102A LEARN: Create a Two-Column Document

1. Start *Word.* Open *CD-102-Career Fair* found in your data files. This file contains handwritten notes that you will use to create a document. Print the file and then close it.

2. Open a new document in *Word.* Set the alignment to **Justify**.

3. Choose **Format, Paragraph** from the menu bar. Under **Special**, choose **First line** and enter **0.25**. This setting will automatically indent the first line of each paragraph.

4. Choose **Format, Columns** from the menu bar. Select **Two** in the Presets section of the Columns dialog box. See Figure 13.18. The **Equal column width** option should be selected. If it is not, select it. Click **OK**.

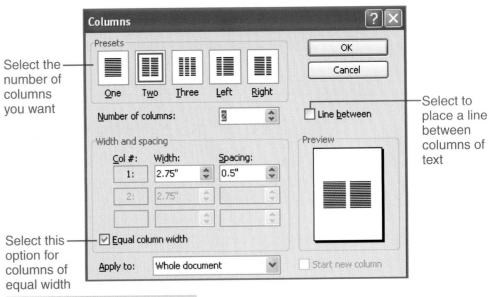

Figure 13.18 Columns Dialog Box

5. Key the text from the handwritten notes that you printed. For the title, use center alignment and bold. Leave one blank line after the title. Do not leave blank lines between paragraphs.

40C PRACTICE: Speed Forcing Drill

Key a 30" timed writing on each line. Your rate in gross words a minute (*gwam*) is shown below the lines.

TECHNIQUE TIP

Reach out with little finger and tap the ENTER key quickly. Return your finger to home key.

1 Jane left.
2 He paid for us.
3 Joel did their wash.
4 Jo may be here next week.
5 Kent went to the game with me.
6 Did the man make the signs for her?
7 Paul may be able to take the exam later.
8 Jason got a new computer before he left town.
9 Felipe was able to key six words faster this week.

| gwam 30" | 2 | 4 | 6 | 8 | 10 | 12 | 14 | 16 | 18 | 20 |

✔ **CHECK POINT** Did you keep your eyes on the copy as you keyed each line?

40D APPLY: Timed Writing

Key each paragraph once. DS between paragraphs. Key a 1' timed writing on each paragraph; determine *gwam*.

 all letters used

```
            •    2    •    4    •    6    •    8    •
      Are you one of the people who often look from
10    •    12    •    14    •    16    •    18    •
the copy to the screen and down at your hands?  If
  20    •    22    •    24    •    26    •    28    •
you are, you can be sure that you will not build a
  30    •    32    •    34    •    36    •    38    •
speed to prize.  Make eyes on copy your next goal.
            •    2    •    4    •    6    •    8    •
      When you move the eyes from the copy to check
10    •    12    •    14    •    16    •    18    •
the screen, you may lose your place and waste time
  20    •    22    •    24    •    26    •    28    •
trying to find it.  Lost time can lower your speed
  30    •    32    •    34    •    36    •    38    •
quickly and in a major way, so do not look away.
```

8. Format the text for Arial 16-point font. In the *Excel* file, click and drag to select data for **Voter Participation** (rows 1–5 in columns A and B). Click **Copy** on the toolbar. Move to the *Word* document. Click in the text box below the sentence. Click **Paste** on the toolbar. Center-align the table.

9. Close *Excel*. Save the *Word* document again using the same name, *101-Election*. Complete the Check Point and then close the document.

✔ **CHECK POINT** Ask a classmate to review your flyer and offer suggestions for improvement. Make changes as needed.

101E APPLY: Create a Course Flyer

1. Work with one or two classmates to complete this activity. Design a flyer your teacher can use to tell others about the value of this course. Review the guidelines for creating flyers on page 459. Include some of the following in your flyer:

   - The name of the course
   - The activities you enjoy
   - Important things you have learned
   - Why others should take the course
   - The computer software you use
   - How the course helps you in other courses or activities
   - WordArt, clip art, or other graphics to make the flyer attractive

2. Save the document as *101-Course Flyer*. Print the file and then close it.

Lesson 102   Multi-Column Documents

Objectives

In Lesson 102, you will:

↘ Create multicolumn newsletter articles.
↘ Insert section breaks.
↘ Change the number and format of columns.
↘ Use portrait and landscape orientations.
↘ Automatically hyphenate text.
↘ Compose and format an article about desktop publishing careers.

Data files: *CD-102-Career Fair, CD-102-Design, CD-102-Conference*

Lesson 41　New Keys / and $

Objectives
In Lesson 41, you will:
↘ Learn reach technique for / and $.
↘ Combine / and $ with other keys.

41A PRACTICE: Warmup

Key each line twice.

Alphabet
1 Jack Vasquez may work for Bill Pagel the next day.

Spacing
2 When did you see the girls go to the lake to work?

Easy
3 She owns the big dock, but they own the lake land.

gwam 1' | 1 | 2 | 3 | 4 | 5 | 6 | 7 | 8 | 9 | 10 |

41B LEARN: New Keys / and $

Key each line twice. If time permits, rekey lines 7–9.

/ Right little finger

$ Left index finger +
RIGHT SHIFT

SPACING TIP

Do not space between a figure and the / or the $ sign.

Learn / (diagonal)
1 ; / ; /|;; // // ;;|;/; /;/|/p; /p/|/;p /;p|p/; /;
2 He keyed the date as 05/17/05 instead of 05/17/06.
3 Toua added 3 3/4 and 4 1/2 and came up with 8 1/4.

Learn $ (dollar sign)
4 f $ f $|f rr $$ f rr $$|f r $ f r $|r$f r$f|$fr $f
5 $102.93 and $48.76 and $547.29 and $9.86 and $1.03
6 I owed $502.78 for February and $416.39 for March.

Combine / and $
7 Rae paid $30 for 2 1/2 lbs. I paid $15 for 1 1/4.
8 On 06/17/05 I paid $898. On 07/15/05 I paid $608.
9 The terms were 2/10, n/30 for the $594.76 he owed.

10. Change the text box size to just fit the contents. Move the text box so it is centered under the clip art. Apply a colored border or fill color to the text box if desired.

11. Save the document as *101-Laptop* and close it.

101D PRACTICE: Create an Election Results Flyer

1. Start *Word*. Open a new document.

2. Create WordArt for the text **WMS Student Government**. Place the WordArt near the top of the page as a heading for a flyer. Size it appropriately.

3. Double-click in the document about 0.5 inch under the WordArt. Click the **Insert Picture** button on the Drawing toolbar. See Figure 13.17. Look in the folder where your data files are stored. Select the file *CD-101-Results* and click **Insert**.

Insert Picture button

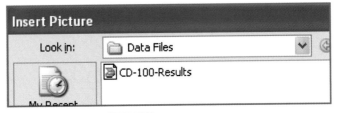

Figure 13.17 Insert Picture Dialog Box

4. Create a text box. Place the text box about 0.5 inch under the Election Results art. Key the text shown below in the text box. Save the document as *101-Election*.
   ```
   President:
   Vice President:
   Secretary:
   Treasurer:
   ```

5. Start *Excel*. Open *CD-101-Election Data* found in your data files. Look at the election results. For each office, find the name of the student who received the most votes. Key the names into the *Word* document in the text box.

6. Select the text in the text box. Change the font to Arial 28-point. Set the Line Spacing to **1.5**. Make other changes to the border or fill color for an attractive text box. Center the box under the WordArt.

7. Create another text box about 1 inch below the first box. In the text box, key:
   ```
   Thanks to all students who took part in the
   election!
   ```

41C PRACTICE: Keying Technique

Key each line twice.

Double letters

1 cook ball green puzzle pepper waffle access quarry
2 Dallas or Minnesota plays Tennessee in four weeks.

One-hand words

3 hook cart noun look agree radar pupil state hookup
4 we are|no regrets|only degree|dress up|pink garage

Shift keys

5 We had delegates from Ohio, Texas, Iowa, and Utah.
6 The New York Yankees play the New York Mets today.

41D PRACTICE: Keying Script

Key each line twice.

TECHNIQUE TIP

Keep up your pace to the end of the line. Tap ENTER quickly and begin the new line without a pause or stop.

1 Try to increase your speed on each of these lines.
2 Keying each word letter by letter takes very long.
3 Keying some of the words as words increases speed.
4 Keeping the eyes on the copy also increases speed.
5 Keep your fingers upright and curved to go faster.
6 Quickly tap the ENTER key at the end of each line.

41E APPLY: Enrichment Activity

MicroType

Use MicroType Numeric Keyboarding Lesson 7 for additional practice.

Unscramble the letters shown below to create eight words. If you have difficulty, key the letters in different orders to unscramble the words.

ghis	dtaiu
okto	sufys
eter	rapoe
eethr	slacs

SOFTWARE TIP

If desired, close the Clip Art pane by clicking the **Close** button in the upper-right corner of the pane.

6. Scroll through the results to identify clip art of a laptop computer that you want to use. Click the thumbnail to insert the clip art into your document.

7. Right-click on the clip art and select **Format Picture** from the pop-up menu. Click the **Size** tab. Enter **3** for the height. Do not change the width. Select the **Lock aspect ratio** option. See Figure 13.15. Click **OK**. Because you locked the aspect ratio, the width will change automatically as needed.

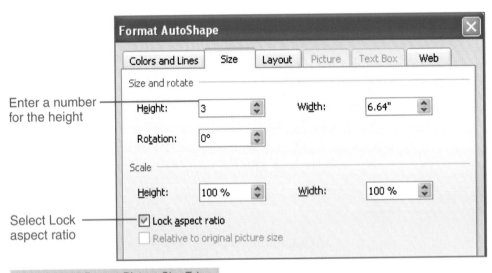

Figure 13.15 Format Picture Size Tab

8. Now you will center the picture horizontally on the page. Right-click on the clip art and select **Format Picture** from the pop-up menu. Click the **Layout** tab. Select **Center** in the Horizontal alignment section of the Format Picture dialog box. See Figure 13.16. Click **OK**.

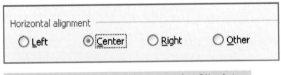

Figure 13.16 Select an Alignment for Clip Art

9. Double-click near the left margin below the clip art. Insert a text box. Set the font to Arial 24-point. Key the following text:

```
Contact: (Your Name)
Phone: 555-0134
Model: Dell Inspiron 1000
Operating System: Microsoft Windows XP Home
Price: $500
Extra Battery Included
```

Lesson 42 New Keys % and –

Objectives

In Lesson 42, you will:
↘ Learn reach technique for **%** and **–**.
↘ Combine **%** and **–** with other keys.

42A PRACTICE: Warmup

Key each line twice.

Alphabet
1 Marjax made five quick plays to win the big prize.

Figures
2 Miguel told us to add 187, 369, 420, 215, and 743.

Easy
3 It is right for the man to aid them with the sign.

gwam 1' | 1 | 2 | 3 | 4 | 5 | 6 | 7 | 8 | 9 | 10 |

42B LEARN: New Keys % and –

Key each line twice. If time permits, rekey lines 7–9.

% left index finger + RIGHT SHIFT

– Right little finger

SPACING TIP

Do not space between a figure and the % or the –.

Learn % (percent sign)
1 f % f %|ff %% ff %%|f%f f%f|%%f %%f|%8% %f%|%f; %f
2 You will give 5%, 10%, or 15% off all sales today.
3 About 45% voted yes to the increase; 55% voted no.

Learn – (hyphen)
4 ; – ; –|;; –– ;; ––|;–; ;–;|––; ––;|–;– ;–;|–;– –;
5 Rebecca rated each film 1-star, 2-star, or 3-star.
6 She has 1-, 2-, and 3-bedroom apartments for rent.

Combine % and –
7 Merely 5% of the 3-bedroom apartments were vacant.
8 The fifteen-story building is 85% to 90% occupied.
9 About 15% of the women read the up-to-date report.

Clip Art

You can insert ready-made pictures called clip art into your document. You can search a collection of clip art files provided with your software to find a file that is right for your document. If desired, you can search the Internet for clip art. You can also add your own clip art to the collection. As with other graphics, you can make changes to the clip art size and placement in your document.

Find and Insert Clip Art

1. Start *Word*. Open *CD-101-Clipart* found in your data files. Position the insertion point below the AutoShape (rounded rectangle).

2. Click the **Insert Clip Art** button on the Drawing toolbar. The **Insert Clip Art** pane opens at the right of your document. (If an Add Clips to Organizer dialog box opens, click **Later** to close it.)

3. You need to find clip art related to laptop computers. Key **laptop computer** in the Search for text box. See Figure 13.14. **All Collections** should be shown in the Search in box. If it is not, click the down arrow for the list box and choose **Everywhere**.

4. Click the down arrow for the Results should be list box and choose **Clip Art**. Click the **Go** button.

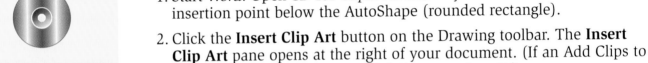

Figure 13.14 Enter a term in the Search for text box.

5. Search results will be displayed as **thumbnails** (miniature pictures) from which you can select.

Keying Technique

Keep fingers curved
and upright.

Tap ENTER quickly and
begin the new line
without a pause or stop.

Key each line twice.

Double letters

```
1 little mall three buffet root quizzed mammal grass
2 Barrett will go off to Mississippi in three weeks.
```

Balanced hands

```
3 worn keys paid name their handy laugh sight island
4 Dixie may visit the big chapel by the dismal lake.
```

Shift keys

```
5 St. Paul, MN|San Diego, CA|Las Vegas, NV|New York,
6 Dr. Chi was in Boise, Idaho, on Monday and Friday.
```

gwam 15" | 4 | 8 | 12 | 16 | 20 | 24 | 28 | 32 | 36 | 40 |

| 42D APPLY:

Timed Writing

Key each paragraph once. Key two 1' timed writings on each paragraph.

 All letters used

```
        •    2    •    4    •    6    •    8    •
     It is okay to try and try again if your first
  10   •   12    •   14    •   16    •   18    •
efforts do not bring the correct results.  If you
  20   •   22    •   24    •   26    •   28    •
try but fail again and again, however, it is foolish
30   •   32    •   34    •   36    •   38    •
to plug along in the very same manner.  Rather,
  40   •   42    •   44    •   46    •   48    •
experiment with another way to accomplish the task
  50   •   52    •   54    •   56    •   58    •
that may bring the skill or knowledge you seek.
        •    2    •    4    •    6    •    8    •
     If your first attempts do not yield success,
  10   •   12    •   14    •   16    •   18    •
do not quit and merely let it go at that.  Instead,
  20   •   22    •   24    •   26    •   28    •
begin again in a better way to finish the work or
30   •   32    •   34    •   36    •   38    •
develop more insight into your difficulty.  If you
  40   •   42    •   44    •   46    •   48    •
recognize why you must do more than just try, try
  50   •   52    •   54    •   56    •   58    •   60
again, you will work with purpose to achieve success.
```

Use MicroType Numeric
Keyboarding Lesson 8 for
additional practice.

101A LEARN: Create an AutoShape

In this activity, you will create the AutoShape shown in Figure 13.13. You will set the size for the shape, select a border width, apply a fill color, and add text to the shape.

1. Start *Word*. Open a new document. Click the **AutoShapes** button on the Drawing toolbar. See Figure 13.13 on page 461. Click **Basic Shapes**. Select the cross shape in row 3.

2. A drawing canvas is inserted. Click in the drawing canvas and drag across and down to create the shape. Release the mouse.

3. Right-click on the shape and select **Format AutoShape** from the pop-up menu. Click the **Size** tab. Enter **1.1** for the height and **1.5** for the width. Click **OK**.

4. Click the shape to select it. Click the **Line Style** button on the Drawing toolbar and select **2 ¼ point (pt)**. Click the **Fill Color** button and select **red**.

5. Right-click on the shape. Select **Add Text** from the pop-up menu. Key **First Aid Station** on two lines as shown in Figure 13.13. Select the text on the shape. Change the font to Arial 14-point. Select **Center** alignment. Select **white** for the font color.

6. Save the file as *101-First Aid*. Complete the Check Point below and then close the file.

 Does your graphic look like the one in Figure 13.13? If not, follow the steps again to create the graphic.

101B PRACTICE: Create an AutoShape

1. Start *Word*. Open a new document. Access the AutoShapes. Select the **Stars and Banners** submenu and choose the **5-Point Star** shape.

2. Set the size for the star so it is **5 inches** tall by **5 inches** wide. Click and drag the shape to move it so it appears centered vertically and horizontally on the page.

3. Add this text so it appears to be centered within the star: **Be a Star!** Use a font, font size, and font color of your choice. Use shading and a border that you choose.

4. Save the file as *101-Star*. Complete the Check Point and then close the file.

Lesson 43   New Keys # and &

Objectives
In Lesson 43, you will:
↘ Learn reach technique for # and &.
↘ Combine # and & with other keys.

43A PRACTICE: Warmup

Key each line twice.

Alphabet
1 Nate will vex the judge if he backs my quiz group.

Figures
2 See Fig. 19 and 20 on page 48 or Fig. 37 on p. 56.

Easy
3 The six girls in the sorority may pay for the bus.

gwam 1' | 1 | 2 | 3 | 4 | 5 | 6 | 7 | 8 | 9 | 10 |

43B LEARN: New Keys # and &

SPACING TIP

Do not space between # and a figure. Space once before and after & used to join names.

*Left middle* finger + RIGHT SHIFT

& *Right index* finger + LEFT SHIFT

Key each line twice. If time permits, rekey lines 7–9.

Learn # (number/pounds)
1 d E # d E # | d # d # | d#d d#d | #d3# #d3# | D e #; D e #
2 Orders #673, #677, and #679 still need to be done.
3 Checks #841, #842, and #845 are still outstanding.

Learn & (ampersand)
4 j U & j U & | j & j & | j&j j&j | &j7& &j7& | J u &; J u &
5 Sanchez & Johnson; Barns & Kennedy; Scott & Fitzer
6 I went to the law firm of Matsui & Alou on Friday.

Combine # and &
7 Purchase orders #824 and #901 were for Dunn & Cey.
8 We ordered 30# of #298 grass seed for G & G Grass.
9 Check #38 was from Brown & Smith, not Cray & Retz.

Lesson 101   AutoShapes and Clip Art

Objectives

In Lesson 101, you will:

- ⇘ Insert and format AutoShapes.
- ⇘ Add text to an AutoShape.
- ⇘ Insert and format clip art.
- ⇘ Create a flyer.
- ⇘ Copy and paste data from an *Excel* worksheet into a *Word* document.

Data files: *CD-101-Clipart, CD-101-Results, CD-101-Election Data*

AutoShapes

AutoShape
Add a shape

AutoShapes are ready-made shapes and a variety of lines that are available from the Drawing toolbar. Some shapes, such as lines, rectangles, and ovals, have their own separate buttons on the Drawing toolbar. Other shapes are options you can select from the AutoShapes pop-up menu. AutoShapes can also be accessed from the Insert, Picture menu.

Figure 13.13 shows the shapes that are available for the Basic Shapes option on the AutoShapes menu. The size, color, border thickness, and fill color of the AutoShape can be changed. Text can placed on some of the shapes.

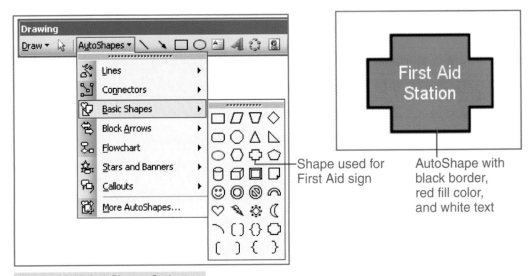

Figure 13.13 AutoShapes Options

Speed Forcing Drill

TECHNIQUE TIP

Quickly tap ENTER at the end of each line and immediately begin the next line.

Key two 20" timed writings on each line.

1 Dick may lend us the map.
2 The firm kept half of the men.
3 Lana may go to the lake with Helen.
4 If the city pays, Elena may do the work.
5 Vivian may do the problems for the six girls.
6 Hal may go with me to make the signs for the city.

| gwam 20" | 3 | 6 | 9 | 12 | 15 | 18 | 21 | 24 | 27 | 30 |

43D APPLY:

Timed Writing

Key each paragraph once. DS between paragraphs. Key a 1' timed writing on each paragraph. Key a 2' timed writing on paragraphs 1–2 combined.

 all letters used

| | gwam | 1' | 2' |

Who was Shakespeare? Few would question that   9   5
he was the greatest individual, or at least one of 19 10
the greatest individuals, to ever write a play. 29 15
His works have endured the test of time. Produc- 39 19
tions of his plays continue to take place on the 49 24
stages of theaters all over the world. Shakespeare 59 30
was an expert at creating comedies and tragedies, 69 35
both of which often leave the audience in tears. 79 39

Few of those who put pen to paper have been   9 44
as successful at creating such prized images for 19 49
their readers as Shakespeare. Each character he 28 54
created has a life of its own. It is entirely 38 58
possible that more middle school and high school 48 63
students know about the tragedy that Romeo and 57 68
Juliet experienced than know about the one that 67 73
took place at Pearl Harbor. 72 75

| gwam 1' | 1 | 2 | 3 | 4 | 5 | 6 | 7 | 8 | 9 | 10 |
| 2' | | 1 | | 2 | | 3 | | 4 | | 5 | |

Use MicroType Numeric Keyboarding Lesson 9 for additional practice.

100C APPLY: Create Flyer

In this activity you will copy and paste a text box. Then you will edit the text box to include new text. You will also create WordArt.

1. Start *Word*. Open the file *100-WMS2* that you created earlier.

2. Click the text box border to select it. Click **Copy** on the Formatting toolbar. Click inside the drawing canvas on a blank area to the right of the text box. Click **Paste** on the Formatting toolbar.

3. Drag the text box to the upper-right corner of the drawing canvas. Select the text in the text box. Key the text below in the box to replace the old text.

Why Join?

Learn Computers
Explore Careers
Be a Leader
Compete
Contribute
Serve
Have Fun

4. Insert **WMSCC Wants You!** as WordArt that matches the style and color of the other WordArt on the flyer. Make the WordArt graphic about 5 inches wide by 1 inch high. Place it about 1 inch below the text boxes. Click and drag the WordArt to center it horizontally.

5. Insert a text box with the same formatting as the boxes you created earlier. Place the text box about 1 inch below the WordArt. Make the text box about 6 inches wide. Key the text below in the box.

   For more information, contact Mrs. Keller in Room 303 or come to the informational meeting on Tuesday, September 14, in the Computer Technology Room 210.

6. Use an Arial Rounded MT Bold, 14-point font. Left-align the text. Resize the height of the box, if needed, so it just fits the contents.

7. Use Print Preview to check the layout of your flyer. If needed, move the graphics to create a balanced look. Experiment with adding shadows to the text boxes, if desired, as described in the Software Tip.

8. Save the document as *100-Flyer*. Print and then close the document.

SOFTWARE TIP

You can add a shadow effect to a text box or other graphic. To do so, select the graphic. Then click the **Shadow Style** button on the Drawing toolbar.

Shadow Style button

Lesson 44   New Keys (and)

Objectives
In Lesson 44, you will:
⬂ Learn reach technique for (and).
⬂ Combine (and) with other keys.

44A PRACTICE: Warmup

Key each line twice.

Alphabet
1 Wusov amazed them by jumping quickly from the box.

Figures
2 The addresses were 1847 Oak, 203 Joy and 596 Pine.

Easy
3 Vivian may handle all the forms for the big firms.

gwam 1' | 1 | 2 | 3 | 4 | 5 | 6 | 7 | 8 | 9 | 10 |

44B LEARN: New Keys (and)

SPACING TIP
Do not space between ( ) and the words they enclose.

(*Right ring* finger + LEFT SHIFT

) *Right little* finger + LEFT SHIFT

Key each line twice. If time permits, rekey lines 7–9.

Learn ((left parenthesis)
1 l o (l o ((|l (l ((|(l (1|1(o(1(o(|19(19(|(l(o(
2 (1, (2, (3, (4, (5, (6, (7, (8, (9, (10, (11, (12,
3 The shift of 9 is (. Use the l finger to key (9(.

Learn) (right parenthesis)
4 ; p) ; p)|;) ;)|););|;)p) ;)p)|;0) ;0)|);) p)
5 1), 2), 3), 4), 5), 6), 7), 8), 9), 10), 11), 12),
6 The shift of 0 is). Use the ; finger to key)0).

Combine (and)
7 He keyed two numbers (2 and 4) and one letter (Z).
8 Juan (Cox) and Stan (Katz) played the entire game.
9 The order (#397) was shipped last Tuesday (May 1).

> The West Middle School Computer Club meets the third
> Tuesday of each month. The meetings begin right
> after school ends. They last about 1 hour. All
> students are invited to join.

3. Format the text using a 16-point, Arial Rounded MT Bold font. Use a dark blue color for the font that matches the WordArt color. Resize the text box, making it longer so it fits its contents. Center-align the text in the box.

4. Format the box to have a 3-point (pt), single-line border. To change the border color, click the down arrow on the **Line Color** button. Select **Blue** for the line color. Apply **Gold** fill color in the box.

5. Save the document as *100-WMS2* and close the file.

Guidelines for Flyers

A **flyer** is an announcement or advertisement usually intended for wide distribution. A flyer is usually one page with large text and graphics. People create flyers for many purposes. They are used to announce activities in school or your community. Flyers may tell people how to register for a soccer, football, or baseball team. They may provide information about a school meeting or party. People use flyers to announce yard sales, apartment rentals, or items for sale. You may make flyers to ask for help in finding a lost pet or piece of jewelry.

When you design a flyer, make sure you create a strong visual message. The flyer should:

- Be colorful so it attracts the attention of those seeing it

- Have ample white space so it is easy to read

- Use pictures that relate to the subject of the flyer

- Use all capital letters sparingly because they are difficult to read

- Use fonts that are easy to read

- Use only one or two fonts (You can use bold, italic, and different sizes to vary the appearance.)

Flyers do not follow a standard format like letters and reports do. You can be creative when designing and laying out the various parts of the flyer. Always try to make your flyer send an effective visual message. It should persuade the readers to take the action you desire.

44C PRACTICE: Keying Numbers

Key each line twice.

1 My next games are on May 19 and 20.
2 Beth spent $378,465 on the project.
3 Helen paid $4,378 for 150 shares of USB.
4 Johan paid $8,692 for 100 shares of IBM.
5 The dates were June 18, June 30, and July 27.
6 Gomez was hitting .459 on Thursday, April 26.

44D APPLY: Timed Writing

Key each paragraph once. Key a 1' timing on each paragraph. Key two 2' timings on the paragraphs. Determine *gwam* on each.

 all letters used

	gwam	1'	2'

The Bill of Rights includes the changes to the Constitution that deal with human rights of all people. The changes or amendments were to improve and correct the original document. They were made to assure the quality of life and to protect the rights of all citizens.

	1'	2'
	9	4
	18	9
	28	14
	37	19
	47	23
	54	27

One of the changes provides for the right to religious choice, free speech, and free press. Another addresses the right to keep and bear fire-arms. Another deals with the rights of the people with regard to unreasonable search and seizure of person or property. Two others deal with the right to an immediate and public trial by a jury and the prevention of excessive bail and fines.

	1'	2'
	9	31
	19	36
	29	41
	39	46
	48	51
	58	56
	68	61
	77	66

gwam 1'	1	2	3	4	5	6	7	8	9	10
2'		1		2		3		4		5

Use MicroType Numeric Keyboarding Lesson 10 for additional practice.

44E APPLY: Enrichment Activity

1. Search the Internet with a classmate to learn more about the Bill of Rights. You can find information at the U.S. National Archives Web site at http://www.archives.gov.

2. Compose a paragraph or two about what you learn from the Internet search. Tell what the Bill of Rights is, when it was ratified, and its main purpose. Tell how many amendments were in the original Bill of Rights. Print a copy of these amendments to attach to your paragraphs.

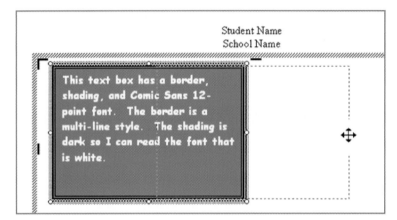

Figure 13.11 Click and drag to move a text box.

10. Now you need to change the size of the drawing canvas. Click and drag sizing handles on the drawing canvas until it fits closely around the text box. Your document should look similar to Figure 13.12.

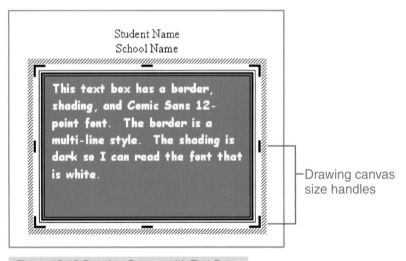

Drawing canvas size handles

Figure 13.12 Drawing Canvas with Text Box

11. Save the document as *100-Text Box*. Close the document.

100B PRACTICE: Create a Text Box

1. Start *Word*. Open the file *99-WMS* that you created earlier.

2. Double-click near the left margin about 1 inch below the WordArt. Insert a text box at the upper-left corner of the drawing canvas. Make the box about 2.5 inches wide by 2.5 inches tall. Key the text on the next page in the box.

Lesson 45 New Keys ' and "

Objectives
In Lesson 45, you will:
- ⬇ Learn reach technique for ' and ".
- ⬇ Combine ' and " with other keys.

45A PRACTICE: Warmup

Key each line twice.

Alphabet
1 Zeb or Jack Gore explained why seven of them quit.

Figures
2 Felipe wrote Check Numbers 268, 297, 304, and 315.

Easy
3 A neighbor paid the men to fix the bicycle for us.

45B LEARN: New Keys ' and "

' *Right little* finger

" *Right little* finger + LEFT SHIFT

Instant Message

On your screen, apostrophes and/or quotation marks may look different from those shown in these lines. Even if they look different, the marks serve the same purpose.

Key each line twice. If time permits, rekey lines 7–9.

Learn ' (apostrophe)
1 ; ' ; ' | ;; '' ;; '' | ;'; ;';| 'p' 'p'| '0' '0' | '9' '9
2 isn't, aren't, can't, don't, you're, what's, let's
3 Isn't the rock 'n' roll troupe performing tonight?

Learn " (quotation mark)
4 ; " ; " | ;; "" ;; "" | ;"; ;";| "p" "p"| "0" "0" | "9" "9
5 Tom said, "I can fix it." Janet said, "So can I."
6 I think the theme for "2005" was "New Beginnings."

Combine ' and "
7 "If it is Pedro's," he said, "I'll ask to use it."
8 I used the contractions "wouldn't" and "couldn't."
9 I said, "Do I use 's or s'?" He replied "Use 's."

Line Style button
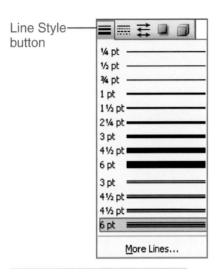

Figure 13.9 Line Style Options

8. You can resize the text box so its height matches its contents. To do so, you drag a sizing handle. A **sizing handle** is one of the small circles or squares that appears on the border of a selected graphic. See Figure 13.10. Click the bottom-center sizing handle on the text box. Drag the border of the box up near the last line of text.

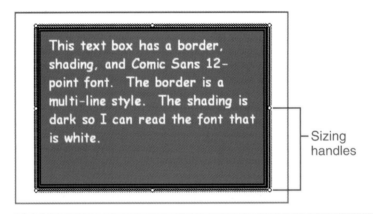

This text box has a border, shading, and Comic Sans 12-point font. The border is a multi-line style. The shading is dark so I can read the font that is white.

Sizing handles

Figure 13.10 A selected graphic object has sizing handles on its borders.

9. You can move the text box to a different position in the drawing canvas. Point to the text box border. When the cursor changes to a four-sided arrow, click and drag the text box so it appears to be centered horizontally and is below the school name. See Figure 13.11.

Keying Technique

TECHNIQUE TIP

Use a down-and-in spacing motion.

Key each line twice.

Letter response

```
1 acres onion bread puppy trade jump saved oil faces
2 are we|my best|minimum tax|are graded|best regards
3 Carter ate a plump plum tart in a cafe on a barge.
```

Word response

```
4 problem right eight bugle shake world cubic mangle
5 is the|eight girls|go to the|if they are|go to the
6 The key is to make the right sign for all of them.
```

Combination response

```
7 box base dusk milk half secret kept best make jump
8 refer to|the average|the award|city tax|big garage
9 Carter and Edward saw the bread and ate all of it.
```

 gwam 20" | 3 | 6 | 9 | 12 | 15 | 18 | 21 | 24 | 27 | 30 |

45D APPLY:

Build Speed

 **MicroType**

Use MicroType Numeric Keyboarding Lesson 11 for additional practice.

1. Turn to 44D, page 163. Key the two paragraphs.

2. Take two 1' timings on each paragraph. Try to increase your speed by two words per minute on each timing. Take two 2' timings on paragraphs 1 and 2 combined.

Ergonomics

Ergonomics is the study of how a person's work environment and tools affect the person. For example, suppose you had to sit and key for hours in a chair that did not allow you to sit up properly. You would become tired and your back or neck would probably ache. If you used this chair every day, you might develop serious back or neck injuries.

By paying attention to ergonomics, people can work more safely. Follow these guidelines to use computers and related equipment safely.

- Do not unplug equipment by pulling on the cord.
- Do not stretch cords across an aisle where someone might trip over them.
- Do not touch frayed electrical cords. Report them to your teacher.
- Keep the area open around the air vents on equipment.
- Adjust the angle of the monitor for comfortable viewing and to reduce glare.
- Grip a mouse or digital pen firmly, but not too tightly.
- Do not put fingers, pencils, pens, paper clips, etc., in disk drives.

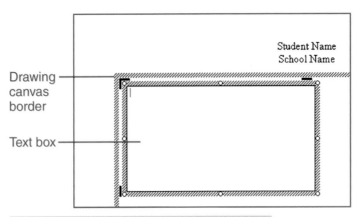

Figure 13.7 Text Box Inside the Drawing Canvas

4. The blinking cursor indicates where text will be inserted when you begin keying. Key the following text in the text box. The text will wrap automatically to the next line until you tap ENTER.

   `This text box has a border, shading, and Comic Sans 12-point font.  The border is a multi-line style. The shading is dark so I can read the font that is white.`

5. The text box should still be selected (with the border and handles displayed). Click the **Fill Color** arrow and select a dark blue-gray color.

6. To format the text, select the text in the text box. Select **Comic Sans** for the font. Select **12** for the font size. Select **Bold**. Click the down arrow on the **Font Color** button on the Drawing toolbar. Select **White** from the palette. See Figure 13.8. Your text box should look like Figure 13.8.

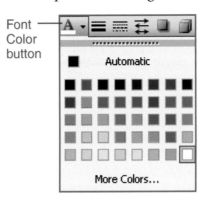

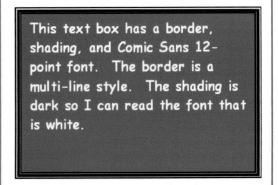

Figure 13.8 Text Box with Dark Shading and White Text

7. To format the border of the text box, select the text box. Click the **Line Style** button on the **Drawing** toolbar. Select the **6-point (pt)**, multiple-line border as shown in Figure 13.9.

Lesson 46   New Keys _ and *

Objectives

In Lesson 46, you will:
↘ Learn reach technique for _ and *.
↘ Combine _ and * with other keys.

46A PRACTICE: Warmup

Key each line twice. If time permits, key the lines again.

Alphabet
1 Jake Win placed first by solving the complex quiz.

Figures
2 The June 15 quiz covered pages 289 and 307 to 426.

Easy
3 The signs by the downtown spa may work for us too.

gwam 1' | 1 | 2 | 3 | 4 | 5 | 6 | 7 | 8 | 9 | 10 |

46B LEARN: New Keys _ and *

Key each line twice. If time permits, rekey lines 7–9.

Learn _ (underline)
1 ; _ ;_|;; __ ;; __|_; ;_;|:_: :_:|_and_ _and_|_;_:
2 1_ 2_ 3_ 4_ 5_ 6_ 7_ 8_ 9_ 10_ 11_ 12_ 13_ 14_ 15_
3 Street Address: _____ City: _____

Learn * (asterisk)
4 k * k *|*K* *K*|k I * k I *|ki* ki*|*k; *k;|*.* *.
5 *abc* *def* *ghi* *jkl* *mno* *pqr* *stu* *vwx yz*
6 Use *(s) in place of unprintable words *********.

Combine _ and *
7 *Cody keyed ___-__-____ for them to key their SS#.
8 Key 6 x 8 equals ___ rather than 6 * 8 equals ___.
9 Jack said, "This symbol (*) is called an _____."

_ Right little finger +
LEFT SHIFT

* Right middle finger +
LEFT SHIFT

Lesson 100   Text Boxes and Flyers

Objectives

In Lesson 100, you will:
- ↘ Create text boxes in *Word*.
- ↘ Format, copy, and edit text boxes.
- ↘ Study guidelines for creating flyers.
- ↘ Create a flyer.

Text Boxes

A **text box** is a drawing object that can hold text or graphics. Text boxes are used to call the reader's attention to specific text or a graphic. They are also used to position several blocks of text on a page. The text box can be moved or made larger or smaller. The text box may have borders and/or shading. Also, the text within the box may be formatted in different ways. A drawing canvas will appear when you insert a text box. In this chapter, text boxes will be placed on the canvas. An example of a text box that has a multiple-line border, shading, and a colored font is shown in Figure 13.6.

> This is a text box that has a border and shading. The text is center aligned. The font is Verdana, bold, 14 point.

Figure 13.6 Text Box Created in *Word*

100A LEARN: Create a Text Box

1. Start *Word*. Open a new document. Select **Center** alignment. Key your name on line 1 and your school name on line 2. Tap ENTER to create a new line.

2. Click the **Text Box** button on the Drawing toolbar. A drawing canvas will appear below your school name.

3. Move the cursor to inside the upper-left corner of the canvas. It will change to a cross. Click and drag to the right and then down until the text box you are drawing is about 3 inches wide and 2 inches tall. Release the mouse button.

46C PRACTICE: Keying Numbers

Use MicroType Numeric Keyboarding Lesson 12 for additional practice.

Key each line twice.

```
1 I was 13 years old in 2005, not 14.
2 Only 98 of the 1,367 kids finished.
3 My phone number was changed to 175-8369.
4 I took 420 feet of pipe for the project.
5 Mr. Dean ordered 140 computers on October 25.
6 He received the bill for $136,786 on April 9.
```

gwam 20" | 3 | 6 | 9 | 12 | 15 | 18 | 21 | 24 | 27 |

46D APPLY: Build Speed

1. Turn to 43D, page 161. Key the two paragraphs.

2. Take two 1' timings on each paragraph. Try to increase your speed by two words per minute on each timing. Take two 2' timings on paragraphs 1 and 2 combined.

Repetitive Stress Injury

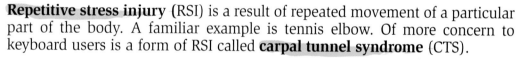

Using proper keying position helps avoid CTS.

Repetitive stress injury (RSI) is a result of repeated movement of a particular part of the body. A familiar example is tennis elbow. Of more concern to keyboard users is a form of RSI called **carpal tunnel syndrome** (CTS).

CTS develops gradually. CTS can cause numbness or pain in the hand, wrist, elbow, or shoulder. It can also make gripping objects difficult. Computer users can reduce the risk of developing CTS by taking these precautions:

- Position the keyboard directly in front of your chair. Keep the front edge of the keyboard even with the edge of the desk.

- Place the monitor about 18 to 24 inches from your eyes, with the top edge of the display screen at eye level.

- Use a proper chair and sit up correctly. Keep your feet flat on the floor while you are keying. Sit erect and as far back in the seat as possible.

- Keep your arms near the side of your body in a relaxed position. Your wrists should be in a flat, neutral position. They should not rest on the desk.

- Keep your fingers curved and upright over the home keys. Tap each key lightly, using the fingertip.

- When using a digital pen, do not use too much pressure when writing. Use good posture when writing as well as when keying.

- Take short rest breaks. Exercise and stretch your neck, shoulders, arms, wrists, and fingers before beginning to key each day and often during keying.

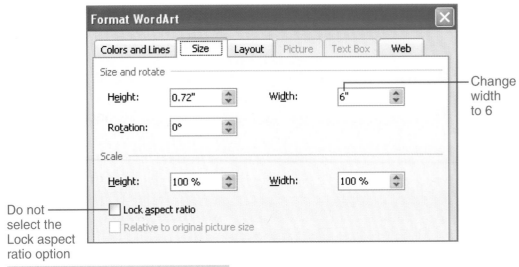

Change width to 6

Do not select the Lock aspect ratio option

Figure 13.5 Format WordArt Dialog Box

8. To deselect the graphic, double-click anywhere on the page outside the graphic. Save the document as *99-September*. Complete the Check Point and then close the file.

 **CHECK POINT** Compare your graphic with that of a classmate. If there are any differences, discuss the reason for the differences and then make any changes that may be needed.

99B PRACTICE: Create WordArt

1. Start *Word*. Open a new document. Change all margins to **1 inch**.

2. Click the **WordArt** button on the Drawing toolbar. Select a WordArt style that places the text horizontally (not vertically) on the page. Key **WMS Computer Club** in the dialog box for your WordArt text.

3. Change the size of the graphic to **1 inch** tall by **6 inches** wide. Horizontally center the WordArt graphic.

4. Change the graphic color. Select **Dark Blue** for the Fill Color and the Line Color.

5. Save the document as *99-WMS* and close it. You will update this document in a later lesson to create a flyer.

Lesson 47 New Keys @ and +

Objectives

In Lesson 47, you will:
⬎ Learn reach technique for @ and +.
⬎ Combine @ and + with other keys.

47A PRACTICE: Warmup

Key each line twice.

Alphabet
1 Jorge F. Bevins quickly swam the dozen extra laps.
Figures
2 Only 2,953 of the 6,780 men attended on August 14.
Easy
3 The men may pay for half of the maps for the city.

47B LEARN: New Keys @ and +

Key each line twice. If time permits, rekey lines 7–9.

@ *Left ring* finger +
RIGHT SHIFT

+ *Right little* finger +
LEFT SHIFT

Learn @ (at sign)
1 s @ s @|ss @@ ss @@|s@s s@s|@s@ @s@|5 @ 25 5 @ 25;
2 yorkmb@nyu.edu, smithj@charter.net, jonesjc@ku.edu
3 50 shares of PEP @ $51.25; 25 shares of INTC @ $27

Learn + (plus)
4 ; + ; +|;; ++ ;; ++| 1 + 2 + 5 + 8|1 + 12 + 5 + 18
5 If you add 30 + 15 + 17 + 8 + 19, you will get 89.
6 Tom and Jay added 6 + 17 + 39 and came up with 62.

Combine @ and +
7 The figures include 16 @ .69 + 10 @ .38 + 7 @ .49.
8 Jonathan added $1.20 (6 @ .20) + $5.80 (4 @ 1.45).
9 Jay's check was for 5 hrs. @ 5.00 + 6 hrs. @ 7.50.

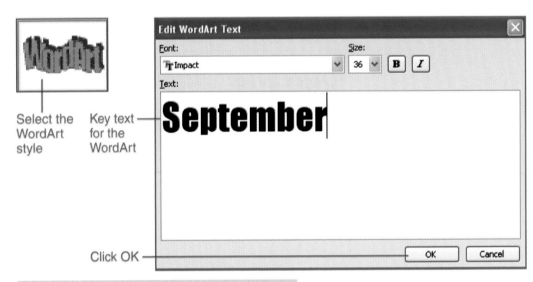

Select the WordArt style

Key text for the WordArt

Click OK

Figure 13.3 Select a WordArt style and key the text.

5. To center the WordArt horizontally, select the graphic by clicking on it. Click the **Center** alignment button on the Formatting toolbar.

6. You can change the color of the WordArt graphic. The graphic should still be selected. Click the arrow on the **Fill Color** button to open a color palette as shown in Figure 13.4. Select a red color. The text color will be changed as shown in Figure 13.4.

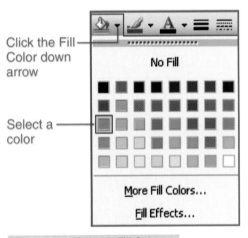

Click the Fill Color down arrow

Select a color

Figure 13.4 Select a Fill Color.

7. You can widen the graphic to extend across the top of the page. The WordArt graphic should still be selected. Right-click on the WordArt to open a pop-up menu. Click **Format WordArt**. Click the **Size** tab in the Format WordArt dialog box. In the Width text box, key **6**. As shown in Figure 13.5, the **Lock aspect ratio** option should not be selected.

Speed Forcing Drill

Key two 20" timed writings on each line.

1 Pamela is to do the work.
2 He may go with me to the lake.
3 Jo may go to the city with the man.
4 Jay may make a profit for the six firms.
5 Helen may go to the island for the oak shelf.
6 He paid the eight men for their work on the forms.

| gwam 20" | 3 | 6 | 9 | 12 | 15 | 18 | 21 | 24 | 27 | 30 |

47D APPLY:

Timed Writing

Key each paragraph once. DS between paragraphs. Key a 1' timed writing on each paragraph. Key a 2' timing writing on paragraphs 1 and 2 combined.

 all letters used

| | gwam | 1' | 2' |

Each President since George Washington has	9	4
had a cabinet. The cabinet is a group of men and	19	9
women selected by the President. The senate must	29	14
approve them. It is the exception rather than the	39	19
rule for the President's choice to be rejected by	49	24
this branch of the government. In keeping with	58	29
tradition, most of the cabinet members belong to	68	34
the same political party as the President.	77	38
The purpose of the cabinet is to provide advice	9	43
to the President on matters pertaining to the job	19	48
of President. The person holding the office, of	29	53
course, may or may not follow the advice. Some	39	58
Presidents have frequently utilized their cabinet.	49	63
Others have used it little or not at all. For	59	68
example, President Wilson held no cabinet meetings	69	73
at all during World War I.	74	75

| gwam | 1' | 1 | 2 | 3 | 4 | 5 | 6 | 7 | 8 | 9 | 10 |
| | 2' | | 1 | | 2 | | 3 | | 4 | | 5 | |

Use MicroType Numeric Keyboarding Lesson 13 for additional practice.

WordArt

WordArt is decorative text that you can create with ready-made effects. A WordArt graphics gallery has several options for text with predesigned font colors, shapes, and other effects. You can apply additional formatting options. For example, the color and shape of the text graphic can be changed.

WordArt can be accessed by clicking the Insert WordArt button on the Drawing toolbar. The Drawing toolbar is shown in Figure 13.2. It is usually displayed across the bottom of the screen.

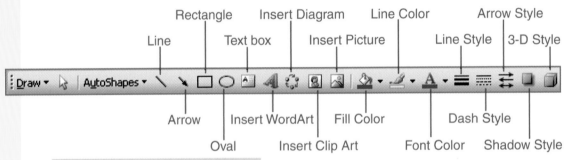

Figure 13.2 Drawing Toolbar in *Word*

99A LEARN: Create WordArt

1. Start *Word*. Open a new document. Display the **Drawing** toolbar if it is not on screen. To show the toolbar, click **View** on the menu bar. Click **Toolbars**. Click **Drawing**.

2. Click the **Insert WordArt** button on the Drawing toolbar. The button is marked in Figure 13.2.

3. Select the WordArt style that is in row 4, column 4. The style is shown in Figure 13.3 on page 453. Click **OK**.

4. In the Edit WordArt Text box, key **September** as shown in Figure 13.3 on page 453. Click **OK**.

Lesson 48   New Keys ! and \

Objectives

In Lesson 48, you will:
↘ Learn reach technique for ! and \.
↘ Combine ! and \ with other keys.

48A PRACTICE: Warmup

Key each line twice.

Alphabet
1 J. Zan quickly removed two boxes from the package.

Figures
2 He bought the house at 5036 Hill on June 24, 1987.

Easy
3 He may make a big profit if he owns the lake land.

48B LEARN: New Keys ! and \

! *Left little* finger +
RIGHT SHIFT

\ *Right little* finger

Key each line twice. If time permits, rekey lines 4–6.

Learn ! (exclamation point)
1 a ! a ! |a! a! a! | |a! !a! |No! No! Yes! Yes! Oh!
2 Don't do that! What a shock! I don't believe it!
3 Leave two spaces after ! at the end of a sentence.

Learn \ (backslash)
4 ; \ ; \|C:\ C:\|D:\tests\Unit 1 D:\Test 12\Unit 23
5 He mapped the drive to access \\spss 25\deptdir56.
6 The complete file name is C:\Unit 1\Lsn 14\Part A.

48C APPLY: Build Speed

1. Turn to 47D, page 169. Key the two paragraphs.
2. Take two 1' timings on each paragraph. Try to increase your speed by two words per minute on each timing. Take a 2' timing on paragraphs 1 and 2 combined.

Lesson 99 — Graphics in Word

Objectives

In Lesson 99, you will:

↘ Learn about types of graphics that can be used in a *Word* document.

↘ Learn about *Word*'s drawing canvas.

↘ Create and format WordArt.

┌ **Help Words** ┐

Graphic
  About graphics
  in *Word*

Graphics

You will learn to use two types of graphics in *Word* documents. A **graphic** is a drawn picture, a photo, or a chart. One type is called drawing objects and the other is called pictures. **Drawing objects** are graphics you draw that are part of your *Word* document. For example, you might include a line or circle in a newsletter.

When you place a drawing object in your document, a drawing canvas is created. The **drawing canvas** is an area in which you can draw several shapes. See Figure 13.1. The canvas helps you arrange the graphics in your document. Shapes in the canvas can be moved as one unit. The canvas has a border that separates your graphics from the rest of the document. By default, the border is visible on the screen when it is selected, but it does not print. The border size can be changed to make the canvas larger or smaller to fit the size of the graphics.

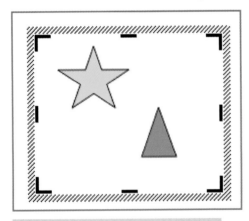

Figure 13.1 Drawing Canvas in *Word*

A **picture** is a drawing or photo in a separate file that you insert into your document. Picture graphics include **clip art** (drawn pictures) that you will use in this chapter.

48D PRACTICE: Keying Numbers and Symbols

Key each line twice.

```
1 About 60% (451 of 752) of the 1983 class attended.
2 The ZIP Code for 382 Hampton Avenue is 97405-1693.
3 Deliver 120 lbs. of #6 nails to project #493-587A.
4 The computer (1849Z3760) was delivered on June 25.
5 She paid $248,739 for the 1560 Michelangelo print.
6 Your check (#1549) for $260.38 arrived on July 17.
```

48E APPLY: Compose Sentences

Use MicroType Numeric Keyboarding Lesson 14 for additional practice.

Key each sentence once, inserting words of your choice to complete the sentence.

```
1 My favorite sport is _____.
2 In my spare time I like to _____.
3 When I grow up, I would like to be a(n) _____.
4 The place I would most like to visit is _____.
5 I would like to have a pet _____.
6 My favorite movie is _____.
```

 **CHECK POINT** Exchange papers with another student. Proofread and mark any needed corrections.

48F LEARN: Finger Gymnastics

Brief daily practice of finger gymnastics will strengthen your finger muscles. Try the drills below that will help you key more easily.

Drill 1

Drill 1

Start with your hands open, fingers wide, and muscles tense. Close the fingers into a tight fist with your thumb on top. Relax the fingers as you straighten them. Repeat ten times.

Drill 2

Drill 2

Clench your fingers against the palm of your hand. Hold them there for a brief time. Then extend your fingers and open your hand. Repeat the movement slowly several times for each hand.

Drill 3

Drill 3

Place your fingers and thumb of one hand between two fingers of the other hand. Spread the fingers as much as possible. Repeat to spread all fingers of both hands.

Chapter **13**

Desktop Publishing

OBJECTIVES

In Chapter 13, you will:

↗ **Use WordArt and AutoShapes.**

↗ **Insert and format text boxes and pictures.**

↗ **Create documents with two or more columns.**

↗ **Create flyers and newsletters.**

Everyone sees or uses newsletters, flyers, brochures, and forms. Your principal may send a school newsletter to students' homes. You may have just read a flyer giving details about the next school event.

All of these documents use desktop publishing. **Desktop publishing (DTP)** is using a personal computer to produce high-quality printed documents. DTP is closely related to word processing. However, the documents produced with DTP often do not follow a standard format like letters and reports do. The documents may have various fonts, text alignments, and columns.

DTP uses graphics with text to make a good visual impression. The graphics features you will learn to use in this chapter include WordArt, AutoShapes, text boxes, and pictures. You will also learn to insert and format graphics.

© Getty Images/PhotoDisc

Lesson 49   New Keys = and [ ]

Objectives
In Lesson 49, you will:
↘ Learn reach technique for = and [ ].
↘ Combine = and [ ] with other keys.

49A PRACTICE: Warmup

Key each line twice. If time permits, key the lines again.

Alphabet
1 Jewel Vikings quickly baked extra pizzas for them.

Figures
2 We met on May 19, 28, and 31 from 6:45 until 7:50.

Easy
3 Hans may go to the lake to work for the eight men.

49B LEARN: New Keys = and [ ]

Key each line twice. If time permits, rekey lines 7–9.

= *Right little* finger

[*Right little* finger

] *Right little* finger

Learn = (equal sign)
1 ; = ; =|;; == ;; ==|;=; =;=|=;= =;=|;/= ;/=|+=; +=
2 If a = b + c and c = 10 and a = 15, what does b =?
3 If 3a = 15, what does a =? If 10b = 30, b = what?

Learn [(left bracket)
4 ; [; [|;; [[;; [[|[a[[B[[c[[D[[e[[F[[g[[H
5 [I [j [K [1 [M [n [O [p [Q [r [S [t [U [v [W [x [Y

Learn] (right bracket)
6 ;] ;]|;;]] ;;]]|1] 2] 3] 4] 5] 6] 7] 8] 9] 10]
7 10a] 11b] 12c] 13d] 14e] 15f] 16g] 17f] 18g] 19h];

Combine [and]
8 My next problem was [a + b/6] + 12/2 = c/6 + 30/3.
9 I used the [and] to set off names [Jay], [Mike].

Sometimes you will need to fill out a job application form *and* submit your resume. Other times you may need to submit only one or the other. However, in all cases, it is important to turn in a neat, complete, and honest document. Your form may be used to run a check on your qualifications. Therefore, you must complete the form honestly. The form should be neat and complete so that you give a good impression of yourself. The way you fill out your form will reflect your ability to follow instructions.

1. In this exercise you will complete a manual and an online job application form. Open the data file *CD-C12-Instructions*, and read more about job applications. Then, open and print the data file *CD-C12-Form*. Use a pen to complete the form. Give the completed form to your teacher.

2. Open the data file *CD-C12-Online Application*. Fill out the form by clicking in each box and entering the information. Save the form as *C12-Online Application*. Print the form and give it to your teacher.

3. Remember to include a sample of your best work from this chapter in your portfolio.

↗ Academic Success Builder

COMMUNICATIONS: ABBREVIATIONS Abbreviations are shortened forms of words or phrases that are used to save time and space. For example, *FBI* is much quicker to write and read and takes much less space than *Federal Bureau of Investigation*. Likewise, writing *B.A.* for a college degree is quicker and shorter than *Bachelor of Arts*. However, notice that FBI is written without periods and B.A. contains periods. In this activity you will learn some of the basic rules for forming and punctuating abbreviations.

1. Start *Word*. Open Open *CD-C12-Abbreviations* found in your data files. Print the file and then close it. Study the Guides and the Learn line(s) for each Guide.

2. For the Practice lines and the Apply lines, key each line using the correct abbreviation. Save your sentences as *C12-Abbreviations*.

READING: READ A CHART Charts are often used to present information in a pictorial format that is easy to understand. Among the most common kinds of charts are bar, column, pie, and line charts. How well can you read a chart? Do you know what the *x* axis is? The *y* axis? Can you read the information and make a decision about what is presented? This activity will give you an opportunity to read a chart.

1. Start *Word*. Open *CD-C12-Chart* found in your data files. Read the chart and key answers to the questions in the file. Save the document as *C12-Chart* and print it.

2. Compare your answers with those of a classmate. Make revisions as necessary.

Speed Forcing Drill

Key each line once at top speed. Then try to complete each sentence in 15".

```
1 Kris may sign to work for the city.
2 He may wish to visit with the maid.
3 A visit by the two men may be a problem.
4 The city auditor may do the work for us.
5 She may make a map of the eight towns for us.
6 The city officials may pay them for the work.
```

gwam 15" | 4 | 8 | 12 | 16 | 20 | 24 | 28 | 32 | 36 |

49D APPLY:

Build Speed

Use MicroType Numeric Keyboarding Lesson 15 for additional practice.

1. Turn to 50D on page 175. Key the two paragraphs.

2. Take two 1' timings on each paragraph. Try to increase your speed by two words per minute on each timing. Take a 2' timing on paragraphs 1 and 2 combined.

49E LEARN:

Finger Gymnastics

Remember to practice finger gymnastics each day to strengthen your finger muscles. Try the drills below that will help you key more easily.

Drill 1

Drill 1

Interlace the fingers of your hands. Wring your hands, rubbing your palms vigorously.

Drill 2

Drill 2

Spread your fingers as much as possible. Hold that position for a few seconds. Then relax your fingers and fold them into the palm of your hand.

Drill 3

Drill 3

Use the fingers and thumb of one hand to rub the other hand. Rub your fingers, your wrist, and the back of your hand.

Drill 4

Drill 4

Hold your hand in front of you with the fingers together. Hold the last three fingers still while moving the first finger as far to the side as possible. Return fingers together. Move the first and second fingers to the side while holding the others in place. Finally, move the little finger to the side while holding the others in place.

ACROSS THE CURRICULUM

Data Files

- *CD-C12-Business*
- *CD-C12-Instructions*
- *CD-C12-Form*
- *CD-C12-Online Application*
- *CD-C12-Abbreviations*
- *CD-C12-Chart*

↗ About Business

OPPORTUNITIES THAT LEAD TO BUSINESS SUCCESS An entrepreneur is a person who owns his or her own business. Have you ever wondered how an entrepreneur gets started in business? How does he or she know what business to be in? One way an entrepreneur may answer this question is by looking for opportunities that lead to business success.

An opportunity to run a business in an area that interests you can help lead to business success. An entrepreneur often needs to spend long hours working in the business. Being very interested in the business helps prevent boredom or frustration when working long hours. For example, someone who enjoys writing computer programs may do well in a business that provides this service.

An opportunity to provide a product or service for which there is a need in the area increases the chances of business success. This can be a new or an existing product or service. For example, if the only dry-cleaning store in a small town closes, this may provide an opportunity for someone to open a dry-cleaning store.

Another opportunity that can lead to business success is purchasing a franchise. A **franchise** is a contract that gives a business the right to sell certain products in a certain region. The entrepreneur benefits by selling products with a known brand name. The company that makes the products usually provides advice to the entrepreneur about how to run the business. This increases chances for success.

An opportunity to go into business with another person who has special skills or talents can lead to business success. For example, one person may be good at making products. The other person may be good at selling products and managing the business. Together, the two partners have a better chance for business success.

1. Start *Word*. Open and print *CD-C12-Business* from your data files.

2. Follow the instructions provided to answer questions related to opportunities that lead to business success.

↗ Career and Life Skills Success Builder

COMPLETE A JOB APPLICATION FORM Chances are, when you apply for your first job, you will need to fill out a job application form. A job application form asks for basic information about you such as your name and address, previous jobs, position desired, and education history. The same form is given to anyone who applies for a job at a certain company. The form allows employers to easily screen each applicant. It also helps employers determine who is best qualified for a job.

Lesson 50 New Keys > and <

Objectives
In Lesson 50, you will:
↘ Learn reach technique for > and <.
↘ Combine > and < with other keys.

50A PRACTICE: Warmup

Key each line twice.

Alphabet
1 Jackie Wilson helped Mary fix the big quartz vase.

Figures
2 Her identification number is 42091; mine is 35768.

Easy
3 Eight of them may form a panel to fix the problem.

50B LEARN: New Keys > and <

Key each line twice. If time permits, rekey lines 7–9.

> *Right ring* finger +
LEFT SHIFT

< *Right middle* finger +
LEFT SHIFT

Learn > (greater than sign)
1 1 > 1>|L>1 L>1|1.> 1.>|15 > 10 15 > 10|3 > 2 3 > 2
2 26 > 25; 108 > 98; a + b is > b + c; 128 + a > 133
3 Use the symbol (>) for greater than (A > C + 8/2).

Learn < (less than sign)
4 k < k <|k,< k,<|k<b, k<b,|1 < 2 1 < 2|2 < 3 2 < 3;
5 16 < 17 < 18 < 19 < 20; 36 < 37 < 38 < 39 < 40 < X
6 Use this symbol (<) for less than. He said a < b.

Combine > and <
7 Yes, 90% of them scored > 76% and 9% scored < 76%.
8 Twelve of the boys understood the < and > concept.
9 Maria and I set the merge fields off with < and >.

Timed Writing

Key each paragraph once. DS between paragraphs. Key a 1' timed writing on each paragraph; determine *gwam*. Key a 2' timing on both paragraphs.

A all letters used   gwam 2'

```
         •    2    •    4    •    6    •    8
     Austria is a rather small country located          4
   •   10   •   12   •   14   •   16   •
between Germany and Italy.  It is about three            8
  18  •   20   •   22   •   24   •   26   •
times the size of Vermont.  The most recognized         14
  28   •   30   •   32   •   34   •   36
city in this country is Vienna.  Over the years         18
 •   38   •   40   •   42   •   44   •   46   •
this city has been known for its contributions to       23
 •   48   •   50   •   52   •   54   •   56
the culture in the region.  It is particularly          28
   •   58   •   60   •   62   •   64   •
known in the area of performing arts.  Another          33
  66   •   68   •   70   •   72   •   74   •
place that has played an important part in the          36
   76   •   78   •   80   •   82   •   84
exquisite culture of the area is the city of            42
                •
Salzburg.                                               43
         •    2    •    4    •    6    •    8
     Salzburg is also recognized as a great city        47
 •   10   •   12   •   14   •   16   •   18
for the performing arts.  This city is known for        52
  •   20   •   22   •   24   •   26   •   28
music.  Just as important, however, is that the         57
       •   30   •   32   •   34   •   36
city is the birthplace of Wolfgang Amadeus              61
  •   38   •   40   •   42   •   44   •   46
Mozart.  Mozart was one of the greatest composers       66
  •   48   •   50   •   52   •   54   •   56
of all time.  Perhaps, no other composer had an         71
    •   58   •   60   •   62   •   64   •   66
earlier start at his professional endeavors than        76
       •   68   •   70   •   72   •   74   •   76
did Mozart.  It is thought that he began playing        81
    •   78   •   80   •   82   •   84   •   86
at the age of four and began composing at the age       86
                •
of five.                                                87
```

gwam 2' | 1 | 2 | 3 | 4 | 5 |

Speed Forcing Drill

Key each line once at top speed. Then try to complete each sentence in 15".

1 Nancy is to go to the city with us.
2 I paid the man for the work he did.

3 Jane paid the men for the work they did.
4 Rick may make them sign the audit forms.

5 Vivian may go to the dock to visit the girls.
6 Cody's dog slept on the chair by the bicycle.

gwam 15" | 4 | 8 | 12 | 16 | 20 | 24 | 28 | 32 | 36 |

Timed Writing

Use MicroType Numeric Keyboarding Lesson 16 for additional practice.

Key each paragraph once. DS between paragraphs. Key a 1' timed writing on each paragraph. Key a 2' timed writing on paragraphs 1 and 2 combined.

all letters used

gwam 2'

Whether you are an intense lover of music or   5
simply enjoy hearing good music, you are more than   10
likely aware of the work completed by Beethoven,   15
the German composer. He is generally recognized as   20
one of the greatest composers to ever live. Much   25
of his early work was influenced by those who wrote   30
music in Austria, Haydn and Mozart.   33

It can be argued whether Beethoven was a   38
classical or romantic composer. This depends upon   43
which period of time in his life the music was   47
written. His exquisite music has elements of both.   53
It has been said that his early works brought to a   58
conclusion the classical age. It has also been   63
stated that Beethoven's later works started the   67
romantic age of music.   70

gwam 2' | 1 | 2 | 3 | 4 | 5 |

Building Keying Skill

Warmup Practice

Key each line twice. If time permits, key the lines again.

Alphabet

1 Fran Vasquez put down the six jackets by my glove.

Figure/Symbol

2 The house at 1768 Oak was decreased 15% ($23,490).

Speed

3 Orlando may keep the turkeys in a box by the dock.

gwam 1' | 1 | 2 | 3 | 4 | 5 | 6 | 7 | 8 | 9 | 10 |

Technique Mastery of Individual Letters

Key each line twice.

A/Z 1 Zach and Anna ate a pizza at the plaza by the zoo.
B/Y 2 Bobby may be too busy to buy Mary a bicycle today.

C/X 3 Chen Xio caught six cod to fix for the six scouts.
D/W 4 Dwight would let Wanda walk the dogs in the woods.

E/V 5 Even Eva had a very heavy box to leave in the van.
F/U 6 Four out of five runners had on fuzzy furry cuffs.

G/T 7 Eight girls tugged on the target to get it higher.
H/S 8 Al's son has his share of those shiny star shapes.

I/R 9 Rick will have their rings shined by Friday night.
J/Q 10 Jacques quit the squad after a major joint injury.

K/P 11 Kip packed a pink backpack and put it on the desk.
L/O 12 Lolita wore the royal blue blouse with gold laces.

M/N 13 Many of those men met in the main entry on Monday.

gwam 1' | 1 | 2 | 3 | 4 | 5 | 6 | 7 | 8 | 9 | 10 |

Lesson 51   Numeric Keypad 4, 5, 6, 0

Objectives

In Lesson 51, you will:

↘ Learn numeric keypad operating position.

↘ Learn to access the Calculator.

↘ Learn reachstrokes for **4**, **5**, **6**, and **0**.

51A LEARN: Numeric Keypad Operating Position

Position yourself at the keyboard as shown at the left. Sit in front of the keyboard with the book at the side—body erect, both feet on the floor.

Curve the fingers of your right hand and place them on the numeric keypad. Use the little finger for the ENTER key as indicated in Figure 5.1. Place the

- index finger on **4**
- middle finger on **5**
- ring finger on **6**
- thumb on **0**

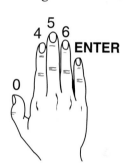

Figure 5.1 Home Keying Position for Numeric Keypad

51B LEARN: How to Access Calculator

You will use the *Calculator* program on your computer to learn and practice the numeric keypad. Follow the instructions given below.

1. Click the **Start** button on the taskbar.

2. Click **All Programs**, then **Accessories**.

3. Click **Calculator**. The *Calculator* window will open, as shown in Figure 5.2.

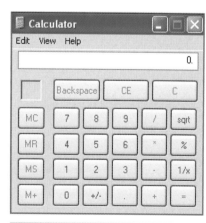

Figure 5.2 *Calculator* Window

Applying *What You Have Learned*

Data File

CD-C12-Table2

Table, Equal Column Widths

1. Start *Word* and open a new document. Create the table below using the Fixed Column Width option. Merge the cells in row 1. Merge the cells in row 9.

2. Horizontally center the title and the column heads. Left-align all other text. Center the table on the page horizontally. Center the page vertically.

3. Shade row 2 and row 9 a light yellow.

4. Remove all border lines from the table. Place a 1 ½-point single line border around the outside edges of the table. Place a ½-point single line border on the top and bottom of the column heading cells.

5. Save the table as *C12-Table1*. Print and close the table.

TEAMS[1]		
Red	White	Blue
Gregg Oslosky	David Ziran	Andy Glover
Betty Konchak	Renny Varghese	Christine Chiripka
Brian Dodd	Charles John	Jennifer Ray
Aida Varner	Robin Alwine	Kathie Kradel
Sharon Pratt	Camerica Quan	Keith Ardash
Juan Vardez	Donna Matessi	Zakir Shaheed
[1]The teams were randomly selected by the coaches.		

Table, AutoFit to Contents

1. Start *Word*. Open *CD-C12-Table2* found in your data files.

2. Make the column widths fit the contents. Center the table horizontally on the page. Center the page vertically.

3. Center all column headings. Apply **Left** alignment for all words and **Right** alignment for all numbers.

4. Change row height for all rows to 0.5". Vertically center all cell entries.

5. Sort the table data by the Number column in ascending order. Save the table as *C12-Table2*. Print the table and then close it.

Supplemental activities for this chapter can be found at www.c21jr.swlearning.com.

51C LEARN: 4, 5, 6, and 0 (home keys)

Use the *Calculator* program to complete the addition drills shown below.

1. Key the first number with the proper finger and tap the + key with the little finger of the right hand.
2. Key the next number and tap the + key.
3. After entering the last black number in the column and tapping the + key, verify your answer with the answer shown in color.
4. Tap ESC on the main keyboard to clear the number. Then do the next problem.

Drill 1

A	B	C	D	E
4	5	6	4	6
4	5	6	5	4
8	10	12	9	10

Drill 2

A	B	C	D	E
44	55	44	45	56
55	66	66	46	45
99	121	110	91	101

Drill 3

A	B	C	D	E
45	54	46	44	64
56	64	65	56	46
64	56	45	65	55
165	174	156	165	165

Drill 4

A	B	C	D	E
40	40	60	506	504
50	60	50	406	406
60	50	40	540	560
150	150	150	1,452	1,470

Drill 5

A	B	C	D	E
54	504	405	605	450
50	605	506	406	406
56	406	604	540	605
160	1,515	1,515	1,551	1,461

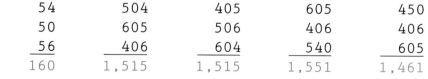 **CHECK POINT** Did you check each answer against the book?

Reviewing   *What You Have Learned*

Answer **True** or **False** to each question to review what you have learned in Chapter 12.

1. A table is information arranged in rows and columns.

2. Table rows run horizontally and columns run vertically.

3. Table titles must be outside the table grid.

4. The place where a row and a column cross each other is called a subrow.

5. A column heading appears at the bottom of a column and describes the data in the column.

6. Words in cells can be centered, right-aligned, or left-aligned.

7. A table on a page that is not vertically centered should have a 2-inch top margin.

8. To select an entire table, click the table move handle.

9. Table markers indicate the end of a cell or row.

10. When the Fixed Column Width command is used, the table grid will have columns of equal width.

11. When the Table AutoFit to Contents is used, the table grid may have varying column widths, but none will be narrower than 1 inch.

12. Tables can be centered horizontally on the page.

13. Tables are centered vertically by selecting Center in the Layout tab of the Page Setup dialog box.

14. Cells in adjacent rows and cells in adjacent columns can be merged.

15. Only cells selected in rows can be split.

16. Rows can be added above or below existing rows.

17. Columns must be deleted before rows can be added.

18. All row heights in a table must be the same size.

19. Tapping ENTER after keying text in a cell will move the insertion point to the next cell in the row.

20. The default placement for data in a cell is left and top alignment.

21. A table can be printed without borders.

22. If desired, shading can be added to just one row.

23. A superscript font places text slightly lower on the line than regular text.

24. Only table columns with numbers can be sorted.

Lesson 52   Numeric Keypad 7, 8, 9

Objectives

In Lesson 52, you will:

↘ Learn reachstrokes for **7**, **8**, and **9**.

↘ Combine the **7**, **8**, and **9** keys with other keys.

52A PRACTICE: Warmup

Use the *Calculator* program to complete the addition drills shown below.

A	B	C	D
4	56	406	440
5	45	504	506
6	64	650	605
15	165	1,560	1,551

52B LEARN: 7, 8, and 9

7 *Index* finger
8 *Middle* finger
9 *Ring* finger

Use MicroType Numeric Keypad Lesson 2 for additional practice.

Use the *Calculator* program to complete the addition drills shown below.

Drill 1 *7*

A	B	C	D	E
577	607	747	667	756
774	575	70	75	707
757	740	675	757	574
2,108	1,922	1,492	1,499	2,037

Drill 2 *8*

A	B	C	D	E
808	680	884	458	800
484	584	480	684	68
586	868	856	880	548
1,878	2,132	2,220	2,022	1,416

Drill 3 *9*

A	B	C	D	E
459	954	496	944	964
596	609	965	596	469
964	596	459	659	595
2,019	2,159	1,920	2,199	2,028

Drill 4 All numbers learned

A	B	C	D	E
409	740	695	509	594
507	964	570	476	807
608	850	409	840	560
1,524	2,554	1,674	1,825	1,961

2. Apply **AutoFit to Contents** to the table cells.

3. In row 2 column 1, select the number **2**. Click **Format** on the menu bar. Select **Font**. Click the checkbox to the left of **Subscript** in the Effects section as shown in Figure 12.17. Click **OK**. The text should now appear as H_2O, with 2 being a subscript.

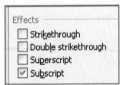

Figure 12.17 Select a Font Style

4. In row 3 column 1, select the first number **6**. Hold down the CTRL key and select the second number **6**. Choose **Format**, **Font**. Select **Subscript**. Click **OK**.

5. Apply **Subscript** font effect to the numbers in the last two chemical formulas.

6. In row 2 column 2, select the number **2**. Click **Format** on the menu bar. Select **Font**. Click the checkbox to the left of **Superscript** in the Effects section. Click **OK**. The text should now appear as $y = x^2$, with 2 being a superscript.

7. Apply **Superscript** font effect to characters in the remaining math formulas as shown in the table.

8. Center the table horizontally and vertically on the page. Save the table as *98-Table3*. Print and close the table.

98C APPLY: Research and Design a Table

1. Working with another student, choose ten first names for people. Do research to find the meaning of the names. Find information about each of the names in your local library or on the Internet. Enter *first name meanings* or similar search terms in a search engine to find information on the Internet. Attempt to find similar information about each name so you can report your findings in a table.

2. Design a table to report your research findings. The table should have a title, column headings, and cell entries to show each name and what you learned about the name from your research.

3. Key the information in the table and then format the table to make it attractive and easy to read.

4. Save the table as *98-Table4*. Print and then close the table.

Lesson 53 — Numeric Keypad 1, 2, 3

Objectives

In Lesson 53, you will:
↘ Learn reachstrokes for **1, 2,** and **3**.
↘ Combine the **1, 2,** and **3** keys with other keys.

53A PRACTICE: Warmup

Use the *Calculator* program to complete the addition drills shown below.

A	B	C	D
549	596	406	740
670	408	809	596
486	758	750	805
1,705	1,762	1,965	2,141

53B LEARN: 1, 2, and 3

1 *Index* finger
2 *Middle* finger
3 *Ring* finger

MicroType

Use MicroType Numeric Keypad Lesson 3 for additional practice.

Use the *Calculator* program to complete the addition drills shown below.

Drill 1 *1*

A	B	C	D	E
171	916	147	415	156
814	151	811	611	417
151	110	901	718	901
1,136	1,177	1,859	1,744	1,474

Drill 2 *2*

A	B	C	D	E
202	289	722	290	256
425	524	208	724	728
726	262	526	282	249
1,353	1,075	1,456	1,296	1,233

Drill 3 *3*

A	B	C	D	E
453	453	303	734	368
396	309	963	583	493
363	396	357	639	735
1,212	1,158	1,623	1,956	1,596

Drill 4 All numbers learned

A	B	C	D	E
429	710	195	325	914
537	264	570	176	827
608	350	432	840	360
1,574	1,324	1,197	1,341	2,101

3. Select **Last Name** from the Sort by drop-down list. This will cause the data to be sorted first by the person's last name. **Text** should appear for the Type. Select **Ascending** for the sort order.

4. Select **First Name** in the first Then by box. This will cause the data to be sorted next by the person's first name. **Text** should appear for the Type. Select **Ascending** for the sort order.

5. Click the radio button by **Header Row** to select this option. This option means that the first row in your table contains column headings that will not be included in the sort. Click **OK**.

6. Save the table using the same name, *98-Table1*, and keep it open.

7. Sort the data by column R (runs) in descending order and then by the Last Name column in ascending order.

8. Save the table as *98-Table2*. Print and close the table.

CHECK POINT Compare your *98-Table2* with that of a classmate. If the data are not sorted correctly, identify what is wrong and sort the table again.

Subscript and Superscript Characters

Superscript is text that is slightly higher than other text on a line. **Subscript** is text that is slightly lower than other text on a line. Both font effects are used frequently in keying information related to math and science.

Key Text with Subscript and Superscript Formatting

1. Start *Word*. Open a new blank document. Key the table below using a regular font for all letters, numbers, and symbols. You will change parts of the formulas to subscript or superscripts in the steps that follow.

COMMON FORMULAS

Chemical Formulas	Math Formulas
H_2O	$y=x^2$
C_6H_6	$a^x a^y = a^{x+y}$
C_3H_6O	$x^2 - 6x - 8 = 0$
C_2H_2	$y = x^2 - 3x - 4$

Lesson 54   Subtraction and Multiplication

Objectives

In Lesson 54, you will:
↘ Learn subtraction on numeric keypad.
↘ Learn multiplication on the numeric keypad.

54A PRACTICE: Warmup

Use the *Calculator* program to complete the addition drills shown below.

A	B	C	D
102	938	476	517
289	304	560	976
854	391	208	645
1,245	1,633	1,244	2,138

54B LEARN: Subtraction

- *Little* finger

Use the *Calculator* program to complete the subtraction drills shown below. Key the first number and tap the – key. Key the second number and tap the ENTER key.

Drill 1

A	B	C	D	E
907	872	614	730	756
- 489	- 312	- 459	- 583	- 621
418	560	155	147	135

Drill 2

A	B	C	D	E
509	847	625	913	810
- 293	- 764	- 501	- 264	- 398
216	83	124	649	412

54C LEARN: Multiplication

* *Ring* finger

Use the *Calculator* program to complete the multiplication drills shown below. Key the first number and tap the * key. Key the second number and tap the ENTER key.

Drill 3

A	B	C	D	E
96	75	84	40	132
x 40	x 46	x 73	x 28	x 19
3,840	3,450	6,132	1,120	2,508

Drill 4

A	B	C	D	E
405	697	803	467	371
x 208	x 50	x 32	x 140	x 62
84,240	34,850	25,696	65,380	23,002

Lesson 98 — Tables, Sorting Data and Applying Font Effects

Objectives

In Lesson 98, you will:

↘ Sort data in a table.

↘ Key text using superscript and subscript fonts.

↘ Research data and design a table.

Data files: *CD-98-Table1*

Sorting in Tables

┌──────────────┐
  Help Words
└──────────────┘
  Sort
   About Sorting

Sort means to arrange or group items in a particular order. You can sort information in a table in ascending or descending order. **Ascending** order means A to Z for words. For numbers, ascending order means from the lowest to the highest number. **Descending** order means Z to A for words. For numbers, descending order means from the highest to the lowest number. You can sort information in the entire table or selected information in one or more columns.

98A LEARN: Sort

1. Start *Word*. Open *CD-98-Table1* found in your data files. Save the table as *98-Table1*.

2. Click a cell in the table. Click **Table** on the menu bar. Select **Sort**. The Sort dialog box will appear as shown in Figure 12.16.

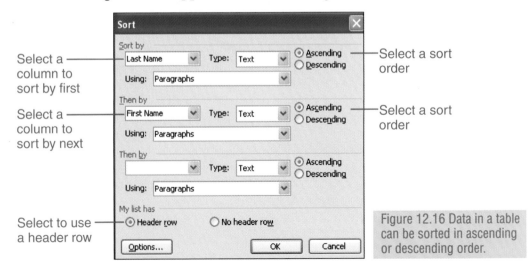

Select a column to sort by first

Select a column to sort by next

Select to use a header row

Select a sort order

Select a sort order

Figure 12.16 Data in a table can be sorted in ascending or descending order.

Lesson 55   Division and Math Problems

Objectives

In Lesson 55, you will:

↘ Learn division on numeric keypad.

↘ Learn to complete math problems on the numeric keypad.

| 55A LEARN: ## Division

/ middle finger

Use the *Calculator* program to complete the division drills shown below. Key the dividend and tap the / key. Key the divisor and tap the ENTER key. Round answers to two decimal places.

Drill 1

A	B	C	D	E
120.6	79	90.33	119	70.8
5/603	11/869	6/542	8/952	10/708

Drill 2

A	B	C	D	E
21.65	64	197.51	95.56	134.58
23/498	79/5,056	43/8,493	62/5,925	67/9,017

| 55B LEARN: ## Math Problems

TEAMWORK

Instant Message

A deposit is an addition to a bank account. A check or service charge is a subtraction from a bank account.

Using the *Calculator* program, work with a classmate to solve the math problems below.

1. Rebecca made four deposits last month. They were for $37.28, $15.91, $45.76, and $50.37. How much money did she deposit for the month?

2. Sarah bought two CDs for $15.99 each. She bought two video games for $59.95 and $49.75. The state sales tax is 5.5%. How much did she spend?

3. Felipe is paid each week. His last four checks were for $49.78, $35.97, $53.76, and $28.73. What did he average per week over this period?

4. Antonio is paid $6.25 per hour. Last week he worked 4 hours on Monday, 3 ½ hours on Tuesday, 5 hours on Wednesday, 2 hours on Thursday, and 4 ½ hours on Friday. How much did he make last week?

5. At the end of last month, Brandon had an ending bank balance of $153.37. During the month, he made one deposit for $97.68. He wrote five checks ($7.98, $15.83, $38.53, $17.21, and $49.76). His service charge this month was $3.25. What is his current balance after recording these amounts?

 **CHECK POINT** Compare your answers with a classmate's answers. If they do not agree, do the problem again to find the correct answer.

6. Select row 1 of the table. Click **Format** on the menu bar. Select **Borders and Shading**. If needed, click the **Borders** tab to open it.

7. Select **Box** for the Setting. Select **Cell** from the Apply to list. Click **OK**.

8. Select row 1 of the table. Click **Format** on the menu bar. Select **Borders and Shading**. If needed, click the **Shading** tab to open it.

9. Select the **Light Green** color in the Fill section as shown in Figure 12.14. Select **Cell** in the Apply to list. Click **OK**.

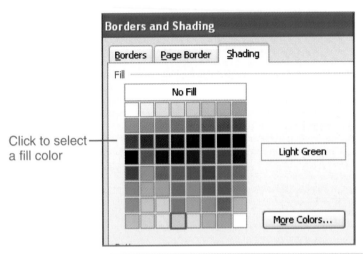

Figure 12.14 The Shading tab allows you to select a fill color for cells.

10. The table should have a black border and light green fill applied to row 1 as shown in Figure 12.15. Save the table as *97-Table4*. Print the table.

NOTABLE INVENTIONS			
Invention	**Date**	**Invention**	**Date**
Aerosol spray	1926	Seat belt	1959
Bubble gum	1928	Audio cassette	1963
Helicopter	1939	Compact disc player	1979
Contact lens	1948	Minivan	1983
Disposable diapers	1950	Laptop computer	1987

Figure 12.15 Table with Shading and Border around Row 1

11. Experiment with applying borders and shading to other cells, rows, and columns in the table. Close the table without saving changes.

Reviewing *What You Have Learned*

Answer these questions to review what you have learned in Chapter 5.

1. When keying numbers, where should you keep the fingers not being used to tap the number key?

2. What does the proofreaders' mark for transpose mean?

3. What is the proofreaders' mark for delete? for close up?

4. Another name for handwritten copy is _____.

5. When keying numbers on the top row, reach up without moving your _____ away from you.

6. To make TAB characters display on the screen, click the _____ button.

7. When keying, keep your forearms _____ to the slant of the keyboard.

8. Do not _____ between a figure and the / or the $ sign.

9. Do not _____ between a figure and the percent sign (%) or the hyphen.

10. Space _____ before and after & used to join names.

11. The study of how a person's work environment and tools affect the person is _____.

12. List three guidelines for using computers and related equipment safely.

13. What is carpal tunnel syndrome (CTS)?

14. List three precautions you can take to help prevent CTS.

15. Describe home keying position for the numeric keypad.

16. When using the *Calculator* program, you may need to tap the _____ key (located above the 7 on the numeric keypad).

17. When using the numeric keypad, use your _____ to tap the 0 key.

18. List the steps for using the *Calculator* program to do a subtraction problem.

Supplemental activities for this chapter can be found at www.c21jr. swlearning.com.

Shading is a colored fill or background that can be applied to cells in a table. Shading can also enhance the appearance of your table and make it easy to read. You can use varying shades of gray or color for shading cells. Shading covers the selected area. It may be applied to the entire table or to selected cells, rows, or columns.

97C LEARN: Change Borders and Shading

1. Start *Word*. Open *97-Table2* that you saved earlier in this lesson.

2. Click in the table. To format the table without borders, click **Format** on the menu bar. Select **Borders and Shading**. If needed, click the **Borders** tab to open it.

3. Select **None** in the Setting section as shown in Figure 12.13. Select **Table** from the Apply to drop-down list if it is not already selected. Click **OK** at the bottom of the dialog box.

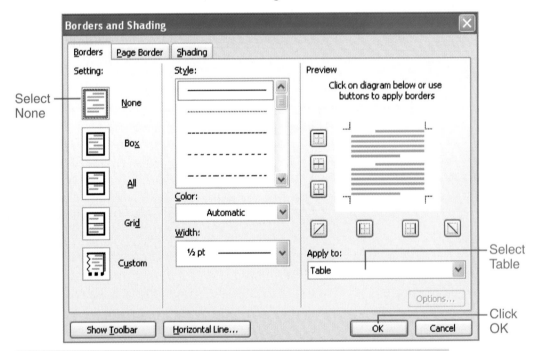

Figure 12.13 Select borders for table cells in the Borders and Shading dialog box.

4. The table should now appear with no border lines. However, the table gridlines may be displayed. The light gray gridlines that appear on the screen will not print. If the gridlines are not displayed, click **Table** on the menu bar. Select **Show Gridlines**. If you want to hide them on the screen, click **Hide Gridlines** on the Table menu.

5. Save the table as *97-Table3*. Print the table, but do not close it.

ACROSS THE CURRICULUM

Instant Message

Review *market economy* on page 141.

TEAMWORK

Data Files

- *CD-C05-Business*
- *CD-C05-Job Discrimination*
- *CD-C05-Apostrophes*
- *CD-C05-Earnings*

↗ About Business

DEMAND AND SUPPLY Demand and supply are the primary forces in a market economy. **Demand** is the amount of a product or service consumers are able and willing to buy. The relationship between a product's price and the demand for the product is called the *law of demand*. Other factors being the same, when a product's price rises, demand will go down. When a product's price goes down, demand will go up. Some of the other factors that affect demand for a product include things such as:

- The amount of money available for buying the product
- The ability to use another product in place of this one
- The buyer's wants or needs for larger numbers of the product

Supply is the amount of a product or service producers (companies) are willing and able to offer for sale. The relationship between a product's price and the amount produced is called the *law of supply*. Other factors being the same, when a product's price falls, the amount produced will go down. When a product's price rises, the amount produced will go up. Some of the other factors that affect supply include things such as:

- The technology used to make a product
- The number of other producers who also make the product
- What products the producer expects consumers to want in the future
- What producers expect the product price to be in the future

Consumers want to buy products at low prices. Producers want to sell products at high prices. Consumers and producers must compromise to reach an agreement on a product's price. The price at which consumers are willing to buy and producers are willing to sell a product is the **market price** of the product.

1. Start *Word*. Open and print *CD-C05-Business* from your data files. Read about the advantages and disadvantages of having a home-based business.

2. Work with a classmate to answer the questions related to demand and supply. Share your answers with the class.

4. To change the text alignment, select the cells in row 1. Click **Table** on the menu bar. Select **Table Properties**. Click the **Cell** tab.

5. Select **Center** under Vertical alignment as shown in Figure 12.12.

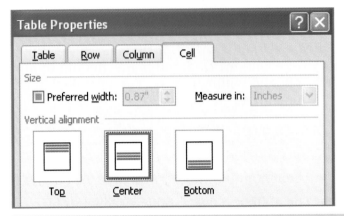

Figure 12.12 Set vertical alignment in the Table Properties dialog box.

6. Using the process you learned in steps 2 and 3, set the height for rows 2 through 6 to **0.3"**. Set the vertical alignment for the cells to **Center**.

7. Save the table as *97-Table1*. Print and close the table.

 **CHECK POINT** Does your table look like Figure 12.10? If not, make corrections as needed.

97B PRACTICE: Change Row Height and Alignment

1. Start *Word*. Open *CD-97-Table2* found in your data files.

2. Change the height of row 1 to 0.7". Change the height of row 2 to **0.5"**. Change the height of the remaining rows to **0.3"**.

3. Change the vertical alignment for all rows to **Center**.

4. Save the table as *97-Table2*. Print and close the table.

Borders and Shading

Borders are the printed lines around cells in a table. Borders can enhance the appearance of your table and make it easy to read. By default, tables are printed with a black 0.5-point, solid line black border around all cells. You can change the border color, thickness, and style. You can choose to have the border around all cells in the table or only selected cells. You can also choose to print the table without any borders.

⬈ Career and Life Success Builder

EMPLOYMENT DISCRIMINATION The workplace has changed dramatically over the years. Today, there are more women, minorities, and seniors working than ever before. As the workforce evolves, so does the culture. People with different backgrounds, ideas, and views create a more *diverse* workplace.

Many companies have policies that protect their employees against discrimination. **Discrimination** is the unfair treatment of people due to factors such as race, ethnic group, age, religion, disability, or gender. These company policies reflect labor acts passed by the U.S. government. In this activity, you will learn more about overcoming discrimination barriers on the job.

1. Start *Word*. Open the data file *CD-C05-Job Discrimination*.

2. Conduct research on job discrimination using the U.S. Equal Employment Opportunity Commission's web site as directed in the data file. Save your work as *C05-Job Discrimination*.

⬈ Academic Success Builder

COMMUNICATIONS: APOSTROPHE An apostrophe (') is used to show possession or to indicate that letters have been left out, as in a contraction (isn't) or a shortened date ('06). People who read your writing will stumble over its meaning if you do not use apostrophes correctly. You will practice using apostrophes in this activity.

1. Start *Word*. Open *CD-C05-Apostrophes* found in your data files. Print the file and then close it. Study the Guides and the Learn line(s) for each Guide.

2. For the Practice lines and the Apply lines, read the sentences and add apostrophes where needed.

READING: READ AN EARNINGS STATEMENT If you are paid $6.00 an hour for working at a restaurant and work 15 hours during the week, you will earn $90.00 for your work. Yes, you earned a gross pay of $90.00. However, did you know that your employer is required to deduct several taxes from your pay? The taxes are sent to various government agencies. In addition, if you receive benefits such as medical, dental, and disability insurance, you may have to pay a portion of the costs. These amounts, too, are deducted from your pay. Therefore, you will receive a net pay that is less than $90.00. In this activity, you will read an earnings statement that lists the amount earned, the amounts deducted from earnings, and the net pay (amount received).

1. Start *Word*. Open *CD-C05-Earnings*. Print the file and then close it.

2. Study the earnings statement and then answer the ten questions. Compare your answers with those of a classmate. If you disagree, decide which answer is most likely to be correct and make any changes needed. Give your answers to your teacher.

in Figure 12.10 is set to Center. In this lesson, you will learn to set row heights to exact measurements and align text in cells vertically.

MEN'S SOCCER WORLD CUP WINNERS

Row 1 ——

Year	Winner	Final Opponent
1986	Argentina	West Germany
1990	West Germany	Argentina
1994	Brazil	Italy
1998	France	Brazil
2002	Brazil	Germany

Figure 12.10 This table has changed row height and vertically centered cells.

97A LEARN: Change Row Height and Alignment

1. Start *Word*. Open *CD-97-Table1* found in your data files.
2. To change the row 1 height, click in row 1. Click **Table** on the menu bar. Select **Table Properties**. Click the **Row** tab, if needed.
3. Click the checkbox to select **Specify height** as shown in Figure 12.11. Key **.5** in the **Specify height** text box. Click **OK** at the bottom of the dialog box.

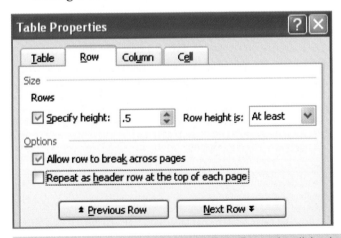

Figure 12.11 Set row height using the Table Properties dialog box.

UNIT 3
Alternative Input Technologies

In Unit 2, you learned to use a keyboard to input data quickly and correctly. Typing on a keyboard is a traditional input method. In this unit, you will learn about new and exciting ways to input data. Handwriting and speech recognition software let you enter data with little keyboard use. Using scanners and digital cameras allows you to place images in documents and presentations. PDAs (small, handheld computers) allow you to take your data with you wherever you go. Data that you input into your PDA can later be transferred to a laptop or desktop PC.

The activities provided at the end of each chapter in this unit will help you: review the concepts you have learned, apply the software skills you have learned, improve your keyboarding skills, learn about business trends and issues, improve math and communication skills, and develop career-related skills.

5. Add a row at the top of the table. Merge the cells in row 1. Key the following title in row 1 using a 14-point font and bold.

STOCK CLUB TOP PERFORMERS

6. Save the table as *96-Table8* and keep the table open. Open *CD-96-Memo1* from your data files.

7. Make *96-Table8* the active window. Click the table move handle to select the entire table. Click the **Copy** button on the toolbar.

8. Make *CD-96-Memo1* the active window. Click in the memo on the blank line below the first paragraph. Click **Paste** on the toolbar. The table should now appear in the memo.

9. Adjust vertical spacing so there is one blank line above and one blank line below the table. Center the table horizontally. Save the memo as *96-Memo1* and print it. Close *96-Memo1* and *96-Table8*.

✔ CHECK POINT Is the table centered between the margins? Compare your % Gain answers with those of a classmate and correct any that are wrong.

Lesson 97 — Tables, Changing Row Height, Borders, and Shading

Objectives

In Lesson 97, you will:
↘ Change row height.
↘ Vertically align text in cells.
↘ Format tables using borders and shading.

Data files: *CD-97-Table1, CD-97-Table2*

Changing Row Height and Vertical Alignment

Row height is the vertical amount of space in a row. Row heights adjust automatically to allow room for text in large font sizes. Row heights can also be set to a certain measurement. The height for row 1 in the table shown in Figure 12.10 is set to 0.5 inch.

By default, text is placed in the upper left of a cell. In previous lessons, you have changed the horizontal alignment of text in a cell. You can also change the vertical alignment of text in a cell. The text may be aligned at the top, center, or bottom of a cell. The vertical alignment for text in the table shown

Chapter 6

Lessons 56–63

Handwriting Tools and OneNote

OBJECTIVES

In Chapter 6, you will:

↗ Resize and move the Language bar or Tablet Input Panel.

↗ Write and take notes with digital ink.

↗ Write with cursive and printed characters.

↗ Turn handwriting into typed text and correct handtyping errors.

↗ Use on-screen keyboards.

↗ Format and edit documents using a digital pen.

↗ Create and name *OneNote* folders, sections, and pages.

↗ Enter and reorganize notes into *OneNote* containers.

↗ Create bulleted lists and outlines in *OneNote*.

↗ Add extra writing space in *OneNote*.

↗ Use color and formatting features to accent notes.

↗ Copy text and pictures from Web files and place in *OneNote*.

↗ Search in *OneNote*.

↗ Insert pictures and sketch pictures in *OneNote*.

For many years computer developers tried to make computers as easy and as fun to use as a box of colored pencils. After years of hard work and many failed attempts, they succeeded. Today, you can use a pencil-like device called a digital pen to write, take notes, and draw on a computer screen. You can also handtype. Handtyping is a process that turns handwriting into typed words.

Phone Number
555-678-0134
555-678-0179
555-348-0144
555-374-0156
555-678-0184
555-472-0172
555-678-0141
555-348-0166
555-374-0112
555-384-0199
555-374-0139

2. Delete the **E-Mail Address** column.

3. Delete row 10 (Yarborough, Pam) and row 4 (Guitterez, Maria). Add a row after row 2 (Aceto, Jill). (To add the row, click in row 2, choose **Table, Insert, Rows Below**.) Key the data below.

Bauer, Brianne	Left Back	10/14/94	555-678-0163

4. Add a row after row 5 (Lei, Su) and key the data below in the new row:

McCoy, Kim	Right Mid	03/01/95	555-348-0118

5. Add a row at the top of the table. Merge the cells in row 1. Using a 14-point font, key the title below in the new row:

TREESDALE ROSTER FOR SOCCER TOURNAMENT

6. Center the page vertically. Save the table as *96-Table7* and close it.

Memo with Table

1. Start *Word*. Open *CD-96-Table8* from your data files.

2. Add a column to the right of column 3 (Room). Key **% Gain** for the column heading.

3. Start the *Calculator* program. Find the percent of gain for each student by dividing the number in the Gain column by the number in the Beginning Amount column. Key the answers in the appropriate cells in the % Gain column. (Round numbers to one decimal place.)

4. Delete the last three columns (Beginning Amount, Ending Amount, and Gain).

© Getty Images/PhotoDisc

You can use your digital writing tools in *Word*, *PowerPoint*, *Excel*, and a variety of other applications. A new application ideally made for handwriting and note-taking is called *Microsoft OneNote*. You can use *OneNote* with the keyboard. It's also fun to take notes in *OneNote* with a digital pen. *OneNote* is a great place to practice your penmanship skills.

You can add and delete rows and columns to change your table grid. Rows can be added above or below the row where you have placed the insertion point. Columns can be added to the left or right of the column where you have placed the insertion point. You will practice adding and deleting rows and columns in the following activity.

96F LEARN: Add and Delete Columns and Rows

1. Start *Word*. Open *CD-96-Table6* found in your data files.

2. To delete row 2, first click in a cell in row 2. Click **Table** on the menu bar. Choose **Delete**. Choose **Rows** from the submenu.

3. To add a row below the last row, click in the last cell in the last row. Tap TAB to add a new row to the bottom of the table.

4. Key the data below in the last row:

2002	Brazil	Germany

5. To add a column between the first and second columns, click in column 1. Click **Table** on the menu bar. Choose **Insert**. Choose **Columns to the Right**.

6. Key the data below in the cells in the new column.

Site
Mexico
Italy
United States
France
Japan/South Korea

7. To delete the last column, click in the last column. Click **Table** on the menu bar. Choose **Delete** and then choose **Columns**.

8. Save the table as *96-Table6* and close it.

96G PRACTICE: Add and Delete Columns and Rows

1. Start *Word*. Open *CD-96-Table7* from your data files. Insert a new column between the **Birth Date** and **E-Mail Address** columns. Key the data below in the new column.

Lesson 56 | Using a Digital Pen

Objectives

In Lesson 56, you will:

➘ Learn about computers and digital tablets that allow handwritten input.

➘ Learn basic digital pen actions.

➘ Start and close programs using a digital pen.

➘ Learn about settings that can be changed for a digital tablet or a Tablet PC.

➘ Draw images in *Paint* using a digital pen.

Handwriting DigiTools

In Chapters 4 and 5, you learned to use a keyboard to input data. In this chapter, you will learn to input data by handwriting. Tablet PCs and PDAs are two types of computers that allow handwritten input directly on the computer screen. A **Tablet PC** is a powerful notebook computer. It has the speed and power of other notebook computers. Unlike other notebook computers, it allows handwritten input. Tablet PCs are small enough to put in your backpack and carry from class to class. A **PDA (personal digital assistant)** is a very small, handheld computer. PDAs can fit in your pocket. You will learn about using PDAs in Chapter 9. A Tablet PC and a PDA are shown in Figure 6.1.

Figure 6.1 A Tablet PC and a PDA

Both Tablet PCs and PDAs let you write directly on the computer screen! Don't try writing on any old computer monitor. Tablet PCs and PDAs have specially designed screens and durable glass surfaces.

To use handwriting input on a desktop or laptop computer, you will need a digital tablet. A **digital tablet** attaches to a desktop or laptop computer.

7. Use the AutoFit to Contents command to change the column widths. Center the table horizontally and center the page vertically.

8. Save the table as *96-Table3* and close it.

96D PRACTICE: Merge and Split Cells

1. Start *Word*. Open a new blank document. Create a table grid with four columns and five rows, using the Fixed Column Width option.

2. Use the Merge Cells and Split Cells commands to make your table grid look like the one below. Then key the data in the table as shown. Use center alignment within all cells. Use a 12-point font for all text.

3. Center the page vertically. Save the document as *96-Table4* and close it.

All cells in row 1 were merged into one cell that spans all the columns.				
These four cells were merged into one cell.	The cell above was split into two cells.		The cell below was split into four cells.	These two cells were merged.
					These two cells were merged.

96E APPLY: Center Table, Merge Cells, and Split Cells

1. Start *Word*. Open a new blank document. Create a table grid with four columns and eight rows, using the Fixed Column Width option.

2. Merge and split cells and format cell entries as shown below. Center the table on the page horizontally. Center the page vertically.

3. Save the table as *96-Table5*. Proofread and correct errors. Print and then close the table.

REFRESHMENT STAND STAFFING					
Saturday	8-10 a.m.		10-11 a.m.	11 a.m-1 p.m.	
September 5	J. Triponey		M. McKeever	B. Hohn	
September 12	D. Ford	M. Lu	G. Bauer	A. Carr	V. Dee
September 19	C. Rickenbach			D. Mars	Z. Sia
September 26	A. Kopolovich			B. Gordon	
October 1	S. Creely	D. Sanchez	M. Nash	R. Janson	
October 8	I. Che	A. Jaso	R. Dolphi	A. Berger	

When you write on the surface of a digital tablet, the writing appears on your computer screen. A digital tablet is shown in Figure 6.2.

Photo courtesy of
Wacom Technology Corporation

Figure 6.2 A Digital Tablet

Using a Digital Pen

The technology that allows handwritten computer input is called **digital ink**. With digital ink, writing on your computer is almost as easy as writing on a piece of paper. To use digital ink, you'll need a digital pen. A digital pen is also called a stylus. A **digital pen (stylus)** is a device used for pointing, drawing, and writing on a special type of computer screen or digital tablet. No ordinary pen will do. You'll need a digital pen that gives input your computer understands. A digital pen is shown in Figure 6.3.

Wacom Technology Corporation

Figure 6.3 A Digital Pen or Stylus

Merge and Split Cells

1. Start *Word*. Open a new blank document. Insert a table grid with three columns and three rows, using the **Fixed Column Width** option. Use the Show/Hide button to display table markers.

2. Using the mouse, point outside the gridlines and to the left of row 1. Click to select the row as shown in Figure 12.8.

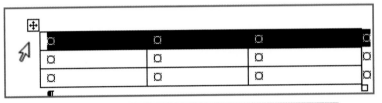

Figure 12.8 You must select cells before you can merge them.

3. To merge the three cells in row 1, click **Table** on the menu bar. Select **Merge Cells**. Row 1 should now have only one cell.

4. To split each cell in row 3 into two cells, select row 3. Click **Table** on the menu bar. Choose **Split Cells**. The Split Cells dialog box will appear as shown in Figure 12.9.

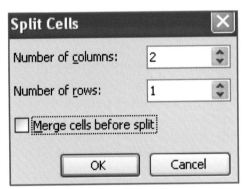

Figure 12.9 Split Cells Dialog Box

5. Key **2** in the Number of columns text box. Key **1** in the Number of rows text box. Remove the check mark from the **Merge cells before split** box. Click **OK**. Row 3 should now have six cells.

6. Key the data below in your table grid. The grid should match the grid below. Format text in the cells as shown.

ELECTED CO-CAPTAINS					
Team Red		Team White		Team Blue	
Mary	Mark	Jose	Prajakar	Mario	Lynora

Hovering is an important skill for digital pen users. Just like a helicopter hovers above the ground, you can hover (hold) your digital pen about ¼ inch above the surface of the computer screen or digital tablet. This will allow you to see the cursor, also called the pen pointer. The pen pointer shows your position on the screen. Depending upon what you're doing, the cursor will take on different shapes. It may be an arrow, a vertical bar, an hourglass, a multisided arrow, a hand, or a pen. Common pen pointer shapes are shown in Figure 6.4.

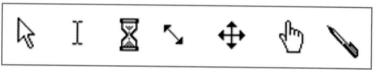

Figure 6.4 Common Pen Pointer Shapes

56A LEARN:

Hover Around Your Tablet

1. Start your computer. If you are using a digital tablet, it should be connected to your computer.

2. The *Windows* desktop should appear on your screen. Hold your digital pen about ¼ inch above the surface of your computer screen or digital tablet. Do not touch your pen to the surface. The pen pointer should appear.

3. Move the digital pen around in a slow circle. Watch the pen pointer move around the screen. Does the pen pointer keep up with your hand movements?

4. Using the digital pen, move the pen pointer to these locations:
   * The top right-hand corner of the screen
   * The bottom left-hand corner of the screen
   * The top left-hand corner of the screen
   * The bottom right-hand corner of the screen
   * The center of the screen

Tiptop Tapping Tips

You can tap, double tap, and touch and drag with your digital pen. Review the following table to compare tapping a pen with clicking a mouse.

4. Save the table as *96-Table1*. Complete the Check Point below and then close the document.

 **CHECK POINT** Is your table centered vertically and horizontally? Use Print Preview to check the layout of the document.

96B PRACTICE:

Center a Table

┌─────────────────┐
Help Words
└─────────────────┘

Merge
  Merge cells into
  one cell in a table
Split
  Split a cell into
  multiple cells in
  a table

1. Start *Word*. Open *95-Table5* that you created in Lesson 95.

2. Change the top margin to 1 inch. Center the page vertically. Center the table horizontally. Use Print Preview to check the placement.

3. Save the table as *96-Table2* and close it.

Merging, Splitting, and Selecting Cells

While formatting tables, you can **merge** (join) cells that are next to each other in the same row or the same column. You can use this feature when information in a table needs to span more than one column or row. You can **split** (divide) a cell into two or more cells. Merging and splitting cells allows you to create tables that are more useful or creative than those that use a standard grid.

When you want to merge or split cells in a table, you must first select the cells. You can always click and drag over cells to select them. However, the table below tells how to select parts of a table quickly.

To Select	Move the Cursor
Entire table	Over the table and click the table move handle
Column	To the top of the column until a solid down arrow appears; then click
Row	To the left area just outside the table until an open arrow appears; then click

Use the Show/Hide button to display table markers as shown in Figure 12.7. These markers are helpful when moving a table or selecting parts of a table.

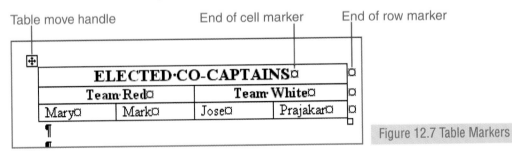

Figure 12.7 Table Markers

BASIC PEN SKILLS		
Pen Action	**Description**	**Mouse Action**
Tap	Touch your pen on the screen or tablet and lift up quickly.	Like a single mouse click
Double-tap	Quickly tap the screen or tablet twice on the same spot.	Like a double-click with a mouse
Touch and drag	Touch the screen or tablet and move while gently maintaining contact with the surface.	Like clicking and dragging with a mouse
Tap, touch, and drag	The first tap selects a graphic or activates an inactive window. The next touch-and-drag action will move or resize windows and graphics.	Like clicking the object first and clicking it again while holding the mouse button down to move or resize an object

56B LEARN: Tap with a Digital Pen

1. Start your computer. If you are using a digital tablet, it should be connected to your computer. The *Windows* desktop should appear on your screen.

2. Using the digital pen, tap once on the **Start** button. When the Start menu opens, tap **All Programs**. Tap **Microsoft Office**. Then tap **Microsoft Word** to open the program.

3. Tap the **Minimize** button to close the open window. The Minimize button is shown in Figure 6.5.

Minimize   Maximize   Restore

Figure 6.5 Control Buttons

4. Tap the **Microsoft Word** button on the taskbar as shown in Figure 6.6. This will open the *Word* window again.

Figure 6.6 Minimized *Microsoft Word* Button on the Taskbar

5. Tap the **Maximize** button (shown in Figure 6.5) to enlarge the *Microsoft Word* window to its largest possible size.

Lesson 96   Tables, Merging and Splitting Cells

Objectives

In Lesson 96, you will:
- Center tables vertically and horizontally.
- Merge and split cells in tables.
- Add and delete rows and columns in tables.

Data files: *CD-96-Table6, CD-96-Table7, CD-96-Table8,* and *CD-96-Memo1*

Table Alignment

Help Words

Center
Position a table on
a page

Tables are usually centered horizontally on a page. However, tables can be aligned at the left or right margin. Tables, like letters and other documents, can be centered vertically on a page. When a table is used in the body of a report, letter, or memo, center it between the left and right margins. Leave one blank line above and below the table.

96A LEARN:

Center a Table

1. Start *Word*. Open *95-Table4* that you created in Lesson 95. In the steps that follow, you will center the table vertically and horizontally.

2. Change the top margin to 1 inch. Change the vertical alignment for the page to **Center**. (To review how to set vertical alignment, refer to Chapter 11, Lesson 93A.)

3. Click in a cell in the table. Click **Table** on the menu bar. Select **Table Properties.** Click the **Table** tab if it is not displayed. Click the icon for **Center** in the Alignment section as shown in Figure 12.6. Click **OK** at the bottom of the box. The table should now be centered horizontally between the left and right margins.

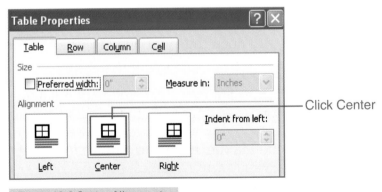

Figure 12.6 Center Alignment

Instant Message

The title bar is found at the top of the program window. It shows the program name. See Chapter 1, Figure 1.9 to review the title bar location.

6. Tap the **Restore** button (shown in Figure 6.5) to shrink the size of the window.

7. Resize the *Word* restored window. Move the digital pen to the bottom right-hand corner of the *Word* window. When a double-sided arrow appears, touch and drag the corner of your window in or out until the window appears about half its original size.

8. Now that you have created a smaller *Word* window, touch and drag the window by the title bar. Move it up, down, left, and right on the screen.

9. Close *Word* by tapping the **Close** button on the *Word* window or by choosing **File**, **Exit** from the menu bar. Tap **No** if you are asked to save.

56C PRACTICE: Open and Close Programs Using a Digital Pen

SOFTWARE TIP

To close the program, tap the **Close** button on the program window or choose **File**, **Exit** from the menu bar.

1. Using your digital pen, start *Microsoft PowerPoint*. (Tap **Start**, **All Programs**, **Microsoft Office**, **Microsoft PowerPoint**.) Minimize the *PowerPoint* window.

2. Maximize and then restore the *PowerPoint* window. Practice moving the window by tapping on the title bar and dragging the window. Close *PowerPoint* without saving.

3. Using your digital pen, start *Microsoft Excel*. (Tap **Start**, **All Programs**, **Microsoft Office**, **Microsoft Excel**.) Practice using your digital pen to minimize, maximize, restore, and resize the window. Close *Excel* without saving.

Instant Message

If you do not have *OneNote*, skip step 4.

4. Using your digital pen, start *Microsoft OneNote*. (Tap **Start**, **All Programs**, **Microsoft Office**, **Microsoft *OneNote***.) Practice using your digital pen to minimize, maximize, restore, and resize the window. Close *OneNote*.

Adjusting Settings

You can adjust various settings related to your pen and tablet or screen. Some settings are chosen when a tablet is installed. Settings can also be changed in the Control Panel. For example, you may be able to indicate whether you are right-handed or left-handed. Doing so will improve the recognition for your writing. You may be able to adjust your pen settings so your tapping is more accurate. These adjustments can be made under options such as Calibrate or Tip Feel. Several options for settings on a Wacom tablet are shown in Figure 6.7 on the next page.

8. Key **1.5** in the Preferred width box to make the column 3 width 1.5". Click the **Next Column** button.

9. Key **1** in the Preferred width box to make the column 4 width 1". Click the **OK** button at the bottom of the box.

10. This table also will not be centered horizontally. Save the table as *95-Table 4* and close it.

95D PRACTICE: Change Column Widths

1. Start *Word*. Open *CD-95-Table5* found in your data files. Use the AutoFit to Contents option to change the column widths. Save the table as *95-Table5*. Print the table and then close it.

2. Open *CD-95-Table5* again. Set the width for columns 1 and 3 to 1.6". Set the widths for columns 2 and 4 to 0.6". Save the table as *95-Table6*. Close the table.

95E APPLY: Create a Basic Table

1. Start *Word*. Open a new blank document. Set the top margin to 2 inches. Create the table shown below. Use the AutoFit to Contents option to set the column widths. Format the data as shown.

2. Proofread the table and correct all errors. Save the table as *95-Table7*. Print the table and then close it.

MONTHS OF THE YEAR IN SPANISH AND ENGLISH

English	Spanish	English	Spanish
January	enero	July	julio
February	febrero	August	agosto
March	marzo	September	septiembre
April	abril	October	octubre
May	mayo	November	noviembre
June	junio	December	diciembre

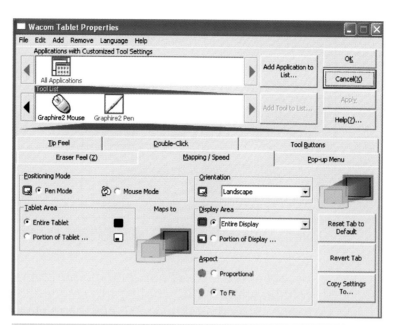

Figure 6.7 Pen and tablet settings can be changed in the Control Panel.

You may be able to change the **orientation** (direction) of your screen or digital tablet. In **landscape** orientation, the long side of your screen or tablet is positioned at the top. In **portrait** orientation, the short side of your screen or tablet is positioned at the top. Figure 6.8 shows an example of each setting. The default setting is typically landscape. You might want to use portrait orientation instead if you find it more comfortable for taking notes or using drawing programs.

Landscape Screen Orientation

Portrait Screen Orientation

Figure 6.8 Screen Orientations

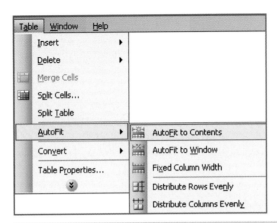

Figure 12.4 Use AutoFit to adjust column widths.

3. Note that the table is not centered horizontally after the change in column widths. You will learn to center a table horizontally in a later lesson. Save the table as *95-Table3* and close it.

4. Open the table *95-Table1* that you created in 95A. Click in a cell in column 1 in the table.

5. Click **Table** on the menu bar. Choose **Table Properties**. Click the **Column** tab. The checkbox by **Preferred width** should be selected. If it is not, click in the box to select it.

6. Key **1.5** in the Preferred width box as shown in Figure 12.5. Click the **Next Column** button.

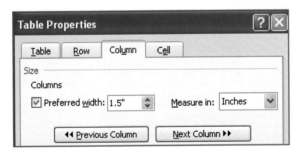

Figure 12.5 Set column widths in the Table Properties dialog box.

7. Key **1** in the Preferred width box to make the column 2 width 1". Click the **Next Column** button.

Screen brightness is another option that you can change easily on a Tablet PC. The monitor setting for brightness on a desktop PC can be changed also. Having the brightness set at a comfortable level helps avoid eye strain and can make reading the screen easier.

Changing pen, tablet, or screen settings may make your writing easier and more accurate. However, do not change the settings on a computer at school without first getting permission from your teacher.

56D APPLY: Use a Digital Pen with Paint

In this activity, you will draw in *Paint* to improve your pen skills.

1. To start *Paint*, use your digital pen to tap **Start**, **All Programs**, **Accessories**, **Paint**.

2. Practice using your digital pen to resize the window to a size that is comfortable for drawing.

3. Using your digital pen, choose the **Rectangle** tool on the toolbar. Tap a **red square** on the color palette. Draw a red rectangle using your digital pen.

4. Using your digital pen, choose the **Ellipse** (oval) tool on the toolbar. Tap a **blue square** on the color palette. Draw a blue circle or oval using your digital pen.

5. Using your digital pen, choose the **Line** tool on the toolbar. Tap a **green square** on the color palette. Draw a green line using your digital pen.

6. Using your digital pen, tap **File** on the menu bar. Tap **Save**. In the Save in box, choose the folder where you save work for this class. Key **56-Paint** for the filename. Click **Save**.

7. Complete the Check Point below. Then close *Paint* by tapping the **Close** button on the *Paint* window.

 **CHECK POINT** Does your *Paint* screen have only three objects? It should have a red rectangle, a blue circle/oval, and a green line. If it has other marks, use the Eraser tool to remove them.

Create a Table

1. Start *Word* and open a new blank document. Set the top margin to 2 inches.

2. Key the table title shown below. Insert a table grid that is four columns by six rows. Key the data in the cells.

3. Apply 14-point font size and bold for the title. Center the column heads and apply bold.

4. Set the alignment for the data under the column heads. Use left alignment for words and right alignment for numbers.

5. Save the table as *95-Table2*. Close the file.

SPRING VALLEY HIGH SCHOOL FBLA OFFICERS

Name	Office	Room	Telephone
Jo Longo	President	218	555-245-0110
Bobbi Kite	Vice President	119	555-678-0134
Brent Diaz	Secretary	214	555-892-0159
Katie Verez	Treasurer	101	555-245-0122
Jerry Wilson	Parliamentarian	116	555-892-0147

Changing Column Widths

Column widths can be changed in different ways. In this lesson, you will use the **AutoFit to Contents** feature. This feature adjusts the column widths to be just wide enough for all of the contents to fit within the cells.

Another way to change column widths is by entering numbers on the Column tab in the Table Properties dialog box. In this box, you can set a column to an exact width, such as 1 inch.

95C LEARN:

Change Column Widths

Help Words

Column
Resize all or part of a table

1. Start *Word*. Open the table *95-Table2* that you created in 95B.

2. Click inside a cell of the table. Click **Table** on the menu bar. Choose **AutoFit**. Choose **AutoFit to Contents** as shown in Figure 12.4.

Lesson 57   Using Handwriting Tools

Objectives

In Lesson 57, you will:
- ⬎ Access the Language bar or Tablet Input Panel.
- ⬎ Locate the Writing Pad tools and adjust settings.
- ⬎ Practice handtyping.
- ⬎ Write for accuracy.

Software Handwriting Features

The software features and tools you use for handwriting input will vary depending on the type of computer you use. Instructions are given for each set of tools. If you use a digital tablet with a desktop or notebook PC, you will use handwriting tools that are provided with *Microsoft Office*. Follow the instructions marked **Office**. If you use a Tablet PC, you will use instructions that are part of the *Windows* operating system. Follow the instructions marked **Tablet PC**.

57A LEARN: Open the Handwriting Tools and Writing Pad

Office

The **Language bar** contains handwriting tools that you can use in *Microsoft Office* programs. You can use them with a digital tablet connected to a desktop or laptop PC. The Language bar is shown in Figure 6.9. You will learn to access the Language bar in this activity.

1. Start *Word* and open a new blank document. To install your *Office* handwriting software, tap **Tools** on the menu bar. Choose **Speech**. If a message about using speech recognition software appears, tap **Cancel**. If a message about the microphone appears, tap **OK** to close the box.

2. Tap the **Microphone** button on the Language bar to turn off the microphone. Your Language bar should look similar to Figure 6.9.

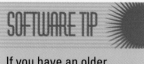

SOFTWARE TIP

If you have an older version of *Windows*, the minimized Language bar will appear as an **EN** in the taskbar. To open it, tap the button and select **Show the Language bar.**

Handwriting button — Minimize button

Figure 6.9 Language Bar

Figure 12.2 Insert Table Dialog Box

4. In the Insert Table dialog box, key **4** for the **Number of columns**. Key **5** for the **Number of rows**. The **Fixed column width** radio button should be selected. Click **OK**. A table grid should appear in your document.

5. Click in the first cell in column 1 row 1. Key the column heading **Name**. Apply bold and center alignment to the column heading. Tap the TAB key one time to move to the next cell (column 2 row 1).

6. Key the other column headings in columns 2, 3, and 4. Apply bold and center alignment to each one. Use TAB or click in a cell, using the mouse to move from cell to cell.

7. Beginning in column 1 row 2, key data in the cells. Use the default alignment.

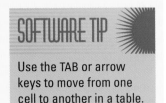

Use the TAB or arrow keys to move from one cell to another in a table.

8. Now you will change alignment for some cells. Click and drag over the cells under the column head in column 2 to select them. Selected cells are shown in Figure 12.3 at the left. Click **Align Right** on the Formatting toolbar. The cells should now appear as in Figure 12.3 at the right.

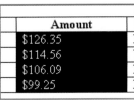

Selected cells   Right-aligned cells

Figure 12.3 Select cells to apply formatting.

9. Right-align the cells under the column head in column 4.

10. Save the table as *95-Table1*. Close the document. Close *Word* or continue to the next activity.

3. Tap the **Minimize** button to minimize the Language bar. Look for the minimized Language bar on the taskbar. It should appear similar to Figure 6.10.

—Restore button

Figure 6.10 Language Bar on the Taskbar

4. Restore the Language bar by tapping the **Restore** button on the bar. (If the Language bar fails to reappear, try reinstalling it by choosing **Tools, Speech** from the menu bar.)

5. Move the Language bar around the screen by tapping and dragging on the far left side of the Language bar. Then move it to the center at the top of your screen.

6. Tap the **Handwriting** button on the Language bar (marked in Figure 6.9). Choose the **Writing Pad** option from the menu. The Writing Pad will appear as shown in Figure 6.11.

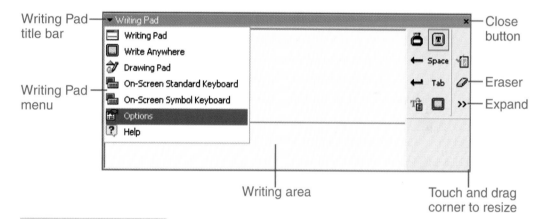

Figure 6.11 Writing Pad

7. When the Writing Pad opens, touch and drag it by its title bar. Move it to a convenient spot, perhaps near the bottom of your screen. Note the features marked in Figure 6.11 that you will use in later steps.

8. Tap the **Expand** icon on the toolbar to view all of the handwriting tools.

9. Make the Writing Pad window an appropriate size by touching and dragging the bottom-right corner of the window.

10. Tap the down arrow by the words **Writing Pad** on the title bar to open a menu. Choose **Options** from the menu as shown in Figure 6.11.

- A **column heading** appears at the top of a column and describes the data in the column. Key column headings in a 12-point font. Apply bold and center alignment to column heads.

- Key data in cells using a 12-point regular font. Data in cells can be aligned left, aligned right, or centered. Usually, numbers are aligned right and words are aligned left.

- Center tables horizontally on the page. Center tables vertically on a page or set a 2-inch top margin.

- Tables can be printed with the cell border showing (the default) or without cell borders showing. Unless directed otherwise, print tables with cell borders showing.

95A LEARN: Create a Table

1. Start *Word* and open a new blank document. Set the top margin to 2 inches. You will key the table below as you complete the remaining steps.

FUND-RAISING RESULTS FOR ROOM 202

Name	Amount	Name	Amount
Harry Xidas	$126.35	Mary Henry	$93.66
Julio Clemente	$114.56	Vinnie Werner	$91.42
Kerri Gorski	$106.09	Naomi Quinonnes	$89.98
Lawrence Miller	$99.25	Betty Upton	$82.50

2. Key the title **FUND-RAISING RESULTS FOR ROOM 202**. Tap ENTER twice. Select the title and apply 14-point font size. Apply bold and center alignment to the title.

3. Now you will create a table grid of four columns and five rows. Click **Table** on the menu bar. Choose **Insert**. Select **Table** from the submenu. The Insert Table dialog box will appear as shown in Figure 12.2.

Instant Message

Learning to use handwriting tools is easier with Automatic Recognition turned off. You may want to turn this feature on later.

11. Tap the **Common** tab. Locate the **Automatic Recognition** option (marked in Figure 6.12). If this option is selected (has a check mark in the box), tap the checkbox for **Automatic recognition** to turn off this option. The box should not be checked as shown in Figure 6.12. Choose **OK** to close the dialog box.

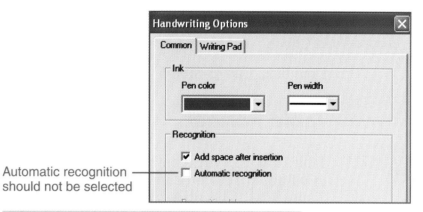

Automatic recognition should not be selected

Figure 6.12 Turn Off the Automatic Recognition Option

12. Tap the **Close** button on the Writing Pad window to close it. Minimize the Language bar. Close *Word*.

Tablet PC

The **Tablet Input Panel** contains the handwriting tools for a Tablet PC. You will learn to use these tools in this activity.

1. Your Tablet PC comes with the TIP (Tablet PC Input Panel) ready to go. To see it, tap the TIP icon on the taskbar. See Figure 6.13.

TIP icon

Figure 6.13 Tablet Input Panel Icon on Taskbar

2. Your Tablet PC Input Panel will open as shown in Figure 6.14. Writing Pad is the option that is selected. Writing Pad allows you to handtype text into documents. Find the parts of the TIP that are labeled in the figure on your screen.

Lesson 95 Basic Tables

Objectives

In Lesson 95, you will:
- ⬆ Create a table.
- ⬆ Insert and key information in a table.
- ⬆ Change widths of columns in a table.

Data files: *CD-95-Table5*

Table Format

Tables are used to organize information. Information is arranged vertically in **columns** and horizontally in **rows**. Columns and rows are marked in Figure 12.1. The place where a row and a column cross each other is called a **cell**. Text, numbers, and formulas for calculating amounts can be entered in a cell. When text is keyed in a cell, it wraps within that cell—instead of moving to the next row. **Gridlines** mark the outline of the area for each cell and are not printed. By default, tables also have cell borders, which do print.

SPRING VALLEY HIGH SCHOOL FBLA OFFICERS — Table title

Name	Office	Room	Telephone
Jo Longo	President	218	555-245-0110
Bobbi Kite	Vice President	119	555-678-0134
Brent Diaz	Secretary	214	555-892-0159
Katie Verez	Treasurer	101	555-245-0122
Jerry Wilson	Parliamentarian	116	555-892-0147

Row 2 — Column heads — Cell borders — Cell — Left-aligned data — Column 3 — Right-aligned data

Figure 12.1 Data in a table is arranged in columns and rows.

Table Format Guidelines

Refer to Figure 12.1 as you read the following formatting guidelines for tables:

- A **table title** describes the content of a table. Key the title in all capital letters using a 14-point font. Apply bold and center alignment to the title. The title may be keyed as the first row in the table grid or a double space above the table grid, as shown in Figure 12.1.

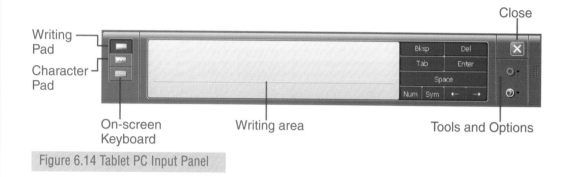

Writing Pad

Character Pad

Close

On-screen Keyboard

Writing area

Tools and Options

Figure 6.14 Tablet PC Input Panel

3. Start *Word*. In the TIP, click the **Tools and Options** icon and choose **Dock at Top of Screen**. Your TIP will move to the top of the screen.

4. Choose the **Tools and Options** icon again. Then choose the **Dock at Bottom of Screen**. Your TIP will move to the bottom of the screen.

5. Choose the **Tools and Options** icon one more time. Choose the **Undock** option. Your TIP will disappear.

6. To display the TIP again, hover over the *Word* window. You will see the floating TIP icon as shown in Figure 6.15. Tap the floating icon to open the TIP.

Figure 6.15 Tablet PC Input Panel Icon

7. Close the TIP by choosing the **Close** button in the top right-hand corner of the TIP.

8. Practice reopening and closing the floating TIP several times.

Handtyping

Inputting data using handwriting recognition is called **handtyping**. Handtyping is easy, if you have good penmanship. For example, in Figure 6.16, the sentence has been converted from handwritten words into the typed words below. Part of the sentence was written in cursive, and the other part was printed. Both printing and cursive can be turned into typed words.

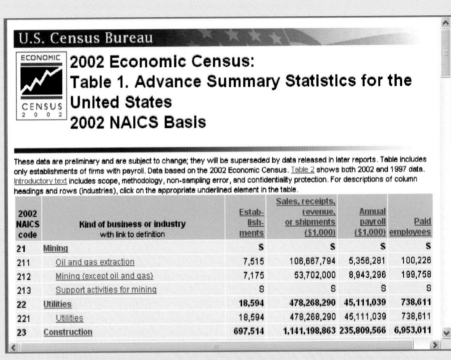

Source: http://www.census.gov/econ/census02/advance/TABLE1.htm

Think about how you use tables. Do you have a schedule of classes that shows your subjects, days and times, room numbers, and teacher names? Do you have a To Do list that shows what you plan to do each day? Do you have a list of frequently called phone numbers? In this chapter, you will learn to create tables to show information in a format that is simple and easy to understand.

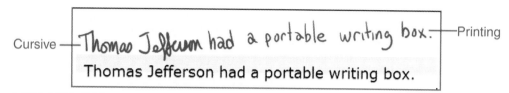

Cursive — Thomas Jefferson had a portable writing box. — Printing

Thomas Jefferson had a portable writing box.

Figure 6.16 Handwriting is converted to typed text.

Microsoft analyzed hundreds of thousands of handwriting samples from all over the world. They used the samples to discover the most common writing styles. Because of this research, if you write clearly, the handwriting software should recognize your writing.

Handtyping Tips

Many people can handtype at 15 to 30 words per minute. But you shouldn't worry about handtyping speed. Think about accuracy instead. To handtype accurately, form each letter carefully. Penmanship truly matters! Read these additional tips for handtyping:

- Separate words by at least ½ inch of blank space.
- Enter punctuation marks immediately after a word.
- Do not try to write too many words on a line.
- When you have finished writing, send the text by tapping the appropriate command.

Handtyping with Printed Characters

In the next few activities, practice printing using block-style letters. Use the same printing or blocked letter style that you learned in elementary school. Examine how these letters should look in the chart that follows.

Chart 6.1 Printed Characters
a b c d e f g h i j k l m n o p q r s t u v w x y z
A B C D E F G H I J K L M N O P Q R S T U V W X Y Z

Chapter 12

Lessons 95–98

Tables

Web Resources:
www.c21jr.swlearning.
com/studentresources

- Data Files
- Vocabulary Flash Cards
- Beat the Clock, Tables
- *PowerPoint* Reviews
- More Activities
- References

OBJECTIVES

In Chapter 12, you will:

↗ Create and print various kinds of tables.

↗ Change column widths and row heights in tables.

↗ Add and delete columns and rows in tables.

↗ Align cell contents and tables.

↗ Merge and split cells in tables.

↗ Apply borders and shading in tables.

↗ Sort information in tables.

↗ Use superscripts and subscripts.

A **table** is information arranged in rows and columns so readers can easily understand the information. Your textbooks use tables to show information that supports what you are learning. The table may contain dates and events. It may contain names of famous people and their inventions. It may show states and their capital cities. Newspapers often use tables. Tables show the rankings of sports teams and players. Television programs and daily temperatures are usually reported in tables.

57B LEARN: Practice Printing

Instant Message

Do not press hard with your digital pen on the surface of the tablet. Pressing hard may damage the tip of the pen and the surface of the tablet.

Office

1. Start *Word*. Open or maximize the Language bar if needed. Open the Writing Pad.

2. Select text mode by tapping the **Text** button on the Writing Pad toolbar. The Text button is marked in Figure 6.17.

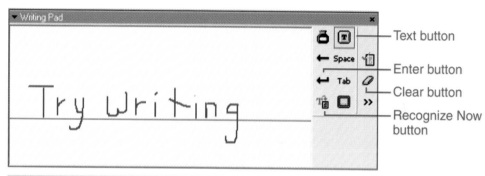

Figure 6.17 Write using printed characters.

3. Print the words **Try writing** above the line on the Writing Pad as shown in Figure 6.17. Tap the **Recognize Now** button.

4. Write the words **as carefully** above the line on the Writing Pad. Leave about ½ inch of space between the words. Don't put too many words on a line. Tap the **Recognize Now** button.

Instant Message

Write punctuation marks directly after the word.

5. Write the words **as you can**. Place a little dot (.) immediately after the word *can* to create a period. Tap **Recognize Now**. Tap the **Enter** button twice to leave a blank line before the next sentence.

6. Practice printing the next two sentences. Tap **Recognize Now** after each group of words.

   ```
   You should | practice your | penmanship | every day.
   [Enter] [Enter]

   Learning to | write clearly | takes practice, | and
   lots | of it! [Enter] [Enter]
   ```

7. Save the document as *57-Printing Practice*. Close *Word*.

need to speak clearly when giving instructions to others. When taking orders, you need to listen closely and follow directions without mistakes. When writing letters or e-mail messages, you should use clear language with error-free grammar and spelling. When talking with customers, you may need to convince others to do or buy something. If you can do all of these things well, you can consider yourself a good communicator.

In previous chapters, you learned about what employers are looking for in an employee. You also learned what about your own personal strengths. In this exercise, you will practice your communication skills. You will use your skills to try to convince someone to do something for you.

1. Open the data file *CD-C11-Message*. Read the instructions to create and send a message to someone.

2. Remember to include a sample of your best work from this chapter in your portfolio.

↗ Academic Success Builder

STUDENT ORGANIZATIONS: KEYBOARDING COMPETITION Organizations such as FBLA have competitions for students. For example, FBLA has a Middle-Level Achievement Program (MAP). There are many competitive events in MAP that relate to what you have learned in this course. Two such events are the Keyboarding Applications I and II.

In the keyboarding events, students are judged on their ability to prepare mailable copy. **Mailable copy** describes a document that is formatted and keyed correctly. If the document is a letter, you should prepare a letter that is arranged correctly. It should contain no errors and be ready to be "mailed." You must use your formatting and proofreading skills to create a mailable letter. You must be able to find and correct all kinds of errors.

In this activity, you will practice skills needed to create a mailable letter. These skills will help you do well in a keyboarding competitive event.

1. Start *Word*. Open *CD-C11-Letter3* found in your data files.

2. Arrange and format the letter parts as a business letter in block style. Use word processing features as needed to make the needed changes. Proofread and correct all spelling, punctuation, and grammar errors.

3. Save the document as *C11-Letter3*. Print the letter and then close it.

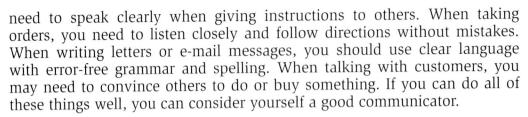

Tablet PC

1. Start *Word*. Open the TIP. Tap the **Character Recognizer** button as marked in Figure 6.18.

2. In the first space on the line, print a capital **A**. TIP will attempt to recognize your handwriting and a letter will appear, replacing what you wrote. If your handwriting was recognized correctly, a capital A will appear. If not, some other letter may appear. If the letter that appears is not the one you were trying to write, try again in the same space.

3. Practice printing the letters of the alphabet. Try to form your letters like the ones shown in Chart 6.1 on page 15. Leave a blank space between letters. Practice both capital and small letters as shown in Figure 6.18.

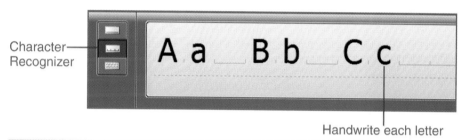

Character Recognizer

Handwrite each letter

Figure 6.18 Practice your printing skills using the Character Recognizer.

4. Tap the **Writing Pad** icon to open the Writing Pad.

5. Print the words **Try writing** above the line on the Writing Pad as shown in Figure 6.19. Tap the **Insert** button.

Leave about ½ inch of space between words

Insert button

Figure 6.19 Write using printed characters.

6. Write the words **as carefully** above the line on the Writing Pad. Leave about ½ inch of space between the words. Don't put too many words on a line. Tap the **Insert** button.

↗ About Business

INCREASING PROFITS IN THE SHORT TERM Businesses forecast a certain amount of sales for certain periods, such as the coming year. This lets managers plan for operations of the business. For example, the number of employees needed, the amount of inventory to purchase, and the amount of supplies to have on hand must be planned. Based on planned sales and expenses, a budget is created. This budget helps managers see whether the business is likely to make a profit.

Sales may not be as high as the amount forecasted. This may be because of factors such as increased competition, a weak economy, or poor product quality. When sales are low, companies may take steps to increase profits in the short term. Increasing profits in the short term allows businesses to stay within the planned budget. Some ways to increase profits in the short term are:

• Reduce expenses, such as advertising or charitable donations

• Reduce the number of employees

• Lower the selling price of the product in an effort to sell more products

• Reduce the cost of making products

• Reduce the cost of products bought for resale

Companies must consider carefully the methods used to increase profits in the short term. Some of these methods may actually reduce profits in the long term. For example, a company may cut its number of employees to lower payroll costs. However, when more employees are needed, the company may have to pay to train new employees. Reducing advertising costs may reduce the number of products sold (and profits) in the long term.

1. Start *Word*. Open and print *CD-C11-Business* from your data files.

2. Follow the instructions provided to complete the problems related to increasing profits in the short term.

↗ Career and Life Skills Success Builder

DEMONSTRATE COMMUNICATION SKILLS Do you have good communication skills? Most people would answer *yes* to that question. However, good communication skills take practice. Acquiring them may be more difficult than you think. For example, as a good communicator, you

7. Write the words **as you can**. Place a little dot (.) immediately after the word *can* to create a period. Tap **Insert**. Tap the **Enter** button twice to create a blank line before the next sentence.

8. Practice printing the next two sentences. Tap **Insert** after each group of words (separated by vertical lines).

   You should | practice your | penmanship | every day. [Enter] [Enter]

   Learning to | write clearly | takes practice, | and lots | of it! [Enter] [Enter]

9. Save the document as *57-Printing Practice*. Close *Word*.

Handtyping with Cursive Letters

Cursive is a faster, smoother way to write than block printing. In the next activity, you will use the cursive style to handtype. If you are a bit rusty on your cursive characters, review the letters in the chart that follows.

Chart 6.2 Cursive Characters
a b c d e f g h i j k l *m n o p q r s t u v w* *x y z*   *A B C D E F G H I J* *K L M N O P Q R S T* *U V W X Y Z*

Speed Forcing Drill

TECHNIQUE TIP

Quickly tap the ENTER key and immediately begin the next line.

Key each line twice. Key a 30" timed writing on each line.

1 Ann and I had a perfect score.
2 The drive to Atlanta takes an hour.
3 Charles attended the Olympics in Athens.
4 My first jump was longer than my second jump.
5 Dan has checked his answers to the problems again.

gwam 30" | 2 | 4 | 6 | 8 | 10 | 12 | 14 | 16 | 18 | 20 |

Timed Writing

Key each paragraph once. DS between paragraphs. Key a 1' timed writing on each paragraph; determine *gwam*.

 all letters used

        •   2   •   4   •   6   •   8
    Money is much harder to save than it is to
    • 10   •   12   •   14   •   16   •
earn. Somebody is always willing to help you
18 •   20   •   22   •   24   •   26   •
spend what you make. If you confuse your needs
  28   •   30   •   32   •   34   •   36
and wants, you can quickly spend much of it
    •   38   •   40   •   42   •   44   •
yourself. Often, friends and relations can
  46   •   48   •   50   •   52   •   54
become an additional major drain if you allow
    •   56   •   58
them to assist you.
            •   2   •   4   •   6   •   8
    And, of course, many politicians at all
    •   10   •   12   •   14   •   16   •
levels think that they can spend your money for
18 •   20   •   22   •   24   •   26   •
you much better than you can do it yourself. It
  28   •   30   •   32   •   34   •   36   •
is really amazing how ready some are to spend the
  38   •   40   •   42   •   44   •   46   •
money of others. At times their motives may be
  48   •   50   •   52   •   54   •   56
excellent; at other times, just selfish. So
    •
beware.

57C LEARN: Handtype Using Cursive Letters

Office and Tablet PC

1. Start *Word*. Open the Writing Pad. Write the sentences shown below, using cursive letters. Remember to write a few words at a time. Then tap the button to insert the text into the document. Leave one blank line between sentences.

```
When do you think you will go?
Tara just finished taking her exam.
Nancy told the man to fix the car brake.
Val could see that he was angry with the boy.
Karen may not be able to afford a new car.
Jay took three hours to complete the project.
```

2. Save the document as *57-Cursive Practice*. Close *Word* or continue to the next activity.

57D PRACTICE: Handtype a Paragraph

Office and Tablet PC

1. Start *Word*. Open the Writing Pad. Write the paragraph shown below. Use printed letters, cursive letters, or a combination of the two as you wish. Remember to write a few words at a time. Then tap the button to insert the text into the document.

```
Thomas Jefferson was a very persuasive writer.
Perhaps his most persuasive piece of writing was the
Declaration of Independence.  He prepared this
document with John Adams and Benjamin Franklin.
This document explains the need for independence.
We should all recognize parts of that document.  For
example, "We hold these truths to be self-evident,
that all men are created equal" is a famous phrase.
```

2. Use your keyboard to correct any mistakes in the document. You will learn to correct using handtyping in the next lesson. Save the document as *57-Jefferson*. Close *Word*.

Building Keying Skill

Warmup Practice

Key each line twice. If time permits, key the lines again.

Alphabet

1 Dr. Kopezy will give Jacques the exam before noon.

Figure/Symbol

2 They received 25% ($164.87) off their order #8390.

Speed

3 Rodney kept the shamrock in the box by the mantel.

gwam 1' | 1 | 2 | 3 | 4 | 5 | 6 | 7 | 8 | 9 | 10 |

Improve Keying Technique

Key each line twice.

Space Bar

1 and the but can may when them lake high find were;
2 Stan may do the work for the six men on the audit.

Shift keys

3 Idaho (Boise) Minnesota (St. Paul) Ohio (Columbus)
4 Sam was sure that the capital of Oregon was Salem.

Adjacent keys

5 buy fire went said ruin were same tree open walked
6 We opened a shop by the same spot as Sandy Merton.

Word response

7 bus when both dial duck held worm soap them signal
8 Jen is to handle all the forms for the small town.

gwam 1' | 1 | 2 | 3 | 4 | 5 | 6 | 7 | 8 | 9 | 10 |

Lesson 58   Correcting Errors

Objectives

In Lesson 58, you will:
- ⇘ Use erasing features to delete words.
- ⇘ Correct handwritten errors using the correction tools.
- ⇘ Use the Space and Backspace buttons to correct mistakes.

Erasing Mistakes

When you handtype, you may sometimes make mistakes. You can erase these mistakes easily. If you are using *Office* handwriting tools, tap the Clear button to erase in Writing Pad. The Clear button is shown in Figure 6.20. If you are using the Tablet PC Writing Pad, quickly swish back and forth four or five times across the word with your digital pen to erase a mistake. In other words, cross it out as shown in Figure 6.20. In a moment after you stop moving the pen, the word will disappear.

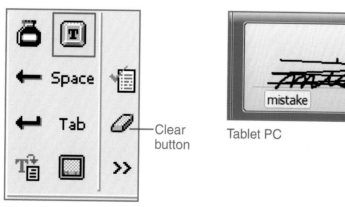

Office Tools   Tablet PC

Figure 6.20 Erase a Mistake in Writing Pad

58A LEARN: Erase Mistakes in Writing Pad

Office and Tablet PC

1. Start *Word*. Open the Writing Pad. Using cursive letters, write **Penmanship**. Do not insert the text in the document.

2. Erase the word. (*Office* users, tap the **Clear** button. Tablet PC users, swish back and forth quickly four times over the word.)

Personal-Business Letter in Block Format

1. Key the following personal-business letter in block format. Use default margins and center the letter vertically on the page. Save the letter as *C11-Letter1*.

2. Create and print a No. 10 envelope with return and mailing addresses for the letter. Close *C11-Letter1*.

853 North Highland Avenue
Atlanta, GA 30306-0403
October 15, 20--

Ms. Amy Mazanetz
4505 Ashford Rd.
Atlanta, GA 30346-0346

Dear Ms. Mazanetz

Thank you for speaking to our Community Service Club. Your points on the importance of giving back to the community were very well received. They will help motivate us to do as much service work as we can.

I enjoyed learning about the projects you have worked on. Our members plan to adopt at least two of the projects you described. Your thoughts about what it takes to plan and carry out service projects will be helpful to us.

Again, thank you for sharing information with our club and agreeing to work with us in the future.

Sincerely

Alex Neu, Secretary

Business Letter and Label

1. Open *CD-C11-Letter2*. Format the letter in block format, using a 2-inch top margin, 1-inch side margins, and a 12-point font. Insert the current date.

2. Use Replace to make changes in the letter. Change *Doe* to *Ford*, *June* to *July*, *team* to *squad*, and *games* to *matches*.

3. Correct all spelling and grammar errors. Save the letter as *C11-Letter2*.

4. Create and print a single label for the letter mailing address. Choose **Avery, 5160 - Address** for the type of label. Print the label in the row 1, column 1 position. Close the letter.

Supplemental activities for this chapter can be found at www.c21jr. swlearning.com.

3. Write the following sentence. If you don't like how you've written a segment of text, erase the words and try again. Insert the text into the document when you are satisfied with it. (To insert the text, tap **Recognize Now** or **Insert**.)

```
Correct mistakes | before they | happen!
[Enter] [Enter]
```

4. Write the next three sentences in cursive. Practice correcting each and every mistake. Remember to write a few words at a time. Then tap the button to insert the text into the document. Leave one blank line between sentences.

```
Try to keep the letters in each word together.
Leave plenty of space between words.
Write so your computer can read your writing!
```

5. Save your writing as *58-Correct*. Close *Word*.

 **CHECK POINT** How was your spacing and penmanship? Do you leave at least ½ inch of space between words? Did you write clearly?

Making Edits

When creating a letter or report, you may change your mind and want to rewrite something. This is called editing. To make edits, select the word or phrase in your document that you wish to change. To select words, touch and sweep over them with your digital pen. Once the words are selected, write the new word or phrase in the Writing Pad. Tap the Recognize Now or Insert button to send the new text to your document.

Sometimes when you handtype, extra spaces may appear where you don't want them. Also, you may accidentally find two words scrunched together with no space between them. You can add and delete spaces using the Space and Backspace buttons. These buttons are shown in Figure 6.21.

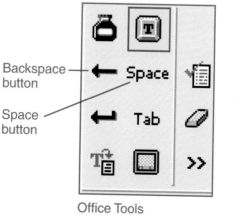

Office Tools

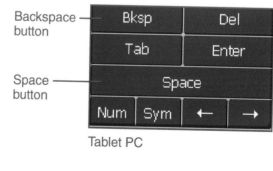

Tablet PC

Figure 6.21 Use the Space and Backspace buttons to make edits.

Applying What You Have Learned

Data File

CD-C11-Letter2

E-Mail Message

1. Key the following information as an e-mail message. Use an address provided by your teacher if the message is to be sent. If e-mail software is not available, format the information as a memo to your instructor from you, using the current date.

2. Save the document as *C11-E-mail* and close it.

SUBJECT: MATH REASONING SKILLS CHALLENGE

A meeting to discuss the Math Reasoning Skills Challenge has been set. The meeting will be on Tuesday, April 17, in Room 23 at 2:30 p.m. Vice Principal Arlo Rome will join us.

The main purpose of the meeting is to discuss the rules for taking part in this competition. We will also talk about program awards and future meeting dates.

Memo in Standard Format

1. Key the following memo. Insert the current date and select the option to have the date update automatically.

2. Save the memo as *C11-Memo*. Print the memo and close it.

TO: FBLA Officers and Committee Heads   *align*

FROM: Marqus Ellerbee, FBLA President

SUBJECT: MEETING NOTICE

All FBLA officers and committee heads will *meet* next Thursday at 2:45 p.m. in Ms. Johnson's room. We will decide the service projects we want to conduct this year. The attached list describes all the *lc* Projects that were identified at the last meeting.

Please review the list and discuss *it* with members you talk with before the meeting. We need to select at least two *projects* from the list. In addition, we need to decide who will enter the competitive events that will take place in the next month. Some of the events require us to form teams.

Attachemnt

Substitution: A Capital Idea

1. Start *Word*. Open the Writing Pad. Use either printed or cursive letters for this activity.

2. In the Writing Pad, write **Olympia, Washington**. Be sure to include a comma (,) after the name of the city. Send the text to your *Word* document.

3. Select the word **Olympia** in your *Word* document. In the Writing Pad, write **Richmond**. Send the text to your *Word* document.

4. Select the word **Washington** in your *Word* document. In the Writing Pad, write **Virginia**. Send the text to your Word document.

5. Using the same steps, replace **Richmond, Virginia** with **Charlotte, North Carolina**.

6. Replace **Charlotte, North Carolina** with **Indianapolis, Indiana**.

7. Finally, replace **Indianapolis, Indiana** with **Jackson, Mississippi**.

8. Move your insertion point just before the **M** in **Jackson, Mississippi**. Tap the **Backspace** button in the Writing Pad to remove the space between **Jackson,** and **Mississippi**. Restore the space by tapping the **Space** button.

9. Close the document without saving.

Improving Correcting Techniques

No one's penmanship is perfect. We all make mistakes from time to time. Fortunately, both *Office* handwriting recognition and the Tablet PC Input Panel offer alternative ways to make corrections.

An effective way to correct handtyping errors is to select the misrecognized word and choose the correct alternative from a list. You will practice this method for correcting errors in the next activity.

Correct Errors Using the Correction List

Office

1. Start *Word*. Open the Writing Pad.

2. Write the words below, spelling **good** incorrectly as shown.

   This was a god day.

Reviewing *What You Have Learned*

Answer these questions to review what you have learned in Chapter 11.

1. Written messages sent in printed form and used by people within an organization to communicate with one another are _____.

2. What are the four heading lines used in a memo?

3. What part tells the reader that other material is enclosed with a letter or memo?

4. When a person besides the writer keys a memo or letter, the typist's _____ are keyed on the letter or memo.

5. In the body of a memo, all lines begin at the _____.

6. What top and side margins should be used for a one-page memo or a letter?

7. What two *Word* features allow you to see a document on screen in a reduced size?

8. A company that provides customer connections to the Internet is a(n) _____.

9. An e-mail address contains a _____ and a domain name separated by the *at* sign (@).

10. List four guidelines you should follow when writing e-mail messages.

11. A program that destroys or harms data on a computer and can arrive as attachments to an e-mail message is a(n) _____.

12. What document is usually sent via United States mail to conduct business of a personal nature?

13. List and describe the seven parts that should be included in a personal-business letter.

14. Describe the spacing generally used for the lines of paragraphs in e-mails, memos, and letters.

15. For a letter in block format, all lines begin _____.

16. Instead of keying a date in a letter, you can use the _____ feature to place the date in the letter.

17. The feature used to find errors such as *its* instead of *it's* in a document is called _____.

18. What options are available in *Word* for aligning a page vertically? Which two options can be used for a letter?

19. How does a business letter differ from a personal-business letter?

20. You can select the letter address in a document and it will appear automatically in the address box when you use the _____ feature.

21. Use the _____ feature to locate words in a document quickly.

22. Use the _____ feature to locate words in a document and change them to other words.

3. In your *Word* document, select the word **god**. Tap the **Correction** button in the Writing Pad. A list of possible corrections will appear as shown in Figure 6. 22.

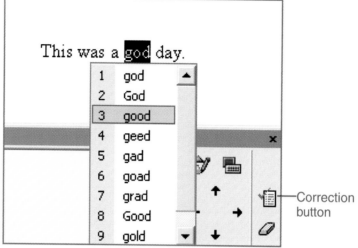

Figure 6.22 Correction List in Writing Pad

4. Tap the word **good** in the correction list. The word will appear in your document.

5. Write two or three more misspelled words of your choice. Try to correct the words using the correction list. Sometimes, none of the words in the correction list will be the word you want. In that case, tap a blank area to close the list. Select the word and rewrite it as you learned earlier.

6. Close the document without saving.

Tablet PC

1. Start *Word*. Open the Writing Pad. Undock the Writing Pad.

2. Write the words below, spelling *hot* incorrectly as shown.

   This is a hoot day.

3. In your *Word* document, select the word **hoot**. A list of possible corrections will appear above or below the Writing Pad. See Figure 6.23.

CHECK POINT How many times does *pay* appear in the document? Compare your answer with a classmate's answer.

5. Place the insertion point at the beginning of the document. Click **Edit** on the menu bar. Select **Replace**.

6. Key **assessments** in the Find what box. Key **taxes** in the Replace with box as shown in Figure 11.19.

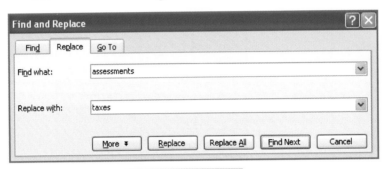

Figure 11.19 Find and Replace Dialog Box

7. Click the **Replace All** button. All instances of *assessments* will be replaced with *taxes*. Click **OK** when the message box indicates the search is completed and the number of replacements made.

8. Use Replace to find and replace all occurrences of **social security** with **Social Security**.

9. Save the file as *94-Replace* and close the document.

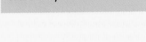

SOFTWARE TIP

Click the **Replace** button to replace the found word only once.

| 94E PRACTICE: Edit Labels with Find and Replace

1. Open a new blank document in *Word*. Access the Envelopes and Labels dialog box. (Select **Tools, Letters and Mailings,** and then **Envelopes and Labels**.)

2. Click the **Labels** tab. Key the following name and address in the Address box:

   Maria Perez
   128 Apple Street
   Monticello, KY 42633-0128

3. Click the **Options** button. Select **Avery standard** from the Label products drop-down list. Select **5160 - Address** for the label size.

4. Select **Full page of the same label** in the Print section. Click the **New Document** button. A new document filled with labels will open.

5. Use Find and Replace to change all instances of *Street* to *Lane*. Use Find and Replace to change all instances of *Maria* to *Miss Maria*.

6. Save the document as *94-Labels* and close the document.

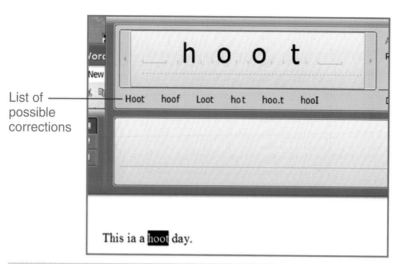

List of possible corrections

This ia a **hoot** day.

Figure 6.23 Possible Corrections in Writing Pad

4. Tap the word **hot** in the correction list. The word will appear in your document.

5. Write two or three more misspelled words of your choice. Try to correct the words using the correction list. Sometimes, none of the words in the correction list will be the word you want. In that case, select the word and rewrite it as you learned earlier.

6. Close the document without saving.

58D PRACTICE: Correct Your Writing

SOFTWARE TIP

When TIP is undocked, Writing Pad will add extra lines as you handtype.

1. Start *Word*. Open the Writing Pad.

2. Write the following short paragraph. Begin your paragraph by tapping the **Tab** button to indent the first line of the paragraph. At the end of the paragraph, tap the **Enter** button twice.

> Outside Williamsburg's Kimball Theatre you can find a statue of Thomas Jefferson sitting on a park bench. He has a curious box on his knee. It is a writing box. The writing box was as handy then as the Tablet PC or portable computer is today. Inside the box were several bottles of ink, several quill pens, and sheets of parchment. Parchment is a type of paper.

3. Proofread the paragraph and correct all mistakes. Save your paragraph as *58-Williamsburg*. Complete the Check Point below. Then close *Word*.

 **CHECK POINT** Ask a classmate to proofread your document on the screen. Correct any errors that are found and save again, using the same name.

Instant Message

Labels are placed in a table in a grid of rows and columns.

Row 1 Column 1	Row 1 Column 2
Row 2 Column1	Row 2 Column 2
Row 3 Column 1	Row 3 Column 2

Help Words

Replace
Find and replace
text or other items

94D LEARN:

SOFTWARE TIP

The word you wish to find can appear as part of other words. For example, *pay* may appear in *payment*. To prevent this, click the **More** button. Select **Find whole words only**.

6. Click the **Single label** radio button to select this option in the **Print** section. Select **Row 1** and **Column 1** as shown in Figure 11.17. This setting will place the label at the top left of the page.

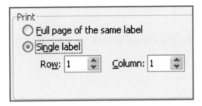

Figure 11.17 Print Placement Options for Labels

7. Your teacher will tell you whether to print on labels or plain paper. After the labels or plain paper are placed in the printer, click the **Print** button. After printing, close the document without saving the changes.

Find and Replace

You can quickly search for a word or phrase in a document by using the **Find** feature. The **Replace** feature not only finds the text, but then replaces the text with other text. All occurrences of the text in the document can be replaced at one time. Replacements can also be made each time the text is found.

Find and Replace Text

1. Open *CD-94-Replace*. Place the insertion point at the beginning of the document.

2. Click **Edit** on the menu bar. Select **Find**.

3. Key **pay** in the Find what box. Click **Find Next**. The word *pay* will be highlighted the first time it is found in the document.

Figure 11.18 Find and Replace Dialog Box

4. Tap the **Find Next** button after each time *pay* is found. Click **OK** when the message box indicates that *Word* has finished searching the document.

1. Start *Word*. Open *58-Williamsburg* that you created earlier. Open the Writing Pad.

2. Move your insertion point two lines below your existing paragraph (to leave a blank line).

3. Continue to handwrite the paragraphs below. Indent the first line of each paragraph. Leave a blank line between paragraphs. Correct any mistakes you make.

```
     Williamsburg, Virginia, was an important
capital city in colonial times.  Hundreds of years
ago, many famous colonial leaders walked its
streets.  If you travel to Williamsburg today, you
just may be able to have your picture taken sitting
next to one of these famous people.

     The lid of Jefferson's writing box was tilted
upward so Jefferson could handwrite on a solid
surface and in a comfortable position.  Just like
the Tablet PCs of today, his handwriting box allowed
Jefferson to write wherever and whenever he needed
to.  If an idea came into his mind, he could stop,
sit under the shade of a nearby tree, and write his
notes, important documents, or letters.
```

4. Save your expanded story as *58-Williamsburg2*. Close *Word*.

Lesson 59   Writing Extras

Objectives

In Lesson 59, you will:

↘ Use the on-screen keyboards.

↘ Format with the digital pen.

↘ Copy and paste with the digital pen.

↘ Use on-screen keyboard shortcuts.

On-Screen Keyboards

Your writing tools come with **on-screen keyboards**. You can tap keys on these keyboards to enter characters. Using a keyboard is helpful for entering symbols such as the @ symbol in an e-mail address. They are also helpful for entering words that are not easily recognized, such as names.

94C LEARN: Create a Label

1. Open *CD-94-Letter1* from your data files. Select the lines of the letter mailing address.

2. Click **Tools** on the menu bar. Select **Letters and Mailings.** Select **Envelopes and Labels** from the submenu. Click the **Labels** tab.

3. The address from the letter should appear in the Address window as shown in Figure 11.15.

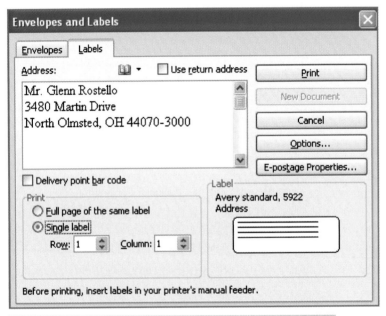

Figure 11.15 Labels Tab of Envelopes and Labels Dialog Box

4. If needed, remove the check mark from the **Use return address** box.

5. Click the **Options** button. Select **Avery standard** from the Label products drop-down list as shown in Figure 11.16. Select **5160** - **Address** from the Product number list. Click **OK.**

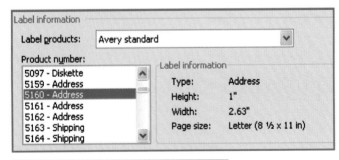

Figure 11.16 Label Options Dialog Box

The Standard on-screen keyboard looks similar to your computer keyboard. It is used for tapping lowercase letters and numbers. The Shifted on-screen keyboard contains capital letters and some symbols. You access the Shifted keyboard by tapping the Shift or Caps key on the Standard keyboard. Standard and Shifted on-screen keyboards are shown in Figure 6.24.

Office Standard On-Screen Keyboard

Tablet PC Shifted On-Screen Keyboard

Figure 6.24 On-Screen Keyboards

To access on-screen keyboards, choose options on the Language bar or Input Panel. You will practice using on-screen keyboards in the next activity.

59A LEARN: Open On-Screen Keyboards

Office

1. Start *Word*. Tap the **Handwriting** button on the Language bar. Select **On-Screen Standard Keyboard** from the menu. Close the keyboard by tapping the **Close** button.

3. If needed, remove the check mark from the Omit box (by Return address). Key the sender's name and address in the Return address window.

Ms. Valerie E. Lopez
207 Brainard Road
Hartford, CT 06114-2207

4. Click the **Options** button. Click the **Envelope Options** tab as shown in Figure 11.14. Click the **Envelope size** down arrow and select **Size 10 (4 ⅛ x 9 ½ in)** from the list. Click **OK**.

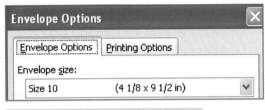

Figure 11.14 Envelope Options Tab

5. Click the **Print** button. (Print the envelope on plain paper unless instructed otherwise by your teacher.) Close the document without saving the changes.

| 94B PRACTICE: | Create an Envelope and Key Addresses

1. Open a new blank document in *Word*. Open the Envelopes and Labels dialog box. (Click on **Tools, Letters and Mailings**, and then **Envelopes and Labels**.)

2. Key your instructor's name and school address in the Delivery address window.

3. If needed, remove the check mark from the **Return Address, Omit** checkbox. Key your name and home address in the Return address window.

4. Select a Size 10 envelope. (Click **Options** and select from the drop-down list.)

5. Print the envelope. When it has printed, close the file without saving.

┌ ─ ─ ─ ─ ─ ─ ┐
Help Words
└ ─ ─ ─ ─ ─ ─ ┘
Label
  Create and print
  labels for a single
  item or address

Labels

Many different sizes of labels can be created and printed by using *Word*'s **Label** feature. You can create labels to place on envelopes, folders, and other items. In this lesson you will learn to print a single Avery 5160 Address label. This is a frequently used label size for No. 10 envelopes.

2. Open Writing Pad. Tap the **On-Screen Keyboard** button on the Writing Pad. See Figure 6.25.

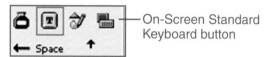
On-Screen Standard
Keyboard button

Figure 6.25 On-Screen Keyboard Button

3. Tap the **Caps** key to access the Shifted keyboard. Taps the **Caps** key again to return to the Standard keyboard. Close the keyboard by tapping the **Close** button.

4. Close *Word* or continue to the next activity.

Tablet PC

1. Start *Word*. Open the Input Panel. Tap the **On-Screen Keyboard** button on the Input Panel. See Figure 6.26.

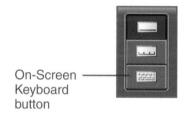
On-Screen
Keyboard
button

Figure 6.26 Tablet PC Input Panel Buttons

2. Tap the **Caps** key to access the Shifted keyboard. Tap the **Caps** key again to return to the Standard keyboard. Close the keyboard by tapping the **Close** button.

3. Close *Word* or continue to the next activity.

59B PRACTICE: Use On-Screen Keyboards

SOFTWARE TIP

Tap the **Caps** key to go to the Shifted keyboard (with all capital letters). Tap the **Caps** key again to go back to the Standard keyboard.

1. Start *Word*. Open *58-Williamsburg2* that you created earlier. Access the Standard on-screen keyboard as you learned to do in Lesson 59A.

2. Move to the very beginning of the *Word* document. Tap the **Enter** key on the on-screen keyboard twice to create two blank lines. Go to the beginning of the document on the first blank line.

3. Tap the **Caps** key on the on-screen keyboard. The Shifted keyboard will appear. Tap keys on the on-screen keyboard to enter the following words in capital letters. Tap the Space Bar to leave a space between words.

THOMAS JEFFERSON

Lesson 94   Envelopes and Labels

Objectives

In Lesson 94, you will
↘ Create envelopes and labels.
↘ Use the Find and Replace feature.

Data files: *CD-94-Letter1, CD-94-Replace*

Envelopes

You have learned how to create letters. Now you need envelopes in which to mail the letters. Many different sizes of envelopes can be created by using *Word's* **Envelope** feature. In this lesson, you will learn to create a No. 10 envelope. This is the most frequently used envelope size for letters printed on 8.5" × 11" paper.

94A LEARN: Create an Envelope from a Letter Address

1. Open *CD-94-Letter1* from your data files. Select the lines of the letter mailing address.

2. Click **Tools** on the menu bar. Select **Letters and Mailings.** Select **Envelopes and Labels** from the submenu. Click the **Envelopes** tab. The address from the letter should appear in the Delivery address window as shown in Figure 11.13.

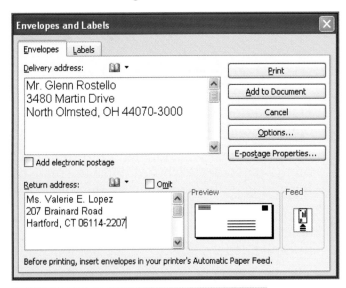

Figure 11.13 Envelopes and Labels Dialog Box

4. Tap the **Caps** key to go back to the Standard keyboard. Tap the **apostrophe** key. Tap the **Caps** key again and finish tapping out the title shown below.

   THOMAS JEFFERSON'S PORTABLE WRITING BOX

5. Tap in the document on the space after Thomas Jefferson's name the first time it appears in the first paragraph. Tap the **Shift** key. The Shifted keyboard appears. Tap the (key. Notice that after you tap the key, the Standard keyboard returns. Tapping the Shift key allows you to key one capital letter.

6. Tap numbers for Jefferson's birth year: **1743**. Tap a **hyphen**. Tap numbers for Jefferson's year of death: **1826**. Tap the **Shift** key and then the) key. The text should now appear as: **Thomas Jefferson (1743-1826)**. Adjust spacing as needed to have one space between words.

7. Save the document as *59-Williamsburg*. Close *Word*.

Formatting and Editing with On-Screen Keyboards

Keyboard shortcuts are available for giving many commands in *Word* and other *Office* programs. These commands work with on-screen keyboards as well as with your PC keyboard. Some keyboard shortcuts you can use to format and edit text are shown in the chart below. To give a command, tap the first key (such as Ctrl) followed by the second key.

CHART 6.3 KEYBOARD SHORTCUTS	
Command	**Action**
Ctrl + b	Applies **bold** format
Ctrl + i	Applies *italic* format
Ctrl + u	Applies <u>underline</u> format
Ctrl + x	Cut selected text
Ctrl + c	Copy selected text
Ctrl + v	Paste copied or cut text

59C LEARN: Use Keyboard Shortcuts

Office and Tablet PC

1. Start *Word*. Open a new blank document. Access the Standard on-screen keyboard as you learned to do in Lesson 59A.

Create Business Letter with Center Alignment

Instant Message

You will print business letters on plain paper. If you were working for a business, you would use letterhead paper.

1. Open a new blank document in *Word*.
2. Choose **File** from the menu bar. Choose **Page Setup**. On the Layout tab, click the down arrow for vertical alignment. Choose **Center**. (See Figure 11.11 on page 407.) Click **OK**.
3. Key the business letter shown in Figure 11.12 on page 408. Use block format, starting with the date, as shown in the figure.
4. Check spelling and grammar. Proofread carefully and correct all errors. Save the letter as *93-Letter1*.

 **CHECK POINT** Ask a classmate to check your printed letter. Discuss any errors found and make corrections.

Create Business Letter

1. Open a new document in *Word*. Key the business letter below in block format. Change the vertical alignment to Center. Insert the current date.
2. Check spelling and grammar. Correct all errors. Save the letter as *93-Letter2*.

```
Mr. Edward Pudlowski
465 Saddler Drive
Bay Village, OH 44140-0465
Dear Mr. Pudlowski
```

Thank you for allowing us to place an ad in your Spring Musical program. A check for $50 for the ad is enclosed. The ad should be a full page in the program booklet.

Please use the copy on the enclosed business card for the content of the ad. Also state in the ad that customers who present this ad at our Ohio Street garden center will get a 15 percent discount. (Place the discount information near the bottom of the ad.) This offer is valid for three months. If you have any questions about the content, please e-mail me at hlandscape@quickstar.com.

Our company is happy to support your booster group by placing this ad. Last year's ad generated many sales from first-time customers. I expect this year's ad and discount will do as well.

```
Sincerely

Harry Piper, Owner

xx

Enclosure
```

2. Tap your full name, using capital and lowercase letters. Tap and drag to select your name. Tap **Ctrl + c**. Tap off your name so it is no longer selected.

3. Tap the **Enter** key to go to a new line. Tap **Ctrl + v**. Your name should now appear two times.

4. Select the first copy of your name. Tap **Ctrl + b** to apply bold to your name.

5. Select the first copy of your name. Tap **Ctrl + u** to underline your name.

6. Select the second copy of your name. Tap **Ctrl + i** to apply italic to your name.

7. Select both copies of your name. Tap **Ctrl + c**. Go to a new blank line and tap **Ctrl + v**. Your name should now appear four times.

8. Select the first two copies of your name. Tap **Ctrl + x** to delete the text. Your name should now appear two times. Close the document without saving.

59D PRACTICE: Format and Edit with On-Screen Keyboards

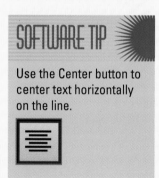
1. Start *Word*. Open *59-Williamsburg* that you created earlier. Access the Standard on-screen keyboard.

2. Select the title of the document (**THOMAS JEFFERSON'S PORTABLE WRITING BOX**). Use a keyboard shortcut command to apply bold to the title. See Figure 6.27 on page 214.

3. Select the title of the document again if it is not already selected. Tap the **Center** button on *Word's* Formatting toolbar to center the title.

4. Select **Williamsburg, Virginia**, in the second paragraph. Use a keyboard shortcut command to apply italic to the text.

5. Select the name **Thomas Jefferson** the first time it appears in the first paragraph. Use a keyboard shortcut command to apply underline to the text.

6. Use keyboard shortcuts to change the order of the paragraphs. Select the first paragraph. Tap **Ctrl + x** to cut the paragraph.

7. Move to the blank line between the two remaining paragraphs. Tap **Ctrl + v** to paste the paragraph. Delete or add lines as needed to have one blank line between paragraphs.

Harry's Landscape, Inc.

247 Ohio Street
Elyria, OH 44035-0280
www.hlandscape.com

Telephone: (442) 351-9847   Fax: (442) 351-9848

November 12, 20--

QS

Ms. Margo Johnson
24168 Squire Road
Columbia Station, OH 44028-0614

Dear Ms. Johnson

Your satisfaction with our products is important to us. I'm sorry to learn that you
are displeased with a few items in the last shipment of plants we delivered to your
home last week.

We will refund your money or replace your plants if you are not fully satisfied with
them. Our delivery person will pick up the plants you want to return. The driver
will stop at your home between 10 a.m. and 1 p.m. next Wednesday. If you will
not be at home then, place the plants by your garage door. The driver will leave a
receipt for what you return.

You have 30 days to stop at our garden center to get replacement plants or a
refund. Just present this letter and your receipt. A gift certificate for $20 that you
can use toward your next purchase is enclosed. Thank you for your business.

Sincerely

QS

Harry Piper, Owner

xx

Enclosure

Figure 11.12 Business Letter on Letterhead Paper

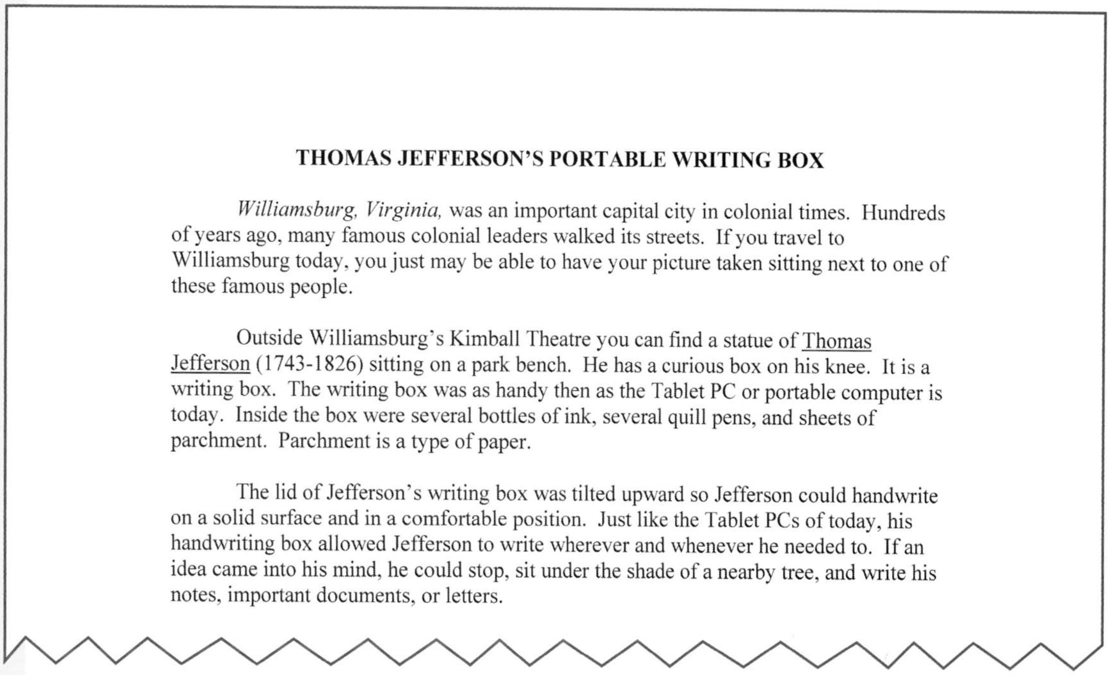

THOMAS JEFFERSON'S PORTABLE WRITING BOX

Williamsburg, Virginia, was an important capital city in colonial times. Hundreds of years ago, many famous colonial leaders walked its streets. If you travel to Williamsburg today, you just may be able to have your picture taken sitting next to one of these famous people.

Outside Williamsburg's Kimball Theatre you can find a statue of <u>Thomas Jefferson</u> (1743-1826) sitting on a park bench. He has a curious box on his knee. It is a writing box. The writing box was as handy then as the Tablet PC or portable computer is today. Inside the box were several bottles of ink, several quill pens, and sheets of parchment. Parchment is a type of paper.

The lid of Jefferson's writing box was tilted upward so Jefferson could handwrite on a solid surface and in a comfortable position. Just like the Tablet PCs of today, his handwriting box allowed Jefferson to write wherever and whenever he needed to. If an idea came into his mind, he could stop, sit under the shade of a nearby tree, and write his notes, important documents, or letters.

Figure 6.27 Documents can be formatted using keyboard shortcuts.

8. Save the document as *59-Williamsburg2*. Print the document.

✔ **CHECK POINT** Ask a classmate to check your printed document. Correct any errors that are found, and save again, using the same name.

Lesson 60   Using OneNote

Objectives

In Lesson 60, you will:
↘ Create and name *OneNote* folders, sections, and page headers.
↘ Enter notes into *OneNote* containers.

OneNote Basics

OneNote is a program that allows you to take notes and organize them in a way that is easy to use. You can key data into *OneNote* using your computer keyboard. You can handtype data into *OneNote* using Writing Pad or an on-screen keyboard. You can dictate data into *OneNote* using speech recognition tools (covered in Chapter 8). You can also use a type of digital ink that leaves your notes in handwritten form. With *OneNote*, you can handwrite your notes just like you would write on a piece of paper.

Lesson 93   Business Letters

Objectives

In Lesson 93, you will:

↘ Format a business letter in block style.

↘ Learn to set vertical page alignment.

Business Letters

In the previous lesson, you learned to create a personal-business letter. In this lesson, you will create a business letter. **Business letters** are sent from a person within a business to another person. The other person may work at another business, or he or she may be a customer or client.

A business letter is the same as a personal-business letter with one change. A return address is not keyed in a business letter. It is not keyed because business letters are printed on special paper. This paper is called letterhead paper. **Letterhead paper** has the business name and address printed on the paper. Letterhead paper often has the company's phone and fax numbers. Web addresses are often included, too. A business letter printed on letterhead paper is shown in Figure 11.12 on page 408.

Vertical Alignment

The **Vertical alignment** feature sets how text will be placed on a page. You can set text to begin at the top, end at the bottom, or be centered on the page. The Center option places about the same amount of white space above and below the text. The Center option can be used for letters (rather than a 2-inch top margin).

Vertical alignment can be changed before or after text is keyed. To change the alignment setting, choose File from the menu bar. Select Page Setup. Choose an option for vertical alignment on the Layout tab as shown in Figure 11.11.

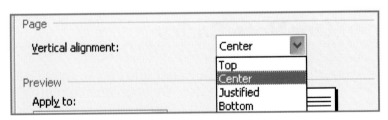

Figure 11.11 Page Setup Dialog Box

Help Words

Center
Change vertical
alignment of text

OneNote takes note-taking to an exciting, new level. *OneNote* can change the way you learn, study, and work. *OneNote* also provides an opportunity to practice your penmanship and handtyping skills.

60A LEARN: Open OneNote

1. Start *OneNote* by choosing **Start**, **All Programs**, **Microsoft Office**, **Microsoft Office *OneNote***.

2. Look at the parts of a *OneNote* screen in Figure 6.28. Find each of these parts on your screen.

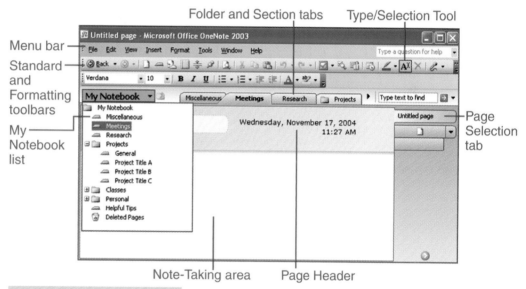

Figure 6.28 *OneNote* Window

3. If the Standard and Formatting toolbars appear on one line, change the setting. Click the down arrow at the end of either toolbar. Choose **Show Buttons on Two Rows** as shown in Figure 6.29.

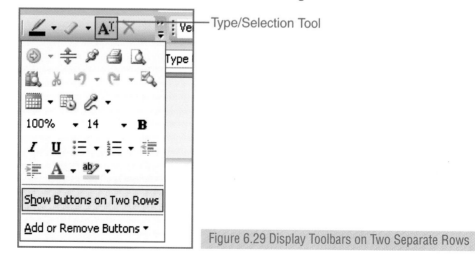

Figure 6.29 Display Toolbars on Two Separate Rows

- **Close.** If you want to stop before the entire document has been checked, click the Close button. Otherwise, click OK when the checker is finished. You will see the message "The spelling and grammar check is complete."

92D LEARN: Grammar Check

1. Open *CD-92-Grammar1*. Position the insertion point at the beginning of the text, if needed.
2. Click **Tools** on the Menu bar. Click **Spelling and Grammar**. The Spelling and Grammar dialog box opens.
3. If the Check grammar option in the lower-left corner is not selected, click in the checkbox to select this feature. See Figure 11.10.
4. The first possible error shown should be *was*. The word *were* should be in the Suggestions list. If so, click **Change**. If not, change *was* to *were* in the top box and then click **Next Sentence**.
5. The second possible error identified should be *whomever*. *Word* questions the use of words, such as *who* and *whom*, that are often misused. *To whomever* is correct, so no change is needed. Click **Next Sentence**.
6. The third error is a sentence fragment. To correct the error, click outside the dialog box and correct the error in the document. Change the text to be one sentence: **We marveled at the players when they scored the winning goal.**
7. Click **Resume** in the Spelling and Grammar dialog box. Click **OK** to close the message box telling you that the spelling and grammar check is complete. Save the file as *92-Grammar1* and close it.

92E PRACTICE: Check Grammar

1. Open *CD-92-Grammar2* found in your data files. Use Spelling and Grammar Check to find and correct spelling and grammar errors.
2. Proofread the text to see if all errors were found and corrected. Correct any remaining errors.
3. Save the file as *92-Grammar2* and close it.

92F APPLY: Format Personal-Business Letter

1. Open *CD-92-Letter3* found in your data files. Print the document. Key this handwritten text as a personal-business letter in block format.
2. Use Spelling and Grammar Check to find and correct spelling and grammar errors. Proofread the text and correct any remaining errors.
3. Save the document as *92-Letter3* and close it.

4. Close *OneNote* by clicking **Close** button on the *OneNote* window or by choosing **File, Exit** from the menu bar.

OneNote Folders, Sections, and Headers

Information in *OneNote* is organized in folders. All *OneNote* folders are stored in the *My Notebook* folder. You can tell which tabs are for a folder by the folder icon as shown in Figure 6.30. Inside folders you'll find sections. A **section** is a computer file like any other computer file. It can have as many pages as you care to create. To say it another way:

- You will write your notes on pages.

- Pages are organized in sections (files).

- Sections are stored in folders.

Pages, sections, and folders can be opened by choosing tabs. Several tabs are shown in Figure 6.30. In the next activity, you'll create a new folder and add several new sections.

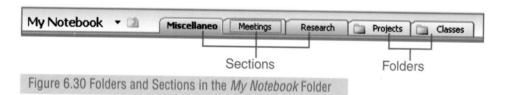

Figure 6.30 Folders and Sections in the *My Notebook* Folder

Name and Rename Folders, Sections, and Headers

1. Start *OneNote*. Open the Writing Pad. Tap or click the **Text/Selection Tool** on the Standard toolbar.

2. To create a new folder, choose **Insert** on the menu bar. Choose **New Folder**. A new tab will appear on the screen. It will be named New Folder. The name should be highlighted. (If it is not, right-click the name and choose **Rename** from the menu.)

3. Key **History** for the folder name and tap Enter. The new folder name will appear on the tab as shown in Figure 6.31.

Figure 6.31 New Folder in *OneNote*

3. Save the file as *92-Form*. Close the document and wait a minute or so.

4. Open the file *92-Form* that you just edited. Look at the date and time. The date should be the same as earlier, but the time should have been updated. Close the file.

Check Grammar

Help Words

Grammar
  Check spelling and
  grammar

Letters should be free of errors. You learned earlier how to check for spelling errors. You can also check for grammar errors when you check for spelling errors. To do so, the **Check grammar** option on the Spelling and Grammar dialog box must be selected. The Check grammar option is selected (checked) in Figure 11.10.

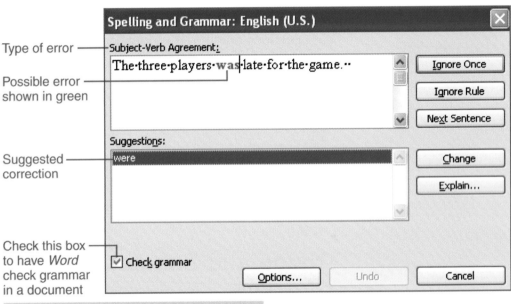

Type of error

Possible error
shown in green

Suggested
correction

Check this box
to have *Word*
check grammar
in a document

Figure 11.10 Spelling and Grammar Dialog Box

Word starts checking grammar in a document at the insertion point location. When a possible error in grammar is found, it is shown in green in the top window. You can do one or more of the following:

- **Ignore Once.** If you want to keep the text as it is, click the Ignore Once button. This will leave the highlighted words unchanged in the text.

- **Ignore Rule.** If you want to ignore the rule this time and all other times that it occurs in the document, click the Ignore Rule button.

- **Change.** If you want to accept a correction shown in the Suggestions list, click the Change button. *Word* will correct the text. In Figure 11.10, *were* is suggested to be used in place of *was*.

- **Other changes.** You may want to make a change that is not in the Suggestions list. If so, click in the top text window and key the correction. Click the Next Sentence button to continue. (You can also click outside the dialog box and correct the error in the document.)

4. Practice renaming a folder. Right-click on the folder tab to open a pop-up menu. Choose **Rename**. Key **Presidents** and tap Enter.

5. Click or tap the new *Presidents* folder tab. You will see the message telling you that there are no sections open in this folder. Click or tap in the middle of the message and a new section will be created. The tab will read **New Section 1**.

6. To change the name of the section, double-click on the tab to select the name if it is not already selected. Enter the new name **Washington**. Tap Enter to record the name.

7. Practice renaming a section. Right-click on the section tab to open a pop-up menu. Choose **Rename**. Key or handtype **George Washington** as shown in Figure 6.32. Tap Enter.

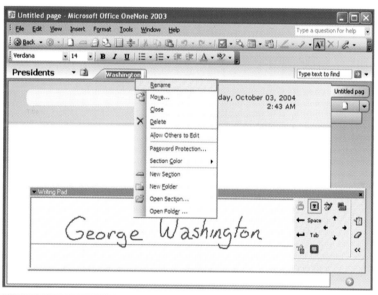

Figure 6.32 Rename a section in *OneNote*.

8. Click or tap in the page header title box. Enter **1st President** for the title as shown in Figure 6.33.

Title box ———

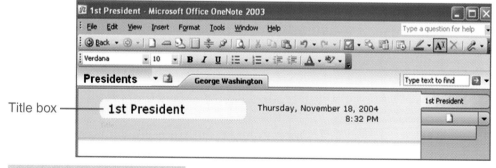

Figure 6.33 Create a page title.

Help Words

Date
  Insert the current
  date and time

Insert Date and Time

The **Insert Date and Time** feature is used to insert the date and/or time into a document. This feature can be helpful when keying letters and other documents that have dates. The format for the date and time can be selected. An option can be selected to have the date and time updated automatically each time the file is opened. The Date and Time command is found on the Insert menu.

92B LEARN: Insert Date in a Personal-Business Letter

1. Open *CD-92-Letter2* found in your data files. On line 3, select the text **Insert date here**.

2. Click **Insert** on the menu bar. Choose **Date and Time**. The Date and Time dialog box will appear as shown in Figure 11.9.

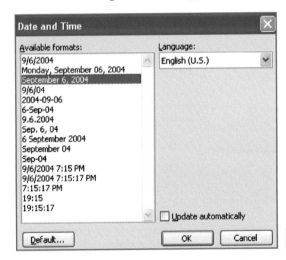

Figure 11.9 Date and Time Dialog Box

3. Choose the month, day, and year format for the date. An example is shown in Figure 11.9. If a check mark appears in the Update automatically box, click the box to remove the check. Click **OK**. The current date should now appear in your letter.

4. Format the text as a personal-business letter in block format. Refer to the guidelines on pages 401–402 and Figure 11.8 as needed. Save the document as *92-Letter2* and close the document.

92C PRACTICE: Insert Date in a Journal Form

1. Open *CD-92-Form* from your data files. Select the text **Date here**.

2. Access the Date and Time dialog box. Choose a date and time format such as **9/6/2004 7:15 PM**. Select the checkbox by **Update automatically**.

9. When you have made several changes, you would normally plan to save those changes. With *OneNote*, all changes are saved automatically every 30 seconds and each time you exit. You don't have to give a Save command. Now that's comforting! Close *OneNote*.

60C PRACTICE: Open and Navigate Around OneNote

1. Start *OneNote*. Click or tap the down arrow to the left of the tabs to display the folder list (marked in Figure 6.34). This will display all the folders and sections in your *My Notebook* folder.

2. Notice that your *Presidents* folder can be distinguished from a section by the folder icon.

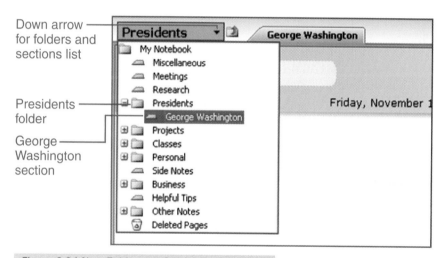

Down arrow for folders and sections list

Presidents folder

George Washington section

Figure 6.34 New Folder and Section in *OneNote*

3. Tap or click the *George Washington* section in the list to open the George Washington section.

4. The George Washington section has one page. The page title or the page number can be displayed numerically along the side of a section. The **Hide/Show Page Titles** button is used to switch between the two views. This button is at the lower right of the *OneNote* window as shown in Figure 6.35.

2. Open a new blank document in *Word*. Set the top margin to 2 inches. Use the default for side margins. Use left alignment and single line spacing.

3. Key the letter shown below. Check the spelling and proofread the letter carefully. Correct all errors. Save the letter as *92-Letter1*.

✔ **CHECK POINT** Use Print Preview to check the format of a classmate's letter. Have that classmate check the format of your letter. Discuss any errors either of you find and then correct them.

```
207 Brainard Road
Hartford, CT 06114-2207
May 15, 20--

Mr. Justin A. Alaron
Brighton Life Insurance Co.
I-84 & Route 322
Milldale, CT 06467-9371

Dear Mr. Alaron

Your job in actuarial science is of great interest to
me.  I am a student at Milldale School and participate
in the Shadow Experience Program (SEP).  I learned
about actuarial science while researching jobs related
to mathematics.  Math is my favorite subject, and I
have done very well in all of my math classes.  Math
appears to be one of my strengths.

SEP encourages students to "shadow" a person who is
working in a career field they are exploring.  I would
like to "shadow" you for one or two days so that I can
learn more about what an actuary does.  A brochure with
more information about SEP is enclosed.

I can arrange to be with you at your office for one or
two days during the coming month.  Please send your
written response to me so that I can present it to
Ms. Michelle Kish, SEP Coordinator.  Thank you.

Sincerely

Ms. Valerie E. Lopez

jas

Enclosure
```

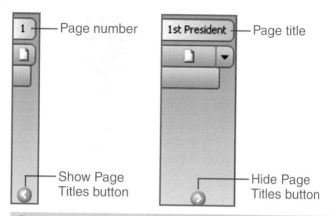

Figure 6.35 *OneNote* can display page numbers or page titles.

5. Click or tap the **Show/Hide Page Titles** button twice to see both views. Then display the full page titles. Close *OneNote*.

Taking Notes in OneNote

OneNote will allow you to enter your notes in any order anywhere in the note-taking area. This is a great way to get facts and ideas down quickly before you forget what you are trying to record!

OneNote organizes notes in areas called **containers**. Think of these containers as blocks of text. Each container can be moved around as needed. In Figure 6.36, notes have been entered in five containers. When you click or tap in a container or move the pointer over a container, a handle (colored bar) appears at the top. See Figure 6.36. This handle allows you to move or resize the container. In Lesson 60D, you will practice writing notes in containers.

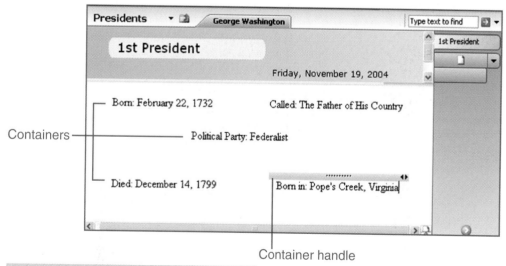

Figure 6.36 Five Note Containers in *OneNote*

- **Alignment.** Begin all lines of the letter at the left margin.
- **Line spacing.** Use single (1) line spacing. Leave blank lines after certain letter parts as noted below.
- **Return address.** A personal-business letter begins with the writer's address. This is called the **return address**. It includes a line for the street address and a line for the city, state, and ZIP Code.
- **Date.** Key the date on the line below the return address. Use the month/day/year format (January 4, 2006). Leave three blank lines (QS) after the date.
- **Letter address.** The name and address of the person to whom you are writing is called the **letter address**. Key a personal title (Miss, Mr., Mrs., Ms.) or a professional title (Dr., Lt., Senator) before the receiver's name. Leave one blank line (DS) after the letter address.
- **Salutation.** A **salutation** is a greeting. Key a salutation, such as Dear Mr. Roberts, after the letter address. Leave one blank line (DS) after the salutation.
- **Body.** The paragraphs or message of a letter are called the **body**. Single-space the paragraphs in the body. Double-space between them and after the final paragraph.
- **Complimentary close.** Key the **complimentary close** (farewell for a letter) a double space after the last paragraph. *Sincerely* is an example of a complimentary close. Leave three blank lines (QS) after the close.
- **Writer's name.** Key the writer's name below the complimentary close. A personal title (Miss, Mrs., Ms., Dr.) may be used before the name if desired. A position or job title (President, Manager), if used, should be keyed after the name. The title can be on the same line as the typed name or on the next line.
- **Reference initials.** A letter is sometimes keyed by someone other than the writer. In this case, key the typist's initials in small letters a double space below the writer's name.
- **Copy notation.** If someone will receive a copy of the letter, key **c** and the person's name a double space after the writer's name (or below the reference initials if they are used).
- **Attachment/Enclosure notation.** If another document is attached to a letter, the word *Attachment* is keyed a double space below the preceding letter part. If the additional document is not attached, the word *Enclosure* is used.

92A LEARN: Create a Personal-Business Letter

1. Review the sample letter in Figure 11.8 and the guidelines for keying letters on pages 401–402.

60D LEARN: Enter Notes

1. Start *OneNote*. Open the *George Washington* section. The *1st President* page will be displayed. Click or tap in the top-left corner of the note-taking area and enter **Born: February 22, 1732**. See Figure 6.36.

2. Notice that the text is entered into a small container. Click or tap in the top-right corner of the note-taking area to create a new container. Enter **Called: The Father of His Country**.

3. Click or tap in the bottom-left corner of the note-taking area and enter **Died: December 14, 1799**.

4. Click or tap in the bottom-right corner of the note-taking area and enter **Born in: Pope's Creek, Virginia**.

5. Click or tap in the center of the note-taking area and enter **Political Party: Federalist**.

6. Complete the Check Point below. Then close *OneNote* or continue to the next activity.

 **CHECK POINT** Compare your *1st President* page with the one shown in Figure 6.36. Do you have notes in five containers?

60E PRACTICE: Create Sections and Notes

1. Work with a classmate to research information about the second U.S. President. Use the Internet or your local library to find the following information:
   - Name of the second U.S. President
   - His date of birth
   - His date of death
   - Where he was born (city and state)
   - Years served in the office of President

2. Work alone to finish this activity. Start *OneNote*. Open the *Presidents* folder. Create a section with the second U.S. President's name.

3. Enter **2nd President** for the page title. Enter each item of information you found in a separate note in the note-taking area.

4. Create a new section in the *Presidents* folder. Name the section **Thomas Jefferson**. Enter **3rd President** for the page title. You will add notes to this page later.

5. Create another new section in the *Presidents* folder. Name the section **James Madison**. Enter **4th President** for the page title. You will add notes to this page later. Close *OneNote*.

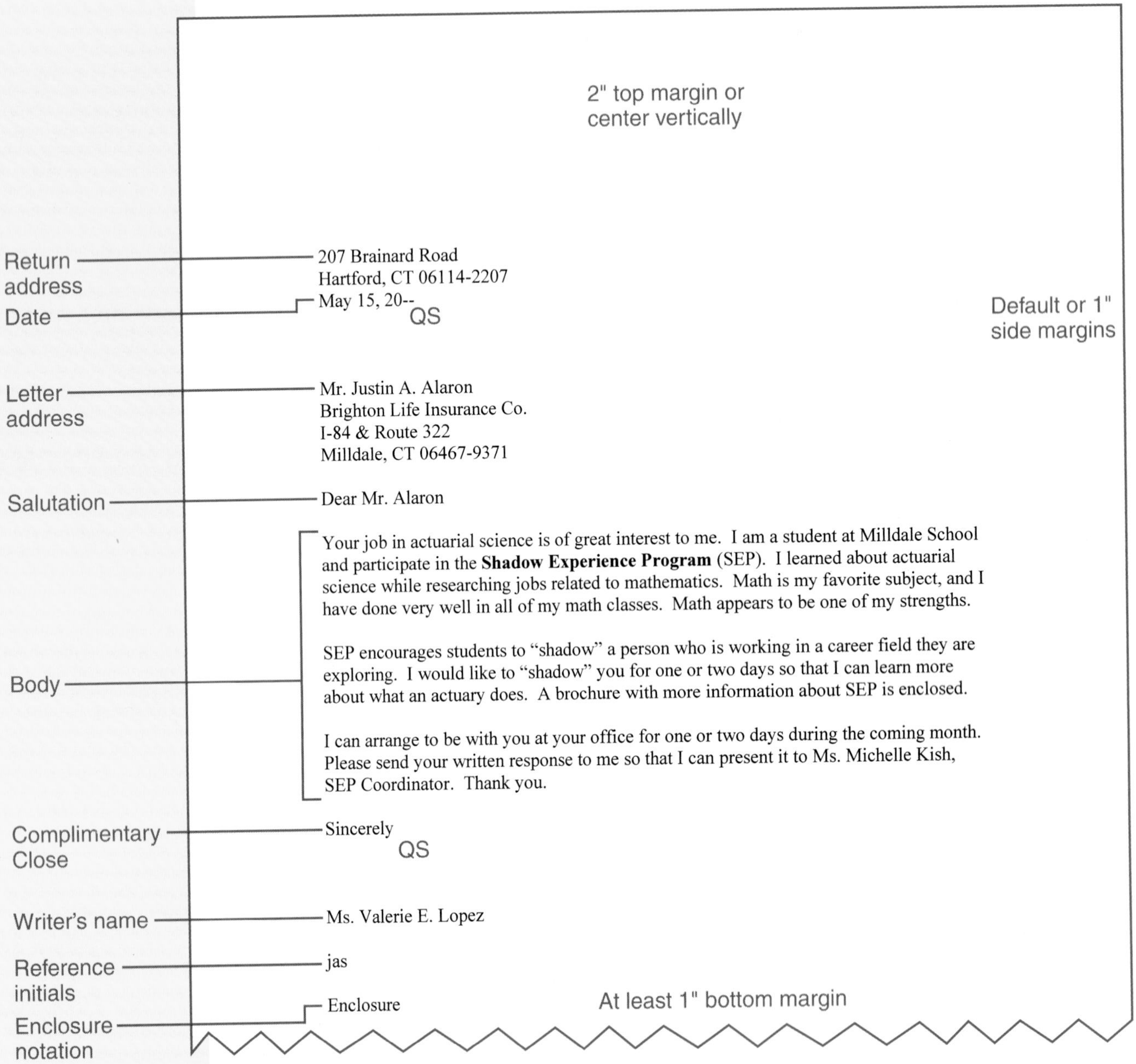

207 Brainard Road
Hartford, CT 06114-2207
May 15, 20--

Mr. Justin A. Alaron
Brighton Life Insurance Co.
I-84 & Route 322
Milldale, CT 06467-9371

Dear Mr. Alaron

Your job in actuarial science is of great interest to me. I am a student at Milldale School and participate in the **Shadow Experience Program** (SEP). I learned about actuarial science while researching jobs related to mathematics. Math is my favorite subject, and I have done very well in all of my math classes. Math appears to be one of my strengths.

SEP encourages students to "shadow" a person who is working in a career field they are exploring. I would like to "shadow" you for one or two days so that I can learn more about what an actuary does. A brochure with more information about SEP is enclosed.

I can arrange to be with you at your office for one or two days during the coming month. Please send your written response to me so that I can present it to Ms. Michelle Kish, SEP Coordinator. Thank you.

Sincerely

Ms. Valerie E. Lopez

jas

Enclosure

2" top margin or center vertically
Return address
Date
QS
Default or 1" side margins
Letter address
Salutation
Body
Complimentary Close
QS
Writer's name
Reference initials
Enclosure notation
At least 1" bottom margin

Figure 11.8 Personal-Business Letter in Block Format

Guidelines for a Personal-Business Letter in Block Format

A personal-business letter is shown in Figure 11.8. Refer to this example as you read the guidelines for keying letters that follow.

- **Margins.** Use a 2-inch top margin. Or, you may use the default top margin and select center alignment for the page. Use the default or 1-inch side margins. Use at least a 1-inch bottom margin.

Lesson 61   Organizing Notes

Objectives

In Lesson 61, you will:

⬎ Reorganize notes.

⬎ Break and merge note containers.

⬎ Change the width of a note container.

⬎ Create a new page.

⬎ Rename a page.

⬎ Create bulleted lists in *OneNote*.

Reorganizing Containers

In Lesson 60, you learned to enter information into *OneNote* containers. Containers can be large or small. The length of the container will grow, as needed, to fit the information you enter. *OneNote* permits you to edit and move containers after you have written notes.

In addition to moving notes, you can merge (join) notes. For example, all of the notes you wrote on the *1st President* page can be merged into one note. Just as easily, you can drag text from a note to create a new note. This means that you can jot notes anywhere without worrying about the order. You can always rearrange them later. In the activity, you will rearrange your notes about George Washington.

61A LEARN: Reorganize Notes

Help Words

Move notes
  Rearrange notes on
  a page

1. Start *OneNote*. Open the *George Washington* section.

2. Move the cursor over the top left side of the note that contains information about Washington's political party. The cursor will become a four-sided arrow as shown in Figure 6.37. Click the container handle and drag the container from the center of the page to the bottom left, well below the date-of-death note.

Click and drag the container handle to move a note

Political Party: Federalist

Click and drag to change the width of a note

Figure 6.37 Selected *OneNote* Container

Learn More About Computer Viruses

1. Access the Internet. Use a search engine to find sites or articles that give information about computer viruses that are spread through e-mail.

2. Record the name and source information for the article or site. A sample source record is shown below. Key a summary or list of the main points you learned from reading the article. Save the documents as *91D-Summary*.

Jay Munro, "Breaking Virus News: MyDoom Hobbles Internet E-mail," *PC Magazine*. January 27, 2004, http://www.pcmag.com/article2/0,1759,1463885,00.asp.

Lesson 92   Personal-Business Letters

Objectives

In Lesson 92, you will:

❯ Create personal-business letters in block format.

❯ Use the Insert Date and Time features.

❯ Use the Grammar Check feature.

Data files: *CD-92-Letter2, CD-92-Form, CD-92-Grammar1, CD-92-Grammar2, CD-92-Letter3*

A **personal-business letter** is used to deal with personal matters. For example, you might write this kind of letter to request information for a trip. You might send this kind of letter to praise a friend for winning an award. A letter is considered more formal than a memo or e-mail.

Personal-business letters are often arranged in block format. Block format means that every line of the letter starts at the left margin. Paragraphs, for example, are not indented as they are in reports. A personal-business letter is shown in Figure 11.8.

3. Click and drag the note that contains what Washington was called to the bottom right of the screen.

4. Make the note wider by clicking and dragging the arrows on the container handle to the right. Make the note smaller by clicking and dragging the arrows on the container handle to the left.

5. Now you will merge five notes into one note. The note with the date of Washington's birth should be in the upper-left corner of the note-taking area. Click and drag the note that contains Washington's place of birth onto the bottom of that note. The two notes will merge into one note as shown in Figure 6.38.

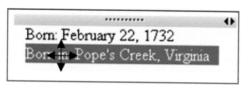

Figure 6.38 Merged Notes

6. Drag the note that contains **Political Party: Federalist** onto the bottom of the note with Washington's date and place of birth.

7. Drag the note that contains **Called: The Father of His Country** onto the bottom of the merged note.

8. Drag the note that contains **Died: December 14, 1799** onto the bottom of the merged note. You should now have one note container that holds all the facts about Washington.

9. You may find that you want to move part of a note into a separate container. To practice breaking out a note, point to the last line of text in your note. A paragraph handle will appear to the left of the text. See Figure 6.39. Click this handle and drag to the right, away from the note. Release the mouse and the text will appear in a separate container.

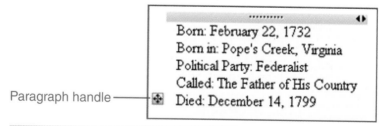

Paragraph handle

Figure 6.39 Click and drag a paragraph handle to move text to a separate note.

10. You can move more than one line of text. Click and drag to select the last two lines of the note on the left. Click and drag the paragraph handle to move this text to a separate note. You should now have three notes.

4. One of your classmates should send an e-mail message to you. When the messages arrives, it will appear in your Inbox folder. An example is shown in Figure 11.7.

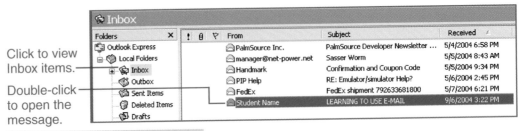

Click to view Inbox items.

Double-click to open the message.

Figure 11.7 *Outlook Express* Inbox

5. Click the Inbox folder to show the messages in the folder. Double-click the message to open it. Read the message.

6. Click the **Reply** button. Information in the To box and the Subject box will be filled in for you.

7. Click in the message area. Key a sentence or two thanking your classmate for helping you learn to use e-mail. Click the **Send** button.

8. Practice forwarding a message. Once again, open the **LEARNING TO USE E-MAIL** message you received. Click the **Forward** button.

9. Key the e-mail addresses of two classmates in the To box. Separate the addresses as you learned to do earlier. Click the **Send** button.

10. Classmates may have replied to your message or forwarded a message to you. Click once on one of these messages to highlight/select the message. Click the **Delete** button to delete the message.

11. Deleted messages may be moved to the Deleted Items folder. Click the **Deleted Items** folder to see if the message appears there. If so, you may need to select the message and click the **Delete** button again to remove the message.

12. Close any open message windows. Close the e-mail program.

Computer Viruses and E-Mail

A **computer virus** is a program that destroys or harms data on a computer. It can be loaded without the user knowing it is present. Some viruses arrive as attachments to e-mail messages. If you receive a message with an attachment from someone you do not know, do not open it.

Antivirus programs can be used to find and remove viruses before they do harm. These programs can be set to scan incoming e-mail to look for viruses.

Reply button

Forward button

Delete button

11. Click and drag to merge the notes back into one note. Place the information in the order shown in Figure 6.39. Close *OneNote* or continue to the next activity.

61B PRACTICE: Merge Notes

1. Start *OneNote*. Open the *Presidents* folder. Open the *John Adams* section.

2. Click and drag notes to create one merged note with all the information about this president. Place the information in this order:

   • His date of birth

   • Where he was born (city and state)

   • Years served in the office of President

   • His date of death

3. Complete the Check Point below. Then close *OneNote* or continue to the next activity.

 **CHECK POINT** Ask a classmate to check your merged note. Does it contain all the information in the correct order? If not, make corrections.

61C LEARN: Create a New Page

OneNote will allow you to add as many pages as you need. You will learn to add a page in this activity.

1. Start *OneNote*. Open the *George Washington* section.

2. Click or tap on the **New Page** button. The button is marked in Figure 6.40.

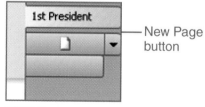

Figure 6.40 Choose the New Page button to add a new page to a section.

3. Enter the word **King** as the title in the new page header. Notice that **King** is also entered automatically on the page title tab.

6. You teacher will tell you whether you should send the e-mail. If permitted, click the **Send** button to send the e-mail message. Close the e-mail program.

```
Please invite all your students to a showing of "The
Story of Science."  This award-winning film will be
shown at 7 p.m. at the Civic Center.  Dates for the
film are Thursday, Friday, and Saturday evenings, March
3-5, 20--.

Students will be admitted without charge on Thursday
evening.  Tell students they will need to present their
school ID card at the door.

Students attending on Friday or Saturday evening must
pay $7.50 with a valid school ID card.  Students
without proper ID and adults will be charged $10.
```

Managing E-Mail Messages

Once you begin using e-mail, you can quickly have many messages in your e-mail inbox. You need to manage the messages to keep your inbox from being too crowded. After you have read messages, you can:

- Reply to the sender.
- Reply to all of the people in the To and Cc fields.
- Forward the message to another person.
- Delete the message.
- File or save the message.

91C LEARN: Receive, Reply, Forward, and Delete E-Mail

Work with your classmates to send, receive, and forward e-mail messages. Write down the e-mail addresses of three classmates to use in the activity. Give your e-mail address to three classmates to use in this activity.

1. Start *Outlook Express*. Create a new blank mail message.
2. Key the address of a classmate in the To box. Key **LEARNING TO USE E-MAIL** in the Subject box. For the body of the e-mail message, compose and key a paragraph telling some points you have learned about e-mail.
3. With your teacher's permission, send the e-mail message.

4. Tap in the top left-hand corner of the note-taking area and enter the following paragraph:

```
George Washington was so popular after the
Revolutionary War that many people wanted him to
become their king.  However, Washington was quite
content to live a peaceful life on his plantation in
beautiful Mount Vernon, Virginia.  This was not to
be.  He was soon elected as the first President of
the United States.
```

5. You have decided that *Popularity* would be a better title for this page. Select the word **King** in the page header. Key **Popularity** and tap ENTER. You should have two pages in the George Washington section as shown in Figure 6.41.

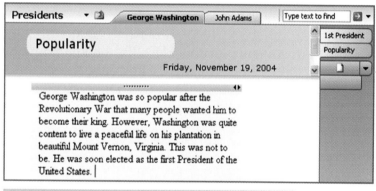

Figure 6.41 Pages in the *George Washington* Section

61D PRACTICE: Create a New Page

1. Start *OneNote*. Open the *Presidents* folder. Open the *John Adams* section.

2. Create a new page in this section. Name the new page **Outline**. You will add notes to this page later.

3. Close *OneNote* or continue to the next activity.

Bulleted Lists

Help Words

Bullets
  Create a
  bulleted list

A **bullet** is a small symbol or graphic used to highlight a line of text. Bulleted lists help a reader focus on key pieces of information. To create a bulleted list, key or handwrite the lines of text for the list. Tap Enter after each item in the list. Select the lines of text for the list. Click the Bullets button on the Formatting toolbar as shown in Figure 6.42. In the next activity, you will create a bulleted list as shown in Figure 6.42.

5. Click in the message portion of the window. Use default margins. Select **12** from the Font Size list on the Formatting bar.

6. Key the e-mail message shown below. Single-space the paragraphs and double-space between them. Proofread the message and correct all errors.

```
My parents and I went to the science open house on
Monday.  We learned a lot.  We agree that I should take
as many science courses as I can before I graduate from
high school.

I plan to major in engineering.  We think that middle
and high school math and science courses will help me
do better in college.
```

7. Choose **File** on the menu bar. Choose **Save As**. The Save Message As box appears.

8. In the Save in box, browse to locate the folder where you save other documents for this class. In the File name box, key **91-e-mail1** as shown in Figure 11.6. Click **Save**.

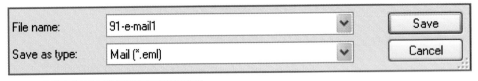

Figure 11.6 Save Message As Box

9. You teacher will tell you whether you should send the e-mail. If permitted, click the **Send** button to send the e-mail message to the address your teacher gave you. Close the e-mail program.

91B PRACTICE: Send E-Mail to Two Recipients

1. Start *Outlook Express*. Create a new blank e-mail message.

2. Key the two addresses your teacher gives you in the To box. (Insert a comma and a space between addresses.) Key an address your teacher gives you in the Cc box.

3. Key **THE STORY OF SCIENCE** in the Subject box.

4. Key the body of the e-mail message as shown on the next page. Use single spacing with double spacing between paragraphs.

5. Proofread and correct errors. Save the document as *91-E-mail2*.

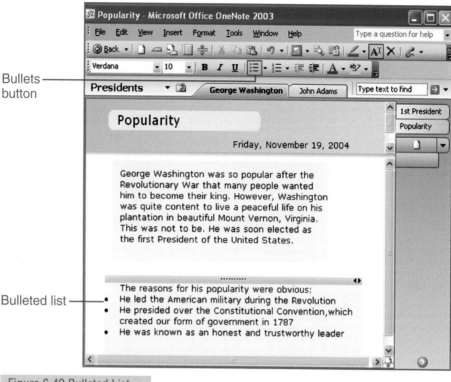

Bullets button

Bulleted list

Figure 6.42 Bulleted List

61E LEARN:

Create a Bulleted List

1. Start *OneNote*. Open the *Presidents* folder. Open the *George Washington* section. Open the *Popularity* page.

2. Click well below the first note to open a new note container. In the new note, key the text shown below. Tap **Enter** where indicated.

   The reasons for his popularity were obvious: [Enter]
   He led the American military during the Revolution. [Enter]
   He presided over the Constitutional Convention, which created our form of government in 1787. [Enter]
   He was known as an honest and trustworthy leader. [Enter]

3. Click and drag to select all of the lines after the first line. Click the **Bullets** button on the Formatting toolbar. Your bulleted list should look like the one in Figure 6.42.

4 Click and drag the arrow on the container handle for the second note (with the list) to make it about the same width as the first note.

Create an E-Mail Message

Instructions for using *Outlook Express* are given in this lesson. If you use a different e-mail program, the steps will be similar.

1. To open *Outlook Express,* click **Start, All Programs, Outlook Express**.

2. Click **File** on the menu bar. Select **New** and then **Mail Message** as shown in Figure 11.4.

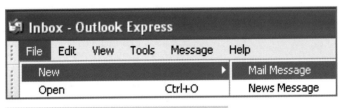

Figure 11.4 Create a New Mail Message

3. The New Message window will open. Key the address your instructor gives you in the To box. An example is shown in Figure 11.5.

4. Click in the Subject box. Key **OPEN HOUSE** in the Subject box. The window name will change from **New Message** to **OPEN HOUSE**.

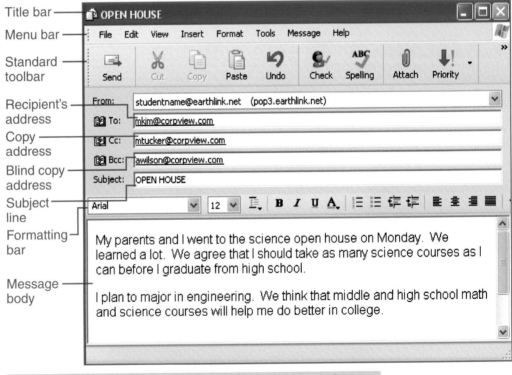

Figure 11.5 *Microsoft Outlook Express* OPEN HOUSE Message Screen

5. You can change the order of items in a list by clicking and dragging the paragraph handle of an item you want to move. Use the paragraph handle to rearrange the items in the list in the order shown below.

- He was known as an honest and trustworthy leader.
- He led the American military during the Revolution.
- He presided over the Constitutional Convention, which created our form of government in 1787.

6. Drag the note container with the list onto the bottom of the other note container to merge the notes. Insert one blank line before the list paragraph. Your merged note should look like Figure 6.43. Close *OneNote*.

George Washington was so popular after the Revolutionary War that many people wanted him to become their king. However, Washington was quite content to live a peaceful life on his plantation in beautiful Mount Vernon, Virginia. This was not to be. He was soon elected as the first President of the United States.

The reasons for his popularity were obvious:
- He was known as an honest and trustworthy leader.
- He led the American military during the Revolution.
- He presided over the Constitutional Convention, which created our form of government in 1787.

Figure 6.43 Merged Note

61F PRACTICE: Format Text as a Bulleted List

1. Start *OneNote*. Open the *Presidents* folder. Open the *John Adams* section. Open the *2nd President* page.

2. Click at the beginning of the note. Handtype or key the text below and choose **Enter**.

   Facts about John Adams:

3. Click and drag to select all of the lines after the first line. Click the **Bullets** button on the Formatting toolbar.

4. Complete the Check Point below and then close *OneNote*.

CHECK POINT Ask a classmate to review your bulleted list. Make corrections as needed.

A file can be attached to the e-mail message. This is done by using the Attachment feature of the software. Common types of attachments include word processing, database, and spreadsheet files.

The paragraphs of the e-mail message are single-spaced. Use a 12-point font and the default margins. Double-space between paragraphs. Align all lines in the body at the left margin.

E-Mail Addresses

Before you can send an e-mail message, you must have an e-mail address. Each e-mail address must be different from all others. Otherwise, e-mail messages could be delivered to the wrong person. An **e-mail address** contains a username and a domain name separated by the *at* sign (@). For example:

Kim@swep.com
Mkim@speakingabout.com
Maria_Bravo@speakingsolutions.com
maria_bravo@corpview.com

Spaces are not used in e-mail addresses. An underline or period is sometimes used to separate parts of a username. The username is also called the mailbox name.

E-Mail Message Guidelines

Follow these guidelines for writing e-mail messages:

- Be courteous to others in your messages.
- Keep your e-mail messages short and to the point, but include all the needed information.
- Place the most important points of the message in the first three or four lines of text.
- Use correct grammar in your messages.
- Use standard punctuation and capitalization in your message.
- Do not use all caps for whole words. Using all caps is viewed as shouting at the reader and is considered rude. Use bold or italic instead of all caps.
- Proofread your message before sending it.
- Do not send private or personal information by e-mail.

Remember that in many cases, e-mail is not private. Always assume someone besides the person to whom you are writing may see the message.

Instant Message

To review domain names, see page 72 in Chapter 3.

Instant Message

If e-mail software is not available, key the e-mail messages in this lesson as memos. Use your teacher's name in the TO: heading. Use your name in the FROM: heading. Use today's date in the DATE: heading.

Lesson 62   Outlines and Formatting

Objectives

In Lesson 62, you will:

⬊ Create an outline in *OneNote*.

⬊ Print a page from *OneNote*.

⬊ Add extra writing space in a note.

⬊ Copy from *OneNote* to a *Word* document.

⬊ Change fonts and use color and formatting to accent notes.

Outlines

┌ **Help Words** ┐

Outline
   Structure notes as
   outlines

An **outline** is a document that organizes facts and details by main topics and subtopics. Outlining is an important note-taking activity. *OneNote* allows you to create outlines and to reorganize outlines after they have been entered. A vertical outline lists each subtopic on a separate line below a main topic. A vertical outline is shown in Figure 6.44.

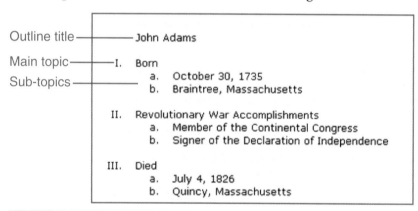

Figure 6.44 Vertical Outline in *OneNote*

| 62A LEARN: Create an Outline

1. Start *OneNote*. Open the *Presidents* folder. Open the *John Adams* section. Open the *Outline* page.

2. Enter the text shown on the next page to create an outline. Tap **Enter, Tab,** or **Backspace** where the command appears in brackets. Your notes should take the form of a simple vertical outline. The Roman numerals (II., III.) and letters (a., b.) will be inserted automatically after you enter the first Roman numeral.

Lesson 91

E-Mail Messages

Objectives

In Lesson 91, you will:

⬎ Create, send, forward, and delete e-mail messages.

⬎ Research information about computer viruses and e-mail.

E-Mail Messages

E-mail (electronic mail) use is growing. This growth is due, in part, to the ease of creating and the speed of sending messages. An e-mail message is often delivered in minutes. Many people now use e-mail rather than memos and letters.

To use e-mail, you must first have an e-mail account. You may also need to set up an account with an Internet service provider. An **Internet service provider (ISP)** is a company that provides customer connections to the Internet. Earthlink and America Online are popular ISPs.

E-Mail Message Format

An e-mail message includes heading lines and the message body. The heading lines include the:

- E-mail address of the person(s) receiving the e-mail

- E-mail address of the person sending the e-mail

- Date the e-mail was sent

- Subject of the e-mail message

The e-mail address of the person receiving the message is keyed in the To box. Use capital and small letters that appear in the addresses given to you. Sometimes a message is sent to more than one person. Separate the addresses with a comma or semicolon and a space. This can vary depending on the program you use.

Always key a subject in the Subject box. Many people delete e-mail messages that do not have a subject line without reading them. Subjects are usually keyed in all capitals.

A copy of an e-mail message can be sent to another person. If a copy is sent, key the addresses in the **Cc** box. If a blind copy is sent, key the address in the Bcc box. A **blind copy** is used when you don't want the person receiving the e-mail message to know that you have also sent the message to another person.

Normally, you do not need to key the sender's name and the date. The software inserts this information.

```
John Adams [Enter]
[Enter]
I. [Tab] Born [Enter]
[Tab]October 30, 1735 [Enter]
     Braintree, Massachusetts
[Enter]
[Enter]
[Backspace]
Revolutionary War Accomplishments [Enter]
[Tab]Member of the Continental Congress [Enter]
     Signer of the Declaration of Independence
[Enter]
[Enter]
[Backspace]
Died [Enter]
[Tab]July 4, 1826 [Enter]
Quincy, Massachusetts [Enter]
```

3. To print your outline, choose **File** on the menu bar. Choose **Print Preview**. Under Print range, choose **Current Page**. Accept the other default settings as shown in Figure 6.45. Click **Print**.

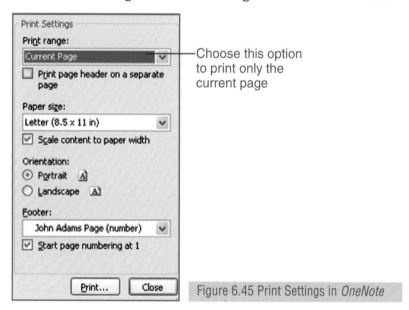
Figure 6.45 Print Settings in *OneNote*

4. Select your printer if it is not already selected. For Pages, **2** will appear because the *Outline* page is the second page in the *John Adams* section. Choose **Print**.

5. Close *OneNote* or continue to the next activity.

✔ **CHECK POINT** Your outline should look like the one in Figure 6.44.

5. You can resize the slide image the same way you learned to resize a program window. Click the image to select it. Click and drag the bottom-right corner of the slide image up and to the left to make it smaller. Use Print Preview to see how the slide looks in the document. Change the size again if desired.

6. Check spelling and proofread the memo carefully. Correct any errors. Use Print Preview to check the format of the memo.

7. Save the memo as *90-Memo2*. Print the memo and close it. Close *PowerPoint* without saving changes to the slide.

```
TO:        (Teacher's name)
FROM:      (Your name)
DATE:      (Current date)
SUBJECT:   CAREER INTEREST
```

The report about one of my career interests is almost finished. An outline of the report is attached. Jim Carney worked with me on this report. We will be ready to give a five-minute talk in class next Friday. We will use six to nine slides when we give the report. You can see the design of the slides from the title slide shown below.

(Paste title slide here.)

As you suggested, we made an appointment with our guidance counselor, Mr. Duncan. We plan to discuss programs at nearby colleges and universities.

Attachment
c Jim Carney

90E APPLY: Compose Memo

1. Open a new document in *Word*. Set the top margin to 2 inches. Set a left tab at 1 inch.

2. Compose a memo to your teacher from you. Use the current date. Key **FIELD TRIP** as the subject. For the body of the memo, tell your teacher about a place you would like to visit for a class field trip. Give the place name and the location or address. Describe the place. Tell why you think this would be a good place to visit with your class.

3. Check the spelling and proofread the memo carefully. Correct any errors. Use Print Preview to check the format of the memo.

4. Save the memo as *90-Memo3*. Print the memo and close it.

 **CHECK POINT** Exchange papers with a classmate. Proofread and mark any errors you find in the memo. Make corrections to your memo, if needed.

62B PRACTICE: Create Abigail Adams Outline

1. Start *OneNote*. Open the *Presidents* folder. Create a new section. Name the section **First Ladies**.

2. Name the new page in this section **Abigail Adams**. Enter the text below to create an outline.

   ```
   Abigail Adams [Enter]
   [Enter]
   I. [Tab] Born [Enter]
   [Tab]November 11, 1744 [Enter]
        Weymouth, Massachusetts
   [Enter]
   [Enter]
   [Backspace]
   Family [Enter]
   [Tab]Parents: Elizabeth Quincy Smith and Reverend
   William Smith [Enter]
        Siblings: Mary, Betsy, and Billy [Enter]
   [Enter]
   [Backspace]
   Marriage [Enter]
   [Tab]Date: October 25, 1764[Enter]
        Husband: John Adams, second U.S. President
   [Enter]
   [Enter]
   [Backspace]
   Died [Enter]
   [Tab] October 28, 1818[Enter]
   Cause of death: Typhoid fever [Enter]
   ```

3. Proofread your outline and make corrections if needed. Print your outline page. Close *OneNote*.

Editing and Formatting

After you have written notes, you may want to edit (change) them in various ways. For example, have you ever taken notes on a pad of paper and discovered you have left something out? Have you ever wished you could just make more space in the middle of your notes? With *OneNote* you can! You will learn to add space in the middle of a note you have written earlier.

You can **highlight** (surround in color) key portions of your notes just as you might highlight notes written on paper. You can also change the style and color of the text used for notes. The style of the text is called the **font**. You can apply different effects to the text such as **bold**, *italic*, and underline. To format text, select the words you wish to format. Then choose an option on the Formatting toolbar. Several formatting buttons are marked in Figure 6.46.

Help Words

Add space
Add more space to a page

Zoom

Sometimes, having a close-up view of your document is helpful. At other times, you might want to see one or more pages at a reduced size. The **Zoom feature** allows you to see close-up or reduced views of a document. You can change the document view using the Zoom command on the Standard toolbar.

90C LEARN: Zoom

1. Open *CD-90-Report* from your data files.

2. Click the **Zoom arrow** on the Standard toolbar as shown in Figure 11.3. Select **150%** from the drop-down list to *zoom in* and make the text larger.

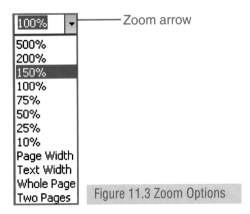

Figure 11.3 Zoom Options

3. Click the **Zoom arrow** and select **Two Pages** from the drop-down list to *zoom out* and display both pages of the document.

4. Click the **Zoom arrow** and select a setting that you want to display. Close the document without saving it.

90D PRACTICE: Memo Format and Print Preview

1. Open a new document in *Word*. Key the memo shown on the following page. Use your teacher's name, your name, and the current date where indicated. Do not key **(Paste title slide here.)**. Leave three blank lines between the paragraphs where you are told to paste the slide.

2. Start *Microsoft PowerPoint*. Open *CD-90-Careers* from your data files. Select **Student Name** on the slide and replace it by keying your name.

3. Click the slide image on the Slides tab at the left of the screen. Click **Copy** on the toolbar.

4. Move to the memo in *Word*. Place the insertion point between the two paragraphs where the slide image should go. Click the **Paste** button.

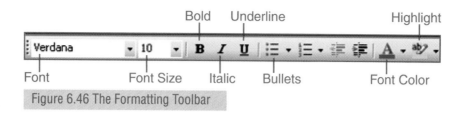

Figure 6.46 The Formatting Toolbar

62C LEARN: Add Space and Edit an Outline

1. Start *OneNote*. Open the *Presidents* folder. Open the *John Adams* section and the *Outline* page.

2. Click or tap the **Insert Extra Writing Space** button on the Standard toolbar. See Figure 6.47.

3. Click or touch between **Braintree, Massachusetts** and **Revolutionary War Accomplishments**. Drag down about 1 or 2 inches to make room for additional notes. An arrow will appear as you do this as shown in Figure 6.47.

Insert Extra Writing Space button

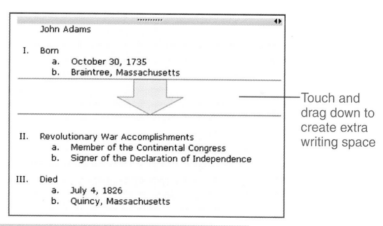

Touch and drag down to create extra writing space

Figure 6.47 You can add space in a note to enter additional text.

4. Click at the end of the fourth line of text, right after the word *Massachusetts*. Enter the text below in the outline. The outline numbers will be adjusted automatically.

```
[Enter] [Enter] [Backspace]
Pre-Revolutionary War Accomplishments[Enter]
[Tab]Attended Harvard University [Enter]
      Lawyer [Enter]
      Married Abigail Smith Adams
[Enter]
```

5. Delete or add lines as needed to leave one blank line before *Revolutionary War Accomplishments*. Close *OneNote* or continue to the next activity.

Instant Message

Save files in the *My Documents\Computers\Chapter 11* folder or where directed by your teacher.

Help Words

Print preview
   Preview a page
   before printing

6. Key the paragraphs in the body of the memo in Figure 11.1. They should be single spaced with double spacing between paragraphs.

7. Tap ENTER twice after the last paragraph. Key your initials at the left margin.

8. Tap ENTER twice and key **Enclosure**. Tap ENTER twice and key **c Maria Castillo**.

9. Check the memo for misspelled words and then proofread carefully. Correct all errors. Save the document as *90-Memo1* and close the document.

Print Preview

You can use the **Print Preview** feature to display several pages of a document in a reduced size. Print Preview also lets you see an entire page on the screen at once. This can be helpful in checking the format of a document. You can make changes to page breaks or correct errors before you print the document. Make a habit of checking every document with Print Preview before printing.

To use Print Preview view, click the Print Preview button on the Standard toolbar. Click Close on the Print Preview toolbar to return to the previous view.

90B LEARN:

Print Preview

1. Start *Word*. Open *CD-90-Report* from your data files.

2. Click the **Print Preview** button on the Standard toolbar. The document will appear in reduced size. A toolbar gives you options for viewing the document.

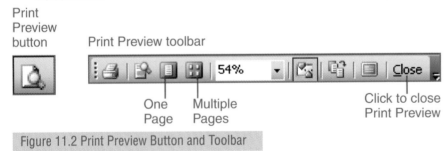

Print Preview button   Print Preview toolbar

One Page   Multiple Pages   Click to close Print Preview

Figure 11.2 Print Preview Button and Toolbar

3. Click the **One Page** button to display one page. Tap the PAGE DOWN key to display the second page.

4. Click the **Multiple Pages** button. Select the first two icons to display both pages of the document.

5. Click the **Close** button on the Print Preview toolbar. Close the document.

62D LEARN: Change Font and Copy Notes

1. Start *OneNote*. Open the *Presidents* folder. Open the *John Adams* section and the *Outline* page.

2. You want to use the updated John Adams outline for a report you plan to write later using *Word*. You will change the font and the font size to match those usually used in *Word*. Click the note container handle to select the entire outline.

3. Click the down arrow by **Font** on the Formatting toolbar. Select **Times New Roman** as shown in Figure 6.48. Click the down arrow for the **Font Size**. Select **12**.

Choose a font   Choose a font size

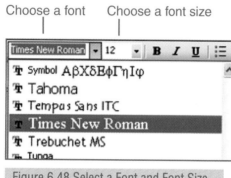

Figure 6.48 Select a Font and Font Size

4. To copy the outline, click the note container handle to select the entire outline. Click the **Copy** button on the Standard toolbar.

5. Start *Word* and open a new blank document. Click the **Paste** button on the Standard toolbar. The outline should now appear in your *Word* document.

6. Save the *Word* document as *62-Adams Outline*. Close *Word*. Close *OneNote* or continue to the next activity.

SOFTWARE TIP

Click the **Copy** button to copy selected text. Click the **Paste** button to paste text.

Copy   Paste
button   button

62E PRACTICE: Copy and Edit Notes

1. Start *OneNote*. Open the *Presidents* folder and the *George Washington* section. Open the *1st President* page.

2. To copy the note on this page, click the note container handle to select the entire note. Click the **Copy** button on the Standard toolbar.

90A LEARN: Create a Memo

1. Open a new blank document in *Word*.

2. Read the memo shown in Figure 11.1 to review the format for a memo.

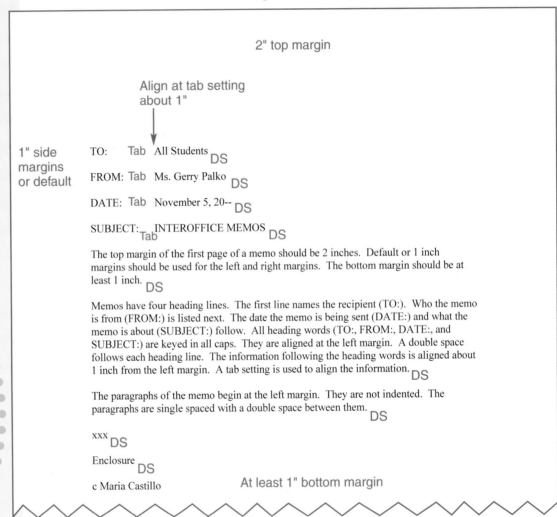

2" top margin

Align at tab setting about 1"

1" side margins or default

TO: Tab   All Students DS

FROM: Tab   Ms. Gerry Palko DS

DATE: Tab   November 5, 20-- DS

SUBJECT: Tab INTEROFFICE MEMOS DS

The top margin of the first page of a memo should be 2 inches. Default or 1 inch margins should be used for the left and right margins. The bottom margin should be at least 1 inch. DS

Memos have four heading lines. The first line names the recipient (TO:). Who the memo is from (FROM:) is listed next. The date the memo is being sent (DATE:) and what the memo is about (SUBJECT:) follow. All heading words (TO:, FROM:, DATE:, and SUBJECT:) are keyed in all caps. They are aligned at the left margin. A double space follows each heading line. The information following the heading words is aligned about 1 inch from the left margin. A tab setting is used to align the information. DS

The paragraphs of the memo begin at the left margin. They are not indented. The paragraphs are single spaced with a double space between them. DS

xxx DS

Enclosure DS

c Maria Castillo   At least 1" bottom margin

Figure 11.1 Memo Format

3. Set a 2-inch top margin. Set a left tab at 1 inch.

4. Key **TO:**. Tap the TAB key and then key **All Students**. Tap ENTER twice to DS.

5. Repeat the process in step 4 to key the remaining heading lines of the memo, as shown in Figure 11.1.

3. Open the *Thomas Jefferson* section and the *3rd President* page. Click the **Paste** button on the Standard toolbar. The note should now appear on the *3rd President* page.

4. Edit the note to contain the facts for Thomas Jefferson as shown below. Start by selecting the text to be changed. Then key or handtype the new text.

```
Born: April 13, 1743
Born in: Shadwell, Virginia
Political Party: Democratic-Republican
Called: A Renaissance Man
Died: July 4, 1826
```

5. Close *OneNote* or continue to the next activity.

62F LEARN: Format Notes

In this activity, you will format and add color to notes to make headings and important facts stand out.

1. Start *OneNote*. Open the *Presidents* folder and the *George Washington* section. Open the *1st President* page.

2. Select **Born:** in the first line. Click the **Bold** button on the Formatting toolbar. Select and apply bold to:

```
Born in:
Political Party:
Called:
Died:
```

3. Select the text **The Father of His Country**. Click the **Italic** button on the Formatting toolbar.

4. Select the text **Federalist**. Click the **Underline** button on the Formatting toolbar.

5. You want to memorize the date of birth for each president. You will highlight this information to make it stand out when you study your notes. Select the text **Born: February 22, 1732**. Click the down arrow for **Highlight** on the Formatting toolbar. Choose the yellow square as shown in Figure 6.49.

SOFTWARE TIP

Use the Bold, Italic, and Underline buttons to emphasize text.

B *I* <u>U</u>

Bold   Italic   Underline
button button button

Lesson 90  Interoffice Memos

Objectives

In Lesson 90, you will:
↘ Create interoffice memos.
↘ Use the Print Preview and Zoom features of *Word*.

Data files: *CD-90-Report, CD-90-Careers, CD-92-Letter2, CD-92-Form, CD-92-Grammar1, CD-92-Grammar2, CD-92-Letter, CD-94-letter1, CD-94-Replace 3, CD-C11-Letter2*

Memo Format

Memos are written messages used by people within an organization. They are sometimes called *interoffice memos*. For example, your school principal might write a memo to your teacher about a staff meeting. A memo is shown in Figure 11.1 on page 390. Refer to this figure as you read about the parts of a memo.

Memos have four heading lines and a body. The paragraphs in a memo are called the **body**. The memo heading lines tell the:

- Name of the person to whom the memo is written

- Name of the person who is writing the memo

- Date the memo is written

- Subject of the memo

A memo may contain these parts after the body:

- Reference initials

- Enclosure note

- Attachment note

- Copy note

Sometimes, one person writes a memo but another person keys the memo. **Reference initials** are the initials of the person who keys the memo. Reference initials are not used if the writer keys the memo. An **enclosure note** or **attachment note** tells the reader that other material is enclosed with or attached to the memo. A **copy note** tells the reader that one or more persons will receive a copy of the memo.

Choose down arrow to reveal highlight color choices

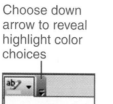

Choose down arrow to reveal font color choices

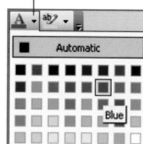

Figure 6.49 Highlight Color Choices and Font Color

6. Select the text **Died: December 14, 1799**. Click the down arrow for the **Font Color** button on the Formatting toolbar. See Figure 6.48. Slowly move the pointer over the palette to see the names of colors. Choose **Blue**.

7. Your formatted note should look like Figure 6.50. Close *OneNote* or continue to the next activity.

Born: February 22, 1732
Born in: Pope's Creek, Virginia
Political Party: Federalist
Called: *The Father of His Country*
Died: December 14, 1799

Figure 6.50 Edited Note for George Washington

62G PRACTICE: Format Notes

1. Start *OneNote*. Open the *Presidents* folder and the *George Washington* section. Open the *1st President* page. Review the formatting you applied to the note on this page.

2. Open the *Thomas Jefferson* section and the *3rd President* page. Apply the same formatting to the note on this page as you did to the note on the *1st President* page.

3. Complete the Check Point below and then close *OneNote*.

 **CHECK POINT** Ask a classmate to review your formatted note. Make corrections if needed.

Memos, E-Mails, and Letters

OBJECTIVES

In Chapter 11, you will:

↗ Learn editing and formatting features of *Microsoft Word.*

↗ Create memos and e-mail messages.

↗ Create personal business letters in block format.

↗ Create business letters in block format.

↗ Create and print envelopes and labels.

People often need to send written messages to others. They may write to others to thank them or invite them to an event. People also send messages to make requests, complain, or persuade. A message may be created as a memo, e-mail message, or personal or business letter. In this chapter, you will learn to create these documents. You will also learn to use features of word processing and messaging software to prepare documents efficiently.

© Getty Images/PhotoDisc

Lesson 63 | Web Content and Pictures

Objectives

In Lesson 63, you will:

⬎ Copy text from Web files.

⬎ Search your notes.

⬎ Insert pictures and sketch pictures.

⬎ Write notes using digital ink.

Data files: *CD-63-Louisiana, CD-63-Indiana*

Copying Web Content

You may need to find information from Web sites as you create notes for reports or other assignments. You can easily copy text from a Web page to *OneNote*. Simply select text that you want to copy in the Web file. Choose the Copy command from the Edit menu. Go to your *OneNote* page and click the Paste button. The text will be placed in your *OneNote* page. You can also drag selected text from the browser window onto the *OneNote* window. When you copy data from a Web site into *OneNote*, the URL for the Web site will automatically be placed under the note as shown in Figure 6.51.

> Adams was born in the Massachusetts Bay Colony in 1735. A Harvard-educated lawyer, he early became identified with the patriot cause; a delegate to the First and Second Continental Congresses, he led in the movement for independence.
>
> Pasted from
> <http://www.whitehouse.gov/history/presidents/ja2.html> —— URL of Web site from which text was copied

Figure 6.51 The URL of copied text displays below the note.

63A LEARN: Copy Text from a Web Page

1. Start *OneNote*. Open your *Presidents* folder and the *James Madison* section. Create a new page named **War of 1812**.

2. Log on to the Internet. Start *Internet Explorer*. In the Address bar, enter **c21jr.swlearning.com**. Click **Links**. Scroll down to find the link **James Madison**. Click the link to open the Web page.

3. Select the title and all of the text on the Web page. Click **Edit** on the menu bar. Click **Copy**.

Instant Message

Notice that the (URL) has been inserted below the article.

What do you see as your personal strengths? Are you a good problem-solver? Are you always on time? Do you work well with a team? Can you plan, organize, and prioritize your work? Are you creative? Are you detail-oriented? Employers are looking for workers with some or all of these strengths. The trick is knowing what you are good at and what you need to work at to land a job that is right for you.

What do you value most in your life? Do you value spending time with friends and family? Is excelling in school or being the best in your favorite sport important to you? Do you value helping others? Understanding your strengths and values will help steer you toward a career that best suits you.

1. Identify your strengths and values. Open the data file *CD-C10-Strengths and Values*. Follow the instructions to rate your personal strengths and values.

2. Remember to include a sample of your best work from this chapter in your portfolio.

↗ Academic Success Builder

MATH AND PERSONAL FINANCE: CHECKING ACCOUNT RECONCILIATION When you have a checking account, you should keep accurate records in your check register. The **check register** is the form on which you record information about your bank account. It includes information such as:

- Checks you have written
- Withdrawals you have made
- Deposits you have made
- Interest you have earned on money in your account
- Service charges the bank deducted from your account

The bank also keeps a record of your checking account transactions. The bank will send you a bank statement each month. The **bank statement** is a report that lists all the transactions in your account during the past month. You should compare the information in your check register with the information in the bank statement. You need to make sure your closing bank statement balance and your check register balance are correct. If the bank made an error, you need to meet with a bank employee to discuss the error. If you made an error, you need to correct it. Otherwise, you may not have as much money in your account as your check register shows. Or, you could have more money than it shows. Both situations can lead to problems.

In this activity, you will use a Reconciliation Form to reconcile your check register balance with the closing balance from a bank statement.

1. Start *Word*. Open *CD-C10-Form* found in your data files. Print the file and then close it.

2. Read the information about bank statements and complete the activities as directed. Compare your answers with those of a classmate.

4. In *OneNote*, click in the upper-left corner of the *War of 1812* page. Click the **Paste** button. The article should now appear in your *OneNote* page. Read the article and insert blank lines between the paragraphs if needed.

5. Close *OneNote* or continue to the next activity.

63B PRACTICE: Download Information on James Madison

1. Start *OneNote*. Open your *Presidents* folder and the *James Madison* section. Open the *4th President* page.

2. Start *Internet Explorer*. Use a search engine to find articles on James Madison. Enter search terms such as *U.S. Presidents* or *President James Madison*.

3. Find three or four important facts about James Madison from the articles you read. Copy each fact and paste it into *OneNote* on the *4th President* page.

4. Close *Internet Explorer* and close *OneNote*.

Searching Notes

Find
    Find notes

You can use the **Find** feature to look for text you have entered in your notes. This can be helpful when you forget which page contains the information you want. It also helps you locate information on a page that contains a lot of text. The Find feature will search both typed and handwritten notes, provided you have written them clearly.

To search for text, choose Find from the Edit menu. Enter a word or term in the box that appears at the right of the tabs. Choose a search area. Click the Find arrow to begin the search. See Figure 6.52.

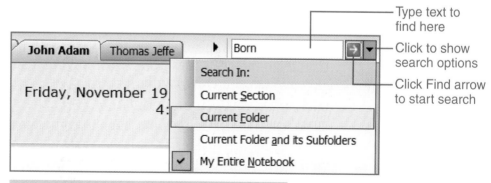

Figure 6.52 Use Find to search for words or terms.

The word or term will be highlighted on the current page as shown in Figure 6.53. You can click the View List button to see a list of pages that

Data Files

- *CD-C10-Business*
- *CD-C10-Strengths and Values*
- *CD-C10-Form*

↗ About Business

ANALYZING COSTS AND BENEFITS Business owners and managers face many decisions. For example, should the limited amount of money available be spent on new equipment or on more advertising? Should the company use its limited store floor space to offer two new products? Should a store stop selling a product that makes no profit? Should it keep selling the product because it brings customers into the store? The choices managers make affect how profitable the business will be.

Each time a choice is made, other options are given up. The best option given up when a choice is made is called the **opportunity cost**. Business owners and managers can use a problem-solving approach to analyze costs and benefits when faced with a decision. A cost is something that decreases the company's profits. A benefit is something that increases the company's profits.

Different managers use different approaches when comparing costs and benefits. A typical approach includes steps such as the following:

1. **Define the problem.** For example, how do we spend our limited advertising funds?
2. **Identify the choices available.** For example, advertising money could be spent on television ads, magazine ads, radio ads, or ads on Web sites.
3. **Gather data about the choices.** For example, what are the costs of the different advertising methods? Which ads are most likely to reach our target customers?
4. **Analyze the data.** For example, compare the expected increase in sales with the advertising funds spent for each type of ad. Determine which ads are likely to increase profits the most.
5. **Make a decision and take action.** For example, choose to use radio and magazine ads.

In this activity, you will use the problem-solving approach described above to analyze the costs and benefits of buying a small copy machine or having copies made at a copy center.

1. Start *Word*. Open and print *CD-C10-Business* from your data files.
2. Follow the instructions provided to complete the cost and benefit analysis.

↗ Career and Life Skills Success Builder

YOUR PERSONAL STRENGTHS VS. EMPLOYABILITY SKILLS Everyone has personal strengths and values that make them unique from everyone else. Your strengths and values help you deal with everyday life. Understanding your strengths and values will help you choose a career that is right for you.

contain the word or term. The page names appear at the right in the Page List pane. Click a page name to go to that page. The term will be highlighted on the page. To end the search, click the Clear Find Highlighting button.

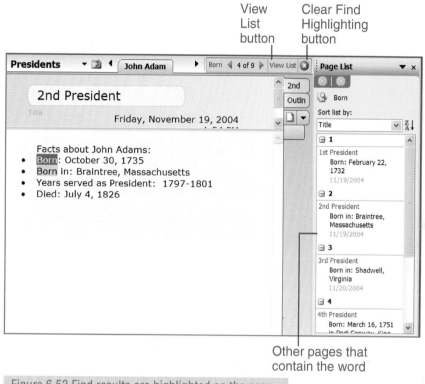

Figure 6.53 Find results are highlighted on the page.

63C LEARN: Use Find to Search Notes

1. Start *OneNote*. Open the *Presidents* folder to any section and page in the folder.

2. Choose **Edit** from the menu bar. Choose **Find**. A box with **Type text to find** will appear to the right of the tabs. Enter **Born** in the Find box.

3. Click the down arrow by the Find box and choose **Current Folder** as shown in Figure 6.52.

4. Notice that *OneNote* highlights the first instance of the word *Born*. Click the **Next Match** and **Previous Match** arrows to move to each instance of the word *Born*. See Figure 6.54.

Speed Forcing Drill

Key a 30" timed writing on each line. Your rate in gross words a minute (*gwam*) is shown below the lines.

1 Paula went out for track.
2 Jan told me to see that movie.
3 Which search engine did Carmen use?
4 Paul bought the video game last weekend.
5 Sandy had a meeting with Mr. Sanchez at noon.
6 My coach told me to be ready for a difficult game.

gwam 30" | 2 | 4 | 6 | 8 | 10 | 12 | 14 | 16 | 18 | 20 |

Timed Writing

Key each paragraph once. DS between paragraphs. Key a 1' timed writing on each paragraph; determine *gwam*.

 all letters used

Risking your own life for the freedom of others has always been considered as an admirable thing. Harriet Tubman, a slave in the South, became a free woman when she escaped to the North. This freedom just did not mean much to her while so many others were still not free.

She quickly risked her own life by going back into the South to help others escape. She was able to help several hundred, an amazingly large number. During the Civil War she continued to exhibit hero-like traits. She served the Union as a spy and as a scout.

TECHNIQUE TIP

Keep your eyes on the copy as you reach out with your little finger and tap the ENTER key quickly.

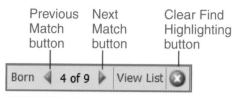

Previous Match button   Next Match button   Clear Find Highlighting button

Born ◀ 4 of 9 ▶ View List ✕

Figure 6.54 View the search results using the Next Match and Previous Match arrows.

5. Click the **View List** button. This will display a list of the pages in the *Presidents* folder that have the word *Born*. Click a page in the **Page List** task pane. Locate the highlighted word.

6. Click the **Clear Find Highlighting** button to clear the search results. Close *OneNote* or continue to the next activity.

63D PRACTICE: Search Notes

1. Start *OneNote*. Open the *Presidents* folder to any section and page in the folder.

2. Use Find to search the current folder for **Madison**.

3. Complete the Check Point below. Then clear the search results and close *OneNote*.

✔ **CHECK POINT** Compare the number of instances of *Madison* you found with the number found by a classmate. If the numbers are not the same, determine why they are different.

Using Pictures and Handwriting in OneNote

You may find having pictures in your notes helpful. For example, you may want to draw or sketch diagrams that relate to your notes. You might want to draw a star by important information. You might want to include a picture or drawing of a person or thing. For example, you might place a picture of each U.S. President on the page with notes about him.

You can place pictures in *OneNote* in several ways. You can insert a picture from a file into a *OneNote* page. You can drag and drop a picture from a Web page or other document onto your *OneNote* page. You can also draw a picture and handwrite notes on the *OneNote* page. To draw or create handwritten notes on a page, you will use the Pen tool.

Building Keying Skill

Warmup Practice

Key each line twice. If time permits, key the lines again.

Alphabet
1 Wesley Van Jantz quickly proofed the biology exam.

Figure/Symbol
2 On 08/13/04 Jorge paid invoice #291 for $2,358.67.

Speed
3 Pamela may hand signal to the big tug by the dock.

gwam 1' | 1 | 2 | 3 | 4 | 5 | 6 | 7 | 8 | 9 | 10 |

Improve Keying Technique

Key each line twice.

Balanced-hand words
1 auto burn dusk kept form half rich pale sign maid;
2 panel quake; right shelf chair; eight elbow giant;
3 enrich handle eighty bushel chapels turkey suspend

Balanced-hand phrases
4 by the end|pay the man|if they fix the| go to work
5 make the sign|right problem|key to the map|to risk
6 with the neighbor|work with the city|sign the maps

Balanced-hand sentences
7 Pay the girl by the city dock for the six bushels.
8 The girls paid for their gowns for the big social.
9 The city officials kept the fox in the big kennel.
10 Jay and Hal may go with us to visit the neighbors.

gwam 30" | 2 | 4 | 6 | 8 | 10 | 12 | 14 | 16 | 18 | 20 |

TECHNIQUE TIP

Think, say, and key the words as words, not letter by letter.

Insert Pictures in OneNote

1. Start *OneNote*. Open the *Presidents* folder. Open the *James Madison* section. Create a new page named **New States**.

2. Indiana and Louisiana became states during the administration of James Madison. You will place pictures that represent these states on the *New States* pages.

3. Click **Insert** on the menu bar. Choose **Picture, From File**. Browse to the folder where your data files are stored. Select the file *C6-Louisiana*. Click **Insert**. The image will be inserted in your page. Drag the image to the upper left of the page if needed.

4. Choose **View** on the menu bar. Choose **Rule Lines, Standard Ruled**. Having these lines displayed on the screen will help you write notes on the page.

Figure 6.55 Picture and Handwriting in a *OneNote* Page

5. Click the arrow for the **Pen** tool on the toolbar. Select **Black (thin)**.

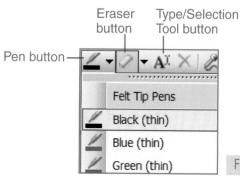

Figure 6.56 Pen and Eraser Buttons in *OneNote*

Report in MLA Format

1. Start *Word*. Open *CD-C10-Report2* and format it in MLA style.

2. The format for this report is based on the MLA style. However, side headings have been added to make finding information easier. Format the side headings as you would for a standard report.

3. Create a Works Cited page with the sources shown below.

4. Use Spelling Check. Proofread the document carefully and correct all errors. Save the document as *C10-Report2*. Print and close the report.

5. Open a new blank document. Create a title page for the report. Save the title page as *C10-title*. Print and close the title page.

Works Cited

Fulton-Calkins, Patsy, and Karin M. Stulz. Procedures & Theory for Administrative Professionals. 5th ed. Cincinnati: South-Western, 2004.

United States Department of Labor. The Bureau of Labor Statistics. "Occupational Outlook Handbook, 2004-2005 Edition." 25 June 2004 <http://stats.bls.gov/oco/>.

University of Waterloo. Career Services. "Step 1: Self-Assessment." Career Development eManual. 25 June 2004 <http://www.cdm.uwaterloo.ca/step1.asp>.

Outline for Report

1. Start *Word*. Open a new blank document. Set all margins to 1 inch. Set a decimal tab at 0.2 inches. Set left tabs at 0.38, 0.63, and .088 inches. Set the Line Spacing to **2**.

2. Key the outline for a report shown below. Use Spelling Check. Proofread the document carefully and correct all errors.

3. Save the document as *C10-Outline*. Print and close the document.

                        The Ear
    I. Parts of the Ear
        A. Outer ear
        B. Middle ear
        C. Inner ear
   II. How We Hear
        A. How sounds reach the inner ear
        B. How the inner ear sends sounds to the brain
  III. Care of the Ear
        A. Preventing ear infections
            1. Keeping fluids out of the ear
            2. Cleaning the ear
        B. Preventing ear injury

Supplemental activities for this chapter can be found at www.c21jr. swlearning.com.

6. Using a digital pen or mouse, click below the state image. Write this note below the image:

```
18th State
April 30, 1812
```

7. If you make a mistake or want to write more clearly, click the **Eraser** button. Move the cursor over the handwritten note to delete a word. Select the **Pen** button and try writing the word again.

8. Your page should look similar to Figure 6.55. Close *OneNote* or continue to the next activity.

63F PRACTICE: Insert Picture and Handwrite Note

1. Start *OneNote*. Open the *Presidents* folder. Open the *James Madison* section. Open the *New States* page.

2. Insert the picture *C6-Indiana* from your data files into the *New States* page. Drag the image to the upper right of the page beside the Louisiana image.

3. Use the **Pen** tool to write the note below under the Indiana image:

```
19th State
December 11, 1816
```

4. Close *OneNote* or continue to the next activity.

63G PRACTICE: Sketch Pictures

1. Start *OneNote*. Open the *Presidents* folder. Open the *James Madison* section. Open the *War of 1812* page.

2. Read the article about the War of 1812. Look for sentences that mention **Native Americans** or **Indian tribes**.

3. Click the arrow for the **Pen** button on the toolbar. Choose **Red (thin)**. Use a digital pen or mouse to underline each use of *Native Americans* or *Indian tribes*. Draw a star in the margin to the right of the paragraph that contains these words.

4. Complete the Check Point below and then close *OneNote*.

   ✔ **CHECK POINT** Compare your *War of 1812* page with that of another student. Did you both find all the words? Do you have the same number of stars?

Applying

What You Have Learned

Data Files

- *CD-C10-Report1*
- *CD-C10-Report2*

Report in Standard Format

1. Start *Word*. Open *CD-C10-Report1* from your data files.

2. Format the report in standard style. Do not number page 1.

3. Add the text shown below to the end of the report. Make the changes indicated by the proofreaders' marks.

4. Use Spelling Check. Proofread the document carefully and correct all errors.

5. Save the document as *C10-Report1*. Print and close the document.

Unfortunately, far too many tires are ^abandoned ~~thrown away~~ rather than recycled. Abandoned tires often litter the sides of our rivers and creeks. Many are ^found ~~hidden~~ in our forests. Too often, worn out tires are stacked in piles that are ugly and provide breeding groudns for pests. These tire piles ⌒ are fire hazards. If they catch fire, they can burn for weeks ruining the air. The ^heat of the fire can cause the rubber to decompose into oil. This oil is likely to _stet_ ^dirty ~~pollute~~ nearby ground and surface water, causing damage to the environment.

The next time you change ~~your~~ tires, even on your bicycle, make sure you dispose ^of them properly. If you can, _lc_ leave them at the ~~S~~tore where you buy the replacment ^e tires. The old tires can be recycled into useful products such as buckets, shoes, mouse pads for your computer, and dust pans.

Reviewing | *What You Have Learned*

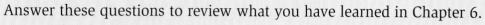

Answer these questions to review what you have learned in Chapter 6.

1. What are two types of computers that allow handwritten input directly on the computer screen?

2. What device can you use to give handwritten input on a desktop computer?

3. The technology that allows handwritten computer input is called _____.

4. The device used for pointing, drawing, and writing on a special type of computer screen or digital tablet is called what?

5. A tap with a digital pen is like what mouse action?

6. The _____ contains handwriting tools that you can use in *Microsoft Office* programs. The _____ contains the handwriting tools for a Tablet PC.

7. Inputting data using handwriting recognition is called what?

8. How can you erase mistakes when handtyping in the Writing Pad?

9. Writing tools come with _____ that you can tap to enter characters.

10. What is the keyboard shortcut for copy? for paste? for bold?

11. What does the *OneNote* program allow you to do?

12. In *OneNote*, a file is called what?

13. How many pages can you have in a *OneNote* section?

14. What button can you use to show or hide page titles?

15. *OneNote* organizes notes in areas called _____.

16. Describe how to merge two note containers that are on the same page. Describe how to split a note into two notes.

17. Describe how to change the width on a note container.

18. How do you create a new page in a *OneNote* section?

19. Describe how to create a bulleted list in *OneNote*.

20. An _____ is a document that organizes facts and details by main topics and subtopics.

21. Name three methods you might use to emphasize the text in a note.

22. Describe two ways to move text from a Web page to a *OneNote* page.

Reviewing | *What You Have Learned*

Answer these questions to review what you have learned in Chapter 10.

1. What are the default settings for margins in *Microsoft Word*?

2. What line spacing is used for a standard or an MLA report?

3. You can look at the _____ bar at the bottom of the screen to see the line position after the word *At*.

4. The style of letters used in a document is called the _____.

5. A(n) _____ contains information that appears at the top of pages in a document. A(n) _____ contains information that is displayed at the bottom of the page.

6. An _____ shows an ordered list of topics to be included in a report.

7. Set locations at which text can be placed are called _____. By default, they are set every one-half inch on the Ruler.

8. What margins and line spacing should be used for a standard report? How should the title be placed for a standard report? Where should the page number appear on the second page of a standard report?

9. What margins and line spacing should be used for an MLA report? How should the title be placed for an MLA report? Where should the page number appear on an MLA report?

10. Notes that are placed in the report body to mark material taken from other sources are called _____.

11. What is the name of the page on which sources used in a report are listed?

12. Use _____ for a list when the items can be considered in any order. Use _____ for a list when the items need to be considered in a certain order.

13. List the parts a title page for a school report usually contains.

14. What does the Cut command do? What does the Copy command do? What does the Paste command do?

15. Describe two ways to move text in a document.

23. You can search for text in *OneNote* pages using the _____ feature.

24. To sketch pictures or make handwritten notes in *OneNote*, use the _____ tool.

Applying **What You Have Learned**

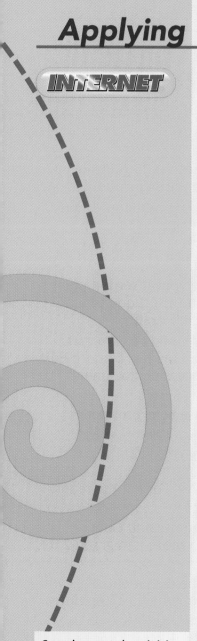

Describe Your Penmanship by Handtyping

How would you describe your penmanship? Is it elegant, artistic, readable, fancy, practical, serious, fun, energetic, or just plain sloppy? Describe your penmanship style as you improve your writing.

1. Start *Word*. Open the Writing Pad.

2. Write a paragraph of 25 words or more that describes your handwriting. Write as clearly as you can, using either printed or cursive letters. A sample paragraph is shown below.

   My handwriting is very sloppy. I write using printed letters most of the time. I write fast, especially when taking notes in class. Sometimes I can't read my own handwriting. I need to practice writing clearly.

3. Save the document as *C06-Penmanship*. Close *Word*.

Create a New Section and Page in *OneNote*

1. Start *OneNote*. Open the *Presidents* folder. Create a new section. Use the name of the current U.S. President as the name of the section. In this section, create a page named **Current President**.

2. Log on to the Internet and open *Internet Explorer*. Go to the White House Web site at http://www.whitehouse.gov. Follow links that lead you to a biography of the current President.

3. On your *Current President* page, record the following information:

   • President's full name

   • President's date of birth

   • President's place of birth

   • Year this President took office

4. Find a photo of the President. Drag the photo of the President onto your *OneNote* page (or use Copy and Paste).

5. Proofread and correct any errors in your notes. Close *OneNote*.

Supplemental activities for this chapter can be found at www.c21jr. swlearning.com.

The **Cut** command removes selected text from a document. The **Copy** command copies selected text so it can be pasted to another location. The original text is unchanged. The **Paste** command places text that has been cut or copied into a document. You can access the Cut, Copy, and Paste commands quickly by clicking buttons on the Standard toolbar. The buttons are shown in Figure 10.23.

Cut   Copy   Paste

Figure 10.23 Cut, Copy, and Paste Buttons

89C LEARN:

Cut, Copy, and Paste

1. Start *Word*. Open *CD-89-Paste1* from your data files. In the steps below, you will use Cut and Paste commands to arrange the steps in order.
2. Select the line numbered 1. Click the **Cut** button. Move the insertion point to the beginning of the first line. Click the **Paste** button.
3. Select the line numbered 2. Drag the text to the beginning of the second line.
4. Select all four lines. Click the **Copy** button. Move your insertion point a double space below line 4. Click **Paste**. Move your insertion point a double space below the second group of lines. Click **Paste**.
5. Open *CD-89-Copy* from your data files in a browser such as *Internet Explorer*. Select the third paragraph and the numbered list. Choose **Edit**, **Copy** from the menu bar. Move to your word processing document. Click at the end of the document. Click the **Paste** button.
6. Save the document as *89-Paste1* and close it. Close your browser.

89D APPLY:

Cut, Copy, and Paste in a Report

1. Start *Word*. Open *CD-89-Report* from your data files. Format the report for MLA style.
2. Use Cut to remove the side headings **E-Mail Etiquette** and **Chat Rooms**. Use Cut and Paste (or select and drag) to move paragraph 2 to make it paragraph 1.
3. Insert a manual page break at the beginning of the document. This will create a new page for a title page. Use Copy to copy the heading lines and report title to the new blank page.
4. Arrange and format the data on the first page as a title page for the report. Select **Different first page** in the **Page Setup** dialog box so the header will not appear on the title page.
5. Check for spelling errors and proofread carefully. Save the document as *89-Report*. Print and close the document.

Building Keying Skill

Warmup Practice

Key each line twice. If time permits, key the lines again.

Alphabet

1 Before leaving, Jexon quickly swam the dozen laps.

Figure/Symbol

2 Our tax increased by 12.7% ($486); we paid $3,590.

Speed

3 Hal and I may go to the social held on the island.

gwam 1' | 1 | 2 | 3 | 4 | 5 | 6 | 7 | 8 | 9 | 10 |

Improve Keying Technique

Key each line twice. If time permits, key the lines again.

Balanced-hand words

1 go if am us to by of he an so is do it go me be or
2 is and the may did man due big for box but oak six
3 with when make such work city down they them their

Balanced-hand phrases

4 big box|pay for|and the|own them|to the end|he may
5 if they|make a|the right|by the|wish to|when did I
6 sign the|for them|make them|when is|and then|to it

Balanced-hand sentences

7 Nancy and I may go to the city for the audit form.
8 Enrique may make a map of the island for the firm.
9 Orlando may work with the men on the bus problems.

gwam 30" | 2 | 4 | 6 | 8 | 10 | 12 | 14 | 16 | 18 | 20 |

TECHNIQUE TIP

Keep your eyes on the copy.

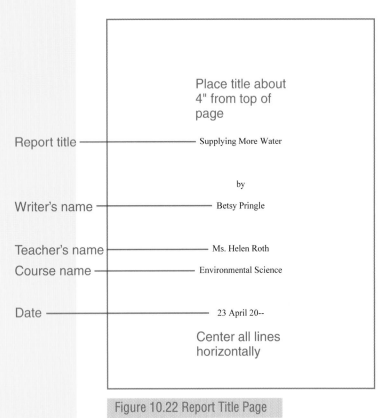

Place title about 4" from top of page

Report title —————— Supplying More Water

by

Writer's name —————— Betsy Pringle

Teacher's name —————— Ms. Helen Roth

Course name —————— Environmental Science

Date —————— 23 April 20--

Center all lines horizontally

Figure 10.22 Report Title Page

2. Create a title page for the report. Open a new blank document in *Word*. Set all margins to 1 inch to match MLA report style. Set the Line Spacing to **2**.

3. Tap ENTER several times to position the insertion point about 4 inches from the top. Refer to the Status bar for correct placement.

4. Click the **Center** button on the Formatting toolbar. Key the title: **Identity Theft**.

5. Tap ENTER twice and key the word **by**. Tap ENTER once and key your first and last name.

6. Tap ENTER twice and key the teacher's name: **Mr. Roman Juarez**. Tap ENTER once and key the class: **Computer Applications**.

7. Tap ENTER twice and key the date: **5 December 20--**.

8. Save the document as *89-Title1* and print it.

89B PRACTICE: Title Page

In Lesson 88, you created a report titled *Supplying More Water*. In this activity, you will create a title page for that report.

1. Locate your printed copy of *88-Report2* that you created earlier.

2. Create a title page for the report. Follow the steps you learned in the last activity. Find the information for the title page on the first page of your printed report.

3. Save the document as *89-Title2* and print it.

Cut, Copy, and Paste

When you create a report, you may write several drafts or versions of the report. You may decide to cut some data that doesn't quite fit with the report subject. You may decide to move a paragraph from page 1 to page 2. You may want to copy a long quote from a Web page into a report. You can use the Cut, Copy, and Paste features to help you make these types of changes to a document.

Speed Forcing Drill

Key a 30" timed writing on each line. Your rate in gross words a minute (*gwam*) is shown below the lines.

1 Pamela may be able to go.
2 You can see the next game too.
3 Mike will be out of town on Friday.
4 Shawn and I can take the exam next week.
5 Nancy will bring your new computer next week.
6 The new version of the video game will be on sale.

gwam 30" | 2 | 4 | 6 | 8 | 10 | 12 | 14 | 16 | 18 | 20 |

Timed Writing

Key each paragraph once. Key a 1' timed writing on each paragraph; determine *gwam*. Key a 2' timed writing on both paragraphs; determine *gwam*.

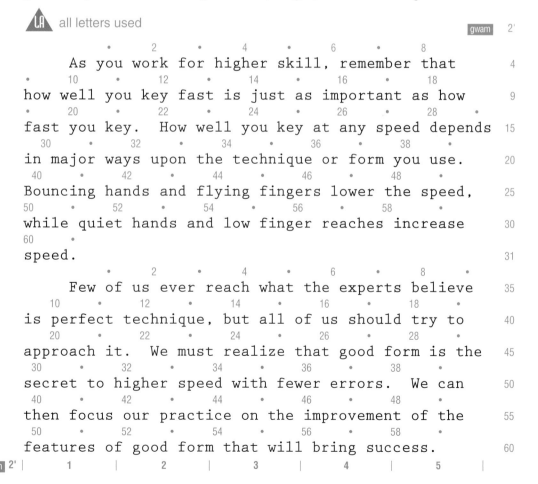

LA all letters used

gwam 2'

As you work for higher skill, remember that   4
how well you key fast is just as important as how   9
fast you key. How well you key at any speed depends   15
in major ways upon the technique or form you use.   20
Bouncing hands and flying fingers lower the speed,   25
while quiet hands and low finger reaches increase   30
speed.   31

Few of us ever reach what the experts believe   35
is perfect technique, but all of us should try to   40
approach it. We must realize that good form is the   45
secret to higher speed with fewer errors. We can   50
then focus our practice on the improvement of the   55
features of good form that will bring success.   60

gwam 2' | 1 | 2 | 3 | 4 | 5 |

MLA Report with Proofreaders' Marks

1. Start *Word*. Open *CD-88-Report2* from your data files. Print this report, which has been marked with proofreaders' marks. Close the document.
2. Open a new blank document in *Word*. Key the report from your printout.
   - Set margins and line spacing for an MLA-style report.
   - Key the writer's last name and insert a page number in a header.
   - Left-indent the long quote 1 inch.
   - Make corrections as indicated by the proofreaders' marks.
   - Insert a manual page break and place the Works Cited on the last page.
3. Save the document as *88-Report2*. Print and close the report.

Instant Message

Long quotations (four or more lines) are indented 1 inch from the left margin. Do not enclose long quotations in quotation marks.

Lesson 89   Title Pages for Reports

Objectives

In Lesson 89, you will:
- ⬎ Create title pages for reports.
- ⬎ Cut, copy, and paste text.
- ⬎ Copy text from another document.

Data files: *CD-89-Paste1, CD-89-Copy, CD-89-Report*

Report Title Page

MLA suggests that a report begin with the first page of the text. However, your teacher may ask you to use a report title page. Standard reports created on the job also often have a title page. Figure 10.22 shows one example of a report title page. Refer to this figure as you read about title pages.

A title page for a school report usually contains these parts:
- Report title
- Report subtitle, if one is used
- Writer's name
- Teacher's name and the course name
- Current date in day, month, and year format

Title Page

In Lesson 88, you created a report about identity theft. In this activity, you will create a title page for that report.

1. Locate your printed copy of *88-Report1* that you created earlier. Note that each item needed for a title page appears on the first page of the report.

Data Files

- *CD-C06-Business*
- *CD-C06-Human Services*
- *CD-C06-Career*
- *CD-C06-Interest*

↗ About Business

ENTREPRENEURS Do you know someone who is an entrepreneur? Will you be an entrepreneur someday? An **entrepreneur** is a person who organizes and manages a business, risking the money he or she invests in the hopes of making a profit. The business may be large or small. The owner may invest a large or small amount of money. The company may make and sell products or offer services.

Successful entrepreneurs need traits such as initiative, responsibility, and creativity. They also need good management skills and the ability to work well with other people. An entrepreneur must be able to identify an opportunity that he or she thinks can lead to a successful business. For example, suppose the owner of the only dry cleaner in a small town plans to retire and close the dry cleaning shop. This creates an opportunity for someone else to open a dry cleaning shop in that town. Next, the entrepreneur must be able to make plans for the business. How much money will be needed to rent or buy a building? Where should the shop be? How many workers will be needed? What equipment will be needed? How will the owner advertise the business to get customers? These are a few of the questions to be answered in a business plan.

Once the business is in operation, the owner may run the company. As the business grows, a manager may be hired. A **manager** is an employee who oversees the daily affairs of a business. If the business is successful, the owner will receive profits from the business. Many small businesses started by entrepreneurs have become large companies. Microsoft Corporation, Hershey Foods Corporation, and Procter and Gamble Company are a few examples.

1. Start *Word*. Open and print *CD-C06-Business* from your data files. Complete the activity to see if you have the traits needed to be a successful entrepreneur.

2. Follow the instructions given to research a large company that was started by an entrepreneur. Be prepared to share the information you find with the class.

↗ Career and Life Skills Success Builder

SOCIAL STUDIES AND HISTORY VS. YOUR CAREER Do you love to study people, places, and cultures? If you enjoy your social studies and history classes, you have many careers to choose from. You may decide to study ancient cultures and be an archaeologist. Maybe you will study family trees and be a genealogist. Maybe you will be an economist and study how people

4. Check for misspelled words and then proofread carefully. Make additional corrections as needed. Save the document as *88-Report1*. Print and close it.

 **CHECK POINT** Did you find errors that Spelling Check did not identify? Compare what you found with what a classmate found. If you do not agree on the errors, proofread again.

Proofreaders' Marks

Every document you create should be checked carefully. You should make sure it does not have spelling, punctuation, or format errors. **Proofreaders' marks** are letters and symbols used to show the errors in a document. These marks make it easier for you or someone else to make the changes. Study the frequently used marks below. Other marks are shown in the resource section of the textbook.

Mark	Action Required	Mark	Action Required
⁋	Begin a new paragraph	*Cap* ≡	Capitalize
⌒	Close up	⅁	Delete
∧	Insert	*stet*	Let it stand
lc	Make lowercase	⊏	Move left
⊐	Move right	∩ *tr*	Transpose

88C LEARN: Proofreaders' Marks

1. Start *Word*. Open a new document. Key the text shown below. Make corrections as indicated by the proofreaders' marks.

2. Save the document as *88-Proof1* and close it.

just how well do you adjust to ^big^ changes in your life? You

should recog nize that change is sa certain as ~~life and~~

death and taxes. You can ^not^ avoid chagne, but your can adjust

lc to it. How Quickly you can do this is a ^good^ index of the

success you are likley to have in the future years. ⁋Can

you think of *stet* ~~changes~~ that have affected your in the past

year? Were you able to adjust too them?

use goods and services. All of these careers are related to your classes in social studies and history.

If you want to be able to help people on a daily basis, you may decide to work in the field of human services. You could choose to work with children in a day care. You could work with the elderly in social services. You could also be a government employee and work as an assistant in your mayor's office. You can begin learning the skills needed for these rewarding careers in your social studies and history courses.

1. Is a career in the field of human services right for you? Open and print the data file *CD-C06-Human Services*. Read the information to see if you are interested in this career path.

2. Open the data file *CD-C06-Career*. Follow the directions given to access the Internet and research a career in the field of human services.

⟋ Academic Success Builder

MATH AND PERSONAL FINANCE: SAVING MONEY Saving money is very important. You may save to buy something you cannot afford today, such as a new CD player. Saving allows you to pay for something in the future. You might save for college or a special vacation. People also need to save so they can live comfortably after they retire from working.

One of the easiest and safest ways to save money is to open a savings account at a local bank. Banks offer different kinds of savings accounts. There are regular savings accounts that pay a fixed rate of interest. **Interest** is money the bank pays you for keeping your money in certain types of accounts. A money market account usually pays an interest rate that varies. These types of accounts let you add money to or take money out of your account whenever you choose. A third kind of account is a certificate of deposit, referred to as a CD. With a CD account, you agree to leave your money with the bank for a stated period of time. The time can be short, such as 30 days, or long, such as 5 years. You cannot add money to a CD. You cannot take money out of a CD for an agreed-upon time without paying a penalty. For this reason, CDs usually pay a higher interest rate than either money market or regular savings accounts.

In this activity, you will learn to compute simple interest and compound interest. **Simple interest** means that interest is paid only on the original amount. With **compound interest**, interest is earned on the original amount and also on the interest you earned during previous interest periods. When the interest rate and the time of the deposit on different CDs are equal, you will receive more interest when interest is compounded than when it is not.

1. Start *Word*. Open *CD-C06-Interest* found in your data files. Print the file and then close it.

2. Complete the math activities as directed. Compare your answers with those of a classmate.

Bulleted and Numbered Lists

You can apply bullets or numbers to text that has already been keyed. Select the items for the list. Click the **Bullets** or **Numbering** button on the Formatting toolbar.

Numbering

Bullets

1. Start *Word*. Open a new blank document. Set the Line Spacing to **1.5**. Key the text below and then tap ENTER.

   I need to take these three books home this evening:

2. Choose **Format** on the menu bar. Click **Bullets and Numbering**. Click the **Bulleted** tab. See Figure 10.21 on page 375. Click a style of bullets you want from the seven styles shown. Click **OK**. *Word* inserts the bullet and moves the insertion point to where you are to begin keying.

3. Key the three lines below. Tap ENTER after each line.

   Math
   English
   Science

4. To end the bulleted list, tap the BACKSPACE key once (or twice if needed) to move the insertion point to the left margin.

5. Key this text below the last bulleted item and then tap ENTER.

   These are my homework priorities for this weekend:

6. Choose **Format** from the menu bar. Click **Bullets and Numbering**. Click the **Numbered** tab. Click a numbering style you want from the seven styles shown. Click **OK**. *Word* inserts the first number and positions the insertion point where you are to begin keying.

7. Key the three lines below. Tap ENTER after each line.

   Write a draft of my English theme.
   Do end-of-chapter math problems.
   Begin science project.

8. Tap BACKSPACE once (or twice if needed) to end the numbered list and move the insertion point to the left margin.

9. Key your name beginning at the insertion point. Save the document as *88-List1*. Print and close the document.

MLA Report with Bulleted List

1. Start *Word*. Open *CD-88-Report1*. Format the document in correct MLA style. Use your name as the person writing the report. Create an appropriate header.

2. Change the numbered list to a bulleted list. (Select the numbered list. Choose **Format**, **Bullets and Numbering**. On the **Bulleted** tab, click a style of bullets you want to use. Click **OK**.)

3. Check the format. Part of this report will appear on a second page. Has a bullet occupying two lines of text been split so that one line is at the bottom of page 1 and the second line is at the top of page 2? If so, insert a manual page break before the bulleted item so that the entire item appears on page 2.

Chapter 7

Lessons 64–66

Digital Imaging, Scanning, and Photography

OBJECTIVES

In Chapter 7, you will

↗ Learn about imaging technologies.

↗ Learn to use and apply various digital image formats.

↗ Learn about file size and image resolution.

↗ Learn when to use low-resolution and high-resolution images.

↗ Learn to care for a scanner.

↗ Scan, crop, view, and save images.

↗ Take digital photographs and change quality and resolution settings.

↗ Save digital photos to a PC.

What if Neil Armstrong and Buzz Aldrin had landed on the moon without a camera? Without pictures this important event wouldn't seem as spectacular. The two astronauts could have spent hours describing their adventures on the moon. However, without photos the story would not be the same.

Pictures such as those shown in Figure 7.1 help capture our imaginations. It would be difficult to describe in words alone these fantastic lunar marvels:

- The amazing black color of the sky in full daylight

- The powdery footprints left by the astronaut's boots that may never blow away

- The earth rising above the lunar horizon

- The stunning reflections off the face masks of the astronauts

Lesson 88   MLA Reports with Lists

Objectives

In Lesson 88, you will:

↘ Create bulleted and numbered lists.

↘ Format a report in MLA style.

↘ Use bullets to list items in a report.

↘ Make changes indicated by proofreaders' marks.

Data files: *CD-88-Report1, CD-88-Report2*

Bulleted and Numbered Lists

┌ ⎤
Help Words
└ ⎦
Bullets
  Add bullets or
  numbering

You may want to include a list in a report or other document. For example, you might list steps for doing a task such as baking a cake. You might want to include a list of points to consider for solving a problem. Lists in a document can be formatted with bullets or numbers. **Bullets** are characters or graphics (squares, circles, pictures) that appear before each item in the list. Use bullets for a list when the items can be considered in any order.

Other lists have a number before each item in the list. Use a numbered list when the items need to be considered in a certain order. For example, when baking a cake you would not give the step about putting the cake in the oven before the steps for adding the flour, milk, and eggs.

The **Bullets and Numbering** feature allows you to select styles for bullets or numbering for lists. The Bullets and Numbering dialog box is shown in Figure 10.21. Note that some styles for an ordered (numbered) list use letters.

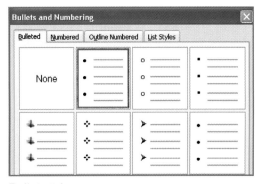
Bullet styles

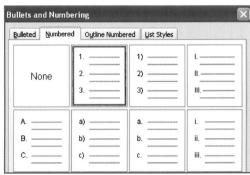
Numbering styles

Figure 10.21 Bullets and Numbering Dialog Box Buttons

Images courtesy of NASA.

Figure 7.1 Sometimes only pictures will do.

Pictures are essential to modern communication. You need to know how to take pictures and images and move them to your PC so you can use them in your future projects. You will learn these skills in this chapter.

7. Your Works Cited page should look similar to Figure 10.18 on page 370 (but with only two Works Cited entries). Save the document as *87-Sources* and close the document.

CHECK POINT Did you place the period after the in-text citations? Is your Works Cited page on a separate page? Does page 2 have a header with the page number? Are the side margins 1 inch?

87D APPLY:

MLA Report with Works Cited

Instant Message

Enter *national parks* or the park name in a search engine to find information on the Internet.

1. Do research and write a report about a U.S. national park. Choose a park. Find information about national parks in your local library or on the Internet. In your report, you should include information such as:

   • The park location

   • A general description

   • Primary attractions

   • Other information that you find of interest

2. Use at least two sources of information about the park. Note the reference information for each source. Use the references shown in Figure 10.18 as examples.

3. Format the report in MLA style. Use an appropriate header, title, and report headings. Write at least three paragraphs for the body. Include at least two in-text citations. Create a Works Cited page as the last page of the report. List all the sources you used on this page.

4. Check for misspelled words and proofread carefully. Save the document as *87-Report* and print it.

CHECK POINT Trade papers with a classmate. Ask your classmate to proofread your paper and mark errors you may have missed. Make corrections, if needed.

Lesson 64   Discovering Images

Objectives

In Lesson 64, you will:

↘ Learn how dots of color can create elaborate computer images.

↘ Zoom in and out on an image.

↘ View and evaluate the resolution of an image with dots per inch or pixels per inch.

↘ Evaluate when to use a low- or high-resolution image.

↘ Learn about image file formats.

↘ Alter an image.

↘ Discover how computers display images.

Data files: *CD-64-Reflection1, CD-64-Message, CD-64-Reflection2, CD-64-Reflection3*

Images, Mosaics, and Pixels

The astronauts were not the only ones who thought pictures were important. Cave dwellers created elaborate images on rock walls to tell of their adventures. Over the centuries, artwork became more spectacular. It took the form of paintings, murals, sculpture, and mosaics. Figure 7.2 shows a mosaic created by ancient Greeks to adorn a public building.

© Roger Wood/CORBIS

Figure 7.2 Greek mosaics were a popular art form 2,000 years ago.

Mosaics are interesting. Mosaics are little dots of color. In years past, they were made of colored pebbles, small pieces of painted pottery, or miniature tinted tiles. The dots were carefully arranged into elaborate images. Mosaics were found in Greek homes, temples, and public buildings. Tiny little dots of color can make very interesting designs!

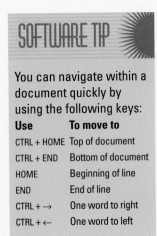
5. The insertion point should be at the end of line 1 of page 3. Look at the Status bar. It should show **Page 3** and **3/3**.

6. Revise the text on page 3 to read:

   This text is also on page 2.

7. Place the insertion point at the beginning of the last line. Tap the BACKSPACE key to delete the manual page break.

8. The last two lines of text should now appear on the second page. Close the document without saving.

87C PRACTICE: Indents and Manual Page Breaks

1. Start *Word*. Open *CD-87-Sources* from your data files. Format the report in MLA style. Add a header for the writer's last name and the page number.

2. Place the insertion point at the end of the third sentence between the end quotation mark and the period. Space one time. Key the citation:

   (Anson and Schwegler 619)

3. Place the insertion point between the last word in the final sentence and the period. Space one time. Key the citation:

   (Hoggatt and Shank 150)

4. Review the example of a Works Cited page in Figure 10.18 on page 370.

5. Place the insertion point at the end of the last paragraph. Hold down CTRL and tap ENTER to insert a manual page break and create a new page. On the new page, center the title **Works Cited** on the first line. Tap ENTER.

6. Set the alignment to Left. Set a hanging indent for the works cited. (Click **Format** on the menu bar. Click **Paragraph**. Click the down arrow for the **Special** drop-down list. Click **Hanging**. Key **0.5** in the By box. Click **OK**. See Figure 10.20 on page 372.) Key the two references shown below.

Anson, Chris M., and Robert A. Schwegler. <u>The Longman Handbook for Writers and Readers</u>. 3rd ed. New York: Addison-Wesley Educational Publications, Inc., 2003.

Hoggatt, Jack P., and Jon A. Shank. <u>Applied Computer Keyboarding</u>. 5th ed. Cincinnati: South-Western, 2004.

Computers also use little dots of colored light to project pictures on screens. Each little dot of light is called a **pixel**. Printers also use dots of ink to make images on paper. For both computer screens and printers, the more dots, the higher the picture quality or **resolution**.

Examine one of the most recognized photographs from the space program shown in Figure 7.3. Astronaut Buzz Aldrin's face mask shows the reflection of the photographer, Neil Armstrong. It also shows a leg of the *Eagle*, the astronauts' lunar module.

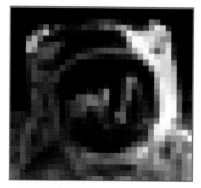

High-resolution Image   Low-resolution Image

Figure 7.3 The same image looks different in high and low resolutions.

Look what happens if you zoom in on the little squares of color in a lower-resolution image. Examine the photo on the right in Figure 7.3. The reflection in the mask is reduced to nothing more than carefully arranged dots or squares of color. You can actually see the little squares by zooming in. The picture looks jagged and rough.

Try this experiment. Zoom out! Set your book up and walk back about 10 feet. As the picture gets smaller, does the image begin to look sharper? Does the picture begin to look as it should?

There are other ways to sharpen the image. You can shrink the size of the picture on your computer by zooming out. You can also increase the picture resolution. You will learn how this works in the upcoming exercises.

64A LEARN: View the Mosaic-like Dots

1. Start *Paint* by choosing **Start**, **All Programs**, **Accessories**, **Paint**.

2. Click **File** on the menu bar. Choose **Open**. In the Open dialog box, browse to the folder where your data files for this class are stored. Select the file named *CD-64-Reflection1*. Click **Open**.

3. Click the *Paint* window **Maximize** button to make *Paint* as large as it can be.

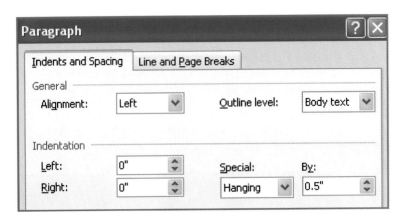

Figure 10.20 Settings for Hanging Indent

7. Click **OK** to close the dialog box. Your Works Cited entries should now be formatted correctly for hanging indent.

8. Save the document as *87-Indents1* and close it.

Manual Page Breaks

Two types of **page breaks** are used to signal the end of a page. *Automatic* page breaks are placed by the software when the current page is full. An automatic page break may move when more text is keyed before the page break. You can enter a *manual* page break when you want to end a page before it is full. Manual page breaks remain in the place they are inserted unless they are deleted.

87B LEARN:

Manual Page Breaks

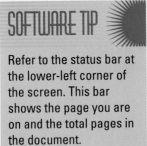
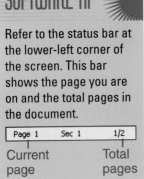

SOFTWARE TIP

Refer to the status bar at the lower-left corner of the screen. This bar shows the page you are on and the total pages in the document.

| Page 1 | Sec 1 | 1/2 |

Current
page

Total
pages

1. Start *Word*. Open a new blank document. Key the line below.

   This text is line 1 on page 1.

2. Hold down the CTRL key and tap ENTER. This will insert a manual page break.

3. Key the line below.

   This text is line 1 on page 2.

4. Hold down CTRL and tap ENTER to insert a manual page break. Key the line below.

   This text is line 1 on page 3.

4. Click the **Magnifier** button on the **Paint** toolbar. Zoom in six times by choosing the **6x** option. See Figure 7.4.

5. Use the bottom scroll bar to center the mask and the American flag on the shoulder patch so they appear centered in the *Start Paint* window. See Figure 7.4.

Click the Magnifier button

Choose 6x

Scroll bar

Image courtesy of NASA.

Figure 7.4 Magnify and center the mask and flag.

6. Examine the rough edges along the space suit. Look at the little squares that make up the flag. Notice how the image of astronaut Armstrong and the lunar module disappear into little squares of color.

7. Step back from your computer about 6 to 10 feet. Does the image look sharper and more realistic?

8. Choose the magnifier button again and return to the **1x** setting. Notice that when you zoom out, the image becomes more realistic. Shrinking an image is just like moving back from your computer several feet. Both actions zoom out from a low-resolution image, making it look sharper.

9. Close *Paint* and do not save the file.

Controlling Dots of Color

Now that you know about the dots or squares of color, you can have some fun manipulating the images. Just like the ancient Greeks used colored pebbles to create elaborate designs and mosaics, you can change the colored squares so that new images appear. For example, wouldn't it have been funny if the *Apollo 11* astronauts had written a message home from space on their face masks? Figure 7.5 shows one possibility.

Paragraph Indents

Help Words

Indent
Indent paragraphs

Long quotes in reports are indented to make them stand out from the rest of the report body. You can see an example of an indented quote in Figure 10.17.

A list of works cited in a report is formatted using hanging indent. The **Hanging Indent** feature begins all lines except the first line away from the left margin. You can see an example of hanging indent in Figure 10.18. With this indent style, the authors' names stand out and are easier to find. The Paragraph dialog box can be used to set these special indents.

87A LEARN:

Paragraph Indents

1. Start *Word*. Open the file *CD-87-Indents1* from your data files.

2. This document contains part of a report. Select the second paragraph of the report, which is a long quote.

3. Click **Format** on the menu bar. Click **Paragraph**. The Paragraph dialog box appears.

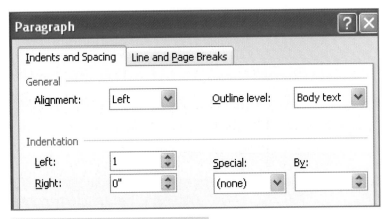

Figure 10.19 Paragraph Dialog Box

4. Under Indentation, in the Left box, key **1**. Click **OK** at the bottom of the box.

5. Move to the next page of the document. This is a Works Cited page. Select all the entries after the title.

6. Click **Format** on the menu bar. Click **Paragraph**. The Paragraph dialog box appears. Click the down arrow for the **Special** drop-down list. Click **Hanging**. Key **0.5** in the By box. This is the distance all lines except the first line are to be indented.

Make a Mosaic on the Mask

1. Start *Paint.* Open *CD-64-Message.*

2. Choose the **Pencil** tool as marked in Figure 7.5. Select **Black** from the color palette.

3. Click or tap your black pencil on each colored square inside the mask. Turn every square inside the face mask black.

4. Choose the **Pencil** tool again. Select **White** or a bright **Yellow** from the color palette.

5. Carefully color just a few squares in the mask at a time to spell out **Hello!** as shown in Figure 7.5.

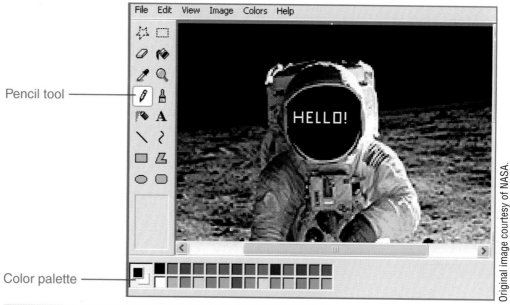

Pencil tool

Color palette

Original image courtesy of NASA.

Figure 7.5 Turn some squares white or yellow to spell out Hello!

6. Click the Magnifier tool and select **1x**. See how the changes you have made will appear in the image. Save your image with the filename *64-Message.* Close *Paint* or continue to the next activity.

Create Mosaics with a Screen Capture

1. Create your own mosaics using screen captures. To capture a picture of anything on your screen, tap the PRTSCRN (PRinT SCreeN) key.

2. Start *Paint.* Choose **Edit** from the menu bar. Choose **Paste**.

Lillian Jackson Braun is a popular mystery writer. Many people enjoy reading her books about an amateur detective and his cats. The cats, Koko and Tum Yum, know how to make themselves at home anywhere.

Indent long quotes 1"

It was their first night in the cabin by the creek. Qwilleran placed the cats' blue cushion on one bunk. They settled down contentedly, while he retired to the other bunk. Sometime during the night, the arrangement changed, in the morning Qwilleran was sharing his pillow with Yum Yum, and Koko was snuggled in the crook of his knee. (Braun 123) ———— **In-text citation**

Figure 10.17 In-Text Citation for a Long Quote

All references cited in a report in MLA style are listed on a separate page. This page is the last page of the report. It is called the Works Cited page. An example of a Works Cited page is shown in Figure 10.18.

This page should have the same margins and header as the report body. The title, Works Cited, is centered at the top of the page. The works cited are listed a double space below the title. The works are placed in alphabetical order by author's last names, if known. If the author is not known, use the title of the work. The paragraphs are formatted for hanging indent.

Title centered

1" top and side margins

Anderson 3

Writer's name and page number in header

Works Cited

Ackerman, Jennifer. "Cranes." National Geographic Apr. 2004: 44.

Anson, Chris M., and Robert A. Schwegler. The Longman Handbook for Writers and Readers.

0.5" hanging indent for paragraphs

3rd ed. New York: Addison-Wesley Educational Publications, Inc., 2003.

Braun, Lillian Jackson. The Cat Who Went Up the Creek. New York: Jove Books, 2003.

Line Spacing 2 for all lines

Hoggatt, Jack P., and Jon A. Shank. Applied Computer Keyboarding. 5th ed. Cincinnati:

South-Western, 2004.

"Mesa Verde." National Park Service. 13 July 2004 <http://www.nps.gov/meve/index.htm>.

At least 1" bottom margin

Figure 10.18 Works Cited Page

3. Click the **Magnify** tool and select the **6x** or **8x** option to see the pixels in the image. In Figure 7.6, an image of flowers has been magnified to expose the colored squares. Use the **Pencil** tool and various colors to alter the image.

4. Click the **Magnify** tool and select **1x** to see the effect of your changes. Save the file as *64-Mosaics*. Close *Paint*.

Figure 7.6 Use the Magnify tool to reveal the pixels in an image.

Resolution and File Size

Computers display images on their screens by passing electrical impulses to little dots of colored light called pixels. You can actually see pixels by taking a magnifying glass and staring closely into a computer monitor.

Printers use dots of ink instead of dots of light. For both computer screens and printed paper, the more dots, the higher the image quality or resolution. Resolution is measured in pixels per inch (PPI) or dots per inch (DPI).

Because higher resolution means better image quality, you may be wondering why all images are not created in high resolution. The reason is that the more dots you have (higher resolution), the bigger the file size is. For images used on the Web, file size must be small to allow rapid downloading to your computer.

Now you may be thinking, "Why not always create low-resolution images?" The reason is that low-resolution images do not look good when printed. Low-resolution pictures may look grainy, blurry, or out of focus when printed. High-resolution printed images can look like high-quality photographs.

1. Start *Word*. Open a new blank document. Compose a short report (one to two pages) about yourself. Format the report in MLA style.

2. Use your name, your teacher's name, your class name, and the current date for the headings. Use your name and the word *Autobiography* for the title. For the body:
   - Tell about when and where you were born.
   - Talk briefly about your parents, brothers and sisters, or other family members.
   - Describe your physical appearance and your personality.
   - Talk about your interests or hobbies.
   - Name one or two jobs that you think you might like to have.

3. Save the document as *86-Report3*. Print the report and close it.

Lesson 87   MLA Reports with Citations

Objectives

In Lesson 87, you will:
↘ Use left and hanging indents to format paragraphs.
↘ Insert manual page breaks.
↘ Format MLA reports with in-text citations.
↘ Create a Works Cited page.

Data files: *CD-87-Indents1, CD-87-Indents2, CD-87-Sources*

Works Cited

In an MLA report, notes are placed in the body to mark material taken from other sources. These notes are called **citations**. For example, you might quote from a magazine article in a report you write. You should cite (give information about) where this material came from.

Citations are placed in parentheses in the report body. Figure 10.17 shows an example of an in-text citation. Citations include the name(s) of the author(s) and page number(s) of the material.

Quotes of up to three keyed lines are placed in quotation marks. Long quotes (four or more keyed lines) are left-indented 1 inch. Summarized material is not put in quotation marks.

File Formats for Graphic Images

Digital images must be saved in a recognizable file format. Different file formats are designed for these very different needs. Four very common image file formats are BMP, TIF, JPEG, and GIF. Common file formats are described in the table below. In the next activity, you will compare high- (TIF), variable- (JPEG), and lower- (GIF) resolution images and file sizes.

Common Graphic File Formats	
BMP (.bmp)	The Bitmap or .bmp file format was created by Microsoft and is used by Microsoft *Windows* and *Office* programs.
JPEG (.jpg)	The Joint Photographic Experts Group is an organization that created the standards for the .jpg format. This format supports millions of colors and can also be compressed. For computer backgrounds and Web graphics, keep the resolution low. For printed documents, increase the resolution and file size.
GIF (.gif)	The Graphics Interchange Format (.gif) is a popular format for images used on the Internet. Images in this format are small and compressed. This format is acceptable for cartoons, logos, Web graphics, graphics with transparent areas, and animations.
TIFF (.tif)	The Tagged Image File format (.tif) (also Microsoft Office Document Imaging File) is a high-resolution format. It is commonly used in desktop publishing and print publishing. Resolution can be increased and decreased in this format. It allows black-and-white and grayscale images as well as color images. It is one of the most widely supported file formats.

64D APPLY: Compare High-, Medium-, and Low-Resolution Images

1. Start *Paint*. Choose **File** from the menu bar. Choose **Open**.

2. In the Open dialog box, browse to the folder where the data files are stored.

3. Click **View** on the menu bar. Choose **Details**. This view shows the file type for each file and the file size. See Figure 7.7.

Kellum 1
Last name and
page number in
header

Sarah N. Kellum

**Heading
lines**

Mrs. Torres

English

Center title

15 February 20--

Formatting School Reports

**Line
Spacing 2
for all
lines**

School reports are often typed using a simple form of the MLA (Modern Language

Association) style.

The top, bottom, left, and right margins on all pages are 1inch. Align right a page

number in a header on each page. The writer's last name should come before the page number.

Double space the entire report. The report heading lines begin 1 inch from the top of the

page. Align left and double space the report heading lines. They include the writer's name,

teacher's name, subject name, and date (day/month/year style) on separate lines.

Center the report title below the date. The title is keyed using rules for capitalizing and

punctuating titles. The report title may be keyed in a slightly larger font size to make it stand

out. However, it should not be underlined or placed within quotation marks.

Figure 10.16 Report in MLA Format

86G PRACTICE: MLA Report

1. Start *Word*. Open *CD-86-Report2* from your data files. Make changes needed to format the report in MLA style.

2. Use Spelling Check to find misspelled words. Proofread to find other errors. Save the document as *86-Report2*. Close the document.

 **CHECK POINT** Did you find two errors that Spelling Check did not identify?

© Getty Images/PhotoDisc

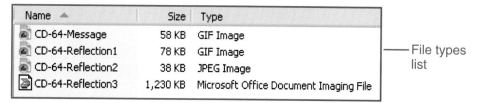

Name ▲	Size	Type
CD-64-Message	58 KB	GIF Image
CD-64-Reflection1	78 KB	GIF Image
CD-64-Reflection2	38 KB	JPEG Image
CD-64-Reflection3	1,230 KB	Microsoft Office Document Imaging File

—— File types list

Figure 7.7 Notice how large the TIFF file is compared with the GIF and JPEG files.

4. Compare the file size of the TIFF image (shown as a Microsoft Office Document Imaging File in Figure 7.7) to the more compressed GIF and JPEG images.

5. In *Paint*, open the file called *CD-64-Reflection3* (which is a larger TIFF image). Choose the **Maximize** button to make *Paint* as large as it can be.

6. Click the **Magnifier** tool and select the **6x** option. Use the bottom scroll bar to center the mask on the screen. Notice that with this larger TIFF image you cannot center the entire mask as you did with the GIF file. This is because there are more dots of color per square inch.

7. Open the *CD-64-Reflection2* found in your data files. This file is a smaller JPEG image. Click the **Maximize** button, if needed, to make *Paint* as large as it can be. Click the **Magnifier** tool and select the **6x** option.

8. Use the bottom scroll bar to center the mask on the screen. Notice that with this smaller (compressed) JPEG image, much of the detail is lost. This is because there are fewer dots of color per square inch. Close *Paint*.

64E PRACTICE: Compare Screen and Print Resolutions

1. Form a team with three or four students. Gather around one computer and open two copies of *Paint*.

2. Open the file called *CD-64-Reflection2* (JPEG) in one *Paint* window. Open the file *CD-64-Reflection3* (TIFF) in the other *Paint* window.

3. Resize the *Paint* windows and place them side by side on the screen. Compare the images. One image has a much higher resolution than the other. Can you see any difference between the two pictures?

4. Start *Word* and open a new blank document. Click **Insert** on the menu bar. Choose **Picture** and then **From File**. See Figure 7.8.

6. The next word shown as a possible error is *Illan*. This name is correct. Click **Ignore Once**.

7. The last word shown as a possible error is *oftne*. This word is incorrect. Click **Change** to accept the suggested correct spelling.

8. When a dialog box appears telling you the check is complete, click **OK**.

9. Carefully read the text after spelling is checked. Write a list of errors you find that Spelling Check did not find. Close the document without saving.

✓ **CHECK POINT** Compare your results with those of a classmate. You should find three errors. What are they?

MLA Reports

Your teachers may tell you to use a certain format when you write a report. You have learned one standard format for reports. In this lesson you will learn to use a format suggested by the MLA (Modern Language Association). The MLA format is used in many schools. A sample report is shown in Figure 10.16 on page 368.

For MLA report format, all margins are 1 inch. The writer's last name and the page number appear in a header. The name and page number are aligned at the right of the header. Line Spacing 2 is used for all lines (except in the header). Report heading lines appear at the top of the report on separate lines and are aligned at the left margin. The headings are the writer's name, teacher's name, subject name, and date (day/month/year style). The report title comes after the headings and is centered.

86F LEARN:

Format an MLA Report

1. Start *Word*. Open *CD-86-Report1* from your data files. Set the margins to 1 inch for top, bottom, left, and right.

2. In a header, key **Kellum** and insert the page number. Use Align Right for the text in the header. See Figure 10.16 on page 368.

3. Select the heading lines above the title. Format these lines for Align Left. Center the title.

4. Select all the lines of the report body. Set the Line Spacing to 2.

5. Use Spelling Check. Proofread and correct all errors. Save the document as *86-Report1*. Print and then close the document.

✓ **CHECK POINT** Exchange reports with a classmate. Check each other's report to see if MLA style guidelines were followed.

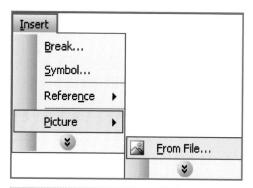

Figure 7.8 Choose commands to insert a picture.

5. Go to the folder where your data files are stored. Select *CD-64-Reflection1* (GIF) and choose **Insert**.

6. After the image appears in your document, tap ENTER twice. Then follow the same steps to insert *CD-64-Reflection3* (TIFF) in the document.

7. Print the document that contains both pictures. Compare them. Look very carefully. Do you see a difference in the resolution? Which format gives the best printed image? Close the file without saving. Close *Word*.

8. Discuss the following questions with your team:

- Which type of image should you use for a Web page to be displayed on a computer screen?

- Which file format should you use for a printed document?

- Why is it hard to tell the difference between the TIFF and GIF formats on a computer screen?

Lesson 65   Scanning Successfully

Objectives

In Lesson 65, you will:

↘ Discover four types of imaging technologies.

↘ Learn how the digitizing process can scan images into a computer image file format.

↘ Learn how to set up and care for a scanner.

↘ Scan an image.

↘ Save an image file that you have scanned.

↘ Display and use an image file you have created.

Spelling Check

The **Spelling Check** feature is used to check text for spelling errors. Spelling Check compares the words typed with words in the software's dictionary. Words that may be wrong appear in red in a dialog box. Suggested corrections and options are given. You can choose to ignore the word or change it.

Spelling Check will not find words that are spelled right but used in a wrong way. For example, the program will not tell you to use *to* if you typed *too*. The software dictionary may not have numbers or many proper nouns or scientific terms. Always read the text carefully and check for errors after using Spelling Check.

86E LEARN: Spelling Check

1. Start *Word*. Open *CD-86-Spell1* from your data files. Position the insertion point at the beginning of the text.
2. Click **Tools** on the menu bar. Choose **Spelling and Grammar**. A dialog box will appear as shown in Figure 10.15.

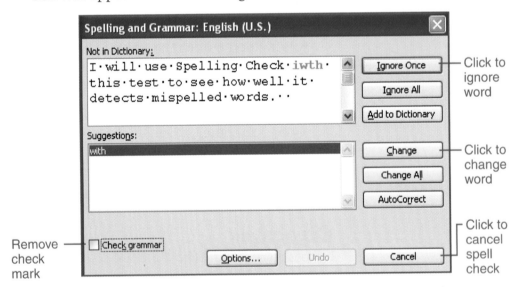

Figure 10.15 Spelling and Grammar Dialog Box

3. A check mark may appear by **Check grammar** in the lower left of the dialog box. If so, remove it by clicking in the box. See Figure 10.15.
4. The first word shown as a possible error is *iwth*. This word is incorrect. Click **Change** to accept the suggested correct spelling.
5. The next word shown as a possible error is *mispelled*. This word is incorrect. Click **Change** to accept the suggested correct spelling.

Imaging Devices

Imaging devices are pieces of equipment that allow users to capture or create pictures. Fax and copy machines are familiar examples of imaging devices. Both of these imaging devices take a picture of an original and make a copy to be printed.

Cameras and scanners are also imaging devices. Cameras are portable. They can capture images of three-dimensional objects such as your soccer team or family pet. A scanner captures images of things such as documents, magazine pages, book covers, drawings, paintings, or printed photographs.

About Scanning

A scanner captures images and converts them into graphics files in formats such as TIFF, JPEG, or GIF. You can scan a variety of things: photos, drawings, articles, and even objects. A scanner creates images through a process called **digitizing**. Digitizing divides an image into tiny squares or grids. Each grid is given a mathematical value. This value is then translated into black, white, gray, red, green, yellow, blue, or other colors.

There are many types of digital scanners. Some examples are shown in Figure 7.9. Some scanners have a glass surface on which you place the document to be scanned. These are often flatbed scanners. Handheld scanners can be moved over the surface of a book or an object to scan the surface. Some scanners have automatic document feeders, which can scan stacks of paper rapidly.

Visioneer, Inc.

Figure 7.9 Various Types of Scanners

Setting up and Caring for a Scanner

Scanners come from the factory with their own software that should be installed before you use the scanner. Once the scanner is properly installed, many programs will let you capture digital images with scanners in *Windows*, *Word*, *PowerPoint*, or *Paint*.

No matter what type of scanner you have, keep it clean. The scanner takes a picture of everything it sees. If there are any fingerprints or pieces of lint

3. Click in the **Tab stop position** box. Key **0.38**. Click the radio button by **Left** under Alignment. Click the **Set** button.

4. Click in the **Tab stop position** box. Key **0.63**. Click the radio button by **Left** under Alignment. Click the **Set** button.

5. Click in the **Tab stop position** box. Key **4.0**. Click the radio button by **Right** under Alignment. Click the **Set** button. Click **OK**.

6. Tap TAB four times until the insertion point is at the right tab you set at 4.0. Key your name. Tap ENTER. Tap TAB four times to move to the right tab again. Key the name of your class.

7. Key the text below that is part of an outline. Tap TAB at each red arrow to indent each level of the text.

```
  ➜     ➜   ➜                    ➜         Student Name
  ➜     ➜   ➜                    ➜          Class Name

  ➜  I. ➜Introduction

  ➜     ➜ A.➜ What is a computer graphics program

  ➜     ➜ B.➜ Why and when should you use one

  ➜ II.➜ Graphics Programs

  ➜     ➜ A.➜ Those that come in a software suite

  ➜     ➜ B.➜ Those that are stand-alone programs
```

8. Your keyed text should be aligned as shown in the example in step 7. If it is not, check your setting in the Tabs dialog box. Close the document without saving.

86D PRACTICE: Set Tabs and Margins for an Outline

1. Start *Word*. Open *CD-86-Outline1* from your data files. Print this handwritten outline. Close the document.

2. Open a new blank document. Click **File, Page Setup** on the menu bar. Set the left and right margins to 1 inch.

3. Click **Format, Tabs** on the menu bar. Click in the **Tab stop position** box. Key **0.2**. Click the radio button by **Decimal** under Alignment. Click the **Set** button.

4. Click in the **Tab stop position** box. Key **0.38**. Click the radio button by **Left** under Alignment. Click the **Set** button. Repeat to set left tabs at **0.63** and **0.88**. Click **OK**.

5. Set the Line Spacing to **2**. Key the outline from the handwritten notes you printed. Center the title. Tap TAB to indent each level of the outline.

6. Save the outline as *86-Outline1*. Print the document and close it.

on the scanned surface, they will show up on your digital image. So, before you start a scanning project, follow the manufacturer's instructions to clean the scanner.

Steps to Scanning

There are three basic steps to capturing an image with the scanner:

- Set up the scanning job and the item to be scanned.
- Preview, adjust, and scan to create an image.
- Save the image.

Set Up the Scanning Job. The first step is setting up the scanner options and the document or object to be scanned. If using a flatbed scanner, place the original facedown on a clean surface. Be sure to put the top of the image at the top of the scanning bed in the direction you wish to see it. If your image is too wide to fit on the bed, you can place it sideways.

The way an image is placed or created is called orientation. When the long side of an image is at the top, it is in **landscape orientation**. When the short side of the image is at the top, it is in **portrait orientation**. See Figure 7.10.

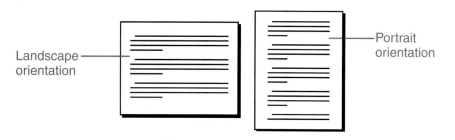

Figure 7.10 Change the orientation to portrait or landscape.

Place your document so it is as straight as possible. This is especially important if you are going to capture text. Use rulers or markers found along the side of the bed to help you place your object in the proper position.

Scan to Create an Image. When the item to be scanned is in place, you can use the Scanner and Camera Wizard provided by *Windows* to scan the image. You can choose the type of image you want to create: color, grayscale, or black and white. The color option will result in a color image close to the original. The grayscale option substitutes colors in images with various shades of gray. The black and white option is used for images or text documents without any color. There may also be a Custom option that allows you to increase resolution and change brightness and contrast settings. Picture type options are shown in Figure 7.11.

86B PRACTICE: Set Margins

1. Start *Word*. Open the file *CD-86-Margins2* from your data files. Read the paragraphs in the document.

2. Practice changing the margin settings as directed in the document. Close the document without saving.

Tabs

Tabs are set locations at which text can be placed. By default, tabs are set every one-half inch on the Ruler. You can change the tab settings using the Tabs dialog box. Tabs can be set to align text at the left, right, center, or a decimal point. Decimal tabs are often used to align numbers in a column. You will use tabs to align levels in an outline.

86C LEARN: Set Tabs

1. Start *Word*. Open a new blank document. Click **Format** on the menu bar. Click **Tabs**. The Tabs dialog box appears as shown in Figure 10.14. You will use this box to set tabs to align parts of an outline.

2. Click in the **Tab stop position** box. Key **0.2**. Click the radio button by **Decimal** under Alignment. Click the **Set** button.

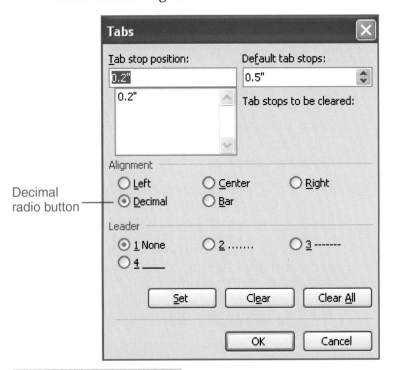

Decimal radio button

Figure 10.14 Tabs Dialog Box

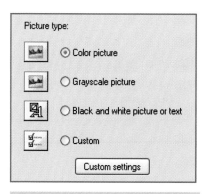

Figure 7.11 Picture Type Options

With many scanners you can preview the scan. This preview allows you to see how the scanned image will appear. Look carefully at the scan preview image. If it doesn't look quite right, reposition the item or adjust the area to be included and preview scan again. Work with the settings until you get just the image you want. Then do a final scan.

If your scanner has a lid, lower it carefully so your image doesn't move out of position. The lid will keep your document in place and will also keep the bright light from your scanner's lamp from hurting your eyes.

Save the Image. After you have adjusted your image to show just the portion you want and scanned the image, you will be ready to save the image. When you save the image, you will be able to give the image a name. Choose a name that will help you identify the image when you see it later in a list of filenames. You will also be able to choose a file format for the image. Choose a format that is best for the use you plan to make of the picture. For example, if you want a high-quality printed image, you could choose the TIFF format. If you want an image with a small file size that will look good on a computer screen, you could choose the GIF format.

65A LEARN: Scan and Save an Image

1. Select an image to copy. Choose the best-quality image available. The better the original, the better the copy. For this exercise, it may be best to choose a color image. This could be a photo, a magazine page, or a book cover—anything that can lie flat on the scanner.

2. Place the original facedown on the surface of a clean flatbed scanner. Orient your document so it is as straight as possible. If the scanner has a lid, lower it carefully.

3. Click the **Start** button and choose **My Pictures**. Under **Picture Tasks**, click **Get pictures from camera or scanner**. This will open the Scanner and Camera Wizard. See Figure 7.12.

settings are indicated on the Ruler by the left and right margin markers, as shown in Figure 10.12.

Some report and outline formats, such as MLA style, require 1-inch side margins. You can change the margins by dragging the margin markers or by using the Page Setup dialog box.

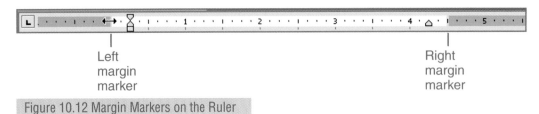

Left
margin
marker

Right
margin
marker

Figure 10.12 Margin Markers on the Ruler

86A LEARN: Set Margins

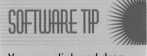

You can click and drag the margin markers on the Ruler to change the side margins quickly. See Figure 10.13.

1. Start *Word*. Open a new blank document. Click **File** on the menu bar. Click **Page Setup**. The **Page Setup** dialog box appears.

2. On the **Margins** tab, click in the box by **Top** and enter **2** as shown in Figure 10.13.

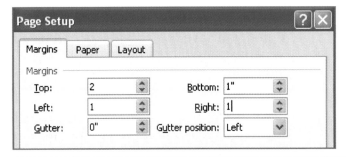

Figure 10.13 Margins can be changed on the Page Setup dialog box.

3. Click the box by **Left** and enter **1**. Click the box by **Right** and enter **1**. Click **OK** at the bottom of the box.

4. Key the following text. Save the document as *86-Margins1*. Close the document.

       This text is keyed on a page that has a 2-inch top margin. The side margins are 1 inch. If the paper being used is 8.5 x 11 inches, each full line of text in the document will be 6.5 inches long. That is about as long a line as most people can easily read.

Select this
option to open
the Wizard

Figure 7.12 Choose Get pictures from camera or scanner.

4. On the **Welcome to the Scanner and Camera Wizard** window, click or tap **Next**.

5. If you have more than one scanner or device connected, you may need to set the Paper Source to **Flatbed** as shown in Figure 7.13. If you are asked, set the Page Size to **Letter**.

6. Select the **Color picture** option as shown in Figure 7.13.

Choose
Color
picture

Select
your
scanner if
necessary

Preview
button

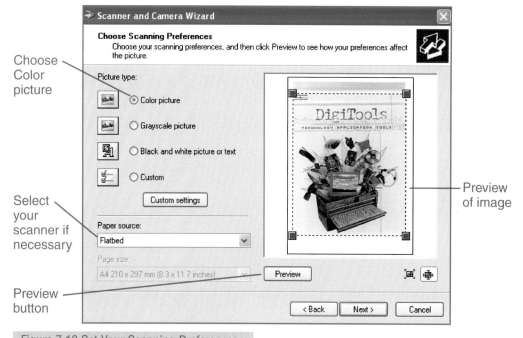

Preview
of image

Figure 7.13 Set Your Scanning Preferences

7. Click the **Preview** button. The scanner will run its lamp down the full length of the scanner's glass bed. A small image of your document will show in the preview screen as shown in Figure 7.13.

8. The wizard will display crop lines around the image as shown in Figure 7.14. **Crop** means to cut or trim. Click and drag inward on one of the sizing handles until you have selected only a part of the image to save.

1" top and side margins

Computer Graphics

Set tabs to indent each outline level

I. Introduction

   A. What is a computer graphics program   Use Line Spacing 2

   B. Why and when should you use one

II. Graphics Programs

   A. Those that come in a software suite

   B. Those that are stand-alone programs

III. Computer Graphics

   A. Bar graphs

      1. Vertical bar

      2. Horizontal bar

   B. Circle graphs

      1. Whole circle

      2. Exploded circle

   C. Line graphs

      1. Without shaded areas

      2. With shaded areas

Figure 10.11 Outline in MLA Style

The margins and line spacing for an outline should match the report body. For an MLA report and outline, the top and side margins are 1 inch. The outline uses Line Spacing 2. Tabs are set at 0.2, 0.38, 0.63, and 0.88 inches to indent the outline levels. The title of the outline is centered. You will learn to set margins and tabs in this lesson. Then you will be ready to key an outline.

Margins

As you learned earlier, the margin is the white space between the text and the edge of the page. The default top and bottom margins are 1 inch. The default left and right margins are 1.25 inches. The left and right margin

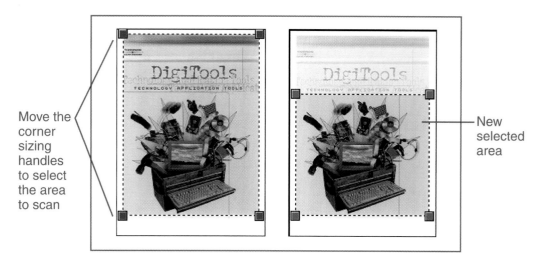

Move the corner sizing handles to select the area to scan

New selected area

Figure 7.14 Crop your image by dragging the sizing handles.

9. Click the **Enlarge** button to see how the scanned image will look. See Figure 7.15. (If you need to change the area that is selected, click the **Show the Entire Image** button and make the change. Then click **Enlarge** again.)

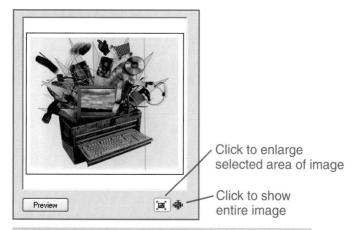

Preview

Click to enlarge selected area of image

Click to show entire image

Figure 7.15 Enlarge your image with the sizing buttons.

10. When you have the image selected as you wish, click **Next**. The Picture Name and Destination window will appear.

11. For the name of the picture, key **65-Color Picture1**. Select **JPG (JPEG Image)** for the file format. Save your image in your *My Pictures* folder or the folder where you save work for this class. See Figure 7.16.

2. Work with a classmate to compose a report using the handwritten notes and the *Excel* worksheet. The report should be about 1 ½ pages long. Add other details that you make up about the project, if needed.

3. Format the report in the standard format. Use three side headings in the report: **Overview of Project**, **Raising Funds**, and **Funds Raised**. Use bold format for the main title and the side headings.

4. Insert a page number in a header to appear on page 2 only. Insert your name and your classmate's name in a footer to appear on page 2 only. Save the report as *85-Team Report*. Print the report and close it.

Lesson 86   MLA Outlines and Reports

Objectives

In Lesson 86, you will:
- ⬊ Change margin settings.
- ⬊ Set decimal and left tabs.
- ⬊ Create an outline for a report.
- ⬊ Use the Spelling Check feature to check reports.
- ⬊ Arrange a short report in MLA format.

Data files: *CD-86-Margins2, CD-86-Outline1, CD-86-Spell1, CD-86-Report1, CD-86-Report2*

Outlines

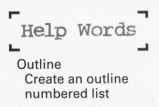

Help Words

Outline
    Create an outline
    numbered list

An **outline** is a document that gives the main points of a subject. Outlines are helpful in planning and organizing reports. Sometimes, an outline may appear in a document so readers can see the report structure. Figure 10.11 on page 362 shows a sample outline prepared for a report in MLA format. Refer to Figure 10.11 as you read about the outline.

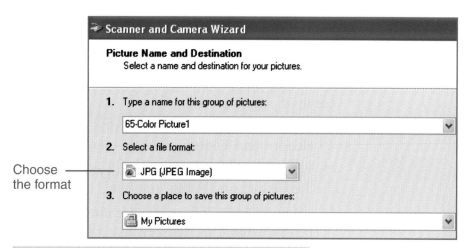

Choose the format

Figure 7.16 Name the file and choose an image format.

12. Click **Next**. The scanner may or may not need to rescan, depending on your scanner. If a rescan occurs, you will see a screen similar to Figure 7.17.

Your scanner may add a number to each image file name

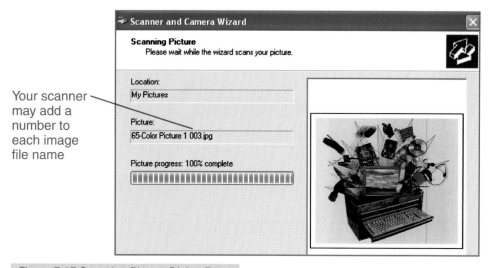

Figure 7.17 Scanning Picture Dialog Box

13. In the Other Options window, select **Nothing. I'm finished working with these pictures.**

14. Click **Next** followed by **Finish**. The Wizard will close and return you to *Windows Explorer* and the *My Pictures* folder (or the folder to which you saved the image).

85C LEARN: Report Footer

Your teacher may want you to add your name in a footer to the reports and other documents you create. Follow the steps below to add your name in a footer.

1. Start *Word*. Open *85-Report2* that you edited earlier. Choose **View, Header and Footer** from the menu bar.

2. The First Page Header box will appear. Click the **Show Next** button on the Header and Footer toolbar. The Header box for page 2 will appear.

3. Click the **Switch Between Header and Footer** button on the Header and Footer toolbar. The Footer box will appear as shown in Figure 10.10.

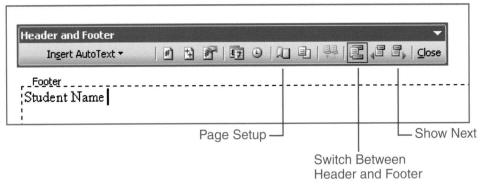

Figure 10.10 Footer Box

4. Key your name in the Footer box. Click the **Close** button on the Header and Footer toolbar.

5. Save the document as *85-Report3*. Print the document.

85D APPLY: Compose a Report

A member of your class, Jerry Populus, was seriously injured in a fall. Members of your class have just completed a project to raise money to help pay for Jerry's medical bills. You took handwritten notes at a class meeting about the project. You will work with a classmate to write a report about the money your class raised. The report will be sent to your principal. It may also appear in the school newspaper.

1. Start *Word*. Open *CD-85-Notes* from your data files. Print the document. Open the *Excel* worksheet *CD-85-Results* from your data files. Print the sheet. Close both files.

65B LEARN: Show Your Image!

1. Click the **Start** button and choose **My Pictures**. Open the folder where you saved your image in Lesson 65A if it was not the *My Pictures* folder.

2. Select the image filename (*65-Color Picture1*).

3. Click the **View as a slide show** link as shown in Figure 7.18.

Figure 7.18 View the image you scanned and saved.

4. To exit the slide show, tap the ESC key on the keyboard or click the **Close** button on the screen.

65C PRACTICE: Scan and View an Image

1. Select another high-quality image to scan. Follow the procedure you learned in Lesson 65A to crop and scan the image.

2. Save the image as *65-Color Picture2*. Select **JPG (JPEG Image)** for the file format. Save your image in the *My Pictures* folder or the folder where you save work for this class.

3. View your image as part of a slide show. Exit the slide show. Close *Windows Explorer*.

Lesson 66   Capturing Photos

Objectives
In Lesson 66, you will:
↘ Learn to capture an image using a digital camera.
↘ Download your digital camera's images to a PC.
↘ View your digital images.
↘ Use your digital images in a variety of applications and situations.

Data files: *CD-66-Log*

2. Choose **View** on the menu bar. Choose **Header and Footer**. The **Header and Footer** box and toolbar appear as shown in Figure 10.8.

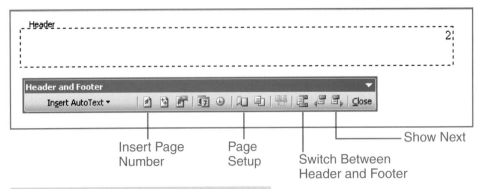

Figure 10.8 Header and Footer Box and Toolbar

3. Click the **Insert Page Number** button on the Header and Footer toolbar. A page number will appear in the Header box. Click the **Align Right** button on the Formatting toolbar to move the number to the right.

4. Click the **Page Setup** button on the Header and Footer toolbar. A dialog box will appear. See Figure 10.9.

5. Click the **Layout** tab. Click the box by **Different first page**. Click **OK** at the bottom of the box. This will prevent the page number from appearing on page 1.

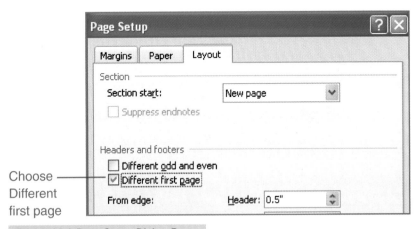

Choose Different first page

Figure 10.9 Page Setup Dialog Box

6. Click the **Close** button on the Header and Footer toolbar.

7. Save the document as *85-Report2*. Complete the Check Point and then close the document.

 **CHECK POINT** Review your document. Your report should show page number **2** in the upper-right corner on page 2. No number should appear on page 1.

It took hundreds of years for the science of photography to fully develop. In 1826, Frenchman Nicéphore Niépce captured an image on photosensitive paper. However, the image was temporary. Sharing his secrets with Louis Daguerre, the duo created the first effective camera. Images were captured on silver-plated copper, coated with silver iodide and mercury. Their image-capturing system was called the Daguerreotype process.

The first cameras were little more than boxes. Glass lenses were added to provide focus and to adjust the detail found in the photographic images. Images were captured on photographic plates. Eventually metal plates were replaced by film.

© Michael Freeman/CORBIS

Figure 7.19 A Daguerreotype is an early form of a photograph.

Digital Photography

Film photography had some serious limitations for the space program. NASA asked, "How can we transmit high-resolution photographs back to Earth from thousands of miles out in space?" To meet NASA's needs, new technologies were developed that converted light into electrical impulses that could be transmitted through space.

NASA's research got many people thinking about a better way to produce photographs without using harmful chemicals. Then in 1981, Sony Corporation came up with a filmless camera that could take digital pictures without film. The new camera was called Mavica. Other companies also began to develop digital cameras. But these new digital cameras delivered images with very poor resolution.

Resolution in digital cameras is measured in **megapixels**. *Mega* means a million. Early digital cameras captured images at a rate of only 1 megapixel or less. At this rate, the resolution was poor. Today, 3-, 5-, 6-, even 8-megapixel cameras are common. These higher-resolution digital cameras finally began to match the image resolution of old-fashioned film photography.

5. Select the second side heading **Funding**. Format this heading with Arial, 14-point, blue font, as you did for the first side heading.

6. Select the report title. Format the title with Arial, 16-point, blue font.

7. Select the name of the first new teacher (**Ms. Anne Hartman**) in the first paragraph. Click the **Bold** button on the toolbar to format the name. Format the other new teacher's name in bold.

8. Select the name of the new program **Essentials Learning System** in the last paragraph. Click the **Italic** button on the toolbar to format the name.

9. On the line below the last paragraph, key **Submitted by** and your name. For example, **Submitted by Juan Perez**.

10. Select your name. Click the down arrow by the font name on the toolbar. Choose a script font, such as **Brush Script**, for the font. Increase the font size, if needed, to make the writing look a realistic size for a signature. Click the **Underline** button on the toolbar to underline your name.

11. Save the report as *85-Report1*. Print the report and close it.

Headers and Footers

Headers contain information that appears at the top of pages in a document. For example, a header is used to display a page number on the second page of a standard report. A **footer** contains information that displays at the bottom of the page. Some report pages are numbered at the bottom in a footer.

In standard report format, no page number appears on the first page. You must indicate that you want the first page to be different from the other pages. This prevents the header (page number) from appearing on the first page.

85B LEARN: Header with Page Number

1. Start *Word*. Open *CD-85-Report2* from your data files. Key the side heading and the paragraphs below at the end of the document. Select the side heading and apply **bold** format.

```
Operation Clean Sweep
     The Science Club volunteered to adopt North
Street for two blocks on each side of the school.
Once each week, club members and their sponsor, Miss
Halley, remove trash from this section of the
street.  They also post signs around the school
asking people not to litter.
```

Neal Ulevich/Bloomberg News /Landov

Figure 7.20 Digital Camera

Capturing Digital Images

Digital cameras are equipped with liquid crystal displays (LCDs) that let you see the pictures you have taken immediately. Digital cameras store pictures as image files on a memory device. The images can then be downloaded to your PC.

Just like scanners, most digital cameras let you select the file type, quality (compression) level, and resolution. Decide what you are going to do with the picture before selecting the settings. If you are going to look at it on a computer screen, post it on a Web site, or e-mail it to a friend, keep the file size small. However, capture as many pixels per inch as your camera will permit to print a large picture in color on expensive photo paper.

Before you can decide the proper setup, you will need to experiment with the camera. In this lesson, you will take a series of pictures of the same image while changing the camera settings. It may be helpful for you (or your team) to keep a log like the one shown in the table below. The entries in this sample record show the file sizes getting bigger as the resolution and picture quality improve.

Picture #	Quality	Resolution	File Size
1	Good	Low	55
2	Better	Low	86
3	Best	Low	123
4	Good	High	100

66A LEARN:

Take Photos of Varying Quality and Resolution

1. Start *Word*. Open *CD-66-Log* from your data files. Print and then close the file. Close *Word*.

2. Turn on your digital camera. Set your camera to the lowest quality and lowest resolution. Enter these settings by Picture 1 on the log. You will record the file size of the images later.

Font Size

You can change the font size. Size is measured in **points**—the larger the point (pt.), the larger the size. A 12-point font is used for the body of most documents. To change the font size, select the text to be changed. Click the down arrow by the font size on the toolbar. Choose a size as shown in Figure 10.6.

Font Color and Formats

You can also change the font color (to red, for instance) and font styles (**bold**, *italic*, underline). To change the font color, select the text. Click the down arrow by the Font Color button on the toolbar. Choose a color as shown in Figure 10.7.

To apply a font style, select the text. Click the Bold, Italic, or Underline button on the toolbar. The buttons are shown in Figure 10.7.

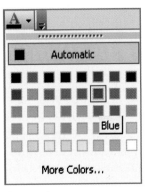

Font colors

Figure 10.7 Font Color Button

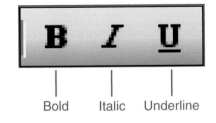

Bold   Italic   Underline

85A LEARN: Change Fonts and Font Styles

1. Start *Word*. Open *CD-85-Report1* from your data files. This report has had side headings added. Side headings make finding information in a report easier. Side headings are placed on a separate line and begin at the left margin.

2. Select the first side heading **New Teachers**. Click the down arrow by the font name on the toolbar. Select **Arial** for the font.

3. Click the down arrow by the font size on the toolbar. Select **14** for the font size.

4. Click the down arrow for font color on the toolbar. Select **blue**. The side heading should now be in Arial, 14-point, blue font.

3. Look through the viewfinder at the object you want to photograph. Hold the camera as still as possible and press the shutter button.

4. Change the quality and resolution settings and take the next picture. Record the settings on the log. Continue to adjust the quality and resolution settings. Take three to six photographs at different settings.

Moving Images to Your PC

There are at least two popular ways to download images from a camera to a computer. First, the camera can be attached by a cable directly to the computer. Second, the camera's memory card can be removed and read by a card reader that is built into or attached to a computer. Adapt the instructions to work with your particular camera.

66B LEARN:

Move Images to a PC

1. If you are using a card reader, connect it to your PC. Remove the memory card from the camera and insert it into the card reader. If you are using a cable, plug your cable into your camera and into the USB port on your PC.

2. Your operating system should sense that you have connected your card reader or camera to the PC and display a screen asking what you want to do next. (**Note:** If this fails to happen, choose **Start**, **My Computer**, and choose your reader or camera device from the list.)

3. Select **Copy pictures to a folder on my computer** as shown in Figure 7.21. Click **OK**. The Scanner and Camera Wizard will begin. Click **Next** on the Wizard welcome screen.

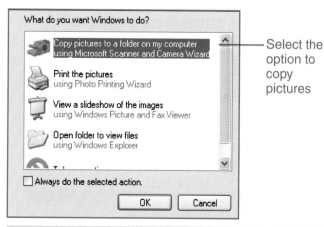

Figure 7.21 Select Copy pictures to a folder on my computer.

4. Select your three to six pictures by making sure there is a check mark in each box as shown in Figure 7.22. Click **Next**.

 **CHECK POINT** Have a classmate check your document to see if it is formatted correctly. If needed, make changes to correct the document.

Lesson 85 | Fonts and Headers in Reports

Objectives

In Lesson 85, you will:

❯ Change fonts, font colors, and font formats.

❯ Create headers and footers in reports.

❯ Arrange a report in standard format.

Data files: *CD-85-Notes, CD-85-Results, CD-85-Report1, CD-85-Report2*

Fonts

A **font** is the style of letters used. You can change the font in a document. Names of common fonts are Times New Roman, Courier New, **Arial**, and **Comic Sans MS**. You may want to change the font used for a report title or headings to make them stand out better.

To change fonts, select the text to be changed to a new font. Click the down arrow by the font name on the toolbar. Select a new font name. Recently used fonts appear at the top of the list.

Font name ——

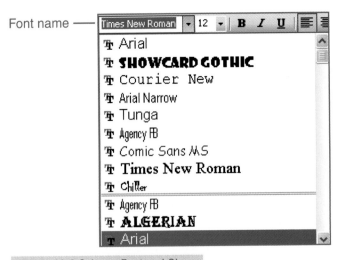

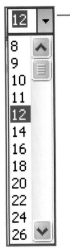 —— Font size

Figure 10.6 Select a Font and Size

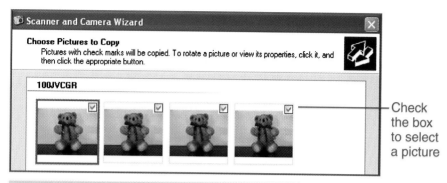

Figure 7.22 Choose the image you wish to download.

5. In the Picture Name and Destination window, key a name for the group of pictures. For example, in Figure 7.23 the name is *66-Bears*.

6. Select a folder in which to save the pictures in the second box. Use *My Pictures* or the folder in which you save work for this class. If you want to select a folder that is not in the drop-down list, use the **Browse** button to find the folder. Click **Next**.

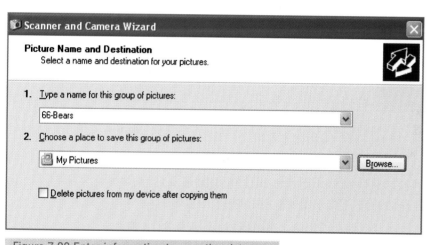

Figure 7.23 Enter information to save the pictures.

7. On the Other Options window, choose **No, I'm finished working with these pictures.** Click **Next**.

8. On the last Wizard screen, click **Finish**. The pictures will be copied to the folder you selected and the folder will open.

9. Click **View** on the menu bar. Choose **Details**. This will allow you to see the file size of each photograph. Use this information to complete the log you began in Lesson 66A.

10. Click **View** on the menu bar. Choose **Thumbnails** to see small images of each picture you have taken.

Line Spacing and Select Text

1. Start *Word*. Open the document *84-Report1* that you edited earlier.

2. Click and drag to select the title and the paragraphs of the report.

3. Click the down arrow on the Line Spacing button and select **2**. See Figure 10.3 on page 354. The report should now be double-spaced. Click in the margin area to cancel the text selection.

4. Notice that one word in the title of the report is not in all capitals. Click and drag to select the word **School**. Tap the CAPS LOCK key and type **SCHOOL**.

5. Place the insertion point at the beginning of the title. Tap ENTER three times. This will place the title at 2.1 inches. Look at the Status bar at the bottom of the screen to see the line position after the word *At*.

Page 1	Sec 1	1/1	At 2.1"

Figure 10.5 Status Bar

6. Save the document as *84-Report2*. You have now edited the report for correct standard format!

84D PRACTICE:

Format a Standard Report

1. Start *Word*. Open *CD-84-Report3* from your data files.

2. Make the changes needed so the text is in standard report format.

3. Save the document as *84-Report3*. Review how to print a document on page 52. Print the report.

 Does your report have double spacing? Is the title centered in all capitals? Is the title positioned about 2 inches from the top?

84E APPLY:

Create a Standard Report

1. Start *Word*. Open a new blank document. Choose a topic from below and compose a short report (less than one page) about this topic. Use an appropriate title. Write at least two paragraphs for the body. Format the document as a standard report.

   Report Topics: my favorite sport, my favorite hobby, my favorite vacation place, my favorite holiday, my favorite pet

2. Save the document as *84-Report4*. Print the report and close it.

 **CHECK POINT** Compare your picture log with that of a classmate. How do the quality and resolution settings on the two cameras compare? How do the file sizes of the images compare at each setting?

66C PRACTICE: Take Digital Photos

1. Use your digital camera to take pictures of a school or community event. Use a quality and resolution setting that will result in medium- to high-resolution images.
2. Move the images to your PC. Save the images in the *My Pictures* folder or the folder in which you save work for this class. Print the images. Make a bulletin board or poster display of the images.

66D APPLY: Use an Image as the Desktop Background

Instant Message

If you do not have an image of your own to use, use *CD-64-Reflection2*. It is a low-resolution image that still has plenty of detail. It can make a stunning background.

In this activity, you will use one of the images you have scanned or snapped with your digital camera as your *Windows* desktop background.

1. Right-click on your *Windows* desktop. Choose **Properties** from the pop-up menu.
2. The Display Properties dialog box will appear. Click the **Desktop** tab.
3. Click the **Browse** button. Go to the *My Pictures* folder or the folder where you have stored your images. Select an image with low resolution (and small file size) so it will load quickly. Click **Open**.

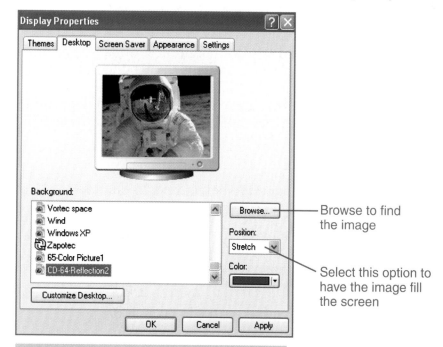

Figure 7.24 Choose a desktop background image.

Instant Message

Save files in the *My Documents\Computers\ Chapter 10* folder or where directed by your teacher.

┌─────────────┐
│ Help Words │
└─────────────┘

Line spacing
 Adjust line or
 paragraph spacing

4. Click anywhere in the first paragraph. Click the **Align Left** button. Click anywhere in the second paragraph. Click the **Align Left** button. The body is now aligned correctly for a standard report.

5. Save the document as *84-Report1* and close it.

Line Spacing

The **Line Spacing** feature is used to change the amount of blank space between lines of text. The default setting is single spacing. Double spacing (2) and one-and-a-half spacing (1.5) are two other options you might use. You can change the line spacing by clicking the down arrow by the Line Spacing button on the toolbar. See Figure 10.3.

Figure 10.3 Line Spacing Options

Select Text

┌─────────────┐
│ Help Words │
└─────────────┘

Select text
 Select text and
 graphics

When you create a report, you may want to change the text in some way. For example, you might change the line spacing or size of the text. To do so, you must first select the text. An example of selected text is shown in Figure 10.4. To select text, click and drag the mouse over the text. Selected text can be deleted by tapping the DELETE key. Selected text can be replaced by keying new text.

You need to select text to change it. Selected text appears dark on the screen.

Selected text looks like this.

Figure 10.4 Selected text appears dark on screen.

4. Select your picture from the Background list as shown in Figure 7.24. Under Position, choose the **Stretch** option. Click **Apply**. Click **OK**. Your image should now be your Desktop background.

66E APPLY: Tell of Your Adventures

You may not have landed on the moon or visited a foreign country, but you certainly have a story to tell. In this activity, you will tell your story using both words and pictures.

1. Start *Word*. Compose and key one or two paragraphs about an adventure you have had. Save the file as *66-Adventure*.

2. Scan images or take photos that relate to your story. Insert one or two images in your *Word* document below the text. Save the file again. Print the document. Close *Word*.

66F LEARN: Research Digital Photography Tips

1. Access the Internet. Use a search engine to find an article or guidelines for how to improve pictures taken with a digital camera. Use a search term such as *digital photos*.

2. In *Word* or in *OneNote*, key the source information for the article. Include the name of the article, the Web site name, the Web site address, and the date you read the material.

3. Key a list of tips or main points from the article.

4. Borrow a classmate's camera and take a picture of your camera. Move the picture to your PC. Insert the picture in your *Word* or *OneNote* document. (The steps for inserting a picture in a *Word* or *OneNote* document are the same. Review these steps in Lesson 64E on pages 254–255.)

5. Save the file if you are using *Word*. If you are using *OneNote*, the document will be saved automatically. Name the *Word* file or the *OneNote* section *66-Digital Photos*.

Standard Report Format

1. Start *Word*. (Choose **Start**, **All Programs**, **Microsoft Office**, **Microsoft Word**.)

2. Open *CD-84-Report1* from your data files. Compare the document with the example report shown in Figure 10.1. List all the changes that should be made to this document to format it as a standard report.

3. Close the document without saving it.

Paragraph Alignment

Paragraph alignment refers to how text is placed on a page. In word processing terms, a **paragraph** is any amount of text that is keyed before the ENTER key is tapped. A paragraph can be one word or several words or lines. Paragraphs can be aligned before or after text is keyed.

Align Left starts all lines of the paragraph at the left margin. Align Left is the default paragraph alignment. **Align Right** ends all lines at the right margin. **Center** places an equal (or nearly equal) space between the text and each side margin. **Justify** starts all lines at the left margin and ends all full lines at the right margin. Figure 10.2 shows the toolbar buttons used to set alignment. Each button also shows how text will be placed on the page.

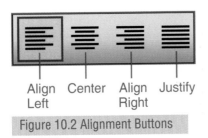

Align Left   Center   Align Right   Justify

Figure 10.2 Alignment Buttons

Paragraph Alignment

1. Start *Word*. Open *CD-84-Report1* from your data files.

2. Click in the report title. Click the **Align Right** button on the toolbar. Notice that the title moves to the right of the page.

3. Click the **Center** button on the toolbar. The title is now aligned correctly for a standard report.

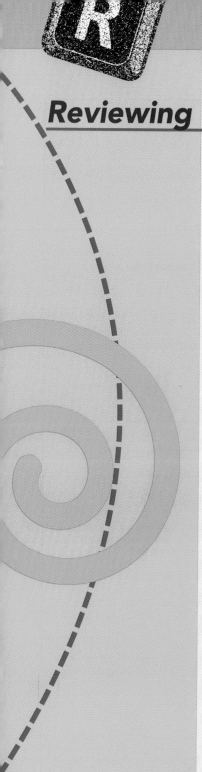

Reviewing What You Have Learned

Answer these questions to review what you have learned in Chapter 7.

1. What is a mosaic image made up of?

2. Each little dot of light in an image on a computer screen is called what?

3. *Resolution* describes what about an image?

4. What tool can you use in *Paint* to show the image larger on the screen?

5. What two measures are used to express resolution?

6. If picture A has more dots per inch than picture B, which one has the higher resolution?

7. What are four commonly used file formats for images?

8. Which of the image file formats discussed in this chapter is commonly used in desktop publishing and print publishing?

9. If you create an image in both GIF format and TIFF format, which format is likely to have the smaller file size?

10. What is an imaging device? Give three examples of an imaging device.

11. A scanner creates images through a process called what?

12. Describe two types of scanners.

13. Explain the difference between landscape orientation and portrait orientation.

14. What does *crop* mean?

15. Resolution in digital cameras is measured in _____.

16. Describe two methods that might be used to move pictures from a digital camera to a PC.

17. Why should you use great care when erasing a picture from the memory card for a camera?

Tap ENTER to place
title about 2" from top

Center title in
ALL CAPS

Title ——————————————— ANSWERING THE SCHOOL TELEPHONE

The telephone is a popular means of communicating in our school. Knowing how

to use the telephone effectively is important.

Answer all incoming calls promptly. Identify yourself and the school office

immediately. Speak in a tone that is relaxed and low-pitched. Keep a writing pad near

the phone to record important parts of the call. Thank the caller at the end of the

conversation.

Knowing how to screen, transfer, and hold calls properly is also important. When

screening calls, first identify who is calling. Then ask the purpose of the call. This

Body ——————— information allows you to decide to take the call or transfer it to another person. Calls

that are not transferred properly can be an annoying experience for callers. Be certain the

caller is transferred to the correct person on the first transfer.

Calls should be placed on hold only when necessary and for short periods of time.

Placing a caller on hold should be handled in a courteous manner. If calls need to be put

on hold for more than a minute or two, callers should be given the option of being called

back.

Use
default
margins

Use Line
Spacing 2

Left-align and
indent paragraphs

Figure 10.1 Report in Standard Format

Applying   *What You Have Learned*

Prepare an Advertisement

1. Think of an item that you might want to sell, such as a bike, a DVD player, a television, or baseball cards.

2. Take digital photos of the item or scan pictures of the item. You need one image with low resolution that you could send by e-mail or place on the Web. You need one image with high resolution that you could place in a printed ad.

3. If taking photos, move the photos to your PC. Place the images in the *My Pictures* folder or the folder where you save your work for this class.

4. Start *Word*. Open a new blank document. Key a description of the item you are selling. The description should contain all the information you think a buyer might want to know. Include a selling price for the item and how a buyer can contact you.

5. Insert the image that is low resolution in the document below the text. Save the file as *C07-Ad Low*.

6. Delete the image from your document. Insert the image that is high resolution in the document below the text. Save the document as *C07-Ad High*. Print the document. Close *Word*.

Scan or Take Photo for Portfolio

In the Career and Life Skills Success Builder activity for this chapter, you will begin a collection of your best work, called a portfolio. Your portfolio will also include a personal information sheet. In this activity, you will create a digital photo to place on your information sheet.

1. Scan a photo of yourself or have a classmate take a digital photo of you. You need a high-resolution file to place in a printed document.

2. Move the photo to your PC. Place the image in the *My Pictures* folder or the folder where you save your work for this class.

3. When you complete your personal information sheet in the portfolio activity, insert your photo at the end of the document.

Supplemental activities for this chapter can be found at www.c21jr. swlearning.com.

Lesson 84   Standard Reports

Objectives

In Lesson 84, you will:
- ⬊ Create reports in standard format.
- ⬊ Set alignment and line spacing for paragraphs.
- ⬊ Select text and delete or replace it.
- ⬊ Print a document.

Data files: *CD-84-Report1, CD-84-Report3*

You will probably write many reports during your school years. Reports are documents that give facts, ideas, or opinions. You might write a report to describe the life of a historical figure, such as George Washington. You might write a report about how to find information on the Internet. You might also write a report to give your ideas about what a poem means.

Many workers also write reports as part of their jobs. A sales associate might write a report discussing items that sold well in a store. A nurse might write a report telling about patient care. A teacher might write a report about a student's progress.

Whatever the type, reports should be written and formatted in a way that makes them easy to read and understand. In this lesson, you will learn a standard format to use for reports. In later lessons, you will learn the MLA format.

Standard Report Format

A short report in standard format is shown in Figure 10.1 on page 352. Refer to Figure 10.1 as you read about a standard report. The **title** or main heading tells what the report is about. The **body** contains the paragraphs that make up the report. Other parts, such as additional headings and page numbers, may also be used.

The default margins settings are used for a standard report. **Margins** are the amount of blank space between the text and the edge of the paper. **Default settings** are those used by the program unless you change them. The default margins are 1.25 inches for left and right margins, and 1 inch for top and bottom margins. You will tap ENTER to move the text down and leave about 2 inches of blank space at the top of the first page of a standard report.

Line spacing refers to the amount of blank space between the lines of text. For a standard report, Line Spacing 2, also called double spacing, is used. This setting leaves one blank line between lines of text. The title of a standard report is centered and keyed in all capital letters.

Building Keying Skill

Warmup Practice

Key each line twice. If time permits, key the lines again.

Alphabet

1 Jack Vasquez placed my next bid for the two gowns.

Figure/Symbol

2 With a 20% discount, Invoice #139 totaled $854.76.

Speed

3 Alan and Glen did half of the problems on the bus.

gwam 1' | 1 | 2 | 3 | 4 | 5 | 6 | 7 | 8 | 9 | 10 |

Improve Keying Technique

Key each line twice.

One-hand words

1 in be we as my at no at up was few see you him get

2 were only date case fact area rate free card aware

3 state hook great link water nylon after puppy best

One-hand phrases

4 as far as|you see|we are|at best|were you|best bet

5 erase my debt|my only rate|upon a hill|hook a bass

6 set a date|free bread|extra pulp|only oil|bad debt

One-hand sentences

7 Get him extra tax cards after you set a case date.

8 As you see, you set only my bad debt fees in July.

9 Only a few cards get you great reserved oil rates.

gwam 30" | 2 | 4 | 6 | 8 | 10 | 12 | 14 | 16 | 18 | 20 |

TECHNIQUE TIP

Keep your fingers curved and upright.

Chapter 10
Reports

Lessons 84–89

OBJECTIVES

In Chapter 10, you will:

↗ Enter, edit, and format text using *Microsoft Word*.

↗ Create reports in a standard format.

↗ Create reports in MLA format.

↗ Create report outlines and title pages.

Reports, reports, reports! Everybody wants one—your science teacher, your math teacher, your English teacher. A **report** is a document that gives facts, ideas, or opinions about one or more topics. A review of a library book you have read is an example of a report. A summary of a science project you created is another example of a report. In this chapter, you will learn to use word processing software to format reports. **Format** means to place text on a page so it looks good and is easy to read.

The reports will be arranged in a standard format or the MLA format. *MLA* stands for *Modern Language Association*. School reports are often prepared in this format.

© Getty Images/PhotoDisc

Speed Forcing Drill

Key a 30" timed writing on each line. Your rate in gross words a minute (*gwam*) is shown below the lines.

1 She may be in her office.
2 He forgot to take their money.
3 Benito won first place in his race.
4 I will have him call you when he leaves.
5 Tryouts for the play take place next Tuesday.
6 Jason and Katie plan on going to the lake to swim.

gwam 30" | 2 | 4 | 6 | 8 | 10 | 12 | 14 | 16 | 18 | 20 |

Timed Writing

Key each paragraph once. DS between paragraphs. Key a 1' timed writing on each paragraph; determine *gwam*.

 all letters used

Students quite often want to know exactly how much they are likely to earn when they start to work either for the summer or after school. Hourly pay varies from company to company and from city to city. It may vary with the worker, also--his or her skills, effort, and attitudes.

Even if you can't earn as much as a seasoned full-time worker, prize the job you acquire. Look upon it as a place to learn all those procedures and skills that can't be provided now by regular classes. Experience is often a helpful teacher because it requires you to work with others.

UNIT 4

Word Processing, Desktop Publishing, and Document Formatting

People use computers a great deal in school, at home, and at work. Being able to enter data quickly and correctly is important. In this unit, you will learn to create documents such as reports, letters, e-mail messages, and tables. You will also create flyers and newsletters. These documents will help you request or share information with others.

The activities provided at the end of each chapter in this unit will help you:

↗ Review the concepts you have learned

↗ Apply the software skills you have learned

↗ Improve your keyboarding skills

↗ Learn about business trends and issues

↗ Improve math and communication skills

↗ Develop career-related skills

Data Files

- *CD-C07-Business*
- *CD-07-My Personal Facts*
- *CD-07-Sample Personal Facts*
- *CD-C07-Colon*
- *CD-C07-Reading*

↗ About Business

ADVANTAGES AND DISADVANTAGES OF BEING AN ENTREPRENEUR
In Chapter 6, you learned that an entrepreneur is a person who organizes and manages a business. You also learned some of the traits needed to be a successful entrepreneur. In this activity, you will learn about some disadvantages and advantages of being an entrepreneur.

Being an entrepreneur has many challenges. One major disadvantage is that you have to risk your money. According to the U.S. Small Business Administration, more than 50 percent of small businesses fail in the first year and 95 percent fail within the first five years.[1] If your business fails, you may lose the money you invested. You may also have to use your own funds to pay debts of the business. The decisions you make also affect others. You may have to lay off or dismiss employees if the business does poorly.

As an entrepreneur, you may have a limited amount of money to invest. This may limit the products or services you can offer. You may need to work long hours. You may feel overwhelmed by the number of decisions that must be made to run the business. You may need to get additional training or learn new skills. You may have to hire a manager or an employee with special knowledge. The cost of this employee's wages reduces profits. All of these are also disadvantages of being an entrepreneur.

In spite of all the challenges and disadvantages, being an entrepreneur can be rewarding. One advantage to being an entrepreneur is that you can be creative and use your talents to help the business succeed. When you are an entrepreneur, you are your own boss. You make the decisions about how the company is run. This is a major advantage that makes people want to be an entrepreneur. Another advantage to being an entrepreneur is that you get all the profits the business makes. If your business is successful, you may make much more money than you could as an employee.

1. Start *Word*. Open and print *CD-C07-Business* from your data files.

2. Complete the activity to help you think about the advantages and disadvantages of being an entrepreneur.

↗ Career and Life Skills Success Builder

DEVELOPING YOUR PORTFOLIO Have you ever saved a group of your papers, reports, or drawings in one place? If you have, you created a type of portfolio. A **portfolio** is a collection of samples of your best work. The reason

---

[1] "Are You Ready?" United States Small Business Administration Web site,
http://www.sba.gov/starting_business/startup/areyouready.htm (accessed November 2, 2004).

What skills do you need to build a bridge or invent a new toy? How can you make a computer process faster, or grow a juicier tomato? Science and math skills are necessary for creating many of the products we use every day. These skills form the foundation of many exciting careers in technology, science, and engineering.

1. Is a career in technology, science, or engineering right for you? Open and print the data file *CD-C09-Science*. Read the information to see if you are interested in this career path.

2. Open the data file *CD-C09-Science and Math*. Follow the directions given to access the Internet and research a career in technology, science, or engineering.

↗ Academic Success Builder

COMMUNICATIONS: NUMBER USAGE Numbers can be expressed as words (three) or as figures (3). When you are writing a paper that includes numbers, do you have trouble deciding whether to write numbers using words or figures? Three guides that will help you make your decisions are shown below.

• Use words for numbers one through ten.

• Use words for numbers that begin a sentence.

• Express related numbers in the same way.

1. Start *Word*. Open *CD-C09-Numbers* from the data files. Print the file and then close it. Study the Guides and the Learn line(s) for each Guide.

2. In a *Word* file, key the Practice and Apply lines, expressing the numbers correctly. Save the document as *C09-Numbers*.

READING: READ A TABLE How good are you at finding specific information? Detailed information is often presented in tables. The title of the table gives clues about the kinds of information in the table. The column headings give major categories of information presented. The rows give specific information that relate to the column headings. Footnotes often provide additional information that is needed to better understand the information in the rows.

In this activity, you will read a table about Presidents and Vice Presidents of the United States. Questions are provided about the information in the table. You will need to read the table for specific information to answer the questions.

1. Start *Word*. Open *CD-C09-Table* from the data files. Print the document.

2. Read the table and answer the questions that follow the table. Compare your answers with those of a classmate. Make revisions as necessary.

you create a class portfolio is to show your teacher the work you created during the class. When you get older and search for a job, you will create a different type of portfolio. A *career portfolio* is a collection of items that show your work abilities. For example, if you wanted to be a photographer, you would include your best photos. Whether you create a portfolio for your class or for a future job search, the items you include should be the best examples of your work.

In this activity, you will begin to develop a portfolio for this class. In future chapters, you will see reminders to add samples of your best work to your portfolio.

1. Get a folder or three-ring binder in which to store items for your portfolio. Include your name and the following title on the cover: **My Class Portfolio**. Decorate the cover with images or words related to this class.

2. Start *Word*. Open and complete the document *CD-07-My Personal Facts*. Save it as *C07-My Personal Facts*. Print a copy to put in your new portfolio. (A completed sample of the document is in the data file *CD-07-Sample Personal Facts*.)

↗ Academic Success Builder

COMMUNICATIONS: COLON AND SEMICOLON Colons are used to introduce or set up a list, example, or quotation. They alert you to pay attention to the words that follow the colon. Colons are also used between hours and minutes that are written in figures. Semicolons are joiners that tell you to pause. They can be used to join related main clauses that are complete sentences. They are also used with transition words such as *however* and *therefore*.

1. Start *Word*. Open *CD-C07-Colon* from your data files. Print the file and then close it. Study the Guides and the Learn line(s) for each Guide.

2. For the Practice lines and the Apply lines, read the sentences and add colons and semicolons where they are needed.

READING: READ A HEADLINE What do you do first when you pick up a newspaper? Do you scan the front-page headlines to see if you want to read any of the articles? Do you turn to the sports section and scan the headlines to find the article that tells you whether your favorite team won their game? Headlines are written to get your attention. Headlines must explain or describe the article so you can quickly decide if you want to read the article. They must develop your interest so you will read the related article. In this activity, you will read a headline and make some predictions about the contents of its article.

1. Start *Word*. Open *CD-C07-Reading* from your data files. Read the headline. Using as much space as needed after each question, key a response to each question.

2. Save the document as *C07-Reading*. Print and close the document. Compare your answers with those of a classmate. Discuss how they differ.

ACROSS THE CURRICULUM

Data Files

- *CD-C09-Business*
- *CD-C09-Science*
- *CD-C09-Science and Math*
- *CD-C09-Numbers*
- *CD-C09-Table*

↗ About Business

FIXED AND VARIABLE COSTS In Chapter 1, you learned that the main goal of a business is to make a profit. Companies try to control expenses, also called costs, to increase profits. Costs are grouped into two categories—fixed costs and variable costs.

Fixed costs are expenses that remain the same regardless of the amount of services or goods that are produced or sold. Fixed costs are also called *overhead*. An entrepreneur might choose to have a home-based business to help keep overhead low. Examples of fixed costs include:

- Rent
- Property taxes
- Insurance
- Salaries for managers
- Equipment purchase or rental payments

Variable costs are expenses that change depending on the amount of services or goods that are produced or sold. Variable costs typically increase as more products are produced or sold. Examples of variable costs include:

- Wages for workers who make products
- Money spent for parts or material to make products
- Shipping costs for delivering products sold

The sum of a company's fixed costs and variable costs is its total cost. Companies are concerned about how much total cost changes as the amount of goods or services produced changes. This is called **marginal cost**. Companies want to find a balance where money spent for producing products gives the greatest profit.

1. Start *Word*. Open and print *CD-C09-Business* from your data files.

2. Answer the questions about fixed, variable, total, and marginal costs. Compare your answers with those of a classmate.

↗ Career and Life Skills Success Builder

SCIENCE AND MATH VS. YOUR CAREER What allows airplanes to fly or boats to float? How is electricity made? Why does aspirin help stop headaches? If you have a love of science and math, a need to understand how and why things work, and strong problem-solving abilities, you may have a future in scientific research or engineering.

Chapter 8

Lessons 67–77

Speech Recognition Tools

OBJECTIVES

In Chapter 8, you will:

↗ Learn how continuous speech recognition software works.

↗ Prepare a headset.

↗ Create a speech recognition profile.

↗ Change the Language bar display modes.

↗ Control the Dictation and Command modes.

↗ Voice-type with speech software.

↗ Correct errors.

↗ Add words and names to a user's dictionary.

↗ Navigate and format documents by voice.

© CORBIS

Wouldn't it be great if your computer could enter everything you say? It can! **Continuous speech recognition** (CSR) software lets you enter data by talking. You can enter data quickly—between 100 and 180 words per minute. You can even tell your computer what to do with special voice commands.

In this chapter, you will create a speech user file that is designed to work just for you. You will dictate text and give voice commands. You will also create letters and reports using speech recognition tools.

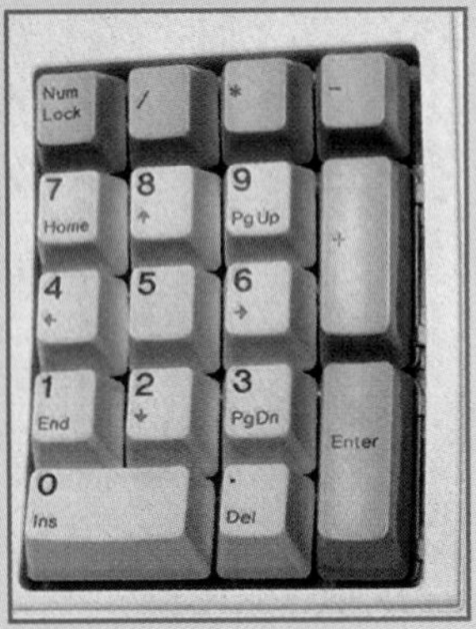

Keypad Practice

Use the *Calculator* program to complete the problems shown below.

Drill 1 Addition

A	B	C	D	E
586	891	379	656	369
+ 374	+ 210	+ 421	+ 41	+ 178
960	1,101	800	697	547

Drill 2 Subtraction

A	B	C	D	E
789	635	406	409	802
- 142	- 78	- 213	- 318	- 576
647	557	193	91	226

Drill 3 Multiplication

A	B	C	D	E
69	47	75	12	798
x 4	x 13	x 24	x 60	x 45
276	611	1,800	720	35,910

Drill 4 Division

A	B	C	D	E
102	132.33	255.11	117	172.8
8/816	43/5,690	28/7,143	76/8,892	25/4,320

Speed Forcing Drill

Key a 30" timed writing on each line. Your rate in gross words a minute (*gwam*) is shown below the lines.

1 Maria took the exam.
2 Jerome lost his overcoat.
3 When will we get the uniforms?
4 Ichiro keyed much faster this week.
5 Hideki had four of the hits in the game.
6 Carlos will take chemistry during the spring.
7 Steven put in a lot of effort to get a good grade.

gwam 30" | 2 | 4 | 6 | 8 | 10 | 12 | 14 | 16 | 18 | 20 |

TECHNIQUE TIP

Press ENTER quickly at the end of the line and immediately begin the next line.

Lesson 67 Discovering How CSR Works

Objectives

In Lesson 67, you will:

- Learn about early speech recognition systems.
- Learn about continuous speech recognition (CSR).
- Discuss the future of speech recognition and other input technologies.

Continuous Speech Recognition Software

Creating programs that allow a computer to understand human speech is very difficult. Research into computer-recognized speech began by using big, expensive computers in the 1950s. At the 1964 World's Fair, IBM demonstrated a computer that could understand simple spoken digits. By the 1980s, some computers could understand single spoken words.

> This — type — of — speech — was —awkward. — Can — you — imagine — talking — like — this?

In 1997, Dragon Systems released *Dragon NaturallySpeaking* software. It was the first continuous speech recognition (CSR) software for personal computers. This type of software lets users speak normally (continuously). To speak continuously means to speak in full sentences and paragraphs. IBM and Microsoft also offer CSR programs. CSR programs are often called *speech engines*. A training screen from *Microsoft Speech Recognition* is shown in Figure 8.1.

Instant Message

Speech software is very helpful for people with disabilities who may have lost the ability to use their hands for typing. It is also helpful for anyone interested in preventing repetitive stress injuries.

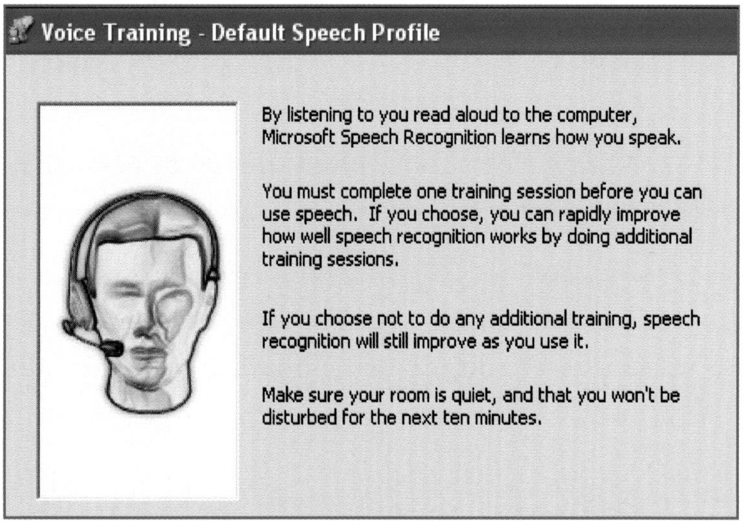

Voice Training - Default Speech Profile
By listening to you read aloud to the computer, Microsoft Speech Recognition learns how you speak.
You must complete one training session before you can use speech. If you choose, you can rapidly improve how well speech recognition works by doing additional training sessions.
If you choose not to do any additional training, speech recognition will still improve as you use it.
Make sure your room is quiet, and that you won't be disturbed for the next ten minutes.

Figure 8.1 *Microsoft Speech Recognition* Training Screen

Building Keying Skill

Warmup Practice

Key each line twice. If time permits, key the lines again.

Alphabet

1 Bill Pax quickly gave away the jazz band uniforms.

Figure/Symbol

2 Please call (736-4895) on May 19 or 20 to confirm.

Speed

3 Turn down the lane by the lake to see the bicycle.

gwam 1' | 1 | 2 | 3 | 4 | 5 | 6 | 7 | 8 | 9 | 10 |

Improve Keying Technique

Key each line twice. If time permits, key the lines again.

Space Bar

1 work when soap sign pays keys maps rush rich proxy

2 Jay and I saw the maid in a big field by the lake.

Shift keys

3 April, May, June, July, August, October, November,

4 Jose and Grant went to see the New York Mets play.

Adjacent keys

5 say top open same were tree dash onion other three

6 I held a sporting equipment sale at the gymnasium.

Long direct reaches

7 much once vice maybe enter cents under check juice

8 Ben brought a recorder to the game to record them.

gwam 30" | 2 | 4 | 6 | 8 | 10 | 12 | 14 | 16 | 18 | 20 |

Popular Speech Engines

After you finish this chapter, your teacher may provide additional study materials for one of the following popular speech engines:

- *Dragon NaturallySpeaking*, which is popular on personal computers.
- *Microsoft Speech Recognition*, which is popular on personal computers running *Office XP* or *Office 2003*.
- *IBM ViaVoice*, which is popular on Macintosh computers. There is also a version for personal computers running the *Windows* operating system.

67A APPLY: Discuss the Future of Input Technologies

The first speech computers, like the ones used at the 1964 World's Fair, weighed hundreds of pounds. Today, a portable PC or Tablet PC weighing less than five pounds can be used to voice-type accurately. Who knows? In the future, a speech recognition device may be as small as a cell phone and weigh a few ounces.

Work in a team with two or three other students. Discuss the following questions in your team:

1. What do you think is the most important input technology: speech recognition, handwriting recognition, or the keyboard? Will your selection always be the most important?

2. What will happen when computers get very small? Will computers ever get too small for keyboards, mice, and digital pens?

3. What kinds of tiny computers do you want to see and use? If you could invent a tiny computer, what would you hope it could do? What would it look like?

Lesson 68   Preparing a Headset

Objectives
In Lesson 68, you will:
↘ Learn about USB and analog headsets.
↘ Properly position a noise-cancellation headset.

Headsets

A **headset** is a device that contains a microphone and speakers and is worn on one's head. A headset is needed to enter data by talking and using speech software. An ordinary headset often does not work well. A special

Applying *What You Have Learned*

Enter Calendar Items

1. Open the *Calendar* application.

2. Enter all your appointments, classes, and deadlines for the next two weeks. Remember that *Calendar* items are scheduled to be done at specific times. Set reminders to help you get things done on time.

Enter Tasks Items

1. Open the *Tasks* application.

2. Enter tasks that you need to complete sometime in the next two to three weeks. These items should be ones that do not necessarily need to be done in any certain order or at a specific time. Nevertheless, they must be accomplished by a certain due date.

3. Check each task as complete after you finish it successfully.

Add Notes to Contacts Entries

1. Open the *Contacts* application. Open the entry for Ronald Evans. Add the notes shown below to the entry. Use any entry method with which you feel comfortable. Close the entry after making the changes.

   ```
   Served in the United States Navy.
   Graduated from University of Kansas with a degree in
   Electrical Engineering.
   Piloted the Apollo 17 command module (CM).
   ```

2. Open the entry for Harrison Schmitt. Add the notes shown below to the entry. Close the entry after making the changes.

   ```
   Nickname: Jack
   Received a Ph.D. in Geology from Harvard University.
   First geologist on the moon.
   ```

Research Applications

1. Work with a classmate to complete this activity. Access the Internet. Use a search engine to find free programs that you can download and use on your PDA.

2. Make a list of the programs you find. Include the name of the program, the type or use of the program, and the Web site address where the program can be downloaded.

Supplemental activities for this chapter can be found at www.c21jr. swlearning.com.

noise-cancellation headset gives the best results. These headsets filter out the background noise or the sounds around you. Background noise can include people talking, a television or radio playing nearby, traffic driving by, or the noise of heating or cooling fans in a building. Noise-cancellation headsets try to block background sounds so that your computer hears only your speech.

There are different types of noise-cancellation headsets. In Figure 8.2 you can see an analog headset. An analog headset transfers sound waves to a PC using a cable. Another headset style is a USB headset. USB models have a digital signal processor (DSP) that converts sound waves into data a computer can understand.

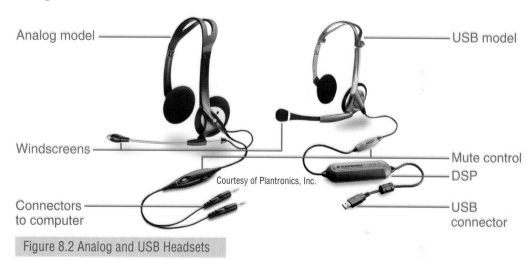

Analog model

USB model

Windscreens

Mute control

DSP

Connectors to computer

USB connector

Courtesy of Plantronics, Inc.

Figure 8.2 Analog and USB Headsets

Microphones on many headsets are covered with a windscreen. A **windscreen** is a shield that helps protect a microphone from sudden blasts of air or from being broken. Many headsets also have a mute button and volume control. The word **mute** means "to silence or to shut off." A mute button turns the microphone off.

Positioning a Headset

Positioning a headset properly is very important. If the microphone is too near your mouth, it may pick up breathing sounds and try to convert them to words. The microphone should be placed about a thumb's width away from the side of your mouth. It should be even with or a bit lower than your lower lip. The microphone should be placed in the same position each time you use it. Avoid touching the microphone with your hands or your mouth. This can cause errors. If you can, get your own personal headset to use every day.

Reviewing | *What You Have Learned*

Answer these questions to review what you have learned in Chapter 9.

1. What is a PDA?

2. What are deadlines?

3. Give three examples of information about contacts that you might enter in a PDA.

4. List three popular operating systems for PDAs.

5. What is a smart phone?

6. Explain the difference between PDA hard buttons and PDA soft buttons.

7. For what purpose is a stylus used?

8. Explain how to change the time zone setting on your PDA.

9. Which onscreen keyboard has capital letters and symbols?

10. Explain how to access the Standard keyboard on your PDA.

11. Explain how to access the Numeric keyboard when you have the Standard keyboard open.

12. What is *Graffiti*? What option that is similar to *Graffiti* is available on the Pocket PC?

13. Besides the Today or Welcome screen, what three views are available in the *Calendar* application?

14. Describe how to move to Day View for a particular date when Month View appears on the screen.

15. Explain how to set a reminder or alarm for a *Calendar* item on your PDA.

16. What is one major difference between *Calendar* items and *Tasks* items?

17. What is the purpose of the Reminder or Alarm options that can be set for *Tasks* items?

Position the Headset

1. Position your headset comfortably on your head as shown in Figure 8.3. Most headsets come with an adjustable headband. Adjust the size of the headset to fit you perfectly.

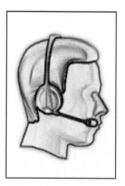

Figure 8.3 Position the headset correctly.

2. Position the listening portion of your microphone (or windscreen) about 1 inch away from your lower lip.

3. Position the microphone to the side of your lower lip if possible.

4. Place your headset in the same position every time you talk to your computer.

5. See if you have a mute button on your headset. Practice turning mute on and off. Mute should be off when you are ready to speak to your computer.

6. Listen to your teacher's tips on how to properly store your headset after you have used it.

Lesson 69 Creating a Speech User Profile

Objectives

In Lesson 69, you will:
- Create a speech recognition user profile.
- Set audio settings.
- Read a training story.

Setting Up a User File

You speak differently from everyone else around you. Many people also speak with a noticeable accent. An accent is a way of speaking that reflects a speaker's regional background. For example, Australians sound very different from Canadians.

6. After the data has been sent, the PDA receiving the information will display a message asking if the data should be accepted. When the user taps **Yes**, the beaming process will be completed. Now both PDAs will have your contact information!

Palm OS

1. Team up with another classmate who also has a PDA. Locate the infrared ports on your PDAs.

2. Open your *Contacts* application by tapping on the icon. Open the entry with your information. Tap **Contact** (or **Address**) at the top of the screen to access a menu.

3. Align the infrared ports on the two PDAs so there are no objects between them.

4. Choose **Beam Contact** (or **Beam Address**) from the menu as shown in Figure 9.28.

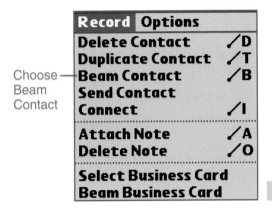

Choose Beam Contact

Figure 9.28 Beam data to another PDA.

5. A screen will appear showing your progress. You will see information about searching for another PDA, sending, and then disconnecting.

6. After data has been sent, the PDA receiving the information will display a message asking if the data should be accepted or saved. When the user taps **Yes**, the process will be completed. Now both PDAs will have your contact information!

83C PRACTICE: Beam Contacts Data

Pocket PC and Palm OS

1. Team up with another classmate who also has a PDA. Align the infrared ports on the two PDAs so there are no objects between them.

2. Open your *Contacts* application. Choose a *Contacts* entry that your classmate does not have on his or her PDA. Beam this data to your classmate's PDA.

3. Check with your classmate to see whether the entry was received.

You must teach your computer to understand your speech. This is accomplished by reading a story to the computer. As you read, the software will create a user profile that only you can use effectively. If another person tries to use your user profile, the software will not understand him or her very well. A user profile collects:

- Your audio volume and background noise settings.
- Information gathered as you read a training story.
- Words you train and correct.
- Information about how you speak.

69A LEARN:

Train a Speech User File

SOFTWARE TIP

Tablet PC users may also choose the **Tools and Options** button on the Input Panel and select **Speech**.

1. Start *Microsoft Word*. Click **Tools** on the menu bar. Select **Speech** as shown in Figure 8.4.

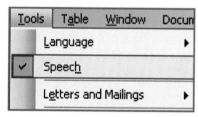

Figure 8.4 Choose Speech from the Tools menu to access the Language bar.

2. The Language bar should appear with buttons similar to those shown in Figure 8.5.

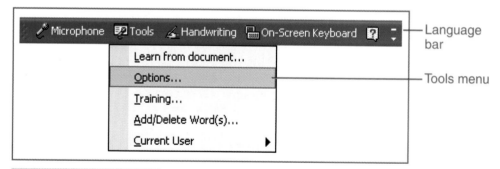

Figure 8.5 Language Bar

3. If you log in to *Windows XP* with your own user name, the following screen may appear. The steps that follow will create a user profile using your login name. If you see the screen shown in Figure 8.6, click **Next**. Then skip to step 7. If not, continue with step 4.

83A APPLY: Enter Contacts Data

Pocket PC and Palm OS

1. Open the *Contacts* application.

2. Place your name, address, phone, and other information into the *Contacts* application to create an electronic business card.

   ✓ **CHECK POINT** Ask a classmate to proofread your entry in the *Contacts* application. Make corrections if needed.

83B LEARN: Beam Your Business Card

Pocket PC

1. Team up with another classmate who also has a PDA. Locate the infrared ports on your PDAs.

2. Open your *Contacts* application by tapping the **Contacts** button or by choosing **Start**, **Contacts**. Open the entry with your information.

3. Align the infrared ports on the two PDAs so there are no objects between them.

4. Choose **Tools**, **Beam Contact** as shown in Figure 9.27.

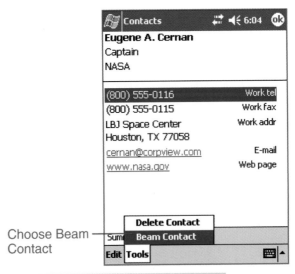

Choose Beam Contact

Figure 9.27 Beam data to another PDA.

5. A screen will appear listing nearby PDAs that you can beam to. If several PDAs are listed, choose the one you want to beam to. Beaming may start automatically. If it doesn't, choose **Tap to send** to start.

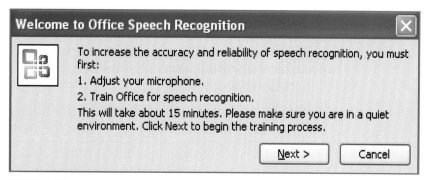

Welcome to Office Speech Recognition

To increase the accuracy and reliability of speech recognition, you must first:
1. Adjust your microphone.
2. Train Office for speech recognition.
This will take about 15 minutes. Please make sure you are in a quiet environment. Click Next to begin the training process.

Next >   Cancel

Figure 8.6 Welcome Screen

4. Click **Tools** on the Language bar and choose **Options.**

5. On the Speech input settings box, click the **Advanced Speech** button.

6. On the Speech Properties box, click the **New** button. The Profile Wizard screen will appear. Key your name in the Profile text box as shown in Figure 8.7. Click **Next** to continue.

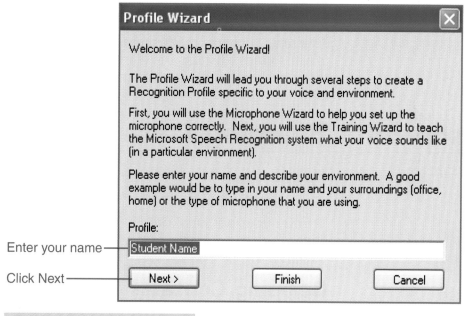

Profile Wizard

Welcome to the Profile Wizard!

The Profile Wizard will lead you through several steps to create a Recognition Profile specific to your voice and environment.

First, you will use the Microphone Wizard to help you set up the microphone correctly. Next, you will use the Training Wizard to teach the Microsoft Speech Recognition system what your voice sounds like (in a particular environment).

Please enter your name and describe your environment. A good example would be to type in your name and your surroundings (office, home) or the type of microphone that you are using.

Profile:

Enter your name —— |Student Name|

Click Next —— Next >   Finish   Cancel

Figure 8.7 Profile Wizard Screen

7. The Microphone Wizard screen will appear. Read and follow the instructions. Click **Next** to continue.

8. The Adjust Volume screen will appear as shown in Figure 8.8. Read the sentences as directed. Click **Next** to continue.

5. Tap the **Alarm** text box. The Set Alarm window will open. Tap the box by **Alarm** to select this option. For the days earlier option, enter **0**. Select an hour option and a minutes option from the lists. For example, select **9** and **30** to have the alarm appear at 9:30. Tap OK to close the Set Alarm window.

6. Tap **OK** to record the date and alarm and to return to the *Tasks* screen. The date should now appear beside the item.

7. Enter the rest of the tasks listed in the *Apollo 17* task items worksheet. Enter an alarm for each item to appear on the day the item is to be completed. Tap the **Home** or **Applications** button to close the program.

82F APPLY: Experience the Mission

If you are lucky enough to be able to keep your PDA for the next two weeks, you will often receive alarms and reminders that will tell you of important events happening aboard *Apollo 17*. Imagine experiencing three days of drifting through space to the moon. Imagine also experiencing the three major expeditions on the surface. Notice that the astronauts had time to rest, eat, and take care of things on the lunar module.

As events happen, mark them completed. For example, when a tasks item alarm sounds, dismiss the alarm or reminder. Open the *Tasks* program. Tap the checkbox by that item to mark it off your list.

Lesson 83 Beaming Data

Objectives
In Lesson 83, you will:
↘ Enter your personal data in the *Contacts* program.
↘ Beam data to another PDA.

Beaming Contacts Data

PDAs have a feature that allows users to transmit data to another PDA using the infrared ports on the PDAs. This process is called **beaming**. Transmitting *Contacts* data is a popular use of this feature. When you beam your personal data, this is called "beaming your business card." A business card on a PDA is an electronic version of the little paper business cards professionals pass out to the people they meet. In this lesson, you will enter data to create your own electronic business card. You will also beam data to a PDA.

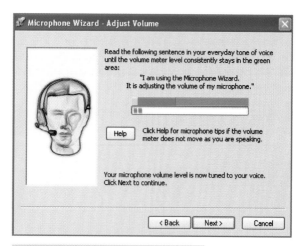

Figure 8.8 Adjust Volume Screen

9. The Test Positioning screen will appear. Read the sentence as directed. Reposition the microphone and read again if needed. Click **Finish**.

10. The first Voice Training screen will appear. Read the screen and click **Next** to continue.

11. On the next screen, click the **Sample** button to hear how you should read your training text. Read the instructions on the screen and click **Next** to continue.

12. Sample text will appear on the screen as shown in Figure 8.9. Read the sample text out loud as directed. This will take several minutes.

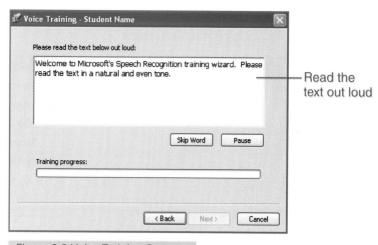

Read the text out loud

Figure 8.9 Voice Training Screen

13. After you finish reading, a screen will indicate that your user profile is being updated. Then a screen will appear that gives you the option of completing more training. You will do more training in a later activity. Click **Finish** to close the screen.

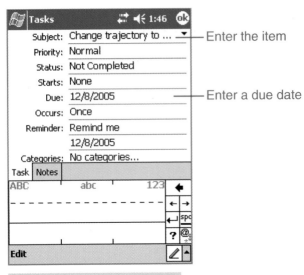

Figure 9.25 Enter Tasks Items

6. Enter the rest of the tasks listed in the *Apollo 17* tasks items worksheet. Enter a reminder for each item to appear on the day the item is to be completed. Tap the **Close** button to close the program.

Palm OS

1. Open the *Tasks* program. Use *Graffiti 2* or the on-screen keyboards to input data in this activity.

2. Tap **New** to open a new item.

3. Enter **Change trajectory to the moon** as shown in Figure 9.26. This is the first task from the *Apollo 17* tasks items worksheet.

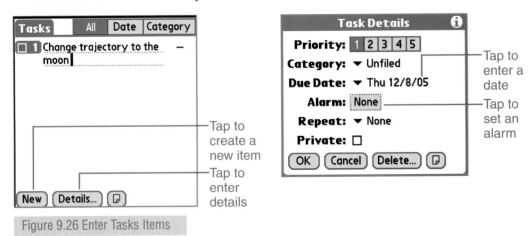

Figure 9.26 Enter Tasks Items

4. Tap the **Details** button. Tap the arrow for **Due Date**. Choose Thursday's date that is listed on the worksheet. (Tap **Choose Date**, if needed, to access the correct date.)

14. When you have completed the training, the Office Speech Training Video may appear. If so, watch and learn from the video. Close the browser window or any dialog boxes that remain open from earlier steps.

69B APPLY: Read More Stories

In this activity, you will read additional training stories. This will make your speech recognition system more accurate.

1. Start *Word*. Click **Tools** on the menu bar. Choose **Speech** to open the Language bar.

2. Click **Tools** on the Language bar and select **Training** from the menu. (Tablet PC users can also choose **Speech Tools**, **Voice Training** from the Input panel.)

3. Select a passage from the list that you have not read before. Follow the instructions displayed on the screen. Read another passage if time allows. Click **Finish** when you are ready to stop training.

Lesson 70 Changing Language Bar Display Modes

Objectives

In Lesson 70, you will:

➘ Learn to use the Language bar.
➘ Restore the Language bar defaults.
➘ Change Language bar display modes.
➘ Select a current user for the speech program.

Help Words

Speech
  Show or hide the
  Language bar

Speech tools are found on the **Language bar**. This toolbar controls the microphone and other features of the speech software. Learning about the commands and options on the Language bar will improve your skill in using speech software.

70A LEARN: Control the Language Bar

1. Start *Word*. Open a new blank document. The Language bar will normally appear. If the Language bar does not appear, choose **Tools**, **Speech** from the menu bar.

About Tasks Items

Tasks items are much like *Calendar* items, except they do not need to be done at a specific time. You can assign tasks to a specific day. You will schedule events and items for several days in your simulated *Apollo 17* mission. Remember, you are the photography expert, so many photo assignments will be found in your list.

82D APPLY: Enter Dates for Tasks Items

1. Start *Word*. Open *CD-82-Tasks Items* from your data files.

2. Enter the dates from your *Apollo 17* calendar items worksheet in this worksheet. For example, if the first Thursday on the calendar items sheet is 12/08/05, enter that date by the first Thursday on the tasks items worksheet.

3. Save the tasks items worksheet as *82-Tasks Items*. Print the tasks items worksheet. Close *Word*.

82E LEARN: Enter Tasks Items

Pocket PC

1. Tap the **Start** icon. Choose **Tasks** from the programs list.

2. Tap the arrow in the bottom-right corner of the screen to open the input Options list. Choose either the **Keyboard** or **Letter Recognizer** option, whichever you want to use.

3. Tap **New** at the bottom of the screen to open a new item.

4. In the Subject field, enter **Change trajectory to the moon** as shown in Figure 9.25 on page 339. This is the first task from the *Apollo 17* tasks items worksheet.

5. Tap the **Due** field and enter Thursday's date that is listed on the worksheet. Tap the Reminder field and choose **Remind me**. Tap the second line for the Reminder field and enter Thursday's date. Tap **OK** to record the item.

2. Locate the move handle on the left-hand side of the Language bar (marked in Figure 8.10). Click and drag the move handle to move the Language bar to the center of the screen.

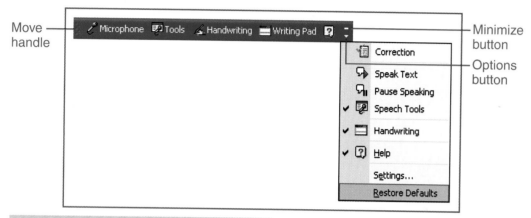

Figure 8.10 Restore the Language bar defaults.

3. The Language bar may show more buttons than you need for speech recognition. To reset the buttons, click the **Options** button (which has a down arrow) in the right-hand corner of the Language bar. Choose **Restore Defaults** from the menu.

4. Click or tap the **Minimize** button to minimize the Language bar. (If a warning box appears telling you the Language bar is being placed on the taskbar, click **OK** to continue.)

5. Look for the minimized Language bar in the *Windows* taskbar. It should look similar to Figure 8.11. To restore the Language bar, click the **Restore** button.

Figure 8.11 Minimized Language Bar

6. Move the Language bar to the top of the screen.

7. Make sure your speech recognition user file has been chosen. Click on the **Tools** button on the Language bar. Select **Current User** from the menu. Your user name should have a check next to it similar to the name shown in Figure 8.12. If it does not, select your name.

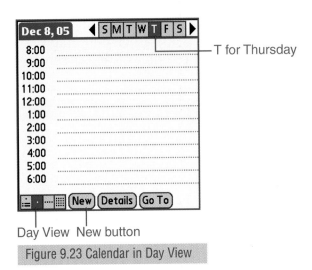

Figure 9.23 Calendar in Day View

2. Tap **New** at the bottom of the screen. A new window will open where you can enter the time for the first event from the *Apollo 17* calendar items worksheet.

3. The time for liftoff is 5:33 a.m. You will enter the time closest to 5:33 a.m. (5:30 a.m.) Tap the **Start Time** box. Tap the up arrow on the hours list. Tap **5**. In the minutes list, tap **30**. Tap the **End Time** box. In the hours list, tap **5**. In the minutes list, tap **30**. (This event happens in a split second.) Your screen should look like Figure 9.24.

4. Tap **OK** to set the time. The Day View screen will appear. On the 5:30 line, enter **Liftoff** as shown in Figure 9.24.

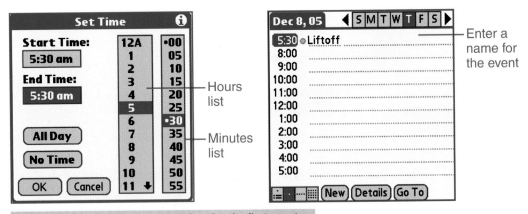

Figure 9.24 Enter a start and end time for the first event.

5. Tap the **Details** button. Tap the box by Alarm to select this option. By Minutes, enter **15** for the alarm time so you won't be late. Tap **OK**. An icon that looks like an alarm clock will appear by the Liftoff entry.

6. Enter the remaining 15 events found on the *Apollo 17* calendar items worksheet. Use the nearest whole hour or half hour for the times. Set an alarm for events for which you think it is appropriate.

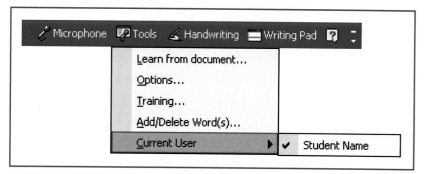

Figure 8.12 Select your speech recognition user profile.

8. Close *Word* without saving the document.

Lesson 71 — Controlling Dictation and Voice Command Modes

Objectives

In Lesson 71, you will:

- Switch between Voice Command and Dictation modes.
- Turn the microphone off using a voice command.
- Practice saying commands.
- Open menus with voice commands.
- Open and close toolbars with voice commands.

Data files: *CD-71-Speech*

Dictation and Command Modes

Help Words

Speech
  Things you can do and say with speech recognition

Microsoft speech recognition provides two different modes in which you can work. **Voice Command mode** allows users to give commands by talking to the system. These commands perform tasks such as opening a menu or moving the cursor to a new line. The words you say are not placed in the document. To use voice commands, the microphone must be turned on and Voice Command mode must be selected.

Dictation mode allows users to enter text by talking to the system. This action is sometimes called *voice-type*. To voice-type, the microphone must be turned on and Dictation mode must be selected. As the user talks, the words will be typed on the screen. You will learn to use Voice Command mode in this lesson. You will learn to use Dictation mode in Lesson 72.

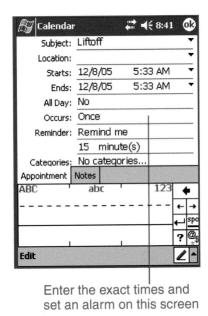

Scroll bar

Choose a time

Enter the exact times and set an alarm on this screen

Tap New to enter data

Figure 9.22 Calendar in Day View

2. Tap **New** at the bottom of the screen. A new window will open where you can enter data from the *Apollo 17* calendar items worksheet.

3. For the Subject field, enter **Liftoff** as shown in Figure 9.22.

4. For the Starts field, tap on the time that is currently showing to select it. Key the new time, **5:33 AM**. For the Ends field, change the time to **5:33 AM** also. (This event happens in a split second.)

5. For the Reminder field, tap the field to reveal options. Choose **Remind me**. On the second line of the Reminder field, tap the field to reveal options. Choose **15** and then **minutes** for the alarm time so you won't be late.

6. The entry should look like the one in Figure 9.22. Tap **OK** to record the entry. The exact time and the subject (Liftoff) will appear on the Day View screen.

7. Enter the remaining 15 events found on the *Apollo 17* calendar items worksheet. Set an alarm (reminder) for events for which you think it is appropriate.

Palm OS

1. Open the *Calendar* application. Tap the **Month View** icon. Tap the date for the first Thursday on your calendar items worksheet. The Day View for that date will open. It should look similar to the screen shown in Figure 9.23.

Saying Commands

Being silent for a second before and after saying a voice command will help the system recognize the command. Your speech software will interpret silence as a signal that a command is coming. For example, the following command will turn the microphone off: < pause > MICROPHONE.

In the activities in this chapter, all the voice commands are shown in UPPERCASE (all capital) letters. Follow these guidelines for saying voice commands:

- Pause briefly before and after saying voice commands.

- Do not mumble when you say a command. Say each word in the command clearly and distinctly.

- Do not hesitate in the middle of a command. If a command has more than one word in it, speak naturally, without pausing between words.

- Say commands in a normal tone of voice. Do not shout and do not whisper commands.

- Wait for a command to be completed before you say the next command.

71A LEARN: Switch between Command and Dictation Modes

1. Start *Word* and open a new blank document. If the Language bar does not appear, choose **Tools**, **Speech** from the menu bar to open it.

2. Click the **Microphone** button on the Language bar. See Figure 8.13. The Language bar will expand to include the Dictation and Voice Command buttons.

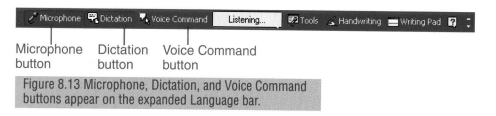

Figure 8.13 Microphone, Dictation, and Voice Command buttons appear on the expanded Language bar.

3. Switch to Voice Command mode by clicking the **Voice Command** button.

4. Switch to Dictation mode by clicking the **Dictation** button.

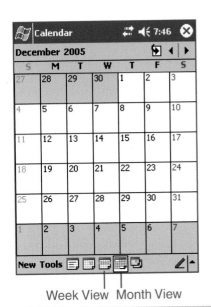

Week View   Month View

Week View   Month View

Figure 9.21 Use the Month View to plan your *Apollo 17* mission.

3. Find the date for the next Thursday after today. Enter that date in your calendar items worksheet for the liftoff date. For example, for Thursday you may enter 9/17/07 if that is the next possible Thursday. Next to Friday, you would key 9/18/07, for Saturday, 9/19/07, and so on. Enter dates for all the days on the worksheet.

4. You will need this file for the next exercise. Save the file as *82-Calendar Items*. Print the document and close *Word*.

82C LEARN: Enter Calendar Items

Pocket PC

1. Open the *Calendar* application. Tap the **Month View** icon. Tap the date for the first Thursday on your calendar items worksheet. The Day View for that date will open similar to the screen shown in Figure 9.22. Use the scroll bar to move up and tap the line for **5** (5:00 a.m.).

5. Switch to Voice Command mode by saying (speaking aloud) **VOICE COMMAND**.

6. Switch to Dictation mode by saying **DICTATION**.

7. Switch to Voice Command mode once again by saying **VOICE COMMAND**.

8. Turn your microphone off by saying **MICROPHONE**. (The microphone can also be turned off by clicking the Microphone button.)

9. The Voice Command and Dictation buttons disappear from the Language bar when the microphone is off. If these buttons still appear, click the **Microphone** button.

Figure 8.14 The Language bar contracts when the microphone is off.

71B LEARN: Use Voice Commands to Open Menus

1. Start *Word* and open a new blank document. Open the Language bar.

2. Turn on the microphone by clicking the **Microphone** button.

3. Activate Voice Command mode with your voice by saying **VOICE COMMAND**.

4. To open the File menu, say **FILE**. Close the menu by saying **ESCAPE**.

5. To open the Edit menu, say **EDIT**. Close the menu by saying **ESCAPE**.

6. To open the View menu, say **VIEW**. Close the menu by saying **ESCAPE**.

7. To open the Help menu, say **HELP**. Close the menu by saying **ESCAPE**.

8. Turn the microphone off by saying **MICROPHONE**. Continue to the next activity or close *Word*.

71C PRACTICE: Use Voice Commands to Open and Close Toolbars

In this activity, you will practice using voice commands as you view and close toolbars.

1. Start *Word* and open a new blank document. Open the Language bar.

2. Turn on the microphone by clicking the **Microphone** button.

Lesson 82   Inputting Calendar and Tasks Items

Objectives

In Lesson 82, you will:

↘ Change time zone settings.

↘ Input *Calendar* items.

↘ Input *Tasks* items.

Data files: *CD-82-Calendar Items, CD-82-Tasks Items*

Preparing to Blast into Space

Apollo 17 lifted off at 5:33 a.m. GMT, on December 7, 1972. It was the last Apollo mission to the moon. The date was a Thursday. You will also begin your PDA simulated journey next Thursday. The journey lasted 12 days, 13 hours, 52 minutes. You will need to keep track of the exact dates for everything on your journey to the moon. You can't afford to be late for liftoff. You certainly don't want to miss the only transport off that rock heading back to Earth. You should also know that all flight times are set at Greenwich Mean Time (GMT).

82A APPLY: Set Your PDA to GMT

Pocket PC and Palm OS

All the *Apollo 17* mission information was recorded according to GMT. Change the time zone and date settings for your PDA to GMT. Remember that London is in the United Kingdom (UK) and is the closest major city to Greenwich, England.

82B APPLY: Complete the Dates Worksheet

Pocket PC and Palm OS

In this activity, you will use the *Calendar* application to find the correct date for each day from Thursday through a 13-day journey.

1. Start *Word.* Open *CD-82-Calendar Items* from the data files.

2. Open your PDA's *Calendar* application. Tap the **Month View** icon as shown in Figure 9.21.

3. Switch to Voice Command mode by saying **VOICE COMMAND**.

4. Say **VIEW** to open the View menu. Say **TOOLBARS** to open a list of toolbars. Say **STANDARD** to close (hide) the Standard toolbar.

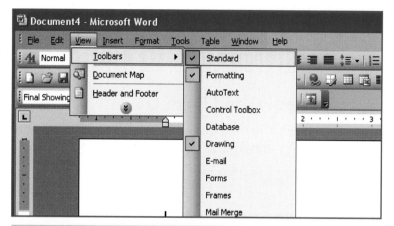

Figure 8.15 Speech users can open and close toolbars by using voice commands.

5. To close the Formatting toolbar, say **VIEW** < pause > , **TOOLBARS** < pause > , **FORMATTING**.

6. To open the Drawing toolbar, say **VIEW** < pause > , **TOOLBARS** < pause > , **DRAWING**.

7. To open the Formatting toolbar, say **VIEW** < pause > , **TOOLBARS** < pause > , **FORMATTING**.

8. To open the Standard toolbar, say **VIEW** < pause > , **TOOLBARS** < pause > , **STANDARD**.

9. To close the Drawing toolbar, say **VIEW** < pause > , **TOOLBARS** < pause > , **DRAWING**.

10. Turn the microphone off by saying **MICROPHONE**. Continue to the next activity or close *Word*.

|71D PRACTICE: Navigate Dialog Boxes

1. Start *Word* and open a new blank document. Open the Language bar.

2. Turn on the microphone by clicking the **Microphone** button.

3. Activate Voice Command mode by saying **VOICE COMMAND**.

4. Open the File menu by saying **FILE**.

5. Open the Open menu by saying **OPEN**. The Open dialog box will appear. To display the *Desktop* folder in the Look in box, say **DESKTOP**.

```
Retired from the United States Navy.
Logged 566 hours and 15 minutes in space.
Spent 73 hours on the surface of the moon.
```

5. Tap **Done** to close the entry.

81D PRACTICE: Enter and Edit Contacts

Pocket PC and Palm OS

1. Open the *Contacts* application. Enter the following information for two other crewmates in the *Contacts* program.

Last Name:	Evans
First Name:	Ronald
(Job) Title:	Pilot
Company:	NASA
Work (Telephone):	800-555-0116
Work Address:	LBJ Space Center Houston, TX 77058
E-Mail:	evans@corpview.com
Web page or site:	www.nasa.gov

Last Name:	Harrison
First Name:	Schmitt
(Job) Title:	Geologist
Company:	NASA
Work (Telephone):	800-555-0116
Work Address:	LBJ Space Center Houston, TX 77058
E-Mail:	harrison@corpview.com
Web page or site:	www.nasa.gov

2. In the *Contacts* list, tap the entry for Eugene Cernan to open it. Tap **Edit** at the bottom of the screen. Change the title (Captain) to **Commander**. Close the entry.

3. Open the entry for Ronald Evans. Edit the entry to add his middle initial **E**. The name should now be Ronald E. Evans. Close the entry. Close the application.

 **CHECK POINT** Ask a classmate to check your *Contacts* entries for accuracy. Make corrections if needed.

Look in box ———

Figure 8.16 Open Dialog Box

Instant Message

Be very quiet for a second before saying **VIEWS**. Wait quietly for a second before saying **ICONS**.

6. To display the *My Computer* folder in the Look in box, say **MY COMPUTER**.

7. To display the *My Documents* folder in the Look in box, say **MY DOCUMENTS**.

8. Change the way you view files and folders by saying the following commands:

   VIEWS < pause >, **ICONS**

   VIEWS < pause >, **DETAILS**

   VIEWS < pause >, **THUMBNAILS**

   VIEWS < pause >, **TILES**

   VIEWS < pause >, **LIST**

9. Close the Open dialog box by saying **CANCEL**.

10. Turn the microphone off by saying **MICROPHONE**.

71E APPLY: Open and Save a Document

1. Start *Word* and open a new blank document. Open the Language bar.

2. Turn on the microphone by clicking the **Microphone** button. Use voice commands in combination with the keyboard and mouse to open the file *CD-71-Speech* from the data files.

3. Use voice commands in combination with the keyboard and mouse to save the file as *71-Speech* in the folder where you save work for this class. Close *Word*.

Instant Message

LBJ stands for Lyndon B. Johnson, the 36th President of the United States.

4. Tap the **Notes** button (marked in Figure 9.19). Enter the following notes about this famous astronaut.

   `Retired from the United States Navy.`

   `Logged 566 hours and 15 minutes in space.`

   `Spent 73 hours on the surface of the moon.`

5. Tap **OK** to accept the changes to the *Contacts* entry.

Palm OS

1. Open the *Contacts* application. Tap **New**. Use *Graffiti 2* to enter data.

2. In the Last name field, enter **Cernan**. In the First name field, enter **Eugene A.** as shown in Figure 9.20.

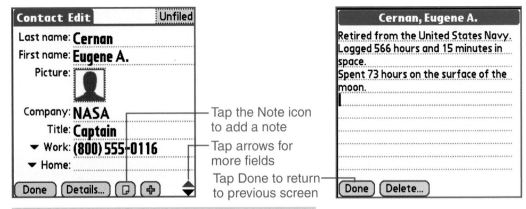

Figure 9.20 Enter a contact name and other information.

3. Continue entering the remaining contact information as shown below. Tap the down arrow to reveal other fields.

Company	NASA
Title:	Captain
Work (Telephone):	(800) 555-0116
Web site:	www.nasa.gov
E-Mail:	cernan@corpview.com
Address (W):	LBJ Space Center
City:	Houston
State:	TX
ZIP Code:	77058

4. Tap the **Note** icon (marked in Figure 9.20). Enter the following information about this famous astronaut. Tap **Done** after you have completed the notes.

Lesson 72 Voice-Typing with Speech Software

Voice-Typing Tips

Help Words

Speech
How to speak to a computer

In this lesson, you will dictate (talk to the system) to enter text and give commands. Follow these tips to improve your voice-typing skills:

- Speak clearly.
- Speak in a normal way.
- Do not speak too loudly.
- Do not whisper. Speak with confidence.
- Do not speak too slowly.
- Do not speak too quickly.

Punctuation and Paragraph Spacing Commands

Some speech programs will insert punctuation automatically as you talk to the system. However, this feature can be somewhat unreliable. It is best to say each punctuation mark to make sure it is entered properly.

For example, the user should say *period* at the end of sentences. Other marks, such as question mark and exclamation point, can also be spoken as needed. The comma is another important punctuation mark that should be spoken when dictating.

Speech users can say voice commands to move the insertion point and to insert blank lines in a document. These commands can be given in Dictation mode. The NEW LINE command inserts a hard return in a document. This is the same action that occurs when the ENTER key is tapped on the keyboard. The NEW PARAGRAPH command inserts two hard returns in the document. This is the same action that occurs when the ENTER key is tapped twice.

Contacts

One of the most powerful programs on a PDA is the *Contacts* application. This software allows you to organize names, addresses, phone numbers, e-mail addresses, and other data with ease.

In a briefing with NASA, you will learn more about the crew you will be joining on *Apollo 17*. Do you have difficulty remembering names? Many people do, so write the crew's contact information in the *Contacts* application.

81C LEARN: Enter Contacts Data for the Crew

Pocket PC

1. Open the *Contacts* application and tap **New**.

2. In the Name field, enter **Eugene A. Cernan** as shown in Figure 9.19. Use *Graffiti 2* or *Letter Recognizer* to enter the data.

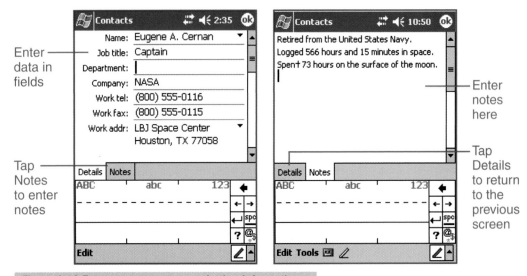

Figure 9.19 Enter a contact name and other information.

3. Continue entering the remaining contact information:

Job Title:	Captain
Company:	NASA
Work Telephone:	(800) 555-0116
Work Fax:	(800) 555-0115
Work Address:	LBJ Space Center Houston, TX 77058
E-Mail:	cernan@corpview.com
Web Page:	www.nasa.gov

72A LEARN: Dictate a Paragraph with Punctuation

1. Start *Word* and open a new blank document. Open the Language bar.

2. Turn on the microphone by clicking the **Microphone** button.

3. Activate Dictation mode by saying **DICTATION**.

4. Dictate the following paragraph. Dictate periods and commas as you come to them.

   Many people use speech software. Historians use speech software to write history books. Police officers use speech software to complete crime reports. Firefighters use speech software to complete accident reports. Doctors, nurses, and medical workers use speech software to transcribe medical records. Scientists use speech software to record the results of scientific experiments. Poets, writers, and authors use speech software to help them communicate with their readers.

5. Correct errors using the keyboard. You will learn to fix mistakes by dictating in the next lesson.

6. Select the entire document by saying:
   VOICE COMMAND
   EDIT
   SELECT ALL

7. The entire document will be selected as shown in Figure 8.17. Say **DELETE**. Undo the delete command by saying **UNDO**. Say **HOME** to move to the beginning of the document.

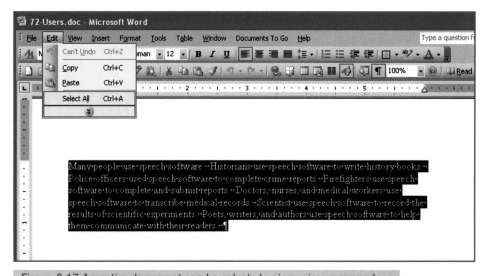

Figure 8.17 An entire document can be selected using voice commands.

5. Tap a letter on the on-screen keyboard to learn how to write that letter. Tap each letter of the alphabet to see how it is written. Notice the placement of the letters on the lines as well as how the letter is formed. After you have finished viewing the demo, tap **OK** to close Help. Close the note.

Palm OS

1. Tap the **Home** or **Applications** button. Open the *Quick Tour* or *Welcome* program. (You may also have a **Graffiti 2** program icon that will provide the same information.)

2. Choose the **Entering Data** option. Read all the information provided about the *Graffiti* writing system. Tap the arrows to move forward and backward through the screens. On the Letters screen, practice writing letters as shown in Figure 9.18. You may have to tap a **Try It!** button to reach the screen.

Letters you write appear here

Tap arrows to move forward and backward

Figure 9.18 Learn the *Graffiti* alphabet.

3. Continue through the practice screens. Also practice writing capital letters and numbers. When you are finished practicing, tap **Done** to close the program.

81B PRACTICE: Write Letters and Numbers in Notes

Pocket PC and Palm OS

1. Open your *Notes* or *Memo* program. Use *Graffiti 2* or *Letter Recognizer* to complete this activity.

2. Write **Alphabet Practice** on the first line. Move down two lines.. Practice writing each letter of the alphabet. First write the letters in lowercase. Then write the letters as capitals.

3. On a new line write **Numbers**. Move to a new line. Practice writing the numbers **1** through **20**. Close the note or memo.

8. Using voice commands in combination with the keyboard and mouse, save the document as *72-Users* in the folder where you save work for this class.

9. Turn the microphone off by saying **MICROPHONE**. Continue to the next activity or close *Word*.

72B LEARN: Dictate Lines and Paragraphs

1. Start *Word* and open a new blank document. Open the Language bar. Turn on the microphone by clicking the **Microphone** button.

2. Activate Dictation mode by saying **DICTATION**. Dictate the following lines. Dictate the punctuation marks as you come to them.

```
Who can use speech recognition?    NEW PARAGRAPH

Historians.            NEW LINE
Police officers.       NEW LINE
Firefighters.          NEW LINE
Doctors and nurses.    NEW LINE
Poets and authors.     NEW LINE
Scientists.            NEW PARAGRAPH

Almost anyone!
```

3. Close the file without saving by saying:

   VOICE COMMAND

   FILE

   CLOSE

   NO

4. Turn the microphone off by saying **MICROPHONE**. Continue to the next activity or close *Word*.

72C PRACTICE: Dictate Lines and Paragraphs

1. Start *Word* and open a new blank document. Open the Language bar. Turn on the microphone.

2. Activate Dictation mode. Dictate the lines on the next page. Dictate the punctuation marks as you come to them.

Table 9.2

Gesture	Action	How to
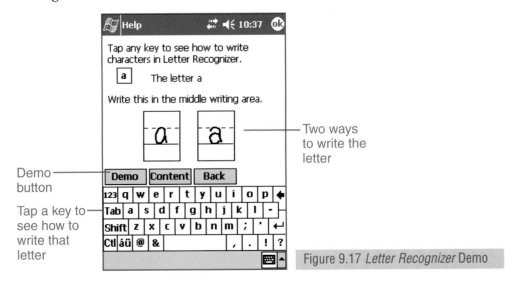	**Backspace gesture**: Erase one character to the left.	Touch the stylus down on the screen and make a quick stroke to the left.
	New line gesture: Create a new line as if pressing the ENTER key on a keyboard.	Touch the stylus down and drag diagonally from right to left.
	Space gesture: Add a space between words.	Touch the stylus down, then slide horizontally to the right.

81A LEARN:

Handwrite Letters and Numbers

Instant Message

Letters used with the *Letter Recognizer* option are similar to *Graffiti 2* letters.

Pocket PC

1. Open the *Notes* program. Open a new note.

2. Tap the up arrow at the lower-right corner of the screen and choose the **Letter Recognizer** option.

3. Tap the **Help** button (marked in Figure 9.16 on page 328). Choose **About Letter Recognizer**. Choose the first link, **Letter Recognizer Overview**. Read the information on this screen. Tap the **Forward** button to access other screens. Read all the information provided about *Letter Recognizer*.

4. Tap the **Demo** button. The on-screen keyboard will appear as shown in Figure 9.17.

Figure 9.17 *Letter Recognizer* Demo

```
Our solar system has nine known planets. How much do
you know about the planets? NEW PARAGRAPH

Which planet is closest to the sun?   NEW LINE
Which planet is farthest from the sun?   NEW LINE
Which planets have rings?   NEW LINE
Which planet is often called "the evening star"?
NEW LINE
Which planet is the largest one in our solar system?
```

3. Read the text in the document. Correct errors using the keyboard.

4. Using voice commands along with the mouse and keyboard, save the document as *72-Planets*.

5. Using voice commands along with the mouse and keyboard, print the document. Close *Word*.

6. Access the Internet. Use a search engine to find information about the planets. Find answers to the questions that you dictated. Write the answers on your printed document.

✔ **CHECK POINT** Compare your answers with those of a classmate.

Lesson 73   Correcting Errors

Objectives

In Lesson 73, you will:
➘ Delete mistakes using voice commands.
➘ Correct errors using the correction list.

Correcting Errors by Voice

Continued practice and completing more training sessions will help you improve your voice-typing skills. However, errors will still occur. If you realize that you have made an error as you are dictating, you can use the SCRATCH THAT command. This command will delete the last word or phrase that you dictated. You can say SCRATCH THAT more than once if needed. The SCRATCH THAT command can be used in Voice Command mode. On some systems, it can also be used in Dictation mode. Experiment with your system to see whether the command works in Dictation mode.

┌ ─ ─ ─ ─ ┐
Help Words
└ ─ ─ ─ ─ ┘

Speech
  Correct speech
  recognition errors

Lesson 81 Using Graffiti and Entering Contacts Data

Objectives

In Lesson 81, you will:

➘ Enter data using *Graffiti 2* or *Letter Recognizer*.

➘ Create and edit *Contacts* entries.

Graffiti and Letter Recognizer

Graffiti is a character recognition program for use on PDAs. It allows users to input information into a PDA by handwriting on the screen. *Graffiti 2* is a later version of the *Graffiti* program. Created by Palm, *Graffiti* allows you to use a shorthand way of writing letters of the alphabet. A similar option, called *Letter Recognizer*, is available on Pocket PCs. If you have good penmanship, you may find using *Graffiti* or *Letter Recognizer* more convenient than using the on-screen keyboards.

The writing area on a PDA is called the input panel or area. When using *Graffiti* or *Letter Recognizer*, letters and numbers are written in different areas. Letters are written on the left side, and numbers are written on the right side. The input area for Palm PDAs and Pocket PCs are similar, as shown in Figure 9.16.

Palm OS Input Area

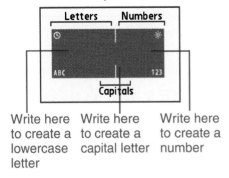

Write here to create a lowercase letter   Write here to create a capital letter   Write here to create a number

Pocket PC Input Panel

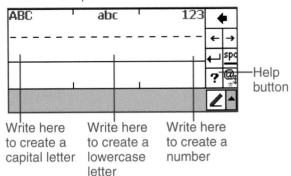

Help button

Write here to create a capital letter   Write here to create a lowercase letter   Write here to create a number

Figure 9.16 PDA Input Panel or Area

Special gestures or strokes make *Graffiti* and *Graffiti 2* easy to use. These gestures are used to add space between words, backspace to erase errors, or create new lines. See Table 9.2 on page 329 for the most popular gestures.

73A LEARN: Use the Scratch That Command

1. Start *Word* and open a new blank document. Open the Language bar. Turn on the microphone.

2. Activate Dictation mode. Dictate the following phrases and then delete them using the SCRATCH THAT command. (You may need to switch to Voice Command mode before saying the SCRATCH THAT command.)

   `Historians use speech   SCRATCH THAT`

   `Police officers use speech   SCRATCH THAT`

   `Firefighters use speech   SCRATCH THAT`

   `Scientists use speech   SCRATCH THAT`
   `Doctors, nurses, and medical assistants SCRATCH THAT`
   (Repeat `SCRATCH THAT` if needed.)
   `Poets and authors can use speech software`
   `SCRATCH THAT`
   (Repeat `SCRATCH THAT` if needed.)

3. Exit Word without saving. Turn off the microphone.

Using a Correction List

Instant Message

If the correct word does not appear in the correction list, key the correct word using the keyboard.

Accuracy can be improved by correcting mistakes using a correction list. A **correction list** is a group of words from which a word can be selected to replace an incorrect word. To open a correction list, select the incorrect word with a digital pen or mouse. Then say the CORRECT THAT command (or right-click the word for Tablet PC users). A correction list will appear as shown in Figure 8.18. Choose a word. The word you select will appear in the document, replacing the error.

The CORRECT THAT and SELECT commands can be used in Dictation mode and in Voice Command mode. The speech software remembers the way you say words when you correct using a correction list. This works to improve your accuracy.

```
Duration: 12 days, 13 hours, 52 minutes
On the Moon: 75 hours
3 EVAs: 22 hours, 4 minutes
```

✔ **CHECK POINT** Your note should look similar to the partial note shown in Figure 9.15, page 326.

6. Tap **Done** to close the keyboard. Tap **Done** again to save the memo. The memo name, *Mission: Apollo 17*, should appear in the *Memos* list. Tap the **Home** or **Applications** button to exit *Memos*.

Organizing Notes and Memos

The notes about the *Apollo 17* mission should be in the *Notes* or *Memos* list. As you create other notes or memos, they will be listed in alphabetical order on a Pocket PC and in numerical order on a Palm PDA. The first line or phrase from each note is generally used as the title. Add a new note and see how it is organized on the list.

80B PRACTICE: Add a New Note

Pocket PC and Palm OS

1. Create a new note or memo. Enter the following information using the on-screen keyboards. Tap the **Enter** key at the end of each line.
   ```
   Landing Site
   Taurus-Littrow highlands
   ```

2. Close the note or memo.

80C PRACTICE: Edit a Note or Memo

Pocket PC and Palm OS

1. Open the *Notes* or *Memos* application. Tap the *Landing Site* memo or note name to open the note. Open the on-screen keyboard.

2. Tap at the end of the first line. Tap the **Enter** key on the on-screen keyboard to add a blank line after the first line.

3. Tap at the end of the last line. Key **and valley**. Tap the **Enter** key. Key **20.16 degrees North, 30.77 degrees East**. Close the note.

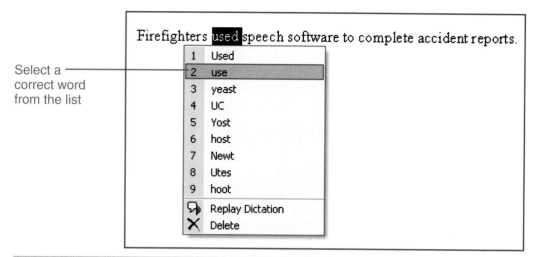

Firefighters **used** speech software to complete accident reports.

Select a correct word from the list

1	Used
2	use
3	yeast
4	UC
5	Yost
6	host
7	Newt
8	Utes
9	hoot
↺	Replay Dictation
✕	Delete

Figure 8.18 Errors can be corrected using a correction list.

73B LEARN: Use a Correction List

1. Start *Word* and open a new blank document. Open the Language bar. Turn on the microphone.

2. Activate Dictation mode. Dictate the following sentence:

   ```
   Many people use speech software to input data.
   NEW PARAGRAPH
   ```

3. If a word is not recognized correctly, select it with your mouse or digital pen. Say **CORRECT THAT**. (Tablet PC users, right-click the selected word.)

4. Locate a correct word on the correction list. Say **SELECT** and the number next to the correct word. (Tablet PC users, say or click the correct word.) If a correct word is not in the list, use the keyboard to key a correct word.

5. Dictate the sentences below. Correct errors in the sentences using a correction list. If a correct word is not in the list, use the keyboard to key a correct word.

   ```
   Historians use speech software to write history
   books. NEW PARAGRAPH
   ```

   ```
   Police officers use speech software to complete
   crime reports.  NEW PARAGRAPH
   ```

   ```
   Firefighters use speech software to complete
   accident reports.  NEW PARAGRAPH
   ```

Palm OS

1. Open the **Memos** (or **Memo Pad**) application. Choose **New** to open a new memo.

2. Tap the **ABC** area of the input panel in the bottom-left corner of the screen. This will open the on-screen keyboard as shown in Figure 9.15.

3. Tap the **Shift** key to switch to the Shifted keyboard. Tap the **Shift** key several times to see how the letters change from uppercase to lowercase. The Shifted keyboard also contains some punctuation marks such as the colon (:) and quotes (").

4. Tap the **123** key at the bottom of the keyboard to reveal the Numeric keyboard. Notice that several symbols and punctuation marks are also on the Numeric keyboard. Tap the **abc** key to return to the Standard keyboard.

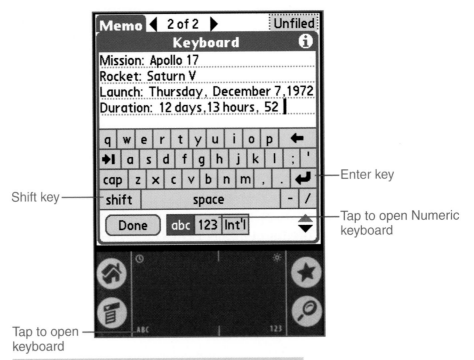

Shift key

Tap to open keyboard

Enter key

Tap to open Numeric keyboard

Figure 9.15 Enter text using the on-screen keyboards.

5. Enter the information shown below using the on-screen keyboards. Switch between the Standard and Shifted or Numeric keyboards as needed. Tap the **Enter** key at the end of each line.

```
Mission: Apollo 17
Rocket: Saturn V
Launch: Thursday, December 7, 1972
```

Doctors and nurses use speech software to transcribe medical records. NEW PARAGRAPH

Scientists use speech software to record the results of their scientific experiments. NEW PARAGRAPH

6. Use voice commands to close *Word* without saving the document. (The commands are **FILE, EXIT, NO**.) Turn the microphone off.

Lesson 74 Adding Words to a User Dictionary

Objectives

In Lesson 74, you will:

↘ Add words to a speech user dictionary.
↘ Add names to a speech user dictionary.

Speech Recognition Dictionary

```
┌ Help Words ┐
└            ┘
```

Speech
Add to or delete from the speech recognition dictionary

A speech program recognizes words by comparing them with those in a dictionary. The number of words that speech software can recognize seems to grow every year. It is unusual to find words that are not in the speech recognition dictionary. However, you may use some unusual words or some names that you wish to add to the dictionary. You will learn to add words to a speech recognition dictionary in the next activity.

| 74A LEARN:

Add Words to a Dictionary

The letters *gwam* stand for *gross words a minute*. You learned this acronym in Chapter 4 when you learned to measure your keying speed. In this activity, you will add *gwam* to the speech user dictionary.

1. Start *Word* and open a new blank document. Open the Language bar.

2. Choose **Tools, Add/Delete Word(s)** from the Language bar as shown in Figure 8.19.

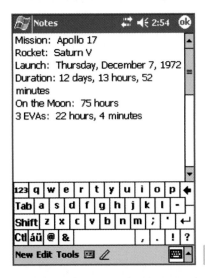

Figure 9.13 Choose Keyboard from the input tools.

Tap for Numeric keyboard

Shift key

Tap the up arrow to select an input tool

Enter key

3. Tap the **Shift** key to reveal the Shifted keyboard. Tap **Shift** several times to see how letters change from uppercase to lowercase. The Shifted keyboard also contains some punctuation marks such as the slash (/) and the colon (:).

4. Tap the **123** key in the upper-left corner of the keyboard to reveal the numeric keyboard. Notice that several symbols and punctuation marks are also on the numeric keyboard. Tap the **123** key to return to the Standard keyboard.

5. Enter the information shown below using the on-screen keyboards. Switch between the Standard and Shifted or Numeric keyboards as needed. Tap the **Enter** key at the end of each line.

```
Mission: Apollo 17
Rocket: Saturn V
Launch: Thursday, December 7, 1972
Duration: 12 days, 13 hours, 52 minutes
On the Moon: 75 hours
3 EVAs: 22 hours, 4 minutes
```

CHECK POINT Your note should look similar to Figure 9.14.

6. Tap **OK** to close the note. The name of the note, *Mission*, should appear in the *Notes* list. Tap the **Close** button to exit *Notes*.

Instant Message

EVA stands for extravehicular activity.

Figure 9.14 Use the on-screen keyboard to enter text.

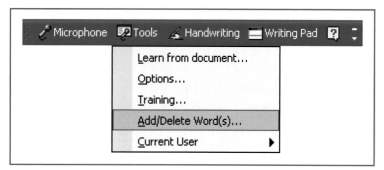

Figure 8.19 Choose Add/Delete Words from the Tools menu.

3. The Add/Delete Word(s) box will appear as shown in Figure 8.20. Key **gwam** in the Word field, using your keyboard.

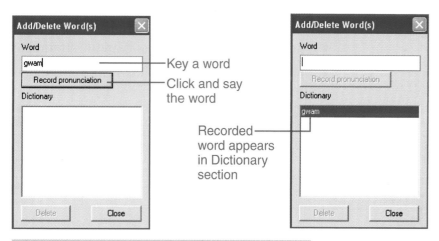

Figure 8.20 Enter a word and record its pronunciation.

4. Click **Record pronunciation** and say **gwam**. When the word is recorded, it moves to the Dictionary section. Click the **Close** button.

5. Try dictating the word in your *Word* document. Turn on the microphone and select **DICTATION** mode. Say **My gwam score is 35**.

6. If the word does not appear correctly, try correcting it using a correction list.

7. Continue to the next activity or close *Word*.

Recognizing Names

Some names are easy for a speech recognition program to understand because they are spelled the way they sound. For example, the name *Rose* is

Lesson 80 Entering Notes and Contacts

Objectives

In Lesson 80, you will:

↘ Enter data using the on-screen keyboards.

↘ Create and edit notes or memos.

On-Screen Keyboards

Data can be input into your handheld computer using a stylus. Both *Palm OS* and Pocket PCs devices provide on-screen keyboards. The following on-screen keyboards are shown in Figure 9.12:

- The **Standard keyboard** has lowercase letters and punctuation marks.
- The **Shifted keyboard** has capital letters and symbols.
- The **Numeric keyboard** has numbers, special characters, and symbols.

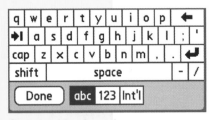

Standard keyboard

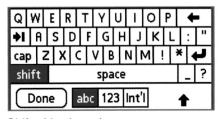

Shifted keyboard

Numeric keyboard

Figure 9.12 On-Screen Keyboards

80A LEARN: Input Mission Notes Using On-Screen Keyboards

Pocket PC

1. Tap **Start** then **Notes** to open the Notes program. Choose **New** at the bottom of the screen to open a new note.

2. Open the on-screen keyboard by tapping the up arrow at the bottom right-hand corner of the screen. This will reveal the input options. Choose **Keyboard** as shown in Figure 9.13. The Standard keyboard will appear on the screen.

one that will usually be recognized. Some names may be recognized incorrectly because they can have more than one spelling. For example, the name *Brown* can also be spelled *Browne*. Sometimes names are not recognized correctly because the speech program tries to use them as regular words (not names) in a sentence.

Names that are used frequently can be added to a speech user's dictionary in the same way that other words are added. Placing a name in the dictionary improves the chances that it will be recognized correctly.

|74B PRACTICE: Add Names to a User Dictionary

In this activity, you will practice adding names to a speech user's dictionary. You will add names of some famous poets and authors.

1. Start *Word* and open a new blank document. Open the Language bar.
2. Choose **Tools**, **Add/Delete Word(s)** from the Language bar.
3. Key **Maya Angelou** into the Word field, using the keyboard. Click **Record pronunciation** and say **Maya Angelou**. When the name is recorded, it moves to the Dictionary section.
4. Click the **Close** button. In Dictation mode, say the name **Maya Angelou**.
5. If the name does not appear correctly, open the Add/Delete Word(s) dialog box. Select the words from the Dictionary, tap **Record pronunciation**, and say the words again. Speak distinctly. Close the box and try dictating the word again.
6. Add these four additional names to the dictionary:
   Lucille Clifton
   Carl Sandburg
   Lewis Carroll
   Catherine Yi-Yu Cho Woo
7. Try dictating the names in your document. Continue to the next activity or close *Word*.

|74C APPLY: Add Words and Names

1. Start *Word* and open a new blank document. Open the Language bar.
2. Choose **Tools**, **Add/Delete Word(s)** from the Language bar.
3. Add your first name and your last name to the dictionary. Try dictating your name in a *Word* document.

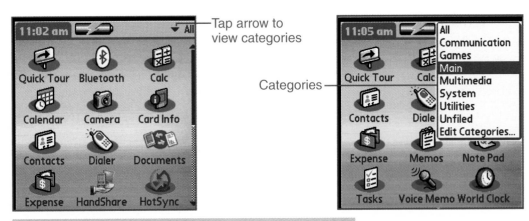

Tap arrow to view categories

Categories

Figure 9.11 Tap the down arrow to view categories in *Palm OS*.

4. Tap the **Home** or **Applications** button several times to reveal several lists of applications. These lists are organized by similar application categories. Continue tapping until you come to the **All** list again.

5. Tap the **Memos** (also **Memo/Memo Pad**) icon. Tap **New** at the bottom of the screen to open a new file. Tap **Done** to close the memo.

6. Tap the **Home** or **Applications** button again. Tap the **Calc** (Calculator) icon. Tap the number **7**. Tap the + symbol. Tap the numbers for **45**. Tap the + symbol. The sum of these two numbers, 52, should appear on the screen. Tap the **C** (Clear) button to clear the numbers. Practice adding, subtracting, multiplying, and dividing numbers as you would using a typical calculator.

7. Tap the **Home** or **Applications** button. Tap the **Quick Tour** (or **Welcome**) icon. Read each screen. Learn as much as you can from the tour.

8. The hard buttons on your PDA open applications. (See Figure 9.2 on page 316.) Press a hard button and make a note of the application that it opens. Return to the **Home** or **Application** screen. Repeat for all the hard buttons on the PDA.

79B APPLY: Calculate Expenses

Pocket PC and Palm OS

You have been asked to join the *Apollo 17* mission to the moon. NASA has given you a $250 expense account to buy a few important items. You will use the *Calculator* program to add the amounts for the items.

1. Start *Word*. Open *CD-79-Expenses* from the data files. Print the document and close *Word*.

2. Follow the instructions in the document to find your total expenses and the amount of money you have remaining.

 **CHECK POINT** Compare your answers with those of a classmate. If they do not agree, add the numbers again.

4. Choose three names of friends or family members. Add them to the dictionary.

5. Think of other words you use that the speech program may have trouble recognizing. Add these words to the dictionary. Close *Word*.

Lesson 75 — Dictating and Correcting Documents

Objectives

In Lesson 75, you will:
↘ Dictate a short report.
↘ Dictate a personal-business letter.
↘ Correct errors in documents.

Dictating Documents

Speech recognition can be used to dictate letters, reports, and other documents. Follow the guidelines below to help improve recognition accuracy.

- Add unusual words or names to the speech user's dictionary before dictating the document.

- Turn the microphone off and think about what you want to say before you begin each paragraph.

- Speak in complete sentences whenever possible.

- Correct mistakes at the end of each paragraph. This way the software will learn how you say words and phrases. The same mistakes will be less likely to happen again.

- Dictate all the paragraphs before you format the document.

75A PRACTICE: Dictate a Report

Instant Message

You will begin by saying the NEW LINE command three times to position the report on the page.

1. Start *Word* and open a new blank document. Open the Language bar. Turn on the microphone.

2. Activate Dictation mode. Dictate the following report. Say the NEW LINE command where indicated.
   ```
   NEW LINE
   NEW LINE
   NEW LINE
   Career Planning      NEW LINE
   ```

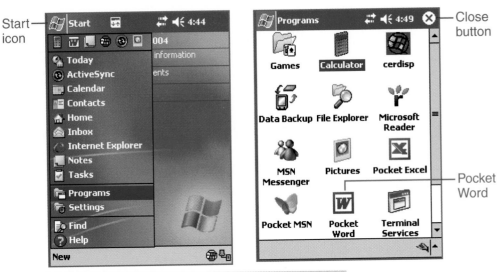

Figure 9.10 Open and view the applications on your Pocket PC.

2. Tap the **Pocket Word** icon. Tap the **New** button at the bottom of the screen to open a new document. Close *Pocket Word* by tapping **OK** and then the **Close** button.

3. Tap the **Start** icon. Tap **Notes** on the list of frequently used programs. Tap the **New** button to open a new document. Close *Notes* by tapping **OK** and then the **Close** button.

4. Tap the **Calculator** icon to open the *Calculator* program. Tap the number **7**. Tap the **+** symbol. Tap the numbers for **45**. Tap the **+** symbol. The sum of these two numbers, 52, should appear on the screen. Tap the **C** (Clear) button to clear the numbers. Practice adding, subtracting, multiplying, and dividing numbers as you would using a typical calculator. Close the *Calculator* by tapping the **Close** button.

5. The hard buttons on your PDA open applications. (See Figure 9.2 on page 316.) Press a hard button and make a note of the application that it opens. Close the application. Repeat for all the hard buttons on the PDA.

Palm OS

1. To access the list of program icons, tap the **Home** or **Applications** button.

2. Tap the down arrow at the top of the screen. This will reveal a list of categories of applications on the PDA. Choose **Main** as shown in Figure 9.11 on page 323.

3. Tap the down arrow again and choose **System** to reveal the system applications. These applications help you manage your operating system.

Career planning is an important, ongoing process. You can never begin planning too early for your career. The career you eventually choose will affect the quality of your life.   NEW LINE

One important step in career planning is to learn about various jobs. One very good resource for learning about jobs is the Occupational Outlook Handbook. This resource is published by the United States Department of Labor. This resource will tell you about thousands of jobs. Some of the jobs described include rock star, athlete, zookeeper, police officer, and reporter.   NEW LINE

Another useful step in career planning is self-assessment. This process will reveal your values and interests. Values help you set priorities in life. They affect the importance you place on family, security, and wealth. You should consider your values when you choose a career.   NEW LINE

Interests are activities that you like or subjects that appeal to you. Listing your interests may help you identify a work setting that you will like. This can be helpful in planning a career.

3. Turn the microphone off. Read the report you dictated, looking for mistakes. Correct errors using the correction list. If a correct word does not appear on the list, key a correct word to replace the mistake.

4. Using voice commands along with the mouse and keyboard, save the document as *75-Report*. You will format the report to make it easier to read in a later lesson. Continue to the next activity or close *Word*.

75B PRACTICE: Dictate a Letter

Instant Message

You will begin by saying the NEW PARAGRAPH command three times to position the letter on the page.

1. Start *Word* and open a new blank document. Open the Language bar. Turn on the microphone.

2. Activate Dictation mode. Dictate the following letter. Say the NEW PARAGRAPH and NEW LINE commands where indicated.
   NEW PARAGRAPH
   NEW PARAGRAPH
   NEW PARAGRAPH
   43 Concord Street   NEW LINE
   Monroe, NC 28110-8233   NEW LINE

Lesson 79 Finding Your Applications

Objectives

In Lesson 79, you will:
↘ Open PDA applications using icons and hard buttons.
↘ Navigate PDA menus.
↘ Calculate expenses with the *Calculator* application.
↘ Close applications.

Data files: *CD-79-Expenses*

Before your first official meeting with NASA, examine some of the tools on your PDA. You need to learn how to use some of them quickly! Like programs on a PC, applications on a PDA allow you to accomplish certain tasks. Here is a short list of popular PDA programs:

- *Notes* or *Memos*
- *Contacts*
- *Calendar*
- *Tasks*
- Camera and video tools
- E-mail
- Instant text messaging
- Phone number dialers (on smart phones)

- Word processors, spreadsheets, and presentation applications
- *Calculator*
- Financial management software
- E-book readers
- Backup and synchronization tools
- Games
- Alarm clock

| 79A LEARN: Open and Close Programs

Pocket PC

1. Tap the **Start** icon. Choose **Programs** from the list. The Programs window will open as shown in Figure 9.10.

May 7, 2005   NEW PARAGRAPH

NEW PARAGRAPH

Miss Laura Roberts   NEW LINE
3601 Rose Drive   NEW LINE
Charlotte, NC 28217-2813   NEW PARAGRAPH

Dear Miss Roberts   NEW PARAGRAPH

Thank you for agreeing to speak to our New Horizons Club. My classmates and I will be very interested in your advice about how to explore careers.
NEW PARAGRAPH

As we discussed, the meeting is at Roper School in the cafeteria. The meeting is at two o'clock on May 18. If you need directions to the school, let me know.   NEW PARAGRAPH

Please plan to stay for a short reception after the meeting. Let me know if you have any questions about the meeting.   NEW PARAGRAPH

Sincerely   NEW PARAGRAPH

NEW PARAGRAPH

Karen Fernandez

3. Turn the microphone off. Read the letter you dictated, looking for mistakes. Correct errors using the correction list. If a correct word does not appear on the correction list, key a correct word to replace the mistake.

4. Using voice commands along with the mouse and keyboard, save the document as *75-Letter*.

✔ **CHECK POINT** Compare the format of your letter with the one in Figure 8.21 on page 302. Make corrections if needed.

5. Using voice commands along with the mouse and keyboard, print the letter. Close *Word*.

4. Tap the **Set Time** text box to open the Set Time window. Tap the hour or minutes. Then tap the up or down arrow to increase or decrease the time. Tap **AM** or **PM** to change this setting. Tap **OK** to close the box.

5. To set the date, tap the **Set Date** box to reveal a calendar as shown in Figure 9.9. Tap the arrows by the year to move ahead or back by year. Tap a month. Tap the current day. Tap **Today** to close the window.

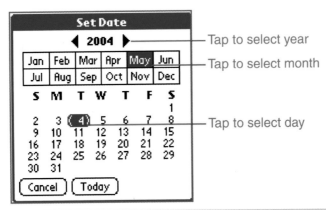

Figure 9.9 Change the year, month, and day settings in the Set Date window.

6. Tap **Home** or **Applications** to return to the list of program icons.

78B APPLY: Calculate Hours Away from GMT

Pocket PC and Palm OS

1. Go to the screen where you can set the time for your PDA. Make a note of the time (that you set to be correct in Activity 78A).

2. Change the time zone to **London** for *Palm OS* or **GMT London** for Pocket PC. Make a note of the time. Subtract the time in your time zone from the time in London to find the number of hours you are away from GMT (Greenwich Mean Time).

3. Reset the time zone to your time zone.

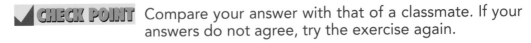 **CHECK POINT** Compare your answer with that of a classmate. If your answers do not agree, try the exercise again.

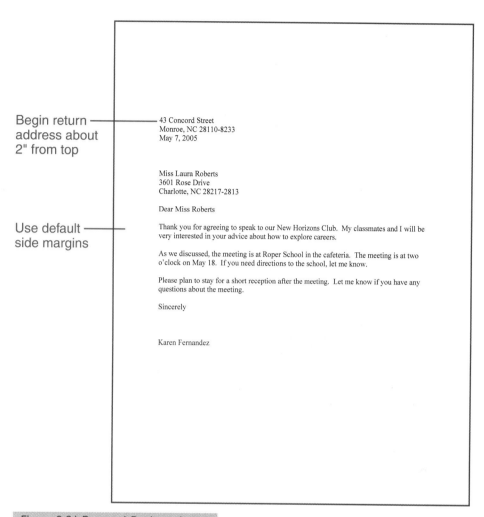

Begin return address about 2" from top

43 Concord Street
Monroe, NC 28110-8233
May 7, 2005

Miss Laura Roberts
3601 Rose Drive
Charlotte, NC 28217-2813

Dear Miss Roberts

Use default side margins

Thank you for agreeing to speak to our New Horizons Club. My classmates and I will be very interested in your advice about how to explore careers.

As we discussed, the meeting is at Roper School in the cafeteria. The meeting is at two o'clock on May 18. If you need directions to the school, let me know.

Please plan to stay for a short reception after the meeting. Let me know if you have any questions about the meeting.

Sincerely

Karen Fernandez

Figure 8.21 Personal-Business Letter

Lesson 76 Text-to-Speech

Objectives

In Lesson 76, you will:
- ↘ Dictate a letter.
- ↘ Use the text-to-speech feature to listen for errors.

Editing with Text-to-Speech

There is more to speech recognition than just dictating. You can also use speech software to listen to the text you have dictated. The **text-to-speech** feature can read your dictated text back to you. It is fun to hear your document being read by a computer. There is a very practical reason to use

Palm OS

1. Start your *Palm OS* PDA. Tap the **Home** or **Applications** button. The options will vary depending on the version of *Palm OS* your PDA uses.

2. Notice that the time is shown at the top of the screen. The **All** category should be shown at the top right of the screen, as in Figure 9.7. If it is not, click the down arrow in the top right of the screen and choose **All**. To access the date and time settings, tap the **Pref** (Preferences) icon marked in Figure 9.7. You may have to scroll down to find the icon.

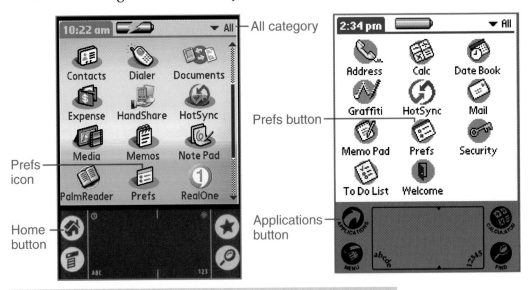

Figure 9.7 Choose the Prefs icon from the Home or Applications screen.

3. Tap the **Date & Time** option. Tap the **Location** arrow or **Set Time Zone** box. Choose a city that is in your time zone. For example, choose **Atlanta** for the Eastern time zone as shown in Figure 9.8.

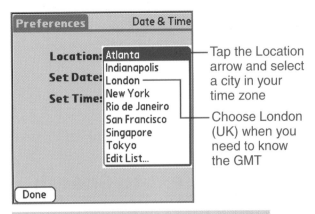

Figure 9.8 Choose a location in your time zone.

text-to-speech—you can listen for mistakes. Listen carefully. If something doesn't sound right, check the text and make corrections as needed.

76A LEARN: Use the Speak Text Command

1. Start *Word* and open a new blank document. Open the Language bar.

2. Before you use the text-to-speech feature, you will display the **Speak Text** and **Pause Speaking** buttons on the Language bar. Click the **Options** button on the Language bar. Select **Speak Text**.

3. Click the **Options** button on the Language bar. Select **Pause Speaking**. The Speak and Pause buttons will display on the Language bar as shown in Figure 8.22.

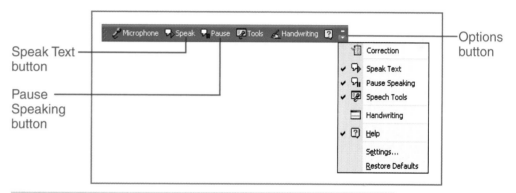

Figure 8.22 The Speak and Pause buttons display on the Language bar.

4. Dictate the following sentences:

   How long does it take to learn to use speech recognition effectively? The answer will be different for each user. Reading training stories and using the correction list to fix mistakes will improve the accuracy.

5. Use voice commands to select the entire document. (**EDIT**, **SELECT ALL**)

6. Click the **Speak Text** button on the Language bar. Listen for mistakes as the text is read. Click the **Pause Speaking** button when you want to stop listening and check for an error. Then click **Resume** to continue.

7. Continue to the next activity or close *Word*.

Instant Message

Always proofread the text carefully, even when you have listened to the dictation. All errors may not be found by listening.

76B PRACTICE: Dictate and Listen to a Letter

1. Start *Word* and open a new blank document. Open the Language bar. Turn on the microphone.

2. Notice that the time is shown at the top of the Today screen. To access the date and time settings, tap the **Clock** icon as marked in Figure 9.4.

3. Locate the time zone setting. Tap the down arrow next to the time zone box. Select your time zone from the list as shown in Figure 9.5.

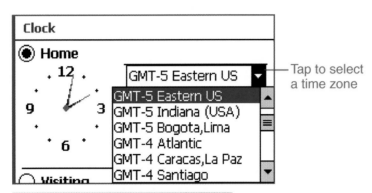

Clock

⦿ **Home**

Tap to select a time zone

GMT-5 Eastern US
GMT-5 Eastern US
GMT-5 Indiana (USA)
GMT-5 Bogota,Lima
GMT-4 Atlantic
GMT-4 Caracas,La Paz
GMT-4 Santiago

Figure 9.5 Update the time zone setting.

4. To set the hours and minutes of the time, tap the hour or minutes. Then tap the up or down arrow until the correct time is shown. Tap **AM** or **PM** to change that setting.

5. Tap the down arrow by the date. Tap the arrows by the month to select the current month. Tap a date on the calendar to select the day as shown in Figure 9.6.

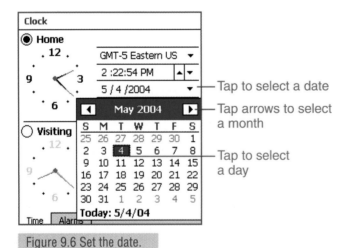

Clock

⦿ **Home**

GMT-5 Eastern US
2 :22:54 PM
5 / 4 /2004 — Tap to select a date

◀ May 2004 ▶ — Tap arrows to select a month

S	M	T	W	T	F	S
25	26	27	28	29	30	1
2	3	4	5	6	7	8
9	10	11	12	13	14	15
16	17	18	19	20	21	22
23	24	25	26	27	28	29
30	31	1	2	3	4	5

Today: 5/4/04

Tap to select a day

○ Visiting

Time Alarms

Figure 9.6 Set the date.

6. Tap **OK** in the upper-right corner of the screen. Tap **Yes** when asked if you wish to save the clock settings.

2. Activate Dictation mode. Dictate the following letter. Say the NEW PARAGRAPH and NEW LINE commands where indicated.

```
NEW  PARAGRAPH
NEW  PARAGRAPH
NEW  PARAGRAPH
27Branson Street      NEW  LINE
Hartford Court, CT  06114-2207      NEW  LINE
May 20, 2005    NEW  PARAGRAPH

NEW  PARAGRAPH

Mr. Joe Chin    NEW  LINE
483 Maple Avenue      NEW  LINE
Hartford Court, CT  06114-0483      NEW  PARAGRAPH

Dear Mr. Chin   NEW  PARAGRAPH

Thank you for inviting us to have our class picnic
at your home.   My classmates and I are excited about
this event.    NEW  PARAGRAPH

As we discussed, several of our parents will attend
to help set up the tables and prepare the food.   We
are planning a menu and games to play after lunch.
NEW  PARAGRAPH

Our teacher, Ms. Lopez, will be in contact with you
soon to discuss details for the picnic.   Thanks
again for offering to be our host.    NEW  PARAGRAPH

Sincerely      NEW  PARAGRAPH

NEW  PARAGRAPH

Alice Park, Class President
```

3. Use voice commands to select the entire document. (**EDIT**, **SELECT ALL**)

4. Click the **Speak Text** button on the Language bar. Listen for mistakes as the text is read. Click the **Pause Speaking** button when you want to stop listening and check for an error. Then click **Resume** to continue.

✓ CHECK POINT Compare the format of your letter with the one in Figure 8.21 on page 302. Make corrections if needed.

Time Zones

The sun doesn't rise and set at the same time everywhere in the world. In fact, at this very moment it may be midnight in one time zone and high noon in another zone on the opposite side of the world. There is an imaginary line from the North Pole to the South Pole. This line stretches past a scientific observatory just outside London in a place called Greenwich, England. Time is measured from that spot. This time setting is called *Greenwich Mean Time (GMT)*.

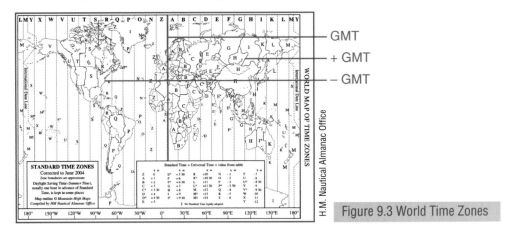

Figure 9.3 World Time Zones

78A LEARN: Change Date and Time Settings

Read and follow the instructions for your PDA. Look for either the ***Pocket PC*** heading or the ***Palm OS*** heading.

Pocket PC

1. Start your Pocket PC. The Today screen should appear as shown in Figure 9.4. If the Today screen does not appear, tap **Start** and choose the **Today** icon.

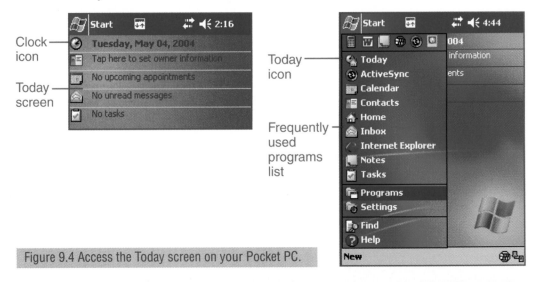

Figure 9.4 Access the Today screen on your Pocket PC.

5. Using voice commands along with the mouse and keyboard, save the document as *76-Letter*.

6. Using voice commands along with the mouse and keyboard, print the letter. Close *Word*.

Lesson 77 Navigating and Formatting Documents by Voice

Objectives

In Lesson 77, you will:
- ➘ Navigate a document using voice commands.
- ➘ Apply formatting using voice commands.
- ➘ Compose, dictate, and format a report.

Formatting is the art of making a document look attractive and easy to read. In this lesson, you will apply formatting to the Career Planning report you created earlier. You will center a title, change the text to all capitals, and double-space paragraphs using voice commands. You will also practice using voice commands to move around in a document so you can find the text you want to change.

77A LEARN: Move around in a Document

SOFTWARE TIP

Hold down the CTRL key and tap HOME to move the insertion point to the beginning of a document.

1. Start *Word*. Open *75-Report* that you created earlier. Move the insertion point to the beginning of the document.

2. Turn the microphone on. In Voice Command mode, say the following commands that will move the insertion point:
```
MOVE TO END OF DOCUMENT
MOVE TO BEGINNING OF DOCUMENT
MOVE TO END OF DOCUMENT
GO TO TOP
GO TO BOTTOM
PAGE UP
PAGE DOWN
PAGE UP
PAGE DOWN
```

take pictures. With many smart phones, users can send text messages, download music files and ring tones, and use the phone like a walkie-talkie. Two smart phones are shown in Figure 9.1.

Figure 9.1 Smart phones have phone and PDA features.

Applications

PDA buttons and software icons are used to start applications. PDAs, like spaceships, have lots of buttons. Fortunately, hitting the wrong button on a PDA won't endanger your life! It's okay to experiment if you are unsure what the button will do.

PDA hard buttons are pressed with your fingers or thumbs. Buttons allow one-press access to important PDA features. Some PDAs also have keyboards or number pads. PDA soft buttons and icons are used with a stylus. A **stylus** is a pencil-like tool that activates the soft buttons when you touch them. A stylus is also used for handwritten input on a PDA.

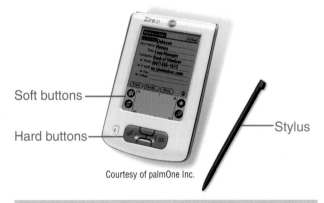

Soft buttons

Hard buttons

Stylus

Courtesy of palmOne Inc.

Figure 9.2 A stylus is used to activate PDA soft buttons.

If you have a brand new PDA, you'll need to set it up for first-time use. Setup instructions for Pocket PCs and Palm PDAs are provided in the user guide that comes with the PDA.

3. In Voice Command mode, say the following commands that will move the insertion point one line at a time.

```
GO UP
UP
GO UP
GO DOWN
DOWN
GO DOWN
GO UP
```

4. In Voice Command mode, say the following commands that will move the insertion point one or more characters at a time.

```
GO LEFT
GO LEFT
LEFT
GO RIGHT
RIGHT
GO RIGHT
```

5. Close the document or continue to the next activity.

77B PRACTICE: Format a Report

┌ ─ ─ ─ ─ ┐
  Help Words
└ ─ ─ ─ ─ ┘

Speech
 Format text by
 using speech
 recognition

1. Start *Word*. Open *75-Report* that you created earlier. Move the insertion point to the beginning of the document.

2. Turn the microphone on. Using the mouse, select the report title **Career Planning**. In Voice Command mode, say **CENTER**.

3. With the title still selected say **FORMAT**, **CHANGE CASE**, **UPPERCASE**, **OK**.

4. To select the entire document, say **EDIT**, **SELECT ALL**.

5. To change the document to double spacing, say **FORMAT**, **PARAGRAPH**, **LINE SPACING**, **DOUBLE**, **OK**.

6. Use voice commands to go to the beginning of the first paragraph. Say **TAB** to indent the paragraph. Use the same steps to indent the other three paragraphs.

7. Using the mouse, select the name **Occupational Outlook Handbook**. Say **ITALIC**.

8. Use voice commands to go to the end of the report. Dictate **By** and your name.

9. Using voice commands along with the mouse and keyboard, save the document as *77-Report*.

 **CHECK POINT** Compare the format of your letter with the one in Figure 8.23 on page 307. Make corrections if needed.

Lesson 78 Learning about PDAs

Objectives

In Lesson 78, you will:

↘ Learn about tasks you can do using PDAs.

↘ Learn about the most popular operating systems for PDAs.

↘ Learn to use a stylus.

↘ Find the Today or Welcome screen.

↘ Adjust date, time, and time zone settings.

Preparing for the Flight

You must learn a few PDA basics before joining the *Apollo 17* team. PDAs require an operating system (OS) to make them work. PDAs are classified by their operating systems. The three most popular operating systems for PDAs are listed in Table 9.1.

Table 9.1

Operating System	Sample PDA Models
Windows Mobile for Pocket PC (from Microsoft)	Pocket PCs HP iPAQ Dell Pocket PC ViewSonic
Palm OS (from PalmSource)	Tungsten Zire
RIM	Blackberry

The OS allows PDA applications to work. Each application allows users to solve a problem or keep track of a different type of information, such as:

- The time, date, and time zone settings

- Meeting notes, communications, and conversations of importance

- Personal contacts: names, phone numbers, e-mail addresses, mailing addresses, phone numbers, and fax numbers

- Task lists

- Deadlines, schedules, meetings, and appointments

- Expenses

PDA features are combined with digital phone features in devices called **smart phones**. With smart phones, users can make calls, play games, and send e-mail. Some smart phones have digital cameras that allow users to

10. Using voice commands along with the mouse and keyboard, print the report. Close *Word*.

Begin title about 2" from top

Use default side margins

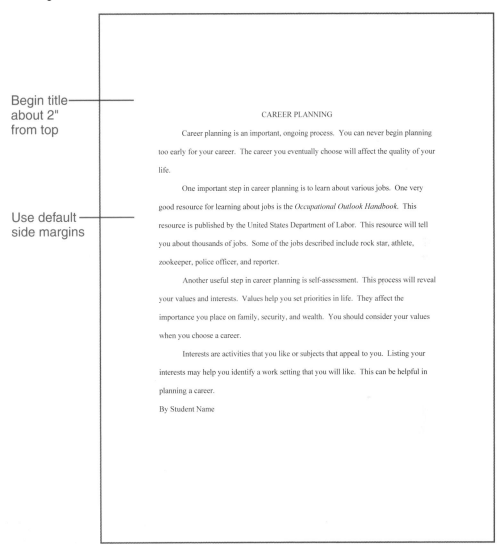

CAREER PLANNING

Career planning is an important, ongoing process. You can never begin planning too early for your career. The career you eventually choose will affect the quality of your life.

One important step in career planning is to learn about various jobs. One very good resource for learning about jobs is the *Occupational Outlook Handbook*. This resource is published by the United States Department of Labor. This resource will tell you about thousands of jobs. Some of the jobs described include rock star, athlete, zookeeper, police officer, and reporter.

Another useful step in career planning is self-assessment. This process will reveal your values and interests. Values help you set priorities in life. They affect the importance you place on family, security, and wealth. You should consider your values when you choose a career.

Interests are activities that you like or subjects that appeal to you. Listing your interests may help you identify a work setting that you will like. This can be helpful in planning a career.

By Student Name

Figure 8.23 Standard Report

77C APPLY: My Biggest Surprises

1. Take some time to think about the biggest surprises in your life.

2. Voice-type a report about your biggest surprise. Create at least two paragraphs. Center the title in all capital letters. Double-space the report and indent the paragraphs. Dictate **By** and your name on the last line.

3. Proofread and correct all errors. Save the report as *77-Surprise*. Print the report.

Chapter 9
Planning with PDAs

OBJECTIVES

In Chapter 9, you will:

↗ Use a variety of input methods to input information into a PDA.

↗ Change time and time zone settings on the PDA.

↗ Access and navigate applications on a PDA.

↗ Make calculations with a calculator on a PDA.

↗ Input notes or memos, task items, contacts, and calendar items into a PDA.

Web Resources:
www.c21jr.swlearning.com/studentresources

- Data Files
- Vocabulary Flash Cards
- Beat the Clock, PDAs
- *PowerPoint* Reviews
- More Activities

Careful planning can help anyone be more successful. Most students and working people have **deadlines**, which are times by which certain things must be done. Many people keep a list of tasks they must complete. Everyone must keep track of contacts. **Contacts** are people you know or communicate with. Contact information includes important names, addresses, e-mail addresses, and phone numbers.

Fortunately, PDAs (personal digital assistants) can help users keep track of information. A **PDA** is a computer that is small enough to fit in your hand. That's why many models are called *Pocket PCs* and others are called *Palms*. They are small, so you can take them anywhere.

Get Aboard Apollo 17

Any important activity or adventure should be well thought out. Think about the Apollo missions. You can't fly to the moon without careful planning.

Let's go "back to the future." Imagine that you have been asked to join the *Apollo 17* astronauts on the final trip to the moon. They will be glad to have you and your PDA along for the ride. You can help them carry out some important experiments and keep track of key deadlines.

Courtesy of NASA

Reviewing   *What You Have Learned*

Answer these questions to review what you have learned in Chapter 8.

1. What type of software lets users enter data into a computer by talking?

2. List three speech recognition programs.

3. A _____ is a device that contains a microphone and speakers and is worn on one's head.

4. Give examples of some types of background noise that might interfere with speech recognition.

5. What is the purpose of a windscreen on a speech recognition headset?

6. Describe how a headset microphone should be placed when using speech recognition.

7. How can a user teach a computer how to understand his or her speech?

8. What type of tools does the Language bar contain?

9. When you want to input data by talking to the computer, what mode should you use?

10. When you want to give commands by talking to the computer, what mode should you use?

11. List three guidelines for saying voice commands.

12. What voice command can be used to close a menu?

13. List three tips to improve voice-typing skills.

14. What action does the NEW LINE command cause?

15. What action does the NEW PARAGRAPH command cause?

16. What voice command can be used to delete the last word or phrase dictated?

17. What type of words might a user add to a speech recognition dictionary?

18. When voice-typing a document, why should you correct mistakes at the end of each paragraph?

19. When you want your dictated text read back to you, what feature can you use to accomplish this?

20. Give three examples of voice commands you can use to navigate in a *Word* document.

If you find it easy to talk to people and show them new things, you may be perfect for a career in sales. If you would rather express yourself through words, maybe a career in advertising is for you. People in business careers need strong communication skills. Studying English and languages can help you succeed in many careers.

1. Is a career in business and management right for you? Open and print the data file *CD-C08-Careers*. Read the information to see if you are interested in this career path.

2. Open the data file *CD-C08-Languages*. Follow the directions given to access the Internet and research a career in business and management.

↗ Academic Success Builder

STUDENT ORGANIZATIONS: ARE THEY RIGHT FOR YOU? Do your activities at school go beyond the classroom? Do you take part in community service projects? Do you help organize after-school events with your classmates? Do you play on a school team? Do you belong to the school band? Do you belong to a school club? Have you been part of a contest where you competed against students from other schools to show what you know and can do? Do you belong to a community-based youth organization? Do you hold a leadership position?

If you can answer *Yes* to some of the above questions, you are on your way to building a foundation for success in:

- Doing well in school subjects
- Working as a member of a team
- Teaching, leading, and serving others
- Working with others from diverse backgrounds
- Showing you can accept responsibility and manage resources
- Building self–esteem

Success in the above areas will help you in many ways. What you learn will carry over to your high school and later studies. Skills you learn from your out-of-class activities are important to future employers. These skills will also help you serve your community to make it a better place to live.

In this activity, you will focus on student organizations and what they have to offer. You will use the Internet to research two student clubs that are available to middle, high school, and/or college students.

1. Start *Word*. Open *CD-C08-Organizations* from the data files.

2. Follow the instructions in the data file to complete the activity.

Applying *What You Have Learned*

Instant Message

Review how to dictate and format a report in activities 75A and 77B.

Dictate a Report

1. Start *Word* and open a new blank document. Voice-type the report shown below. Correct all errors in the document.

2. Format the report using voice commands along with the mouse and keyboard. The report format should be similar to Figure 8.23 on page 307.

3. Using voice commands along with the mouse and keyboard, save the document as *C08-Report*. Print the report. Close *Word*.

PROCRASTINATION

Why are some people so amazingly productive, while others are not? *Procrastination* is the answer to this question. Productive people do not waste time. They maintain that you should not put off until tomorrow what you can do today. People who are successful tend to be those who manage their time well.

A number of things can be done to combat procrastination. First, prepare a list showing each task that should be completed. Many of the tasks that appear on the list will take only a little time. Other tasks may take a great deal of time. As each task is completed, mark it off the list. This gives a person a sense of accomplishment. It also increases the likelihood that the other tasks will be completed.

Another way to combat procrastination is to divide large tasks into several smaller parts. By doing so, the job will not seem overwhelming. A deadline can be set for completing each part of the job. The probability of completing a large job is much greater when it is divided into parts that have assigned deadlines.

Supplemental activities for this chapter can be found at www.c21jr. swlearning.com.

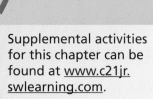

ACROSS THE CURRICULUM

TEAMWORK

Data Files

- *CD-C08-Business*
- *CD-C08-Careers*
- *CD-C08-Languages*
- *CD-C08-Organizations*

INTERNET

↗ About Business

HOME-BASED BUSINESSES A **home-based business** is a company that is run primarily from a person's place of residence. A room or other place at the home is used for business activities. The room may serve as an office for the company. A typical home office is equipped with items such as a desk, telephone, computer, printer, fax/copier, and file cabinets. The office is used for keeping records and communicating with customers.

The work the entrepreneur does may also take place in the home office. For example, an accountant may prepare tax returns for clients in a home office. The work may take place in another area at the home. For example, a home garage may serve as a woodworking shop in which furniture is made. The work of the company can also take place at a client's home or business. For example, in a company that is a cleaning service, the owner and/or other workers go to the client's home or office and do the cleaning. A lawn-care business is another example of a company where the work is done at clients' homes. Home-based businesses may be involved in e-commerce. The owner may use the Internet to advertise or sell products.

Home-based businesses are an important part of the market economy in the United States. According to the U.S. Small Business Administration, more than half the small businesses in the United States are home-based businesses.[1]

1. Start *Word*. Open and print *CD-C08-Business* from your data files. Read about the advantages and disadvantage of having a home-based business.

2. Work with a classmate to describe a home-based business in your community as directed in the data file. Share the information you find with the class.

↗ Career and Life Skills Success Builder

LANGUAGES AND YOUR CAREER Do you enjoy writing and talking with others? You may think that studying English will prepare you only for a career in writing or journalism. Or, you may think that studying languages will help you only to be a teacher or translator. Did you know that these classes can also prepare you for public relations and marketing jobs?

---

[1] "Frequently Asked Questions," U.S. Small Business Administration, http://app1.sba.gov/faqs (accessed October 15, 2004).

Building Keying Skill

Warmup Practice

Key each line twice. If time permits, key the lines again.

Alphabet

1 Jasper amazed Hank by quickly fixing two big vans.

Figure/Symbol

2 Tax (451.38) was added to the invoice (#40-62-79).

Speed

3 Laurie may fish off the bog dock down by the lake.

gwam 1' | 1 | 2 | 3 | 4 | 5 | 6 | 7 | 8 | 9 | 10 |

Technique Mastery of Individual Letters

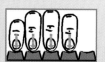

TECHNIQUE TIP

Fingers should be curved and upright.

Key each line twice.

A Abe ate banana bread at Anna's Cafe at 18 Parkway.

B Bob Abbott bobbled the baseball hit by Barb Banks.

C Cecelia can check the capacities for each cubicle.

D Dan added additional games and divided the squads.

E Emery recently developed three new feet exercises.

F Jeff Florez offered the fifty officials free food.

G Gregg gingerly gave the giggling girl a gold ring.

H Herb shared his half of the hay with his neighbor.

I I will live in Illinois after leaving Mississippi.

J Jay, Jet, and Joy enjoyed the jet ride to Jamaica.

K Kay Kern took the kayak to Kentucky for Kent Kick.

L Will lives in Idaho; Lance Bell lives in Illinois.

M Mary Mead assumed the maximum and minimum amounts.

gwam 30" | 2 | 4 | 6 | 8 | 10 | 12 | 14 | 16 | 18 | 20 |

Speed Forcing Drill

Key a 30" timed writing on each line. Your rate in gross words a minute (*gwam*) is shown below the lines.

1 Jan left to go home.

2 They won their last game.

3 Kay's test score was terrible.

4 The next game may not be cancelled.

5 The hurricane struck Florida on Tuesday.

6 The teacher said Jane could make up the exam.

7 She may be able to catch a later flight on Friday.

gwam 30" | 2 | 4 | 6 | 8 | 10 | 12 | 14 | 16 | 18 | 20 |

Technique Mastery of Individual Letters

Key each line twice.

N No one knew Nathan N. Nevins was not here at noon.

O I told Jose and Brook not to mop the floors today.

P Philippe paid for the pepper and paprika for Pepe.

Q Quinton quit questioning the adequacy of the quiz.

R Carrie, correct the two problems before departing.

S Steven and I saw Sam at Sally's session on Sunday.

T Tim bottled the water after talking with the maid.

U He urged us to put the rugs under the four trucks.

V Vivian Von Vogt took the vivid van to the village.

W Will Wesley work on the walnut wall for two weeks?

X The tax expert explained the tax exam's existence.

Y Jay may be ready to pay you your money on Tuesday.

Z Zelda was puzzled by the sizzling heat at the zoo.

gwam 30" | 2 | 4 | 6 | 8 | 10 | 12 | 14 | 16 | 18 | 20 |

Glossary

A

acceptable use policy Rules for computer use

active cell The current location of the insertion point; stores information that is entered

Align Left Software feature that starts all lines of the paragraph at the left margin; is the default paragraph alignment

Align Right Software feature that ends all lines at the right margin

application programs Software that helps users perform tasks

ascending In order from A to Z for words and from the lowest to the highest for numbers

attachment note Tells the reader that other material is attached to a letter or memo

attribute A characteristic, as in a background color, for a Web page

audience People who will listen to a presentation

AutoFit to Contents Feature that adjusts the column widths to be just wide enough for all of the contents to fit within the cells

AutoForm An *Access* feature that creates a form based on an open table and includes all the fields from the table

AutoShapes Ready-made shapes and a variety of lines that are available from *Word's* Drawing toolbar

B

BACKSPACE Key used to delete characters to the left of the insertion point

bank statement Report that lists all the transactions in your bank account during the past month

bar chart Graph that compares values across categories of data

Beaming Transmitting data from one PDA to another by using the infrared ports on the PDAs

blind copy Feature used when you don't want the person receiving the e-mail message to know that you have sent the message to another person

body Contains the paragraphs that make up a report, memo, or letter; main and supporting points of a presentation

borders The printed lines around cells in a table

budget An itemized spending plan

bullet Character or graphic (square, circle, picture) that appears before each item in a list

Bullets and Numbering *Word* feature used to select styles for bullets or numbering for lists

business An entity that sells or rents products or services

business letter Letter sent from a person within a business to another person

C

CAPS LOCK Key used to create a series of capital letters

carpal tunnel syndrome (CTS) A form of RSI that affects keyboard users, causing numbness or pain in the hand, wrist, elbow, or shoulder

category axis Used to plot categories of data in a chart, sometimes called the X-axis

cell Place where a row and a column cross each other in a table

cell reference box Identifies the active cell(s) by the letter of the column and the number of the row where they cross

Center Software feature that places an equal (or nearly equal) space between the text and each side margin

Chat room Internet feature that allows users who are online to type text messages for others in the chat room and display them almost instantly

check A written order to a bank to make a payment from an account

Check Grammar *Word* feature used to check grammar in a document

check register Form on which you record information about your bank account

citations Notes placed in the report body to mark material taken from other sources

clip art Drawn pictures that can be used in documents

close HTML tags Tags that stop commands

column Information arranged vertically in a table

column chart Graph that compares values across categories of data

column head(ing) Appears in a cell at the top of a range of data in a column and describes the data

compact disc (CD) Device used to store computer files

complimentary close Farewell for a letter

compound interest Money earned on the original amount deposited or invested and also on the interest earned during previous interest periods

computer Machine that follows a set of instructions to change and store data

computer interface Means by which users get information and give commands to a computer

computer virus A destructive program that destroys or harms data on a computer and can be loaded onto a computer and run without the computer owner's knowledge

conclusion A summary of points you presented and the action you want the listeners to take

contacts People you know or communicate with

container Object used to organize notes in *OneNote*

continuous speech recognition (CSR) Software that allows users to speak normally and input data into a computer by voice

copy Software command that copies selected text so it can be pasted to another location; original text is unchanged

copy note Tells the reader that another person will receive a copy of the memo or letter

copyright A form of protection for certain works that tells how the work may be legally used or copied

correction list A group of words from which a word can be selected to replace an incorrect word

crop To cut or trim

Cut Software command that removes selected text from a document

D

data Facts and figures

data labels Numbers or words that identify values displayed in the chart

data points Bars, columns, or pie slices that represent the numerical data in a chart

data type Determines the kind of data a field in a database can hold

database An organized collection of facts and figures

deadline Date and/or time by which some task must be completed

default settings Settings used by the program unless you change them

demand The amount of a product or service consumers are able and willing to buy

descending In order from Z to A for words and from the highest to the lowest for numbers

Design template A set of design elements you can apply to slides

desktop On-screen work area on which windows, icons, menus, and dialog boxes appear

desktop publishing (DTP) Using a personal computer to produce high-quality printed documents

D

Dictation mode Allows users to enter text by talking to a computer

digital device Shares data in electronic form (streams of the digits 1 and 0)

digital ink The technology that allows handwritten computer input

digital pen (stylus) Device used for pointing, drawing, and writing on a special type of computer screen or digital tablet

digital tablet A device that attaches to a computer and allows handwritten input

digital video disc (DVD) Device used to store computer files

digitizing Process used by a scanner to create an image

discrimination The unfair treatment of people due to factors such as race, ethnic group, age, religion, disability, or gender

distribution Refers to sending information to the people who need it

double-space Tapping the ENTER key twice to move the insertion point down two lines

drawing canvas An area in which you can draw several shapes

drawing objects Graphics you draw that are part of your *Word* document

E

E-commerce Selling and buying of products on the Internet

economic indicators Measurements that describe how well the economy is doing

edits Changes and corrections made to a database or other document

E-mail The electronic transfer of messages

e-mail address Contains a username and a domain name separated by the at sign (@)

employee benefits Payments other than wages that are made to workers in the form of cash, goods, or services

enclosure note Tells the reader that other material is enclosed with a memo or letter

ENTER Key used to return the insertion point to the left margin and move it down one line

entrepreneur Person who organizes and manages a business, risking the money he or she invests in the hopes of making a profit

Envelope *Word* feature used to create envelopes

ergonomics The study of how a person's work environment and tools affect the person

ethics Moral standards or values

expenses Items for which money is paid, such as rent, utilities, or labor

export To send goods to another country for sale there

F

Favorites Browser feature that allows you to create a list of links for sites

field Contains one piece of information about a person or item in a database

file Digital information in a form that can be read by a computer

file extension A three- or four-letter code that identifies a particular file type, for example .doc for a *Word* file or .html for a Web file

fill handle The small square in the bottom-right corner of the cell used to copy or fill data

Filter A database feature that hides records in a table that do not match the set criteria

Find Feature used to search for a word or phrase in a document; *OneNote* feature used to search notes

firewall Hardware and software used to help prevent unauthorized users from getting to data

fixed costs Expenses that remain the same regardless of the amount of goods or services that are produced or sold

floppy disk Device used to store computer files

flyer An announcement or advertisement usually intended for wide distribution

folder Used by *Windows OS* to organize computer files

font Style of text/letters used

footer Contains information that displays at the bottom of pages in a document

form An object used to enter or display data in a database

format To place text on a page so it looks good and is easy to read

formula An equation that performs calculations on values in a worksheet

formula bar Displays the contents of the active cell and is used to enter or edit text or numbers

function A predefined formula that can be used to perform calculations

G

global marketplace Worldwide area where products are bought and sold

Graffiti or Graffiti 2 Character recognition program for use on Palm PDAs

graphic A drawn picture, a photo, or a chart

graphical user interface A computer interface that displays pictures, icons, and other images

gridlines Marks the outline of the area for each cell in a table and are not printed

gross pay The sum of the regular pay and overtime pay

gross words a minute (gwam) The number of standard words keyed in 1 minute

H

hacker Person who accesses computers or networks without the proper permission

hacking Accessing computers or networks without the proper permission

handwriting Inputting data using handwriting recognition

Hanging Indent Software feature that begins all lines except the first line away from the left margin

hard drive Common storage device located inside a computer

hardware Physical parts of a computer

header Contains information that appears at the top of pages in a document

headset A device that contains a microphone and speakers and is worn on one's head

highlight Surround in color

History Browser feature that shows you a list of links for sites you have visited recently

hits Items in a search results list

home keys The keys where you place your fingers to begin keying: a s d f for the left hand and j k l ; for the right hand

HTML (HyperText Markup Language) Language used to create and display Web pages

hyperlink Text or a graphic in an electronic document that, when clicked, takes you to a new location

I

identity theft The taking of a person's private data and using it to pretend to be that person, especially in making illegal purchases

imaging devices Pieces of equipment that allow users to capture or create pictures

income Money a business receives for products or service

information processing Putting facts or numbers into a meaningful form

input Refers to the way you give data to a computer

Insert Date and Time *Word* feature used to insert the date and/or time into a document

interest Money a bank pays customers for keeping money in certain types of accounts

Internet A web of computer networks that spans the Earth

Internet service provider (ISP) A company that provides customer connections to the Internet

introduction Opening remarks that tell listeners what your talk will be about

J

Justify Software feature that starts all lines at the left margin and ends all full lines at the right margin

L

Label *Word* feature used to create labels

landscape Orientation in which the long side of your screen or tablet is positioned at the top

Language bar A toolbar that contains hand-writing and speech tools that you can use in *Microsoft Office* programs

leader A person who guides, directs, or commands

legend A key (usually with different colors or patterns) used to identify a chart's data categories

letter address Address of the person to whom you are writing a letter

Letter Recognizer Character recognition program for use on Pocket PC PDAs

letterhead paper Paper that has a business name and address printed on the paper

Line Spacing *Word* feature used to change the amount of blank space between lines of text

login name Series of letters and/or numbers that identify you to the computer

M

mailable copy A document that is formatted and keyed correctly and is acceptable for mailing to the recipient

manager An employee who oversees the daily affairs of a business

margin the blank space between the edge of the paper and the print

marginal cost The amount total cost changes as the amount of goods or services produced changes

margins The amount of blank space between text and the edge of the paper

market A company's customers or potential customers

market price The price at which consumers are willing to buy and producers are willing to sell a product

marketplace The geographical area in which a company sells products

megapixels Measurement used for resolution for digital cameras; millions of pixels

memo Written message in printed form used by people within an organization

merge Join

microprocessor Small circuit board that controls all work done by the computer

mute To silence or shut off

N

nested Organized in pairs moving from the outside in; used for some HTML tags

net pay The difference between gross pay and the deductions

netiquette Rules for proper online behavior

network One computer linked to one or more other computers

Newsgroup Internet feature that allows users to post messages about a certain topic for others to read

Notes pane A pane that allows you to key notes about the slide

Numeric keyboard On-screen PDA keyboard with numbers, special characters, and symbols

O

objects Elements of a database such as a form or table

on-screen keyboard Keys that appear on the computer monitor that you can tap to enter characters

open HTML tags Tags that start commands

operating system Software that controls basic operations of the computer

orientation Direction

outline Document that organizes facts and details by main topics and subtopics

Outline tab Displays the number of each slide and the text that is included on each slide

output Refers to the way you get data from a computer

overtime The number of hours worked beyond 40 hours in a week

overtime hourly rate A multiple of your regular pay rate, such as 1.5 or 2 times your regular pay rate

overtime pay The number of overtime hours worked times your overtime pay rate

P

page breaks Used to signal the end of a page

paragraph Any amount of text that is keyed before the ENTER key is tapped; can be one word or several words or lines

password Series of letters and/or numbers that you enter to gain access to a computer

Paste Software command that places text that has been cut or copied into a document

path Drive and series of folders and subfolders that describe the location of a computer file

PDA (personal digital assistant) A very small, handheld computer that is small enough to fit in your hand and allows handwritten input

peripherals Devices that can work with a computer

personal computer A small computer designed for an individual user

personal-business letter Type of letter used to deal with personal matters

picture A drawing or photo in a separate file that you insert into your document

pie chart Graph that shows how much each value is of a total value

pixel Tiny dots of light or ink that make up images

placeholders Boxes with dotted borders that are part of most slide layouts and hold title and body text or objects such as charts, tables, and pictures

plagiarism Using material created by another person and claiming it as your own

points Measurement used for font size

portfolio A collection of samples of your best work

portrait Orientation in which the short side of your screen or tablet is positioned at the top

post Upload a page to the Web for sharing

presentation A talk or speech given to inform, persuade, and entertain

primary key A field that uniquely identifies each record in a database table

Print Command that allows you to print a document

Print Preview Command that allows you to see how a document will look before you print it; *Word* feature used to display several pages of document in a reduced size

privacy policy A document that tells how personal data collected by a company will be used

processing Refers to how data is changed or used

productivity A measure of how much work can be done in a certain amount of time

profile Description

profit The amount of income that remains after expenses are paid

proofreaders' marks Letters and symbols used to show the errors or changes needed in a document

Q

quadruple-space Tapping the ENTER key four times to move the insertion point down four lines

query A database object that displays certain data that meets the set criteria

R

range A group of two or more cells on a worksheet

record Contains all the information about one person or item in a database

reference initials Initials of someone other than the writer who keys a memo or letter

regular pay The number of regular hours worked times your regular hourly rate

repetitive stress injury (RSI) A condition that is a result of repeated movement of a particular part of the body

Replace *Word* feature used to find text and then replace the text with other words

report A document that gives facts, ideas, or opinions about one or more topics; A database object used to format and display data from tables or queries

Resolution Picture quality as measured in dots per inch or pixels per inch

return address Writer's address keyed at the beginning of a personal-business letter

row Information arranged horizontally in a table

row height The vertical amount of space in a row

S

salutation Greeting of a letter

scam A scheme used to take money under false pretenses or for a product that does not work as advertised

Search Browser feature that allows you to look for information related to a word or term

search engine A Web site that allows you to enter search criteria and find Web sites

section A computer file in *OneNote*

Server Powerful computers that store files for the Internet

shading A colored fill or background that can be applied to cells in a table

Shifted keyboard On-screen PDA keyboard with capital letters and symbols

simple interest Money paid only on the original amount deposited or invested

single-space Tapping the ENTER key once to move the insertion point down one line

sizing handle A small circle or square that appears on the border of a selected graphic and can be dragged to change the graphic size

Slide pane Displays the current slide or the slide that you click on in the Slides tab

Slide Sorter A view that shows small images of the slides and allows the user to rearrange slides easily

Slides tab Displays small images of the slides that have been created

smart phone A device that has both PDA features and digital phone features

software Programs that give instructions to a computer

Sort To arrange or group items in a particular order; an *Access* feature that is used to arrange the information in a table or query in a certain order

SPACE BAR Key used to place a space between words

spam Unsolicited e-mail messages sent to many addresses; "junk" e-mail

spreadsheet software Computer program used to record, report, and analyze data in worksheets

Spelling Check *Word* feature used to check text for spelling errors

split Divide

Standard keyboard On-screen PDA keyboard with lowercase letters and punctuation marks

standard word In keyboarding, five characters (letters, numbers, symbols, or spaces)

storage Refers to saving the data for later use

stylus Pencil-like tool used to activate PDA soft buttons and to write on the screen

subfolder Folder stored inside another folder

subscript Text that is slightly lower than other text on a line

superscript Text that is slightly higher than other text on a line

supply The amount of a product or service producers (companies) are willing and able to offer for sale

T

TAB Key used to move the insertion point to a specific location on the line

table Information arranged in rows and columns so readers can easily understand the information; a database element used for organizing and storing data

table title Describes the content of a table

Tablet Input Panel Contains the handwriting tools for a Tablet PC

Tablet PC A powerful notebook computer that allows handwritten input

tabs Set locations at which text can be placed; by default, set every one-half inch on the Ruler

team A group of people working together to achieve a common goal

text box A drawing object that can hold text or graphics

text editor A simple word processing program such as *Notepad*

text-to-speech Feature used to have dictated text read back to the user

thumbnails Miniature pictures that represent graphic files

title Main heading that tells what a report is about

U

uniform resource locator (URL) An address for a Web site

USB Flash drive Device used to store computer files

V

value A number or a word assigned to an attribute, as in a blue Web page background

value axis Used to plot values associated with the categories of data, usually called the Y-axis

variable costs Expenses that change depending on the amount of services or goods that are produced or sold

Vertical alignment *Word* feature that sets how text will be placed on a page vertically

visual aid Something you show the audience to help them understand your message

Voice Command mode Allows users to give commands by talking to a computer

W

Web browser A program that lets you find and view Web pages

Web site A collection of related Web pages that are connected using hyperlinks

Windows Explorer Program used to manage files and folders

windscreen A shield that helps protect a microphone from sudden blasts of air or from being broken

WordArt Decorative text that you can create with ready-made effects

wordwrap Causes text to move automatically to a new line when the current line is full

workbook A spreadsheet file that may contain one or more worksheets, usually with related data

worksheet A section in a workbook (spreadsheet file) where the user can enter data

worksheet title Describes the content of a worksheet table

World Wide Web A system of computers on the Internet that can handle documents formatted in HTML.

Z

Zoom Feature that lets you see your document in smaller or larger sizes (close-up or reduced views)

Index